HISTORICAL DICTIONARY OF THE KOREAN WAR

HISTORICAL DICTIONARY OF THE KOREAN WAR

Edited by
JAMES I. MATRAY

GREENWOOD PRESS
New York • Westport, Connecticut • London

Library of Congress Cataloging-in-Publication Data

Historical dictionary of the Korean War / edited by James I. Matray.
    p. cm.
    Includes bibliographical references and index.
    ISBN 0–313–25924–0 (alk. paper)
    1. Korean War, 1950–1953—Dictionaries. I. Matray, James Irving,
1948–   .
DS918.H536   1991
951.904′2—dc20   90–22833

British Library Cataloguing in Publication Data is available.

Library of Congress Catalog Card Number: 90–22833
ISBN: 0–313–25924–0

First published in 1991

Greenwood Press, 88 Post Road West, Westport, CT   06881
An imprint of Greenwood Publishing Group, Inc.

Printed in the United States of America

The paper used in this book complies with the
Permanent Paper Standard issued by the National
Information Standards Organization (Z39.48–1984).

10 9 8 7 6 5 4 3 2 1

To Benjamin and Amanda

Contents

Preface

Few events in modern world history have deserved more attention and received less than the Korean War. Callum McDonald provides an excellent illustration of this point in the title of his book, *Korea: The War Before Vietnam*. In many ways, however, the Korean conflict was more important than the Vietnam War. Both countries sustained huge losses in resources and population, while suffering massive physical damage. Yet in contrast to Vietnam, Korea remains divided, and its internal cold war continues along with the real possibility of renewed fighting. With respect to world politics, the Korean War was arguably the watershed event in militarizing the Soviet-U.S. clash for predominant influence in international affairs after World War II.

This historical dictionary provides students, scholars, and those casually interested in what Clay Blair has dubbed the forgotten war with a helpful tool to assist in understanding the conflict. Its primary focus is on diplomatic and political developments, with a secondary emphasis on military affairs. Chronologically, this book concentrates on the period of conventional war from the start of the North Korean invasion of South Korea on June 25, 1950, to the signing of the armistice agreement on July 27, 1953. However, recent studies of the Korean War share the view that the conflict had important domestic and international origins prior to the formal outbreak of hostilities. Key developments before 1950 therefore receive attention.

The dictionary allocates a substantially larger portion of space to the U.S. and South Korean side of the story. Until Communist leaders in North Korea, the Soviet Union, and China practice archival *glasnost,* this imbalance in the historical record will persist. The descriptive essays cover all the significant people, controversies, military operations, and policy pronouncements of the era. In certain subject areas, entries appear in groups, such as battles, military operations, United Nations resolutions, and the activities of major participants, most notably Douglas MacArthur, Harry S. Truman, and Syngman Rhee. References at the end of each entry provide guidance to sources for readers desiring more information. Entries appear in alphabetical order, with cross references in the text of each, designated with an asterisk, assisting users interested in learning about related items. This book also contains a list of acronyms, a selection of maps, three appendixes (providing statistical information, a personnel summary, and a chronology of events), and a selected bibliography.

Completion of this valuable research tool would have been impossible without the participation of an outstanding collection of contributors from eight different countries. Following each entry is the name of its author; brief biographical summaries of all contributors appear in the "About the Contributors" section. I have written all the unsigned entries.

This dictionary uses the spelling of Korean and Chinese names that was common at the time of the war to minimize confusion among non-specialists. With respect to Korean-language references and to Korean cities and other places, Michael Robinson of the University of Southern California provided valuable assistance in the effort to ensure grammatical accuracy. I received help in acquiring maps from Susan Piland of Houghton-Mifflin Company, Tim Morris at the U.S. Government Printing Office, and Stuart Rochester of the Office of the Secretary of Defense.

Larry Beck served as editorial assistant for the project, and Cynthia Harris of Greenwood Press deserves credit for providing excellent advice and showing great patience. Most important, Juanita Graves devoted many hours to the dictionary, typing the entire manuscript. My wife, Karin, persuaded me to undertake this project and provided encouragement until its completion. I am dedicating this dictionary to my two children, who share with this volume a common parentage.

Acronyms

ADCOM	Advance Command and Liaison Group in Korea
CCF	Chinese Communist Forces
CCP	Chinese Communist party
CIA	Central Intelligence Agency
CINCFE	Commander-in-Chief, Far East
CINCPAC	Commander-in-Chief, Pacific
CINCPACFLT	Commander-in Chief, Pacific Fleet
CINCUNC	Commander-in-Chief, United Nations Command
CNO	Chief of Naval Operations
CPVA	Chinese People's Volunteers Army
DMZ	demilitarized zone
DPRK	Democratic People's Republic of Korea
ECA	Economic Coordination Administration
EDC	European Defense Community
EUSAK	Eighth U.S. Army, Korea
FEAF	Far East Air Force
HE	high explosive
HEAT	high explosive anti-tank
JCS	Joint Chiefs of Staff
KATCOM	Korean Augmentation Troops, Commonwealth
KATUSA	Korean Augmentation of the U.S. Army
KMT	Kuomintang party
MAC	Military Armistice Commission
MDAP	Mutual Defense Appropriations Program

MLR	main line of resistance
MSA	Mutual Security Act
NATO	North Atlantic Treaty Organization
NAVFE	U.S. Navy, Far East
NKPA	North Korean People's Army
NNRC	Neutral Nations Repatriation Commission
NNSC	Neutral Nations Supervisory Commission
NSC	National Security Council
POW	prisoner of war
PPS	Policy Planning Staff
PRC	People's Republic of China
RAAK	Resist America Aid Korea Movement
RCT	Regimental Combat Team
ROC	Republic of China
ROK	Republic of Korea
ROTC	Reserve Officer Training Corps
SANACC	State–Army–Navy–Air Force Coordinating Committee
SKLP	South Korean Labor party
SWNCC	State–War–Navy Coordinating Committee
UNC	United Nations Command
UNCOK	United Nations Commission on Korea
UNCURK	United Nations Commission for the Unification and Rehabilitation of Korea
UNKRA	United Nations Korean Reconstruction Agency
UNRC	United Nations Reception Center
UNRRA	United Nations Relief and Rehabilitation Administration
UNTCOK	United Nations Temporary Commission on Korea
USAFIK	United States Armed Forces in Korea
WSB	War Stabilization Board

Maps

Map 1
Korea

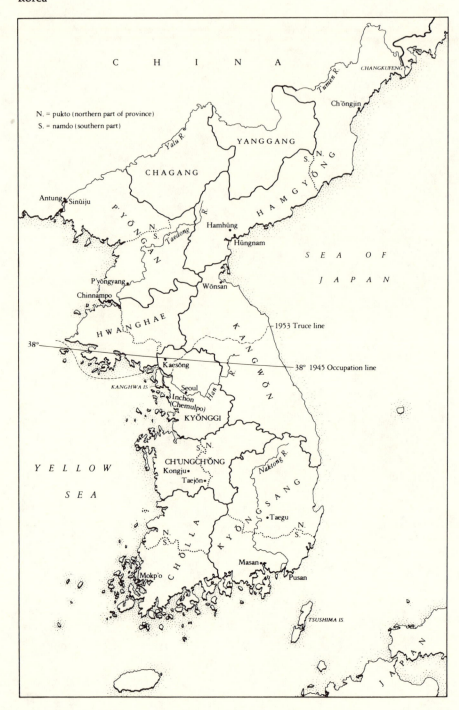

N. = pukto (northern part of province)
S. = namdo (southern part)

Source: J. K. Fairbank, et al., *East Asia: Tradition and Transformation* (1978).

Map 2

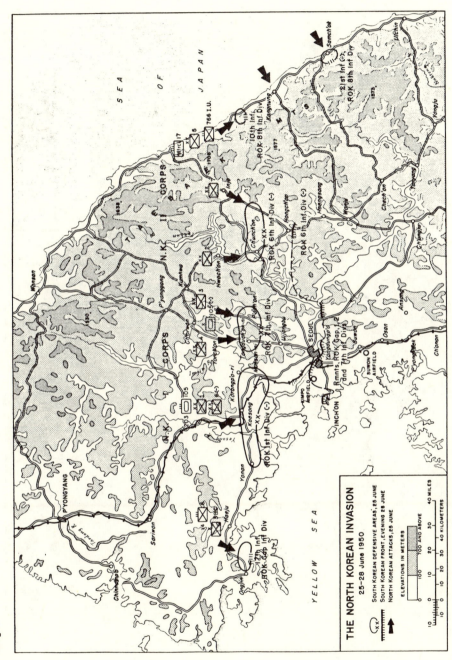

THE NORTH KOREAN INVASION
25–28 June 1950

SOUTH KOREAN DEFENSIVE AREAS, 25 JUNE
SOUTH KOREAN FRONT, EVENING 28 JUNE
NORTH KOREAN ATTACKS, 25 JUNE

ELEVATIONS IN METERS

100   700 AND ABOVE

0   10   20   30   40 MILES

0 10 20 30 40 KILOMETERS

Source: R. E. Appleman, *South to the Naktong, North to the Yalu* (1961).

Map 3

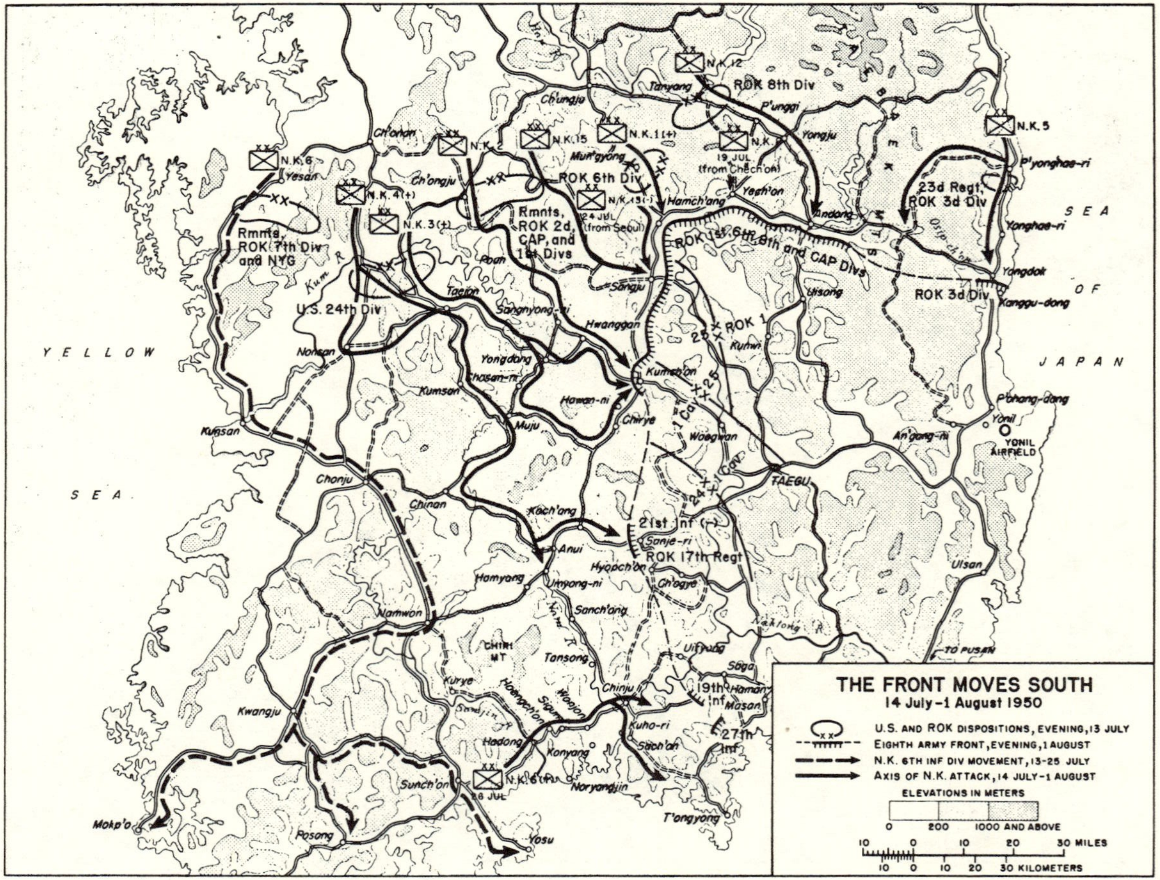

Source: R. E. Appleman, *South to the Naktong, North to the Yalu* (1961).

Map 4

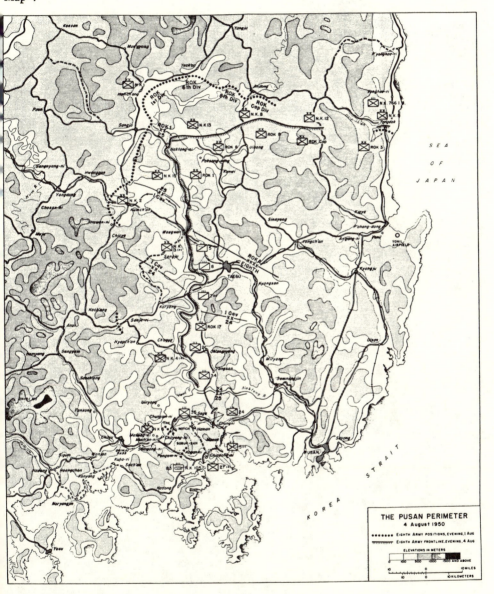

Source: R. E. Appleman, *South to the Naktong, North to the Yalu* (1961).

xvii

Map 5
The Inch'on Assault: 15 September 1950

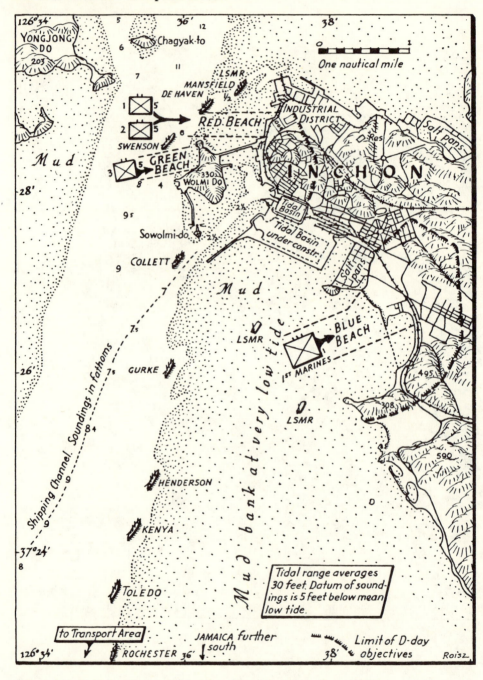

Source: J. A. Field, Jr., *History of United States Naval Operations, Korea* (1962).

Map 6

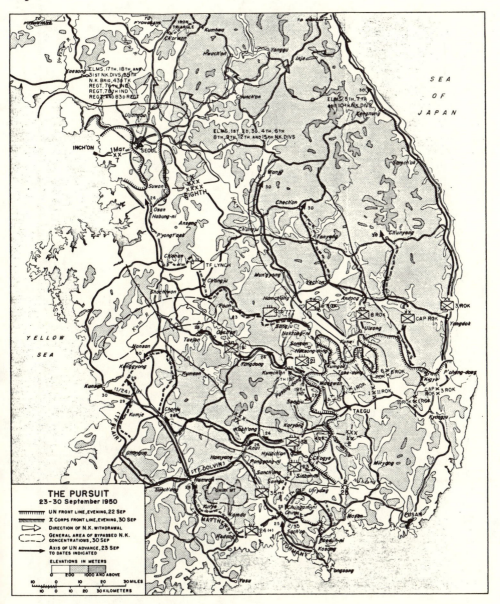

Source: R. E. Appleman, *South to the Naktong, North to the Yalu* (1961).

Map 7
The Clearance of Wŏnsan: 10 October–2 November 1950

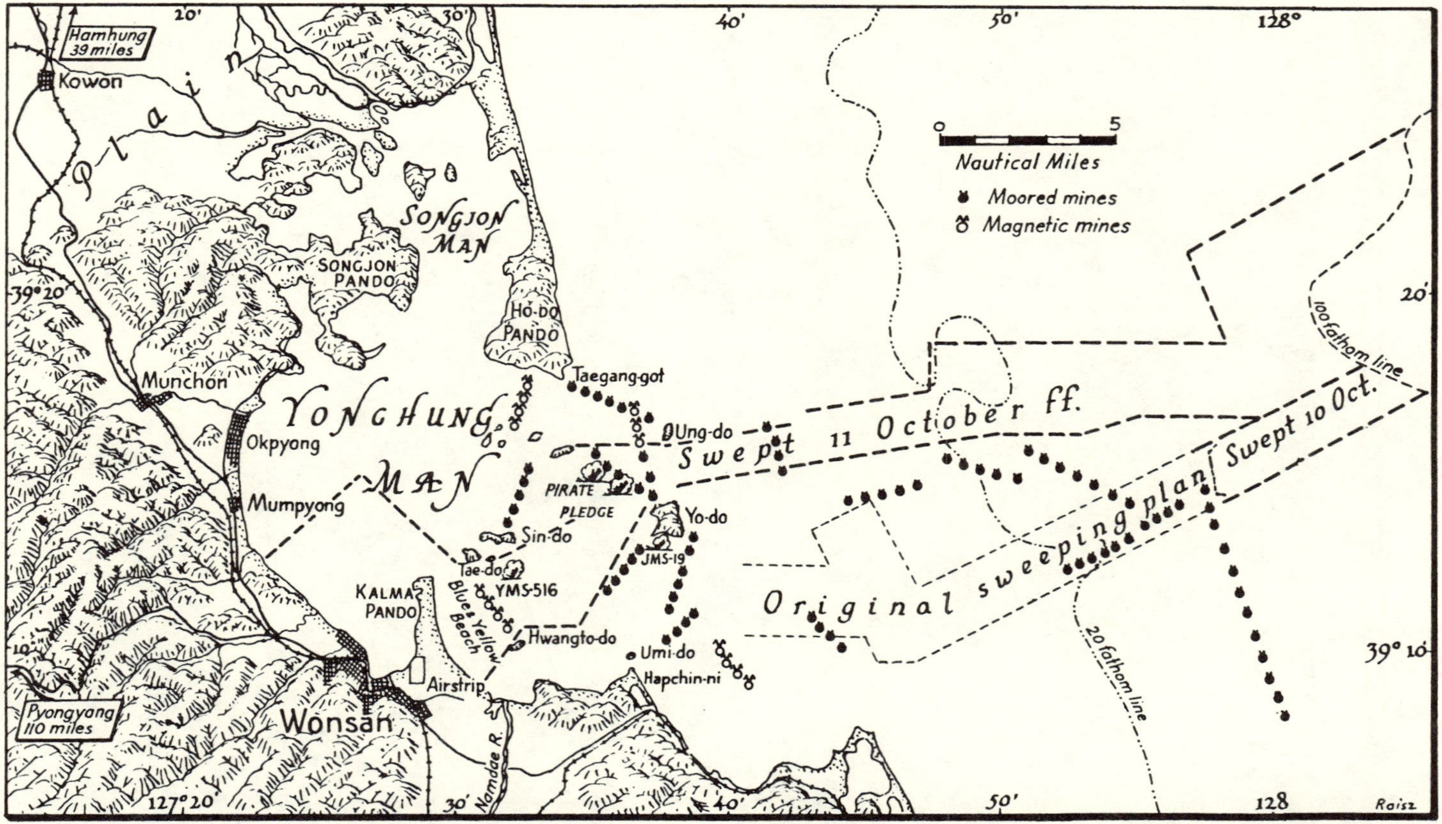

Source: J. A. Field, Jr., *History of United States Naval Operations, Korea* (1962).

Map 8

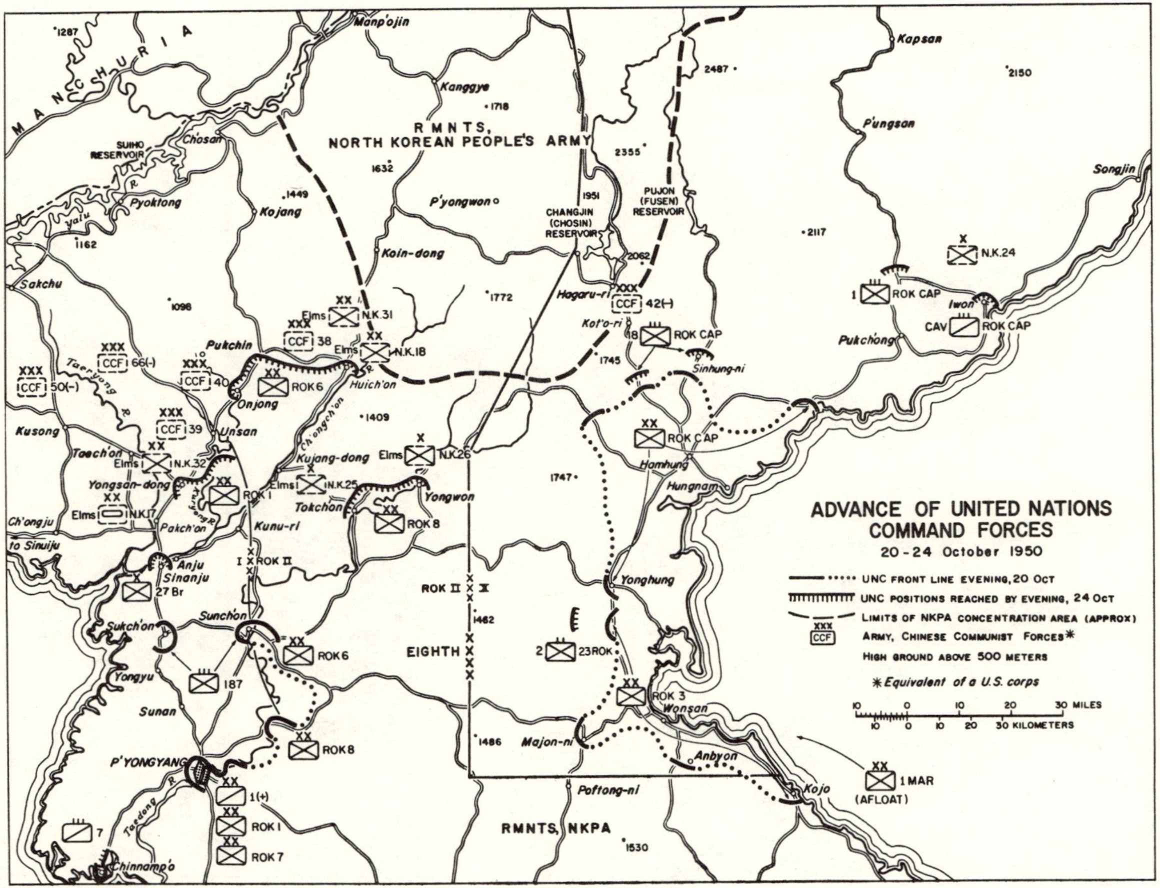

Source: R. E. Appleman, *South to the Naktong, North to the Yalu* (1961).

xxi

Map 9

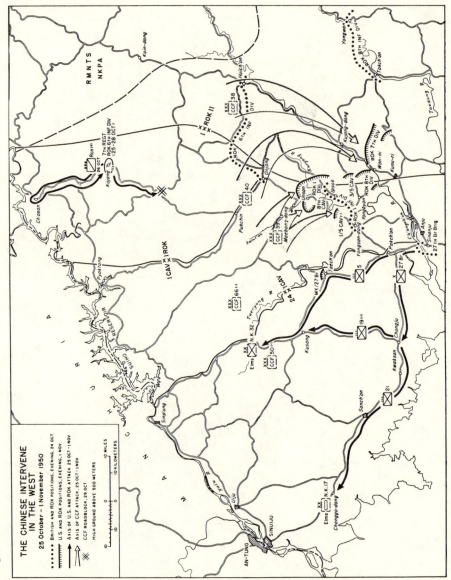

THE CHINESE INTERVENE
IN THE WEST
25 October – 1 November 1950

••••• BRITISH AND ROK POSITIONS, EVENING, 24 OCT
∿∿∿∿ U.S. AND ROK POSITIONS, EVENING, 1 NOV
↑↑ AXIS OF U.S. AND ROK ATTACK 25 OCT – 1 NOV
↑↑ AXIS OF CCF ATTACK, 25 OCT – 1 NOV
⊗ CCF ROADBLOCK, 29 OCT
High ground above 500 meters

Source: R. E. Appleman, *South to the Naktong, North to the Yalu* (1961).

Map 10

THE **NOVEMBER OFFENSIVE**
6–26 November 1950

UN CO ADVANCE, 8 NOV
UN CO ADVANCE, DATE INDICATED
POINT OF CONTACT, DATE INDICATED
US Eighth ARMY LINE, EVENING 23 NOV
US X CORPS ADVANCE, UNTIL 26 NOV
US CO POSITION, EVENING 25 NOV (US EIGHTH ARMY)
UN CO POSITION, EVENING 26 NOV (X CORPS)

ELEVATIONS IN METERS
0   200   500   1000 AND ABOVE

0   10   20   30   40 MILES
0 10 20 30 40 KILOMETERS

Source: J. F. Schnabel, *Policy and Direction* (1972).

xxiii

Map 11

Source: J. F. Schnabel, *Policy and Direction* (1972).

Map 12
The Evacuation of Hŭngnam: 10–24 December 1950

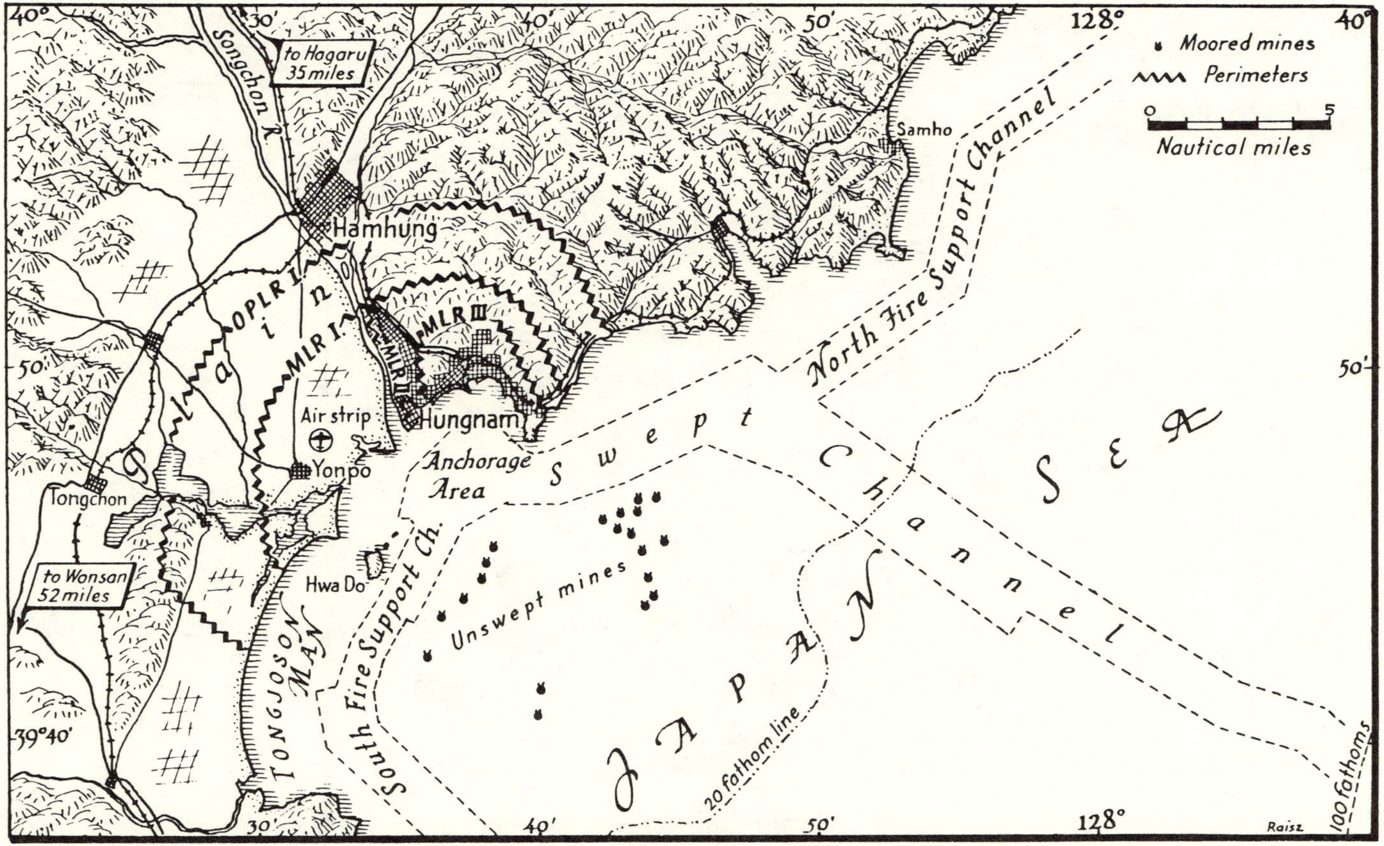

Source: J. A. Field, Jr., *History of United States Naval Operations, Korea* (1962).

Map 13

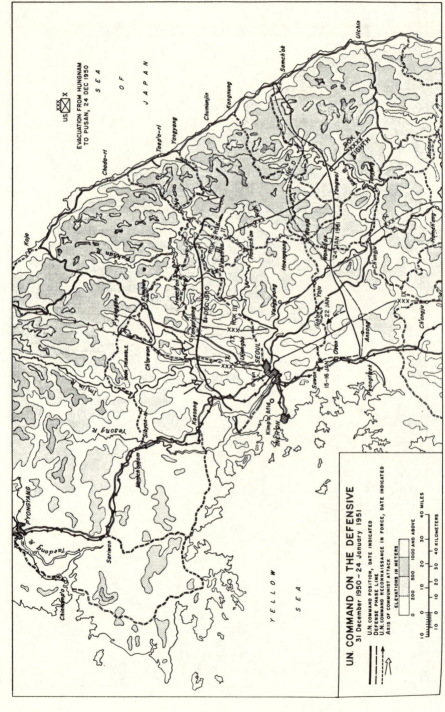

U.N. COMMAND ON THE DEFENSIVE
31 December 1950 – 24 January 1951

U.N. COMMAND POSITION, DATE INDICATED
DEFENSE PHASE LINE
U.N. COMMAND RECONNAISSANCE IN FORCE, DATE INDICATED
AXIS OF COMMUNIST ATTACK

ELEVATIONS IN METERS

200   500   1000 AND ABOVE

0   10   20   30   40 MILES
0   10   20   30   40 KILOMETERS

Source: J. F. Schnabel, *Policy and Direction* (1972).

xxvi

Map 14

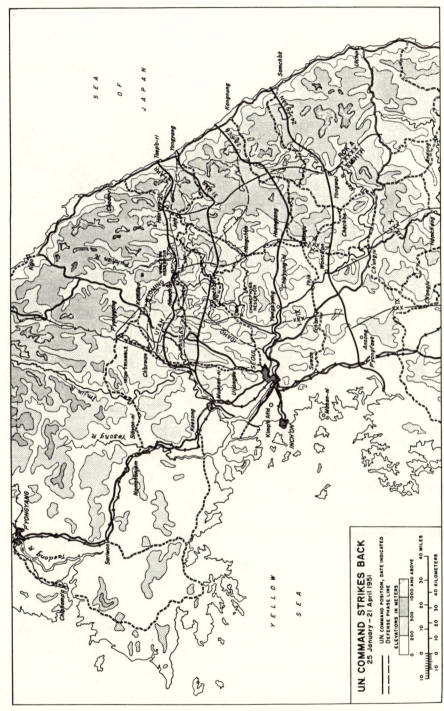

UN. COMMAND STRIKES BACK
25 January – 21 April 1951

—— UN. COMMAND POSITION, DATE INDICATED
- - - DEFENSE PHASE LINE

ELEVATIONS IN METERS

200   500   1000 AND ABOVE

10   0   10   20   30   40 MILES
10   0   10   20   30   40 KILOMETERS

Source: J. F. Schnabel, *Policy and Direction* (1972).

xxvii

Map 15

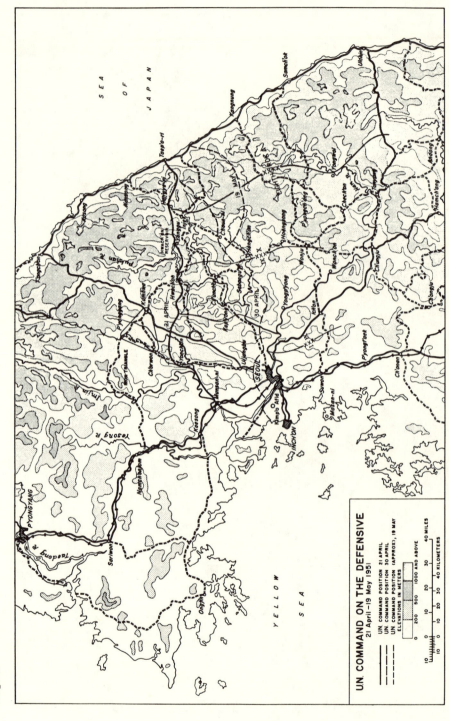

UN. COMMAND ON THE DEFENSIVE
21 April–19 May 1951

UN COMMAND POSITION 21 APRIL
UN COMMAND POSITION 30 APRIL
UN COMMAND POSITION (APPROX), 19 MAY

ELEVATIONS IN METERS

0   200   500   1000 AND ABOVE

0   10   20   30   40 MILES
0 10 20 30 40 KILOMETERS

Source: J. F. Schnabel, *Policy and Direction* (1972).

xxviii

Map 16

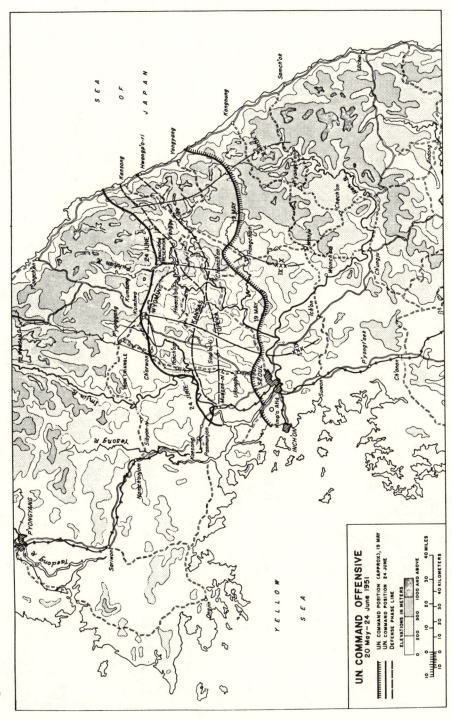

U.N. COMMAND OFFENSIVE
20 May – 24 June 1951

UN COMMAND POSITION (APPROX), 19 MAY
UN COMMAND POSITION 24 JUNE
DEFENSE PHASE LINE

ELEVATIONS IN METERS

| 200 | 500 | 1000 AND ABOVE |

0   10   20   30   40 MILES
0   10   20   30   40 KILOMETERS

Source: J. F. Schnabel, *Policy and Direction* (1972).

Map 17

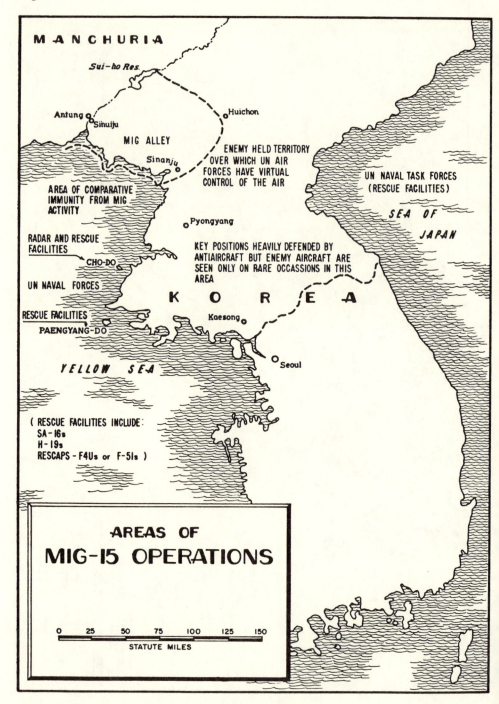

MANCHURIA

Sui-ho Res.

Antung ○
○ Huichon
Sihuiju
MIG ALLEY
Sinanju ○
ENEMY HELD TERRITORY
OVER WHICH UN AIR
FORCES HAVE VIRTUAL
CONTROL OF THE AIR

UN NAVAL TASK FORCES
(RESCUE FACILITIES)

SEA OF
JAPAN

AREA OF COMPARATIVE
IMMUNITY FROM MIG
ACTIVITY

○ Pyongyang

RADAR AND RESCUE
FACILITIES

CHO-DO

KEY POSITIONS HEAVILY DEFENDED BY
ANTIAIRCRAFT BUT ENEMY AIRCRAFT ARE
SEEN ONLY ON RARE OCCASSIONS IN THIS
AREA

UN NAVAL FORCES

KOREA

RESCUE FACILITIES
PAENGYANG-DO

Kaesong ○

YELLOW SEA

○ Seoul

(RESCUE FACILITIES INCLUDE:
SA-16s
H-19s
RESCAPS - F4Us or F-51s)

AREAS OF
MIG-15 OPERATIONS

0   25   50   75   100   125   150
STATUTE MILES

Source: R. F. Futrell, *The United States Air Force in Korea 1950–1953* (1983).

Map 18
The Kaesŏng Conference Site: 1 July 1951

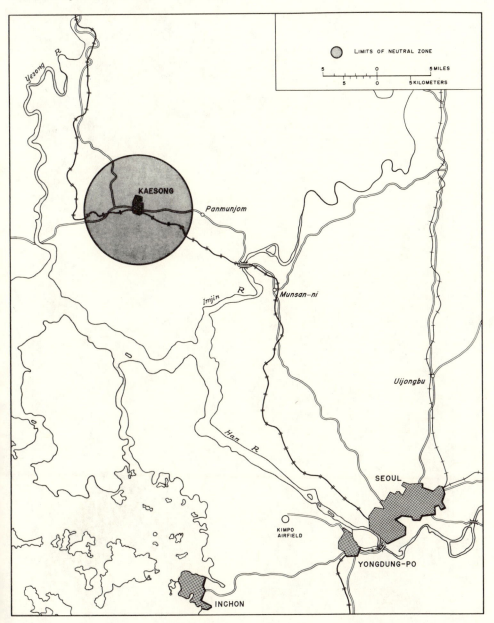

Source: W. G. Hermes, *Truce Tent and Fighting Front* (1966).

Map 19

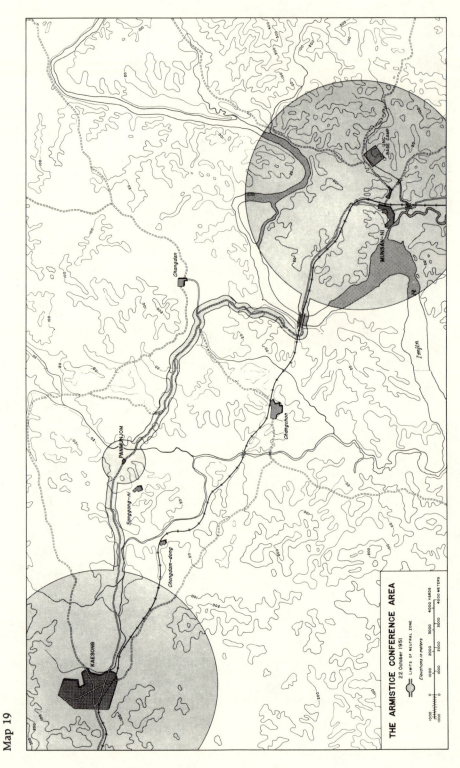

THE ARMISTICE CONFERENCE AREA

22 October 1951

LIMITS OF NEUTRAL ZONE

Elevations in meters

Source: W. G. Hermes, *Truce Tent and Fighting Front* (1966).

Map 20
The Demarcation Line: 27 July 1953

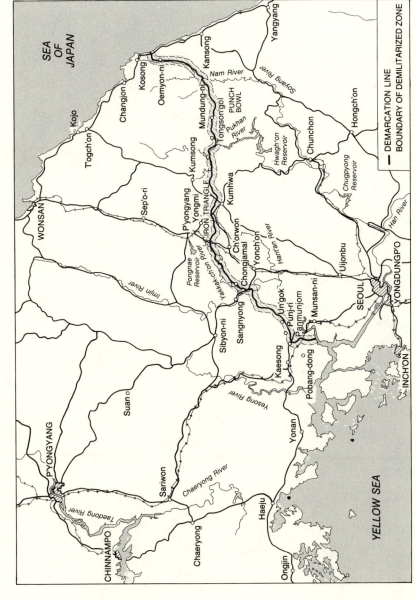

Source: D. M. Condit, *The Test of War, 1950–1953* (1988). Historical Office, Office of the Secretary of Defense, U.S. Dept. of Defense.

HISTORICAL
DICTIONARY
OF THE
KOREAN WAR

A

ACHESON, DEAN G. (1890–1971)

Secretary of State Dean G. Acheson was one of the most important officials of the U.S. government in prosecuting the Korean War, second only to President Harry S. Truman*. He was born in Middletown, Connecticut, and after education at Yale University and Harvard Law School was a clerk for Justice Louis D. Brandeis. Following nearly two decades as a successful Washington lawyer, with a short interval in 1933 as under secretary of the treasury, he became assistant secretary of state in 1940 and then under secretary (1945–1947) and secretary (1949–1953). His relations with Secretary of State James F. Byrnes were correct but not close, but with Secretary of State George C. Marshall* they were intimate. So was his association with President Truman, and it is safe to say that most of his authority as secretary came from the full confidence that Truman placed in his judgment and advice.

Acheson's disdain for the United Nations became well known, as did his belief that Asia was a secondary theater of U.S. policy, compared to Europe. After taking office as secretary in January 1949, he did little to secure the U.S. diplomatic position in Korea, delivering his later well-known National Press Club speech* in January 1950, which excluded the Republic of Korea* from the U.S. defense perimeter. This decision, however, had already been reached by the JCS and was evident anyway in U.S. military withdrawal from Korea* prior to the Korean War.

When the war commenced with the North Korean invasion of South Korea*, Acheson shared completely the view of Truman: that the attack was Soviet inspired but not at the point of major danger, which was Western Europe. Like Truman, he saw the UN endangered but did not think the UN could be a major factor in U.S. policy; he was glad, however, to use its facilities. Also, like Truman, Acheson did not believe it necessary to ask for a declaration of war. Indeed, he thought it dangerous, for it would produce hearings and argument and give opportunity to the "primitives" in Congress.

In subsequent military operations, Acheson constantly kept in mind the weakness of NATO and therefore the danger of drawing a major part of U.S. strength to a peninsula of Asia. He endorsed Truman's authorizing the UN offensive across the thirty-eighth parallel* in September, afterward admitting that, like the JCS, he had given in to the logic of CINCUNC General Douglas MacArthur* that he, MacArthur, was carrying out the UN policy of unifying the Korean nation. Chinese military intervention* much surprised Acheson; he was not present at the Wake Island Conference*, hence not persuaded personally by MacArthur that Chinese intervention in force was impossible, but rather could not believe the Chinese army, an Asian force, could cause such havoc. Again like Truman, he refused to escalate the war, doubtless because of fear of exposing the weak NATO position in Europe. He entirely agreed on the need for Truman's recall of MacArthur* in April 1951.

Acheson's critics pointed out at the time and later that the Korean War hardened his general policy outlook, made him an intense cold warrior, and also exposed him to further attacks from the McCarthyite right. It is difficult to see any hardening of judgment. Acheson always looked upon international relations as a Bismarckian exercise of power.

D. Acheson, *Present at the Creation* (New York, 1969); D. S. McLellan, *Dean Acheson* (New York, 1976); G. Smith, *Dean Acheson* (New York, 1972); H. S. Truman, *Years of Trial and Hope* (Garden City, N.Y., 1956).

Robert H. Ferrell

ACHESON-MORRISON MEETING (September 11, 1951)

Secretary of State Dean G. Acheson* and British Foreign Secretary Herbert S. Morrison* met to discuss future courses of action in Korea following the truce talks suspension of August 23, 1951*. Acheson remarked that if there was an armistice, the United States planned to proceed with political discussions on Korea without bringing in other issues, like Taiwan. Washington would not retreat from the goal of a free, united, and democratic Korea, although the prospect of an agreement along such lines was not bright. Morrison agreed that discussions should be restricted to Korea, keeping in mind, however, "the possibility of a comprehensive approach to settlement of problems in the area." In the back of his mind was British public opinion on China.

Acheson then read a JCS position paper setting forth proposed courses of action if there was no armistice. He emphasized that in this event there was clearly an increased danger of general war and the free nations must accelerate their defense preparations. The JCS paper proposed to give the UNC* tactical freedom to advance to the waist of Korea* in the north. The training and equipping of Japanese troops was to be expedited and additional South Korean forces raised. Restrictions on attacks against the North Korean power installations along the Yalu River were to be lifted. Attacks on the city of Rashin would be approved on an individual case basis, taking every precaution against violating the Soviet border. A complete UN economic blockade of China was recommended. In the event of large-scale air attacks against UN troops, the UNC was to carry out standing orders to inform Washington, which would consult Great Britain and other allies to the extent permitted by the situation, after which retaliation might be authorized. At the UN, Washington intended to make it clear that responsibility for the collapse of armistice negotiations lay with the Communists and to request support for greater military and economic measures.

Morrison responded that Britain was anxious not to become involved in a wider war with the People's Republic of China* and emphasized that dangers existed elsewhere, particularly in the Middle East. While there would be no alternative to retaliation if UN forces were bombed, nothing should be done needlessly. He quoted his predecessor, Ernest Bevin,* on the need to avoid forcing the PRC to rely on the Soviet Union, remarking that it was not yet "a slavish satellite." As for specific measures, he agreed on the need to allow the UNC tactical freedom. There was no problem about increasing South Korean forces, but he had reservations about Japan, stressing the impact of Japanese rearmament on British public opinion and, as later remarks revealed, on the Soviets. Acheson replied that there was no intention of employing Japanese troops in Korea, which Morrison replied greatly improved the situation from his point of view. He raised no problem about bombing the Yalu power stations but pointed out the difficulties involved for Britain in sending more troops to Korea. Morrison was clearly reluctant to endorse economic sanctions even when Acheson emphasized that the United States did not envisage a naval blockade.

D. Acheson, *Present at the Creation* (London, 1970); R. Foot, *The Wrong War* (Ithaca, N.Y., 1985); C. A. MacDonald, *Korea: The War Before Vietnam* (London, 1986).

Callum A. MacDonald

ACHESON'S NATIONAL PRESS CLUB SPEECH (January 12, 1950)

In this speech, Secretary of State Dean G. Acheson* sought to refute Republican charges that the Truman administration had not done enough to prevent the Communist takeover in China during 1949. In addition, since the summer of 1949, Congress had been reluctant to approve the Korean Aid Bill of 1949–1950*, and he wanted to build enough support for authorization. With U.S. aid, Acheson claimed, South Korea had "a very good chance" for successful resistance to Communist expansion. But he refused to pledge U.S. military protection for the Republic of Korea* because it was outside the "defensive perimeter" of the United States. In the event of open aggression beyond Japan, the Ryukyus, and the Philippines, "the initial reliance must be on the people attacked to resist it and then upon . . . the United Nations which so far has not proved a weak reed to lean on by any people who are determined to protect their independence." After the outbreak of the Korean War, critics blamed Acheson for the North Korean invasion of South Korea*, alleging that his National Press Club speech constituted a green light for the attack, since he implied the United States would not act to prevent Communist military conquest of South Korea.

While the impact of Acheson's speech on North Korea is a speculative matter, prior emphasis on this portion of the address has obscured its real significance as a definitive statement of U.S. policy objectives and expectations in Asia. For Acheson, the Soviet-inspired Communist military threat was not as immediate as the challenge of subversion and penetration. Since communism thrived on social upheaval and economic dislocation, Asian nations could best withstand Communist political pressure by developing strong democratic institutions and stable economies. The United States could contribute to political and economic stability in Asia through providing economic aid, technical knowledge, and administrative advice. To substantiate his argument, he pointed to China, explaining that Chiang Kai-shek* had failed to satisfy popular needs and wants, causing the Chinese people to "brush him aside." By contrast, the South Koreans not only wanted American help but would use it effectively. Acheson based his assessment on the key assumption that South Korea would not face open armed aggression. His National Press Club speech sought to persuade the American people that despite the fall of China, local strength and self-reliance would preserve stability in Korea and elsewhere in Asia beyond the defensive perimeter.

D. Acheson, *Present at the Creation* (New York, 1969); J. I. Matray, *The Reluctant Crusade* (Honolulu, 1985); D. Rees, *Korea: The Limited War* (New York, 1964).

ACTIVE DEFENSE STRATEGY

In November 1951, active defense became the foundation for the military strategy of the UNC* in the Korean War. This was the result of an agreement on agenda item 2*, establishment of a demarcation line and demilitarized zone, at the P'anmunjŏm truce talks*. After the truce talks resumption on October 25, 1951*, the negotiators accepted the existing line of battle, or main line of resistance (MLR), as the final demarcation line for a DMZ on the condition that there would be a truce agreement signed within thirty days. On November 12, CINCUNC General Matthew B. Ridgway* therefore sent a new directive to General James A. Van Fleet*, commander of the 8th Army*, instructing him that once there was agreement at P'anmunjŏm on the location of the MLR, he was not to undertake any major ground offensives during the next month since this would not alter the cease-fire line. Rather, he was to limit the size of operations to no more than one division and restrict the scope to capturing outposts in terrain suitable for temporary instead of permanent defense. At the same time, Van Fleet's forces were to inflict maximum casualties on the enemy while the UNC increased air and sea attacks on North Korea. On November 13, the JCS approved implementation of Ridgway's new strategy.

During the last weeks of 1951, a pattern emerged of patrolling and small-scale fighting with the UN forces merely reacting to enemy contacts. Van Fleet tried to limit unnecessary casualties, ordering counterattacks only to regain lost territory. Press reports began to appear in American newspapers that the United States was observing a de facto cease-fire. This was an embarrassment for President Harry S. Truman*, who knew that this would make it much more difficult to resume fighting when the thirty-day period ended. He therefore issued a statement denying that the UNC had ordered a halt to fighting in Korea while condemning the press for "issuing false reports." Nevertheless, active defense in essence became the UNC's strategy for the balance of the conflict as Korea developed into a monotonous war of position and attrition. This was the case because when the thirty-day time limit expired on December 27, the UNC had not formulated plans for offensive operations. The existing MLR was strong and easy to defend, while the costs of forward movement seemed to outweigh the benefits. As the wartime priority shifted to pursuit of an early cease-fire, the Korean War soon resembled World War I, with a static battlefield and armies depending on barbed wire, trenches, artillery, and mortars. Both sides emphasized the achievement and maintenance of defense in depth, increasing troops, and stockpiling equipment behind the front line.

Some U.S. Air Force officers, such as the FEAF commander, Lieutenant General Otto P. Weyland*, supported the active defense strategy, arguing that moving the MLR northward would reduce the size of the enemy territory and make air assaults more difficult. By contrast, Van Fleet strongly opposed fighting a military stalemate that consisted almost exclusively of routine patrols, probing actions, and occasional forays against enemy positions. He developed and proposed many plans for offensive action, but Ridgway and the JCS rejected all of them. Van Fleet became increasingly frustrated, eventually arguing his case to newsmen. An angry Ridgway then reprimanded Van Fleet, delivering a stern reminder that such public criticism was a "function entirely outside" his "field of responsibility." In addition, it undermined the purpose of active defense, which was to maintain pressure on the enemy. Critics at the time charged that the active defense strategy unnecessarily lengthened the war because it allowed the Communists to build permanent defenses in North Korea and thus prolong the armistice negotiations. While Ridgway disagreed, his successor, General Mark W. Clark*, shared these views but was unable to persuade the Eisenhower administration to abandon the strategy.

C. Blair, *The Forgotten War* (New York, 1987); J. L. Collins, *War in Peacetime* (Boston, 1969); W. G. Hermes, *Truce Tent and Fighting Front* (Washington, D.C., 1966); B. I. Kaufman, *The Korean War* (Philadelphia, 1986); M. B. Ridgway, *The Korean War* (Garden City, N.Y., 1967).

ADVANCE COMMAND AND LIAISON GROUP IN KOREA
See Church Survey Mission

AGENDA CONTROVERSY (July 1951)

When the Communist and the UNC* delegations met for the first time at Kaesŏng, just north of Seoul, on July 10, 1951, each presented a different version of the agenda for the truce talks, creating the first of a series of controversies requiring compromise and delaying an end to the war. Vice-Admiral C. Turner Joy*, the chief UNC delegate, asked the other side to agree to his proposal that discussions be confined purely to military matters related to Korea and presented a draft agenda:

1, Adoption of agenda; 2, Location of, and authority for representatives of the International Red Cross to visit prisoner of war camps; 3, Limitation of discussions at this and all subsequent meetings to purely military matters related only to Korea; 4, Cessation of hostilities and of acts of armed force in Korea under conditions which would assure against resumption of hostilities and acts of armed force in Korea; 5, Agreement on a demilitarized zone across Korea; 6, Composition, authority, and functions of a Military Armistice Commission*; 7, Agreement on the principle of inspection within Korea by military observer teams, functioning under a Military Armistice Commission; 8, Composition and functions of these teams; 9, Arrangements pertaining to prisoners of war.

After a recess of three and a half hours, the Communist delegation submitted its version of an agenda:

1, Adoption of agenda; 2, Establishment of the 38th parallel as the military demarcation line . . . and cessation of hostilities in Korea; 3, Withdrawal of all armed forces of foreign countries from Korea; 4, Concrete arrangements for the realization of a cease-fire and armistice in Korea; 5, Arrangements relating to prisoners of war following the armistice.

Both sides spent the rest of the first meeting arguing whether the withdrawal of foreign troops from Korea would be a precondition for negotiations and the thirty-eighth parallel would be a line of demarcation for a cease-fire.

At a meeting on July 16, Admiral Joy presented a revised UNC agenda:

1, Adoption of agenda; 2, Establishment of a demilitarized zone as a basic condition for the cessation of hostilities in Korea; 3, Concrete arrangements for a ceasefire and armistice in Korea . . . ; 4, Arrangement relating to prisoners of war.

But the stumbling block of foreign troop withdrawal prevented its immediate adoption. On July 24, *Radio P'yŏngyang* broadcast the Communist demand for withdrawal of foreign troops as a precondition for a cease-fire. Secretary of Defense George C. Marshall* reiterated the U.S. position that the withdrawal issue was not one to be negotiated in the field; however, he hinted that the issue would pose no problem if the Communists were sincere in settling the conflict in Korea. Quite possibly impressed by Marshall's apparent eagerness to discuss substantive matters, Lieutenant General Nam Il* of the Democratic People's Republic of Korea*, the chief Communist delegate, proposed to add a fifth item—''Recommendation to the Governments of both sides'' calling for a post-armistice conference to negotiate the withdrawal question.

At the tenth session on July 26, the two sides formally approved five agenda items:

1. Adoption of agenda. 2. Fixing a military demarcation line, between both sides so as to establish a demilitarized zone as a basic condition for a cessation of hostilities in Korea*. 3. Concrete arrangements for the realization of a cease-fire and an armistice in Korea, including the composition, authority, and functions of a supervising organization for carrying out the terms of a cease-fire and armistice*. 4. Arrangements relating to prisoners of war*. 5. Recommendations to the governments of countries concerned on both sides*.

The brief clash over the agenda provided little warning that the negotiators had started down what would be a tortuous road to the end of fighting in Korea.

J. L. Collins, *War in Peacetime* (Boston, 1969); W. G. Hermes, *Truce Tent and Fighting Front* (Washington, D.C., 1966); M. B. Ridgway, *The Korean War* (Garden City, N.Y., 1967).

Chang-il Ohn

AGENDA ITEM 1: ADOPTION OF AGENDA
See Agenda Controversy

AGENDA ITEM 2: DEMARCATION LINE AND DEMILITARIZED ZONE

On July 28, 1951, the UNC* delegation at the Kaesŏng truce talks* proposed a DMZ of 20 miles in depth with the current line of battle as a demarcation line. The Communists flatly rejected the proposal and accused the delegation of arrogance and the lack of good faith. They instead presented reasons favoring the thirty-eighth parallel as the military demarcation line. These positions appeared too divergent to permit reconciliation. Unable to draw UN consent for the thirty-eighth parallel, the Communists unilaterally called off the meeting on August 23, 1951, under the pretext of an alleged UN bombing violation, based on clumsily fabricated evidence, of the neutral meeting place. Another formal meeting was not held for over two months until the two delegations met at P'anmunjŏm, a tiny village about 6 miles east of Kaesŏng, on October 25, 1951.

Although their version of the DMZ was substantially different from the one the UNC suggested, the Communists gradually abandoned their insistence on the thirty-eighth parallel for the demarcation line, but according to the Communist compromise plan, UN forces still would give up most of their holdings above the parallel. The UN delegation flatly rejected the proposal. At this point, the Communists proposed a 2-kilometer-wide DMZ on either side of their version of the existing line of contact. Washington, closely monitoring the P'anmunjŏm truce talks*, was growing impatient and applied pressure for obtaining a tangible result. The JCS formally ordered CINCUNC General Matthew B. Ridgway* to settle the issue as early as possible on the basis of the actual line of contact, suggesting a time limit of one month. If both sides could not sign an armistice within thirty days, the UN proposal suggested, the line should be provisional and subject to revision based on the combat actions.

So instructed, the UNC delegation made this proposal to the Communist side on November 17, 1951. The Communists did not accept the proposal in its entirety. Insisting that the line, once agreed, must not be revised even after the specified period, they asked time to study the proposal carefully. After tangled back-and-forth arguments, the subdelegations agreed on November 25 to a specific line of contact. Two days later, both parties accepted the principle that the battleline would be the demarcation line with a DMZ of 4 kilometers for the one-month period. The provisional demarcation line would become a real one if both sides signed the armistice within thirty days. If they did not, this line would be subject to revision. Since neither side raised the questions about the period of grace even after it was over, this provisional line and zone became a de facto demarcation line and zone, which became final with slight change at the last stage of the fighting. *See also* Truce Talks Resumption of October 25, 1951, Truce Talks Suspension of August 23, 1951.

Foreign Relations of the United States, 1951, vol. 7: *Korea and China* (Washington, D.C., 1983); W. G. Hermes, *Truce Tent and Fighting Front* (Washington, D.C., 1966); W. S. Poole, *History of the Joint Chiefs of Staff*, vol. 4: *The Joint Chiefs of Staff and National Policy, 1950–1952* (Wilmington, 1979).

Chang-il Ohn

AGENDA ITEM 3: CEASE-FIRE ARRANGEMENTS AND INSPECTION PROVISIONS

On November 27, 1951, negotiators at the P'anmunjŏm truce talks* began discussing the third agenda item calling for "Concrete arrangements for the realization of a cease-fire and an armistice in Korea including composition, authority, and functions of a supervising organization." In its initial proposal, the UNC* delegation outlined firm measures to guard against any military buildup on the peninsula after the armistice. It called for the creation of a Military Armistice Commission* (MAC) and a supervisory body with "free access to all parts of Korea" for observation and inspection to ensure respect for the cease-fire. In accordance with plans developed the prior August, the UNC proposal would permit only one-for-one replacement of men and worn-out equipment, while placing limits on rehabilitation of airfields, thus maintaining the UNC's predominance in airpower. Lieutenant General Nam Il*, the chief of the Communist delegation, countered with a five-point plan that was less restrictive, although it did support the idea of a MAC. When the armistice was signed, there would be a cease-fire and, three days later, withdrawal of all armed forces from the DMZ. Within five days, the UNC would evacuate coastal islands north of the demarcation line, and all foreign troops would withdraw. The Communist delegation rejected the proposal for troop rotation and replacement, while denouncing the concept of supervision as "a brazen interference in the internal affairs" of North Korea. In addition, Nam Il objected to the prohibition on airfield improvements, dismissing the UNC's argument that this was necessary for preserving the cease-fire.

On December 3, Nam Il presented a new proposal that appeared to break the deadlock. His plan called for no increase by either side of military forces, supplies, equipment, or facilities following the armistice and the establishment of a supervisory body comprised of neutral nations to inspect mutually agreed upon ports of entry and to report its findings to the MAC. Since this proposal acknowledged the necessity for inspections and limits on augmentation of military capabilities, the UNC recommended referral of the plan to the subdelegates to negotiate the details. In subsequent bargaining, the UNC dropped its demand to retain coastal islands north of the demarcation line but insisted that the MAC would supervise both the neutral supervisory group conducting inspections outside the DMZ and joint inspection teams executing the armistice provisions within the DMZ. Both sides would have to agree on members of the supervisory body, which would have the right of aerial observation and photoreconnaissance when conducting inspections. Although CINCUNC General Matthew B. Ridgway* strenuously opposed compromise, Washington instructed the UNC delegation to drop its demand for aerial reconnaissance and, on January 27, 1952, to shelve the airfield rehabilitation issue. As a substitute for stronger inspection provisions, the United States planned to issue with its allies a Joint Policy (Greater Sanctions) statement* threatening to retaliate against the People's Republic of China* if it violated the cease-fire.

During February 1952, the negotiators engaged in genuine bargaining, for the most part resolving agenda item 3. There would be a ceiling of 35,000 on monthly rotation of troops, splitting the difference between the UNC demand for 75,000 and the Communist proposal of 5,000. Compromising as well on the UNC's desire for twelve and the Communist insistence on three, troop movement would occur through five ports of entry on each side (in the north, Sinŭiju, Sinanju, Manp'ojin, Chŏngjin, and Hŭngnam and in the south, Pusan, Inch'ŏn, Kunsan, Kangnŭng, and Taegu). After the Communists dropped their demand for unanimity on the Neutral Nations Supervisory Commission* (NNSC), the negotiators decided not to restrict the items eligible for inspection. A serious dispute then emerged when the Communist delegation proposed the Soviet Union as a member of the NNSC, as the UNC rejected the claim that the Soviet Union was neutral. U.S. leaders soon concluded that the Communists were attempting to use Moscow's candidacy as leverage with respect to the airfield rehabilitation controversy*. On April 25, the negotiators met in plenary session after sixty subdelegation meetings and over seventy at the staff officer level regarding agenda item 3. The UNC delegation submitted its package proposal*, which resulted in the Communist delegation's dropping its demand for Soviet membership on the NNSC in return for the absence of limits on airfield rehabilitation. With agreement on agenda item 3, only agenda item 4, repatriation of POWs, remained as a barrier to the achievement of a truce agreement. *See also* NSC-95.

J. L. Collins, *War in Peacetime* (Boston, 1969); W. G. Hermes, *Truce Tent and Fighting Front* (Washington, D.C., 1966); B. I. Kaufman, *The Korean War* (Philadelphia, 1986); D. Rees, *Korea: The Limited War* (New York, 1964); J. F. Schnabel and R. J. Watson, *History of the Joint Chiefs of Staff*, vol. 3: *The Korean War* (Wilmington, 1979).

AGENDA ITEM 4: PRISONER OF WAR REPATRIATION

The most controversial issue at the P'anmunjŏm truce talks* was agenda item 4: the question of how to deal with POWs when the armistice was achieved. Initially it was proposed in late spring 1951 by the UNC* under Vice-Admiral C. Turner Joy* that there be an agreement to discuss permission for Red Cross representatives to visit POW camps as a prelude to deliberation on their release plus an agreement on the principle of supervisory inspection teams. By November

27, 1951, the Red Cross issue was dropped, and a "little armistice" on other agenda items achieved. For the next twenty months, the POW issue remained the most bitterly contested obstacle to a conclusive peace settlement.

Behind all the camouflage of item 4 at P'anmunjŏm was the UNC demand for voluntary repatriation*—that no prisoner from either side should be forced to return to his own country against his wishes—as opposed to the Communist concept of forced repatriation, championed by the chief of the Communist delegation, Lieutenant General Nam Il*. At the first subdelegate meeting on December 11, 1951, both sides, as previously agreed, produced lists of prisoners, and one-for-one exchange to begin effective January 2, 1952, was proposed. All prisoners would be subject to an interview (screening), which was of primary concern to both sides. When this proposal was refused by the Communists, who charged that UNC POW administration* precluded a free choice, the issue settled into a debate over the UNC conception and definition of voluntary repatriation versus the Communist forced repatriation, as well as the screening of repatriated prisoners and how to deal fairly with the non-repatriated.

By May 1952, negotiators reached a deadlock on the issue. On September 28, Joy's replacement, Major General William K. Harrison, Jr.*, proposed (1) that all non-repatriated prisoners, after identification in the DMZ, be given the right to return to their captors if desired; (2) that all non-repatriated prisoners be interviewed by a neutral representative in the zone and be free to go to the side of choice; or (3) that all non-repatriates be placed in the DMZ without any screening and be able to go to the side of their own choice. After this was rejected by the Communists, the United States reluctantly accepted the V. K. Krishna Menon* POW settlement proposal*, which suggested that a Neutral Nations Repatriation Commission* (NNRC) be established to deal with non-repatriates and the issue of screening them. Considerable debate followed in the UN, and finally in late November its First Committee proposed a compromise amendment to the resolution. A workable commission would be set up, and it was reaffirmed that three months after the armistice was signed, the repatriation procedure would end. In addition, it was stated that provisions for remaining prisoners would be determined by either the political conference provided for under agenda item 5* or the UN. Although approved by the United States, the amended Menon proposal was soundly rejected by the Chinese and North Koreans on December 13, 1952.

A break seemingly came in February 1953 when CINCUNC General Mark W. Clark* proposed that each side participate in an exchange of sick and wounded prisoners. Surprisingly, the Communists agreed, and Operation Little Switch* went into effect in April. Although a worthwhile proposal, it did not address the main issues in the debate: the concept of screening, the issue of non-repatriated prisoners, and the government's right to convince them, within a specified time frame, to return home. It did pave the way for the truce talks resumption of April 26, 1953*. In May 1953 Nam Il proposed that all non-repatriated prisoners be sent to a neutral state outside Korea within three months of the truce with the provision that the governments would have six months to convince the prisoners to return home. This was refused by the UNC. Finally, after four neutral commission states were accepted by the Communists, the UNC proposed that Korean prisoners be released to civilian status but that Chinese non-repatriates be turned over to the NNRC. After sixty days, these non-repatriates would be granted civilian status and freedom. This too was rejected by the Communists.

Exasperated by the Communist rejection and the interference of South Korean leader Syngman Rhee* at this critical juncture, Clark submitted the UNC final POW settlement proposal of May 25, 1953*, prefacing it with the ultimatum that the Communists accept or face the risk that the United States would broaden the war effort, implying that this would include a resort to nuclear means. Under these provisions, all prisoners would be transferred to the NNRC, there would be a sixty-day period for repatriation with a ninety-day period after that to be used as an "explaining" time for non-repatriates either to become citizens or to be referred to the UN. On June 4, 1953, the Communists accepted the plan, and the Terms of Reference for Neutral Nations Repatriation Commission were drawn up with the additional provisions that after 120 days in custody of the NNRC, all non-repatriates would become civilians and that no prisoner would be held more than six months after the truce. Four days later, the agreement was approved settling agenda item 4, and on July 27, 1953, the armistice agreement* was signed. Repatriation would then begin that fall under the terms agreed. *See also* Chou En-lai POW Settlement Proposal; Dulles's Atomic Warning to China; Geneva Convention of 1949; NSC–147; Operation Scatter; POW Transfer Location Question; POW Unilateral Release Proposal.

D. Acheson, *Present at the Creation* (New York, 1969); *Foreign Relations of the United States, 1951,* vol. 7: *Korea and China* (Washington, D.C., 1983); C. T. Joy, *How Communists Negotiate* (New York, 1955); H. S. Truman, *Years of Trial and Hope* (Garden City, N.Y., 1956); W. H. Vatcher, *Panmunjom: The Story of the Korean Military Armistice Negotiations* (New York, 1958).

Kathleen F. Kellner

AGENDA ITEM 5: REFERRAL OF POLITICAL QUESTIONS

This item was added to the agenda at the request of the Communists. In the course of the agenda controversy*, the Communists had urged including the item that called for "withdrawal of all armed forces of foreign countries from Korea," whereas the UNC* delegation had stood firm in its position that the withdrawal issue was not a proper military topic when negotiating a cease-fire. Unable to alter the UN stand, the Communists proposed a constructive approach toward agreement on the agenda by suggesting a fifth item: recommendation to the governments of both sides to call for a political conference by the nations involved in the conflict within a specified time limit after an armistice to negotiate the withdrawal question. With the approval of Washington, the UNC delegation accepted the Communist proposal, which became agenda item 5.

By early 1952, stalemate had emerged not only on the battle front but also at the negotiating table. At this juncture, CINCUNC General Matthew B. Ridgway*, to break the deadlock, proposed to the JCS on January 22, 1952, that should there be no progress within a few days, he would recommend beginning discussion of item 5. This measure appeared to be the only way short of ultimatum to expedite the negotiating process. Washington approved the suggestion, and the UNC made its proposal on January 31, receiving Communist approval the same day. Discussion on item 5 began February 5 and produced results in a comparatively short time. After exchanging several proposals and counterproposals, the UNC delegation finally accepted a revised version of the Communist plan submitted on February 16, 1952. The agreed provision recommended that the governments of the countries involved hold a political conference within three months after the armistice in order to negotiate "the questions of the withdrawal of all foreign forces from Korea, the peaceful settlement of the Korean question, etc." Further, the chief Communist delegate clarified that "foreign forces" meant "non-Korean forces," and that "etc." did not apply to any matters outside Korea. The UNC delegates then suggested that the agreement and clarification be made one article of the armistice agreement*. This breakthrough on item 5 contributed importantly to hastening the negotiating process. *See also* Geneva Conference of 1954; NSC–157/1.

J. L. Collins, *War in Peacetime* (Boston, 1969); *Foreign Relations of the United States, 1952–1954,* vol. 15: *Korea* (Washington, D.C., 1984); W. G. Hermes, *Truce Tent and Fighting Front* (Washington, D.C., 1966); W. S. Poole, *History of the Joint Chiefs of Staff* vol. 4: *The Joint Chiefs of Staff and National Policy, 1950–1952* (Wilmington, 1979).

Chang-il Ohn

AGREEMENT ON ECONOMIC COORDINATION
See Meyer Mission

AIR PRESSURE STRATEGY
Air pressure strategy was developed during the spring of 1952 in an attempt to find an independent role for air power, which U.S. Air Force planners thought had been tied for too long to supporting ground forces. The aim was to bring decisive pressure to bear on the Communists at the P'anmunjŏm truce talks* by attacking North Korean targets of economic importance to the Soviet Union and the People's Republic of China*, thus raising to an unacceptable level the costs of continuing the war. This meant bombing installations along the Yalu and Tumen rivers, such as the Suiho power plant, previously untouched for political reasons. It also encompassed attacking targets of political importance to North Korea to undermine enemy morale and increase the demands of the North Koreans on their Communist allies.

By May 1952, the talks had stalled on the POW issue, agenda item 4*, and CINCUNC General Mark W. Clark* seized upon "air pressure" as a means of hitting the enemy without incurring the large casualties involved in ground offensives. The campaign opened with the great raids on Suiho and the rest of the North Korean hydroelectric system in June 1952. Other targets included Aoji and Hoeryŏng on the Soviet border and the monzanite mines, which provided ore for the Soviet atomic bomb program. Mass air strikes were also launched against the Democratic People's Republic of Korea's* capital, P'yŏngyang, on July 11, and August 27, 1952, using napalm as well as high explosives. The second of these attacks, timed to coincide with a visit by Mao Tse-tung* to Moscow, was the biggest air raid of the Korean War.

Clark, meanwhile, was opposed to a possible compromise at P'anmunjŏm in the belief that air pressure would soon force the enemy to accept UN terms. Despite the raids, however, the Communist position remained inflexible, and the UNC* indefinitely suspended the talks on October 8, 1952, an event that coincided with the exhaustion of air pressure targets in North Korea. The following spring, FEAF planners came up with a new target system—the dams that supplied water for rice cultivation. The first attacks on this complex took place in May 1953, and the FEAF regarded the compromise that emerged at P'anmunjŏm shortly afterward as a vindication of air pressure strategy. In fact, the breakthrough owed more to political factors than to bombing. By June 1953 the air pressure campaign had reached stalemate, and planners were contemplating the next possible step, the employment of tactical atomic weapons on targets in Manchuria. *See also* Dam Raids of 1953; Suiho Bombing Operation; Truce Talks Suspension of October 8, 1952.

M. W. Cagle and F. A. Manson, *The Sea War in Korea* (New York, 1980); M. W. Clark, *From the Danube to the Yalu* (London, 1954); R. F. Futrell, *The United States Air Force in Korea* (New York, 1961); C. A. MacDonald, *Korea: The War Before Vietnam* (London, 1986).

Callum A. MacDonald

AIRFIELD REHABILITATION CONTROVERSY

This was a central issue in negotiations regarding agenda item 3*, "Concrete arrangements for the realization of cease-fire and armistice in Korea, including the composition, authority, and functions of a supervising organization for carrying out the terms of a cease-fire and armistice." CINCUNC General Matthew B. Ridgway* advocated formation of a joint ground, aerial, and photoreconnaissance team for all Korea, including a more complete joint observation team in the DMZ in order to inspect how the truce terms were implemented. Problems included how far the Communists would be allowed to increase their military capability by rebuilding airfields, railroads, and roads and how effectively a joint inspection team could perform its mission in North and South Korea.

While the UNC* delegation tried to limit rehabilitation of military facilities, the Communists desired no restriction. Washington planners in fact excluded airfields from the list of military facilities that could be rehabilitated after the armistice. President Harry S. Truman*, however, expressed doubt about the wisdom of allowing the Communists to rehabilitate military facilities other than airfields. By contrast, Secretary of State Dean G. Acheson* and his associates argued that it would be impractical and impossible to prevent the rehabilitation of military facilities other than airfields in North Korea. Furthermore, they argued that any such prohibition would work both ways and thereby prevent needed rehabilitation in South Korea. President Truman was persuaded, authorizing the UNC delegation to oppose airfield rehabilitation alone.

The Communists interpreted the UN insistence on prohibition of airfield rehabilitation as a clear interference in their internal affairs, castigating this position as "a clear infringement of other's sovereign rights." The UNC delegation countered that the Communist intention to develop military airfields indicated the lack of interest in achieving peace in Korea. As the talks continued without any sign of progress, the incompatibility of the two positions on the issue sometimes touched off emotional tirades during early 1952. However, the UNC delegation attempted with its package proposal* to use its position on the airfield rehabilitation issue to obtain Communist concessions on the composition of the Neutral Nations Supervisory Commission* (NNSC) and agenda item 4*, the POW issue. On May 2, 1952, the Communists formally abandoned their insistence on Soviet membership on the NNSC for the UN compromise on airfield rehabilitation. Then the only remaining obstacle to a truce was the principle of forced versus voluntary repatriation* of war prisoners.

Foreign Relations of the United States, 1951, vol. 7: *Korea and China* (Washington, D.C., 1983) and *1952–1954*, vol. 15: *Korea* (Washington, D.C., 1984); W. G. Hermes, *Truce Tent and Fighting Front* (Washington, D.C., 1966).

Chang-il Ohn

ALEMÁN PLAN
See Mexican POW Settlement Proposal

ALEXANDER-LLOYD MISSION OF JUNE 1952
Britain dispatched Minister of Defense Lord Alexander and Minister of State for Foreign Affairs John Selwyn Lloyd* to Tokyo and Korea in June 1952 to reassure the British public that it was able to restrain U.S. military operations in Korea and avoid widening the war. The prior month, the UNC* had sent Commonwealth units to help suppress the Kŏje-do POW uprising* without obtaining British approval. In addition, rumors spread about the rising influence of Chiang Kai-shek* over U.S. policy toward China, while the P'anmunjŏm truce talks* remained deadlocked. Arriving in the Republic of Korea* in the midst of the South Korean political crisis of 1952*, Lloyd was critical of President Syngman Rhee's* declaration of martial law*. He thought it was necessary for the United States to implement strong measures for the restoration of political freedom. Lloyd also visited the POW compounds for non-repatriates and talked with camp administrators, publicly expressing concern over the existence of strong anti-Communist organization behind the gates. He was shocked to find that beatings and intimidation occurred each night. Nevertheless, Lloyd voiced satisfaction with the rescreening of POWs* then underway and thereby avoided a confrontation over this sensitive issue.

In Tokyo, Alexander and Lloyd held talks with CINCUNC General Mark W.

Clark* and raised the possibility of placing a British representative on his staff for the purpose of influencing policy formulation and keeping London informed of developments. Also, they proposed that Great Britain have a representative on the UNC delegation at P'anmunjŏm. Clark refused to alter the composition of the armistice negotiating team, explaining that to do so "would only be an indication of weakness and indecision to the Communists." It also would prompt other nations with troops in Korea to demand similar representation. However, he did agree to add a deputy chief to his staff. For the United States, this was a meaningful step toward restoring public faith in the Anglo-American alliance since General Matthew B. Ridgway*, Clark's predecessor, had opposed the change. On July 1, 1952, Prime Minister Winston Churchill* announced that he had selected Major General Stephen N. Shoosmith to serve on Clark's staff. He emphasized, however, that the British officer would serve in a normal staff capacity rather than as a liaison, providing the same information made available in the past. Thus, the Alexander-Lloyd mission successfully achieved its objective of relieving domestic political pressure on the Conservatives.

M. W. Clark, *From the Danube to the Yalu* (New York, 1954); *Foreign Relations of the United States, 1952–1954,* vol. 15: *Korea* (Washington, 1984); W. G. Hermes, *Truce Tent and Fighting Front* (Washington, D.C., 1966); C. A. MacDonald, *Korea: The War Before Vietnam* (New York, 1986); J. F. Schnabel and R. J. Watson, *History of the Joint Chiefs of Staff,* vol. 3: *The Korean War* (Wilmington, 1979).

ALLISON, JOHN M. (1905–1978)

John Moore Allison participated extensively in U.S. policymaking toward Korea both before and during the war as chief, State Department Division of Northeast Asian Affairs (1947–1950); special assistant to John Foster Dulles* (1950–1951); and assistant secretary of state for Far Eastern affairs (1952–1953). Born in Holton, Kansas, he taught English in Japan after graduating from the University of Nebraska in 1927. Allison began his diplomatic career in 1930 in the U.S. consulate in Shanghai and held a variety of posts in China and Japan before U.S. entry into World War II. Stationed in London during the war, he returned to Washington in 1947.

That same year, the Truman administration adopted Allison's recommendation for handling the impasse between the United States and Soviet Union over the trusteeship issue. In keeping with this plan, SWNCC 176/30*, the United States turned the Korean question over to the United Nations after the Soviets rejected the final U.S. proposal. With the United States and Soviets unable to reach an agreement and the Truman administration seeking to minimize its commitment to Korea, the passage of the UN resolution of November 14, 1947*, paved the way for the emergence of two separate states on the peninsula.

At the time of the North Korean invasion of South Korea*, Allison was in Japan assisting Dulles in the Japanese Peace Treaty* negotiations. After learning of the attack, both men sent a telegram to Washington urging the use of U.S. forces if South Korea were about to be overrun. On returning to Washington in the summer of 1950, Allison figured prominently in the State Department's internal debate over the question of crossing the thirty-eighth parallel. As a leader of the group favoring the continuation of military operations above the line, Allison argued forcefully that there could be no lasting peace as long as the peninsula was divided. With the completion of the Japanese Peace Treaty in September 1951, Allison became acting assistant secretary for Far Eastern affairs and then assistant secretary in February 1952. From 1953 to 1957, he served as ambassador to Japan. In 1960, after appointments as ambassador to Indonesia and Czechoslovakia, he retired to Honolulu and taught at the University of Hawaii.

J. M. Allison, *Ambassador from the Prairie* (Boston, 1973); R. J. Donovan, *Tumultuous Years* (New York, 1982); W. W. Stueck, *The Road to Confrontation* (Chapel Hill, 1981).

Marc Gallicchio

ALMOND, EDWARD M. (1892–1979)

When the Korean War began, Major General Edward M. Almond was chief of staff for CINCFE General Douglas MacArthur*, making him the second most important man in the U.S. occupation of Japan. Later he commanded the X Corps* that spearheaded the Inch'ŏn landing*. Born in Luray, Virginia, he graduated from Virginia Military Institute in 1915 and the following year received his commission as a U.S. Army second lieutenant. During World War I, Almond fought in the Aisne-Marne and Meuse-Argonne campaigns as the commander of a machine gun battalion. In 1919, he left occupation duty with the 4th Division in Germany to become a professor of military science and tactics at Marion Institute in Alabama. Thereafter, Almond graduated from Infantry School (1924) and Command and General Staff School (1928), assuming command of a Philippine army battalion in 1930. Almond was at the Army War College in 1933, with the War Department General Staff in 1934, and subsequently graduated from the Air Corps Tactical School (1939) and the Naval War College (1940). He then served with the VI Corps, becoming its chief of staff. After the outbreak of World War II, Almond gained promotion to brigadier general, receiving the difficult assignment of reorganizing the 92d Infantry, the only black division slated for commitment to combat. Amid close scrutiny in 1944 and 1945, Almond commanded the unit in Italy, transforming one diversionary operation into a successful offensive through Pisa and Genoa to the French border. But the 92d Infantry's performance failed to match expectations, resulting in the breakup of the unit and damaging the advancement of Almond's career.

In 1946, after a brief stint with the 2d Division, a still-ambitious Almond joined MacArthur's staff in Japan as assistant chief of staff for personnel. Three years later, he became chief of staff for the Far Eastern Command, remaining in that post until President Harry S. Truman's* recall of MacArthur* in April 1951. MacArthur, who disliked staff meetings and administrative matters, came to rely heavily on Almond to implement his directives. But aware of Almond's need to obtain combat experience to gain promotion, MacArthur appointed him in September 1950 as commander of the X Corps for the successful landing at

Inch'ŏn. Following the Wŏnsan landing*, Almond led his troops in the Chosin Reservoir Campaign*. Chinese military intervention* forced the UNC* to retreat from North Korea, and Almond earned a third star for his skillful direction of the Hŭngnam evacuation*, as the X Corps lost little equipment and suffered only light casualties. On December 26, the 8th Army* absorbed the X Corps, but Almond continued to serve as its commander until he returned to the United States in July 1951.

Almond was a controversial figure during the Korean War. One fellow officer labeled him "a brilliant human dynamo," but his own chief of staff admitted that Almond "could precipitate a crisis on a desert island with nobody else around." His relationship with Lieutenant General Walton W. Walker*, commander of the 8th Army, was always stormy. This situation became worse after the creation of the X Corps as a separate unit. While this action angered Walker, others questioned MacArthur's decision to place an army officer in command of the amphibious Inch'ŏn operation with a force that included the 1st Marine Division. But MacArthur wanted to reward Almond, who had been a loyal and efficient subordinate. Almond's service in Europe rather than the Pacific during World War II meant that he was unique in being able to penetrate MacArthur's inner circle of confidants and earn the general's complete confidence. Although often tactless and generally dictatorial, Almond was an effective and aggressive combat officer. His experiences in Korea persuaded him of the importance of tactical air support for success on the battlefield, as well as the value of helicopters. After leaving Korea in July 1951, he became commandant of the Army War College, remaining in this post until retirement in January 1953. He then worked for the Executive Life Insurance Company in Alabama in a public relations capacity and from 1961 to 1968 served as president of Virginia Military Institute.

C. Blair, *The Forgotten War* (New York, 1987); *Current Biography,* 1951; *National Cyclopedia of American Biography,* vol. 1: *1953–1959* (New York, 1960); *New York Times,* June 13, 1979; R. Spiller (ed.), *Dictionary of American Military Biography* (Westport, Conn., 1984).

AN HO-SANG (1902–   )

An was the first minister of education for the Republic of Korea* but resigned from the post one month before the outbreak of the Korean War. He participated in organizing Syngman Rhee's* Liberal party in 1952 and was active as president of the Taehan Youth Corps*. He also helped organize the campaign to press the National Assembly to revise the constitution so that Rhee could be reelected through a direct election by the population as president during the South Korean political crisis of 1952*. But after achieving his aims, Rhee purged the Jokchong (Yi Pŏm-sŏk's* faction) to which An belonged, as he had done before with the others. An was also active in a national campaign opposing the armistice toward the end of the Korean War.

Educated initially in Japan, China, and Germany, An completed his doctorate in philosophy at the University of Jena in 1929. After his return to Korea, he taught in different colleges and became the first president of the Korean Association of Philosophy in 1933. Involved in the anti-Japanese Chosŏn Ŏhakhoe 33-in sagŏn incident, he hid in the mountains to evade police arrest. To the end of the Japanese rule, he resisted pressures to collaborate and to change his name after the Japanese fashion, which many leading Koreans found hard to emulate.

After liberation, An worked for the U.S. military government mainly in matters of education and science. During this period, he was known as a major ideologue on the side of the right-wing nationalists. Although he has been out of government since 1950, he remains active in cultural fields in various capacities, espousing nationalist causes, which many regard as extreme.

An Ho-sang, *Minjok Chongnon* (Seoul, 1983); *Nara Yŏksa 6 Chŏn'yŏn* (Seoul, 1985).

J. Y. Ra

ANGLO-AMERICAN MILITARY AND POLITICAL CONSULTATIONS OF JULY 1950

The government of Prime Minister Clement R. Attlee* gave strong support to the UN Security Council resolutions of June 25* and June 27, 1950*, urging withdrawal of North Korean forces and assistance for the Republic of Korea*. The British immediately placed elements of their Far East fleet at the disposal of the U.S. Navy and committed a brigade-strength force to Korea's defense. Despite these gratifying manifestations of solidarity for UN-U.S. military operations, the United Kingdom was fearful of the possible strategic and economic implications of an extended Korean conflict. Struggling with desperate economic problems, the British Labour government resisted any diversion of U.S. financial aid and raw materials from European defense. British representatives therefore undertook an aggressive diplomatic campaign designed to reaffirm the primacy of the Anglo-American partnership and to limit or end hostilities in what was in their view a strategic backwater.

In early July, Sir David Kelly, British ambassador to the Soviet Union, discussed with Andrei A. Gromyko* a status quo ante basis for peaceful settlement of the conflict in Korea. At the same time, Prime Minister Attlee proposed talks covering the whole field of Anglo-American military and political cooperation. Air Marshal Lord Tedder and Oliver Franks*, Britain's ambassador in the United States, met with General Omar N. Bradley*, the JCS chairman, and Ambassador Philip C. Jessup*. Despite clear signals of Washington's unhappiness about British meddling, Foreign Minister Ernest Bevin* pressed for concessions (such as America's abandonment of Taiwan) to obtain Soviet endorsement of an immediate cease-fire. Bevin argued that the Soviets desired to restore the status quo ante but only if linked with modification of U.S. support for Chiang Kai-shek*. This reflected the British Foreign Office's support for the People's Republic of China's* entry into the United Nations.

Although the initial U.S. reaction to London's "unsolicited initiative" had been tolerant skepticism, Bevin's proposal produced a swift, stern rebuke. On

June 10, Secretary of State Dean G. Acheson*, with President Harry S. Truman's* approval, informed Bevin that the United States would not agree to a swap of Taiwan for Communist withdrawal north of the thirty-eighth parallel. While accepting the UN as a possible venue for discussion of Taiwan's status and settlement of the PRC UN representation question*, these issues had to be "considered on their merits" and not under circumstances of duress and blackmail. Bevin was warned of the serious implications for Anglo-American cooperation should the British persist in their current course.

The British got the message. With a final warning against forcing Peking into the Soviet camp, Bevin ceased mediation efforts in favor of discreet support for Indian peace initiatives*. The military conversations had no practical results but did apparently reassure Britain that the United States did not intend to widen the war or end the Anglo-American condominium for allocation of vital raw materials. Overall, the flurry of British diplomatic activity in July 1950 affirmed the basic unity of purpose of the two historic allies while establishing the groundwork for subsequent British efforts to achieve a negotiated settlement. *See also* British Peace Initiatives.

D. Acheson, *Present at the Creation* (New York, 1969); A. Bullock, *Ernest Bevin: Foreign Secretary, 1945–1951* (New York, 1983); W. W. Stueck, *The Road to Confrontation* (Chapel Hill, 1981).

Theodore A. Wilson

ANGLO-INDIAN FIVE POINT PLAN
See Rescreening of POWs

ANZUS (AUSTRALIA–NEW ZEALAND–UNITED STATES) TREATY
The ANZUS Treaty, signed in San Francisco on September 1, 1951, and taking effect in April 1952, reflected U.S. concern over deteriorating security conditions in Korea, and in East Asia generally, and was closely related to the simultaneous Japanese Peace Treaty*. The war in Korea, and particularly Chinese military intervention*, prompted U.S. policymakers to shorten their timetable for the revival of Japan, now seen as a potential bulwark against Chinese expansionism. Many of the nations of Asia, however, recently victims of Japanese aggression, looked with distrust on anything that might strengthen their erstwhile antagonist. To ease Australia's and New Zealand's fears in this regard, Washington offered a guarantee against a resurgent Japan, as well as against aggression from other quarters. At the same time, U.S. leaders hoped to trade a pledge of U.S. help in the southwestern Pacific for assistance from Australia and New Zealand in the Middle East in case trouble broke out there. Although all three members of ANZUS participated in the UN defense of South Korea, the treaty organization as such played no particular role. *See also* New Zealand and the Korean War.

G. St. J. Barclay, *Friends in High Places: Australian-American Diplomatic Relations since 1945* (Melbourne, 1985); R. G. Menzies, *The Measure of the Years* (London, 1970); R. J. O'Neill, *Australia in the Korean War 1950–53* (Canberra, 1981); P. C. Spender,

Exercises in Diplomacy (Sydney, 1969); J. G. Starke, *The ANZUS Treaty Alliance* (Melbourne, 1965).

                                                                    H. W. Brands

ARAB-ASIAN PEACE INITIATIVES

Mediation efforts on Korea by an Arab or Asian nation commenced in July 1950 when President Jawaharlal Nehru* of India approached the Soviet Union, the United States, and the People's Republic of China* with a proposal for a cease-fire on the peninsula. However, Arab-Asian peace initiatives are here defined as those that involved a simultaneous effort at the UN by several—at one time as many as thirteen—Arab and Asian delegations. Such efforts began in December 1950 and were never far below the surface for the rest of the war, playing a significant role in limiting and eventually ending the conflict. On some occasions, these Arab-Asian delegations could muster a sizable number of votes in the General Assembly, which at a minimum could prevent the United States from building a strong anti-Communist consensus behind its policies. At its peak, the group could combine with occasionally rebellious U.S. allies to threaten the U.S. majority altogether.

The group first came together in early December 1950 at the beckoning of Sir Benegal N. Rau*. As a result, the General Assembly passed the UN resolution of December 14, 1950*, calling for creation of a group of three members to "determine the basis on which a satisfactory ceasefire can be arranged." The initial efforts of this group—Iran's Nasrollah Entezam*, India's Rau, and Canada's Lester B. Pearson*—proved fruitless, as the Communist Chinese, buoyed by their military successes in Korea and signs of disarray in the enemy camp, rejected all overtures. Nonetheless, the UN Ceasefire Group* continued its efforts into the new year. As U.S. pressure increased for a resolution condemning the PRC as an aggressor and the Communist offensive in Korea bogged down in the central mountains south of the thirty-eighth parallel, Peking showed signs of interest. Under intense U.S. pressure, the Western allies and the bulk of the Arab-Asian group supported the UN resolution of February 1, 1951*, condemning the PRC as an aggressor, but they also delayed UN sanctions against China. When sanctions were finally implemented in May, they were limited to an embargo on strategic goods.

The other major Arab-Asian peace initiative came during the Seventh Session of the General Assembly in the fall of 1952. By this time, armistice talks had dragged along for over a year and had resolved all issues except agenda item 4*, repatriation of POWs. U.S. frustration over the Communist refusal to give way on this issue was so great that six days before the General Assembly convened, Washington was responsible for the truce talks suspension of October 8, 1952*. This action produced a flurry of mediation efforts, including discussion of the Mexican POW settlement proposal* and presentation of the Peruvian POW settlement proposal*, in addition to draft resolutions from the Arab-Asian delegations of Indonesia, India, and Iraq.

In early November, these activities began to center around V. K. Krishna Menon* of the Indian delegation. After intense and at times acrimonious negotiations in which Canadian and British diplomats served as intermediaries between Menon and Secretary of State Dean G. Acheson*, the United States finally agreed to give priority to the Menon POW settlement proposal* over its own twenty-one-power UN resolution*. In amended form, the Indian draft resolution passed the General Assembly as the UN resolution of December 3, 1952*, with the support of all but Soviet bloc delegations. Although in an immediate sense Communist opposition prevented the mediation effort from ending the fighting in Korea, the Indian resolution provided the framework for agreement on the POW issue during the following spring. When in the midst of a softening of the Communist line in the aftermath of Joseph Stalin's* death the United States adopted a position that went beyond the terms of the resolution, effective international pressure was quickly brought to bear on Washington to adjust its stance. *See also* NSC-95.

Foreign Relations of the United States, 1950, vol. 7: *Korea* (Washington, D.C., 1976), *1951*, vol. 7: *Korea and China* (Washington, D.C., 1983), and *1952–1954*, vol. 15: *Korea* (Washington, D.C., 1984); G. H. Jansen, *Non-Alignment and the Afro-Asian States* (New York, 1966).

William Stueck

ARMISTICE AGREEMENT (July 27, 1953)

The Korean Armistice Agreement of July 27, 1953, marked the end of negotiations for a cease-fire that had been underway for two years. Four issues figured centrally when representatives of the belligerent parties commenced the Kaesŏng truce talks* on July 10, 1951: the location of the cease-fire line, the composition of a supervisory commission, repatriation of POWs, and the procedure for transforming a truce into a permanent settlement. Although the talks started slowly, by the end of 1951, the two sides had located the line of demarcation near the thirty-eighth parallel and had agreed to supervision by a group of neutral nations. For the next eighteen months, the P'anmunjŏm truce talks* stuck on agenda item 4*, the repatriation question. The difficulty arose from the unwillingness of thousands of POWs held in South Korea to return to North Korea and China. The Communists adhered to the Geneva Convention of 1949*, which specified swift repatriation without reference to prisoners' wishes; the Americans insisted that the POWs have the opportunity, in essence, to defect.

A breakthrough awaited the January 1953 inauguration of the administration of Dwight D. Eisenhower*, which hinted at nuclear escalation if the talks failed, and the death of Joseph Stalin* the following March, whose successors indicated a desire to ease Soviet-U.S. tensions. Three weeks after Stalin's death, the North Koreans and Chinese accepted the principle of voluntary repatriation*, subject to neutral supervision. South Korean president Syngman Rhee*, deeming a cease-fire leaving Chinese troops in North Korea incompatible with his hope of reunifying the country, attempted to sabotage the arrangement in June 1953 by allowing the escape of 27,000 prisoners. But the Communists refused to be provoked, Rhee agreed to be persuaded, and the deal, which included a call for a political conference to seek a final and comprehensive settlement of the Korean questions, went through. The *Department of State Bulletin* of August 3, 1953, has the text of the accord. *See also* Armistice-Signing Procedures Controversy; Dulles's Atomic Warning to China; Geneva Conference of 1954; NSC-147; NSC-154/1; NSC-156/1; NSC-157/1; Rhee's Release of North Korean POWs; Robertson Mission.

A. E. Goodman (ed.), *Negotiating While Fighting: The Diary of Admiral C. Turner Joy at the Korean Armistice Conference* (Stanford, Calif., 1978); W. H. Vatcher, *Panmunjom: The Story of the Korean Military Armistice Negotiations* (New York, 1958).

H. W. Brands

ARMISTICE-SIGNING PROCEDURES CONTROVERSY

After completing work on the armistice agreement*, the two delegations at the P'anmunjŏm truce talks* had a final series of arguments in late July 1953 about how to sign and exchange the armistice documents. On July 24, 1953, the Communists insisted that if the top commanders were to sign the truce documents, newsmen from the Republic of Korea* and Taiwan should be barred from the ceremony. President Syngman Rhee*, who had prohibited the ROK's representative from attending the last sessions of the negotiation for cease-fire as a symbolic gesture of South Korean opposition to the armistice, did not desire to send a representative to P'anmunjŏm, solving one problem. But after careful scrutiny of the Communist demands, CINCUNC General Mark W. Clark* instructed Lieutenant General William K. Harrison, Jr.*, the chief UNC* delegate, that he would not take part in the signing ceremony unless all correspondents were allowed to attend. Instead, he told Harrison that he would have the documents flown to Tokyo and sign there. However, Washington informed Clark that President Dwight D. Eisenhower* "desired him to sign the armistice on the Korean soil," thus restoring the deadlock. Both sides eventually accepted a compromise regarding procedures. According to the plan, the senior delegates were to sign the armistice at P'anmunjŏm at 10 A.M. on July 27, 1953. After that, Clark was to sign the documents at his headquarters in Munsan, and Kim Il Sung* and Peng Teh-huai*, commander of the Chinese People's Volunteers Army*, would affix their signatures in Kaesŏng. A cease-fire would be effective at 10:00 P.M. that same day.

Even on trivial matters, both sides were obstinate. Since six of the eighteen copies of the armistice were to remain in the hands of the UNC, a UN staff officer suggested that the Communists take six copies to Kim and Peng while the UN delegates took the twelve copies intended for the Communist side to be signed by Clark. The Communist side rejected this proposal and insisted on complete equality to the end, arguing that each side would have nine copies for countersignature despite the fact that this method would require two exchanges of the documents. The UN delegation agreed to the Communist proposal. The UNC objected to the structure of the building housing the ceremony. In the original plan, the only door lay on the north side, which meant that the UN delegates would have to pass through the Communist sector in order to enter the building. The UN delegation insisted on the provision of a south entrance to the building. The south gate of the building was constructed, and the two Communist peace doves from the gables of the peace pagoda were removed.

Having resolved the seemingly simple matter of signing procedures, the stage was set for final action. It took only 12 minutes for the two chief delegates, General Harrison and Lieutenant General Nam Il*, to finish signing the armistice documents. At 10 A.M. on July 27, 1953, the two senior delegates entered the room and began to sign the documents in a ''businesslike manner.'' Cold silence was the order of the day. They signed eighteen copies of the armistice agreement and eighteen copies of the supplementary agreement—twelve each in English, Chinese, and Korean. When they completed signing at 12 minutes after the hour, the two delegates glanced at each other for a moment and simultaneously departed. General Clark signed the documents at Munsan three hours later. The signing procedures controversy fittingly reflected how tortuous the road to the armistice had been.

M. W. Clark, *From the Danube to the Yalu* (New York, 1954); *Foreign Relations of the United States, 1952–1954,* vol. 15: *Korea* (Washington, D.C., 1984); W.G. Hermes, *Truce Tent and Fighting Front* (Washington, D.C., 1966).

Chang-il Ohn

ARMY–AIR FORCE CLOSE SUPPORT CONTROVERSY

This controversy emerged in the early days of the fighting and at times became so bitter as to be common knowledge even to the enemy. Many U.S. Army officers believed that the U.S. Air Force had neglected tactical air power since 1945 in favor of strategic bombing and that its concept of tactical air operations ignored the requirements of the ground forces. The army wanted air power concentrated at the front and favored the marine model where close support aircraft were directly controlled by ground commanders. A leading proponent of this view was Lieutenant General Edward M. Almond*, who had experienced the marine system as commander of X Corps*, but sympathy with the idea reached as high as the Army chief of staff, General J. Lawton Collins*.

Although the air force devoted a large part of its effort to close support operations, particularly in the early days of the fighting, it preferred distant interdiction, which attempted to isolate the battlefield by cutting off the enemy from supplies and reinforcements. While offering various reasons to justify its reticence, the air force in fact was fearful for its independence, resisting anything that might again subordinate it to the army. In what became known as the great debate over close support, the air force defended the existing system by which, under the theater commander, co-equal air and ground commanders decided in consultation the assignment of aircraft to various types of operations.

In December 1951, the air force blocked approval when General James A. Van Fleet*, commander of the 8th Army*, requested assignment of a fighter-bomber squadron to each of his corps commanders. CINCUNC General Mark W. Clark* did order a series of close support experiments but only within the parameters of the established system. These ended in controversy with Operation Smack*, an infantry attack on T-Bone Hill supported by fighter-bombers on January 25, 1953. The troops suffered sixty-four casualties, and the press condemned the tests as a waste of lives. There was an element of scapegoating about the close support controversy, which was at its worst when the war was going poorly.

M. W. Cagle and F. A. Manson, *The Sea War in Korea* (New York, 1980); R. F. Futrell, *The United States Air Force in Korea* (New York, 1961); M. B. Voorhees, *Korean Tales* (London, 1953).

Callum A. MacDonald

ATTLEE, CLEMENT R. (1883–1967)

Leader of the British Labour party since 1935, Attlee became prime minister after the Labour victory in 1945. His government was reelected in February 1950 and in power during the early period of the Korean War. During his second term, Attlee presided over a tired and aging cabinet with a narrow majority in Parliament. His foreign secretary, Ernest Bevin*, was frequently incapacitated by illness, forcing Attlee to take a larger role in foreign affairs. When the Korean War broke out, Attlee supported President Harry S. Truman's* call for collective action through the United Nations. He believed that the North Korean invasion of South Korea* was a Soviet probe and feared that the world would relive the experience of the 1930s if nothing were done to resist aggression. He also wanted to confirm Britain's position as the major ally of the United States by supporting Washington in the first armed conflict of the cold war.

In July 1950, he committed British troops to the fighting despite the reluctance of his chiefs of staff. At the same time, Attlee was anxious to prevent the United States from going too far and dragging its allies into a wider war with the People's Republic of China* or a global war with the Soviet Union. Not only would a war with China divert Anglo-American power from the vital areas of Europe and the Middle East, but it would also split the Commonwealth by alienating India and cause political problems within the Labour party. Attlee was thus careful to distance Britain from such American decisions as the neutralization of Taiwan*. Despite these reservations, Attlee supported the UN offensive across the thirty-eighth parallel*, believing that the Soviets would not intervene and that China could be reassured about the intentions of the UN.

When China intervened, Britain faced the threat of a wider war, a fear crystallized in December 1950 by Truman's atomic bomb press conference comment*. At the beginning of December 1950, Attlee flew to Washington in an attempt to reassure domestic opinion, restrain the United States, and reassert the British position within the Atlantic alliance. Although Truman and Secretary of State Dean G. Acheson* agreed that the UNC* must hold a position in Korea and attempt to conclude an armistice, Attlee won no support for his arguments in favor of political concessions to the PRC as the price of a cease-fire. When Attlee returned to London, he exaggerated his success, and the myth gained hold that he had prevented the Americans from escalating the war. Attlee's government never recovered from the shock of Chinese military intervention*, which split the Labour party and led many on the Left to question the wisdom of a policy regarded as too deferential to the Americans. *See also* Attlee's Visit to the United States.

E. Barker, *The British Between the Superpowers 1945–50* (London, 1983); K. Harris, *Attlee* (London, 1982); K. O. Morgan, *Labour in Power* (London, 1985).

Callum A. MacDonald

ATTLEE'S VISIT TO THE UNITED STATES (December 4–8, 1950)

This visit was hastily arranged, on Prime Minister Clement R. Attlee's* in- itiative, after President Harry S. Truman* at a press conference on November 30 had responded to a question about the possible use of atomic weapons in Korea by stating that there had "always" been "active consideration of [the bomb's] use." Coming at the time of a serious deterioration in battlefield fortunes for UNC* forces at the hands of the Chinese People's Volunteers Army*, the British government believed it probable that the Korean hostilities were about to develop into a wider, nuclear war, embracing the territory of the People's Republic of China*.

Although issues other than the Korean conflict were discussed at this summit meeting, including Washington's policy on the stockpiling of raw materials and the rearmament of West German forces, the future conduct of the war dominated discussion. Britain's leaders urged negotiation of a cease-fire with the inducement to the Chinese of the resolution of the status of Taiwan and the PRC UN representation question*. London also argued against Washington's tentative proposal for direct retaliatory action against Chinese territory—possibly to in- clude a naval blockade and air action against certain points in northern China. Attlee raised as well the delicate issue of the seemingly autonomous nature of CINCUNC General Douglas MacArthur's* actions, which the British saw as essential to curtail.

Prime Minister Attlee was able to reinforce the doubts of those within the administration who were apprehensive about the outcome of a "limited war" against China. However, Truman and Secretary of State Dean G. Acheson* would consider a cease-fire in Korea only provided it had no political strings attached and had been preceded by an orderly UNC retreat into beachheads. The U.S. administration reacted badly to the attacks on MacArthur's behavior, per- ceiving these remarks as an indirect criticism of its conduct of the war. On the question of the possible future role for nuclear weapons in the conflict—the original spur for the visit—Attlee achieved little of what he wanted, since Pres- ident Truman declined to put into writing his oral promise to consult with Great Britain before any use of atomic weapons. *See also* Truman-Attlee Joint Com- muniqué; Truman's Atomic Bomb Press Conference Comment.

A. Bullock, *Ernest Bevin: Foreign Secretary, 1945–1951* (New York, 1983); R. Ding-man, "Atomic Diplomacy during the Korean War," *International Security* (Winter 1988–1989); R. Dingman, "Truman, Attlee, and the Korean War Crisis," *International Studies* (Winter 1982); R. Foot, "Anglo-American Relations in the Korean Crisis: The British Effort to Avert an Expanded War, December 1950-January 1951," *Diplomatic History* (Winter 1986); *Foreign Relations of the United States, 1950,* vol. 7: *Korea* (Washington, D.C., 1976).

Rosemary Foot

AUSTIN, WARREN R. (1877–1962)

Warren Austin, U.S. representative to the UN from 1946 to 1953, was a passionate defender of U.S. policy toward Korea before and during the war. Born in Highgate Center, Vermont, he graduated with a B.A. from the state university in 1899. After being admitted to the Vermont bar in 1902, he established a successful law practice and occasionally served in public office. A Republican, Austin was elected in 1931 to an unexpired term in the U.S. Senate and in 1934 and 1940 to full terms. A critic of the New Deal, he nonetheless supported the White House in advocating U.S. action to halt Japanese and German expansion. His advocacy of bipartisanship in foreign policy and his role during World War II in supporting creation of the UN made him a logical choice for appointment as the U.S. representative to the new international organization in 1946.

When hostilities began in Korea, Austin was at his home in Vermont, but he returned to New York in time to push through the UN Security Council resolution of June 27, 1950,* calling on member states to assist in repulsing the North Korean invasion of South Korea*. In early July, his adamance in pressing for a resolution creating a unified command on Korea under the U.S. strained relations with several allied delegations. Austin's inclination to regard the Korean enterprise as a moral crusade and to treat the UN and U.S. roles in it as synonymous continued to irritate colleagues from friendly and neutral nations.

In August, Austin earned accolades from the American press and public when Soviet representative Jacob A. Malik*, who returned to the Security Council after a boycott of nearly seven months, attempted to shift the agenda away from Korea to the question of Chinese representation. Austin held his own in the furious debate, and the anti-Communist majority supported the U.S. position. He also hinted that the UN should not settle for a simple restoration of the status quo ante bellum in Korea but rather should press on to unify the peninsula. Austin continued to play a prominent role in Security Council debates into the fall, but the end of the Soviet UN Security Council boycott* made concrete action by that body impossible. As the United States shifted attention to the General Assembly, he took a back seat to Secretary of State Dean G. Acheson* and John Foster Dulles*, another representative of the State Department, on such key measures as the UN Uniting for Peace resolution of November 3, 1950*. Austin returned to the forefront, however, when the Security Council took up the issue of Chinese military intervention*. Austin expressed outrage over Communist China's flaunting of the UN in Korea and rebutted charges of U.S. aggression coming from the Chinese Communist representative who appeared before the Security Council later that month.

Activity soon shifted to the General Assembly. Not without impatience, Austin led the U.S. campaign to contain allied and Arab-Asian efforts to end the Korean conflict through concessions to the People's Republic of China* regarding Taiwan and the PRC UN representation question*. In January 1951, after Chinese troops crossed the thirty-eighth parallel, he centered on the successful U.S. drive to win passage of the UN resolution of February 1, 1951*, condemning Communist China. Austin's last major involvement with Korea came in the spring of 1951 when he stood behind President Harry S. Truman's* decisions to recall CIN-CUNC General Douglas MacArthur* and limit the war. Although he led the successful U.S. efforts to pass resolutions at the General Assembly sessions during the fall of 1951 and 1952, his declining health plus the direct involvement of Acheson relegated him to a secondary role.

Current Biography, 1944; G. T. Mazuzan, *Warren R. Austin at the U.N., 1946–1953* (Kent, Ohio, 1977); Records of the Australian Department of External Affairs, Mitchell, A.C.T., Australia; Records of the Canadian Department of External Affairs, "War in Korea File," Hull, Canada; "The Reminiscences of Ernest Gross," Oral History Project, Columbia University; W. R. Austin papers, University of Vermont, Burlington.

William Stueck

B

BAILLE, HUGH (1890–1966)

Hugh Baille was a well-known journalist when the Korean War began and gained notoriety because of his published interviews with CINCUNC General Douglas MacArthur*. He was born in Brooklyn, New York, the son of a prominent political correspondent for the *New York World* and *New York Tribune*. After graduating from the University of Southern California in 1910, he worked as a reporter in Los Angeles until 1915 when he joined the United Press Associations (UP). Baille served as general news manager, business and sales manager, and vice-president, implementing innovations to speed the process of news collection. He became president of UP in 1935; however, he remained active as a reporter, traveling to Europe to conduct interviews with Adolf Hitler and Benito Mussolini in 1935 and Neville Chamberlain after the Munich Conference in 1938. During World War II, Baille covered events at the front in Sicily and Belgium, later gaining interviews with Chiang Kai-shek* and Emperor Hirohito. In 1946, Baille obtained exclusive interviews with Joseph Stalin* and General Douglas MacArthur. Subsequently, Baille campaigned vigorously for international action at the UN to guarantee worldwide freedom for exchange and dissemination of news but failed to achieve his goal.

In 1944, *Look* magazine observed that wherever Baille appeared, "big things happen." This certainly was true following the North Korean invasion of South Korea*, as Baille covered various events during the war. He was on hand when MacArthur restored administrative control over the capital of the Republic of Korea* to President Syngman Rhee* after the successful recapture of Seoul operation*. In the aftermath of Chinese military intervention*, Baille had an exclusive interview with MacArthur in which the general declared that the United States should bomb Manchuria as part of a plan for achieving total victory in Korea. Responding to this interview and other public comments, Washington moved to muzzle the general with the JCS directive of December 6, 1950*. But MacArthur would not remain silent; his criticism of U.S. strategy in another interview with Baille in March 1951 led to President Harry S. Truman's* recall of MacArthur*. By 1952, public and press apathy regarding the Korean War prompted Baille to order a series of photographs and interviews with soldiers in the field to revive interest in the conflict. He also insisted that news correspondents accompany Dwight D. Eisenhower* on his trip to Korea*. Three years later, Baille retired as president of UP but remained active as its chairman of the board. Highly competitive and always the "seeker of the spectacular and the human-interest angle," Baille wrote two books, his *High Tension* appearing in 1959.

Current Biography, 1946; *National Cyclopedia of American Biography*, vol. G (Clifton, N.J., 1984); *New York Times*, March 2, 1966; *Who Was Who in America*, vol. 4: *1961–1968* (Chicago, 1968).

BAJPAI, GIRJA S. (1891–1954)

As secretary-general of India's Ministry of External Affairs, Sir Girja S. Bajpai played a primary role in India's Korean War diplomacy. Born to an upper-cast Brahmin family in the city of Lucknow in northern India, he received his education at Oxford University and entered the Indian civil service in 1914. Bajpai quickly won a reputation for being a loyal and dependable servant of the British raj and gained his first foreign policy experience in 1921 when he went to London as secretary to the Indian delegation to that year's imperial conference. After serving in a number of overseas posts, he was sent to Washington, D.C., in 1941 to act as agent general for India in the United States. Although Prime Minister Jawaharlal Nehru* preferred to appoint Congress party activists to positions of authority once India gained its independence in 1947, he turned to the conservative Bajpai to head the Ministry of External Affairs due to the latter's extensive experience and competence in international relations. Bajpai helped lay the foundation for the building of India's modern diplomatic service and served in the ministry until 1952, when he stepped aside due to health reasons.

As was the case with Indian foreign policy in general, Bajpai exerted his influence on the conduct of India's Korean diplomacy rather than its formulation. Loyal to Prime Minister Nehru's nonaligned posture in the cold war, Bajpai nonetheless worked as a moderating influence in Indian circles. Sympathetic to both British and U.S. perspectives due to his previous service in those two countries, the Indian bureaucrat tried to soften Nehru's outspokenness against colonialism and U.S. cold war policies in Asia.

Bajpai figured most prominently in the history of the Korean War during the fall of 1950 when he transmitted warnings from Peking to London and Washington—passed on by India's ambassador, K. M. Panikkar*—concerning the People's Republic of China's* possible entry into the war. The movement of UN troops north of the thirty-eighth parallel, Chou En-lai* reportedly told Panikkar, would evoke a Chinese response. British and U.S. policymakers looked somewhat askance at Panikkar's views since the Indian ambassador had already earned a reputation for his strong advocacy of normalized relations with China. Bajpai, however, lent considerable credence to Panikkar's reports when he personally endorsed them in a late September meeting with Loy W. Henderson*, the U.S. ambassador in New Delhi. In the end, Bajpai's efforts came to no avail. Although British officials in particular respected Bajpai's moderate credentials and were inclined to take him seriously, President Harry S. Truman*, Secretary of State Dean G. Acheson*, and other senior U.S. officials rejected any course of action that might be viewed as a sign of hesitation or weakness.

M. Brecher, *Nehru: A Political Biography* (London, 1959); S. Gopal, *Jawaharlal Nehru: A Biography* (New Delhi, 1979); *London Times,* December 6, 1954; P. Lowe, *The Origins of the Korean War* (London, 1986).

Dennis Merrill

BALDWIN, HANSON W. (1903–   )

Baldwin was born in Baltimore and graduated from the U.S. Naval Academy in 1924. In 1927, he resigned from the navy in favor of newspaper work. By June 1950, when Baldwin's long list of articles on the Korean War began to appear in the *New York Times,* he was in his eighth year as the paper's military correspondent. His recently published series of lectures, *Power and Politics,* set forth his general view that conflict between nation-states was a normal, not an exceptional, phenomenon. Accordingly, since the United States was newly arrived to the status of superpower and no longer partially insulated by geography from geopolitical competition, it should augment its military establishment on a permanent basis. Baldwin was skeptical of the practical utility of atomic weapons. He prescribed a much stronger ground capability while simultaneously cautioning against indiscriminate unilateral guarantees of real estate around the world.

These ideas equipped Baldwin well for the task of analyzing this particular war, and his views undoubtedly had an impact on public opinion regarding Korea. While strongly supporting President Harry S. Truman's* and Secretary of State Dean G. Acheson's* initial decisions on the ground that the nature of North Korea's provocations gave the United Nations no choice but to resist in order to preserve Western credibility, he was a frequent critic of preparation, strategy, and tactics. Throughout the war, he argued that the atomic bomb was useless in Korea for lack of proper targets and because of the moral revulsion that would result from its use. At the height of UN success in late October 1950, Baldwin was pointing out, in a series of seven articles, the deficiencies in ground forces, air tactics, and logistics that had made the situation so desperate during the summer. In December 1950, Baldwin was able to weigh carefully the pros and cons of total withdrawal from a tactical point of view with an appearance of impartiality, but on balance he was passionately committed to continuance of the struggle. He flatly announced that Americans faced "the greatest danger in our history," warning that "Western Civilization and our American way of life" might be destroyed if "the danger from the East" was not met boldly.

Truman's recall of CINCUNC General Douglas MacArthur* found Baldwin examining arguments for and against. Just prior, he had not believed the general guilty of outright insubordination or responsible for Chinese military interven- tion* but criticized him and his command for arrogance, a byzantine structure, and poor intelligence capability. Just after, he rejected what he saw as Truman's overly defensive policy, as well as the Manchurian-atomic adventurism of MacArthur's plan for victory*. Instead, he recommended greater aid to Chiang Kai-shek's* Republic of China*, the end of interdiction of Chinese efforts against the mainland, aid to Chinese guerrillas, a speed-up of Japanese rearmament, and continued military aid to selected non-Communist Asian governments, all de- signed to broaden the U.S. strategy to defeat communism in Asia without wid- ening the Korean War. Baldwin welcomed the truce signed in July 1953 as the best way out of an impasse. Many years later, in *Strategy for Tomorrow,* he described the result as both "triumph and despair": triumph because a prosperous and "fairly stable" nation had risen from the ashes of war, despair because there was still "no end in sight" on reunification and regional stabilization.

H. W. Baldwin, *Power and Politics: The Price of Security in the Atomic Age* (Clare- mont, Calif., 1950); H. W. Baldwin, *The Price of Power* (New York, 1948); H. W. Baldwin, *Strategy for Tomorrow* (New York, 1970); *New York Times,* July 2, 17, 1950, October 29, 30, 31, 1950, November 1, 2, 3, 4, 1950, December 1, 10, 17, 1950, March 28, 29, 30, 1951, April 16, 17, 1951, May 13, 1951, July 8, 1951, January 6, 1952, July 26, 1953, August 2, 17, 1953, September 10, 1953.

                                                                    David W. Mabon

BARR, DAVID G. (1895–1970)

Major General David G. Barr was commanding officer of the 7th U.S. Army Infantry Division during the Korean War. His unit became part of the X Corps* after the successful Inch'ŏn landing*, participating in the recapture of Seoul operation* and later spearheading the advance to the Yalu following the Wŏnsan landing*. Born in Nanafalie, Alabama, Barr was attending Alabama Presbyterian College when the United States entered World War I. In 1917, he received a commission as a second lieutenant in the U.S. Army Reserve, serving in France with the 1st Infantry Division. Barr graduated from Infantry School in 1924 and the Army War College in 1939 and then joined the I Armored Corps as supply officer. After U.S. entry into World War II, he held a number of staff posts, ultimately becoming chief of staff for the 6th Army in 1945.

Following World War II, Barr served as assistant chief of staff with Army Ground Forces until 1948. Then Army Chief of Staff General Dwight D. Ei- senhower* dispatched him to China as head of the Army Advisory Group, a 1,000-man military mission advising the Republic of China*. This two-year term coincided with Mao Tse-tung's* defeat of Chiang Kai-shek* in the Chinese Civil War. Barr's reports were important in undermining the Truman administration's support for the Kuomintang because they criticized the Nationalists for inept military leadership and policies protecting the privileged classes. He recom- mended termination of U.S. military aid after concluding that Chiang's regime had little or no popular support. In 1949, Barr left China for Japan, where he assumed command of the 7th infantry.

When the 7th Infantry came ashore at Inch'ŏn on September 18, 1950, its mission was to advance inland toward Seoul on the right of the 1st Marine Division, providing protection against a North Korean attack from the south. Barr was not a dynamic or forceful combat commander and had had little battlefield experience. One of his aides later observed that contrary to the image of a commanding general, he "was rumpled and round, a super guy, but more like a father figure. He was not the best leader or field general." Although Major General Edward M. Almond*, commander of the X Corps, considered him a liability, Barr nevertheless continued to command the 7th Infantry Division until 1951 when he returned to the United States to become commanding general of the Armored Center. Barr was one of the few lower-ranking officials to testify at the MacArthur Hearings*, presumably because he had experience fighting both the North Koreans and the Chinese Communists. Significantly, he voiced opposition to General Douglas MacArthur's* plan for victory*, expressing his opinion that a naval blockade against the People's Republic of China* would be ineffective and bombing in Manchuria would risk another world war. He also advised against a Nationalist diversionary assault against the mainland unless the United States was prepared to provide substantial support for such an operation.

C. Blair, *The Forgotten War* (New York, 1987); *Military Situation in the Far East*, 5 vols. (Washington, D.C., 1951); *Who Was Who in America*, vol. 5: *1969–1973* (Chicago, 1973).

BATTLE OF BLOODY RIDGE (August 18–September 5, 1951)

Bloody Ridge consisted of three hills—numbers 983, 940, and 773—and their connecting ridges in a region known as the Punchbowl*, which became the scene of intense fighting in the late summer of 1951. The side holding the ridge, which was parallel to the battle line, would have a better observation vantage point but little else. When the war stalemated at the end of June 1951, it was not along any preplanned battle line. While the Kaesŏng truce talks* continued, the 8th Army* made limited attacks here and there to straighten out bulges and salients in the line. The objective of these limited offensives was twofold: to put pressure on the enemy to negotiate in good faith and to keep the 8th Army sharp and in fighting condition. The 8th would "lean against the enemy in order to keep the enemy from leaning against it." The option of total war with the People's Republic of China* had been rejected in Washington. The last two years of the war saw UN forces engage the Chinese and North Korean People's Army (NKPA) for title to largely insignificant pieces of real estate.

On August 17, 1951, orders arrived to the Republic of Korea's* 36th Regiment, 7th Division, to take and hold the ridge. It was to be supported by the 72d Tank Battalion, by American air, and 2d Division Artillery. After heavy fighting, the 36th Regiment took the ridge on August 25 but then had to withdraw the next day due to North Korean pressure. On August 27, the 2d Battalion, 9th Infantry, in support of the ROK forces, attacked the dug-in NKPA positions on Hill 983 but was stopped cold. The 3d Battalion of the 9th struck toward peak 773 but failed to reach even its initial objective. At nightfall, the North Koreans counterattacked. On August 30, the 1st and 2d Battalions attacked the ridge frontally. Supporting artillery fired 451,979 rounds, turning the ridge into a flaming inferno. The North Koreans were so well dug in, though, that shelling alone could not dislodge them, and the attacking battalions had to deal with them at close range with rifles, grenades, and flamethrowers. Casualties on both sides were heavy. The slow progress of the 9th Infantry led to a reorganization of the entire 2d Division; new attacks and flanking maneuvers finally drove the tiring North Koreans to relinquish Bloody Ridge on September 5. The NKPA had not fled; it had merely retreated to Heartbreak Ridge, some 1,500 yards to the north. The effort cost the ROK and UN forces nearly 3,000 casualties. The enemy forces suffered over 15,000 casualties. *See also* Battle of Heartbreak Ridge.

T. R. Fehrenbach, *This Kind of War* (New York, 1963); R. A. Gugeler, *Combat Actions in Korea* (Washington, D.C., 1970); W. G. Hermes, *Truce Tent and Fighting Front* (Washington, D.C., 1966).

Tami D. Biddle

BATTLE OF CHIP'YŎNG (February 13–15, 1951)

The small central Korean crossroads town of Chip'yŏng became the center of one of the most important battles of the war when Lieutenant General Matthew B. Ridgway*, 8th Army* commander, decided to make a stand there against the Chinese Communist forces. In early February 1951, the 23d Regimental Combat Team under Colonel Paul L. Freeman set up a tight perimeter defense about 1 mile in diameter around the town. They were joined by the French Infantry Battalion, the 37th Field Artillery Battalion, an anti-aircraft artillery automatic weapons battery, and another 155mm howitzer battery. Freeman spent ten days building his defense: sowing antipersonnel mines, registering mortars, and digging in machine gun positions and foxholes. By February 13, the 8th Army offensive had bogged down, and a determined Chinese counterattack flowed south, threatening to encircle Chip'yŏng. Freeman requested permission to withdraw his forces to Yŏju, 15 miles south. The corps and divisions commanders agreed, but Ridgway adamantly refused to abandon Chip'yŏng (the printable portion of his reply was "No"). Freeman strengthened his perimeter and requested air strikes and airdrops for the next day. He warned his unit commanders that they would soon be surrounded, saying, "We'll stay here and fight it out."

The first Chinese attacks began at about 10:00 p.m., and the first close action came four hours later when a Chinese platoon with fixed bayonets attacked the French battalion's position. The French countered the Chinese bugles and whistles with a hand-cranked siren. One squad ran toward the attackers throwing grenades, causing the larger Chinese force to turn and run. The enemy launched four separate attacks during the night, but all activity stopped by morning. The soldiers then rebuilt their defenses based on their overnight experience. Many of the artillerymen were raw replacements who found that their first attempts at digging foxholes and personnel trenches around their howitzers had been inadequate. Air strikes hit positions along the perimeter where enemy activity seemed to be increasing, and twenty-four airdrops of ammunition replenished supplies expended in the night's battle. Mortar rounds landed in the perimeter sporadically, but soldiers were able to rest and eat hot meals.

Shortly after dark, bugles and whistles signaled renewed enemy attacks. Although they suffered heavy losses, the Chinese gradually chipped away at the U.S. defenses, taking one foxhole at a time until they had breached the perimeter. At one point, a company commander attempted to fill a gap by organizing a group of artillerymen. Some refused to go, and the rest fled when the first mortar round burst among them. But the Chinese lacked modern communications that would have allowed them to exploit their hole in the perimeter. A counterattack reached the top of the abandoned hill, but the Americans were able to use artillery and machine gun fire to inflict heavy casualties and hold them at bay. The artillerymen had failed to fight as infantry, but they did not abandon their howitzers, which continued to pound the enemy position with the help of cannons and machine guns of three tanks. The Chinese did not withdraw at daylight as usual. They held their ground against a determined attack supported by air strikes, artillery, and tanks. But by early evening, the Chinese withdrew, suffering their first tactical defeat since entering the war.

The Battle of Chip'yŏng was as important psychologically as it was militarily. The morale of the American fighting man, which had plummeted since Chinese military intervention*, rebounded dramatically. The Chinese offensive ran out of steam; the Chinese human wave attacks could be stopped. British Air Vice-Marshal C. A. Bouchier reported that the "myth of the magical millions of Chinese in Korea has been exploded." General Ridgway's revitalized 8th Army regained the offensive. *See also* Operation Roundup.

T. R. Fehrenbach, *This Kind of War* (New York 1963); R. A. Gugeler, *Combat Actions in Korea* (Washington, D.C., 1970); M. Hastings, *The Korean War* (New York, 1987); H. J. Middleton, *The Compact History of the Korean War* (New York, 1965).

Larry R. Beck

BATTLE OF HEARTBREAK RIDGE (September 13–October 15, 1951)

The U.S. 2d Division's struggle to take the line of jagged, north-south hills known as Heartbreak Ridge began just eight days after completion of the Battle of Bloody Ridge*. There were mixed views among American officers as to whether the North Koreans would put up much resistance to this new push to round out the defenses of the Punchbowl*. Aerial reconnaissance showed the enemy bringing artillery and mortar units into the valleys flanking the ridge. What the cameras did not show, however, was that after withdrawing from

Bloody Ridge, the North Koreans had fallen back to well-camouflaged inter-locking bunkers and dug-in artillery positions covering the wooded approaches to Heartbreak.

Heartbreak Ridge, just north of Bloody Ridge, was dominated by three hills—on the north by Hill 851, in the center by Hill 931, and on the south by Hill 894. The plan called for battalions of the 23d Regiment to split the Heartbreak Ridge line by cutting between Hills 931 and 851 and then circling north and south to capture each hill. Elements of the 9th Infantry would advance on Hill 894. Following a thirty-minute artillery barrage on September 13, 1951, battal-ions from the 23d Regiment of the 2d Division launched their initial assault on Heartbreak. As these units moved up the valley floor toward an east-west spur that would take them to their initial objective, they came under heavy artillery and mortar fire from the concealed 1st Regiment of the North Korean People's Army (NKPA) 6th Division, and the prospects of an easy campaign quickly faded.

While the 23d Regiment was bogged down in its effort to penetrate the central-northern sector of the ridge line, the 9th Infantry's 2d Battalion sought to ease some of the pressure on it by attacking Hill 894 on the southern flank. By September 15, the 2d battalion had cleared Hill 894 while taking only eleven casualties; during the next two days, however, it would lose more than 200 men resisting fierce North Korean counterattacks. This success had little impact on the bitter struggle to take Hills 851 and 931. Men and supplies moving through the narrow Pia-ri Valley, southwest of Heartbreak, toward these hills were ex-posed to enemy artillery and mortar fire. On September 23, elements of the 23d Infantry reached the crest of Hill 931 but could not withstand the enemy's counterattack.

After nearly two weeks of trying to take Heartbreak Ridge, further assaults were called off and the original plan was vastly augmented. The new plan (code-named Touchdown) would broaden the offensive to include assaults on key adjacent hills, thereby forcing the NKPA to spread its forces and leaving few reserves to reinforce Heartbreak. Additionally, the 2d Engineer Combat Battalion was to prepare the road along the Mundŭng-ri Valley to allow M-4 tanks to provide mobile support for U.S. forces attacking the two remaining hills on Heartbreak. On October 5, Operation Touchdown began with its series of flanking attacks allowing the 23d to clear Hill 931 the next day. On October 13, elements of the 23d, including the French Battalion, succeeded in taking Hill 851, and the costly offensive was completed two days later when the final objective of Touchdown, hill 1220, fell.

Losses were high on both sides during this month-long campaign. The U.S. 2d Division suffered over 3,700 casualties, with the 23d Regiment and its attached French Battalion incurring almost half of this total. The NKPA 6th, 12th, and 13th divisions and the Chinese 204th Division also had taken heavy losses, estimated at nearly 25,000 men.

V. E. Craven, "Operation Touchdown Won Heartbreak Ridge," *Combat Forces Journal* (December 1953); W. G. Hermes, *Truce Tent and Fighting Front* (Washington, D.C., 1966).

Richard Dean Burns

BATTLE OF THE IMJIN RIVER (April 22–25, 1951)

This was a major Commonwealth action during the Chinese Fifth Phase Offensive. The 29th British Infantry Brigade occupied a position from Chŏksŏng to the junction of the Imjin and Hant'an rivers, a frontage of about 12,000 yards, having reached the area during one of the phases of the 8th Army's* renewed advance northward in the spring of 1951. The brigade's position was an important one because it lay across a natural avenue of approach to Seoul, and the hinge between the 29th Brigade and the Republic of Korea's* 1st Division on its left covered the important road junction at Ŭijŏngbu, which in turn controlled all the roads in the I Corps area. To the right, the UNC* line turned north, and a successful enemy attack would have far-reaching implications by allowing them to cut off UN forces to the east. It was a logical focus of Chinese attention in their attempt to crack 8th Army's front.

The Imjin was easily fordable at that time of year and proved no obstacle to the Chinese, who began their assault on the night of April 22. The forward companies were unable to prevent penetration of their positions by strong, well-organized enemy forces. Confused fighting continued throughout the following day, and on the evening of April 23, some UNC forces withdrew to the east. To the west, other Commonwealth troops still held a frontage of about 2,000 yards. On April 24, the enemy committed a second division to the battle in order to gain a result. On that afternoon, attempts were made to relieve the Gloucestershire Regiment, which was completely surrounded and had concentrated on point 235 for a final stand. After several efforts failed, the remainder of the brigade were ordered to withdraw that night to new positions north of Seoul, which they did with some difficulty.

Early on the morning of April 25, the Gloucesters were advised that with the artillery no longer able to provide fire support, the battalion was to break out toward their own lines if possible. The attempt to regain their own lines was largely unsuccessful; most of the survivors and the wounded who had been left in place before the attempt was made were captured by the Chinese. Only thirty-nine men returned successfully to UN lines. The 29th Brigade suffered over 25 percent casualties in the Imjin battle; one entire battalion was virtually wiped out. Large quantities of equipment were lost or destroyed, as were several of the new Centurion tanks. The brigade was withdrawn to a rear area for rest and refitting, and it was more than a month before it returned to the line. On the positive side, the three-day stand of the brigade had frustrated entirely the enemy's attempts to break through to Seoul and had inflicted disproportionately heavy casualties upon its forces. *See also* Chinese Spring Offensives of 1951.

C. N. Barclay, *The First Commonwealth Division* (Aldershot, 1954); A. H. Farrar-

Hockley, *The Edge of the Sword* (London, 1954); M. Hastings, *The Korean War* (London, 1987); R. O. Holles, *Now Thrive the Armourers: A Soldier's Story of Action with the Gloucesters in Korea* (London, 1952).

Jeffrey Grey

BATTLE OF KAP'YŎNG (April 23–25, 1951)

This was a major Commonwealth action during the Chinese Fifth Phase Offensive. After some months of concerted activity during the winter retreat, followed by the UNC's* renewed advance northward, the 27th Commonwealth Brigade had been withdrawn into a reserve position near Kap'yŏng for rest and refitting. The brigade was on three hours' notice to move in support of the 1st Marine, the Republic of Korea's* Division, or 24th Infantry Division. On the night of April 22, the Chinese attacked the right flank of the 6th ROK Division in strength, and the division began to collapse, although some elements held out overnight. By early the next morning, the brigade commander, Brigadier B. A. Burke, was ordered to move his units to defend the northern approaches of the town, which guarded one of the main east-west communication routes south of the battle line. Burke positioned his units in a naturally strong defensive position along a line of hills around the confluence of the Kap'yŏng River.

The battle was in fact a succession of actions as the Chinese attempted to break through the defending battalions' positions. The 3d Battalion, Royal Australian Regiment, repulsed successive Chinese assaults beginning in the evening of April 23 and lasting until the morning of April 25. Although the Australian battalion was forced to give ground on April 24, the Chinese were unable to penetrate the main positions and broke off the action in the middle of the third day. A single brigade outfought an entire Chinese division in difficult circumstances, made more so because the two British battalions in the brigade were in the process of being relieved, and one of these played no part in the action at all. The Canadians lost ten killed and twenty-three wounded, the Australians thirty-two dead, fifty-nine wounded, and three missing, taken prisoner. For the first time in the war, the Australians took large numbers of prisoners, many of them not wounded. The Chinese failure at Kap'yŏng demonstrated that the enemy had exhausted his resources of men and material, leaving them little option but to retreat. *See also* Chinese Spring Offensives of 1951.

R. J. O'Neill, *Australia in the Korean War 1950–53* (Canberra, 1985); H. F. Wood, *Strange Battleground* (Ottawa, 1966).

Jeffrey Grey

BATTLE OF THE KŬM RIVER (July 14–20, 1950)

The Kŭm River affair opened the defensive phase of the war for the U.S. and Republic of Korea*. Early in July 1950, ROK and U.S. forces had been forced out of the Inch'ŏn-Seoul area and were steadily being pushed toward the tip of the Korean peninsula by no fewer than five full North Korean divisions. Hoping to impede the North Korean advance, as well as to protect the South Korean temporary capital of Taegu and the city of Taejŏn, Lieutenant General Walton

H. Walker*, commander of the 8th Army*, ordered a defensive line established along the Kŭm River just north of Taejŏn.

On July 12 and 13, U.S. Army engineers destroyed all bridges across the Kŭm. The U.S. 21st Regiment took up positions outside the city of Taejŏn to act as a reserve force. The U.S. 24th Division and 34th Infantry Division were positioned along the Kŭm River just north of Taejŏn, the latter charged with protecting the high ground adjacent to the Kŏngju-Nonsan road. On July 14, the North Korean 4th Division employed barges to cross the river downstream from the U.S. 34th Division and promptly overran its defensive positions. Although the 34th Division managed to counterattack, the North Korean 4th Division successfully repelled it and continued its assault, pushing the U.S. 34th Division back toward Taejŏn. On July 16, the North Korean 3d Division crossed the Kŭm and challenged the U.S. 24th Division. From July 17 to 20, the two North Korean divisions pressed their assault against the city of Taejŏn. The U.S. 34th Division was withdrawn to Yusŏng, northwest of Taejŏn, leaving the U.S. 24th Division to defend Taejŏn alone. Although the 24th Division fought valiantly, it was forced to withdraw from the city, leaving behind its commander, Major General William F. Dean*, who became a prized prisoner of war for the Democratic People's Republic of Korea*.

Whether it was the intention of General Walker to employ the Kŭm River line to halt the North Korean advance or just to slow it remains unclear. What did occur was a delaying action to buy Walker enough time to set up the Pusan Perimeter* around Pusan along the Naktong River. There has been some speculation that if the U.S. 34th Division had been better employed at Kŏngju, the North Korean 4th Division might have been halted at the Kŭm. *See also* Battle of the Naktong Bulge.

R. E. Appleman, *South to the Naktong, North to the Yalu* (Washington, D.C., 1961); R. A. Gugeler, *Combat Actions in Korea* (Washington, D.C., 1970); D. Rees, *Korea: The Limited War* (New York, 1964); J. F. Schnabel, *Policy and Direction* (Washington, D.C., 1972).

David J. Wright

BATTLE OF THE MINES
See Wŏnsan Landing

BATTLE OF THE NAKTONG BULGE (August 5–19, 1950)

The first Naktong River engagement was initiated by the North Korean People's Army (NKPA) seeking to break the will of Lieutenant General Walton H. Walker's* 8th Army* and Republic of Korea* forces, which, after failing to hold the NKPA at the Battle of the Kŭm River*, had taken up defensive positions along the Naktong River. Walker's defensive perimeter extended from Taegu to Yŏngdŏk in the north—where vital railway lines linking northern and southern South Korea were situated—and then south from Taegu down the Naktong River, past Masan to the coast. Up to this time, the momentum of battle was clearly on the side of the North Korean forces. They knew, however, that they could not maintain this advantage for long. It became apparent to them that if the 8th Army could hold the line against them long enough to obtain adequate reinforcements to mount a large-scale counteroffensive, the momentum would swing against them. Thus, the North Koreans concluded that it was imperative for them to force the 8th Army to abandon the Korean peninsula before reinforcements arrived.

The Battle of the Naktong Bulge lasted from August 5 to 19, 1950, although it resumed briefly again in early September. The NKPA attacked along a broad front spanning the entire perimeter. Only in two sectors, however, did the North Koreans possess sufficient forces to cross the Naktong. In the north, they crossed near Waegwan bent on capturing Taegu, only to run head-on into the U.S. 1st Cavalry Division and the ROK 1st Division. The NKPA 1st and 3d divisions were met with combined air and land counterattacks in fighting so fierce that by August 19, the 3d Division no longer existed.

In the south, the North Korean 4th Division had better fortune. From August 7 to 11, the North Korean 4th Division, commanded by Major General Lee Kwon Mu*, successfully pummelled the U.S. 24th and 25th divisions along the Obong-ri Ridge. The North Korean 4th Division on August 11 gained control of the access road linking Yŏngsan with Masan, severing communications between the two cities. The U.S. 25th Division was sent to bolster defenses around Masan in the event that the North Korean 4th Division should turn its immediate attention in that direction. That left the weary and beleaguered U.S. 24th Division to stop the North Korean 4th Division's main assault, which it did. The North Korean 4th Division still had considerable fight left in it and consequently launched a small-scale offensive in early September. This attack was rebuffed. By September 17, 1950, Obong-ri and all other previous North Korean acquisitions in the bulge were eliminated, and the Pusan Perimeter* was secure. By the end of the Battle of the Naktong Bulge in August 1950, the momentum had shifted from the NKPA to the UNC*. With the defeat of North Korean forces along the perimeter, reinforced UN forces could mount a counteroffensive. *See also* Defense of Taegu.

R. E. Appleman, *South to Naktong, North to the Yalu* (Washington, D.C., 1961); J. A. Field, *The History of the United States Naval Operations, Korea* (Washington, D.C., 1962); H. J. Middleton, *The Compact History of the Korean War* (New York, 1965); D. Rees, *Korea: The Limited War* (New York, 1964); W. Sheldon, *Hell or High Water* (New York, 1968).

David J. Wright

BATTLE OF NAMSI (October 24, 1951)

Namsi was the biggest air battle of the Korean War. At first, the UNC* had enjoyed almost unchallenged air superiority in the skies over Korea. This situation changed, however, when China intervened and the first MiGs appeared. The jets were based mainly at Antung, across the Yalu from Sinŭiju, and operated in an area of northwest Korea between the Yalu and Ch'ŏngch'ŏn rivers that became known as MiG Alley*. Counter-air attacks on Chinese bases were ruled out by the limited nature of the war, but in November 1950 the U.S. Air Force rushed a wing of modern F-86 Sabres to Korea to counter the threat. These aircraft flew blocking patrols in MiG Alley in order to prevent the Communists from interfering with interdiction operations between Sinanju and Sinŭiju.

Despite the appearance of the Sabres, the MiGs in April 1951 destroyed three B-29 bombers and badly damaged ten others on daylight raids in MiG Alley. The UNC's worst losses, however, were suffered in October 1951 when daylight raids against the North Korean airfields at Ta'ech'ŏn, Saamch'ŏn, and Namsi provoked large-scale resistance. On October 24, 1951, 150 MiGs, despite the provision of close escort by 55 Thunderjets, broke through and destroyed 4 bombers over Namsi. Of the remaining 4, only 1 escaped serious damage. By the end of the week, 5 B-29s had been shot down and 8 seriously damaged, almost doubling the losses suffered by Bomber Command since July 1950. Alarmed military leaders in Washington suspended B-29 daylight raids over northwest Korea and rushed a second wing of scarce Sabres to East Asia by aircraft carrier to preserve air superiority between the Yalu and the Ch'ŏngch'ŏn. Namsi also underlined the attrition rate that the UNC would face in any attempt to extend the air war into Manchuria and increased the reluctance of the JCS to stir up what the chairman, General Omar N. Bradley*, described as the MiG hornet's nest around Antung.

R. Jackson, *Air War Over Korea* (London, 1973); B. I. Kaufman, *The Korean War* (Philadelphia, 1986); C. A. MacDonald, *Korea: The War Before Vietnam* (London, 1986).

Callum A. MacDonald

BATTLE OF OLD BALDY (June 26, 1952–March 26, 1953)

Old Baldy (Hill 266), which lay west of Ch'ŏrwon, was chosen in early June 1952 as one of a number of outposts in front of the U.S. 45th Division and became the site of an off-and-on struggle from that time until the spring of 1953. The Communist forces resisted the establishment of the outposts, but the 45th Division was able to secure the hills. On June 16, the 179th Infantry Regiment relieved the 180th and took over outpost positions at Old Baldy, Pork Chop, and Eerie hills. Enemy attacks began, and the contest for Old Baldy was in full swing by the end of June. On the night of June 27, the Chinese People's Volunteers Army* (CPVA) tried three times to break through the defensive fire. The Chinese repeated their efforts, without success, on the nights of June 28 and July 3.

A CPVA battalion finally overran the Old Baldy outpost on July 17 (after the 45th had been relieved by the 2d Division), and for several days a battle raged for possession of the small, denuded mound of earth. Torrential rains kept UN forces from retaking the hill until August 1, when the 23d Infantry Regiment was successful. In September, the Chinese tried for Old Baldy again after pounding it heavily with artillery. They took the crest, but by September 21 control changed hands again when the elements of the 38th Infantry, supported by a platoon of tanks, were able to launch a two-pronged drive to regain the real estate. The back-and-forth pattern was similar to the fighting that had raged in the battles of Bloody Ridge* and Heartbreak Ridge* a year earlier and was typical of the savage, apparently endless struggles for hills that would go on through the autumn of 1952 and into 1953.

On the night of March 23, 1953, the Chinese staged simultaneous attacks on Old Baldy and Pork Chop Hill. UNC* troops were driven off Old Baldy as the Chinese showed themselves willing to expend manpower freely to take and hold the hill. Plans to regain Old Baldy were called into question by the new 8th Army* commander, Lieutenant General Maxwell D. Taylor*. After considering the likely casualties for limited gain, Taylor decided that the hill was not essential to the defense of the sector. The Chinese used the possession of Old Baldy to assist in their April attacks, resulting in the Battle of Pork Chop Hill*.

T. R. Fehrenbach, *This Kind of War* (New York, 1963); M. Hastings, *The Korean War* (New York, 1987); W. G. Hermes, *Truce Tent and Fighting Front* (Washington, D.C., 1966).

Tami D. Biddle

BATTLE OF OSAN (July 5, 1950)

The first engagement between U.S. and North Korean soldiers in the Korean War took place at a roadblock set up across the main north-south highway about 3 miles north of Osan on the morning of July 5, 1950. Task Force Smith*, about one-half of a 24th Infantry Division battalion commanded by Lieutenant Colonel Brad Smith, had arrived from Japan to delay the North Korean advance and show the U.S. flag. Smith's 406 men were joined by 134 men from the 52d Field Artillery Battalion under Lieutenant Colonel Miller O. Perry, who had crossed from Japan on a landing ship, tank. They had almost 1,200 rounds of 105mm ammunition, but only six of these were high explosive anti-tank (HEAT)—one-third of the anti-tank rounds in Japan. There were no anti-tank mines in Korea. Rain and low clouds precluded air support. The North Korean forces consisted of thirty-three Russian-made T-34 medium tanks of the 107th Tank Regiment leading the infantry of the 4th Division southward.

Smith deployed his forces along a 1-mile front on high ground commanding the highway and railroad. One of the howitzers with all of the HEAT rounds was set up on the highway about 1,000 yards south of the infantry, and the remaining guns were in a wooded area off the road about 1,000 yards farther back with only high explosive (HE) rounds. These rear guns and the mortars opened fire on the advancing column of North Korean T–34 tanks at 8:16 A.M., killing enemy soldiers clinging to the outside of the tanks. But this did not cause the tanks themselves to slow their advance, deploy from their column formation, or even leave the road. Colonel Smith ordered the recoilless rifles to hold their fire until the tanks reached 700 yards, but even at that range direct hits had no effect. The bazookas were similarly ineffective. After they had passed through the infantry position, the two lead tanks were finally crippled by HEAT rounds from the forward howitzer, but they merely pulled off the road, allowing the third tank to destroy the gun with its 85mm cannon as HE rounds bounced off its armor. Two other tanks were eventually stopped and three others slightly damaged, but the rest of the column continued southward, passing through the U.S. roadblock by 10:15 A.M. Although the Communists had inflicted fewer than thirty casualties, they had badly shaken the confidence of the cocky Americans.

There was no communication between the infantry and their artillery when the enemy infantry came down the road about two hours later because the tank's treads had chewed up the telephone lines laid along the road and the task force's radios were old and wet. Smith's mortars, recoilless rifles, and machine guns stopped the truck column about 1,000 yards in front of their position. The unsuspecting North Koreans would have been easy targets for artillery or air attacks. Instead, the small, green task force now faced two regiments of well-trained combat veterans who dismounted from their trucks to assault the blocking position. As the enemy took the high ground to the west and began flanking movements on both sides, Colonel Smith ordered a withdrawal in mid-afternoon. Withering close-range machine gun fire soon turned the withdrawal into a rout. Crew-served weapons, the dead, and even the seriously wounded were abandoned to the enemy. Task Force Smith suffered its heaviest casualties during the withdrawal, the infantry sustaining about 150 men killed, wounded, or missing, while the artillery lost 31. The North Koreans did not pursue, content to gather the weapons and equipment that the Americans had abandoned.

At the Battle of Osan, the soldiers of Task Force Smith fought well for nearly seven hours although they were badly outnumbered and lacked the proper weapons to fight tanks. The casualties were light compared to later battles. Perhaps the heaviest casualty of the Battle of Osan was the chauvinistic arrogance that presumed the North Koreans were no match for Americans.

R. E. Appleman, *South to the Naktong, North to the Yalu* (Washington, D.C., 1961); D. Detzer, *Thunder of the Captains* (New York, 1977); T. R. Fehrenbach, *This Kind of War* (New York, 1963); D. MacArthur, *Reminiscences* (New York, 1964).

Larry R. Beck

BATTLE OF PORK CHOP HILL (March 23–July 11, 1953)

As negotiations dragged on in 1953 at the P'anmunjŏm truce talks*, isolated outposts such as Pork Chop Hill (Hill 234) became the scene of intense fighting more for their political or symbolic value than their military significance. On the night of March 23, elements of the 67th and 141st Chinese divisions launched assaults on Pork Chop and neighboring Old Baldy. On Pork Chop Hill, a dug-in U.S. rifle company first came under heavy artillery and mortar fire and then an assault by two Chinese companies. After being forced off the summit during the initial attack, the hastily reinforced U.S. unit recaptured Pork Chop early the next morning. On Old Baldy, however, the Chinese overran the Colombian Battalion*, which had been holding the crest. Unsuccessful American counterattacks continued on Old Baldy through March 26, when Lieutenant General Maxwell D. Taylor*, 8th Army* commander, decided it was not essential to the defense of the sector. The Chinese People's Volunteers Army* (CPVA) lost between 600 and 800 men in the two days of fighting for Old Baldy and Pork Chop, but it was also costly for the U.S. 7th Division, whose casualties exceeded 300 dead, wounded, and missing.

The Chinese tried again to take Pork Chop Hill on the evening of April 16. They succeeded in reaching the summit, where a deadlock ensued. The battle escalated as the Chinese increased their artillery bombardment and sent up reinforcements while the Americans responded in kind. Finally, late on April 18, the Chinese broke off the assault and left the hill in the hands of the U.S. 7th Division. The 8th Army's artillery units had fired over 77,000 rounds in support of its men on Pork Chop, a new record for such a small front. Chinese artillery had hardly fired less—leaving the hill barren and desolate.

The Chinese, however, were apparently determined to possess the hill. Throughout the summer, they pounded it with artillery and mortar fire rounds as the men of the 7th Division struggled to rebuild bunkers and trenches. Finally on July 6, following a ferocious artillery barrage, a succession of CPVA infantry units again assaulted Pork Chop Hill. The attackers far outnumbered the defenders, and the situation became chaotic as each side introduced companies, battalions, and finally regiments into the fray. Chinese determination may be judged by the fact that they matched each new U.S. company with a battalion. Meanwhile, both sides continued to pound the hill with savage artillery and mortar barrages. By the morning of July 11, five U.S. battalions had been committed to trying to hold a company-sized outpost against at least a full Chinese division. Faced with the prospect of sending additional units into the battle at a time when an armistice was near, General Taylor reluctantly decided to withdraw. Consequently, on July 11, U.S. units withdrew from their positions on Pork Chop Hill, and demolition crews rendered them uninhabitable for the occupying CPVA forces. The sacrifices for Pork Chop had been for naught; the armistice was signed sixteen days later. Today Pork Chop Hill lies partly in the DMZ and partly in North Korean territory. *See also* Chinese Summer Offensives of 1953.

W. G. Hermes, *Truce Tent and Fighting Front* (Washington, D.C., 1966); S. L. A. Marshall, *Pork Chop Hill: The American Fighting Man in Action, Korea, Spring, 1953* (New York, 1956); D. Rees, *Korea: The Limited War* (New York, 1964).

Richard Dean Burns

BATTLE OF TAEJŎN
See Battle of the Kŭm River

BATTLE OF TRIANGLE HILL (October 14–November 5, 1952)

Hill 598 (Triangle Hill) was part of a complex that included Pike's Peak on the left and two smaller hills, Sandy Hill and Jane Russell Hill, on the right. In October 1952, the hill complex became the U.S. IX Corps objective in Operation Showdown*, which was designed to push the enemy back and thus improve corps defense lines north of Kŭmhwa. Though it was intended to be a routine and rather low-profile operation with limited casualties, the Chinese soon turned the Battle of Triangle Hill into something quite different, as the elite regiment defending the area made it clear that it intended to stay.

Preparatory air strikes against the hill complex had to be cut back from five days to two because of resource demands ensuing from the Battle of White Horse Hill*. The 1st and 3d battalions of the 31st Infantry Regiment, 7th Division, were assigned initially to take the right and left arms of Triangle Hill. The rifle companies commencing the attack ran into immediate resistance from the well-dug-in Chinese forces. Both battalions met strong resistance from the elite Chinese 15th Army. By only the second day of fighting, two fresh U.S. battalions had to be committed to the battle.

After U.S. artillery and mortar fire, Hill 598 was taken on October 15. Possession of Jane Russell Hill was taken on the following day, but the Chinese gave U.S. forces more trouble on Pike's Peak. On October 18, the U.S. 3d Battalion, 17th Regiment, fought its way to the top of the hill, but the Chinese, fighting fiercely, reestablished control of the area on the evening of the next day. Heavy artillery fire relieved the pressure on U.S. troops and provided a temporary lull. On October 23, the Chinese rallied in an attempt to clear the U.S. troops out of the complex. Intense fire-fighting took place near Pike's Peak, though Chinese forces made only a slight penetration at Jane Russell Hill. The Chinese still held Pike's Peak when the Republic of Korea's* 2d Division relieved the U.S. 7th Division on October 25.

On October 30, the Chinese were able to dislodge the ROK forces from Hill 598 and were able to seize Jane Russell Hill two days later. Due to mounting casualties, ROK counterattacks on Triangle Hill were suspended on November 5. The ROK forces, however, continued their engagement on Sniper Ridge, which lay a little over a mile northeast of Hill 598 and which had been their initial objective in Operation Showdown. They were finally able to capture a part of Sniper Ridge—for no less than the fourteenth time since the initiation of the operation—on November 18 and coped with the Chinese probes that occurred through the end of the month. As the winter approached, the front settled down into a quieter pattern.

The original plan for a limited attack on Chinese positions turned into six weeks of hard fighting and 9,000 casualties. At Triangle Hill, the Chinese People's Volunteers Army* (CPVA) once again showed a remarkable willingness to incur casualties to defend key positions (they lost over 19,000 men). The CPVA's dogged determination to stay the course caused the UNC* to cancel the attack. Little was gained by the UN forces despite their increasingly large commitments of men and time and resources.

W. G. Hermes, *Truce Tent and Fighting Front* (Washington, D.C., 1966).

Tami D. Biddle

BATTLE OF ŬNSAN

See Chinese Military Disengagement of November 6, 1950; UN Offensive Across the Thirty-eighth Parallel

BATTLE OF WHITE HORSE HILL (October 6–15, 1952)

White Horse Hill (Hill 395), which had been the object of some fighting in 1951, was the scene of an intense battle on the eve of the 1952 U.S. presidential election. Hill 395 lay 5 miles west of Ch'ŏrwon on the Republic of Korea's* 9th Division front. Because it dominated the western approaches to Ch'ŏrwon, loss of the hill would deny the IX Corps the use of the main road net and would open up the entire Ch'ŏrwon area to enemy penetration. In the early autumn of 1952, the Communists began to increase their activity in an effort to improve their defensive positions before the winter. On October 3, the 8th Army* learned through a Chinese deserter that the enemy planned to attack White Horse Hill. IX Corps reinforced the ROK 9th Division with tanks, artillery, and anti-aircraft weapons because other intelligence sources confirmed the deserter's story.

On October 6, the Chinese sent a battalion-sized force against Hill 281 (Arrowhead), which lay 2 miles southeast of White Horse, to pin down the French Battalion there and to keep the 2d Division busy. The Chinese maintained the diversion with attacks on October 9 and 12 against tough French resistance. Meanwhile, two battalions of the 340th Regiment, 114th Division, Chinese 38th Army were sent up to the northwest end of White Horse Hill. The Chinese repeatedly tried to advance against the ROK forces but were repulsed each time. Reinforced the following day, the Chinese forced the ROK troops off the crest, only to be pushed back off two hours later by an ROK counterattack. By the third day, the Chinese were throwing a mighty effort against Hill 395, with heavy supporting fire and rapid reinforcements. The hill crest changed hands twice again on October 8, and the seesawing continued as the enemy continued to send men despite the high casualty rate they were suffering. Over the next three days, the determined enemy sent masses of infantry against the objective. The IX Corps saturated Chinese infantry with massed firepower. A break came on October 12 when the 30th ROK Regiment launched a counterattack that brought extremely heavy casualties to the enemy. On October 15, the battle ground to a halt after the Chinese People's Volunteers Army* (CPVA) suffered close to 10,000 casualties. The battle proved that ROK troops, when properly trained and prepared and provided with strong U.S. fire support, were capable of staving off the most determined CPVA attacks.

T. R. Fehrenbach, *This Kind of War* (New York, (1963); W. G. Hermes, *Truce Tent and Fighting Front* (Washington, 1966); C. A. MacDonald, *Korea: The War Before Vietnam* (New York, (1986).

Tami D. Biddle

BATTLE OF YŎNGCH'ŎN (September 5–13, 1950)

The Battle of Yŏngch'ŏn was one of the most critical battles fought during the time of the Pusan Perimeter* defense. The town of Yŏngch'ŏn, an important transportation center situated at a major road junction, was strategically crucial to the UNC*. North Korean occupation and control of Yŏngch'ŏn would not only cut off the last remaining transportation and communication road on the defense line between Taegu and Kyŏngju but also pose an immediate threat to both cities. The North Korean 15th Division, with a total strength of about 12,000 troops, started the general offensive against the Republic of Korea's* 8th Division north of Yŏngch'ŏn in the early dawn of September 5. On the left flank, the 21st Regiment was able to contain the North Korean advance, thus pinning down two North Korean People's Army (NKPA) regiments and protecting the right flank of the neighboring 6th ROK Division. However, the central front of the 8th Division collapsed as the NKPA's main thrust, spearheaded by tanks, poured along the Ibam-Yŏngch'ŏn road, reaching the edge of the town along the northeast access road. Early the next morning, following heavy artillery bombardments, the North Korean troops stormed into the town, forcing the 8th ROK Division to retreat to the west bank of the Kŭmho River. The North Koreans, however, did not remain in the town. They moved southward across the Kŭmho River, gained control of the railroad station, set up roadblocks on the Yŏngch'ŏn-Kyŏngju-Pusan road, and advanced southeast toward Kyŏngju.

As the situation became desperate, Yu Jai Hyung*, commander of the II ROK Corps, obtained the release of the 19th Regiment from the 6th Division and the 11th Regiment from the 1st Division to be reassigned to fight on the Yŏngch'ŏn front, in addition to the support of five tanks from the 1st U.S. Cavalry Division. On September 7, the 19th Regiment took up a position north of Yŏngch'ŏn and recaptured the town on the following afternoon. Fierce fighting ensued for several days, often involving hand-to-hand combat, and the town changed hands four times. In general, the North Korean troops were inexperienced, fatigued, and low in morale, and their supplies were short and their operations uncoordinated. The ROK troops, on the other hand, regrouped and mounted a counteroffensive on September 10. When six ROK regiments commenced the attack on all fronts, the NKPA 15th Division quickly disintegrated, many of its units trapped and routed. By September 13, the ROK troops had regained all the lost territory and pushed their line some 15 kilometers north of the Yŏngch'ŏn-P'ohang road. It is generally believed that the successful defense of Yŏngch'ŏn by the ROK 8th Division saved the UNC defense line along the north of the Taegu-Kyŏngju corridor road, making possible the swift counteroffensive northward in coordination with the Inch'ŏn landing*.

R. E. Appleman, *South to the Naktong, North to the Yalu* (Washington, D.C., 1961); Chungang Ilbo, *Minjok ŭi Chŭngŏn* (Seoul, 1973); Kukbang-bu p'yŏnch'an wiwŏn-hoe, *Han'guk Chŏnjaeng-sa,* vol. 3 (Seoul, 1970).

Yŏng-ho Ch'oe

BATTLES OF THE HOOK (October 1952–July 1953)

One of two central positions in the Commonwealth Division* line (the other was point 355, or Little Gibraltar), the Hook was a ridgeline 4 miles northwest of the confluence of the Samich'ŏn and Imjin rivers and dominated the Samich'ŏn Valley below it. At least five major actions were fought for possession of the feature, three by Commonwealth units. More Commonwealth casualties were incurred in defense of the Hook than on any other Korean battlefield. The first Chinese attempt to take the Hook was resisted by the U.S. 7th Marine Regiment on the night of October 26–27, 1952. The most costly assault in terms of UN casualties was made on the night of November 18–19, when more than 100 enemy dead were counted, but the cost to the defenders was 13 killed, 72 wounded, and 21 missing. The next Chinese attempt to capture the feature was made on March 21, 1953, against the U.S. 2d Infantry Division, which had relieved the Commonwealth Division in the line in February. The Americans repelled several companies of Chinese troops on this occasion without significant loss to themselves.

Two intensive actions were fought during the final period of negotiation at P'anmunjŏm, the last one almost certainly an attempt to improve the local situation immediately prior to the cease-fire. The climax of the first of these came on the night of May 28–29, 1953, when the Duke of Wellington's Regiment withstood a concerted Chinese attack preceded by a heavy artillery bombardment that placed an estimated 10,000 shells on a defensive position measuring 300 yards by 150. The British battalion lost 23 killed, 105 wounded, and 20 missing, and 170 enemy dead were counted around the ruins of the Commonwealth position. The last Chinese attack was made on the night of July 24–25, preceded by a mortar barrage of approximately 4,000 rounds. The 2d Battalion, Royal Australian Regiment, was involved in bitter hand-to-hand fighting, suffering 5 killed and 25 wounded over two nights of intense action. The supporting defensive fire from American and Commonwealth artillery was so heavy and so effective on this occasion, however, that 2,000 to 3,000 enemy dead were counted in the battalion area. *See also* Chinese Summer Offensives of 1953.

C. N. Barclay, *The First Commonwealth Division* (Aldershot, 1954); A. J. Barker, *Fortune Favours the Brave, the Hook, Korea, 1953* (London, 1974); R. J. O'Neill, *Australia in the Korean War 1950–53* (Canberra, 1985).

Jeffrey Grey

BATTLES OF WŎNJU (July 5, 1950–February 18, 1951)

The small city of Wŏnju lies in the center of the Korean peninsula 46 miles south of the thirty-eighth parallel. This road and railroad hub was the object of several battles as the front fluctuated up and down the peninsula. Interestingly, in all of these battles, UNC* forces were on the defensive.

During the North Korean invasion of South Korea*, Communist forces reached Wŏnju on July 2, 1950, as the Republic of Korea's* 6th Division fought a delaying action down the Ch'unch'ŏn-Hongch'ŏn road against the enemy 7th Division. The North Korean high command relieved the division commander, Major General Chon U, at this time because he was behind schedule, Wŏnju falling on July 5.

As the ROK II Corps advanced northward in late September, North Korean forces withdrew from Wŏnju. The city was II Corps headquarters when a force of 1,000 to 2,000 North Korean soldiers who had been bypassed in the mountains attacked in their attempt to escape to the north. After killing most of the corps headquarters staff (including five American liaison officers), they killed over 1,000 civilians before continuing northward.

After the Chinese People's Volunteers Army* (CPVA) drove the allies south, the U.S. 2d Division was holding Wŏnju against two Chinese divisions on January 2, 1951. The weather was so cold that the air force could not fly close support missions. When the inexperienced ROK III Corps on the east flank collapsed under heavy attack, Lieutenant General Matthew B. Ridgway*, 8th Army* commander, ordered Wŏnju abandoned to consolidate his position.

When the UNC counterattacked with Operation Thunderbolt* in late January, it found Wŏnju deserted. Ridgway assigned the 7th Division to defend the Wŏnju area. The Chinese counteroffensive put heavy pressure on Wŏnju from four North Korean divisions but losses from groundfire, bombardment, hunger, and cold forced the enemy to break contact and withdraw on February 18.

This final Battle of Wŏnju, like its predecessors, was not a vital turning point in the war. Yet the fate of the road and railroad hub in the center of the peninsula was important in each phase of the war as the fighting moved up and down Korea.

R. E. Appleman, *South to the Naktong, North to the Yalu* (Washington, D.C., 1961); J. L. Collins, *War in Peacetime* (Boston, 1969); T. R. Fehrenbach, *This Kind of War* (New York, 1963); R. A. Gugeler, *Combat Actions in Korea* (Washington, D.C., 1970); H. J. Middleton, *The Compact History of the Korean War* (New York, 1965).

Larry R. Beck

BEBLER, ALES (1907–1981)

Ales Bebler was Yugoslavia's permanent delegate at the UN and its representative on the Security Council at the start of the Korean War. Highly intelligent and multilingual, he was known as "Tito's chief diplomatic trouble shooter." Bebler could be witty and suave, but when defending justice for small nations, he was often vitriolic.

Born at Idrija near Trieste, Bebler became politically active as a youth, drawing inspiration from the Soviet Union's program for economic development and its public advocacy for the principle of national self-determination. In 1929, he joined the Communist party while studying for the law degree that he would earn the following year at the University of Paris. Aware that arrest awaited him in Yugoslavia, Bebler instead went to Moscow in 1933, where he met Tito. He was wounded while serving with the International Brigade in the Spanish Civil War and then fought with skill and daring against the Nazis with the Yugoslavian Partisans during World War II.

In 1945, Bebler became finance minister of Slovenia, gaining election to the Constituent Assembly that formed the Federated People's Republic of Yugoslavia. From 1946 to 1949, he served as deputy foreign minister and attended all the major postwar conferences. At the UN General Assembly in 1946, Bebler was alternate delegate, devoting his time to Balkan issues and especially Greece.

On December 3, 1949, Tito appointed him as Yugoslavia's permanent repre-sentative. Thereafter, Bebler worked to build international support for Yugoslavia in its efforts to resist Soviet dictation and obtain economic assistance from the West.

North Korea's attack on the Republic of Korea* placed Yugoslavia in the uncomfortable position of trying to maintain its neutrality without alienating the Truman administration. When the UN Security Council met on June 25, 1950, Bebler proposed contacting representatives of the Democratic People's Republic of Korea* to obtain additional information, but this was rejected. Unable to block passage of the UN Security Council resolution of June 25, 1950*, Yu-goslavia's delegate abstained. Two days later, Bebler urged mediation, to include North Korea's formal participation in the process. After failing to gain approval of this alternative, he cast the only vote against the UN Security Council reso-lution of June 27, 1950*. Tito, attempting to pacify the United States, announced that Bebler had acted on his own initiative and Yugoslavia would no longer attempt to block UN efforts to defend South Korea.

In November 1950, Bebler served as president of the UN Security Council. That month, mounting evidence of Chinese military intervention* prompted the UN to invite the People's Republic of China* to discuss its intentions at Lake Success. Bebler wanted bilateral talks between the United States and the PRC, but the Truman administration refused. Working to prevent a wider war, he urged the PRC's representative to be conciliatory. When the UN Security Council convened on November 27, Bebler recommended that discussions cover together charges of Chinese aggression in Korea and the PRC's complaint against the United States for invading Taiwan. For Washington, it was a relief when in December T. F. Tsiang* of the Republic of China* became UN Security Council president. Bebler later became under secretary of state and served as ambassador to France and Indonesia. He finished his career as a judge on Yugoslavia's constitutional court.

Current Biography, 1950; Foreign Relations of the United States, 1950, vol. 7: Korea (Washington, D.C., 1976); New York Times, August 13, 1981.

BENDETSEN, KARL R. (1907–1989)

During the Korean War, Karl R. Bendetsen was under secretary of the army and, from 1950 to 1952, director general of the U.S. railroad system. After earning a law degree at Stanford University in 1932, he returned to his home town of Aberdeen, Washington, where he practiced law until 1940, defending logging, lumber, and mining interests in matters related to taxes and real property. Simultaneously, Bendetsen served as a captain in the field artillery branch of the U.S. Army Officers Reserve Corps. In 1940, he joined the office of the judge advocate general, helping to draft the Soldier and Sailor Civil Relief Act that same year. After serving briefly as the secretary of war's representative to General Douglas MacArthur*, he joined the War Department General Staff to help direct the relocation of 110,000 Japanese-Americans living on the West

Coast and establish a POW information bureau. Then Bendetsen helped organize the Provost Marshal Office, Army Military Police Corps, and the School of Military Government. Traveling to Europe in 1944, he was part of the combined staff that helped plan the Normandy invasion. After the war, Bendetsen resumed his law career in California.

In 1948, Bendetsen returned to government service, working as special consultant in the Office of the Secretary of Defense. Early in 1950, he became assistant secretary of the army in charge of general management. Bendetsen developed a five-year plan to expand and increase the combat readiness of the U.S. Army Reserve, based on his findings as a member of the Civilian Components Policy Board. In August 1950, railroad workers threatened a nationwide strike after seventeen months of negotiations had failed to resolve a dispute with management over wages and hours. To avoid any adverse impact on the war effort in Korea, President Harry S. Truman* issued an executive order establishing federal control over all U.S. railroads, appointing Bendetsen as general director. The railroads remained under Bendetsen's nominal control until May 1952, when there was a settlement of the dispute. Becoming under secretary of the army that same month, Bendetsen left government service later that year, joining Champion Papers and Fiber Company as general consultant. After service as general manager and vice-president, he became chief executive officer in 1957, remaining in this capacity after Champion merged with U.S. Plywood in 1967. Meanwhile, in 1956, Bendetsen had undertaken advisory missions to Germany and the Philippines for the U.S. government. From 1950 to 1959, he also was chairman of the board for the Panama Canal Company. Although Bendetsen retired in 1973, he served as chair of President Ronald Reagan's panel on the Strategic Defense Initiative.

Current Biography, 1952; International Who's Who, 1988–1989 (London, 1989); National Cyclopedia of American Biography, vol. L (Clifton, N.J., 1972); New York Times, June 30, 1989.

BERENDSEN, SIR CARL A. (1890–1973)

Sir Carl August Berendsen was New Zealand's ambassador to the United States and head of the New Zealand delegation to the UN when the Korean War broke out in 1950 until 1952 when he retired. He was implacably anti-Soviet and an outspoken supporter of U.S. and UN action in Korea. Born in Sydney, Australia, Berendsen moved to New Zealand with his parents in 1900. In 1906, he joined the New Zealand civil service as a cadet in the Department of Education, Wellington. He attended Victoria University College, Wellington, as a part-time law student, receiving the LL.B. (1915) and LL.M. degrees, the latter with honors (1917). He served in the New Zealand army from 1914 to 1915 and 1917 to 1919. In 1916, he became chief clerk in the Labor Department and deputy registrar of industrial unions. In 1926, he was appointed imperial affairs officer and in 1928 became secretary for external affairs and in 1932 head of the Prime Minister's Department. In 1943, he became New Zealand's first high commissioner in Canberra, Australia, was cross-posted to become minister at the New Zealand Legation in Washington, D.C., in 1944, and became ambassador when the legation was raised to an embassy in 1948. Berendsen's experience and his seniority in the New Zealand civil service made him a confident and opinionated ambassador.

Berendsen believed that the UN and the United States had a clear moral responsibility for the Republic of Korea*. He hated appeasement and applauded UN intervention in Korea. He was convinced the Democratic People's Republic of Korea* was under Kremlin control and embarrassed the New Zealand government by saying so on radio networks at a time when such an accusation had been carefully avoided by the U.S. administration. He consistently urged the New Zealand government to stand with the United States, suggesting that the Truman administration might regard Korea as a test of those who could become members of a U.S.-supported Pacific Pact*. He enthusiastically endorsed the New Zealand government's decision of June 29, 1950, to send two frigates to the war zone and praised its reluctant decision of July 26 to supply ground troops. Although required by the New Zealand government to vote in favor of the UN resolution of December 1, 1950*, to set up a three-power committee to determine a cease-fire, he regarded the idea of a cease-fire and the Indian-led Arab-Asian peace initiatives* as "inexcusable appeasement" and "surrender to the aggressor." He urged New Zealand support, ultimately given, for the U.S.-sponsored UN resolution of February 1, 1951*, which would brand China as the aggressor. Berendsen favored the bombing of Chinese bases beyond the Yalu, and he regarded the armistice negotiations as wrong. He retired in January 1952 believing that, over Korea, appeasers among the allies were "hanging onto American coat-tails and holding the United States back."

I. C. McGibbon, "New Zealand's Intervention in the Korean War, June-July 1950," *International History Review* (May 1989); A. Trotter, "Personality in Foreign Policy: Sir Carl Berendsen in Washington," *NZ Journal of History* (November 1986); A. Trotter, "Sir Carl Berendsen and Japan," in I. Nish (ed.), *Aspects of the Allied Occupation of Japan* (London, 1986).

Ann Trotter

BEVAN, ANEURIN (1897–1960)

Influential British minister of labor at the start of the Korean War, Aneurin Bevan began his working life as a miner. After entering politics, he established a reputation as an outspoken and often controversial figure on the left of the British Labour party. He was appointed minister of health in Clement R. Attlee's* postwar Labour government. In his attitude to foreign affairs, Bevan was something of a nationalist, believing that Great Britain must set an example to the rest of the world. While he had no sympathy with Stalinism, he was also unhappy about certain aspects of American capitalism and believed that Britain must avoid subservience to the United States. He opposed the terms of the American loan to Britain in 1946 but supported the Marshall Plan and NATO.

When the Korean War broke out, Bevan, like most of the rest of the Labour party, supported the principle of collective security. He was soon disillusioned, however, by the war and its wider consequences. As early as August 1950, he was expressing concern that the costs of Britain's swelling rearmament budget would limit domestic reforms in areas like health and housing. This concern became acute after Attlee's visit to the United States* in December 1950 when the cabinet discussed further large increases in the rearmament program. Although he accepted the post of minister of labor in January 1951 and defended rearmament in the House of Commons, he continued to believe that the program should not be pursued at the expense of economic stability and social reforms.

Bevan's jaundiced view of U.S. policy deepened after Chinese military intervention* in the Korean War. He opposed sanctions against the People's Republic of China* and feared that the Truman administration might allow CINCUNC General Douglas MacArthur* to drag Britain into a wider Asian conflict. In January 1951, he argued against voting in favor of a U.S. resolution at the UN condemning China as an aggressor. Both issues became entangled in Bevan's uneasy relationship with Hugh Gaitskell, chancellor of the exchequer. Gaitskell won out, gaining a vote in favor of the UN resolution of February 1, 1951*, condemning China by threatening to resign in January 1951, and proposing a budget in March designed to impress Washington by its commitment to rearmament through imposing charges for false teeth and spectacles. According to Bevan, Gaitskell was wildly pro-American and acting as an amateur foreign secretary. Attempts to preserve cabinet unity failed, and Bevan resigned on April 22, 1951. The dispute split the Labour party and helped ensure its defeat in the general election six months later.

J. Campbell, *Nye Bevan and the Mirage of British Socialism* (London, 1987); M. Foot, *Aneurin Bevan* (London, 1973); K. O. Morgan, *Labour in Power* (London, 1984); P. Williams, *Hugh Gaitskell* (London, 1979).

Callum A. MacDonald

BEVIN, ERNEST (1881–1951)

Ernest Bevin was British foreign secretary from 1945 to 1951. An illegitimate child, he left school at 12 and worked in the Bristol docks. He became active in the trade union movement and in the Labour party, and he rose to become minister of labor in the World War II coalition government. A staunch anti-Communist who strove for Anglo-American partnership in the containment of communism, Bevin firmly supported U.S. intervention in Korea in June 1950. He disassociated Britain from U.S. policy regarding Taiwan, however. In early July 1950, Bevin tried to persuade the Soviet government to bring about a North Korean withdrawal to the thirty-eighth parallel. Secretary of State Dean G. Acheson* curtly rejected Bevin's suggestion on July 7 that terms for peace might include U.S. concessions regarding Taiwan and the People's Republic of China's* admission to the UN. Bevin supported the British government's decision to send British troops to Korea and the UN offensive across the thirty-eighth parallel* in October 1950.

When Chinese forces appeared in Korea in late October 1950, Bevin proposed a buffer zone along the North Korean–Chinese border, but the U.S. government disagreed. Following Chinese military intervention* in massive force after November 24, 1950, Bevin proposed a settlement on favorable terms to the Chinese with regard to Taiwan and Communist China's admission to the UN, but Acheson angrily rejected any offer of concessions under duress. Bevin and Acheson also disagreed over the U.S. introduction of a UN resolution condemning China as an aggressor, but Bevin ultimately supported the U.S. position in the vote on the UN resolution of February 1, 1951*.

Bevin's disagreements with U.S. policy arose from his concern to heed Asian Commonwealth countries, especially India, and to protect British interests in Hong Kong. As a result, Bevin wished greater sensitivity toward China, especially over Taiwan. Bevin's primary concern, however, was with Europe, so he endeavored to ensure that the bitter Anglo-American disagreements over East Asian policy in 1950 and 1951 did not imperil overall Anglo-American unity in the face of the Communist threat worldwide. Hence, although Bevin acted as a restraining influence in some respects on U.S. policy in Korea, he generally gave way to the American viewpoint on issues on which the United States was adamant. *See also* British DMZ Proposal.

R. Barclay, *Ernest Bevin: Foreign Office, 1932–69* (London, 1975); A. Bullock, *Ernest Bevin: Foreign Secretary, 1945–1951* (London, 1983); C. A. MacDonald, *Korea: The War Before Vietnam* (New York, 1986).

Peter G. Boyle

BIOLOGICAL WARFARE CONTROVERSY (February–June 1952)

The Soviet Union, the People's Republic of China*, and the Democratic People's Republic of Korea* charged that the United States was engaging in germ warfare in North Korea and China, a claim the United States denied. The Communists had previously alleged that Americans were spreading smallpox germs in South Korea and in Eastern Europe, but their campaign asserting bacteriological warfare began in earnest on February 18, 1952, when the Soviets charged on radio that the United States was deliberately spreading smallpox and typhus and sending lepers into North Korea. PRC premier Chou En-lai* repeated the charges. Chou added on March 8 that the U.S. Air Force was dropping insects, rats, shellfish, and chicken feathers to spread disease in North Korea and northern China. Weeks later the North Koreans published confessions of captured American airmen that the United States did indeed engage in such warfare. The Communists mounted the campaign probably to divert attention from the annual epidemics of typhus and smallpox in China and North Korea that appeared especially threatening in 1952 because scarce medical personnel and supplies had been transferred to Korean battlefields. The Chinese may have wanted to draw notice away from their economy, greatly strained by the war, and from the suffering caused by the broad anti-corruption purge then in progress. The Soviet government used the issue to discredit the United States by warning Soviet citizens about the latest lethal weapon of the scientifically advanced West.

Secretary of State Dean G. Acheson* asked for the International Committee of the Red Cross to investigate in March. The North Koreans and Chinese made no reply to the Red Cross and denied a request by the World Health Organization for a verification visit. The Communists stepped up their propaganda, the Soviets inoculating workers against the supposed menace and Chinese newspapers printing alleged proof of the charges. The campaign reached a zenith in June when Chinese germ-hunting squads covered northern China and Korea. The largest Communist propaganda effort aimed at discrediting the West, the biological warfare controversy caused the State Department much work and frustration and weakened American standing in Europe and in Asia. It also helped put the UN negotiators at the P'anmunjŏm truce talks* on the defensive, although not enough to solve agenda item 4* dealing with prisoner repatriation before 1953.

B. I. Kaufman, *The Korean War* (Philadelphia, 1986); D. Rees, *Korea: The Limited War* (New York, 1964).

Richard W. Fanning

BLAIR HOUSE MEETINGS
See First Blair House Meeting; Second Blair House Meeting

BLOODY RIDGE, BATTLE OF
See Battle of Bloody Ridge

BOATNER, HAYDON L. (1900–1977)

During the Kŏje-do POW uprising*, Brigadier General Haydon L. Boatner was appointed the fourteenth commandant within sixteen months at the UN Kŏje Island POW compounds following the disastrous Dodd-Colson POW incident*. Born in New Orleans, ''Bull'' Boatner enlisted in the U.S. Marine Corps in 1918 as a private following U.S. military intervention in World War I. After the armistice and one year of study at Tulane University, he entered the U.S. Military Academy at West Point, graduating in 1924. Boatner served with the 29th Infantry and graduated from Infantry School in 1929. He then joined the 15th Infantry in Tientsin, China, and after learning the Chinese language, served as assistant military attaché in charge of translation at the U.S. embassy at Peking from 1930 to 1934. Boatner returned to the United States for duty with the 30th Infantry and graduated from Command and General Staff School in 1939. He then served as an assistant on Chinese affairs in the War Department General Staff. During World War II, his China expertise resulted in an appointment to organize and command General Joseph W. Stilwell's headquarters at Lashio, in China and, after a brief stint in the United States, Burma, in 1942. After World War II, Boatner was assigned to the 4th Army as personnel officer.

At the time of the North Korean invasion of South Korea*, Boatner was a professor of military science and tactics and commandant of cadets at Texas A&M College. In 1951, he was appointed deputy commanding general of the 2d Infantry Division. His background in China, along with a reputation for being a tough disciplinarian and proximity, explained his selection to replace Brigadier General Charles F. Colson as Kŏje-do camp commandant on May 14, 1952. When asked about the possibility of negotiations with the prisoners, he stated flatly, "Prisoners do not negotiate." Boatner acted with decisive swiftness to end the POW uprising, using tanks and troops to subdue the militants and restore order and control over the compounds. On September 1, 1952, he left for the United States to become deputy commanding general of the 4th Division at Fort Sam Houston. Boatner's last post was as the Department of the Army's provost marshal general in Washington, D.C., from 1957 to 1960.

In retirement, he was publicly and privately critical of American handling of the POW issue during the Korean War. According to Boatner, U.S. "custodianship of the P.O.W.'s was largely a self-inflicted mess and was run in an inefficient, unintelligent manner and evidently directed at the highest government levels with vacillation, unrealism, and a *lack of knowledge of the Asiatic mentality.*" Efforts at reeducating the Chinese POWs and support for the principle of voluntary repatriation*, he argued, only prolonged the war and created needless U.S. casualties.

H. L. Boatner papers, Hoover Institution, Stanford University, Stanford, California; *Current Biography*, 1952.

BOHLEN, CHARLES E. (1904–1974)

Charles E. Bohlen, a veteran diplomat and Soviet expert, helped shape the U.S. diplomatic approach to the Korean conflict. Born in Clayton, New York, and educated at Harvard University, he entered the foreign service in 1929, serving in positions involving Soviet affairs before, during, and after World War II. Bohlen was a member of the first U.S. delegation to Moscow after President Franklin D. Roosevelt recognized the Soviet Union in 1933, was interpreter and adviser to Presidents Roosevelt and Harry S. Truman* at all the wartime summit conferences, advised at the postwar foreign ministers meetings, and was counselor in the State Department. He was assigned to the Paris embassy when the Korean War began.

"Chip" Bohlen's complex and often open-ended assessment of the Korean situation prompted Secretary of State Dean G. Acheson* to complain that Bohlen, like the other Soviet experts, was hedging his bets. Bohlen argued that the invasion was not a prelude to Soviet expansion elsewhere, particularly in Europe, yet he warned that the Soviets were always probing for weak spots, so the United States should be on guard. Recalled to Washington for consultation, he supported Truman's decision to resist but urged restraint since incursion into North Korea might trigger Chinese or even Soviet intervention.

But Bohlen did not advocate capitulation to Soviet desires. When the UN offensive across the thirty-eighth parallel* brought Chinese military intervention*, he called his colleague George F. Kennan* from Paris and implored him to persuade the policymakers not to seek negotiations with the Soviets or Chinese from a weakened position. In 1951, Bohlen was reassigned to Washington. In

September, he accompanied General Omar N. Bradley* to the Korean front and visited CINCUNC General Matthew B. Ridgway* in Tokyo. The Bradley-Bohlen visit to Korea* convinced Bohlen that a military solution to the conflict was improbable.

In April 1953, after a lengthy confirmation fight with Senate McCarthyites, Bohlen became ambassador to the Soviet Union. With the P'anmunjŏm truce talks* stalemated, he proposed a new strategy to Secretary of State John Foster Dulles*: a direct approach to Soviet foreign secretary Vyacheslav M. Molotov* with a new U.S. proposal. After the UNC* made its final POW settlement proposal of May 25, 1953*, Bohlen approached Molotov with a summary of the proposal on plain paper, impressing on the Soviet diplomat the finality and seriousness of the offer. Shortly after, Molotov verbally informed Bohlen that the Soviets would encourage their allies to come to terms. Unknown to Bohlen at the time, Dulles had concurrently delivered his atomic warning to China,* which may have brought the diplomatic arrangement ending the Korean War.

C. E. Bohlen, *Witness to History* (New York, 1973); W. Isaacson and E. Thomas, *The Wise Men* (New York, 1986); T. M. Ruddy, *The Cautious Diplomat* (Kent, Ohio, 1986).

T. Michael Ruddy

BOLTÉ, CHARLES L. (1895–1989)

When the Korean War began, Lieutenant General Charles L. Bolté was the U.S. Army's assistant chief of staff for operations. Born in Chicago, he graduated in 1917 with a degree in chemical engineering from the Armour Institute of Technology. He earned his commission as a second lieutenant after attending student training camps from 1914 to 1916. Bolté fought in France with the 4th Infantry Division at St. Mihiel, participating as well in the Argonne-Meuse and Aisne-Marne offensives. In 1920, he joined the War Plans Division of the War Department General Staff, later working in the Office of the Army Chief of Staff. Bolté completed courses at the Infantry School in 1930 and the Command and General Staff School in 1932, before an assignment with the 15th Infantry at Tientsin, China. After graduating from the Army War College in 1937, he was an instructor there until 1940, when he became an operations and training officer with the 4th Army Corps. In May 1941, Bolté went to London to assist in the coordination of war planning.

A month after the United States entered World War II, Bolté became chief of staff for U.S. forces in Europe, later fighting in Italy from 1943 to 1945 as commander of the 69th Division and then the 34th Division. Having risen through the ranks to major general, he returned to Washington in October 1945, serving in a variety of posts related to high-level Pentagon planning. In 1949, Bolté participated in developing plans for the U.S. military withdrawal from Korea*. He became assistant chief of staff for operations in March 1950. Appearing before a congressional committee that spring, he testified that the South Korean army was strong enough to repulse an invasion from the north. After the United

States committed combat troops in the Korean War, Bolté strongly advocated National Guard mobilization* but consistently cautioned against an overcommitment of U.S. men and material. For example, he voiced opposition when CINCUNC General Douglas MacArthur* requested four additional combat divisions in July 1950. In response to Chinese military intervention*, he recommended preparations for the outbreak of global war while advocating evacuation of Korea rather than dispatching more troops.

After Major General Clyde D. Eddleman replaced him in 1952, Bolté assumed command of the 7th Army in Germany and later became commander of the U.S. Army in Europe, working to improve its effectiveness. Upon his return to Washington in September 1953, he served as vice-chief of staff, remaining in that position until his retirement in 1955. Both of his sons fought as officers in the Korean War and were wounded. A long-time cohort of Army Chief of Staff General J. Lawton Collins*, Bolté had a reputation for being warm, witty, and tactful.

C. Blair, *The Forgotten War* (New York, 1987); *Current Biography,* 1954; *New York Times,* February 13, 1989; J. F. Schnabel, *Policy and Direction* (Washington, D.C., 1972).

BOND, NILES W. (1916–   )

Niles W. Bond was in charge of the Korean desk in the Department of State's Division of Northeast Asian Affairs during 1949 and 1950. Born in Newton, Massachusetts, he graduated from the University of North Carolina in 1937 and the Fletcher School of Law and Diplomacy in 1938. Bond then joined the foreign service, with his first posting as vice-consul in Havana, Cuba. From there, he went to Tokyo in 1940, where he was interned following the Japanese attack on Pearl Harbor. In 1942, Bond returned to the United States aboard the *Gripsholm,* serving until 1946 in the U.S. embassy in Madrid. After a brief stint in Bern, he returned to Washington in 1947 to work in the Division of Northeast Asian Affairs.

In late 1949, Bond traveled to the Republic of Korea* to assess its need for additional military assistance. After completing this survey, he became a vigorous advocate for expansion of the ROK's military capabilities until the outbreak of the Korean War on June 25, 1950. In July, Bond went to Tokyo to serve as first secretary under William J. Sebald*, political adviser to CINCUNC General Douglas MacArthur*. Two years later, he became counselor at the U.S. embassy in Tokyo and held the same position in South Korea from 1953 to 1954. During the remainder of his career as a diplomat, Bond held postings abroad in Italy and Brazil while serving at home as director of the office of UN Political and Security Affairs. In 1968, he became secretary of the board of trustees for the Corcoran Gallery of Art in Washington, D.C.

Foreign Relations of the United States, 1950, vol. 7: *1950* (Washington, D.C., 1976); J. I. Matray, *The Reluctant Crusade* (Honolulu, 1985); *Who Was Who in America,* vol. 6: *1978–1979* (Chicago, 1978).

BONNET, HENRI (1888–1978)

During the Korean War, Henri Bonnet was France's ambassador to the United States. Born in Chateauponsac, he earned a doctorate in history at the University of Paris, where he taught beginning in 1912. During World War I, Bonnet was a captain in the French army and in 1919 became foreign editor for the *Ere Nouvelle*. From 1920 to 1931, he was a member of the Secretariat at the League of Nations. During the next decade, he served in a variety of capacities, including secretary-general of the permanent conference of the Hautes Etudes Internationales, vice-president of the Center for Studies of Foreign Policy, and member of the Superior Council of Scientific Research. Bonnet fled to the United States in 1940 following the Nazi invasion of France, becoming a professor of political science at the Ecole Libre des Hautes Etudes in New York City. After serving on the executive council of the France Forever Committee, he joined the Free French provisional government as minister of information in 1943. The next year, Charles de Gaulle appointed him ambassador to the United States because of his experience and personality.

Bonnet, the quintessential French diplomat, served as ambassador to the United States until 1955. In this capacity, he signed the UN Charter for France, helped obtain economic aid for Europe under the Marshall Plan, and participated in the establishment of NATO. Following the North Korean invasion of South Korea*, Bonnet worked to ensure that France played a role in the development of policies regarding the war and that the United States considered the impact of events in Korea on Indochina. In June 1951, he proposed a tripartite conference to open armistice negotiations. Later, at the Korean War briefing meetings*, Bonnet advocated postponing discussion of political issues until after achievement of a cease-fire with adequate inspection provisions. Acting on instructions, he pushed for including a reference to Indochina in the Joint Policy (Greater Sanctions) statement*. In retirement, Bonnet was active as vice president of the France-America Friendship Society. He authored a number of books, articles, and studies related to both foreign affairs and assorted cultural subjects.

Current Biography, 1945; *Foreign Relations of the United States, 1951*, vol. 7: *Korea and China* (Washington, D.C., 1983) and *1952–1954*, vol. 15: *Korea* (Washington, D.C., 1984); *New York Times*, November 6, 1978; *Who Was Who in America*, vol. 8: *1982–1985* (Chicago, 1985); *Who's Who in the World, 1976–1977* (Chicago, 1976).

BORDER CLASHES (May 1949–June 1950)

Before the Korean War, there was already a kind of war along the thirty-eighth parallel. Battalion-sized and larger units were often involved, and casualties were heavy. Both sides initiated engagements, and neither considered the parallel an international boundary; opposing forces sometimes penetrated miles into the other's territory. The major battles were carefully orchestrated to drive home political points, gather intelligence, and keep the enemy off balance. In line with President Syngman Rhee's* policy of bluff, the Republic of Korea's* forces began posturing along the parallel in the spring of 1949 as U.S. troops were being withdrawn. North Korea seems to have gotten the worst of it in the initial fighting, since it controlled the border with lightly armed border guards while holding its army in reserve, allowing the ROK to achieve local superiority before it could bring its regular forces into play. Later, P'yŏngyang came down hard on South Korean forces as part of a campaign against Rhee's sabre rattling and talk of a "March North."

Fighting started in early May 1949 with a general consolidation of the parallel by ROK forces in the midst of discussions with the United States about U.S. military withdrawal from Korea*. Rhee called for a "March North," lobbied for U.S. military aid, and turned southern commanders loose along the parallel. The most serious fighting occurred at Kaesŏng, in the Ch'unch'ŏn area in the center of the parallel, and on the isolated Ongjin Peninsula (which lacked overland lines of communication with the rest of South Korea and where U.S. advisers feared southern troops would be trapped if war broke out). The two sides often vied for control of strategic heights that straddled the border, especially Unp'a-san and Hill 488, which dominated Haeju and Kaesŏng, respectively. In one incident in May, two ROK battalion commanders defected to North Korea with the bulk of their soldiers. Other incidents were designed to cover the infiltration of guerrillas, usually Communist partisans but occasionally ROK irregulars. There were also naval engagements. Rhee's visit to Chinhae—the port of the ROK navy—for a summit with Chiang Kai-shek* at the end of July inspired a southern naval offensive in which ROK ships shelled shore installations at the mouth of the Taedong River and sank most of the North Korea's west coast fleet.

The Democratic People's Republic of Korea* started its share of incidents but concentrated on building a revolutionary base while supporting the southern guerrilla struggle. As the military balance tilted in its favor as a result of Soviet arms deliveries, however, P'yŏngyang showed its annoyance at Rhee's needling in a concerted campaign against southern "invasions" of its territory. The campaign opened with the formation on August 1 of a committee to investigate the border incidents. In heavy fighting at Ongjin, Kaesŏng, and Ch'unch'ŏn, the DPRK drove ROK forces from salients north of the parallel. The heavy blows were designed to demonstrate that P'yŏngyang had gained the upper hand; for the first time, it committed its regular army to the fighting. The campaign continued to unfold with a big Liberation Day parade to display its newly acquired weaponry, a show trial for captured ROK guerrillas, and a fund-raising drive to buy more Soviet tanks and planes. The campaign ended with Foreign Minister Pak Hŏn-yŏng* sending the report of the investigating committee to the United Nations, along with a warning that if it continued to ignore the DPRK and interfere on the peninsula, the Korean people would have to rely on their own means to unify the divided country.

Except for a brief flare-up on Ongjin, there were few major border incidents after this until the outbreak of the war. ROK commanders adopted a much lower stance along the parallel, avoiding fights they could no longer win. Nonetheless, the clashes had been a costly diversion. They made it harder to read the purpose of the northern military buildup, whose seriousness the U.S. Korean Military Advisory Group* downplayed. Rhee's policy of bluff reduced the readiness of his forces and squandered American goodwill; suspicion of his intentions led Washington to keep ROK forces on a short leash. P'yŏngyang was able to use its campaign against the border incidents to mobilize domestic support and lay the groundwork for justifying its invasion. Most important, by raising the spectre of a long-term threat from South Korea, the border clashes may have bolstered Kim Il Sung's* arguments to Joseph Stalin* to approve the North Korean invasion of South Korea*.

Chŏnsa p'yŏnch'an wiwŏn-hoe, *Han'guk Chŏnjaeng-sa* (Seoul, 1967); J. Merrill, *Korea: The Peninsular Origins of the War* (Newark, Del., 1989); Harutaka Sasaki, *Han'gukchŏn pisa* (Seoul, 1977).

John Merrill

BOWLES, CHESTER (1901–1986)

As ambassador to India, Bowles encouraged the Indian government in 1952 to pursue efforts to mediate an end to the Korean War. Born in Springfield, Massachusetts, Bowles graduated from Yale University in 1924 and launched a highly successful Manhattan advertising agency with fellow Yale graduate William Benton. During the 1940s, he fulfilled a lifelong ambition by entering government service, first as director of the wartime Office of Price Administration and later as U.S. delegate to the UN Educational and Science Organization. Bowles was elected governor of Connecticut on the Democratic ticket in 1948, and after he narrowly lost reelection in 1950, President Harry S. Truman* appointed him ambassador to India. A New Deal Democrat and a confirmed internationalist, Bowles held a deep interest in the developing nations of Asia and Africa, and he welcomed the opportunity to serve in India. After completing his assignment in New Delhi in 1953, Bowles remained a prominent figure in the liberal wing of the Democratic party. During the Kennedy and Johnson administrations, he served as under secretary of state and then returned to India for a second tenure as U.S. ambassador.

When Bowles first reached India in October 1952, the P'anmunjŏm truce talks* had bogged down on one issue: agenda item 4*, forcible versus voluntary repatriation* of POWs. More supportive of India's nonaligned foreign policy than most other U.S. officials, Bowles urged Prime Minister Jawaharlal Nehru* to make use of his contacts with the People's Republic of China* and the Soviet Union to facilitate negotiations. Convinced that Moscow particularly sought to prolong the war, the ambassador went so far as to warn Nehru that America's extension of the war was inevitable unless a satisfactory settlement was soon reached. At the same time, Bowles reported to Washington on India's view that the PRC appeared more amenable to an armistice than its Soviet ally and counseled that the United States should exploit the differences. As a nonaligned nation and an Asian power, India had already taken the initiative on several occasions to seek a negotiated settlement of the war, and in November 1952, India's UN representative, V. K. Krishna Menon*, introduced a compromise resolution on the emotional POW issue. After the Soviet Union had rejected the Menon POW settlement proposal* and the addition of a number of amendments that effectively ensured voluntary repatriation, the United States followed Bowles's advice and endorsed the Menon plan, voting for the UN resolution of December 3, 1952*. Following the death of Joseph Stalin* in March 1953, China did accept a modified version of the Menon resolution, and an armistice agreement* was signed in July. Although it is unlikely that Bowles's activities substantially contributed to the settlement, many of his views did prove to be accurate. *See also* Indian Peace Initiatives.

C. Bowles, *Ambassador's Report* (New York, 1954); C. Bowles, *Promises to Keep: My Years in Public Life, 1941–1969* (New York, 1971); C. Bowles papers, Sterling Library, Yale University, New Haven, Connecticut.

Dennis Merrill

BOWLING ALLEY

This was the nickname for a straight stretch of road that ran through a narrow valley 13 miles northwest from Taegu. U.S. soldiers assigned this label to the area in August 1950 while defending the Pusan Perimeter* because solid shells from enemy tanks at the head of the valley ricocheted down the road with thunderous reverberations. During fighting in the Bowling Alley, the UNC* was able to inflict major losses on the North Korean army, contributing to the successful defense of Taegu*.

BRADLEY, OMAR N. (1893–1981)

General of the Army Omar N. Bradley was chairman of the Joint Chiefs of Staff throughout the Korean War. Born in Clark, Missouri, he graduated from the U.S. Military Academy in 1915 and served in various domestic posts during World War I and the interwar period. He rose swiftly during World War II, ending the war as a four-star general. He saw his first combat as deputy corps commander in North Africa in 1943, was a corps commander in North Africa and Sicily, and commanded the 1st U.S. Army in the Normandy invasion. As commander of the 12th U.S. Army Group in 1944 and 1945, he oversaw U.S. ground operations in the defeat of Nazi forces on the Western Front. After the war, he headed the Veterans Administration for two years and was army chief of staff from February 1948 until August 1949, when President Harry S. Truman* appointed him JCS chairman. Although the newly created position of JCS chairman was technically non-voting, Bradley's opinions carried much weight. He frequently represented JCS views in meetings at which the other chiefs were not present. Truman liked the unpretentious and plain-spoken general, who became one of his most trusted advisers. Truman raised him to five-star general in September 1950.

Bradley and the other chiefs found themselves in the middle of the developing conflict between Truman and CINCUNC General Douglas MacArthur*. Their reluctance to exercise detailed control over the tactical operations of a field commander was heightened by MacArthur's immense prestige and popularity. The success of the Inch'ŏn landing* added to their hesitancy (shared by other administration officials) to restrain MacArthur in his drive to the Yalu in November 1950, despite their doubts about its military wisdom. After the Chinese intervened in full force, the JCS took a more active role in dealing with MacArthur, in support of Truman's efforts to limit the war. The JCS unanimously supported Truman's recall of MacArthur*, but accounts of Bradley's role differ. According to Truman, Bradley declared at an April 6 meeting with the president and his senior advisers that MacArthur should be fired on grounds of insubordination. According to Bradley's contemporary account, he did not recommend MacArthur's relief at that time. When the full JCS met two days later, he agreed with their unanimous view that MacArthur should be relieved, not on grounds of insubordination but to maintain the principle of civilian control over the military.

At the MacArthur Hearings*, Bradley testified at length and argued effectively against MacArthur's recommendations, declaring that widening the war to China "would involve us in the wrong war, at the wrong place, at the wrong time, and with the wrong enemy." This much-quoted statement did not refer to the Korean War, to which it is sometimes misapplied, but to a possible war with China or the USSR. Bradley's association with Truman's policies made him a target of Republican criticism in 1952, but he remained JCS chairman under President Dwight D. Eisenhower* until the end of his second two-year term in August 1953. *See also* Bradley-Bohlen Visit to Korea.

O. N. Bradley, *A General's Life* (New York, 1983); J. L. Collins, *War in Peacetime* (Boston, 1969); J. F. Schnabel and R. J. Watson, *A History of the Joint Chiefs of Staff,* vol. 3: *The Korean War* (Wilmington, 1979).

Harriet D. Schwar

BRADLEY-BOHLEN VISIT TO KOREA (September 28–October 3, 1951)

This fact-finding mission occurred in response to the truce talks suspension of August 23, 1951*, resulting from the Communist Chinese charge that a U.S. aircraft had allegedly carried out a bombing raid in the neutral areas around Kaesŏng. In the face of this setback, the Truman administration was intent upon resuming these talks at the earliest possible date. When the opportunity presented itself in September, an internal dispute developed between CINCUNC General Matthew B. Ridgway* and some officials in Washington. Ridgway believed that the Chinese Communists were in an unfavorable military position and that a resumption of the talks benefited the Chinese more than the United States. He was adamant that he would not return to the talks unless directly ordered to do so. Furthermore, he did not want to return to the Kaesŏng site.

In response to this disagreement, General Omar N. Bradley*, JCS chairman, and Charles E. Bohlen*, State Department counselor, were dispatched on a fact-finding mission to Tokyo and Korea. After discussions with Ridgway and a two-day tour of the front, the two returned to Washington and made their report. In his memoirs, Bohlen discounts the significance of this trip; however, in some respects, the exchange of views with Ridgway during the visit helped to define U.S. goals and direction.

First, Bradley made it clear to Ridgway that the United States had no intention of committing more divisions to Korea since mobilization would be required. This decision in effect meant that the United States was abandoning a military victory as its goal. Second, both Bohlen and Bradley returned with a clearer and more positive conception of the UNC* position in Korea. This partially affirmed Ridgway's contention that the Chinese position was unfavorable and that they needed a resumption of talks. In fact, Bohlen upon his return to Washington supported Ridgway's demand that he not return to the Kaesŏng site. Ultimately P'anmunjŏm became the new location for the talks. *See also* Kaesŏng Neutral Zone Controversy.

C. E. Bohlen, *Witness to History* (New York, 1973); O. N. Bradley, *A General's Life* (New York, 1983); J. C. Goulden, *Korea: The Untold Story of the War* (New York, 1982); C. A. MacDonald, *Korea: The War Before Vietnam* (New York, 1986).

T. Michael Ruddy

BRAINWASHING AND PRISONER OF WAR MORALE

In the aftermath of the Korean War, an emotional and divisive debate erupted in the United States over allegations of brainwashing of UN, and specifically U.S., prisoners of war by their Chinese captors. Although brainwashing as presented at that time is a myth, Chinese attempts at prisoner indoctrination and ideological persuasion were a significant part of Chinese POW policy. These efforts, however, were generally clumsy, and the political lectures delivered to prisoners were met with derision. This unsuccessful compulsory indoctrination attempt was abandoned by the beginning of 1952, with the Chinese denying that it had ever taken place. Failure of the policy led to reprisals against leading POW "reactionaries" and widespread interrogation of the remainder. The removal of most POW leaders, the existence of a small group of informers and "progressives" in their midst, and the fact that most U.S. prisoners were captured before mid-1951 and had been given little if any preparation in methods of resistance to their captors led many prisoners to cooperate—but in general not to collaborate—with the Chinese. It was this perceived widespread failure to resist strenuously that led to fears of brainwashing and charges of widespread collaboration.

Journalists Eugene Kincaid and W. L. White publicized the brainwashing allegations in the late 1950s but did not provide any substantive body of evidence. Nevertheless, it resulted in changes to the Uniform Code of Military Justice and the general democratization of personnel policy. In particular, they drew attention to an alleged lack of discipline and growing softness in American society. The behavior of U.S. Army personnel was singled out for criticism, and invidious comparisons were drawn with the behavior of the U.S. Marines, the Turks, and the Commonwealth. In none of these cases did Kincaid or White draw the correct conclusions from the higher survival rates or lower cooperation rates among these groups; the marines were volunteers and had been given some training in resistance to their captors, the Turks utilized a language barrier that prevented infiltration by the Chinese and was supplemented by a ruthless policy of executing informers in their midst, and among the British, at least the incidence of cooperation with their captors was far higher than the critics allowed and derived from the same general causes, none of which had anything to do with brainwashing.

Although Albert Biderman and others effectively refuted the brainwashing issue in the early 1960s, the allegations did lead to widespread concern among the armed forces in the West and led to the strengthening of escape and evasion training for service personnel in a number of countries and to the standardization of code of conduct regulations. *See also* Communist POW Administration; UN POW Administration.

A. D. Biderman, *March to Calumny* (New York, 1963); Cyril Cunningham, ''The Origins and Development of Communist Prisoner-of-War Policies,'' *RUSI Journal* (March 1974); J. Grey, ''Commonwealth Prisoners of War and British Policy during the Korean War,'' *RUSI Journal* (Spring 1988); E. Kincaid, *In Every War But One* (New York, 1959); Ministry of Defense, *Treatment of British Prisoners of War in Korea* (London, 1955).

Jeffrey Grey

BRIDGEFORD, SIR WILLIAM (1894–1971)

Lieutenant General Sir William Bridgeford was the commander in chief, British Commonwealth Occupation Force and British Commonwealth Forces, Korea, 1951 to 1953. A graduate of the Royal Military College, Duntroon (1915), Bridgeford served in France during World War I. Between the wars, he held a variety of staff and instructional posts, also attending the Staff College, Quetta, and the Imperial Defence College, London. During World War II, he commanded the 25th Australian Infantry Brigade in England and saw service in the Middle East; after returning to Australia in 1942, he held a variety of senior command and staff posts. From his postwar position as quartermaster-general of the Australian Military Forces, Bridgeford was sent to replace Lieutenant General Sir Horace Robertson* in Japan in October 1951. Robertson had strained relations with the British chiefs of staff and the Foreign Office in the exercise of his command, and Bridgeford's appointment was intended to restore relations to a more even keel. A large, genial man of considerable ability, he quickly smoothed over most of the tensions in the Commonwealth Division's* organization inherited from his predecessor. He had few remaining duties in relation to the occupation of Japan, since this was rapidly approaching its end, but he continued to discharge responsibility for the logistical and administrative needs of the Commonwealth forces.

Bridgeford was unfortunate to preside over a serious rift in Commonwealth

relations in 1952 over the dispatch to the POW compounds at Kŏje-do of Canadian troops for guard duty. The Canadian authorities claimed not to have been
consulted and argued that their forces should not be divided in this way. Bridgeford took the view that meeting the CINCUNC's request for Commonwealth
troops was a legitimate exercise of his command, and the British and Australian
governments backed him on the issue, although the Canadian authorities tried
to have him sacked. This incident aside, his period of command in Japan was
regarded favorably by the British, Australian, and New Zealand governments,
and he was said to have enjoyed particularly good relations with the U.S. high
command.

J. Grey, *The Commonwealth Armies and the Korean War* (Manchester, 1988); R. J.
O'Neill, *Australia in the Korean War 1950–53* (Canberra, 1981, 1985).

Jeffrey Grey

BRIGGS, ELLIS O. (1899–1976)

Ellis O. Briggs was U.S. ambassador to the Republic of Korea* from November 1952 to April 1955. He took over the embassy from John J. Muccio*
whose personal relations with President Syngman Rhee* had soured. One of
Briggs's main tasks was to establish a less adversarial relationship between Rhee
and the U.S. ambassador, a difficult assignment because Rhee's views on key
issues such as the armistice, Korean unification, the size of Korean armed forces,
and Japan clashed directly with U.S. policy. Rhee's tendency to deal directly
with President Dwight D. Eisenhower* and Secretary of State John Foster Dulles*
and to use the U.S. ambassador as a mere conduit complicated Briggs's job.
Nonetheless, Briggs had an important role as an adviser to Washington, albeit
one of many, on U.S.-Korean relations.

Briggs grew up in Riverdale, New York, and graduated from Dartmouth
College in 1921 with an A.B. in international relations. After college, he taught
in Turkey and tried a stint as a freelance writer. In 1925, Briggs joined the
foreign service. He spent most of his career at Latin American postings or in
Latin American jobs at State and then became ambassador to the Dominican
Republic in 1944. Briggs had limited experience in East Asia, serving in 1945
at Chungking, the Republic of China's* wartime capital. Briggs's service with
the Chinese Nationalists was not enough to taint him as one of the "China
hands" who were blamed for the "loss" of China.

During his career as a foreign service officer, Briggs was strongly anti-
Communist and generally conservative in his political outlook. He was ambassador to Czechoslovakia from 1949 to 1952, an experience that he claimed
reinforced to him the dangers and drawbacks of communism. Briggs was appointed as ambassador to Korea with explicit instructions to rush to his new post
before President-elect Eisenhower made his trip to Korea* in December 1952.
Though appointed by President Harry S. Truman*, Briggs worked closely and
well with the new Republican administration. He considered himself a popular

writer, and the reports he drafted from Korea had a distinctive, pungent style. After retirement in 1959, Briggs contributed to popular magazines and wrote two books, *Farewell to Foggy Bottom* (New York, 1964) and *Anatomy of Diplomacy* (New York, 1968), which were combinations of anecdotes and prescriptions for the conduct of diplomacy in the future.

Edward C. Keefer

BRITISH DMZ PROPOSAL (November 1950)

This was a British plan to prevent massive Chinese military intervention in the Korean War following the first evidence of China's entry at the beginning of November 1950. It was feared that CINCUNC General Douglas MacArthur* could not now reach the border without bombing Manchuria, risking the wider war that Britain had consistently wanted to avoid. The British chiefs of staff therefore proposed halting MacArthur's forces on the line Hŭngnam-Chŏngju and creating a DMZ from there to the Yalu River. On November 10, British foreign minister Ernest Bevin* approached the Americans, emphasizing that holding this good defensive position would be a temporary expedient pending Korean unification. The North Koreans in the zone would be asked to lay down their arms, and the area would be run by a UN commission, which would consult the People's Republic of China* on issues of border security. The plan was calculated to reassure Peking, secure the withdrawal of the Chinese People's Volunteers Army*, and open the way to Korean unification without risking a wider war.

While the plan received a favorable response from Canada and India, the United States was unencouraging. MacArthur, who apparently had advance knowledge of British intentions, informed Washington on November 9 that he intended to drive to the Yalu. Although more concerned about the situation than MacArthur, Secretary of State Dean G. Acheson* was unenthusiastic about the British plan and asked Bevin to delay its publication. On November 15, he emphasized that military operations must not be suspended. The only way to ascertain Chinese intentions was by further military probing.

While Washington stalled, Bevin decided to sound out the Chinese. On November 23, the British chargé in Peking saw the Chinese vice–foreign minister and speaking unofficially suggested a DMZ as a means of reassuring China about the security of the border. This approach produced no Chinese response, and the following day the British proposal was finally turned down by Washington. On November 24, as MacArthur's Home-by-Christmas offensive* began, Acheson emphasized to Britain the divisive results if it went ahead and presented its plan at the UN. Five days later, the issue became academic when MacArthur reported that with massive Chinese military intervention* his command faced an "entirely new war." *See also* Chinese Military Disengagement of November 6, 1950; Yalu Bridges Controversy.

E. Barker, *The British Between the Superpowers, 1945–50* (London, 1983); P. Lowe, *The Origins of the Korean War* (London, 1986); C. A. MacDonald, *Korea: The War Before Vietnam* (London, 1986).

Callum A. MacDonald

BRITISH PEACE INITIATIVES

Great Britain's support of a military response to the North Korean invasion of South Korea* and commitment of British naval and ground forces, under UN auspices, to the struggle was the product of sincere popular enthusiasm for checking the Communist advance and pragmatic concern for keeping intact the Anglo-American alliance. Nevertheless, from the beginning of the Korean War, Britain was anxious that the chief focus of the United States not be shifted from Europe to a comparatively insignificant corner of East Asia and that larger goals not be compromised by the Truman administration's inflexible pursuit of military solutions. Thus, British leaders sought from the outset a diplomatic settlement that would restore the prewar situation without dangerous escalation of cold war tensions and reinforce the primacy of Western Europe and Britain's economic resuscitation in U.S. strategic thinking.

Within weeks of the North Korean attack, the British were seeking to mediate between the United States and the Kremlin. The aim was to prevent a Soviet-U.S. confrontation by resolving UN issues and devising a deal over Korea and Taiwan. When these efforts triggered violent American objections, Prime Minister Clement R. Attlee's* government backed off, though it quietly encouraged Indian peace initiatives* during the summer of 1950. In the aftermath of Chinese military intervention* and appalled by CINCUNC General Douglas MacArthur's* bellicosity and President Harry S. Truman's* atomic bomb press conference comment*, the British renewed their efforts to avoid expansion of the war into China by proposing negotiations looking toward a cease-fire. Attlee's position was that the United States not become so enmeshed in East Asia as to open Western Europe to attack. In particular, Britain believed that U.S. support of Chiang Kai-shek* and opposition to seating the People's Republic of China* in the UN were obstacles to resolving the conflict. British and U.S. leaders smoothed over the differences, but their contrasting views on such matters as China's international status were not resolved. In January 1951, the United Kingdom joined with India, Canada, and other states to sponsor a UN resolution espousing "five principles" for a peaceful settlement in Korea. The United States reluctantly supported this initiative but was relieved when Peking rejected the plan, opening the way to passage of the UN resolution of February 1, 1951*, condemning the PRC for aggression in Korea.

British advocacy of a negotiated settlement revived during the discussions, following the UNC* military successes in March 1951, about advancing north of the thirty-eighth parallel. Foreign Secretary Herbert S. Morrison* proposed that all nations contributing to the war effort endorse the goal of an independent, united Korea, withdrawal of all foreign troops, and negotiations to these ends.

Despite Truman's recall of MacArthur* and the U.S. acceptance of cease-fire negotiations—and the return to power of Winston Churchill* as leader of a Conservative government committed at all costs to maintaining the Anglo-American special relationship—Britain continued to maneuver for a UN solution to the conflict. This culminated in October 1952 in British support for Indian diplomat V. K. Krishna Menon's* POW settlement proposal*, to break the impasse over agenda item 4*, prisoner repatriation. Once again, an open break with the United States was avoided, but the most recent British backstage initiative served to confirm the substantial differences between Washington and its major allies over strategic priorities and political realities. *See also* NSC-80; NSC-95; UN Ceasefire Group.

D. Acheson, *Present at the Creation* (New York, 1969); A. Bullock, *Ernest Bevin: Foreign Secretary, 1945–1951* (New York, 1983); W. R. Louis and H. Bull (eds.), *The Special Relationship: Anglo-American Relations Since 1945* (New York, 1986).

Theodore A. Wilson

"BUDDY SYSTEM"
See Korean Augmentation of the U.S. Army

BUFFER ZONE PROPOSAL
See British DMZ Proposal

"BUG-OUT FEVER"
This was the U.S. Army term for unauthorized retreats when troops broke and ran in the face of the enemy. The problem was particularly acute in the early weeks of the fighting when the understrength and poorly trained divisions of the 8th Army* were hurriedly thrown into battle against the North Korean veterans. The Pentagon was seriously concerned by the situation, complaining on August 9, 1950, that American soldiers in Korea "lacked an aggressive fighting spirit" and were "not up to World War Two standards." At times the 8th Army commander, Lieutenant General Walton W. Walker*, resorted to desperate measures, gliding over retreating units in a scout plane and yelling at them to stand fast. Although many white troops performed badly, the U.S. 24th Infantry, a segregated black outfit, was thought to pose a special problem. Although individuals fought bravely, units of the regiment endangered the military position on several occasions by retreating without orders. It was later charged by the National Association for the Advancement of Colored People that soldiers from the 24th Infantry were treated more severely by courts-martial for such offenses than white soldiers from other units.

The problem of "bugging out" reemerged during the winter of 1950 when the People's Republic of China* entered the war. The retreat across the thirty-eighth parallel was known as the "big bug-out," and morale in many units was poor. The situation was quickly taken in hand by the new 8th Army commander, Lieutenant General Matthew B. Ridgway*, who imposed strict standards of discipline and was quick to fire incompetent officers. "Bug-out fever" was attributable less to the supposed poor fighting qualities of the U.S. soldier than to his inadequate training and preparation for the tasks that faced him in Korea. It was never a problem with the marines, whose training and esprit de corps carried them through in the grimmest situations such as the Hŭngnam evacuation* in December 1950.

R. E. Appleman, *South to the Naktong, North to the Yalu* (Washington, D.C., 1961); C. A. MacDonald, *Korea: The War Before Vietnam* (London, 1986); B. C. Nalty, *Strength for the Fight: A History of Black Americans in the Military* (New York, 1986).

Callum A. MacDonald

BURKE, ARLEIGH A. (1901–   )

Rear Admiral Arleigh A. Burke served during the Korean War as deputy chief of staff, commander, U.S. Naval Forces, Far East (1950–1951), a member of the UN Truce Negotiating Team (1951), and director of the Strategic Plans Division of the Office of the Chief of Naval Operations (1952–1954). Born in Boulder, Colorado, he graduated from the U.S. Naval Academy in 1923 and spent six years at sea. After postgraduate work, including an M.S. in chemical engineering from the University of Michigan, he served as a design and production expert in explosives, alternating sea duty with tours in the Bureau of Ordnance. Burke saw his first combat in the South Pacific in early 1943, earning the nickname "31-Knot Burke." In March 1944, he joined Fast Carrier Task Force 58 as chief of staff during the Marianas, Leyte, Iwo Jima and Okinawa campaigns. Burke's postwar service was entwined with the navy's fight to preserve itself in the face of the challenges of defense unification and the cold war. In 1949, he gained national notoriety as head of the Organizational Research and Policy Division of the Office of the Chief of Naval Operations (Op–23), developing navy positions for debates on the National Security Act amendments of 1949 and congressional hearings on the B–36 bomber and unification and strategy. Removed from the promotion list for rear admiral by Navy Secretary Francis P. Matthews*, he was reinstated by President Harry S. Truman* in December 1949.

When the Korean War broke out, Rear Admiral Burke was the navy member of the Defense Research and Development Board. Admiral Forrest P. Sherman*, the chief of naval operations, ordered Burke to Japan as his personal troubleshooter. Working for Vice-Admiral C. Turner Joy*, commander, U.S. Naval Forces, Far East, Burke was in charge of plans and operations. He oversaw preparations for navy support of the invasion and expected occupation of North Korea*, negotiated with the Japanese Maritime Safety Agency for minesweepers to use in the Wŏnsan landing*, and directed navy planning for the withdrawal of UN forces following the Chinese military intervention* in November and for a possible allied evacuation of Korea. Burke also regularly reported to Washington on the situation in Korea via sensitive "Blue Flag" messages for the eyes of only Admiral Sherman.

In late May 1951, Burke took command of Cruiser Division Five off the coast of Korea, but after barely a month of gunfire support operations, he was temporarily detached to serve on the truce negotiating team headed by Admiral Joy. The assignment dragged on into the fall, as the agenda controversy* gave way to service on a subcommittee to establish the military demarcation line and DMZ, agenda item 2*. Burke found Communist procedural delays and propaganda immensely frustrating. In addition, he was alarmed that secret UN negotiating positions were repeatedly anticipated by the Communists. In November, Washington ordered the UNC* to accept the Communist position on the demarcation line in hopes of expediting an early agreement. Burke believed he had outlived his usefulness on the truce team and departed for Washington convinced that "the only thing the Communists pay any attention to is power." This belief, born in the truce tents of Kaesŏng, subsequently guided much of his work as head of the Strategic Plans Division through the end of the Truman administration and the first year of President Dwight D. Eisenhower's* "New Look," and then as chief of naval operations from 1955 to 1961.

M. W. Cagle and F. A. Manson, *The Sea War in Korea* (Annapolis, 1957); W. G. Hermes, *Truce Tent and Fighting Front* (Washington, D.C., 1966).

David Alan Rosenberg

C

CAIRO DECLARATION (December 1, 1943)

Although this document related primarily to Allied intentions after World War II regarding China, it also constituted the public foundation for U.S. policy toward postwar Korea. From November 22 to 27, 1943, President Franklin D. Roosevelt, British Prime Minister Winston Churchill*, and Chiang Kai-shek*, leader of the Republic of China*, met at Cairo in Egypt to discuss future Allied military operations against Japan and Allied global strategy for the remainder of World War II. Roosevelt sought this personal meeting with Chiang primarily because of the deteriorating economic, political, and military situation in China, to include the challenge of the Chinese Communists to the generalissmo's leadership. While Roosevelt refused to satisfy Chiang's requests for additional military and economic assistance, the president attempted to improve Chinese morale with promises of great gains from the disposition of the Japanese empire after the achievement of victory. With respect to Korea, Roosevelt wanted to obtain British and Chinese consent for a three-power trusteeship preparatory to eventual independence.

Issued as part of a public communiqué following the conference, the Cairo Declaration promised that after Allied victory in World War II, "Japan shall be stripped of all the islands in the Pacific which she has seized . . . and that all the territories Japan has stolen from the Chinese, such as Manchuria, Formosa, and the Pescadores, shall be restored to the Republic of China." With respect to Korea, the three Allies, "mindful of the enslavement of the people of Korea, are determined that in due course Korea shall become free and independent." At the Tehran Conference, Roosevelt gained the approval of Soviet leader Joseph Stalin* for a Korean trusteeship. Korean exiles denounced the Cairo Declaration, insisting that the Allies satisfy Korean demands for immediate independence. However, Roosevelt was aware that all indications pointed to Korean unpreparedness for independence and the probability of Sino-Soviet disagreement over the best means for reconstructing the Korean nation. Only joint Allied action regarding the postwar development of Korea and other nations in Asia would ensure peace and stability in the Pacific. The emergence of Soviet-U.S. hostility during the last months of World War II prevented the formulation and implementation of a specific trusteeship plan for Korea, leading instead to postwar military occupation and partition of the peninsula. *See also* March First Movement; Thirty-eighth Parallel Division.

S. Cho, *Korea in World Politics* (Berkeley, 1967); H. Feis, *Churchill, Roosevelt, Stalin* (Princeton, 1967); *Foreign Relations of the United States, The Conferences at Cairo and Teheran, 1943* (Washington, D.C., 1961); J. I. Matray, *The Reluctant Crusade* (Honolulu, 1985).

CASSELS, SIR ARCHIBALD JAMES H. (1907–   )

Field Marshal Sir Archibald James H. Cassels was the first general officer commanding, 1 Commonwealth Division*, 1951 to 1952. Commissioned into the Seaforth Highlanders from Sandhurst in 1926, Cassels served throughout World War II in Europe, commanding the 51st Highland Division at the Rhine crossings as one of the youngest major generals in the British army. He commanded the 6th Airborne Division in Palestine in 1946 and after a succession of command and staff postings assumed command of the Commonwealth Division in July 1951. A distinguished career followed Korean War service, including director of operations during the Malayan Emergency (1957–1959), commander of NATO Northern Army Group (1960–1963), and finally chief of the general staff (1965–1968).

Cassels faced the difficult task of forging a division from three disparate infantry brigades of different nationality and of ensuring that the division operated effectively within a higher command organization of different nationality again. He experienced few serious difficulties with the British, Canadian, and Commonwealth infantry brigades but faced considerable opposition from his U.S. Corps commander, Lieutenant General J. W. "Iron Mike" O'Daniel. There were fundamental differences between the British and American ways of war, and O'Daniel was disinclined to grant Cassels, as a divisional commander, the level of independence and flexibility in operations that is more characteristic of British-pattern armies. He also attempted to impose U.S. operating procedures on the Commonwealth formations, a move that Cassels successfully resisted.

A tall and rather ascetic man with an aristocratic air, Cassels was know as "Gentleman Jim" to his soldiers. A highly successful operational commander, he also possessed the political and diplomatic sense needed to oversee an integrated division within a multinational command. As a divisional commander responsible to five Commonwealth governments for the operational safety of their troops, Cassels was equipped with a directive that empowered him to appeal over the head of his corps commander in situations that he thought endangered his force "to a degree unusual in war." Although he never used the right of appeal, the existence of the mechanism undoubtedly enabled him to argue with and win over his American superiors to his point of view. As a result, the Commonwealth Division was left very much to conduct its operations as its commander saw fit.

C. N. Barclay, *The First Commonwealth Division* (Aldershot, 1954); A. J. H. Cassels, "The Commonwealth Division in Korea," *Journal of the Royal United Services Institute* (April 1953); J. Grey, *The Commonwealth Armies and the Korean War* (Manchester, 1988).

Jeffrey Grey

CHAE BYUNG DOK (CH'AE PYŎNG-DŎK; 1917–1950)

Chae was chief of staff for the armed forces of the Republic of Korea* when the Korean War began. Weighing nearly 300 pounds, U.S. officials in Korea referred to him as "Fat Chae." Born in P'yŏngyang, he graduated from P'yŏngyang Middle School and then entered the Japanese Military Academy. He was excellent in mathematics and was assigned a role concerning the maintenance of armaments. During World War II, he served as an officer of the Japanese imperial army but was never directly exposed to the battlefield, although he attained the rank of major. After the defeat of Japan and the liberation of Korea, he voluntarily entered the Korean National Guard. Chae graduated from Military English School, which was established for the education and production of the Korean army officers in January 1946. Upon graduation, he was commissioned a captain of the Korean Constabulary army. Through several army posts, he became a commander of the 4th Brigade in April 1948.

When the ROK was formally established in August 1948, so too was the regular Korean armed forces. In May 1949, Chae became the chief of staff of the Korean army and remained in that post until October 1949, when he retired due to conflict with General Kim Suk Won* and other matters. However, in April 1950, he returned to the army and became chairman of the ROK joint chiefs of staff. Just five days after the outbreak of the Korean war, "Fat Chae" was removed from his post as chief. He was held responsible for the initial defeat in the war and also for the ill preparation against the North Korean invasion of South Korea*. General Chung Il Kwon* was his replacement as chief of staff. General Chae then became a commander for the Interim Armed Forces. He was killed at the Battle of Hadong on July 26, 1950. When he was the chief of staff just before the outbreak of the Korean War, he made several mistakes, most prominent being unwise personnel changes in the important army posts and underestimation of the warnings of the imminent North Korean invasion filed by lower-ranking officers. *See also* Lee Hyung Keun.

Korean Biographical Dictionary (Seoul, 1980); H. J. Noble, *Embassy at War* (Seattle, 1975); Harutaka Sasaki, *Hidden History of the Korean War* (Seoul, 1977).

Chull Baum Kim

CHANG HAN-FU (ZHANG HANFU; 1905–1972)

During the Korean War, Chang Han-fu was the People's Republic of China's* vice–foreign minister who handled the daily affairs of the Ministry of Foreign Affairs. He had joined the Chinese Communist party (CCP) in 1927 while a student in the United States. After studying at the Chinese Labor University in Moscow, Chang was a researcher at the Oriental Department of the Third International from 1928 to 1931. Returning to China in 1931, he did party work in Kwantung province and at the Central Committee. The Kuomintang government arrested him in 1933 when he was serving as secretary of Kiangsu provincial party committee, but he was released after the outbreak of the Sino-Japanese War in 1937. Chang worked at the *Hsinhua Daily* in Chungking from 1939 to 1945 as its chief of the editorial staff and general editor. He attended the inauguration conference of the UN in San Francisco in 1945 as an assistant to Tung Pi-wu, the Communist member of the Chinese delegation.

During the Chinese Civil War (1946–1949), Chang held leading posts in the party committees of Shanghai and Hong Kong. When Tientsin was liberated in January 1949, he was in charge of foreign affairs in the municipality. Then Chang became the director of the Foreign Affairs Department, Shanghai Military Control Commission, following the liberation of China's largest city in May 1949. After the birth of the PRC in October 1949, he served for many years as senior vice–foreign minister. He was also the chief assistant to Chou En-lai*, premier and foreign minister, in handling the diplomatic aspect of the Korean War. He represented the Chinese government in contacts with Indian ambassador Sarder K. M. Panikkar* and emissaries of other countries. For example, he received Panikkar on October 5 and 10 and November 23, 1950, during the crucial stage of Chinese military intervention*. In charge later of the translation of the first four volumes of the *Selected Works of Mao Tse-tung,* Chang was elected alternate member of the CCP's Central Committee in 1956. He died in 1972 as a result of the purge suffered during the Great Proletarian Cultural Revolution.

Cai Chengwen and Zhao Yongtian, *A Factual Record of the Korean War* (Beijing, 1987); Chinese People's Liberation Army Academy of Military Science, *A Military History of the Anti-U.S. Aid-Korea War* (Beijing, 1988).

Hua Qingzhao

CHANG, JOHN M. (CHANG MYŎN; 1899–1966)

Chang was Korean ambassador in Washington before and during the Korean War. Born in Inch'ŏn, Chang was educated in YMCA English School and Manhattan Catholic College. He was a devout Catholic, and many of his activities were related to Catholic organizations. President Harry S. Truman* wrote in his memoirs that Chang was "downhearted almost to the point of tears" when the latter brought him President Syngman Rhee's* appeal for help immediately after the North Korean invasion of South Korea*. Chang's own account of the meeting is slightly different: he protested vigorously that the United States had neglected providing the Republic of Korea* with adequate military assistance. As a matter of fact, when Secretary of State Dean G. Acheson* delivered his National Press Club speech* six months earlier, Chang called at the State Department to ask for an explanation and appealed personally to Truman for military assistance, pointing out military weakness on the part of the ROK army in vain. When John Foster Dulles* made his trip to Korea* in June 1950, Chang asked him to do two things: to go to the thirty-eighth parallel in person and to make a public commitment during his speech at the National Assembly that in case of invasion by North Korea, the United States would support South Korea. He was satisfied later when Dulles met both of his demands.

Chang was appointed prime minister and returned home in 1951. But he soon found himself in an awkward position. Rhee suspected, with good grounds, that Chang was scheming to succeed him as president. He led the Korean delegation to the 6th UN General Assembly in Paris in November 1951 and returned to Korea at the beginning of the South Korean political crisis of 1952*. Chang resigned as soon as he arrived from Paris, allegedly in protest against Rhee, and took refuge in a U.S. hospital. Dismissing these charges as groundless, Chang explained his resignation as solely the result of hepatitis, for which he was hospitalized. There was no consideration, he insisted, of political asylum. Nevertheless, this was a turning point; Chang split with Rhee politically and participated in organizing a new unified opposition party. Following the student revolution of April 1960, he was swept into power as prime minister. But his government survived only for eight months until overthrown by the coup d'état led by Park Chung Hee next May. Shortlived as it was, it was the first and last period when the ROK had a government based on a parliamentary cabinet system.

Chang Myŏn, *Hanal ŭi Miri Chukchi Ankonŭn—Chang Myŏn Paksa Hoegorok* (Seoul, 1967); H. S. Truman, *Years of Trial and Hope* (Garden City, N.Y., 1956).

J. Y. Ra

CHANG T'AEK-SANG (1899–1969)

After serving previously in the Republic of Korea* as minister of foreign affairs, Chang T'aek-sang was vice-speaker of the National Assembly at the start of the Korean War. Also, he was a member of the Korean delegation to the 5th and 6th UN General Assembly. Liberal U.S. diplomatic representatives in Korea hated him, one critic describing Chang as having "the face of Nero and the manners of Goering." Chang was educated at Waseda University and Edinburgh University. He suffered brief imprisonment under the Japanese colonial government because of his involvement in a nationalist organization but resisted to the end temptations to cooperate with the Japanese war effort toward the end of World War II.

Chang is best known for his role as the chief of Seoul metropolitan police during the tumultuous period after Korea's liberation from Japanese rule in 1945 and later as prime minister during the South Korean political crisis of 1952*. In the former capacity, he worked successfully to keep law and order and suppress leftist elements in southern Korea. He consistently backed Syngman Rhee* politically against explicit instructions from the U.S. occupation commander, Lieutenant General John R. Hodge*, to support moderate Kim Kyu-sik instead. In 1948, Chang was appointed minister of foreign affairs in President Rhee's first cabinet, much to his dissatisfaction. He expected to head the Home Ministry, which, according to his own account, Rhee had tacitly promised to him. In any case, he resigned from the post after only three months in the office after clashing with Rhee. Chang also angered U.S. officials with public statements favoring Korea's reunification through a military offensive northward.

Chang was elected to the National Assembly in the second general election in 1952 after failing twice in by-elections. He was appointed prime minister in April 1952 when the conflict between Rhee and his opposition in the National Assembly was just beginning to develop into a political crisis. Obviously Rhee expected Chang to resolve this test of strength in favor of Rhee. During the crisis, he was the prime mover behind a compromise plan for the revision of the constitution, which combined elements from Rhee's proposal for a presidential system and the cabinet system espoused by his opposition in the National Assembly. Chang ensured that Rhee would be elected for a second term as president through a direct election, but his position was often so ambivalent that it was difficult to discern which side he was supporting. Perhaps he was simply maneuvering to come out on the winning side at the end of the struggle. When, for instance, Rhee began employing high-handed methods to intimidate the National Assembly, Chang protested vigorously, imploring the UNCURK* delegates to "save" Korea by active intervention. There is no doubt, however, that throughout the affair, Chang favored the reelection of Rhee as president. Soon after the South Korean political crisis of 1952 ended, Chang was compelled to resign as prime minister.

Chang Pyong-ye, *Sangnok ŭi Cha Yu-hon* (Taegu, 1973); J. Halliday and B. Cumings, *Korea: The Unknown War* (New York, 1988); Kim Sok-yong, *Chonggye ŭi Hoksŏng Chang T'aek-sang* (Seoul, 1952).

                                                                                                                           J. Y. Ra

CHAUVEL, JEAN M. H. (1897–1979)

Jean Michel Henri Chauvel was France's permanent delegate at the UN Security Council during the Korean War. He was born in Paris and educated in Catholic schools. After earning a law degree in 1921 from the University of Paris, Chauvel embarked on a forty-year career in diplomacy. His first foreign assignment was as third secretary in the French embassy in Peking, China. He then served as secretary-general of the French High Commissariat in Syria and Lebanon. In 1938, Chauvel was consul general at Vienna, but before the year ended, he returned to the Foreign Office in Paris to become subdirector for Asia-Oceania. After the Nazi invasion of France in 1940, he was chief of the Far Eastern division in the Vichy government, resigning two years later and joining the underground resistance. In 1944, Chauvel fled to Algiers, where he became secretary-general of the Commissariat of Foreign Affairs of the Committee of National Liberation, a non-partisan office. He would fill the same position in the Ministry of Foreign Affairs of Charles de Gaulle's provisional government in 1945. His appointment as France's permanent UN delegate in February 1949 came after four years of continuous service under successive premiers, as he participated in the negotiation of such agreements as the Brussels Treaty, the Western Union, and the North Atlantic Pact.

At the UN Security Council, Chauvel soon developed a reputation as a "scholarly diplomat who gives tightly reasoned arguments replete with detail and documentation," often using "Latin adages and other classical material." He participated in the negotiations that ended the Berlin blockade while working for international control over atomic weapons. In response to the Soviet UN Security Council boycott* of January 1950, Chauvel criticized Moscow for damaging the prestige of the international organization. As France's delegate, he cast votes in favor of the UN Security Council resolutions of June 25* and June 27, 1950*, authorizing action in defense of the Republic of Korea* following the North Korean invasion of South Korea*. Chauvel cosponsored the UN Security Council resolution of July 7, 1950*, which established the UNC*, although he was unable to obtain U.S. approval for the creation of a separate UN committee to organize and supervise military contributions from member nations. In August, he spoke against the Soviet charge that the United States was the aggressor in Korea, also rejecting Moscow's claim that the Security Council's actions had been illegal because its delegate was absent.

Chauvel was concerned that if the United States became bogged down militarily in Korea, it would be unable to provide enough assistance to France in its war against the Communists in Indochina. When evidence emerged of Chinese military intervention*, he urged that the United States ban air attacks on the Yalu hydroelectric installations. Chauvel feared that if the United States widened the war, the People's Republic of China* would extend its military operations into Indochina. He therefore opposed condemning the Chinese as aggressors in Korea and instead pressed the United States to seek negotiations with the PRC. After China refused to work with the UN Ceasefire Group*, Chauvel supported the United States in gaining passage of the UN resolution of February 1, 1951*, but then spoke in favor of achieving a cease-fire. In 1952, he left the UN to become ambassador to Switzerland, later serving on France's delegation at the Geneva Conference of 1954*. Thereafter, Chauvel was high commissioner in Austria and ambassador to Great Britain (1955–1962). His last post was as diplomatic counselor to the French government (1962–1963).

Current Biography, 1950; *Foreign Relations of the United States, 1950*, vol. 7: *Korea* (Washington, D.C., 1976) and *1951*, vol. 7: *Korea and China* (Washington, D.C., 1983); *New York Times*, June 1, 1979; *Who's Who, 1976–1977* (New York, 1976).

CHEJU-DO POW UPRISING (October 1, 1952)

In the Cheju-do POW camps, Chinese prisoners who wanted to be repatriated to the People's Republic of China* were detained following the Kŏje-do POW uprising*. They decided in June 1952 not only to ignore deliberately the orders and directions issued from the camp directors but also to continue their demonstrations and to communicate secretly between compounds for the uprising. They planned also to kill the camp commander. When their plot was uncovered, they rose in revolt openly on October 1. UN guards entered the POW camp to restore order, but the prisoners had prepared stones, clubs, and spears to retaliate against the guards. Thus, the UN guards and prisoners came into direct conflict. As a result of these violent clashes, fifty-one prisoners were killed and ninety wounded. Several UN guards were wounded as a result of the confrontation, but the UN had reasserted control on Cheju-do. As in the case of the Kŏje-do POW uprising, the Communists used this incident at the P'anmunjŏm truce talks* to discredit the UNC*, charging brutality in its treatment of POWs. *See also* UNC POW Administration.

   B. Alexander, *Korea: The First War We Lost* (New York, 1986); M. W. Clark, *From the Danube to the Yalu* (New York, 1954); S. Y. Kim, *Panmunjom* (Seoul, 1972); Ministry of Defense of the ROK, *Korea in War: July 1952-July 1953* (Seoul, 1954).

Woo Chul-koo

CHEJU-DO REBELLION (1948–1949)

   The Cheju-do rebellion began without warning on April 3, 1948, when Communist guerrilla bands descended from bases on Halla-san, an extinct volcanic crater dominating the island off the southernmost tip of Korea, to attack police boxes and towns. The guerrillas tapped into widespread opposition, especially strong on the island, to elections for the establishment of a separate government in the U.S. occupation zone in accordance with the UN resolution of November 14, 1947*. Before it was over, a year later, the uprising had claimed some 60,000 victims, or about 20 percent of the island's population. Whole villages in the interior of the island were laid waste, their inhabitants massacred or forcibly relocated to refugee camps along the coast. There is still much about the rebellion that remains unclear. Whatever role the South Korean Labor party's (SKLP) campaign against the elections played in setting the stage, events on Cheju-do soon spun wildly out of control—threatening to undercut northern Korean efforts to build a united front with political opponents of Syngman Rhee* and persuade them to attend a conference of North-South political leaders that opened a few days later in P'yŏngyang. But what started out as a spontaneous popular uprising, touched off by local factors and the intensely politicized atmosphere in the run-up to the scheduled May 10 elections, gradually took on the character of an organized partisan movement.

   U.S. military governor William F. Dean* visited the island in May 1948 and ordered that the rebellion be settled with a minimum of force. The South Korean Constabulary commander on the island opened secret talks with the guerrillas, but these were sabotaged by attacks on towns by police and rightist youth. Fighting tapered off during the summer as the government turned its attention to ensuring the loyalty of the locally raised constabulary regiment; moreover, the SKLP devoted its energy to garnering popular support in the south for establishment of the Democratic People's Republic of Korea*. The insurgency gained new strength in October 1948 after the Yŏsu-Sunch'ŏn rebellion*, as the Cheju-do guerrillas were greatly emboldened and fighting now spread to the mainland. The bloodiest phases in the suppression campaign on Cheju-do came in the autumn of 1949 and in mop-up operations to prepare for the visit of Rhee, now president of the Republic of Korea*, to the island in April 1949.

The rebellion reflected the failure of the U.S. occupation's policies. In the spring of 1947, U.S. authorities allowed a campaign of right-wing terror to develop by sending hundreds of anti-Communist youth group members to Cheju-do after big protests there marking the anniversary of the March First Movement*. U.S. military advisers were on the island throughout the rebellion but were not directly involved in the fighting; the final campaign in the spring of 1949 was personally supervised by top officials in Rhee's cabinet. But the significance of the rebellion stretched far beyond the island. It was one of a number of insurgencies that broke out in other Asian countries as Communist-led nationalist movements resisted attempts to reimpose colonial structures after World War II. The uprising pushed the SKLP into a premature armed struggle it could not hope to win. Defections of soldiers to the Cheju-do guerrillas alerted the government to the problem of leftist penetration of the constabulary and short-circuited plans for a general uprising in the security forces. The suppression of the Cheju-do rebellion foreshadowed the destruction, by similar tactics, of the mainland guerrilla movement the following winter. The rebellion marked a major escalation of the conflict between the Korean Left and Right and forged another link in the chain of domestic political violence that led to the outbreak of the Korean War.

J. Merrill, "The Cheju-do Rebellion," *Journal of Korean Studies* (1980); J. Merrill, *Korea: The Peninsular Origins of the War* (Newark, Del., 1989).

John Merrill

CH'EN YI (CH'EN I; 1901–1972)

Ch'en Yi was chairman of East China military and administrative committee and the mayor of Shanghai during the Korean War. Ch'en was educated in France in his youth and then embraced socialism. In 1923, he became a member of the Chinese Communist party (CCP), working against warlord rule in Peking. In 1926, he joined the Northern Expedition and focused his activities on political affairs. After Chiang Kai-shek* purged the CCP in 1927, Ch'en joined the Nanch'ang uprising and then led the remaining troops to Chingkang Mountain, where the first Red Army was organized and China's first Soviet base was established. Over the next few years, Ch'en remained in the top party leadership, where he was responsible for the military and political development. In 1934, when the Red Army began the Long March, Ch'en was ordered to stay in the south, carrying out guerrilla warfare against Kuomintang (KMT) rule. He overcame many unimaginable difficulties and sustained active resistance during Chiang's White Terror. In 1937, the United Front was formed between the CCP and KMT. Ch'en's troops were reorganized to be the New 4th Army, sent to fight the Japanese. By the end of the war, he had expanded his control over most rural areas in Central and East China. In 1946, the Chinese Civil War started, and Ch'en's 3d Field Army fought many bloody battles with the KMT army. Among those, the Battle of Huaihai was the largest in the modern military history of Asia and decisive in determining the outcome of the war, as Ch'en's forces became famous after shattering Chiang's best troops.

After the establishment of the People's Republic of China* in 1949, Ch'en concentrated on planning the final battle against the KMT, aiming at seizing Taiwan. In June 1950, when the Korean War began, the U.S. neutralization of Taiwan* forced Ch'en to abandon his plan. He urged the PRC government to intervene in the Korean War. American intelligence reports claimed that Ch'en opposed intervention and was potentially disloyal to Mao Tse-tung*, but this was not true. When some Shanghai citizens advised Ch'en not to fight the United States, he replied, "Don't be afraid of nuclear bomb. If they really throw one in Shanghai, as the Mayor, I will be the last one to run!" Ch'en began to move part of his 3d Field Army into Korea during October 1950 in preparation for bloody fighting in November with the UNC*. Although he did not take part in battle planning, Ch'en occasionally visited Korea, inspecting his soldiers and encouraging them to fight better. Throughout the war, about a half-million soldiers from the 3d Field Army were sent to Korea. After the armistice, the Chinese People's Volunteers Army* began to withdraw, and Ch'en went to Korea again to ensure an orderly departure.

In 1955, Ch'en attained the rank of marshal. In 1958, he became foreign minister, assisting Premier Chou En-lai* in China's foreign affairs. Although Ch'en's military career ended, many of his protégés were still in important military posts. Beginning in 1966, Lin Piao* emerged as second only to Mao Tse-tung in military power in the Great Proletarian Cultural Revolution. Ch'en became one of Lin's major rivals and was squeezed out of power, but he did not bend and continued the political struggle against Lin. Mao considered Ch'en's previous contribution and loyalty and decided to protect him. Despite suffering from cancer, Ch'en stayed alive long enough to witness Lin's fall in 1971.

He Shao-lu, *Yuan Shuai WaiJiao Jia* (Beijing,1985); History Division, *Ci Hai* (Shanghai, 1980); Huang Chen-hsia, *Mao's Generals* (Hong Kong, 1968).

Li Yi

CHIANG KAI-SHEK (JIANG JIESHI; 1887–1975)

Chiang Kai-shek, as president of the Republic of China* and head of the Kuomintang party (KMT), sought to influence U.S. policy toward Korea both before and during the war to strengthen his claim to political authority on the mainland of China. At an early age, Chiang determined upon an army career and pursued his military education in Japan. During subsequent years, in association with various central China warlords and the Green Gang of Shanghai, he gained the increasing interest and patronage of Sun Yat-sen. In 1923, Sun dispatched Chiang on a mission to Moscow, where he developed a distaste for Communists. The following year, Sun appointed him the head of the newly established Whampoa Military Academy. Military power rapidly led to acquisition of political authority. After Sun's death, Chiang nominally unified China in 1928 and took control of the KMT and the government. Initially, he did not respond forcefully to Japanese aggression, preferring to eliminate the Communist threat to his regime. The 1936 Sian incident forced Chiang reluctantly to join forces with his erstwhile opponents. War followed quickly.

During the conflict, Chiang's government at Chungking called for Allied recognition of the Korean Provisional Government and its leader, Kim Ku, to block assumption of power by Communist-supported Korean exiles or Syngman Rhee*. In 1943, Chiang signed the Cairo Declaration* providing for the eventual independence of Korea. Despite this, Chiang proved to be determined to reestablish China's preeminence in Korea after the war. But renewed civil strife erupted, distracting Chiang and preventing any serious Nationalist involvement in Korea. Early in 1949, with his forces disintegrating, Chiang fled to his island redoubt of Taiwan. From there he unsuccessfully attempted to engineer a security agreement, the Pacific Pact*, in conjunction with Rhee and Elpidio Quirino of the Philippines during the summer of 1949.

The Korean War came as a blessing to Chiang. President Harry S. Truman* reversed U.S. policy, which had been to accept the impending takeover of Taiwan, and placed the U.S. 7th Fleet in the Taiwan Strait. Capitalizing on this reprieve and hoping to turn the Korean conflict into a war big enough to generate U.S. support for returning his forces to the mainland, Chiang offered Nationalist troops to the UN effort in Korea, but Washington declined. In 1953, newly elected President Dwight D. Eisenhower* appeared more receptive to a role for Chiang Kai-shek. In his first State of the Union address, he threatened to broaden the conflict by announcing the "unleashing" of Chiang*. Although the policy was not new or intended to lead to large-scale military operations, it provoked an outcry among U.S. allies and from the People's Republic of China*. Chiang, in fact, was not interested in having the war end. As agenda item 4, repatriation of POWs, became a key issue preventing settlement, Chiang directed his guard units in the POW camps to create a reign of terror, coercing prisoners to resist repatriation. Chiang used the impending armistice to place strong pressure on the United States to grant Taipei a mutual defense treaty. See also Chiang's Offer of Chinese Troops; Neutralization of Taiwan.

C. M. Dobbs, *The Unwanted Symbol* (Kent, Ohio, 1981); R. Foot, *The Wrong War* (Ithaca, N.Y., 1985); C. A. MacDonald, *Korea: The War Before Vietnam* (New York, 1986); J. I. Matray, *The Reluctant Crusade* (Honolulu, 1985).

Nancy Bernkopf Tucker

CHIANG'S OFFER OF CHINESE TROOPS

On June 27, 1950, following a U.S. appeal for multilateral support of the embattled Republic of Korea*, Generalissimo Chiang Kai-shek* offered to make available some 33,000 Chinese Nationalist troops—if the U.S. government equipped and transported them to Korea. Although President Harry S. Truman* revealed initial interest in accepting the offer, most of his diplomatic and military advisers responded negatively. Secretary of State Dean G. Acheson* and General Omar N. Bradley*, chairman of the JCS, made several critical points. The Nationalist troops had a poor fighting record even while defending their own soil. Weapons, supplies, and support equipment were already in short supply for U.S. troops. Training and integrating Nationalist forces into a U.S. or UN command would also take precious time. In addition, stripping forces from Taiwan would leave the island more vulnerable to attack and might provoke Chinese intervention in Korea. In private, even CINCFE General Douglas MacArthur* dismissed the value of Nationalist troops, describing them as a likely "albatross around our neck." By June 30, Truman relented and rejected Chiang's offer.

Following Chinese military intervention*, MacArthur resurrected the issue in both classified reports and public statements. From December 1950 on, he argued that since the Chinese People's Volunteers Army* had already internationalized the Korean War, Washington was justified, even required, to accept the standing offer of Nationalist troops. MacArthur recommended a two-pronged strategy of using some 50,000 Chinese troops to buttress the UNC* on the Korean peninsula, while the United States assisted Nationalist regular and guerrilla forces in an invasion of south China. As they had months before, the JCS and Acheson faulted this strategy. U.S. planners predicted that any Nationalist troops actually placed on the Chinese mainland would face obliteration, creating pressure for the United States to rescue them and then confront the danger of involvement in a second, even larger, land war in Asia. In the end, the Truman administration rejected all proposals to employ Chiang's troops in Korea or China, although some joint, small-scale covert and guerrilla operations took place.

D. C. James, *Years of MacArthur*, vol. 3: *Triumph and Disaster, 1945–1964* (Boston, 1985); M. Schaller, *Douglas MacArthur: The Far Eastern General* (New York, 1989).

Michael Schaller

CH'IN CHI-WEI (QIN JI-WEI; 1911–   )

Ch'in was the commander of the 15th Army of the Chinese People's Volunteers Army* during the Korean War. Born into a poor peasant family in Hupei province, he developed a reputation as a brave soldier in the Communist army when he was only 17. In 1931, Ch'in was the guard captain for Chinese Communist party (CCP) leaders Chang Kou-t'ao and Hsu Hsiang-ch'ien. With his loyalty and courage, he saved them many times and was quickly promoted to commander of a battalion and then a regiment. In 1937, Ch'in entered the Anti-Japanese University. Three years later, he led an independent brigade to the suburbs of Peking and Tientsin, carrying out guerrilla warfare against the Japanese. During the Chinese Civil War, Ch'in's army expanded into the 9th Column of the 2d Field Army under the command of Lin Piao* and Teng Hsiao-p'ing. His bravery brought him high praise, and, with the establishment of the People's Republic of China*, the 9th Column became the 15th Army.

In March 1951, Ch'in led his 15th Army into the Korean War as a reinforcement unit with orders to launch an offensive on Seoul in the first stages of the Chinese spring offensives of 1951*. He did not have any experience in dealing with a UN army possessing modern equipment and commanded his troops to rush toward enemy lines in mass, where they suffered great losses. In May, Ch'in took one division to penetrate enemy defensive lines, but U.S. tanks and cannon forced him to retreat. Ch'in received the entire blame for these two defeats and was removed from the front to undergo a training program. In October 1952, he was given a second chance; the 15th Army was ordered to defend against an attack from the U.S. 7th Division and the Republic of Korea's* 2d and 7th divisions. Ch'in successfully held the line, although his unit suffered heavy casualties. This engagement won him accolades as one of the heroes of the Korean War.

In 1954, Ch'in was appointed vice-commander of the Yunnan military zone and then commander of the Kunming Force, obtaining the rank of lieutenant general as well. Beginning in 1958, Ch'in was in charge of the PRC's military mission to Southeast Asia. During the Great Proletarian Cultural Revolution, he experienced disgrace and then political recovery. Having been a general in the 2d Field Army, his good fortune returned when Teng Hsiao-p'ing regained prominence and he was appointed political commissar of the Peking Force. Now Ch'in is the PRC's minister of defense.

Huang Chen-hsia, *Mao's Generals* (Hong Kong, 1968); Institute of International Relations, *Chinese Communist Who's Who* (Taipei, 1971); *Who's Who in Modern China* (Tokyo, 1978).

Li Yi

CHINA

See People's Republic of China; Republic of China

CHINA'S HATE AMERICA CAMPAIGN

See China's Resist America Aid Korea Movement

CHINA'S RESIST AMERICA AID KOREA MOVEMENT

Known in Chinese as the *KangMei yuanChao yundong* (RAAK), the movement was a nationwide campaign that mobilized civilian support for the Chinese effort in the Korean War. Kuo Mo-jo* was chairman of the committee responsible for supervising the RAAK. Although formally launched on November 4, 1950, the origins of the campaign may be traced to September, when public meetings in Chinese cities were held around a slogan that added to RAAK two other phrases, *baojia weiguo* ("protect the family and defend the country"). Mao Tse-tung's* lengthy summary of the three-year campaign was dated September 12, 1953. Early themes in the RAAK, prior to the first Chinese military intervention* in the war in late October, stressed the issue of Taiwan and U.S. continued intervention in the Chinese Civil War, more so than the Korean War itself.

The significance and impact of the RAAK are open questions. Most published interpretations in the West slight the campaign as little more than political indoctrination and mass mobilization that would have occurred even without the Korean War. This inattention to the impact of the war on the People's Republic of China* qualified somewhat by eyewitness accounts of Americans who were in China at the time, often as political prisoners, and also by more recent, largely journalistic, reassessments of China's role in the Korean War.

Chinese interpretations of RAAK are by contrast heavily patriotic—long on quantity and short on evidence and argument not clouded by politics. One index to the materials of RAAK, the *KangMei yuanChao ziliao mulu,* published in December 1950, was 358 pages long, and included 25 pages of book titles, 67 pages of periodical titles, and 255 pages of newspaper titles. Bound by the political line that the decisions of the Chinese Communist party (CCP) throughout the war were correct, Chinese descriptions of the RAAK for over three decades have obscured any resistance to China's entry into and behavior during the war, by military leaders, by Chinese intellectuals, and by the families whose members "volunteered" for the war. To be sure, Chinese hostile perceptions of the United States antedated the RAAK, but the bedrock hostility that shaped both official and popular images of the cold war in succeeding decades became enshrined during the years of the RAAK as official and popular perceptions of the outside world. RAAK may be seen as an umbrella campaign under which more specific campaigns, such as the Campaign to Suppress Counterrevolutionaries* (1951) and the so-called three-anti and five-anti campaigns of 1951 and 1952 for suppression of counterrevolutionaries in the party bureaucracy and business community, respectively, were carried out.

However much inclined Western observers have been to dismiss RAAK as propaganda and mass mobilization, it is important to recognize the broad degree of support throughout all of China and among all levels of society for the Chinese war effort. That support is demonstrated by the largely successful thought-reform effort that become more intense after China encountered setbacks in its spring offensives of 1951*, and the willingness, even eagerness, of Chinese students, intellectuals, and writers to volunteer for the war effort out of patriotic feeling and out of their general enthusiasm for the new Peking government.

W. C. Ch'en, *Chinese Communist Anti-Americanism and the Resist-America Aid-Korea Campaign* (Lackland Air Force Base, n.d.); Renmin chubanshe, *Weida de kangMei yuanChao yundong* (Peking, 1954); A. and A. Rickett, *Prisoners of Liberation* (Cameron, 1957); L. S. Weiss, "Storm around the Cradle: The Korean War and the Early Years of the People's Republic of China, 1949–1953" (Ph.D. dissertation, Columbia University, 1981); A. S. Whiting, *China Crosses the Yalu* (Stanford, Calif., 1960).

Philip West

CHINESE CAMPAIGN TO SUPPRESS COUNTERREVOLUTIONARIES (1951)

The launching of this campaign is variously placed in September or December 1950, or in February or March 1951 and its ending sometime later that year. It is regarded as the most violent of all campaigns in the first two decades of Communist rule in China. This violence and the campaign's extensiveness appear to be closely linked with China's fighting in the Korean War. It may be seen as the outcome of genuine fear channeled through and manipulated by the Chinese Communist party (CCP) in the further consolidation of its control over China, especially after the war reached a stalemate in the spring of 1951. The number of Chinese executed in the campaign for the first six months of 1951 according to official Chinese figures was 135,000. The number executed in the whole campaign, according to Western specialists, may have been as high as a million, and the total number of people affected by imprisonment and public humiliation was much higher.

The difficulty in assessing the importance of this campaign lies in the ambiguous definitions of campaigns generally in China and their overlapping with each other. This campaign, officially designated as the Suppression of Counterrevolutionaries (*Zhenya fangeming fenzi*) is not to be confused with the campaign to liquidate (*suqing*) counterrevolutionaries in 1955, although continuities between the two may be found. The 1951 campaign may be seen as part of China's Resist America Aid Korea Movement*. Also associated with the suppression campaign are thought reform, which intensified in the spring of 1951, and the so-called three-anti and the five-anti campaigns, also begun in 1951 and directed, respectively, against the party bureaucracy and the business community. The suppression campaign also overlapped with land reform, which was officially announced on the eve of the Korean War and became noticeably more violent during the war. Thus, in addition to Kuomintang agents, sympathizers, and those generally opposed to the Communist consolidation of power in China, landlords came to be included as counterrevolutionaries and are included in casualty figures for the campaign. Mao Tse-tung's* attention to the campaign can be found in five different official statements about it in 1951.

Because of growing Western hostility towards the government of the new People's Republic of China* and some doubts about the Chinese ability to sustain a prolonged campaign against the military power of the United States, many Chinese intellectuals came under severe pressure during this campaign. Countering the general return of Chinese students, intellectuals, and other urban residents to China in 1949, the Campaign to Suppress Counterrevolutionaries forced hundreds to flee China. Their stories of thought reform, imprisonment, and torture were reported in the West and strengthened U.S. antagonism generally toward China. Throughout modern history, repression typically follows a revolution. The degree to which the repression of this particular campaign can be correlated with China's fears, intervention, and frustrations in the Korean War, quite distinct from earlier patterns in the CCP's control, is an open question.

R. J. Lifton, *Thought Reform and the Psychology of Totalism: A Study of "Brainwashing" in China* (New York, 1961); M. Meisner, *Mao's China: A History of the People's Republic* (New York, 1977); S. Schram, *Mao Tse-tung* (New York, 1966); J. R. Townsend, *Political Participation in Communist China* (Berkeley, 1968); E. Vogel, *Canton Under Communism: Programs and Politics in a Provincial Capital, 1949–1968* (Cambridge, 1969).

Philip West

CHINESE MILITARY DISENGAGEMENT OF NOVEMBER 6, 1950

By November 2, 1950, China's military forces had shattered the Republic of Korea's* II Corps in northwest Korea and halted the 8th Army's* advance to the Yalu River. Heavy fighting continued near Ŭnsan until November 6, when the Chinese suddenly broke contact and retreated mysteriously. That same day, the Truman administration received a report from CINCUNC General Douglas MacArthur* confirming for the first time that large and organized Chinese forces were operating in Korea. Despite the capture of Chinese soldiers in late October, MacArthur had been unwilling to acknowledge the reality of Chinese military intervention*, advising Washington on November 4 "against hasty conclusions which might be premature" because "final appraisement should await a more complete accumulation of military facts." Then, on November 5, the general ordered a bombing mission to destroy all bridges across the Yalu River to hamper the flow of additional enemy forces from Manchuria into North Korea. Because this violated his instructions to stay well clear of China's border, Lieutenant General George E. Stratemeyer*, the FEAF commander, informed Washington. Coming so soon after MacArthur's call for caution, the Truman administration was "puzzled." It also feared that this would lead to a major war with China and might even prompt Soviet entry. Thus, the JCS postponed raids within 5 miles of the Yalu, explaining that the planned missions required British concurrence.

In reply, MacArthur admitted for the first time the extent of China's threat to his command, protesting that the only way to stop materiel and personnel from "pouring across . . . the Yalu" was the "destruction of these bridges and the subjection of all installations in the north area supporting the enemy" to attack. He insisted that the JCS refer the matter to President Harry S. Truman* because he would not take responsibility for a decision courting disaster. In response, Truman approved authorization for MacArthur to hit targets at Sinŭiju and the Korean side of the bridges "provided that . . . you still find such action essential to [the] safety of your forces." Meanwhile, U.S. newspapers were publishing details about the recent fighting. There were reports that Chinese forces had advanced at least 70 miles south of the Yalu and in the process had "chopped up piecemeal" four South Korean divisions. "Chinese hordes," the *New York Times* declared, were "attacking on horse and on foot to the sound of bugle calls" and inflicting "an Indian style massacre" on the UNC* forces.

Rather than maintaining its offensive, however, the Chinese People's Volunteers Army* abruptly broke off the attack, and a three-week lull in the fighting ensued. Perhaps the People's Republic of China* was providing the United States with a chance to reconsider its drive for forcible reunification. On the other hand, the Chinese might have been trying to conceal their strength and deceive the UNC before mounting a sustained drive southward. On November 8, the JCS cabled MacArthur that in view of China's entry, his objective of destroying the North Korean army might "have to be reexamined." Two days later, Foreign Secretary Ernest Bevin* presented the British DMZ proposal*, hoping to forestall massive PRC intervention. MacArthur refused to consider compromise, informing the JCS that to permit Communist China's aggression to prevent achieving reunification of Korea "would be the greatest defeat of the free world in recent times.'' Fearing the political consequences of challenging the general and holding out hope for victory, the Truman administration decided not to alter MacArthur's instructions. However, State Department officials did start to investigate the possibility of negotiations with the PRC and attempted publicly to reassure the Chinese that the United States had no hostile intent. Ironically, the Chinese decision to vanish from the battlefield following November 6 negated the intended impact of the attack because the PRC's intentions and power remained a mystery. Not only did China's withdrawal spur MacArthur's confidence, but it removed any basis for opposing his Home-by-Christmas offensive* on military grounds. See also ''Hot Pursuit''; Manchurian Sanctuary; Yalu Bridges Controversy.

J. L. Collins, War in Peacetime (Boston, 1969); Foreign Relations of the United States, 1950, vol. 7: Korea (Washington, D.C., 1976); Hao Yufan and Zhai Zhihai, ''China's Decision to Enter the Korean War: History Revisited,'' China Quarterly (March 1990); B. I. Kaufman, The Korean War (Philadelphia, 1986); J. F. Schnabel and R. J. Watson, History of the Joint Chiefs of Staff, vol. 3: The Korean War (Wilmington, 1979).

CHINESE MILITARY INTERVENTION

After the birth of the People's Republic of China* in October 1949, the government of the Democratic People's Republic of Korea* requested that the Koreans who fought in the Chinese army be allowed to return. Subsequently, 38,000 Koreans organized in two well-equipped divisions were sent back to Korea in January 1950. These forces played a leading role in the North Korean invasion of South Korea*. After the outbreak of the Korean War, President Harry S. Truman* announced the neutralization of Taiwan* on June 27, 1950, and reopened the question of the island's status. This action directly linked Taiwan with the war in Korea and violated the sovereign rights of China. The PRC leaders were concerned even though the North Korean troops had swept across South Korea in June and July. To prepare for future developments, the Chinese 13th Army Corps was reorganized into Northeastern Border Forces and deployed along the Yalu River. In early August, the PRC's military experts, most notably Teng Hua*, estimated that the U.S. troops would probably perform a rear-flank landing to cut off the North Korean troops from behind. Four Korean ports were considered as possible landing sites, and Inch'ŏn was one of them. In September, five Chinese military attachés were sent to Korea to do topographical surveys.

Truman authorized CINCUNC General Douglas MacArthur* on September 27, 1950, to pursue Communist forces into North Korea. On September 30, the Republic of Korea's* troops crossed the thirty-eighth parallel. The Chinese Political Bureau met from September 30 to October 5 to discuss the threat posed by the UN offensive across the thirty-eighth parallel*. Kim Il Sung* requested on October 1 that the Chinese 13th Army Corps be urgently sent to Korea to fight against the U.S. troops. Mao Tse-tung* convinced his colleagues, most notably Lin Piao* and Kao Kang* who opposed intervention, at a meeting on October 2 that the PRC should send troops to fight in Korea purportedly as ''volunteers.'' Peng Teh-huai* was chosen as the commander and political commissar after Lin Piao, claiming he was ill, refused the post. But the PRC made a last effort to avoid entering the Korean War. Premier Chou En-lai* received the Indian ambassador K. M. Panikkar* at 1 A.M. on October 3 to explain that China wanted to localize the Korean conflict, but if the U.S. forces crossed the thirty-eighth parallel and expanded the war, China would not sit idly by. Although State Department officials U. Alexis Johnson* and O. Edmund Clubb* believed that Chou's warning should be taken seriously, Secretary of State Dean G. Acheson* and most other senior officials thought the PRC was bluffing. The U.S. troops did cross the parallel on October 8, and, on the same day, Mao issued orders for the Chinese People's Volunteers Army* (CPVA) to enter and fight.

China's decision to join the fighting in Korea was a result of careful deliberations. During the Political Bureau meeting discussing the Korean situation, Mao asked the participants to put forward reasons for not fighting in Korea. In the end, Mao concluded, "Your points are all reasonable. But now their country is in a critical moment. Whatever reasons we may have, if we only stand by and watch, we will feel sorry in our hearts." China's decision was difficult because the PRC was not prepared to wage a major war: scars from the trauma of the Chinese Civil War had not yet healed, land reform had not been completed and remnant bandits and secret agents had to be liquidated, the equipment and training of the Chinese troops were not adequate, and a part of the population and the troops were tired of war. Nevertheless, Mao was convinced that a reunited Korea closely allied to the United States would constitute an intolerable threat to Chinese national interests and security. In addition, China intervened to repay the Korean Communists for their assistance during the Chinese Civil War and to supplant the predominant influence of the Soviet Union in North Korea.

Joseph Stalin* was optimistic in the beginning of the Korean conflict, but he became pessimistic after the Inch'ŏn landing* and informed Mao that Kim Il Sung would come to Manchuria to form an exile government. Mao decided to intervene in part to avoid having to shelter Kim's regime on Chinese soil. In response, Stalin promised to send aircraft to Manchuria to assist Chinese ground troops that were fighting in Korea. When Chou En-lai went to Moscow on October 8 to negotiate logistical support, Stalin said that the Soviet air force was not ready to move into Manchuria. The PRC leaders were very unhappy and suspended entry of the CPVA into Korea. They eventually decided, on October 13, that Chinese troops would fight without Soviet air support, and the CPVA moved into Korea on the frozen Yalu on October 19. One week later, the UNC* captured its first Chinese soldiers. During the next week, there was heavy fighting in northwestern North Korea as the CPVA inflicted major losses on mainly South Korean forces. By November 2, the Chinese had forced Lieutenant General Walton W. Walker*, 8th Army* commander, to halt temporarily the advance to the Yalu River.

Kim Il Sung received formal word of the Chinese decisions to enter the Korean War from Chinese ambassador Ni Chih-liang on October 8, 1950. On October 20, CPVA Commander and Political Commissar Peng Teh-huai met with Kim

Il Sung for the first time during the Korean War. He informed Kim that China would send twelve infantry divisions and three artillery divisions (260,000 men) as the first group of troops fighting in Korea, with twenty-four divisions more as the second and the third group. He said that it was not easy for the PRC to fight in Korea, since China had its own difficulties; however, once the PRC had decided, it would try to help settle the Korean question through destroying the U.S. invaders. It had also prepared for the United States to declare war on China, bomb Manchuria and industrial cities, and attack coastal areas. Peng asked Kim the strength of his troops, and Kim told him that at this point North Korea had only three divisions and two regiments in hand. Other troops were cut off in the south and were in the process of withdrawing. China's entry into the Korean War halted the Home-by-Christmas offensive* and forced the Truman administration to accept a cease-fire short of total victory. It also demonstrated the PRC's power, strengthening its prestige and influence in Asia. *See also* Chinese Military Disengagement of November 6, 1950; Chosin Reservoir Campaign; CIA Report: Position of the United States with Respect to Communist China; CIA Report: Soviet Intentions in the Current Situation; NSC-92; NSC-95; NSC-101; Withdrawal from Seoul of December 1950-January 1951.

Cai Chengwen and Zhao Yongtian, *A Factual Record of the Korean War* (Beijing, 1987); Cai Chengwen and Zhao Yongtian, *Panmunjom Negotiations* (Beijing, 1990); Chinese People's Liberation Army Academy of Military Science, *A Military History of the Anti-U.S. Aid–Korea War* (Beijing, 1988); Peng Dehuai, *My Self-Accounts* (Beijing, 1985); A. S. Whiting, *China Crosses the Yalu* (Stanford, Calif., 1960); Yao Xu, *From the Yalu to Panmunjom* (Beijing, 1986).

Hua Qingzhao

CHINESE PEOPLE'S VOLUNTEERS ARMY

This was the official name of the People's Republic of China's* armed forces that fought in the Korean War. The PRC was concerned after the Korean War broke out that the war might expand into China. Chinese Communist leaders felt particularly threatened when on June 27, 1950, President Harry S. Truman* linked Chinese territory to the Korean War when he ordered the neutralization of Taiwan*. During the meeting of National Defense Council on July 7, 1950, chaired by Premier Chou En-lai*, it was decided that a Northeastern Border Forces be established on the basis of the 13th Army Corps. The Central Military Commission issued an order to this effect on July 13, demanding that the troops concerned hasten their concentration in Shengyang and Antung before the end of July. This was the embryo of the Chinese People's Volunteers Army (CPVA).

The PRC chose the euphemism *volunteers* to give the appearance that the government had not ordered Chinese military intervention*. This presumably would foster support for its actions in Asia, while making it more difficult for the United States to justify, in strict legal terms, extending the war to China. After the decision of October 2, 1950, that China, at the request of the government of the Democratic People's Republic of Korea*, would send troops to fight in Korea as volunteers, Chairman Mao Tse-tung* announced on October 8 that the

Northeastern Border Forces would be renamed the Chinese People's Volunteers Army. In addition, he ordered that the force should rapidly advance into Korea, and Peng Teh-huai* was commissioned as commander and political commissar.

Mao was optimistic about the CPVA's ability to halt the advance of the UNC* to the Yalu River and force its withdrawal southward in part because the Soviet Union had agreed to commit its air force in support of Chinese military operations. Even though Soviet leader Joseph Stalin* reversed his decision on October 10, nine days later the CPVA still entered the Korean War. Apparently, Stalin was so impressed with China's military success that he decided to increase Soviet aid. By late 1950, the Soviet Union had sent two air force divisions (less than 200 planes) to defend the bridges across the Yalu and the main transportation lines into North Korea. Dressed in Chinese uniforms, Soviet pilots had instructions to identify themselves as Chinese Russian minority subjects if captured. In addition, Moscow would sell China enough weaponry to equip more than 60 army and 10 air force divisions, as well as 80 percent of the roughly 250,000 tons of ammunition it used during the Korean War.

On March 1, 1951, Mao decided that the Chinese troops should fight in Korea on a rotating basis in three groups. This was aimed at creating the ability to fight a long war of attrition. Most of the field troops of the regular Chinese army saw action in Korea with the label "volunteers," rotating in three groups. Altogether, the PRC deployed more than 2.3 million soldiers as part of the CPVA during the Korean War, including 66 percent of its entire field army (25 field corps), 62 percent of its artillery (70 divisions), 70 percent of its air force (12 divisions), all 3 of its tank divisions, 10 railway engineering divisions, and 2 public security divisions. The death toll for the CPVA officers with the rank of major or higher was 215. The highest ranking was a major general, who died of illness. Total CPVA losses for the entire Korean War—wounded, dead, and missing—was approximately 360,000. When the Korean armistice agreement* was signed on July 27, 1953, Peng signed for the CPVA and, after becoming minister of defense, returned to China in 1954. Those who succeeded him as commander from October 1954 to October 1958 were Generals Teng Hua*, Yang Te-chih, and Yang Yung, while subsequent political commissars were Generals Li Chih-min and Wang P'ing. The CPVA troops withdrew in 1958, the disengagement starting on March 15 and finishing on October 26. However, there are still CPVA representatives to the Military Armistice Commission*.

Cai Chengwen and Zhao Yongtian, *A Factual Record of the Korean War* (Beijing, 1987); Cai Chengwen and Zhao Yongtian, *Panmunjom Negotiations* (Beijing, 1990); Chinese People's Liberation Army Academy of Military Science, *A Military History of the Anti-U.S. Aid-Korea War* (Beijing, 1988); Hao Yufan and Zhai Zhihai, "China's Decision to Enter the Korean War: History Revisited," *China Quarterly* (March 1990); Yao Xu, *From the Yalu to Panmunjom* (Beijing, 1986).

Hua Qingzhao

CHINESE SPRING OFFENSIVES OF 1951

This was the People's Republic of China's* final effort to achieve a decisive military victory in Korea by destroying the UNC* and reunifying the Korean peninsula by force. Its failure, by demonstrating that such a solution to the Korean problem was beyond China's means, opened the way to the initiation of Kaesŏng truce talks*. Indeed, from a Chinese perspective, such talks became imperative as the United Nations, with increasing confidence in its newly demonstrated firepower, threatened to press north once more.

The Fifth Phase Offensive, as the Chinese termed it, was launched on April 22 after a prolonged buildup, its main weight falling on the sectors of I and IX Corps where some 486,000 Chinese were soon estimated to be advancing. The main effort was directed at Seoul, with a secondary thrust at Kap'yŏng, while North Korean forces mounted a smaller supporting offensive at the eastern end of the line. Chinese tactics, which relied as previously on night attacks and weight of numbers to overwhelm the defenses, were quickly revealed to be costly and ineffective against well-prepared forces with adequate artillery and air support. Although a breakthrough was achieved in the Kap'yŏng area when the South Korean 6th Division collapsed, both main thrusts were blunted by resolute action in which Commonwealth units were prominent. UN forces fell back in good order some 35 miles to the No Name Line* just north of Seoul, against which the offensive petered out at the end of April.

Despite having suffered huge casualties, the Chinese prepared for the second step of their offensive. Unexpectedly shifting their concentration eastward during the period from May 10 to 16, they launched twenty-one Chinese and nine North Korean divisions at the UN lines late on May 16. Again South Korean divisions succumbed to the onslaught, but the breakthrough was contained, and the advance of UN forces in the west soon threatened the Chinese with envelopment. In the face of this counteroffensive, the Chinese fell back in disarray. The Fifth Phase Offensive achieved none of its objectives and inflicted upon the Chinese forces their worst losses of the war. By confirming the UNC's ability, through effective organization and concentrated firepower, to overcome tactics relying on massed manpower, it hastened the development of military stalemate. *See also* Battle of the Imjin River; Battle of Kap'yŏng.

Peng Dehuai, *The Memoirs of a Chinese Marshal* (Beijing, 1984); M. B. Ridgway, *The Korean War* (Garden City, N.Y., 1967); J. F. Schnabel, *Policy and Direction* (Washington, D.C., 1972).

Ian C. McGibbon

CHINESE SUMMER OFFENSIVES OF 1953

Once the negotiators at the P'anmunjŏm truce talks* began work on the final terms of an armistice agreement in June 1953, the Communists launched several military thrusts to push the battle line southward because the provisions for resolving agenda item 2* called for the demarcation line and the DMZ to follow the final line of battle. On June 8, after reaching agreement on agenda item 4*, repatriation of POWs, Major General William K. Harrison, Jr.*, the chief delegate of the UNC*, suggested approval of the same demarcation line that the negotiators had adopted in November 1951. Changes in the fighting front since that date, he argued, had been "relatively minor in nature," and this would simplify and expedite the completion of a final armistice agreement. The Communist delegation rejected the proposal, demanding revision of the line to reflect the current situation. The staff officers began work on determining the location of the main line of resistance on June 10. That night the Communists attacked South Korea's 5th Division and then broadened the assault into a general offensive against the Republic of Korea's* II Corps. Their objective undoubtedly was to achieve the propaganda value of at least a symbolic military victory at the end of the Korean War.

On June 18, President Syngman Rhee* brought a halt to the armistice talks with his release of North Korean POWs*. In response to the UNC's denial of complicity, the Communist delegation asked how the UNC could guarantee a cease-fire if it was unable to control Rhee. Harrison then obtained approval for a recess on June 20 for the purpose of securing a pledge from the South Korean government not to disrupt an armistice. Six days later, the Communists opened an offensive against the ROK II Corps in the area of the Kŭmsŏng salient, pushing back the battle line approximately 3 miles along an 8-mile front. On July 6, there was another assault in the Iron Triangle* that inflicted major casualties on the South Koreans. Four days later, after Rhee agreed to accept an armistice, the negotiations resumed at P'anmunjŏm, but the Communist delegation did not rush to finalize the terms. Having in mind political rather than military objectives, the Communists on July 13 launched a massive offensive against the ROK divisions in the Kŭmsŏng area, resulting in the heaviest fighting since the Chinese spring offensives of 1951*. Within less than a week, elements of five divisions of the Chinese People's Volunteers Army* had shattered the ROK Capital and 3d divisions, while nearly destroying three more South Korean divisions. Setting a monthly record for artillery rounds fired, the Communists inflicted 14,000 casualties on the South Koreans.

CINCUNC General Mark W. Clark* observed later that "the main reason" for the Chinese offensive "was to give the ROK's a 'bloody nose' and show them and the world that 'puk chin'—'go north'—was easier said than done." In addition, China was sending Rhee a message that breaking the truce would have fatal consequences while reassuring the Democratic People's Republic of Korea* that the People's Republic of China* would protect it following a cease-fire. For the Eisenhower administration, this offensive revealed that despite two years of intensive effort, the United States had not been able to create a South Korean force capable of defending the ROK against a major Communist assault. When General Maxwell D. Taylor*, commander of the 8th Army*, ordered a withdrawal south from the Kŭmsŏng River, many South Korean soldiers fled in disarray. To avert disaster, the UNC sent U.S. troops from the 3d and 24th divisions to support the South Koreans, as well as committing the 187th Regimental Combat Team from Japan. After halting the offensive, the UNC launched a counteroffensive on July 17 and advanced over the next two days to a position 6 miles south of the original line.

Neither Taylor nor Clark wanted to renew large-scale fighting, thus ordering the UNC forces not to cross the Kŭmsŏng River. By contrast, Secretary of State John Foster Dulles* voiced opposition to allowing the Chinese to finish the war with a victory. Army Chief of Staff General J. Lawton Collins* was unsupportive, arguing that stabilizing the battle line was more important than regaining lost terrain. Once the United States made plain its refusal to respond in kind to China's offensive, the PRC moved quickly at P'anmunjŏm to finish the truce negotiations. On July 19, the Communists accepted assurances from the UNC delegation that if the ROK broke the cease-fire, the UNC would continue to observe the truce and not provide the Rhee government with supplies necessary to sustain an offensive northward. Four days later, the negotiators began work on determining the final demarcation line as the basis for the DMZ. At a cost of 28,000 casualties, the Chinese had pushed the line farther south, but the loss of land was worth it for the United States. There now was greater reason to believe that Rhee would respect the armistice because Communist forces had demonstrated their clear superiority over the South Koreans if the ROK had to fight alone.

C. Blair, *The Forgotten War* (New York, 1987); W. G. Hermes, *Truce Tent and Fighting Front* (Washington, D.C., 1966); B. I. Kaufman, *The Korean War* (Philadelphia, 1986); C. A. MacDonald, *Korea: The War Before Vietnam* (New York, 1986).

CHIP'YŎNG, BATTLE OF
See Battle of Chip'yŏng

CHO PYŎNG-OK (CHOUGH PYUNG OK; 1894–1960)

Cho Pyŏng-ok was the minister of home affairs in the Republic of Korea* during the Korean War and later a presidential candidate. Born at Mokch'ŏn in South Ch'ungch'ŏng province, he received his early education at American missionary schools. In 1914, Cho went to the United States to study and earned from Columbia University a B.A. in 1922 and a Ph.D. in economics in 1925. He returned to Korea to teach at Chosŏn Christian College (now Yonsei University) and in 1929 was imprisoned by the Japanese for his nationalist activities. In 1945, when Korea was liberated from the Japanese rule, Cho became a founding member of the conservative Korean Democratic party. In October 1945, he joined the U.S. military government in Korea as chief of the police bureau, thus becoming the chief architect of the South Korean national police, which played the leading role in suppressing Communist and other leftist influences in southern Korea.

When the ROK was inaugurated in 1948, Cho was appointed by Syngman Rhee* as his special goodwill emissary. He was South Korea's representative to the United Nations in June 1950. The following month, Cho was given the post of minister of home affairs. Forceful and dynamic, Cho reorganized the demoralized Korean national police, increasing its strength from 13,000 to 65,000, equipping it with modern rifles and machine guns, and deploying it to fight the North Korean invaders. This Korean police force was said to have been quite effective in ferreting out North Korean infiltrators disguised as refugees. In September 1950, during the defense of Taegu*, Lieutenant General Walton H. Walker*, the 8th Army* commander, ordered the withdrawal of the ROK Ministries of Defense and Home Affairs from Taegu. Cho, however, is said to have refused the order and told Walker bluntly that he and his men would remain in Taegu to fight until the last man. This statement reportedly moved Walker to countermand his order and redouble his determination to defend the city of Taegu.

In early 1951, disagreeing with Rhee over the handling of the investigation of the Kŏch'ang incident*, Cho resigned his ministerial post. Thereafter, he became the leading critic of Rhee's authoritarian rule. In June 1953, when responding to Rhee's release of North Korean POWs*, Cho publicly criticized Rhee for unnecessarily damaging ROK's diplomatic position. By 1956, he had become head of the Democratic party and in 1960 challenged Rhee for the presidency. He developed cancer that year and died at Walter Reed Hospital. Courageous and straightforward, Cho is admired by many Koreans as a strong leader and also as a champion of democratic rule, in spite of his earlier role in organizing the Korean national police.

Cho Pyŏng-ok, *Na ŭi Hoegorok* (Kunsan, 1986); Ko Hŭng-mun, "Yusŏk Cho Pyŏng-ok P'yŏn," in *Chŏnggye Yahwa* (Seoul, 1966).

Yŏng-ho Ch'oe

CHOI DUK SHIN (CH'OE TŎK-SIN; 1914–1989)

Choi Duk Shin was a general in the army of the Republic of Korea* and a member of the UNC's* armistice delegation. Born in Ŭiju, North Korea, he moved to China with his family in 1921. After graduating from Nationalist China's Central Military Academy and serving in Chiang Kai-shek's* army, Choi joined the Korean Restoration Army, which was active in China to restore Korean independence from Japan. In 1946, he returned to Korea and in March 1947 was commissioned as a major in the South Korean Constabulary upon graduation from its Constabulary Academy. In 1949, Choi was the superintendent of the Korean Military Academy and then the commander of the newly created 3d Division before he was sent to the United States for further military training in July of that year. Shortly after the outbreak of the Korean War, he returned to Korea as chief of staff in the ROK I Corps, serving briefly during August 1950 as commander of the 8th Division that fought the North Korean troops left behind in the Chiri-san area following the UNC counteroffensive in September 1950. Thereafter, he was deputy superintendent of the ROK War College, superintendent of the Army Infantry School, the deputy commanding general of the I Corps, and a member of the ROK military mission to the UNC in Tokyo.

In April 1953, he was appointed as a member of the UNC's armistice delegation. By this time, the P'anmunjŏm truce talks* had reached the final stage, the last remaining stumbling block being agenda item 4*, covering disposition of POWs. As a member of the UNC delegation, Choi represented his government's positions forcefully. Determined to achieve national unification by any means, President Syngman Rhee* strongly opposed a cease-fire that would leave Korea divided, urging the UNC to fight on until the whole of North Korea would come under the authority of the ROK government. Upon being appointed to the UNC delegation, Choi visited Rhee and promised that he would oppose any armistice that would not release the non-repatriate North Korean POWs immediately and would allow the Chinese People's Volunteers Army* to remain in North Korea. When the UNC made its final POW settlement proposal of May 25, 1953*, acceding to the Democratic Republic of Korea's* demand to turn over the non-repatriate POWs to the neutral commission, Choi publicly criticized the UNC position and boycotted the subsequent truce negotiations. The next month, he was one of the few officials Rhee consulted before his release of some 27,000 North Korean POWs*.

In 1956, Choi retired from active military duty, subsequently serving as the first ROK minister to the Republic of Vietnam and ambassador to the Federal Republic of Germany. In the late 1970s, having moved to Canada, he spoke out against the authoritarian government of South Korea and actively promoted the causes of North Korea. In 1987, he moved to North Korea, where he served as vice-chairman of the Committee for the Peaceful Reunification of the Fatherland until his death.

Ch'oe Tŏk-sin, *Naega Kyŏkkŭn P'anmunjŏm* (Seoul, 1955); M. W. Clark, *From the Danube to the Yalu* (London, 1954); W. G. Hermes, *Truce Tent and Fighting Front* (Washington, D.C., 1966).

Yŏng-ho Ch'oe

CH'OI YONG-KON (CH'OE YŎNG-GŎN; 1900–1976)

Ch'oi Yong-kon, alias Ch'oi Sŏk-ch'ŏn, was commander of the North Korean People's Army and national defense minister for the Democratic People's Republic of Korea* when the Korean War broke out. After the North Korean invasion of South Korea*, he became commander for the defense of Seoul and was promoted to deputy prime minister. Born in North P'yŏng'an province as a farmer's son, he was educated in Osan School under Cho Man-sik, a staunch anti-Japanese nationalist leader. After joining the March First Movement* of 1919 as a student, he went to China for the military training. In 1925, after graduating from the Wun'nan Military Academy, he became an instructor of military science at Whampoa Military Academy. His career in the anti-Japanese, Communist guerrilla movement began in 1926, and he served in various capacities after 1936 in the Northeastern Anti-Japanese Allied Army under the leadership of the Chinese Communist party. Through this organization, he became a close comrade of Kim Il Sung*, with whom he fled to exile in the Soviet Union in 1939.

In September 1945, he returned to North Korea with Kim Il Sung, constituting the *Kapsan* (Soviet exile) faction in the post-liberation North Korean politics, playing a major role in the establishment of the DPRK. He also was prominent in the preparation as well as the execution of the attack on South Korea, rising to second place in the North Korean hierarchy of leadership. In December 1955, he was the presiding judge of the military court at the Supreme Court that imposed the death penalty on political rival Pak Hŏn-yŏng*. In 1956, he was elected deputy chairman of the Korean Workers' party and later, in 1957 and 1962, to chairman of the Presidium of the Supreme People's Congress. As ceremonial head of state, he visited the Soviet Union, China, Cuba, Egypt, Algeria, Cambodia, and East European countries, receiving medical treatment in East Germany in 1970 and 1971. Ch'oi retained this post until 1972, when Kim Il Sung, under the newly revised constitution, replaced him.

Nodong Shinmun, September 20, 1976; South Korean Central Intelligence Agency, *Pukkoe Inmul* (1971).

Hakjoon Kim

CHOSIN (CHANGJIN) RESERVOIR CAMPAIGN (October–December 1950)

In October 1950, the remnants of the North Korean People's Army (NKPA) had been pushed by UN forces to the northeast corner of Korea, bordering the Yalu River. The morale of the North Korean forces had been at the lowest point since the conflict began in July. War weary, the NKPA had been reduced to fighting small guerrilla-style engagements against the 8th Army* commanded by Lieutenant General Walton H. Walker*. Meanwhile, the three divisions under the command of Major General Edward M. Almond's* X Corps* arrived at Wŏnsan on the northeast coast and proceeded northward toward the Chosin Reservoir. The objective of this combined Republic of Korea*-UN offensive was to pursue and destroy the remaining effective NKPA divisions in their defensive positions along the Manchurian border. CINCUNC General Douglas MacArthur* and his general staff were optimistic that this last and final push would defeat the North Korean's military resolve by early November.

In support of the beleaguered NKPA, four full armies of the People's Republic of China*—the 38th, 39th, 40th, and 42d—crossed the Yalu River into Korea in mid-October, unbeknown to the UNC*. Throughout October and November, the 8th Army, the ROK II Corps and other UN forces fought seesaw engagements against the Communist Chinese—the NKPA staying out of most of the fighting on the western front. Meanwhile, the Chinese 42d Army, comprised of the 124th, 125th, and 126th Infantry divisions, descended from Manchuria into Korea and advanced toward the Chosin Reservoir area. The 124th Division, upon reaching the town of Hanuru-ri, began probing the area to find out the strengths and weaknesses of the enemy. The 125th and 126th divisions were held at the reservoir as reserves and not deployed. On October 24, the 124th took up defensive positions on the southern tip of the Chosin Reservoir, with the intention of blocking the UNC's access to the road leading to the reservoir. The next day, the 26th Regiment, 3d Division, ROK I Corps engaged the Chinese 124th Division at Koto-ri. Shortly after, the rest of the 3d Division joined the battle. Despite the efforts of the ROK, the Chinese held their ground and managed to repulse the 3d Division. On October 27, the battle-weary ROK 3d Division was relieved by the U.S. 1st Marine Division. The U.S. Marines met and engaged the 124th at Sŭngdong, astride the access road to the reservoir. By October 29, the 124th still maintained its blocking position, denying allied forces an avenue of attack into the Chosin Reservoir basin.

The U.S. 7th Marine Division was brought up from Hŭngnam on the coast to break through the Chinese forces blocking the mountain passes into the Chosin Reservoir basin and north to the Manchurian border. From November 2 to 7, 1950, these units met with intense opposition from elements of the Chinese 124th and 126th divisions at Sŭngdong, as did the 1st Marine Division previously. Slowly the 7th pushed through this opposition and continued northward. From November 8 to 17, elements of 7th and the 1st Marine divisions fought their way in subfreezing weather up the access road from Hŭngnam into the Chosin basin. Aided by marine and naval air support, these elements swept away the Chinese 42d Army units from their entrenched positions. Because the roads to the reservoir were not entirely secure, ammunition and supplies had to be air-dropped to the troops left to protect the plateau and the supply lines to the north. On November 14, the 7th Division moved into Hagaru-ri unopposed, finding the town gutted and the power plant just north of the town in ruins. The 5th Marine Division was moved up to keep the access road clear for supply and communication traffic. By late November, U.S. forces had moved into the upper reaches of the reservoir. During this period, marine units operating in the mountain passes along the Chosin Reservoir found themselves in only sporadic firefights. This lack of opposition was the result of General Lin Piao's* orders to pull the Chinese 42d Army out of the Chosin area and redeploy it on the western front against General Walker's 8th Army. This was to be only a temporary respite for U.S. forces at Chosin.

In late November, U.S. forces in the east were spread out from the tip of the Chosin Reservoir to the coast along the main access road. On November 27, the Chinese 27th Army and several divisions from the 20th Army attacked U.S forces all along the American lines. U.S. Marine regiments engaged and attempted to hold against three full Chinese divisions. Meanwhile, the 7th Division, operating just east of the reservoir, found itself fighting a division from the 27th Army. The remainder of the 27th Army was to disrupt the supply lines from the coast to the reservoir. Cutting off the 7th and 1st Marine's supply lines would leave these forces at the mercy of the Chinese divisions encroaching upon them. From December 1 to 8, the marine divisions at the reservoir were cut off from their landed supply routes. During that week, the 27th Army, through repeated attacks, hoped to break the resolve of the Americans. However, through airdrops, medicine, food and ammunition were received by the trapped marines. Air support and heavy artillery suppression fire kept the pressure on the Chinese. Chinese forces that had made contact with U.S. forces at Chosin found that they could not breach the tight perimeters put up by the marine defenders. By the end of these eight days of fighting, the Chinese controlled the road to Hŭngnam, and the U.S. Marines maintained their positions around the reservoir. *See also* Chinese Military Intervention; Hŭngnam Evacuation.

R. E. Appleman, *South to the Naktong, North to the Yalu* (Washington, D.C., 1961); R. F. Futrell, *The U.S. Air Force in Korea* (New York, 1961); R. A. Gugeler, *Combat Actions in Korea* (Washington, D.C., 1970); L. Montross and N. A. Canzona, *U.S. Marine Operations in Korea, 1950–1953*, vol. 3: *The Chosin Reservoir Campaign* (Washington, D.C., 1957); J. F. Schnabel, *Policy and Direction* (Washington, D.C., 1972).

Richard Dean Burns

CHOU EN-LAI (ZHOU ENLAI; 1898–1976)

Chou En-lai was premier and foreign minister of the People's Republic of China* during the Korean War. Educated in Japan and the American missionary–supported Nankai University at Tientsin, Chou early became a committed student activist, leading to his imprisonment during the May Fourth Movement of 1919. As a worker-student in France during World War I, he participated in the establishment of the Chinese Communist Youth League. Upon his return to China in 1924, he became director of the political department of the Whampoa Military Academy commanded by Chiang Kai-shek*. Although Chiang split with the Chinese Communist party (CCP) in 1927, Chou temporarily stopped the civil war in 1936 by negotiating a united front to fight the Japanese. He then performed as the CCP's main representative to the Republic of China's* wartime government in Chungking and participated in negotiations led by General George C. Marshall* to end the Chinese Civil War. After the founding of the PRC in 1949, Chou's most important responsibilities were as premier (until 1976) and minister of foreign affairs (until 1958). He impressed foreigners as urbane, witty, self-possessed, graceful, and charming.

With the North Korean invasion of South Korea* and U.S. neutralization of Taiwan*, Chou denounced U.S. perfidy for reversing earlier declarations that Washington would not interfere with a CCP attack on Taiwan. During the summer of 1950, however, his primary efforts aimed at trying to avert warfare between Americans and Chinese in Korea. To this end, he issued public statements and summoned Indian ambassador K. M. Panikkar* to a late-night meeting in Peking on October 2, 1950. Chou insisted that South Korean troops would not be considered a threat but U.S. troops' approaching the Yalu River would be intolerable. His warnings unheeded, the UN offensive across the thirty-eighth parallel* triggered Chinese military intervention*.

Chinese participation, which Americans had dismissed as unlikely and insignificant, altered the conflict completely. On December 22, 1950, Chou declared that a settlement necessitated withdrawal of U.S. forces from Korea as well as Taiwan and assumption by Peking of its rightful seat in the UN. Chou also made it clear that China would attempt reunification of the Korean peninsula under Communist rule. To fuel the PRC effort, Chou took a large delegation of military and economic specialists to Moscow in August 1952 to negotiate Soviet assistance but found the Soviets far from generous. Unable to force UN troops to abandon

South Korea, China moved toward an armistice only after the death of Joseph Stalin* in March 1953. Chou traveled to Moscow for the funeral and upon his return to China proved willing to come to an agreement with the UNC* regarding agenda item 4*, the repatriation of POWs, producing an armistice agreement* in July.

At the Geneva Conference of 1954*, Chou emerged as a world statesman. His diplomatic skill vitiated earlier images of a bellicose Chinese leadership. He called for peace in Asia and demanded removal of foreign military bases from the area. He was not, however, successful in discrediting UN jurisdiction over Korean issues or in pursuing unification of the country. *See also* Chou En-lai POW Settlement Proposal; PRC UN Representation Question.

R. Foot, *The Wrong War* (Ithaca, N.Y., 1985); *Foreign Relations of the United States, 1952–1954*, vol. 16: *The Geneva Conference* (Washington, D.C., 1981); W. W. Stueck, *The Road to Confrontation* (Chapel Hill, 1981); A. S. Whiting, *China Crosses the Yalu* (Stanford, Calif., 1960).

Nancy Bernkopf Tucker

CHOU EN-LAI POW SETTLEMENT PROPOSAL (March 30, 1953)

Within a week after Chou En-lai's* return from Joseph Stalin's* funeral and the Communist delegation's agreement to the UNC's* suggestion for immediate exchange of sick and wounded POWs (Operation Little Switch*), the Chinese prime minister made this effort to break the deadlock in the P'anmunjŏm truce talks* over agenda item 4*, POW repatriation. He proposed that on the conclusion of a cease-fire, those POWs who wished to be exchanged should be returned home, with the remainder handed over ''to a neutral state so as to ensure a just solution to the question of their repatriation.'' In Chou's view, members of this latter group were ''filled with apprehensions and are afraid to return home.'' He believed that once they were outside the control of the detaining power and had received ''explanations'' regarding their repatriation rights, many would elect to return after all.

Although the Eisenhower administration reacted cautiously to this statement, certain Western and Asian governments believed it represented a significant breakthrough on the item that had been blocking the conclusion of an armistice agreement since April 1952. Chou's remarks did not represent an unequivocable endorsement of voluntary repatriation* for POWs, but they acknowledged for the first time, and publicly, that there existed detainees whose repatriation could not immediately be effected on the signature of an armistice agreement.

The Soviet foreign minister endorsed Chou's suggestion on April 1, and on April 9 the Chinese and North Korean negotiators at P'anmunjŏm set out this position formally in a letter addressed to the CINCUNC General Mark W. Clark*. This led to the truce talks resumption of April 26, 1953*. A number of difficult issues still remained to be resolved, including the naming of the neutral state and the time period for retention by the neutral. Nevertheless, this proposal was instrumental in moving the negotiations toward the successful conclusion of the armistice agreement* in July 1953.

Department of State Bulletin, April 20, 1953; R. Foot, *A Substitute for Victory* (Ithaca, N.Y., 1990); B. I. Kaufman, *The Korean War* (Philadelphia, 1986); C. A. MacDonald, *Korea: The War Before Vietnam* (London, 1986).

Rosemary Foot

CHOUGH PYUNG OK
See Cho Pyŏng-ok

CHUNG IL KWON (CHŎNG, IL-GWŎN; 1917–   )

Chung was brigadier general and vice–chief of staff in the South Korean army when the Korean War broke out. He graduated from the Japanese Military Academy in Tokyo in 1940 and served in the Japanese Manchurian Army. He heard the news of the North Korean invasion of South Korea* in Hawaii on his way back to Korea from Fort Benning, where he had been sent two months earlier for training. The war marked the beginning of a brilliant career for him. Upon his return to Korea on June 30, he was promoted to major general and appointed commander of all of the Republic of Korea's* armed forces, replacing General Chae Byung Dok*. Over the next year, he was primarily responsible for handling difficulties arising from fighting an unusual war: regrouping and reorganizing defeated soldiers and putting them into the front lines, cooperating with the UNC* and coordinating relations between the forces that had little in common, differing in culture, equipment, discipline, and training.

In July 1951, in the aftermath of an army scandal, Chung left Korea for the United States to study at the Command and General Staff School. Upon his return to Korea in July 1952, he was demoted, to his dismay, to a divisional commander post; however, according to his own account, it was just the first part of a program to give Chung battlefront experience, which was arranged by President Syngman Rhee* himself. After three months in the post, he was transferred to the 9th Corps as deputy commanding officer. Three additional months later, he was appointed commanding general of ROK II Corps, remaining in this post until the truce. Apart from the difficulties of coordinating with the UNC, Chung often found himself caught up in conflict over the conduct of the war between Rhee and Washington. When, for instance, ROK and UN forces were halted at the thirty-eighth parallel in September 1950 pending authorization to cross it, Rhee angrily ordered Chung and several high-ranking Korean generals to ignore the UNC's instructions and immediately advance northward. The dilemma was solved by persuading the 8th Army* commander, Lieutenant General Walton H. Walker*, to order an ROK regiment across the parallel to take a North Korean position that had been shelling ROK troops.

In 1956, Chung was made chairman of the ROK joint chiefs of staff. The next year he retired from the army, after which he filled various diplomatic posts, including ambassadorship to the United States, France, and Turkey. Since 1964,

Chung has had an equally successful career in politics, serving as prime minister, minister of foreign affairs, speaker of the National Assembly, and member of the advisory council on state affairs.

Chung Il Kwon, *Chŏnjaeng kwa Hyuchon* (Seoul, 1986).

J. Y. Ra

CHURCH, JOHN H. (1892–1953)

Major General John Church commanded the 24th Infantry Division after the capture of Major General William F. Dean* in some of the most fearsome fighting in its history, all within the space of the first year of the Korean War. General Church enjoyed an enviable combat record: twice wounded as a young lieutenant in World War I's trenches, then three times in World War II, and he had earned a Distinguished Service Medal and two Silver Stars for heroism. But many would say during 1950 and 1951 that Church, by now frail and sickly, and almost crippled by arthritis, was not the man to lead the efforts to halt the North Korean invasion of South Korea*. Certainly he lacked by then a command presence or any inspiring qualities of personal leadership. Nonetheless, Church was to lead the 24th Division through the dispiriting retreat to the Pusan Perimeter*, the counteroffensive after the Inch'ŏn landing*, the race north through South Korea and the UN offensive across the thirty-eighth parallel* into North Korea, and the retreat once again south after Chinese military intervention*.

General Church actually preceded the 24th Division to Korea; he was dispatched by General Douglas MacArthur* on June 27, 1950, to South Korea on his survey mission* and then to head the newly-created Advance Command and Liaison Group in Korea (ADCOM). In March 1951, with the stabilization of the 8th Army's* lines just south of the thirty-eighth parallel after the disastrous retreat before the Chinese Communist forces, Church was relieved of his command. Lieutenant General Matthew B. Ridgway*, Lieutenant General Walton W. Walker's* replacement as 8th Army commander, had taken the opportunity for a general military housecleaning, particularly of the worn-out 24th Division staff. Returning to the United States, Church became commander of the Army Infantry School at Fort Benning, Georgia, until 1952. He barely survived the Korean War, which had taken so much out of him, dying in November 1953 four months after the signing of the armistice agreement*.

R. E. Appleman, *South to the Naktong, North to the Yalu* (Washington, D.C., 1961); C. Blair, *The Forgotten War* (New York, 1987); D. Detzer, *Thunder of the Captains* (New York, 1977).

Stanley Sandler

CHURCH SURVEY MISSION (June 27, 1950)

At the first Blair House meeting*, President Harry S. Truman* approved the State Department's proposal to send a survey team to Korea in the wake of the North Korean invasion of South Korea*. Acting on this decision, General Douglas MacArthur* appointed Brigadier General John H. Church* to command the group, but before its departure, the JCS had ordered U.S. air and naval support for the Republic of Korea*. MacArthur now redesignated the survey team as Advance Command and Liaison Group in Korea (ADCOM) to serve as a forward headquarters to aid in directing the U.S. military effort in Korea. Church arrived at Suwŏn on the evening of June 27 and, after discussion with Ambassador John J. Muccio*, made contact with ROK Chief of Staff General Chae Byung Dok*, stressing the vital importance of holding the Han River line. His efforts at reorganizing the ROK army at first experienced some success, as Muccio sent a rather encouraging cable to Washington the next morning. "Situation had deteriorated so rapidly," he reported, that "had not . . . Church party become known here, [it is] doubtful any organized resistance would have continued through [the] night." According to Muccio, "Church's orders have had great moral effect."

Nevertheless, North Korean forces occupied Seoul on the afternoon of June 28. As the South Korean army continued its retreat, Church advised MacArthur that extreme measures were essential if the "situation is to be stabilized." At least two U.S. combat teams would be needed to restore the line along the thirty-eighth parallel. In response, MacArthur decided to survey the battle area personally, arriving in Korea on the morning of June 29. Upon his return to Tokyo, MacArthur did not recommend the introduction of U.S. combat forces. However, on the afternoon of June 30, Church sent an extremely pessimistic cable to MacArthur, reporting that the situation had deteriorated further and the South Koreans could not halt the Communist advance. MacArthur immediately requested authority to commit U.S. ground troops, and Truman gave his approval. *See also* Han River Operations; MacArthur's Visit to Korea of June 29, 1950; Truman's Commitment of Ground Troops.

R. E. Appleman, *South to the Naktong, North to the Yalu* (Washington, D.C., 1961); *Foreign Relations of the United States, 1950,* vol. 7: *Korea* (Washington, D.C., 1976); J. I. Matray, *The Reluctant Crusade* (Honolulu, 1985); J. F. Schnabel and R. J. Watson, *A History of the Joint Chiefs of Staff,* vol. 3: *The Korean War* (Wilmington, 1979).

CHURCHILL, WINSTON (1874–1965)

Winston S. Churchill, prime minister of Britain from October 1951 until the end of the Korean War, was born into the Victorian heyday of the British Empire, a duke's grandson, the offspring of a brilliantly warped Conservative politician and a beautiful, languid American heiress. A highly intelligent, self-important maverick, Churchill pursued fame with the avarice of a Midas. Early noted for an all-consuming ambition, he entered Parliament in his mid-twenties and, less than two decades later, unfairly saddled with the debacle at Gallipoli in World War I, he was forced to resign as First Lord of the Admiralty, apparently dashing any hope of further political advancement. After a brief sojourn in the trenches, he forged a second career in politics and then, after losing his seat in Parliament in 1922 because of unfashionable imperialist and elitist views, made himself nearly indispensable to Stanley Baldwin's Conservative government.

In 1931, after an open clash with Baldwin over self-government for India, Churchill again found himself in the political wilderness. He was to reside on the Conservative back benches, any aspirations to higher office hopelessly stymied, until rescued by the onset of World War II. Generally known as the principal advocate of British military preparedness—and the most formidable critic on Neville Chamberlain's appeasement policy— Churchill was grudgingly offered a post (the Admiralty) in Chamberlain's cabinet on the day war was declared. Nine months later, with Britain on the verge of defeat, Churchill became prime minister. For the next five years, he presided over Britain's desperate struggle for survival and the forging of the grand alliance that crushed the Axis.

It may be that Winston Churchill realized intuitively that the British-dominated world he knew and so deeply loved could not, like Humpty Dumpty, be put together again. His oft-repeated statement that he had not become "the King's first minister" to preside over the demise of the British Empire perhaps is appropriately seen as an exercise in wish fulfillment. Churchill wished to see Britain rise from the travail of war to reclaim its position of global leadership and to be capable of exerting decisive military power and political authority in Europe. That fervent desire, along with his wishful faith in the generous nature of the American people and the ability of President Franklin D. Roosevelt to work political miracles, proved to be a potent combination in the determination of British policy at a critical juncture. The U.S. failure to honor Roosevelt's moral commitment to rescue the British economy clearly contributed to Churchill's shocking defeat in 1945, though popular suspicion of "Winnie" and the Conservative party's inability to look beyond the battlefield to the necessities of rebuilding an exhausted nation proved the determining factor. During the years between 1946 and 1949, spent as leader of the opposition and writing his six-volume history of World War II, Churchill established cordial, if not close, relations with President Harry S. Truman*. He endorsed wholeheartedly the increasingly tough U.S. stance toward the Soviet Union, despite pessimism about the possibility of avoiding another world war.

Churchill returned to power in October 1951 on a wave of popular dissatisfaction with Labour's domestic economic record, but he was bored with the minutiae of budgets and social services legislation. He wanted to play a vigorous role in world affairs but, painfully aware of Britain's economic and military decline, pursued this goal through seeking a reaffirmation of the "special relationship" of Britain and America. Among his first important acts during his second stint as prime minister was arranging comprehensive discussions with President Truman. Churchill's visit to Washington* in January 1952 was calculated to remind American leaders of wartime sojourns. But Churchill's dogged efforts to restore some semblance of the wartime Anglo-American parity ultimately met with little success. Both Truman and President Dwight D. Eisenhower*, upon whom in 1954 Churchill pressed his arguments for an Anglo-American condominium and a U.S.-British-Soviet summit conference, preferred to follow a policy of unilateralism and to treat the United Kingdom "just as other nations would be treated." But they had to acknowledge that the septuagenarian Churchill, termed by Truman "the greatest public figure of our age," had done everything possible to revive that myth of Anglo-American unity that was chiefly his own remarkable invention.

R. A. Callahan, *Churchill: Retreat from Empire* (Wilmington, 1984); J. Colville, *The Fringes of Power* (New York, 1985); M. Gilbert, *Winston S. Churchill,* vols. 7, 8 (Boston, 1986, 1988).

Theodore A. Wilson

CHURCHILL'S VISIT TO WASHINGTON (January 5–19, 1952)

Shortly after Winston Churchill* was returned to office as British prime minister in October 1951, he set in motion arrangements for an official visit to the United States. These British-American discussions also inaugurated a period of vigorous diplomacy between the two nations—one of determined British effort to have its concerns taken seriously and to restrain the American tendency toward quick, violent solutions to complex issues. The visit's manifest aim was to assert the principle of British and American equality in world councils and to consider current problems and the future of the Anglo-American relationship. Consumed by the Korean War and the challenges of administering its global commitments, U.S. leaders were less than enthusiastic about a visit but acceded to the old warrior's desire. They sought, however, to control the meeting's agenda and to make it a celebration of British-American amity. While Churchill had to be disappointed that the Truman administration showed little interest in joint approaches to the Soviet Union, the January 1952 visit did inaugurate a period of British-American dialogue and combined action regarding the Middle East. Churchill's pro-American stance undoubtedly proved an effective brake upon the desire of the Foreign Office to assert an even more independent position regarding Asian policy.

In the end, the visit in January 1950 proved both an end and a beginning. Churchill and President Harry S. Truman* along with small working parties dealt with problems stemming from Britain's economic decline (additional Marshall Plan aid, the Suez dispute, Iranian oil) and matters such as the status of U.S. air bases in the United Kingdom, command of NATO forces, and whether to standardize rifle calibers, a problem resulting from the British Empire's displacement by the United States. Deliberately echoing shared wartime experiences, Churchill made a powerful address before a joint session of Congress and reaffirmed his absolute faith in the primacy of the Anglo-American special relationship. He gave a ringing endorsement of the Truman administration's tough stance toward Communist aggression in Korea while supporting the Joint Policy (Greater Sanctions) statement*. But privately, Churchill and Foreign Secretary Anthony Eden* made clear that they had little sympathy for U.S. policy toward Chiang Kai-shek* and the People's Republic of China* and would press, as had the Labour government, for a negotiated settlement of the Korean conflict. In addition, they expressed concern about projected measures, especially bombing targets north of the Yalu and a naval blockade of mainland China, should the Communists renew their aggression in Korea. Secretary of State Dean G. Acheson's* pledge not to take any action without first consulting Britain apparently satisfied the prime minister.

D. Acheson, *Present at the Creation* (New York, 1969); M. Gilbert, *Winston S. Churchill, 1945–1965* (Boston, 1988); C. A. MacDonald, *Korea: The War Before Vietnam* (New York, 1986).

Theodore A. Wilson

CIA REPORT: CURRENT CAPABILITIES OF THE NORTHERN KOREA REGIME (June 19, 1950)

On June 19, 1950, President Syngman Rhee* of the Republic of Korea* pressed State Department adviser John Foster Dulles*, then in Seoul, for some assurance of U.S. aid to offset possible Chinese or North Korean aggression. Dulles responded that formal pacts were unnecessary for common action. More important, South Korea should create conditions within its borders that would discourage the growth of communism. On the same day, the Central Intelligence Agency's memorandum on North Korean capabilities suggested that President Rhee's concerns were not misplaced. For the CIA, the primary objective of the Soviet and North Korean governments was the unification of the Korean peninsula under Communist domination. Perhaps because of administrative and economic weaknesses, the Democratic People's Republic of Korea* had avoided an invasion of South Korea, but the CIA concluded that North Korea was capable, "in pursuit of its major external aim of extending control over southern Korea, of continuing and increasing its support of the present program of propaganda, infiltration, sabotage, subversion and guerrilla operations against southern Korea." To the CIA such activities seemed insufficient to extend Communist control over the south as long as U.S. economic and military aid to South Korea continued at generally the current rate.

The CIA report assumed Soviet control of the DPRK through its Communist-dominated government and the huge Soviet mission. The North Korean government lacked popular support but appeared to exercise complete control over the North Korean population. Although North Korea had experienced some recent economic growth and exported important products to the Soviet Union, productivity was far below the 1944 level, and it continued to rely heavily on Soviet assistance. Its armed forces depended on the Soviet Union almost entirely for logistical support, as well as training and planning. Still, the troops seemed well indoctrinated and possessed good morale. Despite North Korea's superior military preparation, armament, artillery, and aircraft, the CIA believed that North Korea would achieve only limited, short-term military objectives in an invasion of South Korea. With greater sacrifices and continued U.S. aid, South Korea appeared capable of resisting future encroachments of North Korea successfully.

Foreign Relations of the United States, 1950, vol. 7: *Korea* (Washington, D.C., 1976).

Norman A. Graebner

CIA REPORT: FACTORS AFFECTING THE DESIRABILITY OF A UN MILITARY CONQUEST OF ALL OF KOREA (August 18, 1950)

Even as the Republic of Korea* continued to reel under the assault of North Korean forces in July 1950, U.S. officials argued about whether the thirty-eighth parallel should be the basis of a postwar settlement. This report summarized the CIA's position on the matter. A CBS "World News Round-Up" on July 13 quoted President Syngman Rhee* of South Korea to the effect that the North Korean action had obliterated the thirty-eighth parallel and that Korea would have no peace as long as it remained divided at that line. That same broadcast quoted a U.S. Army officer who insisted that U.S. forces would stop at the thirty-eighth parallel. On July 22, the State Department's Policy Planning Staff (PPS) advocated as well a restoration of the status quo alone. It noted that none of the UN resolutions had anticipated more than the withdrawal of North Korean forces to the thirty-eighth parallel. The United States therefore could not anticipate any UN support for military action aimed at Korean unification. The PPS warned, moreover, that the Soviet Union would never tolerate a non-Communist regime in North Korea. Predictably, therefore, UN military operations north of the thirty-eighth parallel would result in conflict with either the Soviet Union or the People's Republic of China*. The risk of a major war with one of the Communist powers, the memorandum concluded, far outweighed any political advantage that might come from military action above the 38th parallel. Two days later, John M. Allison*, director of the Office of Northeast Asian Affairs, entered a strong dissent, insisting that the United States be guided not by its UN allies but by the determination of the South Koreans to unite their country. If the United States failed to unite Korea, wrote Allison, the South Korean people would rightly lose faith in the courage, intelligence, and morality of the United States.

In its memorandum, the CIA acknowledged that conquest of all Korea had advantages for the UN and the United States in terms of prestige; for Korea, it could bring unification. But the CIA agreed with the PPS that the risks of such a military decision would far exceed the benefits. It was doubtful that other UN members would favor any action that ran the danger of a strong Soviet counterattack. Asian nations, such as India, would view an invasion of North Korea as an aggressive action dictated by U.S. self-interest in Asia. Invading forces might become involved with the Chinese Communists, permitting the Kremlin to separate the United States from its allies. Because of its strategic interests in North Korea, the Soviet Union would probably enter the hostilities, directly or indirectly, in response to any UN action that threatened the Democratic People's

Republic of Korea*. If UN forces managed to conquer North Korea, the North Korean People's Army (NKPA) would merely withdraw into Manchuria and the Soviet Union. From such bases, the NKPA would endanger any new government with a renewal of the war. Finally, the CIA memorandum noted, Rhee lacked extensive support even in South Korea; in North Korea he had none. Rhee could scarcely hope to win a free election. To hold him in power without an election would require unending external support.

Foreign Relations of the United States, 1950, vol. 7: *Korea* (Washington, D.C., 1976).

Norman A. Graebner

CIA REPORT: POSITION OF THE UNITED STATES WITH RESPECT TO COMMUNIST CHINA (January 11, 1951)

Mainland China's spectacular advances across North Korea during November and December 1950 compelled the U.S. government to examine the nature of the People's Republic of China*, as well as the long-term prospects of coming to terms with it. To answer these questions, the CIA submitted this intelligence estimate to the JCS that cautioned against any expectation that the United States could eliminate the Chinese problem at any reasonable cost. The Chinese Communist regime, the CIA concluded, would retain exclusive control of the Chinese mainland for the foreseeable future. Its capacity to survive a counterrevolution seemed apparent. As the CIA estimate explained, "The disaffected elements within the country are weak, divided, leaderless and devoid of any constructive political program."

To underscore its estimate of Communist China's political stability, the CIA limited the opposition forces in mainland China to localized bandits, discontented peasants, Nationalist remnants, and ideological critics of the regime—altogether an infinitesimal percentage of the total population that could not be expected seriously to endanger the Communist government. An invasion of Republic of China* forces from Taiwan would not improve the chances of overthrowing the mainland regime. In all probability, the Communists would again defeat decisively any Nationalists operating on the mainland. At the same time, the CIA assumed that the presence of the 7th Fleet in Taiwan Strait was sufficient to ensure the survival of Chiang Kai-shek's* regime. The CIA attributed the close cooperation between Communist China and the Soviet Union to mutual interest in reducing Western power and influence in Asia but detected the potentialities for conflict between the two governments. China would predictably resent any Soviet effort to infringe on its sovereignty by reducing it to a satellite. The two countries, moreover, had conflicting interests in Sinkiang, Manchuria, Korea, and Southeast Asia. Only a dangerous common enemy would keep these potential conflicts from emerging.

Finally, the CIA doubted that any direct economic, naval, or air assault on China would be effective, thus challenging the wisdom of CINCUNC General Douglas MacArthur's* plan for victory*. The Chinese economy was rural and generally impervious to external pressure. The urban economy was dependent on overseas trade, but a third of China's imports came from the Soviet Union.

A naval blockade would compel massive adjustments in the Chinese economy; it would not undermine the regime. If bombing of industrial and transportation facilities would injure the Chinese economy severely and even reduce China's military capabilities, such damage would only incite a massive response. Certainly the Chinese would retaliate by attacking all Western interests within reach with the support of both the Chinese people and the Soviet Union. *See also* NSC-101.

Foreign Relations of the United States, 1951, vol. 7: *Korea and China* (Washington D.C., 1983).

Norman A. Graebner

CIA REPORT: SOVIET INTENTIONS IN THE CURRENT SITUATION
(December 2, 1950)

Chinese military intervention* in the Korean War created the need for this report because it raised the question of Soviet intentions in East Asia. For the CIA, the People's Republic of China's* defense preparations indicated that the Chinese, by intervening, had assumed the risk of a general war with the United States. It seemed equally clear that the Chinese would not have accepted that risk without the promise of effective Soviet support. The CIA predicted that the Soviet Union would continue to underwrite Chinese operations in Korea with materiel, technicians, aircraft and antiaircraft artillery, and trained personnel to defend Chinese targets from attack. In the event of a U.S. or UN invasion of Chinese territory, the Soviets, according to CIA information, would probably come to China's rescue. But if the Soviets had accepted the risk of global war, the CIA doubted that they intended to enter Korea or precipitate a general war in Asia.

A broadened war between the United States and the PRC would be advantageous to the Soviet Union. Such a war would involve the U.S. and allied forces in an indecisive theater where the price of victory would exceed any strategic gains. It would create dissension between the Americans and Europeans, whose perceived interests in Asia were considerably less than those of the United States. A war against China would expand Communist possibilities in Korea and East Asia even as they obstructed plans for the defense of Western Europe. If the United States refused to fight the Communist Chinese altogether, the Soviets could anticipate easy Communist gains in Korea and Indochina. The CIA concluded that the Soviet Union remained a dangerous threat to the peace of Asia and the rest of the world:

The Soviet rulers have resolved to pursue aggressively their world-wide attack on the power position of the United States and its allies, regardless of the possibility that global war may result, although they may estimate that the Western Allies would seek to avoid such a development. Further direct or indirect Soviet aggression in Europe and Asia is likely, regardless of the outcome of the Korean situation. . . .

The possibility cannot be disregarded that the USSR may already have decided to precipitate global war in circumstances most advantageous to itself through the development of general war in Asia. We are unable, on the basis of present intelligence, to determine the probability of such a decision having in fact been made.

This estimate, concurred in by all members of the intelligence advisory committee, was issued by the CIA director as a National Intelligence Estimate, dated December 5, 1950.

Foreign Relations of the United States, 1950, vol. 7: *Korea* (Washington, D.C., 1976).

Norman A. Graebner

CIA REPORT: THREAT OF FULL CHINESE COMMUNIST INTERVENTION IN KOREA (October 12, 1950)

Despite Chinese warnings that a UN invasion of North Korea would bring the People's Republic of China* into the war, the General Assembly adopted the UN resolution of October 7, 1950*, favoring the unification of Korea under the direction of the UNCURK*. As the UN offensive across the thirty-eighth parallel* got underway, the CIA, in this report, raised the burgeoning issue of possible Chinese military intervention* in the Korean War. The CIA document concluded that Communist China, lacking air and naval power, could intervene effectively but not decisively. But it doubted that the PRC, despite statements by Chou En-lai* and other warnings circulating through the embassies of Asia, had any intention of resorting to a full-scale intervention. Yet the CIA acknowledged that certain factors might prompt Chinese involvement. If successful, military intervention could add to the PRC's prestige, confirm China as a major Asiatic power, and constitute a gain for world communism. If the intervention failed, the Chinese Communists could exploit the failure to excuse their inability to carry out economic reforms in China and justify their claims for Soviet military and economic aid. Communist Chinese intervention, successful or not, would trap the United States and its allies in a costly, possibly inconclusive, war in East Asia. But China's abstention from the Korean War could result in the unification of Korea under a non-Communist government—a major defeat for communism in Asia.

For the CIA, those factors that discounted Chinese intervention appeared far more persuasive. The CIA assumed above all that the PRC, with its economy in chaos, would avoid any military confrontation with the United States because this could endanger the very existence of the Communist regime. Any Chinese intervention, unless supported heavily by Soviet air and naval power, promised to be costly in human life. Such aid would make Communist China more dependent on the Soviet Union and increase Soviet control of Manchuria. If the Chinese effort failed, the regime's critics would accuse it of failure to resist the pressures from Moscow. Finally, Chinese intervention would seal that country's exclusion from the UN. The CIA report concluded:

While full-scale Chinese Communist intervention in Korea must be regarded as a continuing possibility, a consideration of all known factors leads to the conclusion that barring a Soviet decision for global war, such action is not probable in 1950. During this period, intervention will probably be confined to continued covert assistance to the North Koreans.

Foreign Relations of the United States, 1950, vol. 7: *Korea* (Washington, D.C., 1976).

Norman A. Graebner

CIVILIAN INTERNEE ISSUE

On November 9, 1951, CINCUNC General Matthew B. Ridgway* received approval for his request to reclassify certain POWs as civilian internees preparatory to their outright release. Most of these were citizens of the Republic of Korea* whom the Communists had impressed into military service during North Korean invasion of South Korea* plus innocent bystanders whom the UNC* had mistakenly incarcerated as security risks or suspected North Korean soldiers. This group also comprised North Korean refugees who had collaborated with the UNC and could expect extreme punishment or death if repatriated. There were other POWs who claimed but were denied civilian status, including South Korean citizens who had fought voluntarily on the Communist side and soldiers impressed into the North Korean army or mistakenly imprisoned as stragglers. Ridgway planned to parole legitimate civilian internees gradually when the situation was opportune and after obtaining the ROK's approval.

Preliminary screening in December 1951 determined that there were 37,500 civilian internees and approximately 10,000 of them would want to return to North Korea. The next month, the UNC segregated this group after a rescreening process to correct errors. It became necessary to use force in Compound 62 on Kŏje-do during February 1952 to end violent resistance, resulting eventually in nearly 200 deaths and the failure to screen perhaps as many as 15,000 POWs. By March 1952, the Communist delegation at the P'anmunjŏm truce talks* had accepted the principle of special treatment for civilian internees. Uncertainty about whether any of the POWs would wish to remain in the ROK persuaded the Communists to approve on April 2 the screening of all POWs, and three days later, the UNC started Operation Scatter*. Subsequently, General James A. Van Fleet*, commander of the 8th Army*, moved those civilian internees wanting to remain in South Korea to the mainland. But Ridgway delayed their release, fearing that to do so would endanger an overall settlement of the POW issue.

By June 1952, the deadlock over agenda item 4*, repatriation of POWs, had eliminated any further reason for delay. In addition, the ROK wanted the civilian internees released, plus it would reduce the demand for guards and the logistical burden on the UNC. President Harry S. Truman* gave his approval, and on June 13 the JCS approved the plan that CINCUNC General Mark W. Clark*, Ridgway's replacement, had submitted for the release. To prevent the press from relying exclusively on information from the ROK and issuing stories "distorted and filled with half-truths," Clark issued a press release on June 22 explaining the reasons for Operation Homecoming. The next day at P'anmunjŏm, Major General William K. Harrison, Jr.*, the UNC's chief negotiator, announced the impending release of the civilian internees. The Communists protested but could do nothing.

From July to August, the UNC gradually released about 27,000 people in coordination with the ROK's ability to process and transport to new homes what Clark described as "a whole miserable grabbag of men, women and some children swept up in the retreat and advance of the first eighteen months of the war." One month later, after rescreening, the UNC classified 11,000 more people as civilian internees, releasing them in October and November. The disposition of this group of POWs provided valuable experience for the UNC when it later released the remainder of the prisoners of war after the armistice.

C. Blair, *The Forgotten War* (New York, 1987); M. W. Clark, *From the Danube to the Yalu* (New York, 1954); J. L. Collins, *War in Peacetime* (Boston, 1969); W. G. Hermes, *Truce Tent and Fighting Front* (Washington, D.C., 1966); J. F. Schnabel and R. J. Watson, *History of the Joint Chiefs of Staff*, vol. 3: *The Korean War* (Wilmington, 1979).

CLARK, MARK W. (1896–1984)

General Mark W. Clark was CINCFE and head of the UNC* from May 12, 1952, until July 27, 1953, when the Korean armistice agreement* was signed. Born in Watertown, New York, he graduated from the U.S. Military Academy at West Point in 1917 and then was a student at the Command and General Staff College at Fort Leavenworth from 1933 to 1935. During World War II, Clark served with distinction in Italy, where he commanded the U.S. 5th Army at Salerno, rising by 1945 to head the 15th Army Group. After the war, he commanded the U.S. occupation forces in Austria and established a reputation as a tough anti-Communist. In June 1950, Clark was head of the U.S. Army Field Forces at Fort Monroe, Virginia, and became responsible for training the troops destined for combat in the Korean War. He tried to make this training as realistic as possible and in February 1951 visited the front to investigate conditions there.

When Clark replaced General Matthew B. Ridgway* as CINCUNC in May 1952, armistice negotiations were bogged down on agenda item 4*, the POW issue. But Clark's problems in Korea were as much political as military, with much of his time initially taken up by the Kŏje-do POW uprising*, which Clark suppressed by force. He also had constant problems with President Syngman Rhee* of the Republic of Korea*, which culminated in Rhee's attempts to sabotage the truce talks in June 1952. Although Clark sympathized with Rhee's anti-communism, he was angered by his tactics and developed a secret contingency plan, Operation Everready*, to overthrow the South Korean leader. Clark believed that the Communists understood nothing but force, a lesson he claimed to have learned in Austria, and stepped up military pressure on the enemy to break the stalemate at P'anmunjŏm. He relied on air pressure strategy* rather than ground offensives because the latter would incur heavy casualties and cause political problems at home.

Although he obeyed the orders limiting the war, Clark shared General Douglas MacArthur's* desire for victory in Korea. Not only did he disagree with a policy that forbade attacks on Manchuria, he developed a contingency plan (OPLAN 8–52) for a drive to the Yalu involving the use of tactical atomic weapons and Republic of China* troops. He hoped that Dwight D. Eisenhower's* election in 1952 would be followed by the rolling back of Asian communism, but after the new president's visit to Korea*, Clark concluded that Eisenhower, like President Harry S. Truman*, was prepared to settle for a draw. On July 27, 1953, by his own account, Clark signed the armistice agreement with a heavy heart, claiming that he had become the first American soldier in history to end a war short of victory. After retiring from the army in October 1953, Clark became convinced that Communist subversion at home had weakened American resolve and made no secret of his right-wing sympathies. He later argued that Vietnam was the inevitable result of the retreat from victory in Korea.

M. Blumenson, *Mark Clark* (London, 1985); M. W. Clark, *From the Danube to the Yalu* (London, 1954); R. Foot, *The Wrong War* (Ithaca, N.Y., 1985); W. G. Hermes, *Truce Tent and Fighting Front* (Washington, D.C., 1966).

Callum A. MacDonald

CLUBB, O. EDMUND (1901–1989)

O. Edmund Clubb was director of the State Department's Office of Chinese Affairs from 1949 to 1951. In this position, he offered advice on U.S. policy toward Korea before and after the outbreak of the war. Along with fellow China expert John Paton Davies*, who served on the Policy Planning Staff, Clubb played a central role in the the Truman administration's efforts to assess the motives and anticipate the actions of the People's Republic of China* regarding Korea. He opposed, for example, the UN offensive across the thirty-eighth parallel*, anticipating Chinese military intervention*, although he did not speak out strongly against the Home-by-Christmas offensive*. Clubb was the only top U.S. official who consistently warned that Chou En-lai's* statement about the PRC's intention to join the fighting was not a bluff. He later opposed extending the war to China, fearing that this would bring Soviet intervention in accordance with the Sino-Soviet Treaty of Friendship and Alliance*.

Born the son of a cattle rancher in South Park, Minnesota, Clubb joined the foreign service in 1928 after graduating from the University of Minnesota, spending the better part of the next twenty-two years in China and other East Asian outposts. He taught Chinese and Russian to his fellows in Peking, wrote the first detailed study of the Chinese Left, spent eight months in a Japanese camp during World War II, and served as general consul in Vladivostok, Mukden, Changchun, and Peking. When Mao Tse-tung's* Red Army hauled down the flag from the U.S embassy in Peking, Clubb was there.

Beyond his status as a "China hand" and an alleged participant in a plot to undermine Chiang Kai-shek*, Clubb had the bad luck of a brief encounter with Alger Hiss's accuser, Whittaker Chambers. This led to FBI interrogations, a subpoena from the House Committee on Un-American Activities, and, finally, a Loyalty Review Board decision in December 1951 labeling him a "poor security risk'' and leading to his suspension. Clubb appealed, winning reinstatement and prompting Secretary of State Dean G. Acheson* to banish him to an obscure desk in the State Department's Division of Historical Research. Clubb turned down his new assignment, taking early retirement at the age of fifty-one. He went on to teach part-time at New York University, Brooklyn College, and Columbia University before joining Columbia's East Asian Institute as a research associate. Over the course of the three decades after he left the foreign service, Clubb wrote several books and dozens of articles on China.

O. E. Clubb, *The Witness and I* (New York, 1974); R. Foot, *The Wrong War* (Ithaca, N.Y., 1985).

Kenneth O'Reilly

COLLINS, J. LAWTON (1896–1987)

General J. Lawton Collins, U.S. Army chief of staff from August 1949 to August 1953, was born in New Orleans. He graduated from the U.S. Military Academy at West Point in 1917. Early in World War II, Collins assumed command of the "Tropic Lightning" 25th Infantry Division, whose soldiers gave him the nickname "Lightning Joe." His distinguished leadership on Guadalcanal and New Georgia attracted the attention of General George C. Marshall*, who selected Collins as one of the few general officers to be transferred from the Pacific to the European theater. Lightning Joe commanded the VII Corps in the Normandy invasion and the victory over Germany. After the war, he served as deputy chief of staff under General Dwight D. Eisenhower* and vice–chief of staff under General Omar N. Bradley* on his way to his own appointment to the JCS.

During the Korean War, Collins was a central figure in Washington's efforts to coordinate strategy with the CINCUNC, General Douglas MacArthur*. Collins played an especially crucial role in JCS efforts to provide MacArthur the men and materiel needed to sustain what was at times a desperate defense in Korea without weakening U.S. military resources elsewhere. This assignment would have been difficult in any case, but Collins faced a special challenge in attempting to communicate Washington's limited war strategy to the imperious MacArthur. Their first meeting came when Collins and Air Force Chief of Staff General Hoyt S. Vandenberg* arrived at MacArthur's headquarters to assess the situation as North Korean forces pushed toward Pusan. In August, Collins was back again, this time with Chief of Naval Operations Admiral Forrest P. Sherman*, to discuss a proposed flanking assault at Inch'ŏn. Collins had a number of reservations about the plan, but he and the other service chiefs ultimately approved it. Collins later reflected that the eventual reverses in North Korea were owed, at least in part, to a failure of the Pentagon to stand up to the formidable MacArthur after his Inch'ŏn landing* success.

In the wake of the Chinese military intervention*, Collins and Vandenberg went again to Tokyo in January 1951 to confer with MacArthur. Collins returned to Washington with a positive report that the 8th Army*, recently placed under the command of his West Point classmate Lieutenant General Matthew B. Ridgway*, exhibited good morale and was regaining its confidence. In MacArthur's ensuing clash with Washington over the scope and direction of the war, Collins joined the other chiefs in supporting President Harry S. Truman's* recall of MacArthur* and in backing the administration's decision to seek to avoid a wider war. During the MacArthur Hearings*, Collins gave key testimony about MacArthur's disagreement with basic U.S. policies and described the Pentagon's concern that MacArthur might seriously and unilaterally violate those policies. After his term as chief of staff, President Dwight D. Eisenhower sent him to Vietnam as U.S special representative from November 1954 to May 1955. Collins retired from the Army in 1956. *See also* Collins-Sherman Visit to Tokyo; Collins-Vandenberg Visit to Tokyo (January 1951 and July 1950).

   J. L. Collins, *Lightning Joe: An Autobiography* (Baton Rouge, La., 1979); J. L. Collins, *War in Peacetime* (Boston, 1969); J. W. Spanier, *The Truman-MacArthur Controversy and the Korean War* (New York, 1965).

David L. Anderson

COLLINS-SHERMAN VISIT TO TOKYO (August 19–25, 1950)

   Army Chief of Staff General J. Lawton Collins* and Navy Chief of Staff Admiral Forrest P. Sherman* traveled to Tokyo on August 19, 1950, to discuss with CINCUNC General Douglas MacArthur* his plans for the Inch'ŏn landing*. They also would consider whether to recommend the relief of the 8th Army* commander, Lieutenant General Walton W. Walker*. When MacArthur first proposed Operation Chromite*, the JCS had expressed grave reservations about the wisdom of the project. Access to the harbor of Inch'ŏn was narrow and dominated by Wolmi Island, plus the port suffered from high tides, mudflats, and seawalls. During their discussions in Tokyo, Collins and Sherman again reminded MacArthur of the serious risks posed by his planned amphibious landing behind enemy lines. All those present during these talks agreed that Inch'ŏn would be an extremely dangerous operation, but MacArthur delivered an extemporaneous speech that by all accounts was a masterful job of persuasion. He convinced his audience that the element of surprise alone guaranteed success. "We shall land at Inch'ŏn," MacArthur perorated, "and I shall crush them." Before returning to Washington, Collins and Sherman visited Korea. Improved battlefield conditions persuaded them not to recommend replacing Walker.

   Perhaps the most significant aspect of the Collins-Sherman visit, however, was that a consensus existed on the need to cross the thirty-eighth parallel. Collins, Sherman, and MacArthur agreed that the United States had to destroy the North Korean army completely, or the threat of invasion would remain. Since the Soviet Union had not yet intervened militarily in Korea, MacArthur expressed confidence that Moscow would not become involved in the future. MacArthur adopted a global perspective when he argued: "The Oriental follows a winner. If we win, the Chinese will not follow the USSR." Upon their return to Washington, Collins and Sherman informed President Harry S. Truman* of Mac-

Arthur's plans. The president gave his consent to Operation Chromite, and the JCS tentatively approved the Inch'ŏn landing project on August 28, setting September 15 as the target date. In addition, Truman instructed his advisers to formulate detailed plans for the UN offensive across the thirty-eighth parallel*, the occupation of North Korea*, and the reunification of the peninsula.

C. Blair, *The Forgotten War* (New York, 1987); J. L. Collins, *War in Peacetime* (Boston, 1969); R. D. Heinl, Jr., *Victory at High Tide* (Philadelphia, 1968); J. I. Matray, "Truman's Plan for Victory: National Self-Determination and the 38th Parallel Decision in Korea," *Journal of American History* (September 1979); J. F. Schnabel, *Policy and Direction* (Washington, D.C., 1972).

COLLINS-VANDENBERG VISIT TO TOKYO (July 13–14, 1950)

On orders from President Harry S. Truman*, the JCS dispatched Army Chief of Staff General J. Lawton Collins* and Air Force Chief of Staff General Hoyt S. Vandenberg* to Tokyo in July 1950 to assess CINCUNC General Douglas MacArthur's* current and future needs for U.S. men, materiel, and money following Truman's commitment of ground troops* in the Korean War. By July 7, MacArthur had doubled his original estimate of troops needed to counter the North Korean People's Army and two days later urgently appealed for four additional divisions, again doubling his force-level estimate. The JCS believed that the emergency in Korea warranted these requests, pledging to provide the theater commander whatever he needed. The problem, however, was finding a way to meet MacArthur's immediate requests without weakening U.S. commitments in Western Europe and drawing down the general reserve necessary to meet unforeseen contingencies worldwide.

When Collins and Vandenberg arrived at MacArthur's headquarters on July 13, the Pusan Perimeter* was not yet established. MacArthur buoyantly assured his visitors that the front would soon be stabilized but declared that his ability to mount a counteroffensive depended on the rate of reinforcement. MacArthur acknowledged that the JCS had problems elsewhere in the world, but he argued that the Communist advance must be defeated in Korea to demonstrate U.S. ability to counter aggression anywhere. Also, a counteroffensive could lead to the reunification of Korea, which might necessitate U.S. occupation of the entire peninsula. This scenario prompted Vandenberg to ask about possible Chinese Communist reinforcement of the North Koreans. MacArthur thought that heavy bombing would destroy supply routes out of Manchuria and even mentioned the possible use of atomic weapons.

Collins traveled to the front with Lieutenant General Walton H. Walker*, commander of the 8th Army*, to observe the terrain and assess problems in the field. Meanwhile, Vandenberg studied the problem of how the FEAF with its B-29 bombers could provide tactical air support for the beleaguered U.S. ground forces. Staff officers accompanying the two chiefs conferred with MacArthur's staff on a host of logistical details and preliminary plans for an amphibious assault to cut enemy supply lines. Collins and Vandenberg left Tokyo on July 14 with a report recommending the prompt deployment of reinforcements, including an infantry division, marine division, and three regimental combat teams. With the commitment of these forces, MacArthur began planning the Inch'ŏn landing*, code-named Operation Chromite*. *See also* Operation Bluehearts.

J. L. Collins, *War in Peacetime* (Boston, 1969); J. F. Schnabel, *Policy and Direction* (Washington, D.C., 1972).

David L. Anderson

COLLINS-VANDENBERG VISIT TO TOKYO (January 15, 1951)

On January 15, 1951, the U.S. Army and Air Force chiefs of staff, Generals J. Lawton Collins* and Hoyt S. Vandenberg*, respectively, arrived in Tokyo to confer with CINCUNC General Douglas MacArthur* about U.S. policy as outlined in the JCS directive of January 12, 1951*. In early December, after UNC* forces retreated southward with heavy losses following Chinese military intervention*, MacArthur had sent warnings to the Pentagon that his troops might have to be evacuated from Korea to avoid destruction. Collins flew immediately to Lieutenant General Walton H. Walker's* 8th Army* headquarters in Seoul, finding the situation difficult but not completely desperate. Walker was confident that at least the Pusan area could be held. Meeting with MacArthur in Tokyo on December 6, Collins listened but did not debate as the UNC commander insisted that substantial reinforcement would be required to avoid evacuation.

After Collins returned to Washington, the JCS sent MacArthur a directive on December 30 to defend Korea in successive positions along twelve specifically designated lines. MacArthur claimed that these new orders were contradictory and did not make clear if he was to defend Korea or withdraw. He proposed instead his plan for victory*, which would have greatly expanded the war with the People's Republic of China*. After discussion by the NSC, the JCS, in its directive of January 12, 1951, reaffirmed its December 30 directive. An accompanying letter from President Harry S. Truman* to MacArthur emphasized that it was U.S. policy to continue to resist aggression in Korea but within prudent limits that did not weaken U.S. defenses elsewhere. The president also sent Collins and Vandenberg to assess the morale of U.S. forces and to make sure that MacArthur understood Washington's policy. They brought with them for discussion, however, a memorandum including MacArthur's proposals for escalating the war. Later, MacArthur claimed that this showed the JCS supported implementation of these steps.

In Tokyo, MacArthur told the two chiefs that he interpreted Truman's letter to mean that he was to hold out in Korea indefinitely. Collins explained that MacArthur was to delay any evacuation as long as possible without risking the destruction of the 8th Army or endangering the security of Japan. Collins and Vandenberg then inspected the battlefront as the new 8th Army commander, Lieutenant General Matthew B. Ridgway*, conducted Operation Wolfhound*. In a daring and incredibly risky action for a man who possessed some of his nation's most sensitive defense secrets, Vandenberg flew a low-level helicopter reconnaissance several miles deep into enemy territory. The two generals returned to Washington with a positive report that the 8th Army could hold its own and that the situation was not as dark as feared. Their optimistic evaluation dispelled the gloom that had pervaded Washington since November and cast aside various contingency plans premised upon a rout of UN forces in Korea. *See also* NCS–101.

J. L. Collins, *War in Peacetime* (Boston, 1969); J. F. Schnabel, *Policy and Direction* (Washington, D.C., 1972).

David L. Anderson

COLOMBIAN BATTALION

A battalion of Colombian troops served in Korea between June 1951 and July 1953. In addition, a Colombian frigate, the *Almirante Padilla,* operated off the Korean coast. The Colombian battalion, a contingent of approximately 1,000 men, was attached to various U.S. infantry divisions and fought in actions such as the Kŭmsan offensive and the Battle of Old Baldy*. The battalion sustained nearly 600 casualties during its two years of combat duty and garnered numerous silver and bronze star decorations.

Colombia was the only Latin American nation to send troops to Korea. Throughout the twentieth century, Colombia has consistently supported international organizations. But Colombia's decision can probably be primarily explained by domestic concerns. During the Korean War era, Colombia was wracked by political warfare, *La Violencia,* and ruled by a right-wing dictator, Laureano Gómez. Gómez may have sent troops to Korea in order to curry favor with the United States, deflect attention from the civil strife, and transfer military opponents out of the country.

H. E. Davis and L. C. Wilson (eds.), *Latin American Foreign Policies* (Baltimore, 1975); A. Ruiz Novoa, *El Batallón "Colombia" en Corea* (Bogotá, 1956); R. W. Ramsey, "The Colombian Battalion in Korea and Suez," *Journal of Inter-American Studies* (October 1967).

Stephen G. Rabe

COMMONWEALTH DIVISION (FIRST)

This was the major British Commonwealth ground force contribution to the UNC*. Activated on July 28, 1951, the division was formed through the integration of three separate infantry brigades then operating independently in Korea: 25th Canadian, 28th Commonwealth (a joint British–Australian–New Zealand–Indian formation), and 29th British. The brigades had earned a high military reputation while operating as part of U.S. divisions, and the formation of the division was intended to maximize the Commonwealth's military contribution in Korea while resolving some of the administrative and logistic problems occasioned by their separation.

The division's first major action after its formation was Operation Commando* in October 1951, involving a push northeast and west of the Imjin River to establish the Jamestown Line. The division then remained in the line during the entire period of the static phase of the war, except for a two-month rotation from

February to March 1953, when its position was taken over by the U.S. 2d Infantry Division. During the static phase, Commonwealth units patrolled regularly for intelligence purposes and, in attempts to snatch prisoners, made several large forays into enemy lines at company strength and above and fought off a number of heavy Chinese assaults on their positions, especially around Little Gibraltar and during the Battles of the Hook*.

The Commonwealth division was widely regarded as one of the best formations in the UNC. Many of its operational and staff procedures differed from those of the U.S. and South Korean units, and it employed a separate line of communication and resupply back to Japan. Total battle casualties for Commonwealth units in Korea, including the period before the formation of the division, were 93 officers and 1,170 men killed, 301 officers and 4,516 men wounded, and 60 officers and 1,128 missing, of whom 1,036 were taken prisoner and later repatriated by the Chinese. *See also* Sir William Bridgeford; Sir Archibald James H. Cassels; Sir Horace C. H. Robertson; Sir Michael M.A.R. West.

C. N. Barclay, *The First Commonwealth Division* (Aldershot, 1954); J. Grey, *The Commonwealth Armies and the Korean War* (Manchester, 1988); R. J. O'Neill, *Australia in the Korean War 1950–53* (Canberra, 1981, 1985); War History Compilation Committee, *History of the United Nations Forces in the Korean War,* vol. 2 (Seoul, 1973); H. F. Wood, *Strange Battleground: The Operations in Korea and Their Effects on the Defense Policy of Canada* (Ottawa, 1966).

Jeffrey Grey

COMMUNIST POW ADMINISTRATION

Chinese and North Korean attitudes to UN prisoners of war differed and were founded on divergent assumptions, although both systems involved political indoctrination, brutality, and torture. The three principal features of North Korean treatment of captured UN service personnel were forced labor, intelligence extraction, and political indoctrination, marked by an appalling level of casual brutality and sadism, which was all the worse because many of those who fell into North Korean hands were sick or wounded. Under the North Koreans, prisoners were set to work in labor gangs in P'yŏngyang while under UNC* air attack or kept in interrogation centers where many died through mistreatment, malnutrition, and disease. North Korean administration was marked also by competition between various agencies of the Democratic People's Republic of Korea*, especially the military and the security services, and Soviet and Chinese authorities.

The Chinese attitude to POWs was based on the so-called lenient policy, which offered prisoners their lives in return for submission to certain political "truths" presented by their captors. This system had enjoyed considerable success with captured Japanese soldiers during World War II and with Nationalist troops during the civil war that followed. The barbarous treatment meted out by the North Koreans was at variance clearly with the tenets of Chinese policy, and the Chinese assumed control of POW administration in April-May 1951. After this, the treatment of prisoners improved substantially, not only because the

Chinese were less inclined to use random violence on prisoners but because the rudimentary facilities the North Koreans had operated were regularized and permanent camps built along the Yalu River.

Control within the camps was maintained through a network of informers among the prisoners themselves, subborned either by promises of better treatment or, in a few cases, by ideological conviction. Officers and noncommissioned officers were separated from the other ranks and "reactionaries," those who refused steadfastly to cooperate in any way, were further separated, the whole being moved repeatedly between camps. As a result, no UN prisoner managed to escape from the camps successfully back to his own lines, although many made attempts. The problem of escape was compounded by the distance between the Yalu camps and the UN front line and by the difficulties faced by Europeans moving in a hostile Asian environment. *See also* Brainwashing and Prisoner of War Morale; UNC POW Administration.

C. Cunningham, "The Origins and Development of Communist Prisoner-of-War Policies," *RUSI Journal* (March 1974); C. A. MacDonald, *Korea: The War Before Vietnam* (London, 1986); Ministry of Defense, *Treatment of British Prisoners of War in Korea* (London, 1955).

Jeffrey Grey

COMMUNIST POW SETTLEMENT PROPOSAL OF MAY 7, 1953

This eight-point proposal was accepted by the UNC* delegation at the P'anmunjŏm truce talks* as a basis for discussion leading ultimately to a resolution of agenda item 4*, the POW repatriation issue, and the signing of a final armistice agreement*. On April 26, 1953, the Communists proposed sending non-repatriate POWs to a neutral state after the armistice, where they could receive explanations from their own side, which presumably would persuade them to return home. The UNC delegation objected that this proposal failed to nominate a neutral state, did not allow for the release of POWs after a period of explanations, and involved moving them out of Korea.

On May 7, the Communists condemned the UNC position as obstinate and obstructive, insisting that their own plan was fair and reasonable. At the same time, however, the chief North Korean delegate, Lieutenant General Nam Il*, put forward a new eight-point proposal. This called for the release of all POWs desiring repatriation within two months of the armistice. The remainder were to be handed over to a Neutral Nations Repatriation Commission* (NNRC) consisting of Czechoslovakia, Poland, Sweden, Switzerland, and India, which would take charge of the prisoners at their original places of detention. The members of the NNRC would provide guards for the camps and ensure that the POWs were freed from intimidation and coercion while they received explanations from their own side that would persuade them to return home. Within four months of assuming control and after explanations, the NNRC would repatriate those POWs who wished to return to their own side. The fate of the remainder would be decided by consultation at the political conference, which was to be held within three months of the cease-fire under Article 4 of the armistice agreement.

On May 10, Nam Il elaborated on some of the details, explaining that the NNRC would reach decisions by majority vote. The Communist plan was close to the terms of the UN resolution of December 3, 1952*, on the POW question but rejected by China and North Korea. *See also* Chou En-lai POW Settlement Proposal; Truce Talks Resumption of April 26, 1953; UNC Final POW Settlement Proposal of May 25, 1953.

M. W. Clark, *From the Danube to the Yalu* (London, 1954); W. G. Hermes, *Truce Tent and Fighting Front* (Washington, D.C., 1966); C. A. MacDonald, *Korea: The War Before Vietnam* (London, 1986).

Callum A. MacDonald

CONGRESS AND THE KOREAN WAR

Congressional support for U.S. military actions to defend the Republic of Korea* was strong during the first months of the Korean conflict. As a result, President Harry S. Truman* decided not to ask for a formal resolution endorsing his actions. Public backing for U.S. intervention at the outset of the war made it difficult for critics of the administration to attack the president openly. In addition, as in prior wars, politicians consistently provided financial support for U.S. soldiers at the front.

Congress indicated its willingness to back the war effort less than a week after the North Korean invasion of South Korea* when it approved the Deficiency Appropriations Act of June 29, 1950*, expanding the amount of assistance to the ROK. It also implemented Truman's suggestions regarding economic mobilization when it passed the Defense Production Act* in September. More important, it would approve the Defense Appropriations Acts* for fiscal 1951 and 1952 in accordance with the administration's recommendations.

Evidence of China's entry into the war destroyed the foundation for cooperation between the executive and the legislature, as Truman's critics renewed attacks on administration policies. Senator Kenneth S. Wherry, for example, called for the resignation of Secretary of State Dean G. Acheson*, declaring that "the blood of our boys in Korea is on his shoulders." After the Democrats suffered key losses in the 1950 midterm elections, Congress was not only more able but more willing to challenge the president's authority. During December, massive Chinese military intervention* resulted in an evaporation of congressional unity behind Truman's policies. In both houses, there was angry and emotional debate as some congressmen argued that the United States should withdraw from Korea and save its resources for a war with the Soviet Union. Senator Robert A. Taft* called for a complete reexamination of U.S. foreign policy, but Truman would not agree to joint consultations regarding the matter. And then there was the Great Debate over the administration's proposal to send U.S. troops to defend Western Europe. Reflecting the deterioration of his relations with Congress, Truman stated publicly, "I don't ask their permission, I just consult them."

Truman's recall of CINCUNC General Douglas MacArthur* was very unpopular in Congress, further undermining support for the Korean War. Shortly after the MacArthur Hearings* ended, Congress refused to approve Truman's proposal to extend and strengthen his powers under the Defense Production Act. Less than a year later, many congressmen called for the president's impeachment after Truman's steel plants seizure*. They argued that his action, like military intervention in the Korean War, constituted an unconstitutional and dictatorial exercise of his powers as commander in chief. However, Congress refused to offer legislation to end the strike in the interests of successfully prosecuting the war. This incident provided an excellent illustration of the attitude of Congress toward Korea once the war developed into a bloody stalemate that was unpopular with the voting public. Congressmen were more than willing to allow Truman to absorb political criticism for high taxes, mounting casualties, and the frustrations of fighting a limited and inconclusive conflict. Truman was unable to share the political responsibility with Congress for the war and would leave office as one of the most unpopular presidents in U.S. history. His successor, President Dwight D. Eisenhower*, would negotiate an armistice agreement* ending the war six months after taking office, thus avoiding any problems with Congress. *See also* Congress and U.S. Military Intervention; Congressional Meetings with Truman of June 1950; Truman's Declaration of a National Emergency.

R. J. Donovan, *Tumultuous Years* (New York, 1982); W. W. Stueck, *The Road to Confrontation* (Chapel Hill, 1981); H. B. Westerfield, *Foreign Policy and Party Politics* (New Haven, Conn., 1955).

CONGRESS AND U.S. MILITARY INTERVENTION

President Harry S. Truman* committed U.S. military power to the defense of the Republic of Korea* without requesting or receiving congressional approval. His critics charged that the president exceeded his constitutional authority because Congress had not approved a declaration of war. To avoid what he considered Truman's mistake, President Lyndon B. Johnson later would obtain passage of the Gulf of Tonkin resolution in the Vietnam War.

At the first Blair House meeting*, Under Secretary of State James E. Webb* raised the issue of domestic politics. "We're not going to talk politics," Truman declared. "I'll handle the political affairs." The next morning, the president met with Senator Tom Connally* and asked him whether he would have to ask for a declaration of war if he sent troops into Korea. "If a burglar breaks into your house," the senator replied, "you can shoot him without going down to the police station and getting permission. You might run into a long debate by Congress, which would tie your hands completely. You have the right to do it as commander in chief and under the U.N. Charter." Undoubtedly Truman was of the same opinion, since he believed in strong executive powers. From this point onward, the administration relied on Connally's interpretation to justify its actions in Korea. Yet Truman was aware of the need for consultations with Congress and met with leaders from both parties on the morning of June 27, 1950, to review with them his decisions regarding Korea.

That afternoon, in the House of Representatives, John W. McCormack, the

Democratic majority leader, read Truman's June 27, 1950, statement*. After he finished, everyone stood and applauded except for New York's Vito Marcantonio. Congress then passed overwhelmingly a one-year extension of the Selective Service Act, including presidential authority for National Guard mobilization*. But in the Senate, James P. Kem, Arthur V. Watkins, and John W. Bricker challenged the president's authority to make decisions leading toward war without either informing or obtaining the consent of Congress. Truman's defenders insisted that the United States was acting to fulfill its commitments under the UN Charter and to avoid making the mistake of not fighting aggression, as had occurred in the 1930s. The next day, Senator Robert A. Taft* delivered a speech charging that Truman was guilty of "a complete usurpation . . . of authority," which "unquestionably has brought about a *defacto* war with the government of northern Korea." Worse, he claimed, the administration had invited the Communist attack, pointing to the U.S. military withdrawal from Korea* and Secretary of State Dean G. Acheson's* National Press Club speech*. But after insisting that military intervention in Korea required congressional consent, Taft declared his willingness "to vote to approve the president's new policy." Outside Congress, political support came from the titular head of the Republican party, Governor Thomas E. Dewey of New York, who sent a wire to Truman stating that his action "was necessary to the security of our country and the free world."

Critics of Truman's Asia policy, such as Senator William F. Knowland*, who publicly spoke against appeasement in Korea on June 26, were so pleased that the president had drawn a line against the Communists that the administration would have gained easy passage of a resolution endorsing its actions. But the president rejected this option, telling Secretary of the Army Frank Pace* that "they are all with me." On June 30, after Truman's commitment of ground troops*, the president met again with congressional leaders. Senator H. Alexander Smith recommended that the administration gain passage of a resolution backing Truman's actions in Korea. Acting on instructions from Truman, Acheson prepared a draft of a joint resolution. At a meeting to discuss the issue on July 3, he recommended to Truman that a congressman should take the initiative on the resolution, while the president should deliver a speech to Congress reporting on his actions in Korea. Since Congress had just begun a ten-day recess for Independence Day, Truman said he would wait to consult with congressional leaders upon their return. In the end, when the president made his address to Congress of July 19, 1950*, he outlined measures to expand the military rather than making an attempt to justify his actions and build support for the war. Later, the State Department issued a report listing eighty-five instances where the president had sent U.S. land or naval forces abroad without gaining congressional approval. But if Truman had obtained a resolution, his critics would have been unable later to label the conflict "Mr. Truman's War." However, the Gulf of Tonkin resolution did not shield Lyndon Johnson from harsh criticism of his decisions in Vietnam. *See also* Congressional Meetings with Truman of June 1950; Police Action.

D. Acheson, *Present at the Creation* (New York, 1969); R. J. Donovan, *Tumultuous Years* (New York, 1982); W. W. Stueck, *The Road to Confrontation* (Chapel Hill, 1981).

CONGRESSIONAL MEETINGS WITH TRUMAN OF JUNE 1950

During the week following the North Korean invasion of South Korea*, President Harry S. Truman* held two meetings with congressional leaders to inform them of the actions he had taken to defend the Republic of Korea*. At the second Blair House meeting*, the president had raised the issue of consultations with Congress and decided to arrange a meeting with leading representatives from both parties for the next day. On the morning of June 27, Truman reviewed his actions in Korea with fourteen congressional leaders. Those present included the Speaker of the House, Sam Rayburn; majority leaders Senator Scott W. Lucas and Congressman John W. McCormack; Senators Tom Connally*, Walter F. George, Elbert D. Thomas, Alexander Wiley, and H. Alexander Smith from the Foreign Relations Committee and Millard E. Tydings and Styles Bridges from the Armed Services Committee; and Congressmen Mike Mansfield, John Kee, and Charles A. Eaton from the House Foreign Affairs Committee and Carl Vinson and Dewey Short from the Armed Services Committee. Secretary of State Dean G. Acheson*, Secretary of Defense Louis A. Johnson*, Ambassador Philip C. Jessup*, the JCS, and the services secretaries also attended.

Acheson opened the meeting with a summary of developments in Korea, emphasizing that two factors demanded that the United States act decisively. First, the ROK seemed incapable of mounting effective resistance in the absence of outside leadership. Second, Western Europe was on the verge of panic watching to see how the United States would respond. Then Truman, after stressing that the most important development was the prompt action of the UN Security Council, read the statement he would issue at noon outlining his decisions to the American people. The president said that he hoped the Soviet Union would not become involved, but the United States "could not let this matter go by default." "If we let Korea down," he explained, "the Soviets will keep right on going and swallow up one piece of Asia after another. We have to make a stand sometime, or else let all of Asia go by the board." After the JCS reviewed military dispositions, Acheson responded to a question about expectations for assistance from other nations, stating that Western Europe would send what little military assistance it could. Senator Wiley appeared to speak for the group when he approved the president's actions as necessary and appropriate. Senator Tydings reported that his committee had recommended that morning a one-year extension of the draft and presidential authorization for National Guard mobilization*. Truman then promised to keep Congress informed of developments. "*All* our actions," he emphasized, "will be brought about by the UN." Following the meeting, Senator Smith told the press that he was "very pleased," while Senator Bridges said that he thought "it is damned good action."

On June 30, after Truman's commitment of ground troops*, the president met with fifteen congressional leaders. General Omar N. Bradley*, the chairman of the JCS, summarized the military situation, and then Truman read a statement being issued to the press during the meeting. Senator Tydings responded that it was vital for other nations to contribute troops because no one then could view Korea as "a private American war." To avoid a leak that would alert the enemy to his plans, Truman said that he had not sent troops to the combat area but to Pusan to keep communications and supply lines open. But it was clear from subsequent comments that the congressmen were aware U.S. troops soon would join the fighting and sustain casualties. Of those present, only Senator Kenneth S. Wherry voiced a sharp objection—not to Truman's actions but to his failure to consult Congress. The president replied that he had implemented emergency measures in a crisis under his powers as commander in chief. "If there is any necessity for Congressional action" or "any large scale actions were to take place," he said, "I will come to you." This comment reflected Truman's belief that the war would be limited in scope and duration. Nevertheless, Senator Smith suggested that Congress pass a resolution approving the president's action. As the meeting ended, Congressman Short said that everyone in Congress was grateful for the high quality of the president's leadership during the crisis. This comment may have persuaded Truman that it was unnecessary to obtain a formal resolution from Congress endorsing his Korean decisions. As a result, his critics later were free to attack the president, especially after he failed to achieve military victory, ultimately branding the conflict "Mr. Truman's War." *See also* Congress and the Korean War; Congress and U.S. Military Intervention; UN Security Council Resolution of June 25, 1950.

R. J. Donovan, *Tumultuous Years* (New York, 1982); G. M. Elsey papers, Harry S. Truman Library, Independence, Missouri; G. D. Paige, *The Korean Decision* (New York, 1968); W. W. Stueck, *The Road to Confrontation* (Chapel Hill, 1981).

CONNALLY, TOM (1877–1963)

Thomas T. Connally was chairman of the Senate Foreign Relations Committee during most of the Korean War. Since 1945, the Texas Democrat had enthusiastically supported U.S. participation in the United Nations and had played a key role in forging the legislation that laid the foundation for U.S. cold war policy. In early May 1950, Connally publicly stated that since the fall of the Republic of Korea* was inevitable and Korea was "not absolutely essential," the United States should prepare to abandon the peninsula. Later, critics would charge that this statement, combined with Secretary of State Dean G. Acheson's* National Press Club speech*, provided the Democratic People's Republic of Korea* with the green light to launch its invasion of South Korea*.

Upon the outbreak of fighting in Korea, he cooperated closely with the Truman administration, urging a swift and firm response to what he considered a Soviet-sponsored challenge to world peace and to the UN. Although generally solicitous of congressional prerogatives, Connally recommended that the president not ask for a declaration of war, lest dissenting Republicans obstruct action. Later he reconsidered, remarking of a request for a war declaration: "As a matter of political strategy it would have been a wise move, despite the delay and hell-raising it might have caused.'' Throughout the conflict, Connally emphasized the importance of working through the UN, and when CINCUNC General Douglas MacArthur* appeared to overstep his authority, Connally urged President Harry S. Truman* to relieve the general. With Republicans agitating for a congressional investigation of Truman's recall of MacArthur*, Connally consented to joint hearings by the foreign relations and armed services committees, but he helped deprive MacArthur of a political platform by insisting that the committees conduct the MacArthur Hearings* in closed session, with subsequent release of nonsensitive testimony. After twenty-four years in the Senate and facing a tough campaign in an increasingly anti-Truman state, Connally decided not to run for reelection in 1952.

T. Connally with A. Steinberg, *My Name Is Tom Connally* (New York, 1954); J. I. Matray, *The Reluctant Crusade* (Honolulu, 1985).

H. W. Brands

CORDIER, ANDREW W. (1901–1975)

Born on a farm near Canton, Ohio, Andrew W. Cordier was executive assistant to UN Secretary-General Trygve Lie* during the Korean War. A high school teacher of math, history, and Latin, in 1922 Cordier graduated from Manchester College in Indiana. After earning a doctorate in medieval history at the University of Chicago in 1927, he returned to Manchester as a professor and eventually chair of the history and political science department. During the 1930s, he studied at the Graduate Institute of International Studies in Geneva while traveling throughout Europe and Latin America. In 1944, Cordier joined the State Department as an adviser on international security and participated in the formation of the UN as a technical expert on the U.S. delegation at the San Francisco Conference the next year. He also served as adviser to the president of the UN General Assembly at its first session in 1946.

As executive assistant to the UN secretary-general from 1946 to 1961, Cordier was responsible for coordinating the implementation of the General Assembly's decisions and recommendations. For example, he supervised the UN political missions in India, Palestine, and Korea. In addition, he was in charge of operations at the Secretariat, which included charting meetings, outlining programs, and supervising a staff of 3,200 people. Prior to the outbreak of the Korean War, Cordier had become extremely influential as a peacemaker, practicing skillful diplomacy in bringing together nations at the UN to settle difficult issues. Hardworking and calm under fire, he was also a ''demon parliamentarian'' who could remember minute details and was therefore especially adept at resolving legal disputes. Cordier played an important role in building international cooperation behind the UN military effort to defend the Republic of Korea* after the North Korean attack.

Recognizing Cordier's value, Dag Hammarskjold*, after replacing Lie as secretary-general in 1953, retained him as executive assistant but was less willing than his predecessor to delegate authority. Consequently, Cordier became more of an executor than an initiator of UN policy. After Hammarskjold died in a plane crash in 1961, the Soviet Union charged that Cordier was attempting to dominate UN affairs. In response, Cordier resigned his post, becoming temporary under secretary in charge of the daily workings of the General Assembly. Nevertheless, he continued to coordinate UN peacekeeping efforts in the Congo. In 1962, he left the UN to become professor of international relations and dean at the Columbia University School of International Affairs. During violent student demonstrations in 1968, Cordier reluctantly agreed to serve as interim president, managing to restore calm through isolating radicals and encouraging communication. He remained president of Columbia University until 1970 when he returned to his prior position as dean. Following retirement in 1972, he focused his activities on the issue of adult education.

Current Biography, 1950; N. Lichtenstein (ed.), *Political Profiles: The Kennedy Years* (New York, 1976); *New York Times,* July 13, 1975.

CORY, THOMAS J. (1914–1965)

As adviser to the U.S. delegation at the UN in May 1951, Thomas J. Cory was responsible for arranging the meetings between Jacob A. Malik*, Soviet permanent delegate at the UN, and George F. Kennan* that resulted in the beginning of armistice negotiations to end the Korean War. Born in San Francisco, Cory earned an A.B. degree from the University of California at Berkeley in 1935. After postgraduate studies at the National University of Mexico, he worked for his father as an agricultural engineer. Cory entered the foreign service in 1938, with his first assignment as vice-consul at Vancouver, British Columbia. Thereafter, he had a variety of postings in Spain, Venezuela, and the Soviet Union from 1941 until 1947, developing a reputation as an expert on Russian affairs.

In 1948, Cory became second secretary at the U.S. embassy in Nanking and assisted in the evacuation of American nationals as the Communists completed their conquest of China in 1949. This experience proved helpful when, after transferring to the U.S. embassy in the Republic of Korea*, he helped with the emergency evacuation of about 100 Americans from Kimp'o Airfield on June 28, 1950, after the North Korean invasion of South Korea*. Before the year ended, Cory was at the UN, serving as an adviser on East Asia and Eastern Europe. In addition to arranging the Kennan-Malik conversations*, he officially extended U.S. condolences to the Soviet mission when Joseph Stalin* died. Following the Korean War, he spent two years as first secretary at the U.S. embassy in Vienna. Cory left government service in 1955 and went to work for the Standard Vacuum Oil Company as a liaison to facilitate cooperation with the U.S. government on issues related to trade, licensing, and research and development. Prior to his death in an automobile accident, he occasionally acted as an adviser for the U.S. government at international meetings on matters that related to oil and minerals.

Foreign Relations of the United States, 1951, vol. 7: *Korea and China* (Washington, D.C., 1983); *National Cyclopedia of American Biography,* vol. 51 (New York, 1969); *New York Times,* September 16, 1965; *Who Was Who in America,* vol. 4: *1961–1968* (Chicago, 1968).

COULTER, JOHN B. (1891–1983)

Lieutenant General John B. Coulter was the last commanding officer of U.S. occupation forces in Korea (USAFIK), a combat commander during the Korean War, and director of the United Nations Korean Reconstruction Agency* (UN-KRA). He was born in San Antonio, Texas, and graduated from West Texas Military Academy in 1911. Coulter received his commission as a second lieutenant in 1912 and served with the 14th Cavalry. In 1917, he was in Washington, D.C., as a National Guard instructor when the United States declared war on Germany. After fighting in France with the 42d "Rainbow" Division and as a battalion commander with the 808th Infantry at St. Mihiel, he returned to the United States and worked in the personnel branch of the War Department General Staff. Coulter graduated from Cavalry School (1922) and Command and General Staff School (1927) before becoming squadron commander with the 8th Cavalry and a training officer with the 1st Cavalry at Fort Bliss in Texas. After graduation from the Army War College (1933) and the Naval War College (1934), he spent time with the U.S. Army military intelligence division and then was commanding officer of the 4th Cavalry in 1940.

Having risen through the ranks to brigadier general in 1941, Coulter was commander of the 3d Cavalry at the start of World War II. In 1942, he assumed command of the 85th Infantry Division, leading it into combat in North Africa in 1943. Coulter then was commander of the first all-draft division to fight in Italy, which led the assault on Rome in 1944 and then secured the strategic Brenner Pass. The next year, he became commander of the Infantry Replacement Training Center at Fort McClellan. After brief service with the 7th Infantry Division in 1948, he joined the USAFIK as deputy to Lieutenant General John R. Hodge*, the commanding officer. With the formation of the Republic of Korea* in August 1948, Coulter became the USAFIK's commander because of Hodge's poor relationship with ROK president Syngman Rhee* and remained with the unit until its deactivation in January 1949. He spent one year in Japan before returning to the United States for service as deputy commander of the 5th Army.

Following the North Korean invasion of South Korea*, Coulter assumed command of the I Corps and, after training at Fort Bragg, North Carolina, arrived with his unit in Korea on August 18, 1950. He owed his appointment in part to the relationship he had developed while fighting in Italy with Major General Edward M. Almond*, CINCUNC General Douglas MacArthur's* chief of staff. Lieutenant General Walton W. Walker*, 8th Army* commander, disliked and distrusted Almond, resulting in Coulter's being shifted to the IX Corps on the eve of the Inch'ŏn landing*. In February 1951, he received a third star and became deputy commander of the 8th Army. Three months later, CINCUNC Lieutenant General Matthew B. Ridgway* appointed Coulter his liaison officer to UNCURK*.

Although Coulter retired in January 1953, because of his extensive experience in Korea, UN Secretary-General Dag Hammarskjold* appointed him to replace J. Donald Kingsley* as director of UNKRA in May 1953 for a two-year term. In this post, Coulter supervised long-range projects in South Korea relating to the restoration of education and medical facilities and the recovery of agriculture, forestry, fishing, and industry. For fiscal 1954, UNKRA received $130 million in U.S. aid. After 1956, Coulter served as adviser to the UN secretary-general on the peacekeeping forces sent to the Middle East after the Suez crisis.

R. E. Appleman, *South to the Naktong, North to the Yalu* (Washington, D.C., 1961); C. Blair, *The Forgotten War* (New York, 1987); *Current Biography,* 1954; J. I. Matray, *The Reluctant Crusade* (Honolulu, 1985); *Washington Post,* March 7, 1983.

CUTLER, ROBERT (1895–1974)

Robert Cutler was special assistant for national security affairs to President Dwight D. Eisenhower*, serving from 1953 to 1955 and again from 1957 to 1958. He graduated with honors from Harvard College in 1916 and from Harvard Law School in 1922, where he was editor of the *Harvard Law Review.* Cutler also taught there briefly. He became a partner in the Boston law firm of Herrick, Smith, Donald & Farley in 1928, was corporate counsel for the city of Boston, and chairman of the board of Old Colony Trust Company.

Serving in both world wars, he was lieutenant in the infantry with the American Expeditionary Forces in Europe from 1918 to 1919 and during World War II served at various posts in the Office of the Secretary of War, rising to the rank of brigadier general. After becoming Eisenhower's special assistant for national security affairs, the president asked him to establish a National Security Council in which representatives of various departments would discuss national security issues as the basis for policy. The organization Cutler established remained through the Eisenhower presidency. He later was U.S. executive director of the Inter-American Development Bank and special assistant to the secretary of the treasury.

In the closing months of the Korean War, Cutler coordinated development of policy dealing with the death of Joseph Stalin* (no contingency plans had been made) and Syngman Rhee's* release of North Korean POWs*. Cutler carried out his presidential mandate not to interpose himself between the oval office and the cabinet secretaries. He was instead principal executive officer, facilitator, and coordinator of the NSC. He advised the president, wrote the council's agenda, presented matters for discussion at meetings, supervised operations of members and staff, and, in relations with the press, kept his promise to the president to "keep my trap shut."

S. E. Ambrose, *Eisenhower, the President* (New York, 1984); J. L. Gaddis, *The Long Peace: Inquiries into the History of the Cold War* (New York, 1987); P. G. Henderson, *Managing the Presidency: The Eisenhower Legacy—From Kennedy to Reagan* (Boulder,

Colo., 1988); *White House Staff Book, 1953–1961,* Dwight D. Eisenhower Library, Abilene, Kansas; *Who Was Who in America,* vol. 6: *1974–1976* (Chicago, 1976).

William B. Pickett

D

DAM RAIDS OF 1953

The attacks on the Korean rice dams represented a final attempt by the FEAF to find a decisive target system and bring the enemy to terms through the air pressure strategy*. In early 1953, FEAF planners noted the importance of rice to the economy of the Democratic People's Republic of Korea* and recommended attacks on the dams that fed the irrigation system in the provinces of South P'yŏng'an and Hwanghae. It was predicted that the destruction of the rice dams would flood the fields and destroy the crops in North Korea's richest rice-growing areas. Peking would be forced to divert its own resources to support the North Koreans, increasing the economic strains of the war on the People's Republic of China*. When the matter was considered in April 1953, however, FEAF Commander Lieutenant General Otto P. Weyland* and CINCUNC General Mark W. Clark* were reluctant to order a general air attack. According to one account, they wished to keep the dams in reserve in case the Communists broke off the P'anmunjŏm truce talks*.

Political factors were also undoubtedly involved. German destruction of the Dutch dikes in 1944 had been condemned as a war crime at Nuremburg. Weyland suggested limiting the bombing to dams in the vicinity of military targets like railway lines since such operations would be easier to justify than direct attacks on the rice crop. On May 13, 1953, the 5th Air Force attacked the Toksan dam on the P'odong River, 20 miles north of P'yŏngyang. No immediate effect was observed, but the structure gave way during the night; the resulting flood washed away 6 miles of railway embankment, five bridges, and 5 square miles of rice. Encouraged by these results, Weyland ordered attacks on the Chasan dam on the Taedong River, 20 miles northeast of P'yŏngyang, on May 15 and 16. Once again the collapse washed away railway embankments, bridges, and rice crops. P'yŏngyang itself was flooded. Subsequent raids were less successful because the Communists reduced the water level behind the dams, but this tactic itself hampered rice production. A U.S. Air Force study later argued that the dam raids brought the Communists to terms on agenda item 4*, the POW issue.

Despite the importance of rice to the North Korean economy, however, the breakthrough probably owed more to political factors. In the end, the FEAF's ability to destroy its targets was matched by the ingenuity of the Communists in patching them up. Despite the sowing of the area with delayed action bombs, a temporary replacement had been erected at Toksan within two weeks.

R. F. Futrell, *The United States Air Force in Korea* (New York, 1961); R. Jackson, *Air War Over Korea* (London, 1973); D. Rees, *Korea: The Limited War* (London, 1964).

Callum A. MacDonald

DAVIES, JOHN PATON (1908–   )

When the Korean War began, John Paton Davies, Jr., was the chief China expert on the State Department's Policy Planning Staff (PPS). He played a central role in the Truman administration's efforts to assess the intentions and anticipate the actions of the People's Republic of China* after the North Korean invasion of South Korea*. In July 1950, Davies warned that the PRC might intervene in Korea because of ''irredentism, expansionism, Soviet pressure and inducements, strategic anxieties, ideological zeal, the enormous demands of internal problems, emotional anti-Americanism—and miscalculation of [U.S.] intentions.'' To deter the Chinese, he recommended a strategy of coercion—informing Peking that the United States would initiate a major bombing campaign against China if the PRC joined the fighting. Davies soon expressed doubts about the likelihood of either Soviet or Chinese intervention, disagreeing with fellow China expert O. Edmund Clubb*. When the United States considered halting the advance into North Korea after the Chinese military disengagement of November 6, 1950*, he advocated continuing the offensive, arguing that retreat would be ''humiliating'' and invite Communist ''exploitation.'' Massive Chinese military intervention* prompted Davies to urge support for the British DMZ proposal* and help arrange the Kennan-Malik conversations* leading to the start of the Kaesŏng truce talks*.

Born in Koating, China, Davies's parents were Baptist missionaries. He studied at Peking's Yenching University and Columbia University before joining the foreign service in 1931. After postings in Kunming, Peking, Mukden, Hankow, and Chungking, Davies served as a political adviser to General Joseph W. Stilwell from 1943 to 1944 and repeatedly raised hard questions about the corruption, reactionary politics, and military foot-dragging of the Republic of China* under Chiang Kai-shek*. When he left China in 1947 to become first secretary at the U.S. embassy in Moscow, questions about Davies's loyalty had begun to circulate. Former U.S. ambassador to China Patrick J. Hurley claimed that Davies and other members of an elite group of foreign service officers known as the ''China hands'' had secretly plotted to undermine Chiang's regime, resulting in the ''loss'' of China in 1949 to Mao Tse-tung's* Communist party. The China lobby then gave wide publicity to these charges. Perhaps in response to these attacks, Davies, after joining the PPS, was more militant than his colleagues in offering advice regarding China. Although he favored U.S. recognition of the PRC, he often scolded Mao's regime for its failure to demonstrate independence from Soviet leadership. Nevertheless, he came to symbolize treason to many Americans, especially when Senator Joseph McCarthy named him as a member of Secretary of State Dean G. Acheson's* "crimson crowd" that supposedly busied itself with Communist subversion while American boys fought and died in Korea.

Beginning in 1950, congressional investigating committees, loyalty review boards, and State Department officials reviewed Davies's security clearance on eight separate occasions. Transferred to an obscure post in Peru in 1953, Davies returned to Washington a year later for yet another security investigation, after President Dwight D. Eisenhower* issued an executive order requiring the dismissal of any person whose continued employment could not meet a "clearly consistent with national security" test. When Davies refused to retire, Secretary of State John Foster Dulles* dismissed him in November 1954, saying that he lacked "judgment, discretion and reliability." Davies went back to Peru and made a modest living in the furniture business before returning to the United States after the 1960 elections. Despite appeals from friends in and around the Kennedy administration (W. Averell Harriman*, Chester Bowles*, George F. Kennan*) to clear him, Secretary of State Dean Rusk* did not push the idea and President John F. Kennedy said rehabilitation would have to wait until the second term. In 1969, Davies received a security clearance after the Massachusetts Institute of Technology hired him for a project contracted through the Arms Control and Disarmament Agency.

J. P. Davies, *Dragon by the Tail* (New York, 1972); R. Foot, *The Wrong War* (Ithaca, N.Y., 1985); D. Halberstam, *The Best and the Brightest* (New York, 1975); E. R. May, "The China Hands in Perspective: Ethics, Diplomacy, and Statecraft," in P. G. Lauren (ed.), *The China Hands' Legacy: Ethics and Diplomacy* (Boulder, 1987).

Kenneth O'Reilly

DEAN, ARTHUR (1898–1987)

Arthur Dean led the UN delegation that negotiated with the Chinese and North Koreans at P'anmunjŏm from October 25 to December 12, 1953, to decide Korea's political future, three months after the signing of the armistice agreement*. The son of a law school professor, he received his law degree from Cornell University and then joined the nation's most prestigious international law firm, Sullivan and Cromwell of New York City, in 1923. After extensive work in German and Japanese affairs for the firm in the 1920s and 1930s, Dean succeeded his close friend, John Foster Dulles*, as senior partner in 1949.

Dulles and President Dwight D. Eisenhower* gave Dean ambassadorial rank to lead the delegation at P'anmunjŏm. The ambassador found himself trapped between his ally, the Republic of Korea's* president Syngman Rhee*, who demanded reunification of Korea under his control, and the Communists, who demanded participation by the Soviets and Asian neutrals in the settlement. Drawing on his legal tricks, Dean argued loudly and bluntly (at one point he cried to the Communist delegates, "Don't you hear what I say"), but to no avail. In December, Huang Hua, a future Chinese foreign minister, claimed

Americans were guilty of "perfidy" because they had allowed Rhee to storm out of the meeting. The talks then ended.

In truth, neither side wanted an agreement unless it united Korea under their control. Given the military stalemate, that was impossible. In 1963, Dean led the U.S. delegation that negotiated the limited nuclear test ban with the Soviets. Later, in 1967 and 1968, he advised President Lyndon B. Johnson against negotiations with the Communists in the Vietnam War, in part because of his bitter experiences at P'anmunjŏm.

J. Halliday and B. Cumings, *Korea: The Unknown War* (New York, 1988); B. I. Kaufman, *The Korean War* (Philadelphia, 1986); *New York Times,* December 1, 1987.

Walter LaFeber

DEAN, WILLIAM F. (1899–1981)

Major General William F. Dean commanded the 24th Infantry Division in June 1950 when that unit was selected to be the first U.S. combat force to respond to the North Korean invasion of South Korea*. Born in Carlyle, Illinois, he joined the ROTC at the University of California, Berkeley, and received a regular commission in 1923. A lieutenant colonel at the beginning of World War II, he rose to two-star rank before the war's end. In October 1947, Dean went to Seoul as military governor of southern Korea and deputy to Lieutenant General John R. Hodge*, commander of U.S. occupation forces. Dean supervised the Korean police, transportation, and communication systems and distribution of food, as well as arranging polling places and making other preparations for the elections creating the Republic of Korea* in 1948. After transferring to Japan, he assumed command of the 24th Division in October 1949 with headquarters on Kyushu.

The proximity of Dean's division to Korea, his combat experience, and his knowledge of Korea made his command the logical choice to spearhead the initial U.S. ground operation of the Korean War. Despite its leader's ability, the division itself was understrength, inadequately equipped, and inexperienced. Thrown into the fray near Taejŏn, the green U.S. troops with their light armament could not withstand the momentum of the enemy's tank assault. Without a sufficient staff of battle-tested officers, Dean himself took direct charge at the rapidly collapsing front. He attempted a rash forward thrust that quickly turned into a chaotic retreat. His tactics may have been questionable, but his personal courage was undeniable. As enemy forces entered Taejŏn, Dean stayed with his men in a fiercely fought rearguard action. Finally, on July 20, he ordered a withdrawal of his last remaining elements. In the ensuing escape, Dean became separated from his men and wandered for thirty-six days eluding the enemy until, weak from hunger, he was captured on August 25.

Dean was the Democratic People's Republic of Korea's* highest-ranking POW. The DPRK kept him in solitary confinement much of the time and did not even reveal his capture until December 18, 1951. In January 1951, while he was still listed as missing in action, President Harry S. Truman* awarded

Dean the Medal of Honor. He survived three years of arduous captivity and resisted numerous efforts to force him into false confessions and other propaganda ploys. His release came on September 3, 1953. He was deputy commander of the 6th Army in San Francisco until his retirement from the service in 1955. *See also* Battle of the Kŭm River.

R. E. Appleman, *South to the Naktong, North to the Yalu* (Washington, D.C., 1961); W. F. Dean, *General Dean's Story* (New York, 1954).

David L. Anderson

DEATH OF STALIN (March 5, 1953)

The death of Joseph Stalin* and the accession of Georgi Malenkov* to general secretary of the Communist party of the Soviet Union brought a new tone to Soviet foreign policy and probably helped bring the Korean armistice agreement*. Upon entering the White House in 1953, President Dwight D. Eisenhower* sought peace in Korea. Armistice negotiations begun in 1951 had broken down over agenda item 4*, POW repatriation. Eisenhower and Secretary of State John Foster Dulles* were determined to press the Soviet Union and the People's Republic of China*, hoping this would make the people under their control tired of communism. For the short term, Eisenhower decided on a similar tactic in Korea. Announcing the "unleashing" of Chiang Kai-shek*, he removed the 7th Fleet from the Taiwan Strait. He also authorized the CIA to increase its support of Nationalist guerrilla raids on the mainland. At the same time, however, in February 1953, he approved an initiative by CINCUNC General Mark W. Clark* to accept an International Red Cross proposal for exchanging sick and wounded prisoners of war (Operation Little Switch*).

Unfortunately, the deadlock at P'anmunjŏm ended only after Stalin's death on March 5. Just ten days after taking office, Malenkov stated that disputes between Moscow and Washington could be "decided by peaceful means, on the basis of mutual understanding." The Soviet government allowed more freedom in Eastern Europe and arrested Lavrenti P. Beria, head of Stalin's secret police. Soviet radio acknowledged for the first time the major roles of the United States and Great Britain in World War II, and the Soviets agreed to help Britain obtain release of its citizens imprisoned in the Democratic People's Republic of Korea*. There is some evidence also that the Soviet leader asked Chinese and North Korean leaders directly to end the war.

On March 28, Premier Kim Il Sung* of North Korea and General Peng Teh-huai*, commander of the Chinese People's Volunteers Army*, accepted General Clark's offer of an exchange of sick and wounded prisoners. They said the exchange should lead to a settlement of the prisoner of war issue and an armistice. A few days later, Kim and Foreign Minister Chou En-lai* announced a willingness to compromise on voluntary repatriation*. Not until July 27, however—after more negotiation and more fighting, Dulles's atomic warning to China*, and a period of confusion caused by Syngman Rhee's* release of North Korean POWs*—was the armistice finally signed. *See also* Chou En-lai POW Settlement Proposal.

S. E. Ambrose, *Eisenhower, the President* (New York, 1984); C. Blair, *The Forgotten War* (New York, 1987); R. Foot, *The Wrong War* (Ithaca, N.Y., 1985); J. C. Goulden, *Korea: The Untold Story of the War* (New York, 1982); B. I. Kaufman, *The Korean War* (Philadelphia, 1986).

William B. Pickett

DECLARATION OF WAR
See Congress and U.S. Military Intervention

DEFENSE APPROPRIATIONS ACTS (1951–1953)

War in Korea produced a dramatic increase in U.S. defense spending, militarizing U.S. foreign policy in the cold war. Beginning with the budget for fiscal 1951, the United States would build an enormous military establishment and, despite the return to peace, would maintain it for the next forty years. After World War II ended, military expenditures had experienced a steady decrease from roughly $84 billion to $13.5 billion for fiscal 1950 (July 1, 1949–June 30, 1950). President Harry S. Truman* was a fiscal conservative who feared that excessive government spending would ruin the economy. But after the Soviet detonation of an atomic bomb and the Communist triumph in China, some administration officials concluded that U.S. security interests demanded a vast increase in military capabilities. This resulted in the formulation of NSC-68*, a policy paper recommending a tripling of the defense budget. However, Truman withheld approval because he shared with Congress a reluctance to authorize major spending increases. When the administration submitted its final proposal for fiscal year 1951, it called for a defense budget of $13.394 billion to fund an overall military strength of approximately 1.5 million men. The North Korean invasion of South Korea* blew off the tight lid Truman had kept on defense spending for the prior four years. By early 1951, military expenditures would be three times greater and the defense establishment two times larger than before the outbreak of the Korean War.

On September 6, 1950, Congress approved the original budget for fiscal 1951, which included $13.278 billion for defense. At that time, the administration already had exceeded its force limitations and had recommended a supplemental military appropriation. In his address to Congress of July 19, 1950*, Truman had indicated that the amount would be approximately $10 billion. On September 27, Congress approved the final request for $11.729 billion and a force level of 2.1 million men. These funds were intended to support operations in Korea and therefore were part of a stopgap measure. Simultaneously, the administration was developing a five-year plan for an increase in U.S. military capabilities to the levels outlined in NSC-68. To begin reaching these goals, the JCS recommended a second supplementary defense appropriation of $20 billion for fiscal 1951, but Truman would not submit the request because he expected an early end to the war following the successful Inch'ŏn landing*. Chinese military intervention* changed the situation entirely; Congress approved on January 6, 1951, a second supplement providing for $16.795 billion in additional defense spending to finance a force level of 2.9 million men. On May 31, Congress passed a final supplement of $6.38 billion.

The Korean War stimulated in one year an expansion of the U.S. military establishment to nearly 3.5 million men, while increasing defense spending to $48.2 billion, a figure equaling all military appropriations for the previous four fiscal years. This expansion was not entirely for Korea; a large part of the money funded a buildup of U.S. forces in Europe and an enlargement of military assistance to NATO, Indochina, the Philippines, and Taiwan. Planning for defense spending in fiscal 1952 began in September 1950, but evidence of China's entry into the war postponed discussions. By February 1951, the JCS was proposing $73 billion for fiscal 1952 to reach the levels projected in NSC-68 two years earlier. Still fearful of excessive spending, Truman submitted a request for $56.3 billion on April 30. Many congressmen wanted to reduce the amount further, especially after the start of the Kaesŏng truce talks* created the hope for an early armistice. In October, Congress approved $55.5 billion, and, after supplementary appropriations, defense spending for fiscal 1952 reached $60.4 billion. By then, it was clear that the American public would not tolerate maintaining a defense budget at this level, while administration plans continually assumed an early end to the war. Consequently, Congress approved $44.3 billion in military expenditures for fiscal 1953 on July 10, 1952, representing a 10 percent reduction in Truman's request. Preliminary plans for fiscal 1954 called for a slight decrease, but for the next four decades the unprecedented pattern of large peacetime defense budgets would continue. *See also* Congress and the Korean War; Defense Production Act; Truman's Declaration of a National Emergency.

D. M. Condit, *History of the Office of the Secretary of Defense*, vol. 2: *The Test of War, 1950–1953* (Washington, D.C., 1988); B. I. Kaufman, *The Korean War* (Philadelphia, 1986); W. R. Schilling, P. Y. Hammond, and G. H. Snyder, *Strategy, Politics, and Defense Budgets* (New York, 1962).

DEFENSE PRODUCTION ACT (September 8, 1950)

The outbreak of the Korean War caught the U.S. economy just emerging from a sharp if brief recession and an inflationary spurt (a 5.3 percent consumer price increase in 1950) resulting from easy credit policies and mushrooming international demand for American goods. To combat inflation and to ensure priority to production of military items in the wake of enormous increases in defense and military assistance appropriations, Congress in September 1950 passed a bundle of measures for placing the economy on a near-wartime footing. This legislation, the Defense Production Act, assigned to President Harry S. Truman* broad authority to requisition and allocate scarce commodities needed for defense and standby powers to effect wage and price controls. The Defense Production Act also made available to the executive branch the power to expand the nation's productive capacity in critical areas and to stockpile strategic raw materials. In addition, the president received the authority to waive the application of antitrust laws when circumstances were deemed essential to the national defense.

After a futile campaign to obtain voluntary compliance with wage and price guidelines, the White House made use of these sweeping powers over the economy in December 1950. Truman declared a state of national emergency. Efforts to achieve a rapid increase in defense production and to impose wage and price controls were announced. Charles E. Wilson*, president of General Electric, was named head of the Office of Defense Mobilization, which was created to oversee these initiatives. Despite bureaucratic confusion and growing conservative opposition to the Truman administration's policy of financing the war in large part by taxes, the Defense Production Act proved successful in stimulating production and controlling inflation. *See also* Defense Appropriations Acts (1951–1953); Truman's Declaration of a National Emergency.

R. K. Donovan, *Tumultuous Years* (New York, 1982); B. I. Kaufman, *The Korean War* (Philadelphia, 1986); W. R. Schilling, P. Y. Hammond, and G. H. Snyder, *Strategy, Politics, and Defense Budgets* (New York, 1962).

Theodore A. Wilson

DEFENSE OF TAEGU (August–September 1950)

Successful defense of Taegu during one month from August to September 1950 completely reversed the trend of the war in favor of the UNC* until the Chinese military intervention* later that year. Situated at the northwestern corner of the Pusan Perimeter*, Taegu, the third largest city in the Republic of Korea*, was critically important strategically and psychologically for the UNC defense. Between August 9 and 14, the North Koreans attempted to cross the Naktong River at two points but were pushed back by the U.S. 1st Cavalry after suffering heavy casualties. Along the north of the lateral road connecting Waegwan and Tabu-dong starting August 14, three North Korean divisions launched an offensive against the thinly spread 1st ROK Division defense line, resulting in a bitter contest that often involved hand-to-hand combat. When North Korean forces, spearheaded by tanks, broke through the 1st ROK defense along the Sangju-Taegu corridor and threatened Tabu-dong, the U.S. 27th Regiment was dispatched in an emergency situation and fought the Battle of the Bowling Alley*. All along the front, the fierce seesaw battles continued, causing heavy casualties on both sides, until August 24 when the UNC forces were able to push back the North Korean advances. During these battles, several North Korean artillery shells landed in downtown Taegu on three different occasions, causing considerable confusion among the civilian population.

Regrouped and resupplied, the North Koreans launched the second attack on September 2. In spite of heavy air, artillery, and infantry assaults by the UNC forces, the North Koreans broke through and moved behind the U.S. defense line, overrunning Tabu-dong and forcing the 1st Cavalry to retreat in disarray and to redeploy in an arc just 6 air miles from Taegu on September 5. At this juncture, the 8th Army* prepared to evacuate Taegu and retreat to the Davidson Line, the last defense line close to Pusan. At the last minute, however, Lieutenant General Walton W. Walker*, 8th Army commander, decided not to withdraw but instead to defend the city to the last man.

Fortunately for Walker, the North Korean troops, many of whom were inexperienced soldiers recruited during the occupation of South Korea*, lacked the stamina to push the UNC defenders any further. On September 12, the 1st Cavalry Division attacked Hill 314, which overlooked the Taegu–Tabu-dong road, and was able to secure the hill after fierce fighting, while the 1st ROK Division successfully warded off the North Korean attempt to penetrate into Mount P'algong and inched its way northward to the walled peak of Kasan (Hill 902), by September 15. When the UNC, after the Inch'ŏn landing*, unleashed a general counteroffensive on September 16, the North Koreans continued to offer stiff resistance north of Taegu. The threat to the city did not completely dissipate until the UNC troops recaptured Tabu-dong on September 21.

R. E. Appleman, *South to the Naktong, North to the Yalu* (Washington, D.C., 1961); C. Blair, *The Forgotten War* (New York, 1987); Kukbang-bu p'yŏnch'an wiwŏn-hoe, *Han'guk Chŏnjaeng-sa,* vol. 3 (Seoul, 1970).

Yŏng-ho Ch'oe

DEFENSIVE PERIMETER
See Acheson's National Press Club Speech

DEFICIENCY APPROPRIATIONS ACT (June 29, 1950)
Less than a week after the North Korean invasion of South Korea*, Congress approved this piece of legislation to increase economic aid to the Republic of Korea*. Under the Far Eastern Economic Assistance Act of 1950*, the United States had appropriated $60 million for the ROK. This bill increased that figure by $50 million, bringing the total assistance package for fiscal 1950 to $110,000. It provided an indication of congressional unity behind President Harry S. Truman's* efforts to prevent the Communists from conquering South Korea. *See also* Korean Aid Bill of 1949–1950.

Foreign Relations of the United States, 1950, vol. 7: *Korea* (Washington, D.C., 1976).

DEMILITARIZED ZONE
See Agenda Item 2

DEMOCRATIC PEOPLE'S REPUBLIC OF KOREA
On September 9, 1948, North Korean leader Kim Il Sung* proclaimed the establishment of the Democratic People's Republic of Korea (DPRK), stating that the new government represented the entire nation and intended to send representatives to the UN. The DPRK's history dates from the waning moments of World War II, when Japanese occupation officials persuaded Yŏ Un-hyŏng, a prominent Korean leftist, to form a transitional government capable of maintaining law and order and protecting Japanese lives and property. Yŏ promptly created 135 local people's committees to assume administrative responsibilities. Reflecting the popular desire for sweeping reform, these bodies expropriated the land of the Japanese and their Korean collaborators while simultaneously releasing all political prisoners. By the end of August 1945, Yŏ had secured

widespread support from landlords, intellectuals, students, and professional people, emerging as the unchallenged de facto leader throughout Korea. But he also allowed the Communist party under Pak Hŏn-yŏng*, who had led the anti-Japanese wartime resistance, to exercise considerable influence in his government, resulting in increasing political repression of wealthy and conservative Koreans. On September 6, Yŏ proclaimed the establishment of the Korean People's Republic (KPR) at a conference in Seoul, promising elections before March 31, 1946. In addition, the Communists engineered the adoption of a platform recommending specific economic and social reforms.

When the Soviet army occupied northern Korea in the middle of August, it encouraged the formation and activities of the people's committees. By contrast, U.S. occupation officials rejected the KPR's legitimacy and worked to destroy the people's committees. In response to repression of leftists and Communists in the south, the Soviets began to install trusted clients in positions of authority during the fall of 1945, among them Kim Il Sung. At a conference in the northern capital of P'yŏngyang in February 1946, representatives from the people's committees elected Kim chairman of the Provisional People's Committee. Recognizing that most Koreans wanted sweeping change, the Soviet Union expropriated land from the wealthy and distributed it without requiring cash payment. In June, Kim's government nationalized all large-scale industry, transportation, communications, and banking, while mandating an eight-hour workday and proclaiming sexual equality. In November 1946, the Provisional People's Committee held elections for representatives who would establish a permanent government. In February 1947, a Congress of People's Committees convened and approved retroactively all previous reforms. It also adopted a national economic plan for completing nationalization and starting rural collectivization. The Congress then created a permanent People's Assembly, which elected a presidium and organized a supreme court.

Meanwhile, a separate governmental structure had emerged in southern Korea. One final effort to achieve reunification through Soviet-U.S. negotiations failed in the summer of 1947, setting the stage for the formal creation of two Koreas. Passage of the UN resolution of November 14, 1947* resulted in internationally supervised elections south of the thirty-eighth parallel and the establishment on August 15 of the Republic of Korea*. Rejecting the ROK's legitimacy, the northern People's Assembly sponsored nationwide elections on August 25 for delegates to a Supreme Korean People's Assembly. During the first week of September, this body met in P'yŏngyang and promulgated a constitution. The legislature also elected a Supreme People's Council and chose Kim Tu-bong*, who had fought with the Chinese Communists, as chairman. Kim selected Kim Il Sung as premier and called upon him to form a cabinet, thereby providing the ruling authority for the DPRK. From the start, Kim Il Sung's government was dedicated to reunification, and built a large and powerful army to achieve this purpose through force if necessary. Kim Il Sung also was chairman of the Korean Workers' party that maintained Communist political control internally. Initially,

Kim had to share power not only with Kim Tu-bong but also Pak Hŏn-yŏng, who served as the DPRK's foreign minister and as vice-chairman of the Workers' party.

On June 25, 1950, the DPRK launched its invasion of the ROK after two years of border clashes*. Kim Il Sung came close to realizing his dream of reunification, only to face the near destruction of his regime after the UN offensive across the thirty-eighth parallel*. But Chinese military intervention* saved the DPRK. During the years immediately following the armistice, Kim Il Sung moved to eliminate his political rivals, resulting in the execution of Pak Hŏn-yŏng for falsely predicting that an attack on the south would spark a popular uprising. Postwar North Korea soon resembled a typical Stalinist state, but there were important differences, most notably the concept of *juche*, or self-reliance. As the self-styled "Great Leader," Kim also created a personality cult far more pervasive in its influence than what Mao Tse-tung* attempted in China or Joseph Stalin* in the Soviet Union. By 1960, North Korea had made great strides in industrialization, urbanization, education, and standard of living. But since that date, the ROK has surpassed the DPRK in all these areas, eliminating Kim's chances to obtain control over all Korea peacefully. To slow the erosion of popular support, North Korea's leaders have systematically isolated the population from information and engaged in a massive fabrication of history, resulting in an almost completely closed society. Yet Kim deserves credit as a political survivor who has pursued for nearly half a century an independent political course for himself and the DPRK, being subservient neither to Moscow nor to Peking. A tight security-conscious state, the DPRK still considers itself a leader in the Third World.

B. Cumings, *The Origins of the Korean War* (Princeton, 1981; 1990); J. Halliday and B. Cumings, *Korea: The Unknown War* (New York, 1988); J. A. Kim, *Divided Korea* (Cambridge, 1975); J. I. Matray, *The Reluctant Crusade* (Honolulu, 1985); G. D. Paige, *The Korean People's Democratic Republic* (Stanford, Calif., 1966).

DEWEY'S VISIT TO KOREA (July 8, 1951)

Governor Thomas E. Dewey of New York visited Korea as part of an extended personal tour of East Asia during the negotiation of the Japanese Peace Treaty*. He traveled as a private citizen at the urging of his fellow Republican, John Foster Dulles*, who was playing a major role in negotiating the peace treaty with the Japanese in San Francisco. Dulles believed that Dewey's trip, including a stop in Japan, would demonstrate bipartisan support of a treaty of reconciliation with Tokyo. Dewey also wanted to pay a courtesy visit to Chiang Kai-shek* on Taiwan, as well as see first hand the effect of Communist insurgencies on East Asian countries. President Harry S. Truman* and Secretary of State Dean G. Acheson* gave grudging approval to the trip. Accepting the consensus administration view that the Soviets had started the war in Korea, Dewey saw the peninsular campaign as just the latest step in Joseph Stalin's* quest for world domination. But he blamed Acheson's National Press Club speech* for permitting Korea to appear vulnerable by leaving it outside the U.S. defense perimeter.

Following a visit to Japan, Dewey on July 8 landed on the dirt-and-gravel landing strip of Pusan, the temporary capital of the Republic of Korea*. There he met with President Syngman Rhee* and other Korean officials and then flew to a devastated Seoul and toured the battlefronts to the north and east with General James A. Van Fleet*, commander of the 8th Army*. He thought little of Korean officials or soldiers but had high regard for the U.S. fighting forces. Leaving Korea, he visited Taiwan, the Philippines, Hong Kong, Saigon, Singapore, Indonesia, Australia, and New Zealand.

Upon his return to the United States, Dewey reported that U.S. military forces in Korea did not exaggerate claims about enemy losses, as had been the case in World War II. South Korean troops, lacking a military tradition, were ill trained and with few exceptions required UN troop support. Without U.S. intervention in Korea, he concluded, UN prestige would have plummeted and all of Southeast Asia would likely have fallen to communism. In a speech to the American Bar Association, he proposed a comprehensive Pacific Mutual Defense Alliance between the United States and non-Communist nations of Southeast Asia that would supplant recent bilateral agreements. His proposal, perhaps suggested by Dulles, foreshadowed the later SEATO treaty with these nations.

T. E. Dewey, *Journey to the Pacific* (Garden City, N.Y., 1952); *New York Times,* July 2, September 19, 1951; R. N. Smith, *Thomas E. Dewey and His Times* (New York, 1982).

Richard W. Fanning

DODD-COLSON POW INCIDENT (May 7–11, 1952)

On May 7, 1952, Communist militants at the Kŏje-do POW camp audaciously kidnapped commandant Brigadier General Francis T. Dodd*. After luring Dodd to the entrance of Compound 76 to discuss grievances, a group of POWs returning from a work detail pushed him inside and closed the gate. Dodd's successor, Brigadier General Charles F. Colson*, acting on his own authority, made a bad situation worse by signing a statement containing the phrase, "I do admit that there has [sic] been instances of bloodshed where many PW [sic] have been killed and wounded by UN forces." In ensuing negotiations, Generals Colson and Dodd, in their desire to avoid casualties, made concessions that gave the Communists even more propaganda advantage. After Dodd's release on May 11, a U.S. Army investigating board found both generals blameless. General James A. Van Fleet*, 8th Army* commander, and CINCUNC General Mark W. Clark* were outraged. A second board later reversed the original finding, causing both Dodd and Colson to be reduced in rank to colonel. With full Department of the Army backing, Clark ordered the new camp commandant, Brigadier General Haydon L. Boatner*, to clean out the compounds and restore UN command authority. On June 10, crack paratroopers routed the militants out from their fortified compounds. Six Patton tanks, their 90mm guns trained on the last holdouts, decided the matter. *See also* Kŏje-do POW Uprising; UNC POW Administration.

B. Alexander, *Korea: The First War We Lost* (New York, 1986); H. L. Boatner, ''The Lessons of Koje-do,'' *Army* (1972); H. Vetter, *Mutiny on Koje Island* (Rutland, Vt., 1965).

Stanley Sandler

DRUMRIGHT, EVERETT F. (1907–   )

It was Everett F. Drumright, counselor at the U.S. embassy in Seoul, who first received word of the North Korean invasion of South Korea* on the morning of June 25, 1950. After waiting for confirmation, he phoned Ambassador John J. Muccio* one hour later with news of the attack. Born in Oklahoma, Drumright earned a B.S. degree at the University of Oklahoma and entered the foreign service in 1931. His first posting was in Ciudad Juarez, Mexico, as vice-consul. In 1931, he went to Hankow, China, and then worked from 1932 to 1933 as a language officer in Peking. He remained in China until World War II, serving as vice-consul in Shanghai (1934–1937) and third and second secretary in the U.S. embassy at Nanking (1938–1941). At Chungking, the wartime capital of the Republic of China*, Drumright was counselor and first secretary, until 1944 when he returned to the United States. After World War II, Drumright spent time at the U.S. embassies in London and, as counselor and first secretary, in Tokyo. By then, he had developed a reputation for being hard-driving, energetic, and dogmatic.

His service in the Republic of Korea* began in 1948. During Muccio's visits to the United States, Drumright was primarily responsible for embassy affairs. Since Muccio disliked writing dispatches, he also was the primary author of cables from Seoul to Washington, D.C., enjoying the power to send telegrams without showing them to Muccio. He worked to strengthen the ROK politically, economically, and militarily but found it difficult to deal with the unpredictable and authoritarian behavior of President Syngman Rhee*. During the U.S. evacuation of Seoul* following the North Korean attack, Drumright was able to persuade a reluctant Muccio to flee south with the rest of the embassy staff.

From July through September 1950, he wrote a series of letters to State Department official John M. Allison* providing details on political and military developments. In general, he lauded the battlefield performance of the South Korean troops, but his remarks about the temperamental Rhee remained disparaging. His reports may have prompted Allison to advocate crossing the thirty-eighth parallel because Drumright suggested that reunification alone would solve Korea's problems. In 1951, he went to India, serving in New Delhi and Bombay before returning to the State Department's Office of Far Eastern Affairs in 1953. After a four-year posting in Hong Kong, Drumright finished his diplomatic career as ambassador to the Republic of China on Taiwan from 1958 to 1962.

E. F. Drumright papers, Hoover Institution, Stanford University, Stanford, California; *Foreign Relations of the United States, 1950,* vol. 7: *Korea* (Washington, D.C., 1976); H. J. Noble, *Embassy at War* (Seattle, 1975); *Who's Who in America, 1966–1967* (Chicago, 1967).

DULLES, JOHN FOSTER (1888–1959)

John Foster Dulles was secretary of state under President Dwight D. Eisenhower* during the last months of the Korean War. He was born in Washington, D.C., and grew up in Watertown, New York. Graduating from Princeton University as valedictorian of his class, he attended the Sorbonne for a year, where he studied under the philosopher Henri Bergson. After two years at George Washington University Law School, he joined the New York firm of Sullivan and Cromwell, with which he was associated until he entered public service. His grandfather was Secretary of State John W. Foster, his uncle Secretary Robert Lansing. From them he easily took interest in foreign affairs. They arranged for him to attend the Second Hague Peace Conference in 1907 and the Paris Peace Conference in 1919. In the late 1930s, he became prominent as a Presbyterian layman, and his friendship with Governor Thomas E. Dewey of New York made him prominent in Republican circles. Dulles briefly represented the United States at the UN, helping gain passage of the UN resolution of December 12, 1948*, regarding Korea. Appointed a State Department adviser by President Harry S. Truman*, he was a natural bipartisan choice to draw up the Japanese Peace Treaty* ending the occupation. The Korean War interrupted his diplomacy with the Japanese treaty. Dulles managed to move ahead with the negotiations, persuading administration officials that the war made the Japanese Peace Treaty even more necessary, for it had denuded Japan of occupation troops.

Korea became of interest to Dulles in part because President Syngman Rhee* was a Christian and marked anti-Communist. In June 1950, he visited the Republic of Korea* just before the North Korean invasion of South Korea*, addressed the National Assembly, and surveyed the thirty-eighth parallel. When the Korean War opened, Dulles was in Kyoto sightseeing. He rushed to Tokyo where he was astonished by the sangfroid of General Douglas MacArthur*, who did not believe the North Korean attack was worth much attention. According to the recollection of Under Secretary of State James E. Webb*, MacArthur told Dulles, "Oh, this is just a bonfire. These tanks will run out of gas pretty soon; this won't amount to anything." At the beginning of the war, Dulles's enthusiasm for the Korean policies of the Truman administration was total, but after some months, he turned critical. At the time of Truman's recall of MacArthur*, he informed an administration official that it was a mistake to have removed the general from Japan before conclusion of the peace treaty. By the time of the 1952 presidential campaign, Dulles was severely critical. Author of the GOP foreign policy planks, he wrote, "With foresight, the Korean war would never have happened."

As secretary of state, Dulles carried out the Eisenhower policy of ending the war—what he later described as the art of "going to the brink" by pressing for a truce or threatening all-out fighting, including use of nuclear weapons. He informed Indian prime minister Jawaharlal Nehru* of this policy, information that presumably was passed to Peking. The Korean War seems to have changed Dulles's thinking about communism. Korea, he believed, showed that the Soviets were willing to take increased risks. His enthusiasm for the UN lessened. He became much concerned over the possibility of Soviet miscalculation abetted by hasty American action. His well-known ideas about deterrence, and support of the domino theory, almost certainly came out of his experience with the Korean War. *See also* Dulles-Rhee Correspondence; Dulles's Atomic Warning to China; Dulles's Trip to Korea; "A Policy of Boldness."

J. Beal, *John Foster Dulles* (New York, 1959); L. L. Gerson, *John Foster Dulles* (New York, 1966); M. A. Guhin, *John Foster Dulles* (New York, 1972); T. Hoopes, *The Devil and John Foster Dulles* (Boston, 1973).

Robert H. Ferrell

DULLES-RHEE CORRESPONDENCE (June–July 1953)

The exchange of letters and messages between President Syngman Rhee* and Secretary of State John Foster Dulles* during the last phase of the fighting and the period immediately after the cease-fire was significant in the process of shaping postwar relations between the Republic of Korea* and the United States. The Dulles-Rhee correspondence clearly revealed how the United States wanted to secure Rhee's support for the armistice agreement* without concluding a NATO-type treaty with South Korea. Faced with Rhee's opposition to the armistice, on June 12, 1953, Dulles invited Rhee to come to Washington for a meeting with President Dwight D. Eisenhower*. President Rhee declined the offer, saying that he was "busy" directing the fighting, and instead he invited Dulles to come to Korea. Secretary Dulles proposed instead sending Assistant Secretary for Far Eastern Affairs Walter S. Robertson* to solve "some misunderstandings as to our post-armistice policies." Rhee's unilateral release of North Korean POWs* on June 18, 1953, added another dimension to the Robertson Mission* to Korea.

When Robertson arrived in South Korea, he carried a strongly worded letter from Dulles that the ROK had no right to disrupt the prospective armistice won by the blood and lives of so many UN soldiers. Serious discussions then followed from June 26 to July 12 between Rhee and Robertson on the substantial matters relating to postarmistice policies. After serious bargaining and skillful bluffing, President Rhee obtained in a series of letters from Dulles four U.S. pledges in return for his promise not to disrupt the armistice. The United States pledged a security pact, long-term economic aid, assistance to build and maintain twenty South Korean army divisions with navy and air force, and close consultation and cooperation before, during, and after the postarmistice political conference, including simultaneous withdrawal from the conference should it produce nothing substantial after ninety days. For these, Robertson carried a letter from Rhee to Eisenhower in which the ROK president said, "I have decided not to obstruct, in any manner, the implementation of the terms, in deference to your requests."

Because an armistice seemed to be imminent, however, President Rhee appeared to retreat from his pledge. On July 24, 1953, Rhee sent a message to Dulles requesting definite answers about two "vital questions"—the inclusion of "immediate and automatic military support" in the proposed security pact and the U.S. participation in resuming military efforts to eject "the Chinese invaders from Korea" if the political conference failed to find a viable solution for the future of Korea. Secretary Dulles sent a lengthy reply the same day. Expressing his disappointment about the "uncertain" attitude of Rhee, Dulles complained "that the attitude of your government toward a truce was already decided." Proposing discussion of the matter during a personal visit to Korea immediately after the signing of the armistice, Dulles proclaimed, "Never in all its history had the U.S. offered to any other country as much as it offered to you." Rhee was not satisfied and sent another letter to Dulles on the day of signing the armistice, July 27, 1953, again asking for the treaty that could ensure immediate and automatic response against future Communist attacks. Fulfilling its promise, the U.S. initialed the U.S.-ROK Mutual Defense Treaty* on August 8, 1953, which is still in effect.

Foreign Relations of the United States, 1952–1954, vol. 15: Korea (Washington, D.C., 1984); R. T. Oliver, *Syngman Rhee and American Involvement in Korea, 1942–1960: A Personal Narrative* (Seoul, 1978); W. S. Poole, *History of the Joint Chiefs of Staff*, vol. 4: *The Joint Chiefs of Staff and National Policy, 1950–1952* (Washington, D.C., 1979).

Chang-il Ohn

DULLES'S ATOMIC WARNING TO CHINA (May 1953)

Secretary of State John Foster Dulles* and President Dwight D. Eisenhower* publicly and privately credited the conclusion of the armistice agreement* in Korea to a "series of subtle and calculated moves" on their part that convinced the Communists that the alternative to peace in Korea was an expanded war, employing atomic weapons. In May 1953 on a visit to New Delhi, Dulles had informed Prime Minister Jawaharlal Nehru*, assuming that the message would be relayed to the People's Republic of China*, that "if armistice negotiations collapsed, the United States would probably make a stronger rather than a lesser military exertion, and that this might well extend the area of conflict." According to Eisenhower's memoirs, the administration had also earlier in the year "dropped the word, discreetly," at the P'anmunjŏm truce talks* and in the Taiwan Strait area, "of our intention . . . to move decisively without inhibition in our use of weapons." Concurrently with these hints and warnings, the U.S. government had decided to present the UNC* final POW settlement proposal of May 25, 1953*, at P'anmunjŏm. If the Communists rejected it, the administration had determined that the negotiations would not simply be recessed but would be broken off entirely, as a prelude to more intensified warfare.

Analysts of this period have been divided over whether the Eisenhower administration did attempt nuclear coercion. If it did, the question remains concerning the probable impact of such threats—some agreeing with Eisenhower and Dulles that the warnings did serve to break the impasse and others raising doubts about the clarity and timing of the signals. Furthermore, Nehru subsequently denied vehemently that he had ever passed on any threatening messages to the PRC. Though atomic coercion may have played some role in resolving agenda item

4*, the POW issue, other factors are also likely to have been important to the decision to end the stalemate, including domestic economic pressures within the Communist states, the Soviet bloc's growing attention to peaceful coexistence with the West (evident since October 1952), and the death of Joseph Stalin*, which increased the political vulnerability of the socialist bloc and with it its interest in diminishing international tensions. *See also* NCS-147; "Unleashing" of Chiang.

R. K. Betts, *Nuclear Blackmail and Nuclear Balance* (Washington, D.C., 1987); R. Dingman, "Atomic Diplomacy during the Korean War," *International Security* (Winter 1988–1989); D. D. Eisenhower, *Mandate for Change* (Garden City, N.Y., 1963); R. Foot, "Nuclear Coercion and the Ending of the Korean Conflict," *International Security* (Winter 1988–1989); E. C. Keefer, "President Dwight D. Eisenhower and the End of the Korean War," *Diplomatic History* (Summer 1986).

Rosemary Foot

DULLES'S TRIP TO KOREA (June 15–20, 1950)

This visit was to convince President Syngman Rhee* that the Japanese Peace Treaty* would not be negotiated at the expense of the Republic of Korea*. On May 18, 1950, John Foster Dulles* was given the responsibility by President Harry S. Truman* of negotiating the Japanese Peace Treaty and serving as a liaison between the Democratic administration and the Republican party. Throughout the month, in personal and interdepartmental communiqués, he continued to emphasize his view that Taiwan or Indochina was on the brink of Communist takeover, a disaster that could be prevented only by dramatic and strong political or military action.

On June 14, accompanied by John M. Allison*, director of the Office of Northeast Asian Affairs, he left for Japan via Korea. There he toured the thirty-eighth parallel near Ŭijŏngbu and received encouraging reports on the strength of the ROK's army and reassurances from CINCFE General Douglas Mac-Arthur*. Dulles greatly admired Rhee, whose cause he had championed since the end of World War II. After discussions with the ROK president, he delivered an address to the South Korean National Assembly on June 19. In this speech, he declared that Korea was "in the front line of freedom," facing the "dangers of communism." He denounced the actions of the North Koreans in attempting to reunify and issued vague assurances of American moral support and unspecified help in time of trouble. South Korea, he pontificated, was "not alone." For Rhee, the Dulles speech may have led him to believe that the United States would support his plans for reunification at any price. Dulles himself portrayed that speech as simply a message of assurance to the Koreans, albeit a deliberately vague one. He was careful to avoid any concrete promises of positive action for Korea and simply referred to several trouble spots in Asia. Dulles had no intention of permitting an abandonment of U.S. interests in Asia or Korea, and his trip served as an affirmation of that belief.

The following day, he continued on to Tokyo and met with MacArthur to discuss the need to hold Taiwan and protect U.S. interests in East Asia. He also conferred with Prime Minister Yoshida Shigeru and members of the Diet, industrialists, labor union leaders, and foreign diplomats about the proposed treaty during the next four days. On June 27, 1950, he returned to the United States, fortified and comforted by Truman's decision to provide military and economic aid to the ROK following the North Korean invasion of South Korea*. For the North Koreans, his trip clarified the threat of U.S. attack and support of the corrupt regime of Rhee, perhaps convincing the leaders of the Democratic People's Republic of Korea* to attempt forcible reunification. Some writers have pointed to the Dulles trip to support the charge that South Korea either attacked first or provoked the start of the Korean War.

J. M. Allison, oral history interview, Princeton University Library, Princeton, New Jersey; M. A. Guhin, *John Foster Dulles* (New York, 1972); T. Hoopes, *The Devil and John Foster Dulles* (New York, 1973); J. and G. Kolko, *The Limits of Power: The World and United States Foreign Policy, 1945–1954* (New York, 1972); *New York Times*, May–June 1950.

                                                                                Kathleen F. Kellner

E

EDEN, ANTHONY (1897–1977)

In October 1951, Sir Robert Anthony Eden became foreign secretary in the first postwar Conservative government under Prime Minister Winston Churchill*. A strong supporter of the Atlantic Alliance, he had an unrivaled knowledge of world affairs, having served twice previously at the Foreign Office. In opposition, Eden had endorsed UN intervention in Korea and as foreign secretary was less sympathetic towards the People's Republic of China* than his predecessors. Despite these facts, friction continued in the Anglo-American alliance because Britain was still anxious to avoid a wider war with the PRC, remaining fearful that domestic political pressures might push the United States into rash actions.

In December 1951, to speed up the cease-fire negotiations, Eden agreed to a U.S. proposal for issuing a Joint Policy (Greater Sanctions) statement* threatening China with retaliation in the event of postarmistice aggression. He was unwilling to specify the kind of measures Britain would support and in fact opposed any form of blockade, citing the familiar British concern about Hong Kong and a possible clash with Soviet shipping using Port Arthur and Dairen. Eden was worried by the impasse that developed at the P'anmunjŏm truce talks* in the spring of 1952 over agenda item 4* regarding POWs, especially after the United States staged the Suiho bombing operation* without consulting Britain, which embarrassed him politically. He asked Secretary of State Dean G. Acheson* for "no more surprises" and attempted to find a compromise on the POW issue that would avert the risk of further U.S. escalation. Although unwilling to endorse forcible repatriation, Eden suspected that the United States was being unnecessarily rigid on the POW issue in order to embarrass China and to avoid political criticism in an election year.

At the UN General Assembly in November 1952, Eden supported the V. K. Krishna Menon* POW settlement proposal*, which Acheson opposed. Although Acheson eventually accepted the UN resolution of December 3, 1952*, in modified form, the relationship between the two men ended on a sour note. In dealing with the new Eisenhower administration, Eden was suspicious of the influence of the Republican right wing and had little faith in the judgment of the Secretary of State John Foster Dulles*. He was openly critical of President Dwight D. Eisenhower's* "unleashing" of Chiang Kai-shek* in February 1953 and in talks with Dulles insisted on prior consultation in the event of any move to escalate the war in Korea. After the truce talks resumption of April 26, 1953*, Eden, who had continued his efforts to promote a cease-fire, was worried because the United States seemed more concerned with appeasing President Syngman Rhee* of the Republic of Korea* and the Republican right wing than with reaching a settlement. In this situation, he pressed strongly for a compromise and went as far as to threaten withdrawal of British approval for the "Greater Sanctions" statement.

D. Acheson, *Present at the Creation* (London, 1970); D. Carlton, *Anthony Eden* (London, 1981); R. Foot, *The Wrong War* (Ithaca, N.Y., 1985); C. A. MacDonald, *Korea: The War Before Vietnam* (London, 1986).

Callum A. MacDonald

EIGHTH ARMY

The 8th U.S. Army in Korea (EUSAK) was the principal U.S. ground force responsible for conducting ground military operations in Asia during the Korean War. Following World War II, it was stationed in Japan as an occupation and security force. At the outbreak of the Korean War, the 8th Army consisted of four infantry divisions (1st Cavalry, 2d, 24th, and 25th Infantry) under the command of Lieutenant General Walton H. Walker*. Although lacking training in basic infantry skills and large-scale maneuvers, a young, inexperienced 8th Army expected easy victory in Korea. After establishing the EUSAK Command, Walker's troops quickly found themselves fighting a defensive war. The EUSAK was constantly outflanked and attacked from the rear, and North Korean infiltration tactics initially hampered organization and effectiveness. Soon U.S. forces grew hesitant to leave roads or their vehicles, and morale and confidence suffered.

Following Walker's untimely death in December 1950, Lieutenant General Matthew B. Ridgway* assumed command of the EUSAK. Under Ridgway, the EUSAK developed into a disciplined and aggressive fighting unit. Slowly and methodically, EUSAK advanced northward up the Korean peninsula. Ridgway's successor, Lieutenant General James A. Van Fleet*, also demanded a strict and determined military effort. Gradually, however, the war developed into a "sitzkrieg," and an increasingly disenchanted Van Fleet retired in February 1953. His replacement, Lieutenant General Maxwell D. Taylor*, strengthened defensive positions as ground advances stalled and a stalemate developed. By the end of the war, a rotation of troops system* and gradual racial integration had changed the composition of the 8th Army. Moreover, the first U.S. war fought not for victory but for negotiating table influence deeply affected EUSAK's purpose, ability, and mission. Still, the 8th Army played a critical and significant role in carrying out the U.S. war effort and preventing Communist conquest of the Republic of Korea*. *See also* "Bug-Out Fever"; Korean Augmentation of the U.S. Army.

J. C. Goulden, *Korea: The Untold Story of the War* (New York, 1982); R. A. Gugeler, *Combat Action in Korea* (Washington, D.C., 1954); C. A. MacDonald, *Korea: The War Before Vietnam* (New York, 1986); J. B. Wilson, *Armies, Corps, Divisions, and Separate Brigades* (Washington, D.C., 1987).

John Neilson

EISENHOWER, DWIGHT D. (1890–1969)

Eisenhower was president of the United States during the last six months of the Korean War and used a threat of atomic attack on the People's Republic of China* to obtain the armistice agreement*. Attaining the rank of general of the army before his election as president in 1952, he was chief of staff, following General George C. Marshall*, from November 1945 until May 1948 and supreme commander of Allied Forces in Europe (SHAPE) from January 1951 until March 1952. Between these two appointments to the nation's most important army commands, he served unofficially as chairman of the JCS, commuting from his duties as president of Columbia University.

Born in Denison, Texas, he attended the U.S. Military Academy at West Point beginning in 1911 and graduated with the class of 1915. Thereafter, he had a series of assignments, reaching the rank of lieutenant colonel at the end of World War I and command of the tank training post at Camp Colt; he was slated for overseas assignment when the war came to an end. He served afterward in Panama, Washington, and elsewhere, with two years at staff school at Fort Leavenworth. In the early 1930s, Eisenhower was a staff assistant to General Douglas MacArthur*, then chief of staff. When MacArthur went to the Philippines in 1935, Eisenhower accompanied him as chief of staff. Returning in 1939, he was a brigadier general at the time of Pearl Harbor, in charge of war plans in Washington by the spring of 1942, and thereafter became commanding general of Allied forces in England, North Africa, and Italy. Placed in command of the Allied invasion of France in 1944, he saw the war through to the defeat of Germany on May 8, 1945.

In his high positions of command during wartime, he gained an extraordinary reputation as a conciliator, gaining the cooperation of U.S. and British officers and troops while allaying trouble with General Charles de Gaulle's Free French. Although Eisenhower had no combat experience prior to 1942, he made several decisions in regard to the invasion of Europe—to invade on June 6, 1944, to bomb the French transport system, not to try for Berlin near war's end—that showed strategic good judgment. As chief of staff after Marshall and during the months of virtual chairmanship of the Joint Chiefs (the post did not then officially exist), he said very little about Korea, and his contribution to policies was either concerning the occupation of Germany and Austria or the gnawing problems of demobilization or unification of the three services. As commander of NATO, he spent all of his time attempting to unify his disparate forces and cajole the European governments into increasing them.

Eisenhower's single contribution to Korean policy was arrangement of the armistice in 1953. Here his hand was seldom clear but his purpose obvious.

During the 1952 presidential campaign, he promised to visit Korea, implying that this would speed an armistice on terms acceptable to the United States. After the trip, he decided first against expanding the ground war, rejecting MacArthur's recommendations for such a course in a December memorandum. The Eisenhower administration ultimately decided that, failing a Korean armistice, it would bomb Chinese bases and supply sources, blockade the mainland, and possibly use tactical nuclear weapons. Eisenhower told his presidential chief of staff, Sherman Adams, that what brought the armistice was ''danger of an atomic war.'' Such a warning, conveyed to Indian Prime Minister Jawaharlal Nehru*, may have sufficed, although the death of Joseph Stalin* may have been of near equal importance. *See also* Dulles's Atomic Warning to China; Eisenhower's Trip to Korea; MacArthur's Victory Proposal; NSC-147.

S. Adams, *Firsthand Report* (Westport, Conn., 1974); D. D. Eisenhower, *Mandate for Change* (Garden City, N.Y., 1963).

Robert H. Ferrell

EISENHOWER'S TRIP TO KOREA (December 2–5, 1952)

Four weeks after winning the presidential election in 1952, Dwight D. Eisenhower* fulfilled a campaign promise by taking a three-day trip to the battlefront in Korea. He had made the original commitment in a speech in Detroit on October 24, 1952. Exploiting the growing national frustration over the bloody stalemate in Korea, the Republican candidate announced that if elected, his goal would be ''to bring the Korean War to an early and honorable end.'' He then added that to reach that goal, he would take ''a personal trip to Korea.'' Most observers credited this pledge, made by the man widely viewed as the architect of victory in World War II, with clinching Eisenhower's victory over Adlai E. Stevenson* two weeks later.

During his stay in Korea, President-elect Eisenhower met only briefly with President Syngman Rhee* of the Republic of Korea* and CINCUNC General Mark W. Clark*, both of whom favored an all-out offensive to the Yalu. Instead, clad in heavy winter gear, Ike visited front-line units to get a firsthand understanding of the realities of the Korean battleground. What he saw convinced him of the futility of more ground assaults; as he put it later, ''Small attacks on small hills would not end the war.'' He preferred a renewed effort at diplomacy, combined with subtle hints to China of the possible use of nuclear weapons, to break the deadlock at P'anmunjŏm. These tactics, together with the death of Joseph Stalin* in early March, finally led to the signing of the armistice agreement* that brought the Korean War to an end. *See also* Dulles's Atomic Warning to China; K1C2.

S. E. Ambrose, *Eisenhower, the President* (New York, 1984); R. J. Caridi, *The Korean War and American Politics* (Philadelphia, 1968); R. A. Divine, *Foreign Policy and U.S. Presidential Elections, 1952–1960* (New York, 1974); B. I. Kaufman, *The Korean War* (Philadelphia, 1986); D. Rees, *Korea: The Limited War* (New York, 1964).

Robert A. Divine

ELSEY, GEORGE M., JR. (1918–   )

As administrative assistant to President Harry S. Truman* from 1949 to 1952,

George M. Elsey was often present when U.S. leaders formally or informally discussed developments during the Korean conflict. His papers at the Harry S. Truman Library in Independence, Missouri, which contain the notes he took on these discussions, comprise one of the richest archival collections containing materials on the war. Elsey was born in Palo Alto, California. He graduated from Princeton University in 1939 and then earned an M.A. in history at Harvard University in 1940. That same year he went on active duty with the U.S. Naval Reserve and worked in the White House Map Room with Clark Clifford. Following World War II, Clifford became Truman's special counsel, and Elsey served as his civilian administrative assistant and speechwriter. In 1946, the two men wrote an influential report, "American Relations with the Soviet Union," explaining how Moscow used espionage and subversion to promote Communist expansion in Asia and Europe. Urging steps to confine Soviet influence, this paper paved the way for adoption of the containment strategy the next year. In 1947, Elsey replaced Clifford as special counsel. When the Truman administration left office in 1953, Elsey joined the American Red Cross and served as vice-president from 1958 to 1961. He then advised large corporations and worked for public welfare groups such as the American Food for Peace Council. In 1970, Elsey became president of the American Red Cross.

E. W. Schoenebaum (ed.), *Political Profiles: The Truman Years* (New York, 1968).

EMMONS, ARTHUR B. III (1910–1962)

One of the few State Department officials who had spent time in Korea before the war began, Arthur B. Emmons III was in charge of the Korean desk from July 1950 until 1952. Born in Boston, he earned his B.S. from Harvard University in 1933. From 1931 to 1933, he was in Tibet as a member of the American expedition that mapped and made the first ascent to the top of Mount Minya Konka. After mountain climbing in the Himalayas, Emmons joined the foreign service in 1939, beginning his career as vice-consul in Montreal, Quebec. He had a brief posting at Hankow, China, in 1940, before moving to Seoul. After Japan's attack on Pearl Harbor, Emmons returned to the United States with other American diplomats aboard the *Gripsholm*. His firsthand report on internal conditions in Korea emphasized that the isolation and economic exploitation of the average Korean had created incredible political apathy. Emmons warned that the peninsula might reemerge after World War II as the object of an international rivalry. The Emmons report helped persuade the State Department to advocate a postwar trusteeship for Korea.

During most of World War II, Emmons served as third secretary and vice-consul in Montevideo, Uruguay. In 1945, he went to Tokyo and worked on the political advisory staff under CINCFE General Douglas MacArthur*. The next year, he served briefly as U.S. consul in Seoul. Emmons then became second secretary at the U.S. embassy in Madrid. He returned to Washington less than a month after the North Korean invasion of South Korea* to become the officer in charge of Korean affairs at the State Department. Emmons, like his predecessor, Niles W. Bond*, would play a secondary role in policy formulation because his superiors had assumed primary responsibility for decisions regarding Korea. However, he was the principal architect of the U.S. policy regarding war crimes trials*. In 1952, he served in Paris with the U.S. delegation to the UN General Assembly. From 1953 to 1958, he held postings in Australia, Ireland, and Malaya. Author of *Men Against the Clouds,* Emmons finished his career at the State Department as deputy director of Southwest Pacific Affairs and special assistant on SEATO affairs.

J. I. Matray, *The Reluctant Crusade* (Honolulu, 1985); *New York Times,* August 23, 1962; *Who Was Who in America,* vol. 4: *1961–1968* (Chicago, 1968).

END-THE-WAR OFFENSIVE
See Home-by-Christmas Offensive

ENTEZAM, NASROLLAH (1900–   )

Nasrollah Entezam, Iranian foreign minister, ambassador to the United States, and permanent delegate to the UN, played an active role in UN dealings with the Korean issue during 1950 and 1951. Born in Tehran, he received a B.A. from the University of Tehran in 1918 before following in his father's and grandfather's footsteps by pursuing a diplomatic career. During the 1920s, Entezam served in Paris, Warsaw, and London, and from 1929 to 1938 he was Iran's representative to the League of Nations. Returning to his native land in 1938, he held a variety of important government posts during World War II, rising to minister of state for foreign affairs in 1944. In April and May 1945, he represented his nation at the San Francisco Conference, and early the following year he attended the First Session of the UN General Assembly. Gaining prominence through his work on several important UN committees, Entezam was a candidate for president at the Fourth Session of the General Assembly but withdrew in the interest of unity among Asian nations.

Entezam was elected president of the General Assembly at the Fifth Session, almost simultaneously with his appointment as Iranian ambassador to the United States. At a time when Iran was trying to improve relations with the Soviet Union and gain economic assistance from the United States, Entezam's two positions put him in an extremely delicate situation. A mild-mannered, gracious man, Entezam avoided his country's alienation from either the Americans or the Soviets. In December 1950, he became embroiled in the effort by Arab and Asian nations to bring about a cease-fire in Korea. Midway through the month, he became chairman of an ad hoc cease-fire group created by the General Assembly to explore with the Americans and the Chinese an end to the fighting. After this effort failed and the UN General Assembly established a UN Good Offices Committee* through its resolution of February 1, 1951*, Entezam became chairman of the new group, which continued the effort to contact the People's Republic of China* in order to commence negotiations. Again the effort failed, but the committee's activities helped stall until mid-May U.S. efforts to apply "additional measures" against Communist China. After the armistice, Entezam went on to serve in a variety of political, diplomatic, and legal positions in the Iranian government. *See also* Arab-Asian Peace Initiatives; UN Ceasefire Group.

Current Biography, 1950; *Foreign Relations of the United States, 1950,* vol. 7: *Korea* (Washington, D.C., 1976) and *1951,* vol. 7: *Korea and China* (Washington, D.C., 1983); *Who's Who in the United Nations and Related Agencies,* 1975.

William Stueck

F

FAR EASTERN ECONOMIC ASSISTANCE ACT OF 1950 (February 14, 1950)

This legislation authorized U.S. aid to the Republic of Korea* and to the Republic of China* on Taiwan. Its passage demonstrated the strength of congressional support for the Chinese Nationalists and corresponding weakness of support for Korea and made a political linkage between the two for the first time. On January 19, 1950, the House rejected H.R. 5330, which provided economic aid to Korea for the remainder of fiscal 1950, by a single vote. The outcome was in part an expression of anger at President Harry S. Truman's* declaration of U.S. disengagement from the Chinese Civil War and in part an alliance between Republicans and economy-minded southern Democrats. Truman and Secretary of State Dean G. Acheson* quickly took steps to obtain reconsideration of the bill. In particular, Acheson indicated the administration's willingness to extend the China Aid Act to permit the expenditure of over $100 million in previously approved funds. In early February, the House Foreign Affairs Committee reported out a revision of S. 2319, the Senate version of H.R. 5330, authorizing $60 million in aid to Korea and extending the China Aid Act until June 30. The House approved the bill on February 9 by a vote of 240 to 134. The Senate concurred the following day, and President Truman signed it into law four days later. *See also* Korean Aid Bill of 1949–1950.

R. M. Blum, *Drawing the Line: The Origin of the American Containment Policy in East Asia* (New York, 1982); J. I. Matray, *The Reluctant Crusade* (Honolulu, 1985); H. B. Westerfield, *Foreign Policy and Party Politics: Pearl Harbor to Korea* (New Haven, Conn., 1955).

Harriet D. Schwar

FATHERLAND FRONT UNIFICATION PROPOSAL (June 7, 1950)

Less than one month before the North Korean invasion of South Korea*, the Democratic People's Republic of Korea* attempted to accomplish the reunification of the peninsula through peaceful means. On June 7, the Democratic Front for the Unification of the Fatherland (a Communist-led organization that the

DPRK had created a year earlier to build mass support for reunification in the south and thereby weaken the Republic of Korea*) issued a a public statement denouncing the May 1950 elections in South Korea and ridiculing the ROK as a U.S.-sponsored police state. Furthermore, it proposed a meeting to discuss peaceful unification and the formation of a committee to organize an election early in August for delegates to a national legislature. The proposal called for the exclusion, however, of ROK President Syngman Rhee* and Yi Pŏm-sŏk* from participation, while prohibiting the UN Commission on Korea (UNCOK) from observing the elections. South Korea scornfully rejected the plan, announcing its intention to boycott the proceedings. But acting UNCOK chairman, A.B. Jamieson* of Australia, greeted the proposal with enthusiasm, recommending in a public broadcast a meeting to discuss possible international consultation and observation.

On June 10, North Korean representatives met with members of the UNCOK at the thirty-eighth parallel. They presented the commission with copies of a DPRK appeal to the South Korean people to support the proposal of the Fatherland Front but would not discuss the matter in detail. After an exchange of gunfire and considerable confusion, the North Koreans ruled out any UN participation in the process leading to reunification. The next day, three men crossed the thirty-eighth parallel and entered South Korea carrying a ''Peace Manifesto.'' South Korean troops promptly arrested these representatives of the Fatherland Front, indicating again the ROK's unswerving hostility to any North Korean proposal for reconciliation. In a final demonstration of its sincerity, the Fatherland Front on June 19 proposed merging the two legislatures for the purpose of drawing up a new constitution and supervising national elections. Undoubtedly, the DPRK anticipated a favorable public reception for its initiatives in the south because the recent May elections had resulted in defeat for many of Rhee's political allies. Rhee would have to accept its proposal or risk a popular insurrection. The failure of these efforts may have persuaded the North Koreans that reunification was possible only through a resort to force, although the DPRK might have been attempting to mask its invasion plans.

Foreign Relations of the United States, 1950, vol. 7: *Korea* (Washington, D.C., 1976); J. A. Kim, *Divided Korea* (Cambridge, 1975); J. I. Matray, *The Reluctant Crusade* (Honolulu, 1985); *New York Times,* June 10, 11, 1950; J. F. Schnabel, *Policy and Direction* (Washington, D.C., 1972).

FECHTELER, WILLIAM M. (1896–1967)

Admiral William M. Fechteler became U.S. Navy chief of staff in August 1951 after the unexpected death of Admiral Forrest P. Sherman*, serving in this position until the end of the Korean War. He was born in San Rafael, California, and, following in the footsteps of his father, Admiral Augustus F. Fechteler, he attended the U.S. Naval Academy, graduating in 1916. In World War I, Fechteler served aboard the U.S.S. *Pennsylvania,* the flagship of the Atlantic Fleet, as aide to the fleet commander. After nearly two decades of alternating tours at sea and duty in Washington, D.C., and as an instructor at the U.S. Naval Academy, he became commanding officer of the U.S.S. *Perry* in 1935. Fechteler was assistant naval chief of staff for operations in 1941, but following the start of World War II, he became assistant director of the U.S. Navy's personnel bureau. Remaining in this post until July 1943, his duties involved the implementation of decisions regarding the procurement, education, training, discipline, promotion, distribution, and demobilization of naval officers and enlisted men. For the last two years of the war, Fechteler held various command positions in the Pacific, directing amphibious operations in the Gilbert, Marshall, and Admiralty islands and at the Battle of Leyte Gulf. By 1945, he was a rear admiral and had become assistant chief of naval operations.

Fechteler returned to sea duty with the Atlantic Fleet in 1946 as a vice-admiral. From 1947 to 1950, he was deputy naval chief of staff in charge of personnel and spent considerable time representing the U.S. Navy before congressional committees and speaking in favor of wage increases. During these hearings, Fechteler won considerable respect for being honest, knowledgeable, and straightforward. Also, as one observer noted, he "knew how to turn on the charm." However, Fechteler was the only admiral not to testify during the Revolt of the Admirals controversy. When the Korean War began, Fechteler was commander of the Atlantic Fleet. In August 1950, he represented the United States during NATO meetings for coordination of military operations in response to possible new acts of aggression in Europe. In February 1951, Fechteler was to become supreme NATO commander of the North Atlantic region, but Winston Churchill* favored a British officer instead. Before Fechteler assumed his responsibilities, President Harry S. Truman*, to avoid friction, selected him as chief of naval operations upon the death of Sherman. By then, the Korean War had become a bloody stalemate, and the naval chief of staff had limited involvement in decisions about military operations, aside from enforcing the blockade of North Korea and China. However, Fechteler did voice consistent opposition to compromising with the Communists at the P'anmunjŏm truce talks*. After serving as commander of Allied forces in southern Europe from 1953 to 1956, Fechteler retired and went to work for General Electric Company.

Current Biography, 1951; *Foreign Relations of the United States, 1952–1954*, vol. 15: *Korea* (Washington, D.C., 1984); *New York Times*, July 5, 1967; *Who Was Who in America*, vol. 4: *1961–1968* (Chicago, 1968).

FINLETTER, THOMAS K. (1891–1980)

Thomas K. Finletter became secretary of the air force in early 1950 and faced the difficult assignment of following an aggressive, controversial figure, Stuart Symington, and serving under three powerful secretaries of defense: the even more aggressive and controversial Louis A. Johnson*, the august George C. Marshall*, and the powerful, assertive Robert A. Lovett*. His tenure coincided with a period of unprecedented adjustment for the newly independent U.S. Air Force. Born in Philadelphia, Finletter served in France during World War I. He earned his law degree at the University of Pennsylvania in 1920 and for the next two decades worked at Wall Street brokerage firms. In 1941, Finletter joined the State Department's office of international economic affairs. Two years later, he became executive director and later deputy director of the office of foreign economic coordination, serving in the organizational phase of UNRRA under Governor Herbert Lehman. President Harry S. Truman* appointed him chairman of the Air Policy Commission in July 1947, which held a series of public hearings and submitted a report stressing the need to develop fully the potential of the air force over the next five years, including the hydrogen bomb. In May 1948, he became head of the Economic Cooperation Administration mission to Britain, acquiring an appreciation for the challenge of integrating Western Europe economically and militarily within a developing North Atlantic community but having little direct involvement with strategic questions.

In 1949, Finletter returned to Washington and practiced law briefly before becoming secretary of the air force. He took office at a time of severe budgetary constraints, but war in Korea opened the floodgates for expansion of strategic and tactical capabilities. Organizational imperatives arising from the unification of the armed forces and the National Security Act of 1947 assigned primary responsibility for budgeting and policymaking to the secretary of defense. Once Truman replaced the disastrous Johnson, Finletter and his colleagues enjoyed little independence. He attended the first Blair House meeting* and spoke against the commitment of ground troops. Finletter also essayed counsels of moderation during the events surrounding Truman's recall of CINCUNC General Douglas MacArthur*. Finally, he negotiated with his counterpart, Frank Pace*, secretary of the army, the Finletter-Pace agreement on the role of "organic aviation," which would permit the U.S. Army's acquisition of helicopter transports. In 1953, he returned to private life, working closely with W. Averell Harriman* in New York politics. During the Kennedy administration, Finletter returned to public service as permanent U.S. representative to NATO. The author of several books on corporate reorganization, he also contributed articles during World War II devoted to the "One World" cause to the *New Republic* and *Commonweal*.

C. W. Borklund, *Men of the Pentagon: From Forrestal to McNamara* (New York, 1966); *Current Biography,* 1948; R. F. Futrell, *The United States Air Force in Korea* (Washington, D.C., 1961); *New York Times,* April 25, 1980; S. L. Rearden, *History of the Office of the Secretary of Defense,* vol. 1: *The Formative Years, 1947–1950* (Washington, D.C., 1984).

Theodore A. Wilson

FIRST BLAIR HOUSE MEETING (June 25, 1950)

This was a meeting of President Harry S. Truman* and his top advisers less than twenty-four hours after the North Korean invasion of South Korea* to discuss the crisis. It convened in the evening at Blair House, across the street from the White House, because the executive mansion was undergoing renovation. In preparation for this meeting, State Department officials had formulated a list of policy options reflecting a preference for restraint in initially reacting to the Korean War. The report included such limited alternatives as sending South Korea all essential equipment and permitting the U.S. Korean Military Advisory Group* to remain with the South Korean army. If necessary, the United States would use naval and air power to establish a protective zone around Seoul and the port of Inch'ŏn for the evacuation of all Americans. If South Korea's survival demanded drastic steps, the United States might commit ground forces "to stabilize the combat situation including if feasible the restoration of original boundaries at 38 degree parallel." The State Department also recommended that CINCFE General Douglas MacArthur* send a survey team to South Korea to determine the minimum amount of aid necessary to enable the Republic of Korea* to defend itself without undermining the security of Japan.

Informally during dinner, conversation centered on the global nature of the Soviet challenge in Korea. While ruling out appeasement, many participants voiced fears that Soviet or Chinese intervention would create a wider war. Everyone shared the hope that South Korea could defend itself. After dinner, Secretary of State Dean G. Acheson* summarized the State Department's recommendations, also suggesting that Truman order the 7th Fleet into the Taiwan Strait to prevent an attack on either the island or the Chinese mainland. Truman's other military and civilian advisers registered immediate support for Acheson's proposals. They advised against the dispatch of ground forces to Korea, favoring instead the use of U.S. air and naval power to halt the North Korean advance. After approving the State Department's recommendations, Truman instructed Air Force Secretary Thomas K. Finletter* to make preparations for the destruction of all Soviet air bases in Asia; State and Defense were to formulate contingency plans for reacting to the next probable location of Soviet aggression. After approving a press release, the president told his advisers to stress in public comments that the United States was acting under international authority and would limit its military activity to protecting the U.S. evacuation of Seoul*. He would consider more drastic action only if North Korea defied the UN request for cease-fire and withdrawal. *See also* Johnson's Visit to Tokyo; Neutralization of Taiwan; Second Blair House Meeting; UN Security Council Resolution of June 25, 1950.

G. D. Paige, *The Korean Decision* (New York, 1968); W. W. Stueck, *The Road to Confrontation* (Chapel Hill, 1981); H. S. Truman, *Years of Trial and Hope* (Garden City, N.Y., 1956).

FIVE PRINCIPLES
  See UN Ceasefire Group; UN Resolution of February 1, 1951

FORMOSA (TAIWAN)
  See Republic of China; Neutralization of Taiwan

FOURTH MEETING OF CONSULTATION OF MINISTERS OF FOREIGN AFFAIRS OF AMERICAN STATES
See Washington Conference

FRANKS, SIR OLIVER (1905–   )

Oliver Franks was British ambassador to the United States from 1948 to 1952. His close relationship with Secretary of State Dean G. Acheson* helped to smooth out Anglo-American differences on many issues during the Korean War. Franks and Acheson met regularly, on average once per week, for an informal, off-the-record discussion of world events. At the outbreak of the war in June 1950, Franks conveyed British backing of U.S. policy, including the British decision to contribute naval support. Less welcome was Franks's communication of British views on Taiwan, which diverged from the U.S. position. Franks's message from Foreign Secretary Ernest Bevin* on July 7, 1950, proposing peace terms, including concessions to the Chinese government regarding Taiwan and admission of the People's Republic of China* to the United Nations, received a curtly dismissive reply from Acheson.

Franks believed strongly that Britain should send ground troops to Korea as an expression of solidarity with the Americans. He wrote an untypically impassioned personal letter advancing this view to Prime Minister Clement R. Attlee* on July 15, and this influenced the British cabinet decision of July 25 to send two British brigades to Korea. Although the British military contribution was relatively slight and tended to be overlooked by the Americans, Franks thought that the token gesture of British and U.S. soldiers fighting shoulder to shoulder was valuable when differences on policy arose between the two countries. Franks needed to exercise all of his diplomatic skill in crises over such matters as the British DMZ proposal* of November 1950, President Harry S. Truman's* atomic bomb press conference comment* in late November 1950, British proposals for peace negotiations on conciliatory terms to China from December 1950 to January 1951, U.S. insistence on support for a UN resolution of February 1, 1951*, condemning China as an aggressor, and frequent American criticisms of British trade with China.

Franks was not a career diplomat but an Oxford University professor of philosophy, who served in the Ministry of Supply in World War II and as chairman of the Committee on European Economic Cooperation in 1947. After his term as ambassador in Washington, he returned to private life, first in banking and then in a renewed academic career at Oxford University. Elevated to the peerage, Lord Franks chaired various government commissions, such as the inquiry into the origins of the Falklands War in 1982. *See also* British Peace Initiatives.

D. Acheson, *Present at the Creation* (New York, 1969); P. G. Boyle, "Oliver Franks," in J. Zametica (ed.), *British Officials and British Foreign Policy, 1945–55* (Leicester, 1990); A. Bullock, *Ernest Bevin: Foreign Secretary, 1945–1951* (London, 1983).

Peter G. Boyle

G

GENEVA CONFERENCE OF 1954

The Geneva Conference of 1954 represented the final act of the Korean War. Article 4 of the armistice agreement* specified the calling of a conference of interested parties to negotiate the evacuation of foreign troops from Korea and "the peaceful settlement of the Korean question." The Geneva Conference began on April 26, 1954, after considerable haggling among the participants, especially the United States and the Republic of Korea*. ROK President Syngman Rhee* several times threatened to boycott the conference, arguing that it would lead to the abandonment of South Korea and the end of all hopes of Korean unification. Eventually Rhee agreed to send representatives to the conference but only after eliciting a pledge of increased military assistance from the Eisenhower administration, to augment a previous commitment to a U.S.-ROK Mutual Defense Treaty*.

The conference itself proved sterile. Part of the difficulty followed from the fact that by the time it began, the great powers were distracted by events in Indochina. Concurrently with the conference on Korea, the powers negotiated the partition of Vietnam. Equally to the point, Washington, Moscow, and Peking did not deem a settlement of the Korean problem sufficiently desirable to apply the requisite pressure on their clients to force a solution. Unification of Korea would have required country-wide elections and the withdrawal of foreign forces. Rhee refused to accept the results of elections in North Korea until the Communists laid down their arms and the Chinese People's Volunteers Army* left. Not surprisingly, P'yŏngyang and Peking rejected this demand. The Communists also vetoed supervision of elections by the United Nations, which they logically considered unneutral in the Korean affair. Before the French defeat at Dienbienphu, the Eisenhower administration might have encouraged the South Koreans to compromise, but with communism victorious in Vietnam, Washington decided to let Rhee be Rhee—unpredictable in some matters yet anti-Communist to the core. On June 15, delegates from the United States and its UN allies announced that further discussion of the Korean question would be fruitless, and the conference ended. *See also* Agenda Item 5; NSC-157/1.

H. W. Brands, "The Dwight D. Eisenhower Administration, Syngman Rhee, and the 'Other' Geneva Conference of 1954," *Pacific Historical Review* (February 1987)

H. W. Brands

GENEVA CONVENTION OF 1949

The Geneva Convention of 1949 was an enlarged version of the Geneva Convention of 1929, which it replaced. During the Korean War, controversy centered on Convention IV, which covered the treatment of POWs, specifically Article 118, ensuring their right to repatriation. The UNC* insisted upon the POW's ability to refuse return to his homeland, while the Communists viewed voluntary repatriation* as a violation of the Geneva Convention. The United States had signed but not ratified the convention when the Korean War broke out. In July 1950, CINCUNC General Douglas MacArthur* announced that the UNC would adhere to the humanitarian provisions of the convention. In September 1950, the United States assumed responsibility for all POWs on behalf of the UNC. Although the Democratic People's Republic of Korea* had not signed the convention, the foreign minister, Pak Hŏn-yŏng*, informed Trygve Lie*, UN secretary-general, that his side would observe the Geneva principles. The People's Republic of China* had not signed the convention, and the Chinese People's Volunteers Army* at first made no pretense of observing its provisions. In July 1952, however, China announced that it too would apply the Geneva rules.

In fact, neither side strictly observed the convention, and there were many cases of mistreatment and brutality, particularly in the early stages of the war. Moreover, both sides employed POWs as tools of political and psychological warfare. While the Communists tried to indoctrinate their POWs, the United States introduced an educational program for prisoners designed to demonstrate the superiority of capitalism and Western values. The Geneva Convention first became an issue at the P'anmunjŏm truce talks* in December 1951 when the UNC proposed non-forcible repatriation of POWs after the armistice. Under this principle, nobody would be returned to his own side against his will. This provision was intended to protect anti-Communist POWs in American hands, while also designed as psychological warfare against China and North Korea. Displaying a legal literalism never applied to other sections of the convention, the Communists rejected the proposal and cited Article 118, which stated that "Prisoners of War shall be released and repatriated without delay after the cessation of active hostilities." They denied any right of asylum, appealing to Article 7, which stated that "Prisoners of War may in no circumstances renounce in part or in entirety the rights secured to them by the present Convention." They refused to concede that their men would freely choose to reject repatriation, insisting that the UNC position amounted to "forcible detention." After the most divisive issue of the talks had delayed an armistice by over a year, the first steps toward a compromise came early in 1953 when both sides agreed to an exchange of sick and wounded POWs, Operation Little Switch*, under Article 109 of the convention. *See also* Agenda Item 4; Brainwashing and POW Morale; Communist POW Administration; UNC POW Administration.

B. J. Bernstein, "The Struggle over the Korean Armistice: Prisoners of Repatriation?" in B. Cumings (ed.), *Child of Conflict* (Seattle, 1983); M. W. Clark, *From the Danube to the Yalu* (London, 1954); W. G. Hermes *Truce Tent and Fighting Front* (Washington, D.C., 1966).

Callum A. MacDonald

GRAFSTROM, SVEN (1902–1955)

Grafstrom was a member of the UN Good Offices Committee* and later the Neutral Nations Supervisory Commission* during and after the Korean War. He entered the Swedish Foreign Service in 1928, serving in Norway, Great Britain, the Soviet Union, Iran, and Turkey. At the outbreak of World War II in Europe, he was stationed in Warsaw. He took part in the effort to evacuate the diplomatic corps from Poland. From 1939 to 1948, he served in a number of positions in the Swedish foreign office, including minister plenipotentiary in the diplomatic service in 1945. In 1948, the government appointed him to lead the Swedish delegation at the United Nations. Grafstrom believed that the UN had to respond to the North Korean invasion of South Korea*, though he did not think blame should be placed on the Soviet Union for the outbreak of war. In December 1950, he suggested that a small UN delegation go to Peking for discussions with the Chinese on the Korean War. He believed, in addition, that this would reemphasize UN support for the Republic of Korea*.

In early 1951, after India decided against serving on the UN Good Offices Committee, Grafstrom agreed to be appointed as the Swedish representative on the three-person committee. The purpose of the UN Good Offices Committee was to approach the Chinese to find some method for working toward a peace settlement in Korea. It was thought that because of Swedish diplomatic representation in Peking, the Swedes could be used as a communications connection between the UN and the People's Republic of China*. Grafstrom believed it was important to find some basis for a cease-fire with the PRC as an initial step toward a conference for negotiations. He maintained close contact with the U.S. delegation at the UN because of its importance in any final UN decision on discussions with the PRC. But after three months, the UN Good Offices Committee had been unable to make any headway with the PRC. In 1954, he was appointed Swedish minister to Mexico. He held this position until his death from a fall off a train in France.

Foreign Relations of the United States, 1950, vol. 7: *Korea* (Washington, D.C., 1976) and *1951,* vol. 7: *Korea and China* (Washington, D.C., 1983); L. M. Goodrich, *Korea: A Study of U.S. Policy in the U. N.* (New York, 1956); Utrikespolitska Institutet (Sweden), *Sweden and the United Nations* (New York, 1956).

Paul J. Morton

GREATER SANCTIONS STATEMENT
See Joint Policy Statement

GROMYKO, ANDREI A. (1909–1989)

When he retired from government service in 1988, Andrei Andreyevich Gromyko had served the Soviet Union as minister of foreign affairs (1957–1985), member of the Politburo (after 1973), and both president of the Soviet Union and chairman of the Presidium of the Supreme Soviet (1985–1988). As deputy foreign minister at the time of the Korean War (1949–1952), he helped to bring about the Kaesŏng truce talks* that began on July 10, 1951, and, after moving to P'anmunjŏm, brought the war to an end two years later.

After graduating from a teachers' college in 1931, Gromyko received M.A. degrees from the Moscow Agricultural Institute and the Institute of Economics, where he studied foreign politics and economics. Later, he served as senior research scientist at the Academy of Sciences of the U.S.S.R. and lectured at various Moscow universities. He gained a reputation as an austere individual who did not drink, smoke, or socialize with women. After serving from May until October 1939 as head of the division for American countries in the Commissariat of Foreign Affairs, he became counselor to the Soviet embassy in the United States. For a brief period he served as chargé.

In August 1943, he succeeded Maxim Litvinov as ambassador to the United States. He participated in the Teheran, Yalta, and Postdam conferences and was chairman of the Soviet delegation at the Dumbarton Oaks Conference. Later, he was a member of the delegation to the UN conference in San Francisco in 1945 and a delegate to the first UN General Assembly meeting in London and New York, eventually becoming official Soviet representative. After serving briefly as ambassador to Great Britain, he became foreign minister in February 1957.

Gromyko helped move the war in Korea toward armistice when, in June 1951, he told Alan G. Kirk*, the U.S. ambassador to Moscow, that a speech by Soviet UN ambassador Jacob A. Malik* reflected official Soviet policy and that the Soviet Union desired peace in Korea—something he earlier had conveyed to the UN secretary-general and to the governments of Great Britain and India. He recommended that the belligerents begin discussions, limiting themselves to military matters. This was accepted by Secretary of State Dean G. Acheson* as the basis for negotiations.

C. Blair, *The Forgotten War* (New York, 1987); *Current Biography*, 1958; R. Foot, *The Wrong War* (Ithaca, N.Y., 1985); *International Who's Who* (London, 1988); B. I. Kaufman, *The Korean War* (Philadelphia, 1986).

William B. Pickett

GROSS, ERNEST R. (1906–   )

As deputy U.S. representative to the United Nations, Gross played a key role in U.S. diplomacy at the UN during the Korean War, especially at its beginning. Born in Brooklyn, New York, he received a B.A. from Harvard College in 1927 and, after stints at Oxford University in England and the Geneva School of International Studies in Switzerland, an L.L.B from Harvard Law School in

1931. After serving as assistant legal advisor to the State Department, Gross worked during the New Deal era for a variety of public and private agencies, including the National Recovery Administration, the National Association of Manufacturers, and the National Labor Relations Board. Commissioned a captain in the U.S. Army in 1943, he served in the economic section of the Civil Affairs Division of the War Department General Staff, centering his efforts on plans for occupied and liberated areas in the postwar era. In 1946, he was transferred to the State Department as a deputy to the assistant secretary of state for occupied areas. Thus from 1943 to 1947, when he became legal advisor to the State Department, Gross developed a familiarity with the Korean issue.

In early 1949, Gross became assistant secretary of state for congressional relations, dealing with, among other things, the effort to secure appropriations for economic and military aid for the Republic of Korea*. Later in the year, he asked Secretary of State Dean G. Acheson* for the position of deputy representative to the UN. Receiving the post, Gross worked smoothly with his immediate superior, Warren R. Austin*. When Austin, a much older and frail man, was away from the UN, Gross possessed the authority to act as his replacement. On the evening of June 24, 1950, therefore, with Austin at his home in Vermont, the State Department contacted Gross in New York after it received word of the North Korean invasion of South Korea*. Throughout the night and the following day, he strove to contact delegates to the UN Security Council and mobilize them behind the resolution of June 25, 1950*, calling on North Korea to cease fire and withdraw above the thirty-eighth parallel. Because of the Soviet UN Security Council boycott*, Gross gained passage of the measure, persuading nine of the ten members in attendance to vote for it. Upon Austin's return to New York two days later, Gross retreated from the spotlight, although his superior energy and skill in diplomacy made him a crucial instrument later in guiding several key resolutions through the General Assembly. Gross left government service in 1953 for private practice in law but continued to take an interest in UN affairs, publishing *The New United Nations* and *The United Nations: Structure for Peace*.

Current Biography, 1951; *Foreign Relations of the United States, 1950*, vol. 7: *Korea* (Washington, D.C., 1976) and *1952–1954*, vol. 15: *Korea* (Washington, D.C., 1984); G. D. Paige, *The Korean Decision* (New York, 1968); "The Reminiscences of Ernest Gross," Oral History Project, Columbia University; *Who's Who in America, 1954–55, 1984–85* (New York, 1954, 1984).

William Stueck

H

HAMMARSKJOLD, DAG (1905–1961)

Three months before the end of the Korean War, Dag H. A. C. Hammarskjold replaced Trygve Lie* as secretary-general at the United Nations. At this time, the negotiators at the P'anmunjŏm truce talks* were in the process of resolving the prolonged deadlock over agenda item 4*, POW repatriation, and Hammarskjold therefore played a limited role in the achievement of the armistice agreement*. Born in Jonkoping, Sweden, he earned a B.A. (1925) and an M.A. (1928) from Uppsala University. While a professor of political economics at Stockholm University, Hammarskjold completed his doctorate in 1934. The next year, he became secretary of the Bank of Sweden and later was chairman of the board from 1941 to 1948.

In 1936, Hammarskjold joined the Swedish Ministry of Finance, serving as under secretary of state. Beginning in 1946, he was a financial advisor for the Ministry of Foreign Affairs, assuming the post of assistant foreign minister in 1949. As Sweden's top monetary expert, Hammarskjold attended a variety of European conferences and UN General Assembly meetings during the postwar period. In 1951, he became minister of state, at the same time serving as vice-chair and then chair of Sweden's delegation at the UN. After two years of wrangling over a successor to Lie, the UN Security Council chose Hammarskjold as secretary-general, then considered by many the "darkest of the dark horses." Until his death in a plane crash, he sought to play an activist role in inaugurating a new era of reduced international tensions. Hammarskjold developed a reputation for being witty, showing ease in personal relationships and brilliance in oratory.

Current Biography, 1953; *New York Times*, September 19, 1961; *Who Was Who in America*, vol. 4: *1961–1968* (Chicago, 1968).

HAN PYO-WOOK (1916–   )

Han, currently professor of international relations at Korea's Kyung Hee University, was first secretary at the Korean embassy in Washington from its opening in 1949 to 1951, promoted to counselor in 1951, and then to minister in 1954. Following the North Korean invasion of South Korea*, he was delegate to the UN Security Council. Thus, Han was in a position to participate on a working level in most of the important transactions between Seoul and Washington throughout the Korean War. He accompanied Korean ambassador John M. Chang* when the latter was received by President Harry S. Truman* on the afternoon of June 27, 1950. According to Chang's recollection, Han nudged to restrain him when he was becoming emotional at the beginning of the meeting in protesting that the United States had neglected providing enough military assistance to the Republic of Korea* and should share the blame for precipitating the North Korean attack. Toward the end of the war, Han was originally on the list of Korean delegation to the Geneva Conference of 1954* but remained in Washington upon instruction from President Syngman Rhee* to coordinate contacts with the State Department since Ambassador Yang You Chan* was to go to Geneva.

Han earned his M.A. at Harvard University and Ph.D. at the University of Michigan, both in political science. He had met Rhee while studying in the United States and worked for him in his campaign to obtain U.S. support for Korean independence toward the end of World War II. He remained in diplomatic service, successively filling important posts, including the Korean ambassadorship to Thailand and to the United Kingdom until he retired in 1981.

Han Pyo-wook, *Han Mi Oegyo Yŏramgi* (Seoul, 1984); Chang Myŏn, *Hanal ŭi Miri Chukchi Ankonŭn—Chang Myŏn Paksa Hoegorok* (Seoul, 1967).

J. Y. Ra

HAN RIVER OPERATIONS (June 29–July 3, 1950)

While General Douglas MacArthur* had hoped to seize the initiative early against the invading North Korean People's Army (NKPA), his visit to Korea of June 29, 1950*, for the inspection of the Seoul region convinced him of the necessity of halting the North Korean drive and of reorganizing the thoroughly demoralized army of the Republic of Korea*. To accomplish the first of these objectives, he sought to establish a defensive line along the Han River, just south of Seoul. U.S. support of this defensive system was largely limited to air and naval strikes against North Korean airfields, port facilities, and advancing forces. On June 29, U.S. planes from the FEAF flew 172 combat sorties, while the U.S.S. *Juneau* shelled North Korean ports along the eastern coastal corridor. Air support at the Han River line was meager, and even this was accomplished with great difficulty. After the NKPA captured Kimp'o Airfield on June 28, the FEAF had to use Suwŏn Airfield—the last remaining airstrip in central Korea—under the most desperate of circumstances. Without direct communications with its planes or adequate maps, American planes at Suwŏn sought to provide air support for the ROK forces along the Han River. As the enemy approached Suwŏn on June 30, American units were forced to evacuate the airstrip and bring planes from more distant points to provide close air support along the Han River line.

The NKPA had not paused after its capture of Seoul but immediately challenged the ROK's new defenses along the Han River. While the main attack was directed on July 1 at the industrial center of Yŏngdŭng-p'o immediately across the Han from Seoul, other NKPA units on the right and left flanks had already begun crossing the river. Because most of the bridges had been destroyed, North Korean units initially had to leave their tanks on the northern shore and swim or raft across. The hastily regrouped, lightly armed ROK defenders were able to put up effective resistance for two days. When the port city of Inch'ŏn on the west coast and Yŏngdŭng-p'o fell to the North Korean forces, the main bridges across the Han were repaired, and the enemy began pushing its armor units south toward Pusan. One of the immediate results of the collapse of the Han River line was that General MacArthur had to reassess his needs. Initially he had implied that two U.S. divisions would be adequate to stabilize the front in Korea. Now he warned the JCS that at least four full-strength U.S. divisions, plus support units, would be required to stop the NKPA. He was just beginning to grasp the true strength and quality of his enemy. *See also* Truman's Commitment of Ground Troops; Withdrawal from Seoul of June 1950.

R. F. Futrell, *The United States Air Force in Korea* (New York, 1961); H. J. Middleton, *The Compact History of the Korean War* (New York, 1965); W. Sheldon, *Hell or High Water* (New York, 1968).

Richard Dean Burns

HARRIMAN, W. AVERELL (1891–1986)

When the Korean War began, W. Averell Harriman had just become President Harry S. Truman's* special assistant for national security affairs. Son of railroad tycoon Edward H. Harriman, he was educated at Yale University. He compiled an impressive record as a business entrepreneur in his own right—with the Union Pacific Railroad, in shipping and on Wall Street—before signing on with the National Recovery Administration during the early days of the New Deal. An associate of Harry Hopkins, he performed as a White House troubleshooter in Britain dealing with Lend-Lease and then as U.S. ambassador to the Soviet Union from October 1943 to February 1946. Harriman accepted the post of secretary of commerce in the wake of Henry A. Wallace's resignation. He performed a crucial role in the Marshall Plan era, heading the "non-partisan committee" that drafted the domestic component of the European Recovery Program and then going to Paris as U.S. special representative for the Economic Cooperation Administration. In February 1946, Harriman visited southern Korea. When he returned to the United States, he recommended a policy of firmness toward the Soviet Union, while reporting that he was "favorably impressed" by the "ability and diplomacy" of Lieutenant General John R. Hodge*, the occupation commander.

Harriman returned to Washington to assume his responsibilities as Truman's special assistant just days after the North Korean attack. Thus, he was at the pivot of history in the critical first months of the war. His role cannot be ex-

aggerated in such questions as the selling of NSC–68*, protecting Secretary of
State Dean G. Acheson* against the sniping of right-wing Republicans, mediation
between CINCUNC General Douglas MacArthur* and the JCS over the proposed
Inch'ŏn landing*, and masterminding the massive military assistance programs
undertaken in 1950 and 1951. Perhaps most important was Harriman's visit to
Tokyo* in August 1950 to persuade MacArthur to cooperate with Truman's
policy toward China. In many ways, he performed as the prototypical national
security adviser. After an ineffective bid for the Democratic presidential nomination in 1952, Harriman was governor of New York and later served the
administrations of John F. Kennedy and Lyndon B. Johnson as a roving ambassador.

W. A. Harriman and E. Abel, *Special Envoy to Churchill and Stalin, 1941–1946* (New
York, 1975); W. Isaacson and E. Thomas, *The Wise Men* (New York, 1986); L. S.
Kaplan, *A Community of Interests: NATO and the Military Assistance Program* (Wash-
ington, D.C., 1980).

Theodore A. Wilson

HARRIMAN'S VISIT TO TOKYO (August 6–7, 1950)

W. Averell Harriman*, who returned from Europe immediately after the North
Korean invasion of South Korea* to take the position of special assistant for
national security affairs, served President Harry S. Truman* as a troubleshooter.
Among his first assignments was a journey to Tokyo in early August 1950 to
investigate conditions there, especially CINCUNC General Douglas Mac-
Arthur's* mental and physical state. He also was instructed to assure MacArthur
of Truman's total support for his conduct of the Korean War but to emphasize
that nothing be done to provoke a war with the People's Republic of China*.
The latter task resulted from MacArthur's visit to Taiwan* late in July 1950,
which had created confusion about the U.S. defense commitment to the Republic
of China*. It implied that the United States intended to replace its policy of
neutralization of Taiwan* with a more aggressive approach. Harriman was to
caution MacArthur against unauthorized encouragement of Chiang Kai-shek's*
aspirations to invade the mainland. Also, he was to avoid giving the appearance
that the Truman administration sought any long-term commitments with Chiang's
regime.

On August 6, Harriman arrived in Tokyo with Lieutenant Generals Matthew
B. Ridgway* and Lauris Norstad*. During the ride from the airport, the general
spoke in general terms about the Japanese and the impact of American occupation.
Subsequently the ambassador had three long conversations with MacArthur and
visited Korea briefly before his departure the next afternoon. Their first formal
discussion covered events in Korea. After Harriman conveyed the president's
message of support, MacArthur declared that Truman's commitment of ground
troops* had been ''an historic decision which would save the world from Communist domination.'' He then emphasized the importance of achieving a quick
military victory, warning that delay would create discouragement at the UN and
in Asia while benefiting Soviet and Chinese plans for expansion. MacArthur

then lectured Harriman on the superior fighting ability of Asians, explaining that for Orientals "life begins with death." If the administration provided more troops, he would restore President Syngman Rhee's* government in Seoul, and two months later, there would be elections in the north to fill the 100 seats in the National Assembly of the Republic of Korea*. Moscow and Peking, MacArthur said, would not intervene to prevent Korea's reunification.

In accordance with his instructions, Harriman summarized at length Truman's policy on China. Chiang, he said, was determined to regain power on the mainland, but the United States was committed only to denying Taiwan to the Communists. Harriman pointed to the dangers of becoming involved in fighting a war on the Chinese mainland, among them the loss of support for the United States in the UN. MacArthur replied that he would, of course, "as a soldier, obey any orders from the President," but "without full conviction," Harriman later noted. The general then insisted that he had refused to discuss political matters with Chiang and rejected the generalissimo's offer of control over Nationalist military forces. However, MacArthur told Harriman that the United States should be doing more to weaken the Chinese Communist regime instead of undermining the Nationalist government on Taiwan. Upon his return to Washington, D.C., Harriman reported to Truman that "for reasons which are rather difficult to explain, I did not feel that we came to a full agreement." The general had the "strange idea" that the United States should back any leader who was anti-Communist. In his memoirs, MacArthur wrote that Harriman's visit had provided additional evidence of how Asian affairs were "little understood and mistakenly downgraded in high circles in Washington." Before August ended, MacArthur's VFW message* would reveal that the ambassador's efforts at persuasion had failed miserably.

D. Acheson, *Present at the Creation* (New York, 1969); W. Isaacson and E. Thomas, *The Wise Men* (Boston, 1986); D. C. James, *The Years of MacArthur,* vol. 3: *Triumph and Disaster, 1945–1964* (Boston, 1985); H. S. Truman, *Years of Trial and Hope* (Garden City, N.Y., 1956).

Theodore A. Wilson

HARRISON, WILLIAM K., JR. (1895–1987)

On May 19, 1952, Major General William K. Harrison, Jr., replaced Vice-Admiral C. Turner Joy* as the UNC's* chief delegate at the P'anmunjŏm truce talks* and would remain in this position until the end of the Korean War. A direct descendant of President William Henry Harrison, he was born in Washington, D.C. Along with J. Lawton Collins*, Matthew B. Ridgway*, and Mark W. Clark*, Harrison graduated from the U.S. Military Academy at West Point in 1917. During World War I, he fought in France with the 1st Cavalry Division. Harrison then studied language for three years in France and Spain before returning to West Point in 1922 as an instructor. After graduating from Cavalry School in 1923, he served with the 7th Cavalry, the 26th Cavalry School in the Philippines, and the 2d Cavalry. From 1932 to 1934, Harrison attended the Command and General Staff School, remaining there as an instructor until he went to the Army War College in 1937. In 1939, he joined the War Plans Division of the War Department General Staff, three years later becoming deputy chief for the strategic plans and policy group.

During World War II, Harrison served with the 78th and 30th Infantry Divisions and in 1944 was wounded fighting in France. In 1945, he became commander of the 2d Infantry Division in Czechoslovakia before returning to the United States to command the 38th Regimental Combat Team while it underwent mountain and winter weather training at Camp Carson, Colorado. In 1946, Harrison went to Japan and there served as CINCFE General Douglas MacArthur's* assistant in charge of administrative affairs and reparations. Promoted to brigadier general in 1948, he returned to the United States the following year to assume responsibility for troop information and education in the office of the chief of staff. Harrison worked for the secretary of defense during 1950 and then was with the 9th Infantry Training Division. In December 1951, he went to Korea as deputy commander of the 8th Army*, joining the UNC negotiating team at P'anmunjŏm in January 1952.

After replacing Joy as the UNC's chief delegate, Harrison attended sessions wearing an open-collar khaki shirt rather than a dress uniform because he viewed the Communists with contempt as "common criminals." An opponent of compromise, he had "a style of talking bluntly or not at all." During the summer of 1952, Harrison was calm and unruffled in response to Communist denunciations regarding the Kŏje-do POW uprising* and the biological warfare controversy*. After these angry exchanges, he recommended that the Truman administration approve an indefinite recess if the Communists refused to accept the UNC position on agenda item 4*, POW repatriation, the final issue preventing an armistice. Approval of this recommendation led to the truce talks suspension of October 8, 1952*. During March 1953, however, the Chinese modified their position on the repatriation question, thus ending the stalemate and reducing Harrison's role to merely working out the details of the final settlement. After he signed the armistice agreement*, Harrison remained with the 8th Army until April 1954 when he became commander of the new U.S. Army Caribbean Forces. A deeply religious man, Harrison was a Baptist lay evangelist who often preached to the troops and frowned on drinking, smoking, and swearing. He returned to prominence during the 1960 presidential campaign when he voiced concern about whether John F. Kennedy, a Catholic, should be president, fearing he would be open to pressure from the pope.

J. L. Collins, *War in Peacetime* (Boston, 1969); *Current Biography,* 1952; *New York Times,* May 29, 1987; D. Rees, *Korea: The Limited War* (New York, 1964); E. W. Schoenebaum (ed.), *Political Profiles: The Eisenhower Years* (New York, 1977).

HEARTBREAK RIDGE, BATTLE OF
See Battle of Heartbreak Ridge

HENDERSON, LOY W. (1892–1986)
Loy W. Henderson held the post of U.S. ambassador to India at the time the Korean War began. He was born in Arkansas and educated at Northwestern

University. After serving with the Red Cross during World War I, he entered government service in 1921 and held numerous diplomatic posts, including a tour in Moscow from 1934 to 1938. While assigned to the State Department's European desk during World War II, he gained a reputation as a hardliner, suspicious of Soviet intentions. Since his views did not coincide with the position of the Roosevelt administration, he was transferred to Iraq in 1943, where he became chief of mission. After serving in Washington from 1945 to 1948, he was appointed ambassador to India (1948–1951) and then to Iran (1951–55).

Henderson found himself in a diplomatically sensitive position when the Korean War began. Since there were no formal diplomatic relations between the United States and the People's Republic of China*, India became a diplomatic conduit between the two nations. For its part, India as a neutral nation feared that events in Korea could escalate and create problems. Henderson endeavored to exploit India's diplomatic position to find a settlement for the conflict. On one occasion, on orders from Washington, he urged Prime Minister Jawaharlal Nehru* to allow the Indian UN delegation to support the UN Security Council resolution of June 27, 1950*, condemning the North Korean attack. India was sitting on the Security Council at the time, and Nehru worried about angering the Soviet Union and China. Nevertheless, it took little persuading to secure Nehru's support.

On another occasion, during July 1950, Indian diplomats tried to arrange a cease-fire. But for the United States, this was poor timing, since the UNC* was on the defensive. Furthermore, the plan the Indians proposed would have linked a cease-fire to U.S. guarantees that the PRC would receive a seat on the Security Council and that support for the Republic of China* would cease. Henderson concurred with Washington's position that a cease-fire could not be linked to such conditions, conveying this to Indian officials. In late September 1950, after UN forces had staged a counterattack, Henderson learned from Indian diplomats that Chinese forces would undoubtedly intervene if UN forces pushed north of the thirty-eighth parallel. Henderson urged that this information be taken seriously, but Washington discounted his and other warnings. After transfer to Iran, Henderson had little further direct involvement in the Korean conflict. *See also* Indian Peace Initiatives.

D. Acheson, *Present at the Creation* (New York, 1969); G. Baer (ed.), *A Question of Trust* (Stanford, Calif., 1986); L. W. Henderson, oral history interview, Harry S. Truman Library, Independence, Missouri; W. W. Stueck, *The Road to Confrontation* (Chapel Hill, 1981).

T. Michael Ruddy

HICKERSON, JOHN D. (1898–1989)

John Hickerson, assistant secretary of state for UN affairs, played a central role in U.S. policy and diplomacy toward Korea from mid-1949 to July 1953. Born and raised in Texas, he served in the U.S. Army during World War I and completed his B.A. at the University of Texas in 1920. Entering the consular service almost immediately, Hickerson served several years in Latin America.

After receiving appointment in the foreign service in 1924, he worked his way up to the position of assistant chief of the Division of Western European Affairs in six years. In 1947, Hickerson became director of the Office of European Affairs, where he became a key figure in the creation of the NATO. Soon after the United States signed the North Atlantic Treaty in April 1949, Hickerson took over leadership of UN affairs in the State Department, a position for which he was well prepared given his role as adviser to the U.S. delegation to the San Francisco Conference in 1945.

Hickerson was one of the first officers called to the State Department on the evening of June 24, 1950, after word arrived of the North Korean invasion of South Korea*. As indicated in contingency plans, he recommended that the matter be referred to the UN Security Council. Through the night and well into the next day, Hickerson took a prominent role in arranging for an emergency meeting of that body and in preparing a draft resolution to present to it. He also attended the first and second Blair House meetings*. At the second meeting, he read to the group a draft resolution to follow up the UN Security Council resolution of June 25, 1950*. Presented the next day, the UN Security Council resolution of June 27, 1950*, was adopted.

Hickerson continued to play an important part in drafting U.S. resolutions on Korea, in coordinating actions between the State Department and the U.S. delegation at the UN, and in dealing with allied and neutral nations. In January 1951, with dissatisfaction at a peak over U.S. conduct of the war, he became a backup to Dean Rusk*, the assistant secretary for Far Eastern Affairs, in the Korean War briefing meetings* for allied ambassadors regarding the developing situation in Korea. When Rusk left the State Department at the end of the year, Hickerson took over the main responsibility for those briefings. In general, however, he was less influential than Rusk as a policymaker on Korea and less effective as a briefer in mollifying allied concerns. When the war ended in July 1953, Hickerson joined the faculty of the National War College, serving later as ambassador to Finland and the Philippines.

Current Biography, 1950; Foreign Relations of the United States, 1950, vol. 7: Korea (Washington, D.C, 1976), 1951, vol. 7: Korea and China (Washington, D.C., 1983), and 1952–1954, vol. 15: Korea (Washington, D.C., 1984); G. D. Paige, The Korean Decision (New York, 1968); State Department, Biographic Register, 1961–62.

William Stueck

HICKEY, DOYLE O. (1892–1961)

During the Korean War, Major General Doyle O. Hickey was deputy chief of staff under CINCUNC General Douglas MacArthur* and chief of staff under CINCUNC General Matthew B. Ridgway*. He was born in Rector, Arkansas and, after graduating from Hendrix College in 1912, went to work for a lumber company in Memphis, Tennessee. In 1917, Hickey joined the U.S. Army Field Artillery Reserve and, after undergoing officer training from 1917 to 1918, received more artillery training in France during World War I. Beginning in 1919, he spent four years with the 1st Field Artillery at Fort Sill and graduated from Field Artillery School in 1924. After serving with the 10th and 3d Field Artillery, Hickey went to the Philippines and held various positions with the 24th Field Artillery from 1927 to 1930. He was with the 7th Field Artillery for two years before assuming responsibility for park police and building guards in Washington, D.C., as chief of the U.S. Army protection division. Following graduation in 1936 from Command and General Staff School, Hickey served with the 10th Field Artillery and then returned to the Philippines in 1938 as aide to the commander at Fort Stotsenburg. In 1940, he was at Fort Bragg with the 9th Field Artillery.

When the United States entered World War II, Hickey was executive officer at the Field Artillery Replacement Training Center. Subsequently, he served with the office of the chief of field artillery and the Army Ground Forces headquarters at Fort Knox. In 1944, Brigadier General Hickey traveled to France as commander of the 3d Armored Division, leading the 1st U.S. Army in its advance from St. Lo to the Siegfried Line during July and August. His unit played a key role in halting the German offensive at the Battle of the Bulge and then led the 1st Army across the Remagen Bridge. Following World War II, Hickey spent time with U.S. Army Ground Forces and Army Field Forces before he went to Tokyo in 1949 as deputy chief of staff for the Far Eastern Command. In September 1950, he became acting chief of staff when MacArthur appointed Major General Edward M. Almond* as commander of the X Corps*. Not only did he help plan military operations in the Korean War, but Hickey was able to persuade MacArthur not to resign after Washington refused to approve bombing of the Yalu bridges early in November 1950. In April 1951, Hickey, now a lieutenant general, was in effect acting CINCUNC prior to Ridgway's arrival in Japan after President Harry S. Truman's* recall of MacArthur*. For the rest of the Korean War, Hickey served as chief of staff, retiring in 1953 and devoting his time thereafter to horse training.

C. Blair, *The Forgotten War* (New York, 1987); *National Cyclopedia of American Biography*, vol. 50 (Ann Arbor, Mich., 1971); *New York Times,* October 21, 1961.

HIGGINS, MARGUERITE (1920–1966)

A war correspondent for the *New York Herald,* Marguerite Higgins was the only female reporter during the Korean conflict. In 1951, she won a Pulitzer Prize for her warfront reports and also wrote a book based on her experiences, *War in Korea: Report of a Woman Combat Correspondent.* Higgins was born in Hong Kong and educated in France and Britain. In 1941, she graduated from the University of California at Berkeley and earned an M.A. the following year from Columbia University's School of Journalism. Already a reporter on campus affairs for the *New York Herald,* Higgins went to work for the newspaper full time on the city staff, although she was more interested in obtaining an assignment overseas to report on World War II. In 1944, she went to London and then accompanied the 7th U.S. Army's advance through France and Austria, filing battlefield reports along the way. By 1945, Higgins was chief of the Berlin bureau for the *New York Herald* and covered the Allied liberation of the concentration camps at Buchenwald and Dachau. Subsequently, her stories focused on a variety of topics, including wives of Nazi officers, the Nuremburg trials, and the Polish elections.

In 1950, Higgins went to Tokyo as a correspondent on events in East Asia. As a result, she was one of the first journalists to arrive in Seoul following the North Korean invasion of South Korea*. She fled the city with other American nationals on June 27, crossing the Han River on a raft and returning to Tokyo. However, Higgins was at Suwŏn when General Douglas MacArthur* made his visit to Korea of June 29, 1950*. Flying back to Tokyo aboard the *Bataan,* MacArthur told Higgins, during an exclusive interview, that the South Korean Army was in good condition but lacked effective leadership. He therefore intended to recommend the commitment of U.S. ground forces. Lieutenant General Walton W. Walker*, commander of the 8th Army*, wanted to bar her from entering combat zones, but Higgins appealed to MacArthur, who lifted the ban. "Korea," as she later explained, "was more than just a story. It was a personal crusade. I felt that my position as a correspondent was at stake. . . . I could not let the fact that I was a woman jeopardize my newspaper's coverage of the war."

After Chinese military intervention*, her reports made the Hŭngnam evacuation* famous in the United States. Higgins was smart, tough, determined, and courageous, helping save the lives of many wounded soldiers and earning much praise and respect. One U.S. officer commented that "Maggie wears mud like other women wear make-up." After the Korean War, she stayed in Asia until 1958, then returning to Washington, D.C., as a diplomatic correspondent. Higgins died of a rare tropical disease she contracted during a tour of Vietnam, Pakistan, and India. Her book on Korea does not offer a broad perspective, but it nevertheless includes valuable firsthand information on a personal level about the war.

C. Blair, *The Forgotten War* (New York, 1987); *Current Biography,* 1951; *New York Times,* January 4, 1966; *Who Was Who in America,* vol. 4: *1961–1968* (Chicago, 1968).

HODGE, JOHN R. (1893–1963)

Lieutenant General John R. Hodge was commanding officer of U.S. Armed Forces in Korea (USAFIK) during the period of military occupation from September 1945 until the formal establishment of the Republic of Korea* in August 1948. Born in Golconda, Illinois, he began his military training in May 1917 at Fort Sheridan's Advanced Officers Training School. After seeing combat in France during World War I, he became a professor of military science and tactics at Mississippi A&M College in 1921, leaving that post to begin intensive advanced military training in 1925 at army staff schools and the Army War College. Hodge served five years on the War Department General Staff prior to Pearl Harbor and then fought with distinction in World War II. Wounded at Bougainville, he also saw heavy action as commander of the Americal Division in the Solomons. In April 1944, Hodge assumed command of the XXIV Corps and prepared it to conduct amphibious operations against the Japanese in the Marianas and the Carolines. After a change in strategy, his unit fought at Leyte and on Okinawa. Hodge had a reputation as a "soldier's soldier," sharing hardships with his troops at the front.

During August 1945, the War Department separated Hodge and his XXIV Corps from the 10th Army and instructed it to occupy Korea south of the thirty-eighth parallel. Hodge received no more occupation guidelines from Washington for six months, making more difficult his task of responding to the revolutionary climate existing in Korea upon his arrival. From the start, Hodge's highest priority was the preservation of law and order. Because of his lack of administrative training, political experience, or familiarity with Korean history and culture, he committed numerous errors while occupation commander. Most significant was his reliance on wealthy and conservative landlords and businessmen, including some Koreans who had collaborated with the Japanese. Hodge also worried constantly about Soviet occupation of northern Korea and the military threat it posed to his command. Simple, blunt, and direct in approach, he advocated early U.S. military withdrawal from Korea* and was a persistent opponent of trusteeship.

Although Hodge assisted Syngman Rhee* and other Korean conservative exile leaders in their return to Korea in late 1945, they later became bitter enemies. This occurred because Hodge tried to fashion a moderate political coalition in 1946 and then refused to hold quick elections for a separate government in the south. In another key blunder, Hodge proceeded to undermine the moderates but without placating the conservatives. Rhee never forgave Hodge, and it led to his relief and return to the United States. Following his recall, Hodge assumed various posts until President Harry S. Truman* appointed him commander of Army Field Forces in June 1952, a post he held until his retirement the next year.

B. Cumings, *The Origins of the Korean War* (Princeton, 1981); C. M. Dobbs, *The Unwanted Symbol* (Kent, Ohio, 1981); G. Henderson, *Korea: The Politics of the Vortex* (Cambridge, 1968); J. I. Matray, *The Reluctant Crusade* (Honolulu, 1985); *New York Times*, November 13, 1963.

HOME-BY-CHRISTMAS OFFENSIVE (November 24, 1950)

CINCUNC General Douglas MacArthur* planned and executed this massive campaign to end the Korean War, restore peace and unity to the peninsula, and allow the gradual withdrawal of United Nations forces. Following the victorious Inch'ŏn landing* and recapture of Seoul operation*, UN troops crossed the thirty-eighth parallel. The Yalu River and Manchuria appeared within easy striking distance as the UN offensive across the thirty-eighth parallel* got underway. In late October and early November 1950, Communist Chinese soldiers were captured in several engagements, demonstrating the reality of Chinese military intervention* in the war. MacArthur, however, viewed full Chinese participation as unlikely and disregarded the incidents. On November 24, 1950, the Home-by-Christmas offensive (as it later came to be known) was launched to force the Democratic People's Republic of Korea* to capitulate and end the war. MacArthur may have picked this date to intimidate the People's Republic of China*, since the PRC's representative arrived at the UN that same day to discuss China's intentions regarding the war. The principal UN forces, consisting of the 8th Army* (EUSAK) and the X Corps*, were each to strike separately toward the Yalu River before linking to engulf the North Korean People's Army (NKPA). EUSAK attacked first, driving north from Sinanju to Kangji and Chasan, and northeast to Sinŭiju. Three days later, on November 27, the X Corps launched an attack on the western front from Changjin, cutting off the main road to the Yalu and striking the NKPA from the rear.

Initially, little resistance was encountered. However, fighting intensified as the Chinese People's Volunteers Army* struck the UN line, driving a deep wedge into the center and dividing EUSAK and the X Corps. The campaign to end the war turned into a rout as an entirely different war developed. In retrospect, the Chinese were compelled to act given the presence of large numbers of U.S. armed forces near the Manchurian border. Still, while reconnaissance failed to convince MacArthur of the scope of Chinese involvement, the early warning signs were clearly ignored by the veteran commander. The EUSAK and the X Corps were the real losers in this ill-fated debacle. Its failure ultimately persuaded President Harry S. Truman* to abandon reunification as a war aim in favor of restoring the division at the thirty-eighth parallel. *See also* Chosin Reservoir Campaign; CIA Report: Threat of Full Chinese Communist Intervention in Korea; MacArthur's Reconnaissance in Force; NSC-81.

R. E. Appleman, *East of Chosin: Entrapment and Breakout in Korea, 1950* (College Station, Texas, 1987); R. E. Appleman, *South to the Naktong, North to the Yalu* (Washington, D.C., 1961); J. F. Schnabel, *Policy and Direction* (Washington, D.C., 1972); J. W. Spanier, *The Truman-MacArthur Controversy and the Korean War* (Cambridge, 1959); I. F. Stone, *The Hidden History of the Korean War* (New York, 1952).

John Neilson

HOOK, BATTLES OF THE
See Battles of the Hook

HOOVER'S GIBRALTAR AMERICA ADDRESS (December 20, 1950)
In this radio address, former president Herbert Hoover suggested that the United States curb its commitments in Europe and concentrate on making the Western Hemisphere a "Gibraltar of Civilization." His timing was auspicious; he gave the speech shortly after the powerful Republican senator, Robert A. Taft*, gave a speech questioning the Truman administration's policy in Europe and two days after Dwight D. Eisenhower* had been named commander of expanded NATO forces in Europe. Further, he spoke at a time of great public uneasiness in the United States about foreign affairs and about the chance of a new world war—U.S. and UN forces were reeling from the new Chinese military intervention* in the Korean War, the debate inside and outside the government

about atomic weapons continued, and Americans feared Soviet intentions in Asia and Europe.

Hoover argued that the United States could not afford to act as the world's policeman; other nations would have to assume primary responsibility for their defense against Communist aggression—with U.S. encouragement. The main Communist foes, the United States and Britain, Hoover noted, had a population of 300 million and 60 combat divisions, whereas the Communist nations had 800 million and 300 combat divisions. Americans could not possibly stop communism everywhere without destroying their already-strained economy. Instead, he proposed that the nation use its naval and air power to control the Western Hemisphere and such island outposts as Britain, Japan, the Philippines, and Taiwan. After initial spending on improved sea and air forces, military expenditures would drop because of decreased spending on a land army. The nation could then balance its budget, halt inflation, and spend money on domestic uses, such as education. In short, he implied, Europe and Asia could come under Soviet influence without undermining U.S. security.

Reaction to the speech was swift; telegrams and telephone calls began pouring into Hoover's office even before he returned from the broadcast studio. Congress was also deluged with mail. Positive responses outnumbered the negative, but influential critics blasted Hoover's proposals. President Harry S. Truman*, the *New Republic,* and the liberal historian, Arthur M. Schlesinger, Jr., described the suggestions as isolationism. Hoover had opened the so-called Great Debate over foreign policy that would occupy politicians during the first half of 1951. Republicans used the issue to hammer the Democrats but also argued among themselves about the Hoover doctrine. The internationalist wing of the party, headed by Governor Thomas E. Dewey of New York and John Foster Dulles*, favored worldwide intervention against the Soviet menace but disliked the means the Truman administration was currently using. *See also* Congress and the Korean War.

G. D. Best, *Herbert Hoover: The Postpresidential Years, 1933–1964,* vol. 2: *1946–1964* (Stanford, Calif., 1983); J. L. Gaddis, *Strategies of Containment* (New York, 1982); B. I. Kaufman, *The Korean War* (Philadelphia, 1986).

Richard W. Fanning

HOT PURSUIT

A JCS directive of September 27, 1950, forbade operations across the Chinese border. On November 7, 1950, CINCUNC General Douglas MacArthur* asked for instructions, implying that he wanted authority to pursue hostile aircraft across the frontier. MacArthur complained that with Chinese intervention, hostile planes based across the Yalu River were operating against his command in increasing numbers. Since the distance between the Yalu border and the main line of resistance was small, it was almost impossible to deal effectively with the "hit and run tactics now being employed." This was having a major adverse effect on the morale of his air and ground forces. On November 13, 1950, Washington sent a message to the UN allies noting that it might become necessary "to permit UN aircraft to defend themselves in the air space over the Yalu River to the extent of permitting hot pursuit of attacking enemy aircraft up to 2 or 3 minutes flying time into Manchuria air space." This would be "a minimum reaction to extreme provocation" and would "add greatly to the morale of UN pilots." The UN allies, however, were strongly opposed to any move that might widen the war or give MacArthur more power, and the proposal was abandoned. On April 28, 1951, MacArthur's successor, Lieutenant General Matthew B. Ridgway*, received JCS authorization to retaliate against Manchurian air bases in the event of an attack that endangered the safety of his command, which the UN allies endorsed in principle.

Hot pursuit was revived by the JCS in July 1951 as part of a series of proposed military moves if armistice negotiations failed. The idea was dropped, however, because of the steady buildup of Chinese air strength in Manchuria. It was feared that hot pursuit would expose the air force to unacceptable rates of attrition and force the diversion of scarce modern jets to Korea. Although the restriction on violating Chinese air space remained in force throughout the war, there is evidence that it was often ignored by pilots who routinely crossed the Yalu in the course of air combat. *See also* Chinese Military Disengagement of November 6, 1950; Manchurian Sanctuary.

R. Foot, *The Wrong War* (Ithaca, N.Y., 1985); C. A. MacDonald, *Korea: The War Before Vietnam* (London, 1986); D. Stairs, *The Diplomacy of Constraint* (Toronto, 1974); H. S. Truman, *Years of Trial and Hope* (Garden City, N.Y., 1956).

Callum A. MacDonald

HSIEH FANG (XIE FANG; 1904–   )

Hsieh Fang, chief of staff of the Chinese People's Volunteers Army* (CPVA) during the Korean War, was born in Chilin province. He started his military career by entering the Northeast Military Academy and then went to Japan for further study. An outstanding student, Hsieh returned home after graduation and served as a staff officer in the Kuomintang (KMT) Northeast Army, which received orders in 1935 to fight the Chinese Communist army in Shensi province. Shrewd as well as knowledgeable in military affairs and public relations, he earned the trust of Chang Hsueh-liang, the young marshal of the army. But in late 1936, when the Sian incident occurred, Hsieh joined the Chinese Communist party (CCP), while remaining in the KMT army. During the Sino-Japanese War, he commanded a brigade fighting around Shantung province. In 1939, he took his troops—some several thousand men—and joined the Communist army. Then Hsieh went to the Soviet Union to study modern warfare tactics and strategy. In 1943, he returned to China and taught in the CCP's Central Party Academy. Two years later, Hsieh was sent to northeast China to contact and organize the Korean Communists, who were fighting in Manchuria. Thus, he established a special relationship with the later leaders of the Democratic People's Republic of Korea*. Throughout the Chinese Civil War, Hsieh made great contributions by instigating many defections of the KMT army. When the war ended, he became garrison commander of the city of Ch'angsha.

In June 1950, Hsieh was called northward and appointed the chief of the 13th Group Army. Soon he received the order to cross the Yalu River as vice-chief and then chief of staff of the CPVA. Hsieh joined in the planning and commanding of all five Chinese offensives, but his special contribution to the war was maintaining cooperation between the Chinese and the North Korean armies by exploiting his personal relations with the DPRK's leadership. In 1951, he joined the Communist delegation at the Kaesŏng truce talks* as the second representative of the CPVA. The North Korean representatives usually looked to Hsieh for guidance on every decision, so he played a much more important role than Teng Hua*, the first CPVA representative. Vice-Admiral C. Turner Joy*, the UNC's* chief delegate, was highly impressed with Hsieh's arguments, considering him to be more powerful than even Kim Il Sung*. In 1953, after the armistice was reached, Hsieh returned to China and became chief of the training department on the general staff of the People's Liberation Army. Two years later, he gained promotion to major general. After 1959, Hsieh became involved in military education, focusing on the cooperation between different types of forces during combat actions. He was dean of the Chinese Military Academy until the start of the Great Proletarian Cultural Revolution.

Huang Chen-hsia, *Mao's Generals* (Hong Kong, 1968); Institute of International Relations, *Chinese Communist Who's Who* (Taipei, 1971); *Who's Who in Modern China* (Tokyo, 1978).

Li Yi

HULL, JOHN E. (1895–1975)

On October 7, 1953, shortly after the Korean War ended, General John E. Hull replaced General Mark W. Clark* as CINCUNC. Remaining in this post until his retirement in 1955, he was responsible for implementing the terms of the armistice agreement*, especially cooperating with the Neutral Nations Repatriation Commission*(NNRC) in disposing of the unrepatriated POWs. Born in Greenfield, Ohio, he graduated from Miami University in 1917 and earned his commission as a second lieutenant in the U.S. Infantry Reserve. That fall, after obtaining a regular army commission, Hull went to France with the 4th Infantry Division, seeing action at St. Mihiel and in the Aisne-Marne and Meuse-Argonne offensives. After World War I, he graduated from Infantry School (1924) and then was an assistant professor of military science and tactics at the University of Wisconsin from 1924 to 1932, holding the same position later at Louisiana State University. Hull graduated from Command and General Staff School in 1936, returning there as instructor in 1938 after completing a tour at the Army War College.

When the United States entered World War II, Hull was disappointed when he did not receive a combat command. Instead, his assignment was with the War Department General Staff. By 1944, he had become assistant chief of staff in charge of the operations division, earning promotion to brigadier general the following year. From 1946 to 1948, Hull was commanding general of the U.S. Armed Forces in the Pacific, supervising the first atomic test on Eniwitok. After returning to Washington, D.C., he served as director of the weapons systems evaluation group (1949–1951), deputy chief of staff for operations and administration (1951), and vice-chief of staff (1951–1953). In 1953, when he became CINCUNC, one writer labeled Hull "the general that nobody knows" because he had been behind the scenes throughout his career. In his first speech in Tokyo, he strongly urged Japan to strengthen itself militarily. Hull adopted a firm position with the NNRC, demanding approval for the release of those POWs resisting repatriation no later than January 22, 1954. Although his relations with K. S. Thimayya*, the NNRC's chairman, were often strained, he regained control of the POWs and released them to civilian status in compliance with his schedule. In 1955, General Maxwell D. Taylor* replaced him as CINCUNC. Modest, self-confident, and easy-going, Hull retired from the U.S. Army that same year and became president of the Manufacturing Chemists Association.

Current Biography, 1954; Foreign Relations of the United States, 1952–1954, vol. 15: *Korea* (Washington, D.C., 1984); *Who Was Who in America*, vol. 6: *1977–1979* (Chicago, 1979).

HŬNGNAM EVACUATION (December 9–24, 1950)

On November 28, 1950, Vice-Admiral C. Turner Joy*, commander of Naval Forces Far East (COMNAVFE), informed Rear Admiral James H. Doyle, commander of Amphibious Force Far East (Task Force 90), that he should begin planning the redeployment of all UN forces from North Korea. The orders reflected the uncertainty of the situation following Chinese military intervention* and the UNC* retreat in North Korea: Doyle was to begin preparation for either an administrative operation or a full-scale emergency withdrawal. The following day, a dispatch from Joy clarified the situation. The military positions of both Lieutenant General Walton Walker's* 8th Army* in the west and Major General Edward Almond's* X Corps*, spread thin around the Chosin Reservoir, were rapidly deteriorating. Joy placed Task Force 90, in Japan for upkeep and replenishment, on six-hour alert. On November 30, with the situation critical, Task Force 90 was ordered to Korean waters.

Not until December 9 did CINCUNC General Douglas MacArthur* formally order the evacuation by sea, despite COMNAVFE's preparations and the retreat of Almond's forces beginning a week earlier when the marines broke out at Yudam-ri. Admiral Joy granted complete responsibility for the east coast evacuation, through Hŭngnam, to Doyle. Rear Admiral Lyman Thackrey, commander Amphibious Group Three (Task Force 90.1), controlled the west coast evacuation of the 8th Army from Inch'ŏn and Chinnamp'o. Almond's operation orders called for the embarkation of the 1st Marine Division, the Republic of Korea's* 3d and Capital divisions, and the U.S. 7th and 3d Infantry divisions in that order. Evacuation began on December 10 as the 1st Marine Division arrived in

Hŭngnam. Departure of the remaining troops followed rapidly: the ROK* forces on December 17, the U.S. 7th Division on December 21, and the U.S. 3d on Christmas Eve.

The military evacuation progressed with little difficulty. Vice-Admiral Arthur Struble's 7th Fleet and Rear Admiral E. C. Ewen's Task Force 77 provided air cover, while Rear Admiral Roscoe H. Hillenkoetter's Gunfire Support Group 90.8 supplied naval gunfire support and night illumination. Military analysts disagree about whether the heavy concentration of support forces or the incredibly heavy losses already sustained by the Chinese People's Volunteers Army*— estimated to be 72,500 battle and nonbattle casualties, or 60 percent of the force—deterred an enemy attack on the Hŭngnam perimeter. Statistics on the evacuation are impressive. Over fourteen days, 105,000 military personnel, 17,500 vehicles, 350,000 measured tons of cargo, and 91,000 Korean refugees, were evacuated from the port. *See also* Chosin Reservoir Campaign; Home-by-Christmas Offensive.

C. Blair, *The Forgotten War* (New York, 1987); M. W. Cagle and F. A. Manson, *The Sea War in Korea* (Annapolis, 1957); L. Montross and N. A. Canzona, *U. S. Marine Operations in Korea 1950–1953,* vol 3: *The Chosin Reservoir Campaign* (Annapolis, 1957).

Lynne K. Dunn

I

IMJIN RIVER, BATTLE OF THE
See Battle of the Imjin River

INCH'ŎN LANDING (September 15, 1950)

This was the key military operation early in the Korean War that resulted in the retreat of the North Korean People's Army (NKPA) north of the thirty-eighth parallel. On D day, September 15, naval vessels under the UNC* along with U.S. naval and marine air units began a shore bombardment of key enemy strongholds—especially Wolmi-do—in preparation for the assault on Inch'ŏn 40 miles west of Seoul. At 7:00 A.M., the 5th Marine Division, constituting the advance force of the X Corps*, landed at Inch'ŏn behind enemy lines, and Operation Chromite* was in motion. By the end of the day, invasion forces were in control of the fortress on Wolmi-do and about a third of the city. In general, the attacking forces had met only slight resistance. By D day plus one, the 5th Marine Division had secured the hilly high ground overlooking Inch'ŏn proper, as well as the access road to Seoul. Early in the morning of September 16, the 1st Marine Division reached the access road and linked up with elements of the 5th Marine Division in preparation for the advance on the capital.

Major General Edward M. Almond* was given command of X Corps; he, in turn, gave the bulk of the responsibility for recapturing Seoul to Major General Oliver P. Smith*, who commanded the 1st Marine Division. The 7th Infantry Division, under Major General David G. Barr*, was to provide protection for the attacking marine division's right flank. The initial objective, Kimp'o Airfield, was cleared and in the hands of the X Corps by September 18. Although the recapture of Seoul operation* would be a much tougher assignment, once accomplished on September 29, the X Corps was free to pursue the fleeing remnants of the NKPA southward into the waiting arms of Lieutenant General Walton H. Walker's* 8th Army*. The Inch'ŏn landing reversed the course of the Korean War, added to CINCUNC General Douglas MacArthur's* reputation as a military genius, and set the stage for the UN offensive across the thirty-eighth parallel*.

H. J. Middleton, *The Compact History of the Korean War* (New York, 1965); L. Montross and N. A. Canzona, *United States Marine Operations in Korea 1950–1953*, vol. 2: *The Inchon-Seoul Operations* (Washington, D.C., 1955); J. F. Schnabel, *Policy and Direction* (Washington, D.C., 1972).

David J. Wright

INDIAN PEACE INITIATIVES (1950)

These consisted of several ill-fated efforts by the Indian government to mediate a negotiated settlement to the Korean War during the early stages of the fighting. Although India in June 1950 supported the UN Security Council resolutions of June 25* and June 27, 1950*, which called for a halt to North Korean aggression and for member state assistance to the Republic of Korea*, Prime Minister Jawaharlal Nehru* never felt entirely comfortable with the military undertaking. Adhering to a nonaligned foreign policy in the cold war and viewing Asia as an area of special interest to India, Nehru sought to minimize the possibility of a superpower conflict and to find a peaceful resolution of the Korean issue.

The Indian leader undertook his first peace initiative during the second week of July when he made coordinated overtures to the governments of the United States, the Soviet Union, and the People's Republic of China*. While the specifics of Nehru's proposal varied somewhat depending upon whom the Indian addressed, it included provisions for seating the PRC, ending the Soviet UN Security Council boycott*, and a concerted effort by those powers to seek a cease-fire in Korea and the eventual reunification of the peninsula. The Nehru initiative coincided with a similar British plan, and in fact the two Commonwealth partners had conferred on the matter. While the Indian peace effort won a polite but noncommittal response from the Soviets and the Chinese, Washington reacted angrily. Over the previous year, the Truman administration had already taken issue with India regarding diplomatic recognition for China. At this point, the administration proved unwilling to accept China's entry into the UN as a precondition for ending the Korean War. Thus, the Indian initiative quickly lost momentum.

In mid-August, India renewed its diplomatic efforts. In an informal meeting of the non-Communist members of the Security Council, Sir Benegal N. Rau*, the Indian delegate to the UN, suggested that a committee of nonpermanent representatives be formed to study proposals for a cease-fire. Neither Washington nor Moscow, however, responded warmly, and the Indian delegate never formally introduced the plan. Sir Benegal made another attempt at conciliation in October 1950—after the UNC* had announced its intention to move troops across the thirty-eighth parallel and China had warned India's ambassador in Peking, K. M. Panikkar*, that the crossing would ensure its entry into the war. Again, the Indians recommended a special subcommittee to explore possible compromises, and again the effort came to no avail. Finally, in December, India led a thirteen-member Asian-Arab bloc in the General Assembly in calling for creation of a three-person committee to seek a cease-fire and a general conference on East Asian affairs to deal with matters such as China's diplomatic recognition. While the United States adamantly opposed the latter, the Soviets refused to consider cease-fire proposals until UN troops had been withdrawn from Korea. *See also* Arab-Asian Peace Initiatives; British Peace Initiatives; NSC-80; NSC-95; UN Ceasefire Group.

D. Acheson, *Present at the Creation* (New York, 1969); B. I. Kaufman, *The Korean War* (Philadelphia, 1986); W. W. Stueck, *The Road to Confrontation* (Chapel Hill, 1981).

Dennis Merrill

IRON TRIANGLE

This label refers to a triangular geographic area located just north of the thirty-eighth parallel roughly in the center of the Korean peninsula. The final demarcation line and DMZ included in the armistice agreement* ending the Korean War ran through this area, with the cities of P'yŏnggang in the north, Ch'ŏrwon in the west, and Kŭmhwa in the east marking each corner of the triangle. The Iron Triangle received its name after the war developed into a bloody stalemate in the spring of 1951 because this area was heavily defended and therefore witnessed some of the fiercest fighting of the entire conflict.

J

JACKSON, C. D. (1902–1964)

C. D. (Charles Douglas) Jackson entered the White House at the beginning of 1953 as President Dwight D. Eisenhower's* special assistant for cold war planning. Formerly an executive with Henry Luce's Time-Life-Fortune chain, Jackson had served with Eisenhower during World War II as an expert in psychological warfare. He brought to his new post a belief that the arts of propaganda and covert operations could go far toward enabling the United States to win the cold war without having to fire a shot. Jackson considered the Korean conflict, as it had developed by the spring of 1953, an obvious field for the application of the principles of psychological warfare. Indeed, he believed the Communists had stolen a march on the United States in this area, with their attempts to convince the world of America's guilt in the biological warfare controversy* and their efforts to manipulate the P'anmunjŏm truce talks* to cloak continued aggression. Jackson warned American negotiators against what he and his associates at the operations coordinating board—Eisenhower's clearinghouse for covert activities—called "war by ceasefire." In addition, he also devised a propaganda program for preventing the demoralization of South Koreans as it became clear that President Syngman Rhee* and his followers would not succeed in liberating the north. This plan also would encourage South Korean compliance with the terms of an armistice and promote democracy in the Republic of Korea*.

After the July armistice agreement*, Jackson organized a public relations campaign for the Geneva Conference of 1954*. Working through CIA-sponsored Radio Free Europe, Jackson's office presented the Geneva meeting as the "China crimes conference" and variants thereof. Jackson plotted schemes for introducing rumors and doctored reports behind Communist lines, thus weakening the cohesion of the Soviet–Chinese–North Korean alliance. Simultaneously, he orchestrated an informational offensive in the United States—making use of leaks, inspired speculation by friendly columnists, and the planting of "Delphic phrases" in speeches by administration leaders—designed to generate maximum support for the U.S. position at the conference. Jackson left the administration in the autumn of 1954 to return to Time, Inc.

H. W. Brands, *Cold Warriors: Eisenhower's Generation and American Foreign Policy* (New York, 1988); H. W. Brands, "The Dwight D. Eisenhower Administration, Syngman Rhee, and the 'Other' Geneva Conference of 1954," *Pacific Historical Review* (February 1987).

H. W. Brands

JAMIESON, ARTHUR B. (1910–   )
During 1949 and 1950, Arthur B. Jamieson was the Australian representative on the UN Commission on Korea (UNCOK) in Seoul, which submitted a report on June 24, 1950, providing evidence that the Democratic People's Republic of Korea* had started the Korean War. Jamieson joined the Australian Department of External Affairs in 1947, after war service in the Royal Australian Navy. In 1948, he succeeded S. H. Jackson as Australia's representative on the UN Temporary Commission on Korea (UNTCOK) established under the UN resolution of November 14, 1947*, and retained that post when the UNTCOK was replaced by the UNCOK under the UN resolution of December 12, 1948*. In that position he was the spokesman for Australian policy, which before the North Korean invasion of South Korea* was often at variance with that of the United States. Australia was opposed to the association of the UNTCOK with the elections of May 1948, held only in the south, but when the Interim Committee of the General Assembly rejected this view, Australia accepted the position. On instructions from his government, Jamieson was absent from the country when the Republic of Korea* was inaugurated in August 1948. This followed the Australian view that consultations between the UNTCOK and Korean representatives should be aimed at the formation of a national government in Korea, not the establishment of a partial authority following separate southern elections.

During 1949, Jamieson was often critical of the means by which ROK president Syngman Rhee* consolidated his position in South Korea, but Australian protests had little effect. In June 1950, Jamieson's reports, in conjunction with the UNCOK report on North Korean attack*, helped to identify the DPRK as the aggressor in the eyes of Australia and other Western countries. Thereafter, his reports contributed to the Australian view that the Rhee government was in many ways reactionary, brutal, and vicious. For that reason, Australian statements emphasized the importance of the UN role in maintaining collective security against aggression rather than supporting the Rhee government.

G. McCormack, *Cold War Hot War* (Sydney, 1983); R. J. O'Neill, *Australia in the Korean War 1950–53* (Canberra, 1981, 1985).

Peter Edwards

JAPANESE PEACE TREATY (September 8, 1951)
The Korean War had a profound and in some ways paradoxical effect on the evolution of the Japanese Peace Treaty. In the months preceding the war, the State Department had begun to push hard for an early treaty, while the Defense

Department and the JCS had resisted on the grounds that a number of security issues, plus JCS doubts about the domestic stability of Japan, could not yet be resolved. Just prior to the outbreak of the war, General Douglas MacArthur* tried to break this logjam by proposing that the peace be structured so that details of base rights and troop dispositions in Japan would be negotiated after the peace treaty was concluded.

During the grim UNC* retreats of the summer of 1950, the JCS insisted that a peace treaty should not go into effect until the Korean conflict was successfully resolved. On the other hand, the JCS received MacArthur's proposal favorably. In addition, they began to take Japanese public opinion into account. In war, Japan became a rear area where popular morale was important. The JCS believed that there was a "dangerous" situation in Japan, owing to the reduction—through removal to the front—of "occupation forces below safe limits." Hence the political appeasement of the Japanese population became a military necessity. Prior military reasoning was almost completely reversed by the fact of war. Instead of waiting for a peace treaty until Japan was pro-Western, it became desirable to begin negotiation of a treaty that would encourage Japan to be pro-Western.

In August 1950, the Defense Department and the JCS assented to the beginning of treaty negotiations. NSC 60/1, approved by President Harry S. Truman* early in September, formalized the government-wide decision. While the JCS were willing for multilateral negotiations to go forward, they still wanted to delay the treaty's effective date until hostilities terminated. General George C. Marshall*, who replaced Louis A. Johnson* as secretary of defense early in the fall, overruled the JCS on this issue in December. In the peace treaty concluded September 8, 1951, Japan, in accordance with the Cairo Declaration*, renounced all "right, title and claim" to Korea and recognized the "independence of Korea." An Acheson-Yoshida exchange of notes (signed along with the treaty itself) provided for certain additional facilities in Japan for U.S. and other UN forces for the duration of hostilities.

Foreign Relations of the United States, 1950, vol. 6: *Asia and the Pacific* (Washington, D.C., 1976) and *1951*, vol. 6: *Asia and the Pacific*, pt. 1 (Washington, D.C., 1977).

David W. Mabon

JCS DIRECTIVE OF DECEMBER 6, 1950

CINCUNC General Douglas MacArthur's* violation of this directive was perhaps the clearest example of his insubordination, providing reason and justification for President Harry S. Truman's* recall of MacArthur* in April 1951. The JCS issued this directive in the aftermath of Chinese military intervention* in response to MacArthur's efforts to shift blame for the military disaster from himself to the Truman administration. His Home-by-Christmas offensive*, MacArthur claimed, had failed because of restrictions on his freedom to prosecute the war. On December 1, 1950, in an interview for publication in *U.S. News and World Report*, he stated that Washington's refusal to permit him to pursue

Chinese forces into Manchuria or to allow unlimited attacks on enemy bases in China was an ''enormous handicap, without precedent in military history.'' That same day, in a letter to Hugh Baillie* of United Press, the general complained about the ''open and notorious'' Chinese support for North Korea from the start of the war ''behind the privileged sanctuary of neutral boundaries.'' He implied that U.S. allies in Europe were primarily responsible for the restrictions that had caused the military disaster.

In a December 5 memorandum to his cabinet members, Truman moved to muzzle MacArthur. ''No speech, press release, or other statement concerning foreign policy,'' the president ordered, ''should be released until it has received clearance from the Department of State.'' Comments on military policy would require approval from the Department of Defense. Although blanket in form, the directive was aimed at MacArthur, as revealed in a separate memorandum from Truman to Secretary of State Dean G. Acheson* and Secretary of Defense George C. Marshall*. ''Officials overseas,'' the president declared, ''including military commanders and diplomatic representatives, should be ordered to exercise extreme caution in public statements, to clear all but routine statements with their departments, and to refrain from direct communication on military or foreign policy with newspapers, magazines or other publicity media.'' The JCS dispatched the new policy to MacArthur on December 6. On March 15, 1951, MacArthur in a press interview argued that the UNC* should not be ordered to halt short of accomplishing its mission—''the unification of Korea''—though he was aware of Truman's planned peace initiative* proposing a cease-fire at the thirty-eighth parallel. MacArthur's ''pronunciamento''* and his letter to Joseph Martin* violated the December 6 directive as well and led to Truman's decision to relieve MacArthur of command. See also Hot Pursuit; Manchurian Sanctuary.

Foreign Relations of the United States, 1950, vol. 7: *Korea* (Washington, D.C., 1976); A. Guttmann (ed.), *Korea: Cold War and Limited War* (Lexington, Mass., 1972); C. A. MacDonald, *Korea: The War Before Vietnam* (New York, 1986).

JCS DIRECTIVE OF JANUARY 12, 1951

This JCS directive reflected Washington's reluctance to make a firm decision either to expand the war or withdraw after Chinese military intervention*. It was approved at a meeting of the NSC on January 12, presided over by President Harry S. Truman*. The meeting was held to consider CINCUNC General Douglas MacArthur's* request for clarification of a JCS directive of January 9, 1951, ordering him to hold successive positions in Korea, inflicting maximum damage on the enemy subject to the safety of his command and his overriding mission to defend Japan. The JCS reply, approved by the NSC on January 12, reiterated the importance of holding a position in Korea for as long as possible and deflating Chinese prestige. It noted that, ''based upon all the factors known to us, including particularly those presented in your recent messages, we are forced to the conclusion that it is infeasible under existing conditions, including sustained major effort by Communist China, to hold for a protracted period in Korea.'' At the same time, it was in the interests of both the United States and the UN to gain time for essential military and diplomatic consultations before initiating the evacuation of troops. It was also important to U.S. prestige, the future of the UN and NATO, and the prospects of anti-Communist resistance in Asia that "Korea not be evacuated unless actually forced by military considerations, and that maximum practicable punishment be inflicted on communist aggressors." The directive emphasized the dangers to morale of a premature decision to withdraw. News would inevitably leak out, perhaps causing a collapse of South Korean forces and hampering the ability of the 8th Army* to hold the bridgehead around Pusan required for an orderly withdrawal. The JCS closed by confirming MacArthur's directive of January 9 and thereby refusing to implement MacArthur's plan for victory*. The message was reinforced by a letter from Truman to MacArthur emphasizing the political importance of holding a position in Korea. *See also* CIA Report: Position of the United States with Respect to Communist China; Collins-Vandenberg Visit to Tokyo (January 15, 1951); NSC-101.

D. Acheson, *Present at the Creation* (London, 1970); R. J. Donovan, *Tumultuous Years* (New York, 1982); D. MacArthur, *Reminiscences* (London, 1964); H. S. Truman, *Years of Trial and Hope* (Garden City, N.Y., 1956).

Callum A. MacDonald

JCS DIRECTIVE OF MAY 31, 1951

In this cable, the JCS outlined new instructions to CINCUNC General Matthew B. Ridgway* for future military operations in Korea that, for the most part, would remain in effect until the war ended. Restoration of the battle lines at the thirty-eighth parallel in the spring of 1951 necessitated a revision of the UNC's* mission, but the Truman administration had not done so because CINCUNC General Douglas MacArthur* was publicly criticizing the strategy of limited war. When Ridgway became CINCUNC, following President Harry S. Truman's* recall of MacArthur*, he began to complain about the ambiguous and contradictory nature of his instructions, especially the JCS directive of January 12, 1951*. To clarify his mission, the JCS dispatched a cable on May 31 rescinding all previous directives and defining a future course of action reflecting the conclusions contained in NSC-48/5*, a policy paper on Asia approved two weeks earlier. Overall, the JCS imposed tighter reins on Ridgway, denying his prior requests to launch retaliatory air strikes on the People's Republic of China* to stave off a battlefield disaster, as well as authorization to withdraw the 8th Army* from Korea at his discretion to ensure the defense of Japan. The directive made no major change in earlier policy regarding possible Soviet intervention in Korea. If there was open or covert involvement of major Soviet units, Ridgway was to assume the defensive, avoid aggravating the situation, and report to the JCS.

Far more important was the Truman administration's new position on war objectives in Korea. Ridgway was to continue to "inflict maximum personnel and materiel losses" on enemy forces "within the geographic boundaries of

Korea," but now the aim was "to create conditions favorable to a settlement of the Korean conflict." This goal would include an enforceable cease-fire that guaranteed the administrative authority and military defense of the Republic of Korea* south of a boundary line at least as far north as the thirty-eighth parallel. Also, there would be provisions for the gradual withdrawal of all non-Korean armed forces from the peninsula coupled with the buildup of sufficient South Korean military power to deter or repel a renewal of Communist aggression from the north. In pursuit of these objectives, the JCS reaffirmed prohibitions against air and naval operations against Soviet territory, Manchuria, and the Yalu hydroelectric plants. Although the UNC was not to undertake a general offensive into North Korea, Ridgway was "authorized to conduct such tactical operations as may be necessary or desirable to insure safety of your command, to maintain contact, and to continue to harass the enemy." In sum, the UNC's mission was to maintain military pressure on the enemy to force acceptance of an agreement that would end the fighting and open the way to political discussions for the achievement of a united, independent, and democratic Korea.

C. Blair, *The Forgotten War* (New York, 1987); D. M. Condit, *History of the Office of the Secretary of Defense,* vol. 2: *The Test of War, 1950–1953* (Washington, D.C., 1988); *Foreign Relations of the United States, 1951,* vol. 7: *Korea and China* (Washington, D.C., 1983).

JCS REPORT ON KOREA'S STRATEGIC SIGNIFICANCE (September 29, 1947)

U.S. military leaders relied heavily on this memorandum to persuade President Harry S. Truman* to authorize U.S. military withdrawal from Korea* after two years of occupation. When the Soviet Union refused to permit reunification, Secretary of State James F. Byrnes had helped to negotiate the Moscow Agreement to remove the division at the thirty-eighth parallel. However, by the summer of 1947, the Joint Soviet-American Commission, set up to implement the Moscow Agreement, was hopelessly deadlocked, and the Truman administration adopted SWNCC 176/30*, providing for the referral of the Korean matter to the United Nations. This pleased Truman's military advisers, who had been applying increasing pressure on the president to approve disengagement from southern Korea since early 1946. Secretary of War Robert P. Patterson consistently emphasized that his department could not continue to bear the cost of occupation, while postwar demobilization meant that U.S. soldiers, unhappy with duty in this remote Asian country, could be deployed in other more important areas. The Policy Planning Staff and the State Department's Division of Northeast Asian Affairs agreed that the global commitments of the United States were so extensive that the Truman administration might have to withdraw prematurely from the peninsula.

Faced with the task of developing future U.S. policy toward Korea, the State-War-Navy Coordinating Committee (SWNCC) on September 15, 1947, requested comments from the JCS on the relationship of Korea to U.S. national security. In its reply, the JCS added weight to the argument for withdrawal when they stated categorically that "from the standpoint of military security, the United States has little strategic interest in maintaining present troops and bases in Korea." While any U.S. offensive on the Asian mainland would bypass Korea, Truman's military experts believed that an enemy position on the peninsula would be vulnerable to air attack. Thus, the United States could contribute more effectively to its national security by deploying the Korean occupation forces in areas of greater strategic importance. The JCS warned that in the absence of a major program for social, political, and economic rehabilitation, disorder and unrest in Korea would undermine Washington's position totally. Forced withdrawal, rather than voluntary disengagement, would be humiliating and inflict infinitely greater damage on U.S. international prestige. This JCS report was influential in the drafting of NSC–8*, which called for U.S. military withdrawal from Korea at an early date. Yet the Truman administration was unwilling to abandon the area to Communist control and did not remove the troops until June 1949.

Foreign Relations of the United States, 1947, vol. 6: *The Far East* (Washington, D.C., 1972); J. I. Matray, *The Reluctant Crusade* (Honolulu, 1985); W. W. Stueck, *The Road to Confrontation* (Chapel Hill, 1981).

JEBB, SIR H. M. GLADWYN (1900–   )

Sir Hubert Miles Gladwyn Jebb was Britain's permanent representative at the UN during the Korean War. Born at Firbeck Hall near Rotheram in Yorkshire, he earned a history degree in 1922 from Oxford University. Jebb entered the foreign service in 1924, spending the next three years as third secretary at the British embassy in Tehran. After two years at the Foreign Office in London, he became secretary to the parliamentary under secretary of state in Ramsey MacDonald's government. As a nonpolitical appointee, Jebb's responsibility in this post was to serve as an advisor and principal assistant. In 1931, Anthony Eden* became the under secretary and retained Jebb's services. After serving briefly in Italy during 1935, Jebb resumed his duties as a secretary in 1937, this time for the permanent under secretary of state. In 1940, he became assistant under secretary in the Ministry of Economic Warfare and, after demonstrating his organizational skill, gained appointment in 1942 as head of the Foreign Office's economic and reconstruction department.

Jebb was an active participant in wartime diplomacy, accompanying Eden as counsellor to the United States for discussions with the Roosevelt administration in 1943 and attending the conferences at Quebec, Cairo, Tehran, Dumbarton Oaks, and Postdam. He served as principal secretary for Winston Churchill* at Yalta in 1945 and participated in the creation of the United Nations at San Francisco. The next year, at the first UN General Assembly session in London, Jebb, also serving as acting UN secretary-general, strongly advocated international control over atomic energy. Later in 1946, he became assistant under secretary of state in charge of UN affairs. After gaining ambassadorial rank in

1948, Jebb went to the UN the next year and became Britain's permanent representative in 1950.

During the Korean War, Jebb vigorously represented British interests at the UN and played a major role in drafting key resolutions. He served as president of the UN Security Council in September 1950, working to obtain approval for the Republic of Korea* to maintain representation in discussion before that body. Acting on his instructions, Jebb urged negotiations with the People's Republic of China* when evidence emerged of Chinese military intervention*. His main concern was that an enlarged military commitment in Asia would weaken the defense of Europe. As Britain's representative on the UN Collective Measures Committee*, Jebb spoke against action that might widen the war. Polished and soft spoken, he earned a reputation for being hardworking and having a sharp intellect. In 1954, Jebb became ambassador to France, remaining in this post until his retirement in 1960. He remained active as the Liberal party's deputy leader in the House of Lords for 1965 to 1988 and as the author of several books, including *The Memoirs of Sir Gladwyn*.

Current Biography, 1948; *Foreign Relations of the United States, 1950,* vol. 7: *Korea* (Washington, D.C., 1976), *1951,* vol. 7: *Korea and China* (Washington, D.C., 1983), and *1952–1954,* vol. 15: *Korea* (Washington, D.C., 1984); *Who's Who, 1990* (New York, 1989).

JESSUP, PHILIP C. (1897–1986)

Philip C. Jessup, as U.S. representative to the UN and Department of State ambassador at large, was involved in implementing U.S. policy toward Korea before and after the North Korean invasion of South Korea*. After graduating from Hamilton College and Yale Law School, Jessup served in World War I. Thereafter, he mixed a career in law with government service and scholarship, resigning a professorship at Columbia University to become the U.S. representative to the UN—a post that brought him some recognition through his verbal sparring with Soviet minister of foreign affairs Andrei Y. Vyshinsky*. When the UN Interim Committee hesitated to authorize international supervision of elections in southern Korea alone, Jessup successfully persuaded the body to instruct the UNTCOK to observe the balloting on May 10, 1948. In January 1950, Jessup visited the Republic of Korea* in an effort to encourage economic reform and progress toward political democracy. Less than six months later, he was present at the first and second Blair House meetings*, preparing minutes for each.

Although Jessup had never served in China, his UN appointment attracted the interest of China lobby czar Alfred Kohlberg, who lumped Jessup with Owen Lattimore and those other State Department employees who had supposedly engineered both the loss of China and American blood in Korea. The China lobby and its friends expressed a particular interest in Jessup's associations in four areas. First, Jessup had been a prominent member of the Institute of Pacific Relations, viewed as a beachhead from which the agents of Joseph Stalin* and

Mao Tse-tung* could go on to infiltrate the State Department. Second, Jessup stood as a character witness for Alger Hiss at both of the former State Department official's perjury trials and he refused to repudiate Hiss even after the jury in the second trial found him guilty of perjury. Third, at Secretary of State Dean G. Acheson's* request, Jessup had edited the State Department White Paper released in August 1949 to counter the charge that the Roosevelt and Truman administrations "lost" China to communism through blunders and betrayal. Finally, Jessup had accompanied President Harry S. Truman* to the Wake Island Conference* for the president's face-to-face confrontation with CINCUNC General Douglas MacArthur*, and he played a minor role in the subsequent events that led to Truman's recall of MacArthur*.

Neither a Communist nor a Communist sympathizer, Jessup became the victim of the partisan political scapegoating of the early 1950s. The most sustained assault on Jessup's integrity and loyalty came not from Alfred Kohlberg but from Senator Joseph R. McCarthy. When the Senate considered Jessup's nomination to serve on the UN delegation in September 1951, McCarthy released a twenty-seven-page brochure arguing against confirmation. Although the Senate had confirmed Jessup five times as UN representative and ambassador at large since 1948, the subcommittee of the Senate Foreign Relations Committee voted against him. Jessup left the State Department to accept a chair of international law at Columbia University and remained active thereafter in the scholarly community and on the fringes of the foreign policy community.

J. I. Matray, *The Reluctant Crusade* (Honolulu, 1985); D. M. Oshinsky, *A Conspiracy So Immense: The World of Joe McCarthy* (New York, 1983); J. N. Thomas, *The Institute of Pacific Relations: Asian Scholars and American Politics* (Seattle, 1974).

Kenneth O'Reilly

JOHNSON, LOUIS A. (1891–1966)

Louis A. Johnson, secretary of defense at the beginning of the Korean conflict, proved to be one of the most controversial figures in President Harry S. Truman's* foreign policy establishment. Born in Roanoke, Virginia, and graduated from the University of Virginia, Johnson served as a captain during World War I. Afterward, he practiced law and became an influential Democratic politician in West Virginia. He served as President Franklin D. Roosevelt's under secretary of war from 1937 to 1940. Johnson attracted Truman's attention in 1948 when, as chairman of the Democratic party's finance committee, he raised $1.5 million. As a reward, Truman appointed him secretary of defense in March 1949.

Johnson's tenure at defense was a stormy one. He eagerly pursued the Truman administration's plans to economize at Defense and to reorganize the military, closing bases, reducing forces, and implementing other measures that prompted critics to contend that these moves contributed to a U.S. lack of preparedness when the Korean War began. More telling for the conduct of wartime diplomacy, Johnson inhibited contact between the Departments of Defense and State, triggering a growing personal animosity with Secretary of State Dean G. Acheson*.

Before and during the war, critical policy decisions were hampered by this personal feud. On March 22, 1950, Acheson invited Johnson and JCS chairman General Omar N. Bradley* to a meeting to discuss a draft reassessment of U.S. national security policy, which would soon become NSC-68*. Acheson was taken aback when Johnson refused to cooperate or discuss the document.

Johnson participated in policy discussion about the conduct of the war beginning with the first Blair House meeting*. Although he largely concurred with the administration's direction, he did have a few differences, such as his advocacy of accepting Chiang Kai-shek's* offer of Chinese troops* for service in Korea. Already concerned about the Acheson-Johnson feud, Truman was further upset by several other Johnson actions. In late August 1950, CINCUNC General Douglas MacArthur*, in an address he sent to the Veterans of Foreign Wars Convention, suggested use of Taiwan as a strategic military base in East Asia. Truman told Johnson to dispatch a formal order to MacArthur to retract that statement. Johnson hesitated to confront the general, and the statement was retracted only after a transcript had been released. Administration opponents seized upon the incident to attack the president's policies. In addition, many suspected Johnson of secretly providing information to Republican politicians, particularly Senator Robert A. Taft*. As a result of Johnson's actions, Truman requested Johnson's resignation, and he complied in September 1950. *See also* Johnson's Resignation as Secretary of Defense; Johnson's Visit to Tokyo; MacArthur's VFW Message.

D. Acheson, *Present at the Creation* (New York, 1969); R. J. Donovan, *Tumultuous Years* (New York, 1982); W. W. Stueck, *The Road to Confrontation* (Chapel Hill, 1981); H. S. Truman, *Years of Trial and Hope* (Garden City, N.Y., 1956).

T. Michael Ruddy

JOHNSON, U. ALEXIS (1908–   )

U. Alexis Johnson served from June 1950 to July 1953 as the executive officer for Korea on day-to-day administrative affairs from positions in the Department of State as both deputy director and director of the Office of Northeast Asian Affairs and deputy assistant secretary for Far Eastern affairs. Johnson's contact with Korean questions began in the 1930s when he served as vice-consul in Seoul. His impression at that time of Syngman Rhee* was not a good one, believing him to be "a hopeless idealist." When Lieutenant General John R. Hodge* was named head of occupation forces in Korea in 1945, Johnson briefed him on Korean politics and culture. Appointed the first State Department representative in Japan under the occupation, Johnson soon found himself back in Korea at the behest of CINCFE General Douglas MacArthur's* chief of staff, who recognized Hodge's need for Korean expertise on a staff largely trained for occupation responsibilities in Japan.

Johnson returned to Washington in 1949, and when war erupted in Korea, he became Assistant Secretary of State Dean Rusk's* primary operator on Korea. Johnson participated actively in discussions leading to the decision to permit the

UN offensive across the thirty-eighth parallel* in an attempt to reunify Korea. Johnson advocated the "move-north" but, unlike his office director John M. Allison*, John Paton Davies*, or Rusk, he took seriously Chinese threats to enter the war. Johnson argued that only South Korean troops should be used north of the parallel. Neither he nor his allies Livingston T. Merchant* or O. Edmund Clubb* proved able to sway Rusk and Allison, who accepted Mac-Arthur's estimate that South Korean forces could not proceed unaccompanied and emphasized that the People's Republic of China* would not intervene.

Johnson welcomed President Harry S. Truman's* recall of MacArthur* from his command position in Korea and advised against retaining him as supreme commander in Japan on the grounds that his prestige would be too severely compromised. Subsequently Johnson prepared Secretary of State Dean G. Acheson's* testimony for the MacArthur Hearings*. Later in the war Johnson, as deputy assistant secretary, attempted to solve the deadlock at the P'anmunjŏm truce talks* over agenda item 4*, the repatriation of POWs. Traveling to Korea, he visited the POW camps and reported that they were increasingly violent places, essentially out of UNC* control. He also returned to Washington agreeing with CINCUNC General Matthew B. Ridgway* that prisoners who would forcibly resist being returned to China should be removed from the POW lists. In response, Truman seriously considered implementing his POW unilateral release proposal*. At the Geneva Conference of 1954*, Johnson was coordinator of all preparations, ensuring compliance with Secretary of State John Foster Dulles's* seating demands, which precluded placement next to Communist delegations.

B. Cumings (ed.), *Child of Conflict* (Seattle, 1983); R. Foot, *The Wrong War* (Ithaca, N.Y., 1985); U. A. Johnson, *The Right Hand of Power* (Englewood Cliffs, N.J., 1984).

Nancy Bernkopf Tucker

JOHNSON'S RESIGNATION AS SECRETARY OF DEFENSE (September 12, 1950)

Secretary of Defense Louis A. Johnson* resigned under pressure from the White House after months of feuding with Secretary of State Dean G. Acheson*. Johnson was an abrasive, aggressive, ambitious man who by June 1950 had become the leader of those administration hardliners favoring a strong commitment to Taiwan. He tirelessly attempted to convince the JCS to agree to military support for Chiang Kai-shek*, despite State Department disapproval and White House reluctance. During his visit to Tokyo* in June 1950, General Douglas MacArthur* confirmed that Taiwan, in his view, was essential in holding back the Communists. After Johnson's return, Senator Robert A. Taft* criticized the administration's foreign policy and called for Acheson's resignation. The next day, Johnson, in the presence of W. Averell Harriman*, then a White House aide, called Taft and congratulated him on his speech. Rumors abounded in Washington that Acheson was out and that the president had reversed his cautious Taiwan policy. A furious Truman muttered that if Johnson kept it up, the administration would soon have a new secretary of defense.

Johnson continued his campaign for closer ties to Taiwan and called for Nationalist preemptive attacks against mainland amphibious troops that threatened either Taiwan or the Pescadores. Acheson icily reminded Johnson that the United States was not at war with the People's Republic of China*. Johnson meanwhile invited attacks from conservative Democrats and Republicans who blamed him for U.S. unpreparedness in Korea because of his budget cutting of the previous year. Repeatedly, Truman had to back his embattled secretary against rumors of impending dismissal. The final straw came on September 11 when Acheson appealed to the president to intervene in his latest battle with Johnson over the Defense Department's bombing in North Korea near the Soviet border. Truman suspended the program and called for Johnson's resignation. He had tired of the Acheson-Johnson feud and of Johnson's tendency to leak his contrary views about Taiwan to the press. The president recognized that Johnson had become a political liability and appointed General George C. Marshall* to take his place. Marshall, Acheson's former boss in the State Department, quickly established better relations between the departments, and Acheson became less combative.

D. Acheson, *Present at the Creation* (New York, 1969); R. Foot, *The Wrong War* (Ithaca, N.Y., 1985); *New York Times,* September 13, 1950; S. Pelz, "U.S. Decisions on Korean Policy, 1943–1950: Some Hypotheses," in B. Cumings (ed.), *Child of Conflict* (Seattle, 1983).

Richard W. Fanning

JOHNSON'S VISIT TO TOKYO (June 18–23, 1950)

Secretary of Defense Louis A. Johnson* traveled to Japan in June 1950 as part of a larger tour of U.S. military facilities in the Pacific. General Omar N. Bradley*, chairman of the JCS, accompanied him on this trip. In Tokyo, Johnson and Bradley had lengthy discussions with General Douglas MacArthur* covering the forthcoming Japanese Peace Treaty* and the future of U.S. military assistance to the Republic of China*. MacArthur gave the secretary a copy of his memorandum on Taiwan's strategic significance* and endorsed a JCS suggestion for the dispatch of a military survey team to Taiwan. Significantly, Johnson and Bradley did not visit the Republic of Korea*, much to the disappointment of U.S. ambassador John J. Muccio*. Upon returning to Washington, D.C., Bradley drafted a memorandum urging an expansion of U.S. military support for Chiang Kai-shek's* regime. Later that same day, news arrived of the North Korean invasion of South Korea*, adding urgency to the task of reassessing U.S. policy regarding Taiwan. Johnson took advantage of the first Blair House meeting* the next night to discuss the contents of MacArthur's Taiwan memorandum with President Harry S. Truman* before dinner. Not only did Johnson's visit to Tokyo pave the way for an increase of military aid to Chiang but also for MacArthur's visit to Taiwan* a month after the outbreak of the Korean War.

Foreign Relations of the United States, 1950, vol. 6: *East Asia and the Pacific* (Washington, D.C., 1976) and vol. 7: *Korea* (Washington, D.C., 1976); J. F. Schnabel and R. J. Watson, *History of the Joint Chiefs of Staff*, vol. 3: *The Korean War* (Wilmington, 1979).

JOINT POLICY (GREATER SANCTIONS) STATEMENT (July 27, 1953)

On July 27, 1953, the sixteen UN member nations whose military forces participated in the Korean War signed a public statement warning the People's Republic of China* that should it attack the Republic of Korea* after the armistice, "in all probability, it would not be possible to confine the hostilities within the frontiers of Korea." The Truman administration first raised the possibility of such a warning with the British in late 1951. The JCS dropped its insistence on inspections in North Korea to ensure Communist observance of cease-fire terms in return for allied public endorsement of the statement. By January 1952, all of the sixteen nations had approved the idea and draft language, with the exception of the French, who wished to modify the text so as to place the PRC on notice that "any other act of aggression," an unspoken reference to Chinese intervention in the war in Indochina, would meet with united and prompt resistance. President Harry S. Truman* insisted that the United States stick to the original statement, and the French withdrew their modification.

The Truman administration's expectation of an armistice in 1952 proved wrong, and the statement was shelved until the spring and early summer 1953, when an armistice again seemed imminent. When the Eisenhower administration revived the statement, it discovered that the British and New Zealanders now considered the language too provocative in the light of the improved international situation in part attributed to the death of Joseph Stalin*. U.S. and Australian diplomats calmed these fears in London and Wellington, but the French once again insisted on inclusion of a section applicable to Indochina. The United States reluctantly agreed to the French demand, and a final sentence was added that the armistice must not "jeopardize the restoration or the safeguarding of peace in other parts of Asia."

When ROK President Syngman Rhee* released North Korean POWs* in June 1953 and threatened that South Korea would not abide by the armistice, Secretary of State John Foster Dulles* had second thoughts about issuing the Joint Policy statement—the new, less provocative name for the Greater Sanctions statement. As a result of Dulles' doubts, the sixteen nations agreed to release the statement as part of a UN report on August 7, 1953, without fanfare and well after the signature of the armistice agreement*. The continuing effect of the Joint Policy statement on the PRC and the Democratic People's Republic of Korea* is difficult to gauge, yet it provided a stop-gap assurance to South Korea that it would be defended until the U.S.-ROK Mutual Defense Treaty* was ratified in 1954 and thus helped convince Rhee to accept the armistice. *See also* Agenda Item 3; Airfield Rehabilitation Controversy; NSC-154/1; Tripartite Meetings of November 1951.

Foreign Relations of the United States, 1951, vol. 7: *Korea* (Washington, D.C., 1983) and *1952–1954,* vol. 15: *Korea* (Washington, D.C., 1984); R. J. O'Neill, *Australia in the Korean War 1950–53* (Canberra, 1981).

Edward C. Keefer

JOOSTE, GERHARDUS PETRUS (1904–   )

During the Korean War, G. P. Jooste was South Africa's ambassador to the United States and an active participant in the Korean War briefing meetings*. He was born in Winburg, Orange Free State, and graduated from the University of Pretoria with a political science degree. After five years in the civil service, Jooste in 1929 became private secretary to the minister of finance. By then, he was a leader in the National party, advancing the interests and viewpoints of the Afrikaaners. Jooste earned an M.A. in 1934 and joined the Department of External Affairs. Thereafter he attended sessions of the League of Nations and imperial conferences, defending apartheid and advocating South Africa's separation from Britain. In 1937, Jooste became chargé in Brussels, fleeing to London in 1940 with the Belgian government in exile. In 1941, he returned to South Africa as head of the economic division in the Department of External Affairs and remained in that post until 1946, when he became head of the political and diplomatic division.

Jooste went to the UN as an alternate delegate in 1948. He became permanent representative the following year and until 1954 vigorously defended South Africa's policy toward South-West Africa and on apartheid. Jooste walked out during one session of the UN Trusteeship Committee in 1949 when the body permitted testimony on internal conditions in South-West Africa. After the North Korean invasion of South Korea*, Jooste delivered a speech condemning the attack as an act of aggression but explained that South Africa had no responsibility for the preservation of peace in East Asia. Nevertheless, South Africa later contributed a fighter squadron and ground forces to the UNC*, undoubtedly to win support from the United States for its inflexible position on retaining control over South-West Africa. In 1950, Jooste had become ambassador to the United States and therefore was even more influential in American discussions with its allies about the Korean War. Following Chinese military intervention*, he spoke in favor of actions that would bring an early cease-fire.

Jooste left the United States in 1954 and went to London, where he was high commissioner for two years. From 1956 to 1966, he was South Africa's secretary for external affairs, serving thereafter until 1968 as special adviser to the prime minister. In addition to being chair of the state procurement board (1968–1971), Jooste has spent time on South African commissions responsible for atomic energy (1956–1966) and for water matters (1966–1990).

Current Biography, 1951; *Foreign Relations of the United States, 1951,* vol. 7: *Korea and China* (Washington, D.C., 1983); *Who's Who, 1990* (New York, 1989).

JOY, C. TURNER (1895–1956)

Admiral Charles Turner Joy was commander, U.S. Naval Force, Far East (NAVFE) and, from July 1951 through May 1952, senior UN delegate to the

Korean Armistice Conference. Born in St. Louis, Missouri, Joy received a private secondary education. Following graduation, he accepted an appointment to the U.S. Naval Academy and was commissioned an ensign in 1916. He served on board the battleship *Pennsylvania,* Atlantic Fleet flagship, during World War I. Following the armistice, he was selected for the naval postgraduate program in ordnance engineering. He received his M.S. from the University of Michigan in 1923. Recognized as an up-and-coming member of the "Gun Club" (a slang term for the naval specialty of ordnance and gunnery), Joy spent the interwar years in a variety of billets ranging from commander of the destroyer *Litchfield* to instructor of ordnance and gunnery at Annapolis. With U.S. entry into World War II, Joy became operations officer on board the carrier *Lexington.* Promoted to captain, he was decorated for his role in the successful planning of carrier task force engagements near Rabaul and New Guinea. In late 1942, Joy was given command of the cruiser *Louisville* and saw combat in the Solomons and Aleutians. After a tour in Washington as head of the Pacific Plans Division, Joy was promoted to rear admiral and returned to combat as commander, Cruiser Division Six. He participated in the Marianas campaign, the capture of the Philippines, Iwo Jima and Okinawa, and fast carrier task force raids against Japanese positions.

When the Korean conflict erupted, Vice-Admiral Joy worked closely with CINCUNC General Douglas MacArthur*, who praised him for his contribution to the planning and execution of both the Inch'ŏn* and Wŏnsan landings*. In July 1951, Admiral Joy was appointed senior UNC* delegate at the Kaesŏng truce talks*. Joy proved himself a grim, determined negotiator. Although he publicly chastised the North Koreans, Joy was relatively discreet about his criticisms of the U.S. posture. He requested that he be relieved of command in May 1952, returning home as superintendent of the U.S. Naval Academy. Following retirement in 1955, Joy became a vocal opponent of President Dwight D. Eisenhower's* policy, publishing *How Communists Negotiate,* a strident indictment of both sides. The posthumous publication of his Korean War diary in 1978 fleshed out his analysis. Joy consistently maintained that Communist promises made during the armistice talks should never have been accepted. Effective negotiations required that the UNC advance a clear, basic position from the outset and then never waver. Joy's diary is replete with complaints about vacillating U.S. political objectives. Joy ultimately opposed the armistice agreement*, believing that the failure to pursue military victory in Korea profited China immeasurably.

A. E. Goodman (ed.), *Negotiating While Fighting: The Diary of Admiral C. Turner Joy at the Korean Armistice Conference* (Stanford, Calif., 1978); C. T. Joy, *How Communists Negotiate* (New York, 1955).

Lynne K. Dunn

K

K1C2 (KOREA, COMMUNISM, CORRUPTION)

Senator Karl Mundt, Republican of South Dakota, coined this phrase during the 1952 presidential campaign to sum up the three central issues to use against the Democrats. Vice-presidential candidate Richard M. Nixon* led the attack on the Truman administration for permitting both communism and corruption to permeate the federal government. Dwight D. Eisenhower* concentrated on growing public dissatisfaction with the Korean War at the climax of the campaign, culminating with his promise to go to Korea if elected to find a way to end the conflict. Contemporary observers, notably Samuel Lubell, argued that frustration over the Korean stalemate was a major reason for Eisenhower's victory in 1952, but political scientists who surveyed voting behavior later concluded that domestic issues were uppermost in the minds of those who elected Eisenhower to the presidency.

C. A. Alexander, *Holding the Line: The Eisenhower Era, 1952–1961* (Bloomington, Ind., 1975); R. J. Caridi, *The Korean War and American Politics* (Philadelphia, 1968); E. F. Goldman, *The Crucial Decade—and After: America, 1945–1960* (New York, 1960); B. I. Kaufman, *The Korean War* (Philadelphia, 1986); D. Rees, *Korea: The Limited War* (New York, 1964).

Robert A. Divine

KAESŎNG BOMBING PROPOSAL

This proposal provided a good illustration of the UNC's* increasing frustration during the last year of the Korean War over the failure to achieve a settlement at the P'anmunjŏm truce talks* and its search for a way to break the deadlock. In December 1952, Colonel Charles W. McCarthy, the senior UNC liaison officer, proposed to the joint strategic plans and operations group that the JCS authorize an air strike against the 28-square-mile sanctuary around Kaesŏng, which had been the first site of the truce talks. This, he said, would be appropriate punishment for the Communist propaganda campaign at P'anmunjŏm regarding agenda item 4*, repatriation of POWs. Since the truce talks suspension of October 8, 1952*, the Communists had been utilizing the P'yŏngyang-Kaesŏng road for daily convoys to the armistice area. The P'anmunjŏm security agreement of October 22, 1951*, did not permit this while the negotiations were in recess; however, the Truman administration was unwilling to grant approval since it was about to leave office.

Thereafter, the UNC began to discuss the possibility of reducing the number of Communist convoys to three or fewer per week in conjunction with the establishment of a tight timetable regulating the hours of passage. Any violations would be met with an air strike. While this would show the American people that the UNC was not passive, it also would send a message to the Communists that they now would pay a higher price for refusing to engage in serious negotiations. Anxious to find a way to end the war, the new Eisenhower administration approved the plan. On January 25, Colonel McCarthy informed the Communist liaison officer that thereafter and as long as the negotiations were in recess, the UNC would permit free passage to the armistice site of only two convoys per week. Every Sunday morning, one convoy could leave P'yŏngyang and another could depart from Kaesŏng, but each had to finish the trip before 8:00 P.M. The Communists vigorously protested this as a unilateral change in the P'anmunjŏm security agreement, but the UNC delegation stood firm.

Early in February, CINCUNC General Mark W. Clark* reported that the Communists were engaged in a major military buildup and planned to stage an offensive prior to the spring thaw. He was particularly concerned over the use of Kaesŏng as an advanced military base, noting that the enemy was moving supplies, equipment, and troops into the area. On February 7, Clark formally requested authority to abrogate the P'anmunjŏm security agreement and, when there was evidence of an impending Communist offensive, stage bombing raids against Kaesŏng. While the JCS opposed the plan, Secretary of State John Foster Dulles* recommended the unilateral ending of sanctuary for Kaesŏng and Munsan, headquarters for the Communist and UNC delegations, respectively. This would permit bombing raids if a large enemy offensive seemed imminent but would not imply any break in the truce talks since P'anmunjŏm's immunity would continue. President Dwight D. Eisenhower*, at the NSC meeting of February 11, suggested that the United States ''should consider the use of tactical atomic weapons on the Kaesong area, which provided a good target for this type of weapon.''

In the end, the president gave approval for ending Kaesŏng's immunity and authorized the JCS to develop plans for air strikes in conjunction with limited ground operations. But justification for an attack disappeared when intelligence reports revealed no enemy buildup around Kaesŏng. Clark received instructions that he could attack Kaesŏng if an offensive started from that location and thereby ended its status as a sanctuary. Offering an alternative, Washington gave approval for an announcement setting a date for terminating Kaesŏng's immunity, though not the roads to P'anmunjŏm. The JCS pointed out that a total abrogation just before the February 24 UN meeting would have ''adverse political implications.'' In response, Clark submitted a draft on February 19 for announcing temporary abrogation of Kaesŏng's immunity while the plenary sessions were in recess. However, the Communists were then indicating a willingness to compromise and resume the talks at P'anumunjŏm, removing necessity to act on the Kaesŏng bombing proposal.

M. W. Clark, *From the Danube to the Yalu* (New York, 1954); *Foreign Relations of the United States, 1952–1954*, vol. 15: *Korea* (Washington, D.C., 1984); W. G. Hermes, *Truce Tent and Fighting Front* (Washington, D.C., 1966); E. C. Keefer, "President Dwight D. Eisenhower and the End of the Korean War," *Diplomatic History* (Summer 1986); J. F. Schnabel and R. J. Watson, *History of the Joint Chiefs of Staff*, vol. 3: *The Korean War* (Wilmington, 1979).

KAESŎNG NEUTRAL ZONE CONTROVERSY

From the beginning of the Kaesŏng truce talks*, there were problems surrounding the maintenance of the neutrality of the conference site. The Communists had suggested Kaesŏng, Korea's ancient capital just below the thirty-eighth parallel and 35 miles northwest of Seoul. Washington had accepted the site over the strenuous objections of CINCUNC General Matthew B. Ridgway* as a demonstration of sincerity to expedite a settlement. In theory, Kaesŏng was in no-man's-land but actually was located within Communist-held territory. This was clear on July 8 when liaison officers held a preliminary meeting at Kaesŏng to finalize arrangements for the opening of the formal negotiation. The UNC's* representative, Colonel Andrew J. Kinney, arrived by helicopter and had to move through heavily armed Communist guards to reach the meeting room. After examining the delegation membership lists, the Communists agreed to clear and secure the road to Kaesŏng from P'anmunjŏm 6 miles to the east so that the UNC delegation could attend the first plenary session on July 10. The UNC convoy was to fly white flags, and military personnel were to wear arm brassards. Kinney obtained assurances that all UNC convoys traveling the road to Kaesŏng would be immune from attack if the Communists received prior notice of the route and time of departure.

Controversy regarding the security arrangements started at the first session when Vice-Admiral C. Turner Joy*, the UNC's chief negotiator, protested having to pass through checkpoints to reach the negotiating site. Worse, Communist newsmen were on hand to photograph the UNC delegation's arrival flying white flags, traditionally symbolic of suing for peace. After resolving the press coverage of truce talks controversy*, Joy insisted on changes. At the third plenary session on July 15, he demanded a circular 5-mile security zone around Kaesŏng and prohibitions against armed troops' passing within a half-mile of the conference site. Within the circle, guards would carry only side arms to perform police functions, and no armed personnel would pass within a half-mile of the conference house. The UNC convoys would have the right of unrestricted movement between Kaesŏng and P'anmunjŏm without notice during daylight hours. Finally, both sides agreed not to stage attacks against each other in the neutral area.

Despite Communist acceptance of these terms, violations of the security agreement began to occur. For example, on August 4, a fully armed company of

Chinese troops marched past the UNC delegation house in the conference area. Following the truce talks suspension of August 23, 1951*, Ridgway agreed to resume the negotiations only at a "new and satisfactory site" that was truly neutral and subject to joint police protection. Washington endorsed this position after the Bradley-Bohlen visit to Korea* and the switch to P'anmunjŏm occurred with the truce talks resumption of October 25, 1951*.

C. Blair, *The Forgotten War* (New York, 1987); *Foreign Relations of the United States, 1951*, vol. 7: *Korea and China* (Washington, D.C., 1983); W. G. Hermes, *Truce Tent and Fighting Front* (Washington, D.C., 1966); D. Rees, *Korea: The Limited War* (New York, 1964); M. B. Ridgway, *The Korean War* (Garden City, N.Y., 1967).

KAESŎNG TRUCE TALKS (July 10–October 24, 1951)

With the relief of CINCUNC General Douglas MacArthur*, the United States sought to end the fighting in Korea. Since October 1950, pressure had been growing in the UN for a negotiated settlement. On June 23, 1951, Jacob A. Malik*, Soviet representative to the UN, proposed a cease-fire in a radio address. Acting upon this initiative, MacArthur's replacement, General Matthew B. Ridgway*, proposed the opening of negotiations for a cease-fire on June 30. Thus, truce talks were begun at Kaesŏng, near the thirty-eighth parallel. Preliminary exchanges began on July 8, with principal talks commencing on July 10. The Republic of Korea* opposed the cease-fire because this would prevent the unification of the Korean peninsula, but its protests were in vain. The truce talks were held among representatives of the UNC*, the North Korean People's Army (NKPA) and the Chinese People's Volunteers Army* (CPVA).

The aims for the cease-fire negotiations, proposed by the UNC, provided for an end to the hostilities, establishment of a demilitarized zone in the area near the thirty-eighth parallel, and supervision of Korea to enforce the cease-fire. The Communists rejected the proposals of the UN, advocating instead withdrawal of all foreign troops, both Chinese and UN, from the Korean peninsula, solving Korean problems by negotiations between the Koreans themselves, withdrawal of U.S. troops from Taiwan, and acceptance of the People's Republic of China* for membership in the UN.

On June 30, 1951, the South Korean government publicly announced its opposition to the armistice negotiations. The ROK demanded withdrawal of the CPVA, disarmament of the army of North Korea, participation of the South Korean government's representative in future conferences, and the acknowledgment that any invasion of the sovereignty and integrity of Korea should be regarded as the action of an outlaw. But as the truce talks went on, despite the opposition of the Korean government, Pyun Yung Tai*, minister of foreign affairs, asked for the participation of South Korea's representative in the armistice talks. The UN agreed, and the Korean representative was accepted to participate in the talks as an observer.

After resolving the press coverage of truce talks controversy*, the two sides clashed immediately in the agenda controversy*. The Communists insisted that the agenda include discussion of the thirty-eighth parallel as a demarcation line and provisions for the withdrawal of all foreign troops. The matter of the thirty-eighth parallel was resolved temporarily on July 16. The issue of foreign troop withdrawals, however, became the critical problem. The insistence on the part of the Communists became the main hindrance to agreement. The United States feared that if UN forces were withdrawn from Korea, the Chinese could send massive reinforcements to North Korea from Manchuria. After the agenda dispute was resolved, the negotiators reached a deadlock over the location of the DMZ, agenda item 2*. After the truce talks suspension of August 23, 1951*, the negotiations were reopened at P'anmunjŏm on October 25, 1951, after Ridgway insisted upon changing sites. This ended the period of the Kaesŏng truce talks.

Vice-Admiral C. Turner Joy* was head of the UN negotiators. To support Joy, the following also served as delegates: Major General Henry I. Hodes, deputy chief of staff, 8th Army*; Major General Laurence C. Craigie, vice-commander, Far East Air Force; Rear Admiral Arleigh A. Burke*, deputy chief of staff, Naval Forces, Far East; and Major General Paik Son Yup*, commanding general, ROK I Corps. The leader of the Communist delegation was Lieutenant General Nam Il*, chief of staff, NKPA, and also vice-premier, Democratic People's Republic of Korea*. Assisting him at the conference table were Major General Lee Sang Cho*, chief of the Reconnaissance Bureau, NKPA and a former vice-minister of commerce; Major General Chang Pyong San, chief of staff, I Corps, NKPA; Lieutenant General Peng Teh-Huai*, commander, 15th Army group, CPVA; and Major General Hsieh Fang*, chief of propaganda, Northeast Military District of China. *See also* Kaesŏng Neutral Zone Controversy; Kennan-Malik Conversations; Li K'e-nung; Malik Radio Address of June 23, 1951; P'anmunjŏm Truce Talks; Ridgway's June 30, 1951, Armistice Message; South Korean Demonstrations for Unification.

Chosŏn Chonsa (P'yŏngyang, 1981); A. E. Goodman (ed.), *Negotiating While Fighting: The Diary of Admiral C. Turner Joy at the Korean Armistice Conference* (Stanford, Calif., 1978); W. G. Hermes, *Truce Tent and Fighting Front* (Washington, D.C., 1966); ROK Ministry of Defense, *Korea in War, July 1952-July 1953* (Seoul, 1954).

Woo Chul-koo

KANG KŎN (1918–1950)

Lieutenant General Kang Kŏn, known as "King Kong" to the Americans, was army chief of staff of the Democratic People's Republic of Korea* before he died in September 1950. Born of a poor peasant family in Sangju, North Kyŏngsang province in southern Korea, he started his Communist career by joining the East Manchurian Communist Youth League in March 1932. When Kim Il Sung* led small partisan bands in Manchuria between 1932 and 1941, he was one of Kim's comrades during part of this time, along with other Manchurian guerrillas, such as Ch'oi Yong-kon*, Kim Ch'aek*, An Kil, and Ch'oe Hyŏn. A veteran guerrilla fighter against the Japanese, Kang followed his leader, Kim Il Sung, into a position of eminence in North Korea after liberation.

Kang was reportedly a Soviet citizen who lived in Kazakhstan and was formerly a captain in the Soviet army. Before coming to North Korea, he first organized and commanded the East Kirin (Manchuria) Peace Preservation Army in September 1945 after the Japanese surrender, a unit subsequently coming under the Northeast Democratic Allied Army (Lin Piao*, commander). In February 1946, he participated in the organization of the North Korean People's Army (NKPA) and became commander of the NKPA 2d Division in Nanam, North Hamgyŏng province. After the first chief of staff of the NKPA, An Kil, died in December 1947, Kang succeeded him as chief of staff.

The NKPA was formally created on February 8, 1948, and top military leadership was in the hands of veteran guerrilla fighters, many of them old partisan comrades of Kim Il Sung. With a few top political figures, these key military leaders were involved in the preparation for the North Korean invasion of South Korea* in June 1950. Kang, for example, reportedly issued an order at an emergency meeting of all divisional commanders and chiefs of staff of June 10, 1950, for all units to be combat ready, which was followed on June 18 by an order from commander in chief Ch'oi Yong-kon for a final precombat inspection, and on June 23 the operational order was issued to attack South Korea on June 25. Kang was killed in action by a land mine in September 1950. He was succeeded by Lieutenant General Nam Il* with Kim Ch'aek serving as NKPA front-line commander.

Chungang Ilbo (ed.), *Pukhan Inmyong Sajŏn* (Seoul, 1981); R. Scalapino and C. Lee, *Communism in Korea* (Berkeley, 1972).

Jinwung Kim

KANSAS-WYOMING LINE

When the 8th Army* pushed back the Communist forces to the thirty-eighth parallel in late March 1951, Lieutenant General Matthew B. Ridgway*, the commander, set as its new objective that of seizing and fortifying defensive positions known as Line Kansas. This line, which lay north of the thirty-eighth parallel, started at the junction of the Han and Imjin rivers and ran northeastward and eastward to Yang-yang. Once this goal was achieved, Ridgway intended to drive 20 miles farther north into North Korea and establish Line Wyoming. From these positions, he intended to maintain contact with the enemy only with heavily armed patrols. And should the enemy counterattack, as Ridgway expected, the 8th Army was to resist strongly along Line Wyoming and, while causing the enemy to suffer heavy casualties, gradually fall back if necessary to the better-fortified Line Kansas.

By early April, U.S. and Republic of Korea* units were at or near their assigned Kansas positions. As UNC* forces were edging toward Line Wyoming, Ridgway on April 12 replaced General Douglas MacArthur* as CINCUNC and Lieutenant General James A. Van Fleet* took over command of the 8th Army. The Chinese and North Koreans launched the first of their anticipated spring offensives of 1951* on April 22, stopping Van Fleet's forces just short of Line Wyoming. The 8th Army grudgingly withdrew to Line Kansas and ultimately to within 5 miles of Seoul while inflicting extraordinary casualties on the enemy. In mid-May, the 8th Army launched its own offensive, catching the Chinese and North Koreans by surprise, and by mid-June it was back at the Kansas-Wyoming Line. Van Fleet's instructions were to fortify Line Kansas and to continue reconnaissance in force and limited attacks to keep the enemy off balance.

At this point, several factors influenced development of the defensive lines originally envisaged. First, Ridgway knew that he could expect no major re-inforcements, and none were likely to become available from U.S. or UN re-sources. Second, U.S. military leaders were aware that an armistice might materialize if the advance into North Korea was modest; however, if the advance was too deep, it would likely prevent serious armistice negotiations. Third, each additional mile of North Korean territory taken would alter the logistical balance, which now favored UN forces. And finally, U.S. leaders—military and politi-cal—were reluctant to accept the casualties that would result from further of-fensive actions.

Realizing that any demarcation line resulting from an armistice would be determined by the positions of the contending armies, Ridgway and Van Fleet agreed that Line Kansas must be held because it offered excellent defensive positions during a cease-fire. Ridgway had hoped to push units out some 20 miles from Line Kansas (that is, Line Wyoming) so that if a 20-mile DMZ was created, his fortified line (Kansas) would have adequate outposts. However, after touring the battlefield, Ridgway and Van Fleet concluded that while such an advance was possible, it would cost too many casualties. By mid-summer 1951, the 8th Army had established its defensive positions by blending the Kansas and Wyoming lines into the UN's new main line of resistance. Much bloody fighting would lie ahead, but the Kansas-Wyoming Line would remain the essential UNC defensive position, with modest revisions, throughout the armistice negotiations.

W. G. Hermes, *Truce Tent and Fighting Front* (Washington, D.C., 1966); J. F. Schnabel, *Policy and Direction* (Washington, D.C., 1972).

Richard Dean Burns

KAO KANG (GAO GANG; 1902–1954)

In 1950, Kao Kang was a top official in the People's Republic of China*, serving as chairman of the government of the semi-autonomous Northeastern Region (Manchuria) and as one of the six vice-chairmen of the Chinese Com-munist party (CCP). Surly and uncouth, the spectacled Kao gained a reputation for being cold-blooded, calculating, and relentless. Along with Lin Piao*, he initially opposed China's entry into the Korean War, but experienced a steady increase in his political power following Chinese military intervention*. Kao facilitated the dispatch of the Chinese People's Volunteers Army* to Korea and played an important role in organizing Manchuria to support the war effort. He moved to Peking during the war, becoming a member of the Politburo in 1952 and chief of the state planning commission. Apparently, Kao had plans to establish an "independent kingdom" in northeast China and even plotted to seize control of the central administrative apparatus in Peking near the end of the Korean War. His ouster in 1954 ranks as perhaps the most celebrated purge in the history of the Chinese Communist movement.

Kao Kang was born into a small landlord family in northern Shensi province. Coming under the influence of Communist teachers, he joined the CCP in 1926 and then attended the Chungshan Military and Political Academy, studying under Teng Hsiao-p'ing. In the early 1930s, he was a key military and political officer with the Communist guerrilla units in Shensi that worked to create a viable, peasant-based movement. Kao lost power briefly in a factional dispute before preparing the base at Yenan for the arrival in 1935 of Mao Tse-tung* and the Chinese Communist forces who survived the Long March. Thereafter, while others went off to fight the Japanese, he focused on building his power inside the party. Having gained election to the CCP Central Committee in 1945, Kao went with other prominent party leaders to establish control over Manchuria. In 1947, he became deputy to Lin Piao, the commander and political commissar of the Northeast Military Region. When Lin Piao led his army southward to defeat Chiang Kai-shek's* forces in the Chinese Civil War, Kao replaced him. In 1949, he became chairman of the Northeast People's Government with broader powers than any other regional leader. That same year, Mao appointed Kao as a vice-chairman on the Central People's Government Council.

After the establishment of the PRC, Kao Kang's influence increased because he was in charge of the most highly industrialized area of China. Manchuria was also the first region "liberated" from Nationalist rule and Kao was responsible for the initial testing of key party policies such as land reform. In addition, the Soviet Union and China jointly administered in Manchuria the Changchun Railway and the strategic naval facilities at Port Arthur and Dairen. Exploiting this privileged and powerful position, Kao became involved with Joseph Stalin* in a scheme to establish a special Soviet sphere of influence in Manchuria. In July 1949, he visited Moscow and negotiated a one-year barter agreement that led to the reorganization of Manchuria's economy along Soviet lines. Stalin evidently lost interest in his plan after the negotiation of the Sino-Soviet Treaty of Friendship and Alliance* in February 1950. Some writers believe Stalin approved the North Korean invasion of South Korea* to recoup his losses in Manchuria. Kao may have opposed Chinese intervention because a united Korea closely allied to the United States would increase the PRC's dependence on his Soviet patron for protection. After the death of Stalin* and the signing of the armistice agreement*, Kao began to quarrel with Mao over matters related to industrial organization, investment priorities, and the role of the old party cadres. This would lead to his ouster and alleged suicide in 1954. However, his purge may have had an international dimension since it coincided with that of Pak Hŏn-yŏng* in the Democratic People's Republic of Korea*. Like Pak, Kao might have served as a convenient scapegoat for the costs of Chinese participation in the Korean War.

D. W. Klein and A. B. Clark (eds.), *Biographic Dictionary of Chinese Communism, 1921–1965* (Cambridge, 1971); J. Merrill, *Korea: The Peninsular Origins of the War* (Newark, Del., 1989); M. Nakajima, "The Sino-Soviet Confrontation in Historical Perspective," in Y. Nagai and A. Iriye (eds.), *The Origins of the Cold War in Asia* (New York, 1977).

KAP'YŎNG, BATTLE OF
See Battle of Kap'yŏng

KATZIN, ALFRED G. (1906–   )

Following passage of the UN Security Council resolution of June 27, 1950*, UN Secretary-General Trygve Lie* appointed Alfred G. Katzin to serve as his personal representative in Korea. He was to act as liaison between Lie and the UNCOK, the Republic of Korea*, and all military forces sent to Korea under the auspices of the United Nations. Katzin was from South Africa and had pursued a variety of business enterprises during the 1930s, becoming a member of the executive board of the South African Chamber of Commerce and later vice-president of the Cape Chamber of Industries. In World War II, he fought with the South African and British armies, rising to the rank of colonel. From 1945 to 1947, Katzin served with the UNRRA and then became special counsel to the UN secretary-general in 1948.

On July 6, 1950, less than two weeks after the outbreak of the Korean War, Colonel Katzin arrived at Taejŏn and presented his credentials to the chairman of the UNCOK. Subsequently, he attempted to establish effective coordination between CINCUNC General Douglas MacArthur* and Secretary-General Lie, while working to maintain a prominent role in Korean affairs for the UNCOK. At the Wake Island Conference*, both MacArthur and John J. Muccio*, the U.S. ambassador to the Republic of Korea, gave Katzin high marks for competence and a cooperative attitude. But Katzin's relations with U.S. officials soured after Chinese military intervention* because he vigorously supported granting a UN seat to the People's Republic of China* in return for a cease-fire. From 1951 to 1952, he was a member of the UN Collective Measures Committee*. After the Korean War, Katzin served in a variety of capacities at the UN, including personnel director (1954) and acting head of the office of public information (1958–1960). In addition, he helped organize conferences on world energy resources, as well as on science and technology from 1961 to 1963. In 1956, Katzin supervised the UN operation that cleared the Suez Canal.

Foreign Relations of the United States, 1950, vol. 7: *Korea* (Washington, D.C., 1976); *Who's Who in the World, 1971–1972* (Chicago, 1970).

KENNAN, GEORGE F. (1904–   )

George F. Kennan, the State Department's premier Soviet expert, provided advice on U.S. policy before and during the Korean conflict in the light of Soviet and Chinese intentions. He would also play a central role in initiating the Kaesŏng truce talks*. Born in Milwaukee, and graduated from Princeton University, he entered the foreign service where he participated in a program to train diplomats conversant in the Russian language and culture. From the time he joined the first U.S. delegation to Moscow after President Franklin D. Roosevelt recognized the Soviet Union in 1933, Kennan served in a number of critical posts before and during World War II. His notorious Long Telegram sent from Moscow in 1946 convincingly analyzed Soviet postwar intentions and attracted the attention of policymakers, prompting Kennan's return to Washington, where he became head of the State Department's Policy Planning Staff. He subsequently became a major architect of the postwar containment policy yet supported U.S. military withdrawal from Korea* in June 1949.

When the war began, Kennan was becoming dissatisfied with his declining influence under Secretary of State Dean G. Acheson*. He was department counselor, but he described himself as a ''floating kidney,'' unable to contribute to policymaking. Nevertheless, he did express his views. At the outset, he argued that the United States had to resist the North Korean invasion of South Korea* but that the country's goal should be limited to restoring the status quo along the thirty-eighth parallel. Contrary to the view of many others, Kennan cautioned that the Soviets had authorized the invasion not as a prelude to a ''grand design'' for the spread of power elsewhere but in response to U.S. moves, such as U.S. military withdrawal, Acheson's National Press Club speech*, and Soviet exclusion from Japanese Peace Treaty* negotiations. Still, he warned that the Soviets might be tempted to exploit weak spots elsewhere, such as in Europe.

Kennan took leave from the State Department in September 1950 to study at the Princeton Institute for Advanced Study, but only after expressing his misgivings about the UN offensive across the thirty-eighth parallel*. After Chinese military intervention*, at the urging of his friend Charles E. Bohlen*, then stationed in Paris, he returned to Washington in December. He argued that the United States should not seek negotiation when on the defensive, but only after the military situation was stabilized because the Soviets would exploit such capitulation. Kennan was asked to approach informally Jacob A. Malik*, Soviet ambassador to the UN, on the possibility of settling the conflict. His meetings with the Soviet diplomat on May 31 and June 5 laid the groundwork for Malik's radio address of June 23, 1951*, signaling Soviet willingness to resolve the conflict and opening the way to the start of the Kaesŏng truce talks*. Although Kennan served as U.S. ambassador to the Soviet Union from May to October 1952, he had little to do with the Korean negotiations, his tenure in office being cut short when the Soviets declared him persona non grata for derogatory remarks he made about the Soviet system. See also Kennan-Malik Conversations.

J. L. Gaddis, *Strategies of Containment* (New York, 1987); W. Isaacson and E. Thomas, *The Wise Men* (New York, 1986); G. F. Kennan, *Memoirs,* 2 vols. (Boston, 1967, 1972).

T. Michael Ruddy

KENNAN-MALIK CONVERSATIONS (May 31, 1951, and June 5, 1951)

These secret conversations were initiated by Washington to investigate the prospects of a cease-fire at a time when UN forces had defeated the Chinese spring offensives of 1951* and had advanced across the thirty-eighth parallel. The conversations were followed by Jacob A. Malik's* radio address of June 23, 1951*, which made the Soviet position official and opened the way to the start of the Kaesŏng truce talks*. It was decided to make the approach through the UN ambassador, Jacob Malik, using the State Department Soviet expert, George F. Kennan*, as an intermediary. Since Kennan was on leave of absence at Princeton University, the contacts could be kept unofficial and disowned if necessary. In adopting this approach, Secretary of State Dean G. Acheson* was influenced by the success of similar unofficial conversations with Malik during the Berlin blockade.

Malik agreed to see Kennan, and two meetings took place in the Soviet compound at Glen Cove on Long Island. The language used was Russian. At the first meeting, Kennan emphasized that there could be no cease-fire in Korea unless the United States and the Soviet Union shared an identity of views on how to proceed. Without binding his government, he suggested that the best solution would be an armistice around the existing battle line with some sort of supervisory commission to guarantee against the renewal of hostilities. Malik repeatedly raised the question of U.S. differences with the People's Republic of China*, which included Taiwan and the UN seat, but Kennan made it plain that a cease-fire must not be related to such wider issues. Although Malik maintained that these statements contained nothing new, he indicated that Moscow would be interested in hearing more detailed proposals. Kennan insisted that this would be pointless in the absence of any indication from the Soviet side on the general desirability of a cease-fire. At Kennan's suggestion, another meeting was arranged for June 5. Malik's repeated references to China led Kennan to conclude that the Soviets felt inhibited about discussing a cease-fire because of their relationship with the PRC.

At the second meeting, Malik, who had obviously received instructions from Moscow, stated that the Soviet Union desired a peaceful settlement of the Korean question at the earliest possible moment. Since Soviet forces were not involved in the fighting, however, the Soviet Union could not participate in discussions about a cease-fire. His personal advice was that the United States should make contact with the Chinese and the North Koreans. Kennan believed that this statement was a hopeful sign. He thought that it was particularly significant that no attempt had been made to link a cease-fire in Korea with a wider political settlement in East Asia, something on which the Chinese had always previously insisted. He doubted if the PRC could maintain this position indefinitely without Soviet support.

D. Acheson, *Present at the Creation* (London, 1969); J. C. Goulden, *Korea: The Untold Story of the War* (New York, 1982); B. I. Kaufman, *The Korean War* (Philadelphia, 1986).

Callum A. MacDonald

KIM CH'AEK (1903–1951)

General Kim Ch'aek served as the North Korean People's Army (NKPA) front-line commander during the period from September 1950 to his death in

January 1951. Born in North Hamgyŏng province, he went to Manchuria and joined the Chinese Communist party in 1925. Kim Ch'aek had a typical *Kapsan* (Soviet exile) faction background and epitomized the type coming to the fore under Kim Il Sung*. He had participated in the anti-Japanese movement in eastern Manchuria in the 1930s, being pushed with Kim Il Sung and others into Siberia by the Japanese in 1941. Trained there by the Russians, he returned to Korea with the Soviet army in August 1945.

As a Kim Il Sung stalwart, Kim Ch'aek was to be the primary organizer and tactician of Kim's faction in northern Korea. He was named a member of the thirteen-member presidium in the North Korean Worker's party in August 1946. When the Second Congress of the North Korean Workers' party was held in P'yŏngyang in March 1948, Kim was added to a membership of seven on the political committee. At the time of the establishment of the Democratic People's Republic of Korea* in September 1948, he became a vice-premier with Pak Hŏn-yŏng* and Hong Myŏng-hŭi under Premier Kim Il Sung. He also held the key cabinet position of minister of industry. When the merger between the South and North Korean Workers' parties came in mid–1949, he became one of the all-important eight-member political committee.

On June 25, 1949, the old Democratic National United Front was renamed the Democratic Front for the Unification of the Fatherland. This new organization was totally dominated by the key leaders of the Korean Workers' party, and Kim held a membership on the leadership committee. The presidium of the Supreme People's Assembly issued on June 26, 1950, an extraordinary decree vesting in the military committee of the party the responsibility for prosecuting the war. Kim was a member of the seven-man committee under Chairman Kim Il Sung. An extremely promising "number two man" in Kim Il Sung's circle, Kim Ch'aek was killed in a U.S. bombing raid in January 1951. Had he survived the war, Kim most certainly would have played a major role in postwar North Korean politics.

Chungang Ilbo (ed.), *Pukhan Inmyong Sajŏn* (Seoul, 1981); J. A. Kim, *Divided Korea* (Cambridge, 1975); R. Scalapino and C. Lee, *Communism in Korea* (Berkeley, 1972).

Jinwung Kim

KIM CHONG-WŎN (TIGER) (1922–1964)

South Korean army officer and a henchman of Syngman Rhee*, Kim was feared by many because he wielded his power without restraint. Unsophisticated and unruly, he served the causes of his superiors with blind faith and symbolized the Rhee government's abuse of power. Kim was born in Kyŏngsan, North Kyŏngsang province, and his formal education ended after the fourth grade. In the early 1940s, he enlisted in the Japanese army as a "special volunteer" and rose to the rank of sergeant, "a rank that epitomized the brutality of the Japanese army at its worst," according to U.S. ambassador John J. Muccio*. After Korea's liberation from Japan, he joined the South Korean Constabulary as an enlisted man when it was established in 1946. He then attended the Constabulary Academy as a member of its first class and became a commissioned officer. As a battalion deputy commander and commander, he took part in the military campaigns to suppress the Yŏsu-Sunch'ŏn rebellion* and in the operations to eliminate the Communist Chiri-san guerrillas in 1948 and 1949. It was during these campaigns that he gained the nickname of "Tiger" for his rough handling of troops and enemies.

Some sources claim that Kim's "Fierce Tiger" unit of the 17th Regiment actually started the Korean War when it attacked North Korean forces first early on the morning of June 25, 1950, on the Ongjin peninsula. After the North Korean People's Army destroyed the 17th Regiment, Kim, as commander of the 23d Regiment, fought along the east coast until late July 1950, when he was relieved of his command because of an incident in which he summarily executed a platoon leader and an enlisted man for losing ground to the enemy near Yŏngdŏk. The following month, Kim had fifty North Korean POWs beheaded. If Kim was rough in dealing with his subordinates and the enemy, he was a man of supreme loyalty and dedication toward his superiors. He was given command of the military police during the UNC* occupation of the capital of the Democratic People's Republic of Korea*, P'yŏngyang, in October 1950. In early 1951, he was concurrently appointed chief of the Civil Affairs Department of the South Kyŏngsang District Martial Law Command, which had jurisdiction over the area that included the city of Pusan, then the temporary capital of the Republic of Korea*.

Kim demonstrated his single-minded loyalty to Rhee in the notorious Kŏch'ang incident*. In February 1951, the ROK troops belonging to the 11th Division massacred several hundred villagers within the county of Kŏch'ang on the charge that they had collaborated with the Communists. In April 1951, when the National Assembly investigation team attempted to visit the site of the incident, it was fired upon by ROK soldiers acting on orders from "Tiger" Kim. Although Rhee tried to protect him, public outcries forced Kim to face a court-martial, which sentenced him to a three-year imprisonment. After serving only three months, he received a special amnesty from Rhee. Upon his release, he was allowed to become chief of police in several provinces until May 1956, when he was appointed head of the national police. In September 1956, Kim was implicated in the assassination attempt on the life of Vice-President John M. Chang*, who belonged to Rhee's opposition party. After long on-and-off trials, he was eventually convicted and sentenced to a fifteen-year imprisonment in July 1961.

R. C. Allen, *Korea's Syngman Rhee: An Unauthorized Portrait* (Rutland, Vt., 1960); J. Halliday and B. Cumings, *Korea: The Unknown War* (New York, 1988); Kukbangbu p'yŏnch'an wiwŏn-hoe, *Han'guk Chŏnjaeng-sa*, vol. 2 (Seoul, 1968); Tonga Ilbosa, *Pihwa Cheil Konghwaguk,* vols. 2, 5 (Seoul, 1975).

Yŏng-ho Ch'oe

KIM IL SUNG (1912–   )

Kim Il Sung was premier of the Democratic People's Republic of Korea*, chairman of the Workers' party of Korea, and supreme commander of the North

Korean People's Army (NKPA) during the Korean War. Born Kim Sŏng-ju to a peasant family near P'yŏngyang soon after the Japanese imposed colonial rule over Korea, Kim completed only eight years of formal education before he was expelled from school in 1929 for joining an anti-Japanese Communist youth organization. Kim adopted the nom de guerre of Kim Il Sung and under that name became a well-known anti-Japanese guerrilla. Kim fought the Japanese from 1932 through 1941 as a member of the Chinese Communist-led Northeast Anti-Japanese United Army in Manchuria. In 1941, Japanese military pressure forced Kim to retreat to the Soviet Union, where he remained until 1945.

Kim returned to Korea in September 1945 and subsequently used both his guerrilla record and the support of the Soviet occupying authorities to outmaneuver older Communist leaders and win control for himself and his *Kapsan* (Soviet exile) faction of both the ruling party and the government of the DPRK by 1949. Kim was committed to uniting Korea under one government, so the initiative for the North Korean invasion of South Korea* probably came from Kim, not from his Soviet sponsors. The timing of the invasion may have been the result of both Syngman Rhee's* threats to march north and internal pressure from Pak Hŏn-yŏng's* domestic faction (Communists who had fought Japanese colonial rule from within the peninsula rather than from guerrilla bases in Manchuria) whose guerrillas in the south had been defeated in early 1950.

Though Kim lost effective control of the conduct of the war in late 1950, when the Chinese People's Volunteers Army* rescued his forces from the successful UN offensive across the thirty-eighth parallel* and assumed the major role in the fighting, he remained in firm control of both North Korea's government and the NKPA. Kim blamed the setbacks suffered in the war on his opponents within the Korean Workers' party and in the years immediately following the war eliminated them and solidified his personal power. Kim today is the general secretary of the Korean Workers' party central committee, as well as chairman of the party's military commission. He is also the president of the DPRK, having abandoned the premiership in 1972 when he introduced a new constitution creating a president above the premier.

B. Cumings, *The Origins of the Korean War* (Princeton, 1981, 1990); C. Lee, "Kim Il-Song of North Korea," *Asian Survey* (June 1967); R. Scalapino and C. Lee, *Communism in Korea* (Berkeley, 1972); R. R. Simmons, *The Strained Alliance* (New York, 1975); D. Suh, *Kim Il Sung: The North Korean Leader* (New York, 1988).

Don Baker

KIM SAE-SUN (KIM TAE-SŎN; 1901–1989)

Kim was a South Korean diplomat stationed in Washington, D.C., during the Korean War. Born at Ch'ŏrwon, Kangwŏn province, he graduated from Waseda University in Tokyo in 1925. The following year, he went to the United States for further studies. After attending Northwestern University, he moved to Columbia University, where he earned an M.A. degree in political science in 1933. After the Japanese attack against Pearl Harbor in 1941, Kim began to work for the U.S. State Department translating Japanese materials. He then worked for the Board of Economic Warfare, which was created in 1942, doing research on the Japanese war economy, until he moved to the Department of Justice a few years later. While in the United States, Kim became a close associate of Syngman Rhee* and worked for the Korean Commission, an agency Rhee created to promote Korean independence from the Japanese rule. In 1948, when the Republic of Korea* was formally inaugurated, Kim became one of its first diplomatic staff members at the Korean embassy in Washington, D.C. While a diplomat, he developed a special relationship with John Foster Dulles* and advised on the now-famous "you are not alone" speech Dulles made before the ROK National Assembly during Dulles's trip to Korea* just before the outbreak of the Korean War.

Following the North Korean invasion of South Korea*, Kim Sae-sun, now the counselor at the South Korean embassy, worked frantically with Ambassador John M. Chang* to gain U.S. support for the ROK. Once the U.S. military intervention in the Korean War was complete, Kim made special efforts to win American assistance—at both the government and private levels—for economic and refugee relief aid for South Korea. After the Kaesŏng truce talks* started in July 1951, Kim, pursuing the policy of his government, worked to oppose an armistice that would not bring reunification of Korea under the authority of the ROK government. A well-liked diplomat, Kim made significant contributions toward reducing tension that arose frequently between the ROK and the United States over various issues during the Korean War.

Personal interview.

Yŏng-ho Ch'oe

KIM SUK WON (KIM SŎK-WŎN; 1893–1978)

When the Korean War broke out, Kim Suk Won was a retired brigadier general of the army of the Republic of Korea*. His retirement as commander at the thirty-eighth parallel in 1949 was a result of his feud with ROK chief of staff Chae Byung Dok*. A leading proponent of invading North Korea for the achievement of reunification, Kim allegedly boasted in May 1949 that a South Korean attack on the Democratic People's Republic of Korea* would bring swift victory, with breakfast in Wŏnsan, lunch in P'yŏngyang, and dinner in Sinŭiju. While he never made this prediction publicly, Chae in fact was the first to do so, and the defense minister, Shin Sung-mo*, repeated it before the National Assembly. P'yŏngyang effectively exploited this comment in June 1950 to substantiate its charge that it was the ROK, not the DPRK, that had violated the thirty-eighth parallel first and instigated the start of the Korean War.

The North Korean invasion of South Korea* provided Kim with the opportunity to serve again in the military. In August 1950, he was appointed commander of the 3d Division and one month later became head of the Taegu Defense Command. Later in the war, Kim commanded the Capital Division. Though a highly capable officer and tough professional soldier, he was unable to halt the North Korean People's Army as it swept southward. Kim fell out of favor with President

Syngman Rhee* after the initial battlefield failures, and, although he gained promotion to major general, he never rose higher than a division commander until his retirement in 1956. Thereafter, he was principal of Sŏngnam Junior High and High School in Seoul, which he founded in 1945, and, from 1960 to 1961, a member of the National Assembly.

Born in Seoul, he was an honor graduate from the Japanese Military Academy in 1916 and served in the Japanese military, rising to the rank of full colonel. Owing to his ''brilliant war record in the China theater,'' Kim, known then as Kaneyama Shankugen, was portrayed as a hero in the early 1940s to attract Koreans into the Japanese army. Emperor Hirohito decorated him for bravery. His heroics included command of the special Korean detachment of the Japanese army that conducted counterinsurgency operations in Manchuria with the special assignment of suppressing Kim Il Sung* and his followers in 1937. In 1945, Kim fled northern Korea. Thereafter, he gained a reputation as an anti-Communist hardliner who was devoted to reunification at all costs. On June 2, 1948, Kim led 2,500 goose-stepping Korean veterans of the Japanese army through the streets of Seoul in their wartime uniforms. After the establishment of the ROK in August 1948, Kim, at Rhee's personal request, assumed command of the 2d Brigade and soon gained promotion to commander of the 3d Division with the rank of colonel. To South Koreans, he is remembered as the ''Kaiser Wilhelm moustache general-principal.''

B. Cumings, *The Origins of the Korean War* (Princeton, 1981, 1990); J. Halliday and B. Cumings, *Korea: The Unknown War* (New York, 1988); S. Kim, *The Politics of Military Revolution in Korea* (Chapel Hill, 1971); personnel records, ROK Ministry of Defense; K. Yi, *Pigŭkŭi Kunindŭl* (Seoul, 1982).

Hakjoon Kim

KIM SUNG SOO (KIM SŎNG-SU; 1891–1955)

Politician, educator, and journalist, Kim was born in Chŏllapukdo, in the southwestern part of the Korean peninsula. He entered the College of Politics and Economy at Waseda University in Tokyo in 1908. After graduating in 1914, he returned to Korea and became a principal of Chung'ang High School, a leading school of the Korean national independence movement. In 1919, he established the Kyŏngsŏng Textile company and in 1920 the *Dong-A Ilbo* (Daily Newspaper), one of the leading Korean newspapers under Japanese colonial rule. In 1932, he founded and became president of Bŏsung College (now Korea University). During the years before liberation, he was a moderate nationalist who devoted his efforts to the education of the younger generation. At the same time, he was a prosperous businessman and industrialist who depended for success upon his close association with the colonial regime. However, Kim was able to rely on his aristocratic dignity to negate for the most part his record as a collaborator.

After World War II, the southern part of Korea was under U.S. military occupation until 1948 when the Republic of Korea* was formed. Kim exerted great influence during these years because he was one of Korea's wealthiest men and owned a considerable amount of land. In the U.S. military government, he assumed the role of head advisor. In September 1946, he became a leader of the conservative Korean Democratic party. In 1947, he was the vice-chairman of the "Association for Fighting Against Trusteeship." After the establishment of the ROK, he became vice-president in 1950. During the Korean War, Kim Sung Soo protested against the dictatorship of President Syngman Rhee* and resigned from the vice-presidency. Until his death, he fought against the political dominance of the presidential Liberal party as one of the opposition leaders.

   Dictionary of Political Science (Seoul, 1975); J. Halliday and B. Cumings, *Korea: The Unknown War* (New York, 1988); G. Henderson, *Korea: The Politics of the Vortex* (Cambridge, 1968).

Chull Baum Kim

KIM TU-BONG (1889–1961?)

Kim Tu-bong was chairman of the presidium of the Supreme People's Assembly of the Democratic People's Republic of Korea* and a member of the Politburo of the ruling Korean Workers' party during the Korean War. Born in southeastern Korea, he moved to China in 1919 after participating in demonstrations against Japanese colonial rule. For most of his two and a half decades in China, Kim was better known as a linguist specializing in the Korean language than as a revolutionary fighting for Korean independence. However, in 1942, he moved to the Chinese Communist base in Yenan and organized the North China Korea Independence League, the political wing of the anti-Japanese Korean Volunteer Corps.

Kim returned to Korea after liberation in 1945 and organized his fellow returned revolutionaries from China into the New Democratic party. Kim's party merged with the North Korean Communist party in 1946 to form the North Korean Workers' party, with Kim as chairman. In 1948, Kim was elected the first chairman of the presidium (the executive committee) of the Supreme People's Assembly of the DPRK, a post he maintained for nine years. In 1949, when the North and South Korean Workers' parties merged, Kim Tu-bong was replaced as chairman of the new Korean Workers' party by Kim Il Sung*, but he remained a member of the powerful Politburo until 1956. Moreover, Kim also served as one of the leaders of the Democratic Front for the Unification of the Fatherland, established exactly one year before the outbreak of the Korean War.

In 1957, in a purge of the Koreans who had worked together in China (the Yenan faction), Kim was accused of siding with enemies of Kim Il Sung. He was ousted from the chairmanship of the presidium of the Supreme People's Assembly in August 1957 and expelled from the Korean Workers' party in March 1958. Kim is reported to have died in 1961 while working as a laborer on an agricultural cooperative not far from P'yŏngyang.

   K. Nam, *The North Korean Communist Leadership, 1945–1965: A Study of Factionalism and Political Consolidation* (Tuscaloosa, Ala., 1974); R. Scalapino and C. Lee, *Communism in Korea* (Berkeley, 1972); D. Suh, *Documents of Korean Communism*

(Princeton, 1970); D. Suh, *Kim Il Sung: The North Korean Leader* (New York, 1988); D. Suh, *The Korean Communist Movement* (Princeton, 1967).

Don Baker

KIM ŬNG (1928–   )

A spectacular soldier, Lieutenant General Kim Ŭng was commander of North Korea's I Corps at the start of the Korean War. After receiving training at the Whampoa Military Academy in China, he fled to Yenan in the 1930s with the Chinese Communists. Kim Ŭng was a division commander with the 8th Route Army during the Chinese Civil War. He returned to northern Korea after World War II, eventually establishing a reputation as the Democratic People's Republic of Korea's* ablest and most energetic field general. His subordinates feared Kim because he was a harsh taskmaster.

During the North Korean invasion of South Korea*, Kim Ŭng was a member of the highest echelon of command at the front. With the death of Chief of Staff Lieutenant General Kang Kŏn* in September 1950, he became chief of staff for General Kim Ch'aek*, the new North Korean army front-line commander. By February 1953, Kim Ŭng had assumed the post of front-line commander. After the war, he served as vice-minister of defense until he became one of Kim Il Sung's* victims in the political purge of 1958. Kim Ŭng resurfaced later as ambassador to South Yemen, serving in that position from 1973 to 1978.

Chungang Ilbo (ed.), *Pukhan Inmyong Sajŏn* (Seoul, 1981); T. R. Fehrenbach, *This Kind of War* (New York, 1963); W. G. Hermes, *Truce Tent and Fighting Front* (Washington, D.C., 1966); J. A. Kim, *Divided Korea* (Cambridge, 1975); *New York Times*, August 25, 1950.

Jinwung Kim

KINGSLEY, J. DONALD (1908–1972)

J. Donald Kingsley was the first agent general of the UN Korean Reconstruction Agency* (UNKRA), serving in this post until 1953 when Lieutenant General John B. Coulter* replaced him. Born in Cambridge, New York, he earned a B.A. (1929), an M.A. (1930), and a Ph.D. (1933) in public affairs from Syracuse University. From 1933 to 1935, Kingsley was professor at Antioch College and coauthored *Public Personnel Administration* (1936). He then spent two years as a postdoctoral fellow at the University of London's School of Economics before returning to Antioch in 1938, where the following year he became assistant to the president. During World War II, Kingsley was with the War Manpower Commission, initially as division chief in Cleveland, Ohio, and then in 1944 as deputy executive director. In 1945, he became the director of manpower and veteran affairs in the Office of War Mobilization and Reconversion, later serving as deputy for fiscal policy, employment, and social security following reorganization of the agency in 1946. That same year, President Harry S. Truman* appointed Kingsley his liaison officer with the Commission on Higher Education and, in 1947, executive secretary of the Scientific Research Council.

In 1947, Kingsley went to work for the UN International Labor Office in

Geneva, Switzerland. Two years later, he became director general of the UN International Refugee Organization and was responsible for the resettlement and repatriation of hundreds of thousands of people who were stateless as a result of war. In addition to maintaining camps and assembly areas, Kingsley devoted considerable attention to lowering immigration barriers, especially for those who were blind, sick, or aged. By 1950, when he became the UNKRA's agent general, he had established an international reputation as an expert on public administration and as a leader in the social service field. Kingsley, after a series of clashes with the UNC* regarding the extent of his authority, was able to achieve considerable progress toward the economic and social rehabilitation of the Republic of Korea*. In 1958, he joined the Ford Foundation, serving as a consultant to the government of Nigeria. From 1963 to 1968, Kingsley was the foundation's director for the Middle East and Africa.

Current Biography, 1950; *Foreign Relations of the United States, 1950*, vol. 7: *Korea* (Washington, D.C., 1976), *1951*, vol. 7: *Korea and China* (Washington, D.C., 1983), and *1952–1954*, vol. 15: *Korea* (Washington, D.C., 1984); *New York Times*, June 2, 1972.

KIRK, ALAN G. (1888–1963)

For the first year of the Korean War, Alan G. Kirk served as U.S. ambassador to the Soviet Union. Born in Philadelphia, Pennsylvania, he graduated from the U.S. Naval Academy in 1909 and spent the next two years at sea with the Atlantic Fleet. In 1911, Kirk was serving aboard the U.S.S. *Wilmington* at Canton when the revolution began that would topple China's last dynasty. After a tour in the Atlantic from 1914 to 1916, he was a gunboat proof and experiment officer before resuming sea duty in 1919 and then spending two years as executive officer and navigator on the presidential yacht. Prior to World War II, Kirk had a variety of ship assignments and was a student and an instructor at the Naval War College (1929–1931), developing a reputation as an expert in gunnery and ordnance. When World War II began, he was operations officer of the U.S. Fleet but went to the U.S. embassy in London, where he served as naval attaché until 1941, when he became director of naval intelligence. In 1942, Kirk was the chief of staff for the commander of the European Fleet. The next year, he became commanding officer of amphibious forces for the U.S. Atlantic Fleet, planning and directing the execution—without the loss of a single ship—of the landing in Sicily. Kirk thus became the logical choice to command U.S. naval forces in 1944, supervising more than a thousand warships, transports, and landing craft during the Normandy invasion and the seizure of Cherbourg. By 1945, Kirk had risen through the ranks to admiral and was serving on the U.S. Navy's general board.

In 1946, Kirk retired from the U.S. Navy and began his career as a diplomat, obtaining appointments as ambassador to Belgium and minister to Luxembourg. Kirk was U.S. representative on the special UN commission on the Balkans from 1947 to 1948 before President Harry S. Truman* selected him in 1949 to replace Walter Bedell Smith* as ambassador to the Soviet Union. His two years and three months in Moscow coincided with one of the worst periods of tension in the cold war. During his tenure, Kirk visited the Kremlin only twice and met Joseph Stalin* once, dealing primarily with Foreign Minister Andrei Y. Vyshinsky*. In response to the North Korean invasion of South Korea*, he was a vigorous advocate of U.S. military intervention, arguing that the United States could not permit this Soviet-inspired aggression to succeed. In November 1951, Kirk left Moscow to become head of the new Psychological Strategy Board. That same year, he became chair of the American Committee for Liberation of the Russian People, remaining active with other anti-Soviet groups for the rest of his life. During the late 1950s, he served as chairman of the board for Mercast Corporation. In 1961, Kirk became the first president of the Belgo-American Development Corporation, a firm interested in exploiting Katanga's mineral resources. President John F. Kennedy sent him to the Congo in 1961 as his personal representative to gather information on the crisis in that African nation. The following year, Kirk replaced Everett F. Drumright* as ambassador to the Republic of China* on Taiwan. *See also* Kirk-Vyshinsky Discussion of October 5, 1951.

Current Biography, 1944; *National Cyclopedia of American Biography,* vol. 50 (Ann Arbor, Mich., 1971); *New York Times,* October 16, 1963; *Who Was Who in America,* vol. 4: *1961–1968* (Chicago, 1968).

KIRK-VYSHINSKY DISCUSSION OF OCTOBER 5, 1951

Two days after this conversation, Communist representatives suggested resumption of the Korean armistice negotiations, yielding to the UNC's* demand to shift the negotiating site from Kaesŏng to P'anmunjŏm. Thus, the discussion between Alan G. Kirk*, the U.S. ambassador to the Soviet Union, and Soviet foreign minister Andrei Y. Vyshinsky* on October 5, 1951, may have been important in gaining the truce talks resumption of October 25, 1951*.

Kirk was scheduled to leave Moscow and become head of the new Psychological Strategy Board in the fall of 1951. Since he had not seen Joseph Stalin* in two years, he thought the Soviet leader might grant a farewell visit. He therefore asked the Department of State if he should request a meeting and, if Stalin agreed, what specific points he should raise. In response, the State Department authorized Kirk to ask Stalin for a farewell visit, informing the ambassador that the only issue of importance at that time was the absence of progress in resumption of the Kaesŏng truce talks*. During the meeting, Kirk was to say that the U.S. government was concerned about the incomprehensible turn in negotiations following Jacob A. Malik's* radio address of June 23, 1951*, which had been a first step toward peace. Then he was to express the hope that Stalin might use his influence to persuade the Chinese and North Koreans to resume the armistice talks.

Acting on these instructions, Kirk requested a farewell meeting with Stalin, but the Soviet leader was vacationing at the Black Sea. Instead, he met with

Vyshinsky on October 5, expressing the U.S. desire for Stalin to use his "good offices and good will" to influence China and North Korean to resume the truce talks. In reply, Vyshinsky blamed CINCUNC General Matthew B. Ridgway* for the truce talks suspension of August 23, 1951*, explaining that he did not understand why the UNC was insisting on a change in negotiating site. Nevertheless, the Soviet leader agreed to convey Kirk's message to Stalin. Following Kirk's departure, the Soviet Union responded formally through its embassy in the United States. Moscow criticized Ridgway for complicating the negotiations, urging that he drop the discussion of petty issues. Though not a participant in the Korean truce negotiations, the Soviets emphasized its full and energetic support for all real efforts to achieve a negotiated settlement ending the war.

C. Blair, *The Forgotten War* (New York, 1987); *Foreign Relations of the United States, 1951,* vol. 7: *Korea and China* (Washington, D.C., 1983).

KNOWLAND, WILLIAM F. (1908–1974)

U.S. senator and advocate of the Asia-first strategy, Knowland emerged as one of the Truman administration's most inflexible critics during the Korean War years. A certified hawk and China lobbyist who liked to end his remarks at dinners and other speaking engagements with the Nationalist toast "Back to the Mainland," Knowland accused the Truman administration of pursuing a policy of appeasement in Korea, which he described as "surrender on the installment plan." His own formula for victory called for strategic bombing, a blockade of the Chinese coast, and the "unleashing" of Chiang Kai-shek*.

Born into a prominent and powerful pioneer family in California, Knowland attended the University of California, graduating in 1929 with a degree in political science, and then went to work for the family newspaper in Oakland. Elected to the state legislature in 1933 at the age of twenty-five and to the Republican National Committee in 1938, he entered the U.S. Army in 1942 as a private and left in 1945 with the rank of major. In September 1945, California Governor Earl Warren appointed the thirty-seven-year-old Knowland to fill the senate seat of Hiram W. Johnson, who died in office, and Knowland won election the following November.

Quickly aligning himself with the Republican party's right wing, Knowland remained at the center of the great debate over the wisdom of New Deal and Fair Deal foreign policy for the next eight years, eventually serving his party as Senate majority leader after Robert A. Taft's* death in July 1953. He called the 1950 congressional elections "a solemn referendum by the American people on our far-eastern policy," provided unqualified support for Senator Joseph R. McCarthy's search for Communists in the State Department, and condemned President Harry S. Truman's* recall of CINCUNC General Douglas MacArthur*. Because he judged all foreign policy by the effect it had on the Republic of China*, Knowland pursued his shrill criticisms throughout the Korean War period—even reportedly bringing Republican Secretary of State John Foster Dulles* to tears once by heckling him at a foreign aid hearing. After losing a bid for the governorship of California in 1958, he returned to the *Oakland Tribune,* taking over the paper in 1965 upon the death of his father. Nine years later, Knowland died, by his own hand.

R. J. Caridi, *The Korean War and American Politics* (Philadelphia, 1968); *Current Biography,* 1947; obituaries in the *Oakland Tribune* and the *New York Times.*

Kenneth O'Reilly

KŎCH'ANG INCIDENT (February 10–11, 1951)

This was an infamous incident where South Korean army soldiers massacred civilians at Sinwŏn-myŏn, Kŏch'ang-gun in South Kyŏngsang province, Republic of Korea*. The tragedy might be called Korea's My Lai. Reportedly, 719 people, 75 percent of them children and elderly, were slaughtered on February 10 and 11 by the 3d Battalion (Major Han Tong-sŏk, commander) of the 9th Regiment (Colonel O Ik-gyŏng, commander) of the ROK 11th Division (Brigadier General Choi Duk Shin*, commander). The division was created on October 2, 1950, to wipe out North Korean People's Army (NKPA) stragglers and Communist Chiri-san guerrillas estimated at about 40,000, who had been active during the war.

The 3d Battalion, which advanced on Sinwŏn-myŏn, first assembled about 1,000 inhabitants at Sinwŏn Elementary School and singled out family members of the army, police, government officials, and the influential. Then the rest of the people were accused of having betrayed the country to the Communists. They were given the death sentence at a summary trial of the military tribunal (Major Han, presiding judge). These civilians were taken to a mountain valley and executed, their bodies burned to destroy the evidence.

This atrocity was revealed by a National Assemblyman, Sin Chung-mok from Kŏch'ang-gun, on March 29, 1951. Thereafter, since reports of ministers of defense, home affairs, and justice on the incident conflicted with one another, the National Assembly dispatched an on-the-spot investigation committee. The investigation team, however, failed to arrive because Deputy Provost Marshal Colonel Kim Chong-wŏn* disguised a platoon of South Korean soldiers as Communist guerrillas and ordered them to attack the investigators on April 7. The National Assembly adopted a resolution censuring the government on the question. As a result, the three ministers resigned, and the investigation resumed in early June on special instruction of President Syngman Rhee*. The provost marshal headquarters arrested O Ik-gyŏng, Han Tong-sŏk, Kim Chong-wŏn, and Second Lieutenant Yi Chong-dae, an intelligence officer in the 3d Battalion, and submitted them for trial by court-martial. Although Yi Chong-dae was found not guilty, the others were convicted. Kim Chong-wŏn was sentenced to a three-year prison term, O Ik-gyŏng to imprisonment for life, and Han Tong-sŏk to ten years in prison. Before long, the three officers were released on a special amnesty. The real truth of the tragedy has never been fully disclosed.

Kukbang-bu p'yŏnch'an wiwŏn-hoe, *Han'guk Chŏnjaeng-sa* (Seoul, 1968); *Wŏlgan Chosŏn* (September 1988); Yŏrŭm Publishing Co. (ed.), *Han'guk Hyŏndae Sahoeundong Sajŏn* (Seoul, 1981).

Jinwung Kim

KŎJE-DO POW UPRISING (May 7–June 10, 1952)

This was the Communist POW uprising that took place at Compound 76 on Kŏje-do (Koje Island). The incident extended settlement of the outstanding issue in the P'anmunjŏm truce talks*, agenda item 4*, POW repatriation, for a considerable period. The UNC* delegation at the P'anmunjŏm truce talks* had taken a stand on the principle of voluntary repatriation* and to this end set out to conduct screening of the prisoners. There was violent resistance, reportedly on direct orders from the Communist high command, against the counting of those both for and against repatriation. Apparently the Communist leaders needed a strong showing in favor of forcible repatriation to strengthen their hands at the bargaining table.

After the first serious bloody incident, which occurred in February 1952 between a battalion of the U.S. 27th Infantry Regiment and Communist POWs, specially trained Communist agents were instructed to be captured at the front to gain access to the UN stockade on Kŏje-do. These agents conveyed to the "loyal" prisoners the latest orders for creating disturbances by all available means. In an excellently planned operation, the POWs of Compound 76 seized Brigadier General Francis T. Dodd, the camp commander, on May 7, and sent out word that as the price for Dodd's release, certain demands had to be met. The terms were directed to Brigadier General Charles F. Colson, next in command at the camps. Colson's main concern was to save Dodd's life. To do so, he agreed to accept many of the conditions. He was forced to sign a humiliating statement in which he admitted that the UN forces killed and wounded many POWs. He assured the prisoners that after Dodd was released unharmed, "in the future POWs can expect humane treatment in this camp," and there would be "no more forcible" screening undertaken. The statement was obtained under coercion, but its effect was devastating on the UNC's international image. The Communist delegation at P'anmunjŏm used Colson's admissions as a propaganda weapon to disrupt the armistice negotiations.

The continued disturbances after the incident led the UNC to authorize firm measures. Brigadier General Haydon L. Boatner*, the new camp commander, took steps swift and effective to recover firm control of the camps on Kŏje-do. The Communist POWs were determined to resist Boatner's efforts to dilute their strength. There was a serious bloody clash on June 10. After over an hour of fighting, Boatner's troops broke the Communist resistance. More than 150 prisoners were killed or injured. One American soldier died, and thirteen were wounded. Thereafter, despite spasmodic violence and acts of defiance, the POW camp was under control. *See also* Dodd-Colson Incident; UNC POW Administration.

J. L. Collins, *War in Peacetime* (Boston, 1969); Kukbang-bu p'yŏnch'an wiwŏn-hoe, *Han'guk Chŏnjaeng-sa* (Seoul, 1968); M. B. Ridgway, *The Korean War* (Garden City, N.Y., 1967).

Jinwung Kim

KOREA
See Democratic People's Republic of Korea; Republic of Korea

KOREAN AID BILL OF 1947

This was a State Department–sponsored bill that focused on building new fertilizer plants in southern Korea to restore and expand rice production. The aid package would have enabled southern Korea to feed itself and resume its critical rice exports to Japan. Initially, the State Department director of Far Eastern Affairs, John Carter Vincent, recommended a $50 million development grant. Under Secretary of State Dean G. Acheson*, however, was already calling for a larger solution to Korea's economic and social problems, advocating planning the regional economic rehabilitation of Asia around what he called "the workshop of Asia"—Japan. Feeding the Japanese people was the first priority. Since much of the Japanese population was receiving food at near-starvation levels in 1947, an enormous drain on the U.S. economy, the restoration of Korea's rice exports (two-thirds of Japan's prewar rice imports) to Japan soon became an urgent concern.

A joint mission from the departments of State, War, and Agriculture went to Korea and Japan. Based on its findings, an interdepartmental committee on Korea recommended an astonishingly large $600 million three-year economic rehabilitation program for Korea. Acheson, who intended to apply the Truman Doctrine in Korea after Greece and Turkey, quickly translated the committee's recommendation into a Korean aid bill and secured support for it from a reluctant War Department. Although he pruned the total package to $540 million, Acheson was unable to bring the bill before the Senate Committee on Foreign Relations. The committee's chairman, Republican Senator Arthur H. Vandenberg, agreed to consider the bill in early 1948 only if the State Department could not get it through the House Armed Services Committee in 1947. Acheson left the State Department on June 30, 1947, and on August 4, 1947, the departments of State, War, and Navy approved a new policy (SWNCC 176/30*), which called for minimizing the commitment of U.S. men and money in Korea. That fall, the Korean aid bill was withdrawn, although Acheson, after becoming secretary of state, pushed through a similar bill in early 1950. *See also* Korean Aid Bill of 1949–1950.

R. L. McGlothlen, "Acheson, Economics, and the American Commitment in Korea," *Pacific Historical Review* (February 1989); J. I. Matray, *The Reluctant Crusade* (Honolulu, 1985); W. W. Stueck, *The Road to Confrontation* (Chapel Hill, 1981).

Ronald L. McGlothlen

KOREAN AID BILL OF 1949–1950

This three-year economic rehabilitation program, signed into law on February 14, 1950, was designed to make the Republic of Korea* nearly self-supporting and to restore its critical trade with Japan. In the spring of 1948, NSC-8* called for the "liquidation of the U.S. commitment of men and money in Korea" and provided only for minimal aid to "forestall economic breakdown." By early 1949, however, the State Department had begun to develop a three-year economic rehabilitation plan, hoping to avoid the collapse of the ROK following U.S. military withdrawal from Korea*. When Dean G. Acheson* became secretary of state in 1949, he strongly endorsed the aid plan, which was modeled after the Korean Aid Bill of 1947*. Making the proposal public, Acheson firmly committed U.S. prestige in Korea.

In June 1949, Acheson presented Congress with a $350 million–$385 million three-year economic rehabilitation program, which concentrated on expanding production facilities for coal, electrical power, fertilizer, and commercial fishing. This would allow South Korea (then essentially an agricultural nation) to restore its high level of rice production and its trade with Japan. In the postwar years, Japan—shorn of the Korea that had provided two-thirds of its imported rice—faced severe food shortages and explosive population growth. By 1949, the United States was supplying 25 percent of Japan's food at a cost of $400 million per year. This was up from $330 million in 1947 and still climbing. In hearings before the House Committee on Foreign Affairs and the Senate Committee on Foreign Relations, Acheson, Under Secretary of State James E. Webb*, and many others strongly urged approval for the assistance package, while a military expert testified that a Communist invasion of the ROK was unlikely.

On January 19, 1950, the House of Representatives defeated the Korean aid bill by a vote of 191 to 192, and Acheson immediately fired off a letter to President Harry S. Truman* saying that this defeat would be "disastrous" for U.S. foreign policy unless it was reversed. Truman began to lobby Congress, while Acheson reduced the cost of the aid plan's first year to $120 million and added limited assistance for the Republic of China* in order to win over the Republican China lobby. The revised aid bill, the Far Eastern Economic Assistance Act of 1950*, passed easily, and Acheson rapidly pushed through another bill providing $100 million for the second year of the plan. Some have pointed to the bill's initial defeat as a factor persuading the Democratic People's Republic of Korea* that it could invade the ROK without risking U.S. intervention. Implementation of the three-year program had barely begun when the Korean War broke out.

R. L. McGlothlen, "Acheson, Economics, and the American Commitment in Korea," *Pacific Historical Review* (February 1989); J. I. Matray, *The Reluctant Crusade* (Honolulu, 1985); W. W. Stueck, *The Road to Confrontation* (Chapel Hill, 1981).

Ronald L. McGlothlen

KOREAN-AMERICAN TREATY OF 1882

This treaty of commerce, amity, and navigation between the Kingdom of Korea and the United States was no longer operative at the time of the Korean War, although Syngman Rhee* invariably referred to it in efforts to increase

U.S. commitments to the Republic of Korea*. Its origins date from 1866, when the American schooner *General Sherman* disappeared after sailing from China to Korea's Taedong River, ostensibly to exchange trade goods with Koreans. To inquire of the ship's fate, Commodore Robert W. Shufeldt in 1867 steered a squadron of U.S. warships to Korean waters. Authorities in Seoul advised him that a local mob had ambushed and burned the *General Sherman* and killed its crew (most members of which were Chinese).

In 1871, the U.S. minister to China, Frederick Low, arrived aboard the flagship of a U.S. flotilla at Chemulp'o (present-day Inch'ŏn) with instructions to negotiate a treaty for the protection of seamen shipwrecked in Korea—also a commercial treaty. Authorities in Seoul turned aside Low's overtures, and when Koreans fired on two American gunboats, Low ordered marines and sailors to undertake a punitive expedition, which claimed the lives of three Americans and perhaps 250 Koreans.

In December 1878, a fleet of American warships under the command of Commodore Shufeldt departed on the first leg of an around-the-world cruise with instructions to arrange a treaty with Korea. When no Korean official would receive him upon arrival at Pusan, Shufeldt attempted to contact the Koreans through the Japanese. The Koreans again rebuffed his overtures, apparently suspecting a Japanese conspiracy aimed at Korea. Delighted when he learned that Shufeldt's attempt had failed, Chinese viceroy Li Hung-chang dispatched a letter to Shufeldt inviting him to visit Tientsin. Shufeldt accepted, conversed with Li, and then returned to the United States. Li thereupon persuaded the Yi court in Seoul to accept a treaty with the Americans; the business of negotiating a treaty binding the United States and Korea began in earnest when Shufeldt returned to China in 1881.

A document that was acceptable to the Koreans eventually emerged. On May 22, 1822, after sailing to Chemulp'o, Shufeldt and Korean emissaries signed a treaty of peace, amity, commerce, and navigation—the Treaty of Chemulp'o—the first article of which provided that "if other Powers deal unjustly or oppressively with either Government, the other will exert their good offices, on being informed of the case, to bring about an amicable arrangement, thus showing their friendly feelings." During the following year, 1883, Lucius M. Foote took up residence in Seoul as the first U.S. minister to Korea.

Unfortunately, the old Hermit Kingdom was becoming caught up in the competition for influence and power in Northeast Asia between Japan and Russia that climaxed in the outbreak of the Russo-Japanese War in 1904. A year later, in 1905, the U.S. president, Theodore Roosevelt, a man who admired the Japanese and felt contempt for Koreans, approved when his secretary of war, in the famous Taft-Katsura memorandum, expressed the view that Japan could establish suzerainty over Korea. The memorandum constituted a repudiation of the spirit, if not the letter, of the Treaty of Chemulp'o. Roosevelt thereupon spurned appeals to save Korea from Japan. Abrogation of the Treaty of Chemulp'o came to pass on August 10, 1910, when the Empire of Japan formally annexed Korea.

M. Deuchler, *Confucian Gentlemen and Barbarian Envoys: The Opening of Korea, 1875–1885* (New York, 1976); F. C. Drake, *The Empire of the Seas: A Biography of Rear Admiral Robert Wilson Shufeldt, USN* (Honolulu, 1984); Y. Lee and W. Patterson (eds.), *One Hundred Years of Korean-American Relations, 1882–1982* (Tuscaloosa, Ala., 1986); D. Suh, "The Centennial: A Brief History," in Y. Koo and D. Suh (eds.), *Korea and the United States: A Century of Cooperation* (Honolulu, 1984); J. E. Wilz, "Did the United States Betray Korea in 1905?" *Pacific Historical Review* (August 1985).

John Edward Wilz

KOREAN AUGMENTATION OF THE U.S. ARMY

In August 1950, the Far Eastern Command (FEC) developed this drastic expedient to overcome the replacement manpower deficiencies in depleted U.S. military units following the North Korean invasion of South Korea*. Implemented concurrently with the rebuilding of the army of the Republic of Korea*, the Korean Augmentation of the U.S. Army (KATUSA) initially provided for the incorporation of between 30,000 and 40,000 ROK recruits into the 24th and 25th Infantry divisions and 1st Cavalry Division in Korea and the 7th Infantry Division in Japan. On August 15, Lieutenant General Walton W. Walker*, the 8th Army* commander, received orders to add 100 Koreans to each company and battery of U.S. troops. Although the ROK would pay and administer these soldiers as part of its own army, the KATUSAs would receive U.S. rations and special service items. To achieve integration, the FEC expected units to adopt the "buddy system." Each KATUSA recruit would pair with a U.S. soldier who would provide training in the use of weapons and equipment, unit drill, and personal hygiene and conduct, at the same time teaching his "buddy" a few words of English.

Before the adoption of the KATUSA program, some U.S. commanders had made unofficial use of South Korean volunteers to strengthen their units. The FEC assigned the first authorized KATUSA recruits to the 7th Division in Japan and they arrived on August 16. The South Korean government had obtained many of these men from the streets of Pusan and Taegu, some boys still carrying their schoolbooks. Starting on August 20, each KATUSA completed five days of training at a center near Pusan. Thereafter, U.S. divisions in Korea received a daily average of 250 recruits. Because the KATUSAs lacked training and could not speak English, U.S. soldiers could not rely on the South Korean recruits during battle. Most units dropped the "buddy system" and organized the KATUSAs into separate squads and platoons with either U.S. or Korean officers. Near chaos accompanied the participation of the KATUSAs in the Inch'on landing*, as the South Korean soldiers, according to one observer, "just didn't know what was going on." Already, many units had asked to receive no more KATUSAs, reporting that they slept on duty, were always hungry, wasted ammunition, panicked under fire, and compromised security by greeting the morning sun with a song. As the UNC* advanced into North Korea in October, many U.S. commanders openly questioned the need for the KATUSAs, insisting that they were a liability rather than an asset.

Chinese military intervention* marked the beginning of success for the KA-TUSA program. While the UNC needed more manpower, the performance of the South Korean recruits improved dramatically once they realized the benefits of serving with the U.S. army. From the start, the KATUSAs had performed valuable menial tasks, such as carrying food, ammunition, and heavy weapons. They also helped dig and camouflage defensive positions. Some made contributions as drivers, welders, and mechanics. But by late 1950, KATUSAs were participating in patrols as scouts, guarding POWs, and helping with refugees. They also provided useful intelligence and had the ability to recognize North Korean operatives among the civilian populace. Soon U.S. soldiers recognized that the South Koreans were their equals in marksmanship and combat skills. During 1952, the UNC began to replace frontline troops with veteran KATUSAs and the program came to occupy an important place in U.S. plans for providing the ROK with the ability to defend itself when the war ended. In July, CINCUNC General Mark W. Clark* obtained approval for the assignment of 2,500 KA-TUSAs per division. From a wartime low of 9,129, the KATUSA force level reached 23,922 just before the armistice. The South Korean government limited recruitment because the program offered prestige and better conditions than existed in the ROK army. The U.S. Army still operates the KATUSA program, providing officer training to carefully selected South Korean recruits.

R. E. Appleman, *South to the Naktong, North to the Yalu* (Washington, D.C., 1961); W. G. Hermes, *Truce Tent and Fighting Front* (Washington, D.C., 1966); D. C. Skaggs, "The KATUSA Experiment: The Integration of Korean Nationals into the U.S. Army, 1950–1965," *Military Affairs* (April 1974).

KOREAN MILITARY ADVISORY GROUP

This U.S. training and instructional group, known more popularly before and during the Korean War by its acronym KMAG, was assigned to assist the Republic of Korea* in developing an army to maintain internal peace and protect its borders. Initially formed as a provisional force following elections for the creation of the ROK, the KMAG was officially established as a training mission on May 2, 1949. Consisting of nearly 500 officers and enlisted men commanded by Brigadier General William L. Roberts*, the KMAG provided military advisors, training teams, and equipment and supplies to the ROK army. One of Roberts's most important subordinates was Major James H. Hausman, who had been the primary architect of the South Korean Constabulary army. Unfortunately, many of the advisors disliked Koreans, and few spoke or understood the language. Training and housing facilities were poor or nonexistent. Moreover, leadership in the ROK army was heavily politicized, and incompetence was rampant. Most ROK units had little platoon or company training, and marksmanship was generally poor. Consequently, the ROK army was largely unprepared for the North Korean invasion of South Korea*.

While the United States hoped that the ROK army could withstand and repel a North Korean attack, the Truman administration was unwilling to supply the

ROK with heavy weapons that could be used to launch an attack to unify the Korean peninsula. Therefore, the ROK had no air force, no heavy artillery, no tanks, and few anti-tank weapons. When North Korean forces crossed the thirty-eighth parallel on June 25, 1950, the ROK army melted in the wake of the attack. As the war progressed and the KMAG was expanded and reinforced, time proved to be the chief enemy in improving military leadership and training opportunities. In July 1951, the South Korean Military Academy was reestablished to help produce a more capable and better-trained officer corps. Advisors were attached to ROK units and assisted in coordinating joint U.S.-Korean operations. Gradually the KMAG played an increasingly important role in the development of the ROK army and in fostering understanding and cooperation between U.S. and Korean military forces.

R. E. Appleman, *South to the Naktong, North to the Yalu* (Washington, D.C., 1961); C. Blair, *The Forgotten War* (New York, 1987); W. G. Hermes, *Truce Tent and Fighting Front* (Washington, D.C., 1966); H. J. Noble, *Embassy at War* (Seattle, 1975); R. K. Sawyer and W. G. Hermes, *Military Advisors in Korea: KMAG in Peace and War* (Washington, D.C., 1962).

John Neilson

KOREAN WAR BRIEFING MEETINGS

These meetings brought together for discussions regarding U.S. conduct of the Korean War representatives from the principal countries contributing military assistance for the defense of the Republic of Korea* under the UN Security Council resolution of June 27, 1950*. The United States arranged for the first of these gatherings at the Canadian embassy on November 30, 1950, following Chinese military intervention*, to provide information on the latest developments in the war. Initially, the meetings were important as a means to counteract press speculation resulting from newspaper reports that arrived from Korea before the receipt of official word from the UNC*. Once the UN forces had halted the Chinese offensive into South Korea during the spring of 1951, however, the United States utilized the Korean War briefing meetings to foster diplomatic and political unity for its policies, such as the establishment of an economic embargo on the People's Republic of China* and later the adoption of the Joint Policy (Greater Sanctions) statement*.

At first, meetings were monthly, but they occurred with greater frequency and irregularity during the last two years of the war. A representative from the JCS always opened the briefing meeting with a summary of current military developments in Korea, after which the United States might raise a major political or diplomatic issue warranting attention. Then there would be questions, answers, and open discussion among the participants. Dean Rusk*, the assistant secretary of state for Far Eastern affairs, usually presided, although John D. Hickerson* or Livingston T. Merchant* chaired the meetings in his absence. Of those attending regularly, the most active participants were Ambassadors Norman J. O. Makin* and Percy Spender*, Second Secretary David W. McNichol and chargé Colin Moodie of Australia, Ambassador Baron Silvercruys and attaché Edmund

Callebaut of Belgium, Ambassador Hume Wrong* of Canada, counselors Jean Daridan and Pierre Millet of France, counselor F. S. Tomlinson* of Great Britain, minister Hughes Le Gallais of Luxembourg, Ambassador Jean Herman Van Roijen and Minister J. G. De Beus of the Netherlands, Ambassador Carl Berendsen* and counselor George Laking of New Zealand, and Ambassador G. P. Jooste* and counselor Basil Jarvie of South Africa. Representatives from Colombia, Ethiopia, Greece, the Philippines, Thailand, and Turkey attended but contributed little to the discussions.

It is doubtful whether the Korean War briefing meetings significantly increased allied unity and support behind U.S. policies during the war. For the United States, these sessions were valuable as a means to anticipate and attempt to resolve in private possible disagreements. The participants discussed the most controversial issues, including UN efforts to achieve a cease-fire in the spring of 1951, President Harry S. Truman's* recall of CINCUNC General Douglas MacArthur*, and the bombing campaign in North Korea. They voiced concern whenever there was a chance that the fighting might not remain localized in Korea but rarely, if ever, raised vigorous objections to U.S. policy. After the start of the Kaesŏng truce talks*, the progress of the negotiations consistently dominated discussions at the briefing meetings, with Washington's allies favoring concessions to obtain an early armistice. Unfortunately, this would result in creating a new controversy, when, on November 17, 1951, the *New York Times* reported the details of an upcoming UNC proposal at the P'anmunjŏm truce talks*. The Truman administration was furious when it learned that a representative at the briefing meetings had leaked the information. On June 28, 1951, the Republic of Korea requested the right to participate in the briefing meetings. The United States already had raised the subject with its allies and, receiving no strong objections, invited the ROK to send a representative. On July 3, Ambassador Yang You Chan* attended his first briefing meeting as an observer.

Foreign Relations of the United States, 1950, vol. 7: *Korea* (Washington, D.C., 1976), *1951,* vol. 7: *Korea and China* (Washington, D.C., 1983), and *1952–1954,* vol. 15: *Korea* (Washington, D.C., 1984).

KŬM RIVER, BATTLE OF THE
See Battle of the Kŭm River

KUO MO-JO (GUO MORO; 1891 [1892?]–1978)
Kuo Mo-jo became chairman of the national committee of the People's Republic of China's* Resist America Aid Korea Movement* (RAAK) in 1952. Kuo was then China's most prominent intellectual speaking out on behalf of the new government in Peking. The outpouring of his articles, public statements, songs, and poems and his frequent appearances at high-level meetings in Peking, already in July and August 1950, are antecedents to the official formation of the RAAK on November 4, 1950. His name frequently appears in the documents of the RAAK. Kuo's assessment of the Korean War in its first year appeared as

a major article in the *People's Daily* on October 1, 1951. It incorporates the pride surrounding the flush of Chinese victories in the early months but disguised the miscalculations that led to the stalemate and the costs that followed. As a vice-premier and after 1952 the president of the Chinese Academy of Sciences, Kuo's language and arguments became enshrined, in effect, in subsequent discussions, both official and scholarly, as the standard Chinese position on the war. Kuo's influence on swaying a part of world opinion favorably toward the PRC during the Korean War must also be noted. As the Chinese spokesman in the World Peace Council, Guo traveled abroad seven different times during the Korean War (twice, within three months' time, to Europe in the winter and spring of 1953), leading Chinese delegations to the various meetings of the World Peace Council to many capitals of Western and Eastern Europe.

Kuo's unqualified attacks on the United States throughout the Korean War and his strident defense of Chinese policies and behavior, in the name of world peace, from 1949 until his death in 1978, are so heavily political as to raise questions about his personal integrity. Such doubts come natural to Western observers, but recently to Chinese critics as well, especially in light of Kuo's emerging from the Great Proletarian Cultural Revolution practically unscathed. It would be easy to dismiss Kuo's behavior as sheer opportunism and fellow-traveling—he never joined the Communist party. His politics gained him titles, positions, and official adulations that fill many pages. As a prolific scholar, (ancient Chinese history and paleography), poet, and writer, Kuo's position in the twentieth-century Chinese intellectual history is impressive. He was not always so patriotic or radical. By the time he was 45, he had spent twenty years studying and teaching in Japan, marrying a Japanese wife who bore him five children. During the war with Japan, furthermore, he lived in Chungking, the wartime capital of the Republic of China*. As late as 1948, he left China to live and write in Hong Kong. Despite the erratic life and the dramatic shifts in his politics, Kuo's patriotism after 1949 illuminates the burdens and dilemmas peculiar to Chinese intellectuals not only during the Korean War but throughout much of modern Chinese history.

H. L. Boorman (ed.), *Biographical Dictionary of Republican China* (New York, 1968); D. W. Klein and A. B. Clark (eds.), *Biographic Dictionary of Chinese Communism, 1921–1965* (Cambridge, 1971); Renmin chubanshe, *Weida de kangMei yuanChao yundong* (Peking, 1954); D. T. Roy, *Kuo Mo-Jo: The Early Years* (Cambridge, 1971).

Philip West

L

LATIN AMERICA AND THE KOREAN WAR

During the Korean War, Latin American nations supported UN efforts to resist the North Korean invasion of South Korea* but generally declined to become directly involved in the struggle. Cuba and Ecuador were members of the Security Council in June 1950 and voted in favor of U.S.-sponsored UN Security Council resolutions on June 25, 1950*, to condemn the North Korean invasion and then on June 27 to assist South Korea. The Cuban and Ecuadorian votes were critical to achieving the two-thirds majority necessary for approval of the UN Security Council resolution of June 27, 1950*. Thereafter, Latin Americans continued to follow the U.S. lead at the UN, although some nations, led by Mexico and its representative, Luis Padilla Nervo*, showed interest in mediation proposals formulated by neutrals like India.

Beyond such expressions of solidarity, however, Latin Americans offered little tangible support other than small quantities of food, clothing, and blankets to the UN and U.S. effort in Korea. The United States, in bilateral meetings and at the Washington Conference* in 1951, repeatedly asked Latin Americans for military contributions, hoping that populous nations like Argentina, Brazil, and Mexico would contribute a division of troops and smaller nations like Chile and Peru a regiment. But only Colombia, which sent the Colombian Battalion* to Korea, responded positively. Led by Brazil, Latin Americans took the position that the best way to combat international communism was through economic development and therefore they should concentrate on internal affairs. This attitude reflected the regional view that Latin American nations had firmly supported the UN during World War II, had reaped little in reward, and had been neglected by the United States during the postwar period.

S. E. Hilton, "The United States, Brazil, and the Cold War, 1945–1960: End of the Special Relationship," *Journal of American History* (December 1981); J. A. Houston, *Latin America in the United Nations* (New York, 1956); S. G. Rabe, "The Elusive

Conference: United States Economic Relations with Latin America, 1945–1952," *Diplomatic History* (Summer 1978).

Stephen G. Rabe

LAY, JAMES S., JR. (1911–1987)

From 1949 to 1961, James S. Lay, Jr., was executive secretary of the National Security Council. Born in Washington, D.C., he earned a B.S. in electrical engineering from Virginia Military Institute in 1933. Two years later, he graduated from Harvard Business School with an M.A. in public utilities and went to work for Stone and Webster Service Corporation. Lay also was a commercial and industrial power sales engineer for the Virginia Electric and Power Company. A member of the U.S. Field Artillery Reserve, he was called to active duty in May 1941 and trained with the 353d Field Artillery Regiment. In August 1942, Lay joined the British empire branch of the War Department's military intelligence service. He served briefly in London in the office of the U.S. military attaché but returned to the United States in December 1943 to become the secretary of the Joint Chiefs of Staff's joint intelligence committee.

Lay, after receiving his discharge in October 1945, joined the State Department as a management analyst for the special assistant in charge of research and intelligence. Before the year ended, he became secretary of the National Intelligence Authority (NIA), serving in 1946 as division chief of the central intelligence group. When the National Security Council (NSC) replaced the NIA in 1947, Lay was appointed assistant executive secretary with responsibility for supervising the NSC staff in assessing national security policy in terms of U.S. potential and actual military power. In December 1949, he replaced Rear Admiral Sidney W. Souers when the first NSC executive secretary resigned. Thereafter, Lay would provide daily briefings for President Harry S. Truman* on intelligence information that the NSC staff had assembled. While not setting policy, he helped draft all NSC papers, including those related to the Korean War. In 1961, Lay became deputy assistant to Allen W. Dulles, director of the Central Intelligence Agency, serving later as executive secretary for the U.S. Intelligence Board. According to one of his colleagues, he was "a master at bringing about organizational change." Lay retired in 1971, although he continued to serve as a presidential consultant until 1977.

Current Biography, 1950; *New York Times*, July 1, 1987.

LEE BUM SUK

See Yi, Pŏm-sŏk

LEE CHONG CH'AN (YI CHŎNG-CH'ŎN; 1916–1983)

Lee Chong Ch'an was chief of staff for the army of the Republic of Korea* at the start of the South Korean political crisis of 1952*. Born in Seoul as a grandson of the Yi dynasty's justice minister, he graduated from the Japanese Military Academy in 1937, reaching the rank of major in 1943. After returning home in 1946, Lee spent a self-imposed period of repentance for three years, rejecting the offer to supervise the formation of the ROK army. One year after the ROK government was established in August 1948, he accepted the post of director of the Information and Education Bureau at the Defense Ministry with the rank of colonel. A week prior to the North Korean invasion of South Korea*, President Syngman Rhee* appointed Colonel Lee commander of the Seoul Security Command. With the outbreak of the Korean War, Lee had to evacuate to Pusan, replacing Brigadier General Kim Suk Won* as commander of the 3d Division in September with the rank of brigadier general. After the Inch'ŏn landing*, he was lucky enough to lead his division when it became the first ROK unit to cross the thirty-eighth parallel on September 30, 1950. Just before the Chinese military intervention*, Lee transferred to the post of chief logistics administrator.

On June 23, 1951, Lee was appointed chief of staff for the ROK army with the rank of major general. In January 1952, he was promoted to lieutenant general. Four months later, President Rhee, in his successful attempt to revise the constitution in his favor, imposed martial law and instructed Lee to redeploy two combat divisions from the front line to reinforce the weak detachment in Pusan. Lee, who had not been consulted with regard to Rhee's declaration of martial law*, rejected the order on the rationale that the military should not be a tool for politicians. He received strong support for his defiance from his staff officers, CINCUNC General Mark W. Clark*, and General James A. Van Fleet*, 8th Army* commander. His decision resulted in Rhee's removing him as chief of staff, but Lee received high praise for an act that reflected the "spirit of the true military man." At that time, Colonel Park Chung Hee, who would later stage a coup d'état and become the president of the ROK, made a futile attempt to persuade Lee to stage a coup against Rhee.

Soon after, Lee was exiled to the United States for further military training. In August 1953, he was appointed president of the ROK Army College. In early 1960, Lee voiced opposition to Rhee's plan to rig the upcoming presidential election. At this time, Park Chung Hee, now a major general, again attempted, in vain, to persuade Lee to stage a coup, but Lee remained firm in his belief that the military should not intervene in civilian politics. In May 1960, after Rhee's ouster following the April student uprising, he joined the interim government led by Ho Chong as defense minister, retiring from the military. One year later, Park Chung Hee staged a successful military takeover. For the subsequent eighteen years of his government, Park treated Lee as a "teacher" and appointed Lee ambassador to Italy and member of the National Assembly.

Kang Song-jae, *Ch'amgun'in Yi Chŏng-ch'ŏn Changgun* (Seoul, 1986); S. Kim, *The Politics of Military Revolution in Korea* (Chapel Hill, 1971); *New York Times,* June 25, 1951, July 24, 1952; K. Yi, *Pigŭkŭi Kunindŭl* (Seoul, 1982).

Hakjoon Kim

LEE HAK-KU (1920–1953)

On September 21, 1950, Colonel Lee Hak-ku surrendered to the UNC* and thereafter was the second-highest-ranking North Korean POW during the Korean War. Trained in the Soviet Union, he returned to Korea following World War II to become an officer in the army of the Democratic People's Republic of Korea*. Lee was operations officer for the 7th Division, II Corps and, at the time of the North Korean invasion of South Korea*, chief of staff for the 13th Division. After his capture, he was most cooperative, providing full information on North Korean military deployments near Tabu-dong, to include the location of the division command post, remaining artillery, the status of resupply efforts, and troop morale. According to Lee, the 13th Division was no longer an effective fighting unit and was suffering a rising number of defections. Subsequently Lee Hak-ku became the leader at POW Compound 76 on Kŏje-do and would receive instructions from Lieutenant General Nam Il* through purposely captured North Korean soldiers. He would play a prominent role in staging the Kŏje-do POW uprising*, resulting in the Dodd-Colson incident*. Under the armistice agreement*, he was repatriated to North Korea in 1953 and was immediately purged.

R. E. Appleman, *South to the Naktong, North to the Yalu* (Washington, D.C., 1961); T. R. Fehrenbach, *This Kind of War* (New York, 1963); W. G. Hermes, *Truce Tent and Fighting Front* (Washington, D.C., 1966).

LEE HYUNG KEUN (YI HYŎNG-GŬN; 1920–   )

When the Korean War began, Brigadier General Lee Hyung Keun was the commander of the Republic of Korea's* 2d Division stationed at Taejŏn. He was a graduate of the Japanese Military Academy and had been a captain in the Japanese army before World War II. Prior to the North Korean invasion of South Korea*, he had attended U.S. Infantry School at Fort Benning, Georgia, and then had served on the bureau of the South Korean Constabulary army. On June 25, 1950, Chief of Staff Chae Byung Dok* ordered Lee to move his forces 120 miles northward to a location east of Ŭijŏngbu where, as part of an envelopment operation, his unit would counterattack with the 7th Division the next day. Lee spent the remainder of the day gathering his men and assuming defensive positions south of the thirty-eighth parallel, but on the morning of June 26, he ignored his instructions and did not attack. The North Koreans assaulted and shattered Brigadier General Yu Jai Hyung's* isolated 7th Division, located to the west and 2 miles north of Ŭijŏngbu, while Lee led his troops in a retreat southward. Although Major James H. Hausman, the U.S. KMAG* advisor, agreed that Chae's plan was foolish, Lee's insubordination guaranteed disaster. Before the end of the second day of fighting, there was no effective force blocking North Korean occupation of Seoul. Later, Lee Hyung Keun became head of the ROK's Field Training Command, served as South Korea's delegate at the P'anmunjŏm truce talks*, and then was the ROK army's chief of staff.

R. E. Appleman, *South to the Naktong, North to the Yalu* (Washington, D.C., 1961); T. R. Fehrenbach, *This Kind of War* (New York, 1963); W. G. Hermes, *Truce Tent and*

Fighting Front (Washington, D.C., 1966); *New York Times,* September 9, 1951; K. Yi, *Pigŭkŭi Kunindŭl* (Seoul, 1982).

Jinwung Kim

LEE KWON MU (YI KWŎN-MU; 1910–   )

A major general in the North Korean People's Army (NKPA), Lee Kwon Mu was commander of the 4th Division at the start of the Korean War. Born in Manchuria, he went to the Soviet Union as a young man to receive officer training. In World War II, he served as a lieutenant in the Red Army, later fighting with the Chinese Communist 8th Route Army against the Japanese. After helping defeat Chiang Kai-shek's* Nationalist forces during the Chinese Civil War, Lee went to the Soviet Union for more military training. In 1948, he returned to North Korea and became army chief of staff in the newly created Democratic People's Republic of Korea*. It was Lee's 4th Division that occupied the capital of the Republic of Korea* on June 28, 1950, thereby earning as its nickname the ''Seoul Division.'' In October 1950, he assumed command of the NKPA II Corps. Following the Korean War, Lee became commander in chief of the DPRK's army. In 1958, Kim Il Sung* purged his political opponents, and Lee became chief of staff for the NKPA, serving in that post until 1960.

R. E. Appleman, *South to the Naktong, North to the Yalu* (Washington, D.C., 1961); Chungang Ilbo (ed.), *Pukhan Inmyong Sajŏn* (Seoul, 1981); T. R. Fehrenbach, *This Kind of War* (New York, 1963); J. A. Kim, *Divided Korea* (Cambridge, 1975).

Jinwung Kim

LEE SANG CHO (YI SANG-JO; 1915–   )

Born at Tongnae, now a part of Pusan, Major General Lee Sang Cho was North Korea's deputy chief delegate to the P'anmunjŏm truce talks*. In 1932, he emigrated to China with his parents. After graduating from a Chinese military officers' training school, Lee fought with the Chinese Communists against the Japanese. Later he became one of the unit commanders of the Korean Volunteer Army, which was supported by the Chinese Communist party (CCP). He returned to northern Korea in 1946 to become deputy chief of the organization department of the North Korean Workers' party and to become an architect of the North Korean People's Army (NKPA).

At the time of the North Korean invasion of South Korea*, he was vice-minister of commerce of the Democratic People's Republic of Korea*. Immediately he became deputy chief of staff of the NKPA. In September 1950, Lee, at the request of Kim Il Sung*, secretly traveled to Peking to appeal for Chinese military intervention* in the war to prevent the destruction of the DPRK following the Inch'ŏn landing*. In 1951, he was transferred to director of the Inspection Bureau. Then during the entire period of the armistice negotiations—July 10, 1951 to July 27, 1953—he served as a member of the North Korean delegation. According to Joseph C. Goulden, ''Chunky and often physically filthy, Lee had one impressive characteristic: He would permit flies to crawl over his face without brushing them away. Apparently he thought this showed iron self-control.''

Following the cease-fire, Lee served as chief of the North Korean component of the Military Armistice Commission*.

In August 1955, after retiring from the army, Lee was appointed ambassador to Moscow. In April 1956, he was elected a candidate member of the central committee of the Korean Workers' party. That same year, encouraged by the de-Stalinization campaign in the Soviet Union, the Chinese exile (Yenan) faction and the Soviet exile (*Kapsan*) faction challenged the personality cult of Kim Il Sung. However, Kim purged the opposition in the so-called Ch'oi Ch'ang-ik incident of 1957, and Lee Sang Cho was one of his victims. Defying a recall order, he sought political asylum in Moscow. Lee never returned to North Korea from the Soviet Union, subsequently serving as a researcher at a Soviet state-run research institute in Minsk where he received his doctorate. He resides in Minsk, living on a Soviet pension. In the summer of 1989, Lee visited South Korea and in a press conference stated that Kim Il Sung initiated the Korean War.

J. C. Goulden, *Korea: The Untold Story of the War* (New York, 1982); *Korea Herald,* September 13, 1989; *Korea Times,* September 10, 1989.

Hakjoon Kim

LEMNITZER, LYMAN L. (1899–1988)

As a major general in the U.S. Army, Lyman L. Lemnitzer served in the Korean War as commander of the 11th Airborne Division in 1950 and then of the 7th Infantry Division from 1951 to 1952. By that time, he was already a founding father of the North Atlantic Treaty Organization. Lemnitzer was one of the new breed of officers whose experience in political-military affairs in World War II led to appointment as high-ranking officials in the Truman administration. But he was also a generalist who accepted rotation from one assignment to another with good grace. Indeed, he welcomed the opportunity to command an airborne division in Korea in 1950. He made his first parachute jump at the age of 51.

Born in Honesdale, Pennsylvania, in 1899, Lemnitzer attended the U.S. Military Academy at West Point during World War I. Graduating in 1919, he rose slowly through the grades from lieutenant to major in the interwar years. World War II accelerated the pace of his career; he served as assistant chief of staff of Field Marshal Sir Harold Alexander's Allied headquarters in the Mediterranean theater. He could manage men as well as plans and won the confidence of his superiors, British as well as American. His ability to deal easily with civilian leaders explains his selection as U.S. representative of the JCS when the newly established Brussels Pact organization began its deliberations. Lemnitzer was the key U.S. military figure in support of European military and political co-operation. Appointed director of the Office of Foreign Military Assistance in 1949, he was as much a lobbyist for aid to Europe as he was an administrator of the aid program.

When he went to Korea in 1950, Lemnitzer left behind a solid infrastructure for the defense of Western Europe. His return to Washington in 1952 as deputy chief of staff for plans and research did not mean his complete disengagement from East Asian affairs. From 1955 to 1957, he was commander in chief of the Far Eastern Command, as well as of the UNC*. His later career in the Eisenhower years followed a conventional path, from army vice-chief of staff to army chief of staff and then to the pinnacle of the military hierarchy, chairman of the JCS from 1960 to 1962. Before his retirement in 1969, Lemnitzer also served as Supreme Allied Commander, Europe.

R. E. Appleman, *South to the Naktong, North to the Yalu* (Washington, D.C., 1961); W. G. Hermes, *Truce Tent and Fighting Front* (Washington, D.C., 1966); K. F. A. Kellner, "Broker of Power: General Lyman L. Lemnitzer" (Ph. D. diss., Kent State University, 1987).

Lawrence S. Kaplan

LEVIERO, ANTHONY (1905–1956)

During the Korean War, Anthony Leviero was bureau chief in Washington, D.C., for the *New York Times,* primarily covering events at the White House. In 1951, he won a Pulitzer Prize for securing and publishing the record of discussions between President Harry S. Truman* and CINCUNC General Douglas MacArthur* at the Wake Island Conference*. Born in Brooklyn, New York, Leviero worked as an office boy and a clerk for the U.S. Shipping Board before becoming an auditor for maritime insurance and shipping firms. He soon realized that he "didn't like figures and ledgers" and in 1926 embarked on a new career when the *New York American* hired him as a copy boy and night police reporter. In 1929, Leviero joined the *New York Times,* subsequently writing stories on crime, the courts, military affairs, and Congress. Meanwhile, he had taken courses at Columbia University and the City College of New York, as well as enlisting in New York's National Guard in 1923. Leviero transferred to the U.S. Army Reserve in 1935 and received training in military intelligence. Called to active duty in 1941, he went to Europe as an intelligence officer, serving later at U.S. Army Field headquarters in North Africa. From 1944 until his discharge in 1945, Lieutenant Colonel Leviero was chief of the publicity branch at military intelligence division of the War Department General Staff.

Leviero returned to the *New York Times* in 1945 and worked at its Washington bureau. Two years later, he became White House correspondent and thereafter was always with President Truman to cover his activities, accompanying him to Wake Island. Leviero reportedly asked the president after the meeting, "How did things shape up?" Truman replied that he was "highly pleased with the results, like an insurance salesman who had at last signed up an important prospect while the latter appeared dubious about the extent of the coverage." Beginning in March 1951, Leviero became a roving reporter on Washington affairs. But after listening to MacArthur's speech to Congress of April 19, 1951*, he remembered the Wake Island Conference and privately asked three administration officials for a transcript of the discussions. Though only able to take notes, Leviero nevertheless reported MacArthur's assurances to Truman that

victory was near and Chinese military intervention* unlikely. MacArthur's supporters immediately charged that he had allowed the Truman administration to
use him for political purposes. A quiet man, Leviero developed a reputation for
being hardworking and diligent. James Reston observed that he was "a man
who taught beavers to be eager." At the time of his death from a heart attack,
Leviero was reporting on the 1956 presidential campaign.

Current Biography, 1952; New York Times, September 4, 1956; D. Rees, Korea: The
Limited War (New York, 1964); Who Was Who in America, vol. 3: 1951–1960 (Chicago,
1960).

LI K'E-NUNG (LI KENONG; 1898–1962)

Li K'e-nung was chief of the Chinese People's Volunteers Army* (CPVA)
delegation at the Korean truce talks and directed both the Chinese and North
Korean military delegates in the negotiations. Throughout his career in the
Chinese revolution and after the birth of the People's Republic of China*, Li
was one of the top leaders in the intelligence and security apparatus. He joined
the Chinese Communist party (CCP) in 1926. In 1928, he became a member of
the special section of the CCP Central Committee in Shanghai, the first intel-
ligence and security organ of the party. Li went to the Central Bases Area in
Kiangsi in 1931 and was appointed the operations chief of the National Political
Security Bureau. Three years later, he was the chief of security of the First Front
Army during the Long March and became the director of liaison bureau, CCP
Central Committee, in 1936.

During the Sino-Japanese War (1937–1945), Li was the CCP armed forces
representative in Shanghai, Nanking, and Chilin, chief secretary of the Yangtze
bureau of CCP Central Committee, and deputy chief of the CCP's social department (the intelligence security apparatus of the party). During the Chinese
Civil War (1946–1949), he became chief of CCP's social department and member
and chief secretary of the CCP delegation to the Executive Headquarters formed
by the representatives of the Kuomintang (KMT), the CCP, and the United
States. He was appointed a vice–foreign minister of PRC government in 1949
and was also a deputy chief of staff in the Chinese People's Liberation Army.
In 1955, he was commissioned a full general. He was also a member of the
CCP Central Committee elected by the Eighth Congress in 1956.

In early July 1951, instructed by Mao Tse-tung*, Li arrived in P'yŏngyang
and met with Kim Il Sung*. With him was a group of associates to work at the
Kaesŏng truce talks*, including Ch'iao Kuan-hua, Pu San, Pi Chi-ung, Shen
Chien-tu, and Ting Ming. At Kaesŏng during July, the original delegation to
the negotiations was divided into two. The North Koreans were to be the major
representatives for the Communist side, while Li K'e-nung and his delegation
were actually in charge of the negotiations. A CPVA Negotiations Delegation
Party Committee was formed with Li as chief; its principal members were Teng
Hua* (deputy commander of the CPVA) and Hsieh Fang* (chief of staff of the
CPVA). Tsai Cheng-wen* (CPVA's liaison officer to the North Korean People's

Army) was the chief secretary of the delegation. Though Li had made great contributions to the conclusion of the Korean War armistice agreement*, he always stayed behind the scenes.

Cai Chengwen and Zhao Yongtian, *A Factual Record of the Korean War* (Beijing, 1987); Cai Chengwen and Zhao Yongtian, *Panmunjom Negotiations* (Beijing, 1990); Chinese People's Liberation Army Academy of Military Science, *A Military History of the Anti-U.S. Aid-Korea War* (Beijing, 1988); Yao Xu, *From the Yalu to Panmunjom* (Beijing, 1988).

Hua Qingzhao

LIE, TRYGVE (1896–1968)

Trygve Lie, the first secretary-general of the United Nations, was a central figure in mobilizing international support behind the defense of the Republic of Korea* after the North Korean attack on June 25, 1950. Born in Oslo, Norway, Lie graduated in 1919 from Oslo University Law School. He spent the next sixteen years in various positions in the Norwegian Labor party and trade union movement. In 1935, he was appointed minister of justice in a coalition government headed by the Labor party. When World War II began, Lie became the minister of shipping and supply, but in June 1940 he fled his country to avoid capture by the Nazis, becoming in February 1941 minister of foreign affairs in the Norwegian government in exile in London. Four years later, Lie headed the Norwegian delegation to the conference on the UN at San Francisco, where he spoke eloquently in favor of a new international order that balanced great power influence with adherence to moral principles. In January 1946, he led his nation's delegation to the first convocation of the UN, where he lost in a close vote for president of the General Assembly but later emerged as a compromise candidate for secretary-general.

Initially, Lie maintained sufficient balance on major issues to avoid alienating either side in the developing cold war. With the North Korean invasion of South Korea*, however, he took an active role in supporting UN action to counter "aggression." In late June, he was instrumental in bringing the Security Council into emergency session and gaining passage of the UN Security Council resolutions of June 25* and June 27, 1950*. He took an active role in the establishing of a UN Command* (UNC) on Korea, although his proposal favoring a more centralized system under the control of a Committee on Coordination on Assistance for Korea was effectively opposed by the United States. These activities produced a sharp reaction from the Soviet Union, which attacked Lie as a partisan of the West, but Lie continued to support UN intervention in Korea.

After the Inch'ŏn landing*, Lie sought to end the conflict quickly. He circulated a plan for UN-supervised elections throughout the peninsula that precluded an immediate move of UN troops into North Korea, but the United States lobbied successfully for the UN resolution of October 7, 1950*, that tacitly approved the UN offensive across the thirty-eighth parallel*. On the other hand, he publicly supported the UN Uniting for Peace resolution of November 3, 1950*, which passed despite Moscow's vociferous objections, as did a resolution extending

Lie's term as secretary-general for three years. Despite increasing Soviet hostility, Lie continued efforts to mediate on Korea. In the midst of the Chinese military intervention* in late 1950, he became involved in negotiations to arrange a cease-fire through the recently arrived delegation of the People's Republic of China*. Those efforts failed, as did Lie's overtures in March 1951 to a number of Western delegates regarding a possible indirect approach to the Democratic People's Republic of Korea*. Lie's next major initiative came in early June, when he circulated a plan that called for talks between military commanders in the field and a cease-fire along the thirty-eighth parallel. This overture may have reinforced the secret Kennan-Malik conversations* leading to the dramatic Soviet initiative on Korea that contributed to the start of the Kaesŏng truce talks.

As time passed, Lie increasingly felt the impact of the Soviet Union's refusal to recognize his extended term as secretary-general. He decided during the summer of 1952 to resign before his term expired, announcing his decision on November 10 but staying on until early April 1953 to give the organization time to choose a successor. By the time Dag Hammarskjold* replaced him, Lie was unpopular with many people at the United Nations, including members of the Secretariat, who resented his handling of the loyalty investigations. On Korea, some delegates had been offended by his pressure in mid–1951 to dismantle the UN Good Offices Committee*, a move that appeared in part to be a result of resentment over the body's preeminence in mediation efforts. After departing from the United Nations, Lie returned to Norway, wrote several volumes of memoirs, including one on his experiences as secretary-general, and held several appointive posts involving both international and domestic activities.

J. Barros, *Trygve Lie and the Cold War* (DeKalb, Ill., 1989); A. W. Cordier oral history, Oral History Project, Columbia University; *Current Biography*, 1946; *Foreign Relations of the United States, 1950*, vol. 7: *Korea* (Washington, D.C., 1976) and *1951*, vol. 7: *Korea and China* (Washington, D.C., 1983); T. Lie, *In the Cause of Peace* (New York, 1956); *New York Times*, December 31, 1968.

William Stueck

LIGHTNER, E. ALLAN (1907–   )

Edwin Allan Lightner, Jr., became the counselor of the embassy in Pusan in March 1951, replacing Everett F. Drumright*. During Ambassador John J. Muccio's* absence from late May to early June 1952, Lightner was chargé d'affaires and became actively involved in the South Korean political crisis of 1952* between President Syngman Rhee* and his opponents in the National Assembly. Born in New York, Lightner graduated from Princeton University in 1930 and joined the foreign service that same year. He spent most of his early career at Latin American posts, and then moved to Europe. After World War II, he handled Central European Affairs for the Department of State. When he arrived in Korea on March 1, 1951, it was his first posting in Asia.

Lightner's sympathies clearly lay with the National Assembly, which he believed had to be protected from Rhee or else democracy would have no chance of survival in Korea. As chargé, Lightner advised Washington to support, even to the point of physical protection, the National Assembly. Instructed by Washington to admonish Rhee for his extralegal action against his opponents, Lightner's meetings with Rhee became increasingly confrontational and on one occasion deteriorated into a shouting match. While he professed few illusions about Rhee's opponents, Lightner considered anyone better than Rhee whose rule he judged to be incompatible with democracy. Lightner also complained that U.S. military men in Korea and Japan were inadvertently passing signals to Rhee that their primary concern was tranquility in the rear echelons, not democracy.

As the most outspoken member of the embassy opposed to Rhee, Lightner was contacted by some Republic of Korea* military leaders who offered to stage a coup against Rhee if the United States agreed to give them the green light. When Washington declined the offer, Lightner reported that it might not be necessary to support the South Korean generals' coup but just to make it known that the United States was talking with them. Then Rhee would be convinced that the United States meant business and might well step down, or at least agree to share real power with the National Assembly. It is impossible to say where Lightner's advice would have taken U.S.-ROK relations. The Truman administration rejected his plan, Rhee overpowered the assembly, won reelection, and became a virtual dictator, as Lightner had predicted. Lightner left Korea in February 1953 and eventually became U.S. ambassador to Libya in 1963.

Foreign Relations of the United States, 1952–1954, vol. 15: *Korea* (Washington, D.C., 1984).

Edward C. Keefer

LIMB, BEN C. (IM PYŎNG-JIK; 1893–1976)

Ben Limb was the Republic of Korea's* minister of foreign affairs from 1949 to 1951. Limb had known Syngman Rhee* for a long time before Rhee, the first president of the ROK, appointed him to this post. He was a student at the YMCA School in Seoul where Rhee was teaching before going into exile in the United States following Japanese annexation of Korea. It was through Rhee's arrangements that Limb went to the United States to study. While a sophomore at Ohio State University, he became secretary to Rhee.

Limb's foremost task before the outbreak of the Korean War was obtaining more U.S. military assistance in the face of growing indications that the Democratic People's Republic of Korea* was stepping up preparations for war. On a number of occasions, he presented the Americans—Ambassador John J. Muccio* and Brigadier General William L. Roberts*, head of the Korean Military Advisory Group*—with evidence collected in the north that the DPRK was rapidly expanding its military preparations and improving on equipment, including tanks and airplanes. But as he recollects, all these efforts were met with cold responses from the American side, which disparaged the information provided by the South Korean government as unreliable. U.S. officials tended to suspect that the South Koreans meant to use the arms they were asking for to

invade the north. He sought explanations from the U.S. government when Secretary of State Dean G. Acheson* excluded South Korea from its defensive
perimeter in his National Press Club speech* but never received any reply. During
John Foster Dulles's* trip to Korea* two weeks before the outbreak of the war,
it was Limb who guided him through his inspection of the thirty-eighth parallel.
In September 1950, he was sent to New York as the chief Korean delegate to
the Fifth UN General Assembly. Later he was relieved of his post as foreign
minister and became ambassador to the UN. Limb finished his diplomatic career
with appointments as ambassador to India and, beginning in 1967, ambassador
at large.

Although a faithful follower of Rhee's foreign policy, Limb told the British
minister in Seoul after he had returned from the Geneva Conference of 1954*
that from then on, it would have to be through economic reconstruction and
prosperity that South Korea should pursue the reunification of the country. This
was a deviation on his part from the orthodox line of policy advocated by Rhee
and the first generation of anti-Communists. It signaled the beginning of South
Korea's shift toward economic development, rather than military means, in
fighting communism in Korea.

B. C. Limb, *Limb Ben Chic Hoegorok* (Seoul, 1964); H. J. Noble, *Embassy at War*
(Seattle, 1975).

J. Y. Ra

LIN PIAO (LIN BIAO; 1907–1971)

Lin Piao was the chairman of the Central-South China military and administrative committee during the Korean War. When Lin was 18, he became
involved in the newly emerged Communist movement in China, entering the
Huangpu Military Academy under the instruction of the Chinese Communist
party (CCP) in 1926. Then he joined the Northern Expedition and started to
build his brilliant military career. After the Kuomintang (KMT) split with the
CCP in 1927, Lin became a general in the Red Army, commanding a division
when he was only 23 years old and contributing to the CCP's defense against
Chiang Kai-shek's* campaigns. In 1937, the Sino-Japanese War broke out, and
Lin again demonstrated his military talent, planning and executing the famous
Battle at P'ing-hsing Pass, where his forces eliminated an entire Japanese di-
vision.

In 1939, Lin was badly wounded and went to the Soviet Union for treatment.
He remained there for three years, studying military theory at a Soviet military
academy, and returned in 1942 to become president of the Anti-Japanese Red
Army College. The next year, Lin went back to the Soviet Union to practice
battlefield tactics. In 1946, when the Chinese Civil War started, Lin got the
chance to apply what he had learned from Soviet generals and played a significant
role in the CCP's final victory. His 4th Field Army was the best of the Communist
troops, fighting its way from Manchuria in the north through Hainan Island in
the south. In 1950, Lin's 4th Field Army was the first unit to cross the Yalu

River as part of the Chinese People's Volunteers Army* (CPVA). At the Battle of Ŭnsan, the Chinese army destroyed a U.S. Marine division and a South Korean division. It failed to expand the victory, however, because of the enemy's superior American-made equipment, and it suffered great losses.

Lin's role in the Korean War remains a matter of debate. Evidence exists that, along with Kao Kang*, he strongly opposed Chinese military intervention* in the Korean War. While some American historians maintain that Lin was the actual commander of the CPVA, the Chinese documents consistently deny this assertion. From the tactics applied in the battles, there can be no doubt that it was Lin's army that was fighting. Even if one assumes that Lin was not in Korea, the field commanders must have executed the military plan that he devised. Controversy also exists regarding his removal from command. According to some accounts, Lin disagreed with Mao Tse-tung's* strategy of fighting a defensive positional war after the failure of the Chinese spring offensives of 1951*, insisting instead on fighting to expel the UNC* from Korea. Another opinion holds that Lin was seriously wounded again and had to leave the battlefield. It is certain, however, that after early 1951, Lin and his army had a minor role in fighting the Korean War.

In 1956, Lin was promoted to the rank of marshal. Three years later, when Peng Teh-huai* was purged, Lin replaced him as the first vice-chairman of the CCP's military committee and the minister of defense. At this point, Lin began to cultivate a special relationship with Mao through encouraging a personality cult. He flattered Mao and won his trust with references to his "four greatnesses," while labeling Maoism a "spiritual nuclear bomb." In 1966, Mao ignited the Great Proletarian Cultural Revolution. Lin was a close ally in Mao's campaign against his main political rival, Liu Shao-chi, who disappeared in 1969. Lin was made Mao's legal successor at the Ninth Party National Congress, reaching the peak of his political career. By early 1971, however, Lin found himself losing favor with Mao and, worried about being purged, plotted a military coup d'état. In September, the conspiracy was discovered. Lin fled to the Soviet Union, but he died when his plane crashed in Mongolia.

M. Ebon, *Lin Piao: The Life and Writings of China's New Ruler* (New York, 1970); Huang Chen-hsia, *Mao's Generals* (Hong Kong, 1968); Research Institute of Chinese Questions, *Lin Piao Chuan Chi* (Hong Kong, 1970).

Li Yi

LLOYD, JOHN SELWYN (1904–1978)

For the last two years of the Korean War, Sir John Selwyn Brooke Lloyd served as Britain's minister of state for foreign affairs. Born in Liverpool, he studied the classics and history at Cambridge before earning his law degree in London at Gray's Inn. During the 1930s, he pursued his law career, mostly pleading insurance cases. In 1939, he joined Britain's Territorial Army but transferred to the Royal Horse Artillery the next year and by 1943 was a lieutenant colonel. Lloyd then served as a staff officer at 2d Army headquarters and participated in the Normandy invasion, becoming one of the few Territorial officers to gain the rank of brigadier. In 1945, as a member of the Conservative party, he was elected to Parliament, representing the Wirral division of Cheshire until 1970. He focused his activities on financial and economic matters, becoming a vocal critic of Clement R. Attlee's* government. Lloyd developed a reputation for skill in organization but was quiet, modest, and a poor public speaker.

From 1948 to 1950, Lloyd was a judge, but he also represented Britain at the Council of Europe meeting in 1949. Returning to Parliament in 1950, he became Foreign Minister Anthony Eden's* principal assistant following the Conservative victory in October 1951. In addition to attending major international conferences, Lloyd assumed leadership of the British delegation at meetings of the UN General Assembly. He was a consistent advocate of firmness in countering Soviet and Chinese aggressive behavior in Asia. At the same time, Lloyd insisted that the United States consult Britain with respect to the conduct of the Korean War. This was a major reason for his trip with Lord Alexander, the minister of defense, to Tokyo in June 1952 for discussions with CINCUNC General Mark W. Clark*. Lloyd found the behavior of Syngman Rhee*, president of the Republic of Korea*, embarrassing. During the South Korean political crisis of 1952*, he urged the Truman administration to take stronger measures to counteract Rhee's dictatorial behavior. Lloyd was also actively involved in efforts to find a method for resolving the impasse at the P'anmunjŏm truce talks* over agenda item 4*, repatriation of POWs. He worked hard to persuade the Truman administration to accept the V. K. Krishna Menon* POW settlement proposal* and the UN resolution of December 3, 1952*.

In 1954, Lloyd served briefly as minister of defense but became Britain's foreign minister the following year. He played a central role in the Suez crisis of 1956, accepting taunts from Labour party critics in the House of Commons. Many observers expected his resignation in the aftermath of the debacle, but Lloyd remained in his position as foreign minister until he became chancellor of the exchequer in 1960. In 1963, he became Speaker of the House of Commons but remained in Eden's political shadow. Lloyd left government service in 1964, working in insurance and investment until 1971. That year, Lloyd was once again Speaker of the House of Commons and won praise thereafter for fairness, humor, and respect for the interests of all parties. In 1976, Lloyd accepted a barony, devoting the remainder of his life to research regarding aging. *See also* Alexander-Lloyd Mission of June 1952.

Current Biography, 1952; *New York Times*, May 18, 1978.

LODGE, HENRY CABOT, JR. (1902–1985)

Senator Henry Cabot Lodge was President-elect Dwight D. Eisenhower's* choice to assist in the transition from the Truman to Eisenhower administrations in late 1952 and early 1953, watching over liaison on all matters save budgetary problems, and thus he was in a position to influence Korea policy. After assuming office, President Eisenhower appointed Lodge to replace Warren R. Austin* as U.S. permanent representative at the UN, a position he held until 1961. Lodge was the grandson of the turn-of-the-century senator, whom he had known well. He graduated from Harvard College in 1924, the year of his grandfather's death, and for a while was a newspaper reporter and member of the Massachusetts General Court. Elected to the Senate in 1936, he served until 1942, when he resigned to enter the army. After the war, during which he achieved the rank of lieutenant colonel, he was reelected to the Senate and served until 1953, being defeated by Congressman John F. Kennedy. Having lost his Senate seat, Lodge was a logical choice for Eisenhower to fill the opening at the UN.

Lodge's influence on Eisenhower is difficult to establish. His two published books are casually written and uninformative. During World War II, he acted occasionally as an interpreter for the supreme commander in the European theater because he was fluent in French. Lodge was very much in favor of U.S. intervention in the Korean War. He was certain that the prompt U.S. response to aggression made for a more peaceful world. His inclination doubtless was to oppose force with force; he was proud of the fact that in World War II he had been the first senator since the Civil War to resign to enter the U.S. Army. Upon taking over the tasks of transition to the Eisenhower administration, he found Korea the most pressing topic. The Truman-Eisenhower transition meeting* revealed that there was much concern by Truman administration officials that their Republican replacements would give in to pressure to repatriate all Chinese and North Korean prisoners. The Republicans desired Eisenhower as president to get the United States out of Korea. At one juncture (January 7, 1953), Lodge heard Eisenhower say that the U.S. Army did not have the ammunition to support conventional military action of a broad, effective nature. Lodge did not say what he, Lodge, advised the president-elect to do.

Again, Lodge's contribution to Korean policy is hard to discern. He did participate in cabinet and NSC meetings in the spring of 1953, when the Eisenhower administration struggled to find a formula for achieving a cease-fire and then a strategy to compel President Syngman Rhee* of the Republic of Korea* to accept the armistice agreement* after his release of North Korean POWs*. It is probable that his influence was not so much in policy formulation as in policy execution at the UN. His well-known name and impressive appearance—he was a tall, rugged man—surely reinforced the messages he carried. In 1960, Lodge was Richard M. Nixon's* choice as a running mate in his unsuccessful campaign for the presidency. President John F. Kennedy appointed Lodge ambassador to South Vietnam to build bipartisan support for his policy in that country. His experiences during the Korean War undoubtedly influenced Lodge's actions in Saigon, especially his tacit support for the ouster of Ngo Dinh Diem in 1963.

Foreign Relations of the United States, 1952–1954, vol. 15: *Korea* (Washington, D.C., 1984); H. C. Lodge, *As It Was* (New York, 1976); H. C. Lodge, *The Storm Has Many Eyes: A Personal Narrative* (New York, 1973).

Robert H. Ferrell

LOGISTICAL REIMBURSEMENT ISSUE

This problem involved compensation to the United States for supplies provided to the armed forces of other UN members that took part in the Korean War. The

United States possessed a fully operational logistical establishment in nearby Japan and alone was capable of meeting all military requirements (even the British were to a degree dependent on U.S. logistical support). As a result, it was logical for U.S. forces to provide food, ammunition, and other items to the contingents from some twenty countries serving in Korea in addition to itself and the Republic of Korea*. At the outset, the U.S. armed services furnished supplies to other UN forces against memorandum receipt. But as the State Department explained, ''It was soon apparent, in view of the volume of support furnished by the United States and the possibility that repayment might not be readily made, that there should be intergovernmental agreements concerning this support.'' Beginning in September 1950, the U.S. military received instructions to furnish necessary supplies and to maintain accounts of the value of goods and services. Though the policy called for immediate reimbursement in U.S. dollars, provision was made for negotiation of the terms of reimbursement on a country-by-country basis.

The amounts involved were relatively small (by one estimate the combined contribution of the twenty nations concerned amounted to 7 percent of the UN ground forces and less than 2 percent of the air forces), but the practical and political aspects of the reimbursement issue proved complicated. Most UN nations sent combat or operational units, relying on the United States for a variety of logistical services; computing the value of these services was difficult. How did U.S. authorities price the items supplied? What standards were applied when calculating usage rates? Was it fair to require payment in scarce dollars? Should the United States avoid the charge that it was hiring mercenaries by taking a hard line on reimbursement? Or, given the push, especially during the first half of 1951 on political grounds, for additional manpower from other UN nations, should the United States write off all costs incurred by UN forces? By December 31, 1952, the United States had advanced approximately $200 million to other than ROK forces and had received some $40 million in payment. Four nations had signed reimbursement agreements; Canada and Denmark were paying on delivery, and only India formally had refused to discuss reimbursing the United States for logistical support.

Foreign Relations of the United States, 1952–1954, vol. 15: *Korea* (Washington, D.C., 1984); W. J. Fox, *Inter-Allied Co-Operation During the Combat Operations* (Washington, D.C., 1952); R. J. O'Neill, *Australia in the Korean War 1950–53* (Canberra, 1981).

Theodore A. Wilson

LOVETT, ROBERT A. (1895–1986)

Robert Lovett was under secretary and secretary of defense during much of the Korean War. Born in Huntsville, Texas, he became general counsel to the Union Pacific Railroad and eventually president of that road. His father worked for railroad tycoon Edward H. Harriman and Lovett himself spent most of his childhood on the Harriman estate after the family moved to New York. Lovett went on to Yale and founded the Yale Unit of the Naval Reserve Flying Corps—

"the millionaires' unit"—dispatched for duty in 1917 with Britain's Royal Naval Air Service. Upon returning home, he entered law school and the business school at Harvard before fleeing Cambridge to join W. Averell Harriman* and his other friends on Wall Street.

As a champion of U.S. air power during the interwar period, Lovett's private study on airplane production in 1940 caught the attention of Assistant Secretary of War Robert P. Patterson and Secretary of War Henry L. Stimson, and he became assistant secretary for air. He also had the ear of General George C. Marshall* and probably did more than any other man to bring the United States into the age of air power. Near the end of the war, he organized the U.S. Strategic Bombing Survey to document the effect and importance of air power. Chosen by Marshall in 1947 to serve as under secretary of state, Lovett worked during the cold war years in securing congressional approval for the Marshall Plan and NATO, plotting the Berlin airlift strategy, and discussing the future of Korea with the Soviets.

With war in Korea and Louis A. Johnson's* resignation*, Lovett joined Marshall, Johnson's replacement, as under secretary of defense. As secretary of defense in 1951, Lovett continued to look ahead and prepare to fight the next war. When the generals asked for more battleships during World War II, Lovett prescribed bombers. When the generals asked for more bombers in Korea, Lovett prescribed missiles. Lovett was no mindless hawk, however. He emerged as one of the Truman administration's harshest critics of CINCUNC General Douglas MacArthur*, particularly MacArthur's reckless plan for victory* regarding the way air power should be used in Korea.

After Dwight D. Eisenhower's* election as president in 1952, Lovett returned to Brown Brothers, Harriman, and to the chair of the Union Pacific and a seat on the CBS television board of directors. After the 1960 elections, President John F. Kennedy offered him a choice of three cabinet posts—State, Defense, and Treasury—but Lovett declined. Thereafter, Lovett continued to advise Kennedy from time to time, on the Cuban missile crisis and other matters of grave importance.

D. Halberstam, *The Best and the Brightest* (New York, 1972); W. Isaacson and T. Evans, *The Wise Men* (New York, 1986).

Kenneth O'Reilly

LOWE, FRANK C. (1885–1968)

President Harry S. Truman* sent Major General Frank C. Lowe to Korea in August 1950 to evaluate the battlefield performance of U.S. National Guard and reserve forces. According to Lowe, he was also "to learn if we [are] still continuing to breed young Americans with guts and virility." "Our soldiers," he concluded in his final report to Truman, "are superb and our Marines are both superior and supreme." But "the old Army that trained you and me, the Army we respected and loved, is dead. Make no mistake about it, it is as extinct as the dodo." This had occurred, he said, because "we have allowed Staff to become the master rather than the servant of command."

Lowe was born in Springfield, Massachusetts, and graduated from Worcester Polytechnic Institute in 1908. Like Truman, he fought in World War I as a reserve artillery officer in France. Lowe then worked for Kennebec Wharf and Coal Company in Maine until he retired as the firm's president in 1938. Two years later, he was recalled to active duty and served as the military attaché on Truman's Senate committee investigating the defense industry, developing a close friendship with the future president. Following U.S. entry into World War II, Lowe became chief of the U.S. Army Reserve. He resumed his prosperous business career in 1945 but remained influential as president of the Reserve Officers' Association and national vice-commander of the American Legion.

Truman conferred with Lowe about the purpose of his mission at the White House on July 11, 1950, and authorized him to "go where he chose, read what he wanted and report what he pleased." The president also wanted to learn about the physical status of CINCUNC General Douglas MacArthur*. In the first of a series of letters to Truman—mostly handwritten—Lowe reported that the general was in good health, providing details on blood pressure, weight, and lifestyle. MacArthur's doctor, Lieutenant Colonel Charles C. Canada, believed his patient "has today the physiological characteristics of a superior physical specimen at fifty years of age." After his first visit to the Korea battlefield in August 1950, Lowe wrote to Truman that "I think this is the Argonne all over again. . . . We *must* break off this action before winter sets in, and that means a deadline of December 1st, *and* we must not break off action short of complete victory. MacArthur has told me of his plan to this end. Success . . . will reflect tremendous and everlasting credit to our country and to all concerned."

Lowe was a Republican and a great admirer of MacArthur. After the Inch'ŏn landing*, he wrote Truman that rather than a rabbit, MacArthur had been able to "pull a pink elephant out of a hat." Thereafter, Lowe agreed with the general that the Chinese Communists would not enter the war. "If they try it," he predicted, "they will get licked, and probably that will solve a lot of future China troubles. However, . . . there is not a chance that China's Tito will be led around by the nose by Moscow." After Chinese military intervention*, Lowe became even more strident in advising against "procrastination or appeasement." "The issue is joined, it is Communism against *all* of the rest of the world; the issue is joined *right over here* and over here is where it must be settled, now, once and for all." Thus, he urged Truman to give MacArthur "a free hand." "Let the U.N. take off the wraps," he advised, and "we will hit these monkeys where it really hurts." As early as November 4, Lowe had begun to advocate approval for bombing of the Yalu hydroelectric plants. During early 1951, he denounced "newspaper embryonic Napoleons" for falsely reporting that UN forces had retreated, evacuated, and been defeated.

While in Korea, Lowe spent most of his time at the front because he wanted to say upon the completion of his mission that "I went, I saw, I *know*." He also followed "ground rule #1" for those representing the president, which meant being "committed to anonymity and to keeping their eyes and ears open and their mouths *shut*.'' His letters to Truman had disparaging remarks for the Korean Military Advisory Group* ''monstrosity,'' the ''unreliability'' and ''viciousness'' of the press, and the South Korean army's lack of training, ''aggressiveness or will to fight.'' Lowe took many risks while he was in Korea, leaving on the last ship during the Hŭngnam evacuation* and being nearly killed in a jeep accident. On March 20, 1951, Truman informed Lowe that he thought it was time for him to ''wind up your affairs there and come home,'' expressing concern ''that you may have used up more than your share of good luck.'' Lowe agreed, confessing that many U.S. officers had come to resent his presence and time with their units. Lowe returned to the United States on April 23 and submitted his final report to Truman the following day, concluding that ''I think we should be very, very careful in drawing any over-all conclusions affecting our national security program by reason of our experiences in Korea; too many factors were distorted and out of proportion over there to permit of drawing logical over-all conclusions.'' Lowe retired in May 1951 but remained very upset about Truman's recall of MacArthur*. He believed that third parties had prevented his letters from reaching Truman and had purposely created an unnecessary clash between the president and the general.

H. S. Truman papers, Harry S. Truman Library, Independence, Missouri; *New York Times,* December 28, 1968; *Who Was Who in America,* vol. 5: *1969–1973* (Chicago, 1963).

LOWE MISSION
See Lowe, Frank C.

M

MACARTHUR, DOUGLAS (1880–1964)

No other American is more identified with the Korean War than General of the Army Douglas MacArthur, who was commander of U.S. and UN forces (CINCUNC) from July 1950 until April 1951. Born in Little Rock, Arkansas, he was the son of General Arthur MacArthur, the U.S. Army's highest-ranking officer from 1906 to 1909. Following his father's example, the younger MacArthur chose a military career, graduating from the U.S. Military Academy at West Point with highest honors in 1903. Before World War I, he served as an engineering officer in the United States, the Philippines, and Panama, eventually joining the War Department General Staff in 1913. MacArthur sailed to France after the United States declared war on Germany, fighting with the 42d Division in the Champagne-Marne, St. Mihiel, and Meuse-Argonne operations. He earned numerous decorations for heroism and promotion to the rank of brigadier general. In 1919, MacArthur began a three-year stint as West Point's superintendent, later serving two command assignments in the Philippines and earning promotion to major general in 1925 and to general five years later. After becoming U.S. Army chief of staff in 1930, he commanded the U.S. troops sent to oust American veterans from the banks of the Anacostia River in Washington, D.C., following the Bonus March in 1932.

In the fall of 1935, MacArthur accepted a position as military adviser with the government of the Philippines, devoting six years to organizing Filipino defense forces. In July 1941, the U.S. government recalled him to active duty and appointed him commander of U.S. Army Forces in East Asia. Following the Japanese attack against Pearl Harbor, MacArthur commanded a stubborn defense of the Philippines but fled to Australia in March 1942. Over the next three years, he supervised Allied military operations in the Southwest Pacific theater, until he was able to liberate the Philippines in 1945 and thus fulfill his pledge of "I shall return." Promoted to general of the army in December 1944, he was named commanding general of U.S. Army Forces in the Pacific in April 1945. When the Japanese capitulated, MacArthur received the additional appointment of supreme commander for the Allied powers (SCAP) to accept formal surrender of the Japanese and then to command the ensuing Allied occupation of Japan. From 1945 until 1951, MacArthur efficiently although occasionally autocratically implemented a series of political, economic, and social reforms in Japan that eliminated militarist, ultranationalist, and feudal vestiges prior to the approval of the Japanese Peace Treaty*.

After World War II, MacArthur, as head of the Far Eastern Command, also presided nominally over Lieutenant General John R. Hodge's* occupation forces in southern Korea (the USAFIK). He rarely played a direct role in policy formulation regarding Korea but was a consistent advocate of early U.S. military withdrawal from Korea*. Following the formal creation of the Republic of Korea* in August 1948, MacArthur never was enthusiastic about the Truman administration's efforts thereafter to provide military and economic assistance. A year before Secretary of State Dean G. Acheson's* National Press Club speech*, he outlined a similar strategy excluding the ROK from guarantees of U.S. protection. In 1949 and 1950, the general lobbied intensively within government circles for a defense commitment to the Republic of China*, outlining his reasons in a June 1950 memorandum on Taiwan's strategic significance*. Nevertheless, following the North Korea invasion of South Korea*, it was MacArthur's recommendation that resulted in President Harry S. Truman's* commitment of ground troops* in the Korean War.

After being appointed head of the UNC* MacArthur consistently advocated a full commitment of U.S. military power. Through the force of his personality, he persuaded the reluctant JCS to authorize the Inch'ŏn landing* of September 15, 1950. After the successful recapture of Seoul operation*, he backed vigorously the administration's decision to destroy the North Korean regime. But already MacArthur's relations with Truman were strained because of the general's pressure for an increase in U.S. support for Chiang Kai-shek*, most notably with his visit to Taiwan* and his VFW message*. He wanted the United States to assist the Kuomintang in an invasion of China because this, he claimed, would reduce the People's Republic of China's* ability to help the Democratic People's Republic of Korea*, as well as the overall Communist threat in Asia. During October, as UN forces pushed northward, MacArthur downplayed the danger of Chinese military intervention*. At the Wake Island Conference*, he assured Truman that the PRC's threat to intervene was a bluff and, even if carried out, would not impede achievement of U.S. war aims. Privately, MacArthur seemed almost to savor the prospect of Chinese intervention in the Korean War because this would provide justification for U.S. attacks on China and assistance for a Kuomintang invasion of the mainland.

After China's massive intervention in late November and the retreat of UN forces south of the thirty-eighth parallel, MacArthur clashed more frequently with both his civilian and military superiors. The general blamed his battlefield problems on restrictions against attacking China, rejecting the wisdom or feasibility of seeking an armistice and restoring the prewar boundary. As the JCS gradually discovered, MacArthur routinely exaggerated the danger to the UNC and fought the war more vigorously in press releases than on the battlefield. Despite MacArthur's dire predictions, battle lines stabilized during March 1951. When the JCS informed him of Truman's proposed cease-fire initiative*, MacArthur sabotaged the effort by issuing a public demand that Chinese forces surrender or risk attacks upon their homeland. Then came his public letter to Joseph Martin* condemning administration policy in Korea as appeasement. These open and highly partisan challenges led to President Truman's recall of MacArthur* on April 11, 1951. Less than two weeks later, the general made his dramatic speech to Congress of April 19, 1951*, in an appeal for public support.

Among the most politically ambitious generals in U.S. history, MacArthur sought the Republican presidential nomination in 1944 and 1948. After Truman fired him from his duties in Korea and Japan, the general looked toward vindication as he took his case directly to the public. However, despite broad popular affection for MacArthur as a war hero and frustration over the Korean stalemate, neither the average citizen nor most civilian and military officials favored a wider war. During the Senate's MacArthur Hearings*, the JCS registered opposition to MacArthur's plan for victory*, while in Korea, Lieutenant General Matthew B. Ridgway*, MacArthur's replacement, succeeded in stopping the Chinese spring offensives of 1951* and thereby opened the way to armistice talks. In 1952, when the American people elected a general as president, it would not be MacArthur but Dwight D. Eisenhower*. After failing to persuade the new president to adopt his victory proposal*, MacArthur dropped out of public life. He accepted a job as chairman of the board of Remington Rand Corporation and made occasional public appearances. *See also* Home-by-Christmas Offensive; JCS Directive of December 6, 1960; MacArthur's "Pronunciamento."

D. C. James, *The Years of MacArthur,* 3 vols. (Boston, 1970–1985); D. MacArthur, *Reminiscences* (New York, 1964); M. Schaller, *Douglas MacArthur: The Far Eastern General* (New York, 1989); R. Spiller (ed.), *Dictionary of American Military Biography* (Westport, Conn., 1984).

Michael Schaller

MACARTHUR HEARINGS (May 3–June 25, 1951)

These were closed-door hearings conducted jointly by two committees of the U.S. Senate relative to President Harry S. Truman's* recall of CINCUNC General Douglas MacArthur* from his commands in East Asia. While MacArthur was en route from Japan to the United States following his relief in mid-April 1951, congressional critics of Truman and his foreign and military policies, most of them Republicans, hit on the idea of an investigation of MacArthur's relief and Washington's policies in Asia. Their purpose was transparent: to discredit the Democratic administration and prepare the way for a Republican victory in the 1952 presidential election. In the light of the popular enthusiasm for MacArthur during those tumultuous days, the Senate could not easily turn aside such demands, and on April 25 its members unanimously approved a resolution providing for a joint inquiry by the armed services and foreign relations committees. Counting on MacArthur's Olympian presence and polished phrases to rally popular support for their views, especially if the hearings were televised, Republicans demanded open hearings. Democrats countered that the inquiry would be dealing with secret documents and sensitive subjects, hence national security required closed hearings and censorship of transcripts of testimony before their release to the communications media. Because the Democrats had a majority of votes in the Senate, their views prevailed.

On May 3, 1951, an eight-week interrogation began of MacArthur, Secretary of Defense George C. Marshall*, the JCS, Secretary of State Dean G. Acheson*, and several lesser individuals who presumably had some expertise on the questions at issue. Appearing first, MacArthur denied that he had made any errors in his conduct of the Korean War. He defended his conviction that only by allowing UN ground forces to drive northward to the Yalu, unleashing UN planes to bomb targets in China, and imposing a naval blockade around China's ports could the war be brought to a successful termination. He doubted that such an expansion of the war would touch off another world war. MacArthur also insisted that he had not been insubordinate, pointing to the Collins-Vandenberg visit to Tokyo of January 15, 1951*, to bolster his claim.

Parrying questions regarding MacArthur's alleged errors and insubordination, Marshall, the Joint Chiefs, and Acheson contended that expansion of the war, if it did not result in a world war, would, in General Omar N. Bradley's* memorable phrase, "involve us in the wrong war, at the wrong place, at the wrong time, and with the wrong enemy." By the time the hearings droned to a conclusion, it appeared that most Americans agreed with Marshall and the others. During their first three days, when the general himself sat in the witness chair, the MacArthur Hearings commanded the front pages of the country's newspapers. But long before Senator Richard B. Russell of Georgia, as chair, announced their termination, most Americans had ceased to give them much thought. As for the senators, they ambled in and out of the hearing rooms, and after the first three weeks, attended hearings only intermittently. The result was a rambling interrogation of witnesses marked by frequent repetition of questions. In truth, the only senator who distinguished himself in the hearings was Senator Russell, who was unfailingly courteous and evenhanded—and unfailingly present. *See also* Congress and the Korean War; MacArthur's Speech to Congress of April 19, 1951; Manchurian Sanctuary.

D. C. James, *The Years of MacArthur,* vol. 3: *Triumph and Disaster, 1945–1964* (Boston, 1985); *Military Situation in the Far East,* 5 vols. (Washington, D. C., 1951); J. W. Spanier, *The Truman-MacArthur Controversy and the Korean War* (New York, 1959); J. E. Wilz, "The MacArthur Hearings of 1951: The Secret Testimony," *Military Affairs* (December 1975).

John Edward Wilz

MACARTHUR'S "DIE FOR TIE" STATEMENT (March 7, 1951)

Following a visit to the Korean battlefront, CINCUNC General Douglas MacArthur* made this statement at Suwŏn during a press conference. It was one of several public utterances that the general made early in 1951 criticizing the Truman administration's limited war strategy in Korea. On this occasion, MacArthur read a written communiqué reporting that the UNC's* military progress had been satisfactory despite "abnormal military inhibitions." The enemy had suffered "exhausting attrition upon both his manpower and supplies," but the flow of ground forces and materiel into Korea was continuing. Given "existing limitations upon our freedom of counter-offensive action, and no major additions to our organizational strength," MacArthur predicted that "the battle lines cannot fail in time to reach a point of theoretical military stalemate." Nevertheless, the enemy had sustained huge losses, and this "cannot fail to weaken his hold upon the Chinese nation and people and materially dampen his ardor for engaging in another aggressive adventure in Asia." MacArthur argued that the decision of the Communists to "continue this savage slaughter despite an almost hopeless chance of ultimate military success is a measure of their wanton disregard of international decencies and restraints and displays a complete contempt for the sanctity of human life."

MacArthur's statement was indiscreet and a wholly unnecessary public review of military strategy. Seizing on the phrases "savage slaughter" and "military stalemate," newsmen dubbed MacArthur's communiqué the "die for tie" statement. It had an unsettling and demoralizing effect on UN troops. MacArthur's communiqué had political importance as well because it ended with a calculated and premeditated attack on the administration's approach in Korea: "Vital decisions have yet to be made—decisions far beyond the scope of the authority vested in me as the military commander, decisions which are neither solely political nor solely military, but which must provide on the highest international levels an answer to the obscurities which now becloud the unsolved problems raised by Red China's undeclared war in Korea." This statement was similar to the general's prior remarks to the press on February 13 at Tokyo and February 20 at Suwŏn, each constituting a clear act of insubordination because they violated the JCS directive of December 6, 1950*, prohibiting unauthorized public comments regarding the war. Coupled with MacArthur's "pronunciamento"* two weeks later, his "die for tie" statement provided reason and justification for President Harry S. Truman's recall of MacArthur* on April 11, 1951.

C. Blair, *The Forgotten War* (New York, 1987); D. C. James, *The Years of MacArthur*, vol. 3: *Triumph and Disaster, 1945–1964* (Boston, 1985); R. Leckie, *Conflict: The History of the Korean War, 1950–1953* (New York, 1962).

MACARTHUR'S LETTER TO JOSEPH MARTIN (March 20, 1951)

President Harry S. Truman* decided to relieve CINCUNC General Douglas MacArthur* shortly after MacArthur's letter to House Republican leader Joseph W. Martin* criticizing Truman's policy in the Korean War became public. As commander of UN forces in Korea, MacArthur vehemently disagreed with many policies the Truman administration pursued in the Korean conflict. He contended, among other things, that the Communists should be driven from Korea at all cost, advocating the use of Nationalist Chinese forces, bombing Communist Chinese installations in Manchuria, and blockading Chinese ports. MacArthur expressed these views publicly, not just through official channels, prompting President Truman to muzzle the general with the JCS directive of December 6, 1950*, an order that all military officials clear any statement on diplomacy and government policy through higher channels. MacArthur chose to defy this order. In February 1951, he criticized administration plans to draw a dividing line across Korea and called positional warfare illusory and unrealistic. In March 1951, after he issued his "die for tie" statement*, he then destroyed Truman's proposed cease-fire initiative* when he issued an ultimatum threatening the Chinese with annihilation if they did not come to terms. Although Truman had hesitated to act against his military commander previously, MacArthur's "pronunciamento"*, the president later claimed, brought the decision for recall.

Early in 1951, Congressman Martin from Massachusetts, an outspoken critic of the Truman administration, sent MacArthur the text of an address he had made on February 12 calling for the use of the Republic of China's* forces in Korea. He asked for the general's comments. In a March 20 letter, MacArthur responded, and Martin on April 5 read the reply on the House floor since MacArthur had not asked for confidentiality. MacArthur concurred with Martin's position, saying that the United States should meet force with counterforce and that it was only logical to utilize Chiang Kai-shek's* forces. The Communists, he said, were moving toward global conquest in Asia, and Europe would not be safe if the free world lost in Korea. He concluded, "There is no substitute for victory." Faced with yet another blatant defiance of orders, Truman, after a series of meetings with his top advisers, signed on April 10 an order removing the general from his command. *See also* Truman's Recall of MacArthur.

R. J. Donovan, *Tumultuous Years* (New York, 1982); W. Manchester, *American Caesar* (Boston, 1978); J. W. Martin, *My First Fifty Years in Politics* (New York, 1960); H. S. Truman, *Years of Trial and Hope* (Garden City, N.Y., 1956).

T. Michael Ruddy

MACARTHUR'S MEMORANDUM ON TAIWAN'S STRATEGIC SIGNIFICANCE (June 14, 1950)

This long memorandum was General Douglas MacArthur's* last warning before the outbreak of the Korean War about the dangers for the United States of a Communist seizure of Taiwan. After it became evident in 1948 that mainland China would fall to the Chinese Communists, MacArthur became concerned over the future of Taiwan. For him, the possible Communist domination of the island would seriously threaten the security interests of the United States. He made his perception of danger known repeatedly to U.S. officials, notably in an estimate forwarded to the Joint Chiefs of Staff on May 29, 1950. In his memorandum of June 14, MacArthur explained that Taiwan was an integral part of the littoral island defense line that extended from the Aleutians to the Philippines. From that line the United States could interdict Communist communications and deny the resources of East and Southeast Asia to the Soviet Union. A Communist-controlled Taiwan would comprise an unacceptable salient at the center of the island defense chain. On Taiwan were air and naval bases superior to any on the Asian mainland south of the Yellow Sea.

MacArthur noted that an enemy could attack Okinawa and the Philippines, both key elements in the U.S. western Pacific defense system, far more readily and effectively from Taiwan than from the mainland. In the hands of the Communists, MacArthur wrote, Taiwan

can be compared to an unsinkable aircraft carrier and submarine tender ideally located to accomplish Soviet offensive strategy and at the same time checkmate counteroffensive operations by United States Forces based on Okinawa and the Philippines. . . . If Formosa should be acquired by the Chinese Communists and bases thereon made available to the USSR, Russia will have acquired an additional "fleet" which will have been obtained and can be maintained at an incomparably lower cost to the Soviets than could its equivalent of ten or twenty aircraft carriers with their supporting forces.

Aside from questions of strategy, MacArthur believed that the United States had a moral obligation to help the Taiwanese develop their own political future unfettered by the dictates of a Communist government. To that end, MacArthur advised, the JCS should direct him as CINCFE to initiate a survey of the military, economic, and political requirements to prevent the Communist domination of Taiwan. That survey should then become the basis of U.S. policy with respect to Taiwan. MacArthur made this visit to Taiwan* shortly after the North Korean invasion of South Korea*, in the process publicizing his differences with the Truman administration over its Taiwan policy. Disagreement regarding the Taiwan issue would contribute to President Harry S. Truman's* recall of MacArthur*. *See also* Johnson's Visit to Tokyo; Neutralization of Taiwan.

Foreign Relations of the United States, 1950, vol. 7: *Korea* (Washington, D.C., 1976).

Norman A. Graebner

MACARTHUR'S PERIODIC REPORTS TO THE UN SECURITY COUNCIL

Under the UN Security Council resolution of July 7, 1950*, General Douglas MacArthur*, President Harry S. Truman's* choice as commander in chief of the UNC* (CINCUNC), was responsible for making periodic reports to the Security Council on developments in the Korean War. At first, the JCS advocated submitting "reports as appropriate" rather than on a "periodic" basis but eventually accepted the latter approach. In reply to a request from Secretary of Defense Louis A. Johnson*, the JCS prepared a memorandum outlining specific procedures for preparation and transmission of these periodic reports. The United States had already blocked the creation of a UN committee that would have had direct access to the UNC. Since the UNC was under U.S. control, the JCS argued that the Security Council should receive reports not from the CINCUNC but from the United States. MacArthur would draft the reports and then submit them to the JCS. Following review and approval, the State Department would transmit them to the Security Council. Both Johnson and Secretary of State Dean G. Acheson* approved this procedure.

To ensure prompt compliance with the July 7 resolution, the JCS had instructed MacArthur to submit his first report before August 4 and at two-week intervals thereafter. They promised to clear changes with MacArthur but reminded the general that "certain political factors which must be determined in Washington" might require amendment. The State Department, without consulting the JCS, lengthened the first report to make it more informative, transmitting it to the Security Council on July 25. However, subsequent reports followed the agreed procedure, with MacArthur sending drafts through the JCS to Army Chief of Staff General J. Lawton Collins*, who, after consultation with the State Department, submitted them to JCS for approval. The secretary of defense then would receive the reports for transmission through the State Department and to the UN Security Council.

Formally adopted on October 3, this process provided clear proof of the nominal role the UN played in the Korean War. MacArthur received his instructions from and reported to the JCS, not the UN. Also, since these reports covered information that newspapers already had reprinted and was therefore common knowledge, they constituted after-action summaries, providing no direct role for UN involvement in events as they transpired. The periodic reports would create an internal political problem for the Truman administration after Chinese military intervention*. With UN forces in retreat, MacArthur sought to use them as a means to defend his Home-by-Christmas offensive* and force approval of his plan for victory*. State Department objections brought significant changes in these reports until MacArthur abandoned his effort at policy manipulation. Reports 2–16 are printed in the *Military Situation in the Far East*.

D. Acheson, *Present at the Creation* (New York, 1969); J. F. Schnabel and R. J. Watson, *History of the Joint Chiefs of Staff*, vol. 3: *The Korean War* (Wilmington, 1979).

MACARTHUR'S PLAN FOR VICTORY

As U.S. and UNC* commander of the Korean theater from June 1950 through April 1951, General Douglas MacArthur* articulated numerous "victory plans," many of which reflected his alternating moods of giddy optimism and bleak despair. In the first hours of the North Korean invasion of South Korea*, he expressed confidence that "all he had to do was send a few Americans over there and the North Koreans would run." The situation changed dramatically in the following weeks as North Korean forces surrounded the Pusan Perimeter*. During August and September 1950, MacArthur's new strategy hinged on the amphibious Inch'ŏn landing* behind enemy lines, combined with a breakout from Pusan. Following the dramatic success of Operation Chromite* and subsequent rout of the North Korean People's Army, the UN offensive across the thirty-eighth parallel* sought to destroy the Communist regime and create a unified Korea, but Chinese military intervention* wrecked this plan for victory.

From the end of December 1950 through his recall the next April, MacArthur recommended a series of moves designed to retake the military initiative, while "liberating" North Korea and creating a unified regime. The general, in private and public, rebuffed administration arguments in favor of holding a line near the thirty-eighth parallel, of accepting the division, of pursuing negotiations with the People's Republic of China*, and of trying to limit the fighting to the Korean peninsula. Instead, he called for a dramatic escalation of the war to avoid destruction of his command and to ensure overall victory. During the winter and spring of 1951, MacArthur pressed the JCS to send more U.S. troops to Korea, to utilize a minimum of 50,000 Nationalist troops there, to support a Republic of China* offensive in south China, to have the 7th Fleet blockade and bombard Chinese coastal cities, and to unleash U.S. air power against civilian and military targets in Manchuria and north China. He also suggested using atomic weapons against China, although he offered no specific plan for their employment. By the spring of 1951, he advocated a renewed major offensive against the Democratic People's Republic of Korea* combined with air and sea attacks to punish and isolate the PRC. This combined strategy, he insisted, would ensure Korean unification with little risk of a wider war.

In January 1951, MacArthur's prediction of imminent doom temporarily led the JCS to consider favorably his call for escalation; however, as they gained a more accurate picture of the battlefield situation, President Harry S. Truman*, as well as his senior civilian and military advisors, dismissed these suggestions as a dangerous fantasy likely to trigger a world war. They guessed, correctly, that once UN forces blunted the Chinese sweep south (as they did by May 1951), China would seek negotiations to restore the status quo. *See also* Collins-Vandenberg Visit to Tokyo (January 15, 1951); JCS Directive of January 12, 1951; MacArthur's Victory Proposal; Manchurian Sanctuary; NSC-101.

D. C. James, *The Years of MacArthur,* vol. 3: *Triumph and Disaster, 1945–1964* (Boston, 1985); M. Schaller, *Douglas MacArthur: The Far Eastern General* (New York, 1989).

Michael Schaller

MACARTHUR'S "PRONUNCIAMENTO" (March 24, 1951)

This was a statement issued by CINCUNC General Douglas MacArthur* after the 8th Army* had driven the Chinese People's Volunteers Army* back to the thirty-eighth parallel calling on the enemy commander to meet him to agree to a cease-fire and acceptance of UN political objectives in Korea. MacArthur's statement destroyed the prospects of peace negotiations, which the Truman administration was about to propose. In his statement, MacArthur scathingly derided Chinese military power, which, he said, lacked an industrial base and had strength only in numbers of men and whose weakness had been exposed in recent Chinese reverses. MacArthur warned that if his ultimatum was not accepted, not only would Chinese forces face destruction, but also the UNC* forces might not continue to show restraint by restricting action to Korea but might attack the People's Republic of China* itself. MacArthur knew of the discussions of the proposed message regarding peace negotiations, although he had not been given the precise details.

As commander in the field, MacArthur possessed authority, in a strictly legal sense, to issue his surrender ultimatum, but his deliberate purpose in issuing his statement at that time was undoubtedly to torpedo the prospects of peace negotiations in which the UN might offer compromise terms. His ultimatum was bluntly rejected, while President Harry S. Truman's* message was not sent, as this would have seemed confusing following MacArthur's ultimatum. The prospects for peace in March 1951 were slim; the Chinese had assembled their forces for the spring offensives of 1951*. Nevertheless, MacArthur's sabotage of the possibility of peace talks was his most substantial act of insubordination.

On receiving news of MacArthur's ultimatum, Truman, according to his memoirs, decided that he would dismiss MacArthur from his command. Truman's immediate response, however, was merely a mild reprimand in a message to MacArthur reminding him of the JCS directive of December 6, 1950*, requiring prior clearance of public statements by Washington, and suggesting that MacArthur seek further information on armistice talks from the JCS. Truman was either preparing the ground for MacArthur's dismissal, or, fearing the political storm that would ensue, he had shrunk from the decision to dismiss MacArthur. MacArthur's letter to Joseph Martin*, read in the House on April 5, 1951, repeated MacArthur's familiar criticisms of administration East Asia policy and was the last straw that led to Truman's recall of MacArthur*. *See also* Truman's Proposed Cease-fire Initiative.

D. C. James, *The Years of MacArthur, vol. 3: Triumph and Disaster, 1945–1964* (Boston, 1985); B. I. Kaufman, *The Korean War* (Philadelphia, 1986); J. W. Spanier, *The Truman-MacArthur Controversy and the Korean War* (Cambridge, 1959).

Peter G. Boyle

MACARTHUR'S RECONNAISSANCE IN FORCE

In military strategy and tactics, this term denotes an offensive operation designed to discover the enemy's strength. The term was used by CINCUNC General Douglas MacArthur* to rationalize his failed Home-by-Christmas offensive* of November 24, 1950. The daily intelligence summary of November 28 first applied the term when it reported that "probing attacks by the Eighth Army* actually turned out to be a reconnaissance in force in which the enemy disclosed his real strength along the entire front." MacArthur later elaborated, writing that "the movement north upset the enemy's timetable, causing him to move prematurely, and to reveal the surreptitious massing of his armies. . . . Had I not acted when I did, we would have been a 'sitting duck' doomed to eventual annihilation." Discovering Communist China's intentions did become important after the Chinese military disengagement of November 6, 1950*. However, the use of one's entire force for reconnaissance was unprecedented. MacArthur's use of this term was an after-the-fact rationalization to avoid having to admit responsibility for the retreat of the UNC* following Chinese military intervention* in the Korean War.

R. E. Appleman, *Disaster in Korea* (College Station, Texas, 1989); T. N. Dupuy, *Dictionary of Military Terms* (New York, 1986); D. MacArthur, *Reminiscences* (New

York, 1964); W. Manchester, *American Caesar* (New York, 1978); R. T. Ruetten, "General Douglas MacArthur's 'Reconnaissance in Force': The Rationalization of a Defeat in Korea," *Pacific Historical Review* (February 1967).

Larry R. Beck

MACARTHUR'S SPEECH TO CONGRESS OF APRIL 19, 1951

General Douglas MacArthur* delivered this televised speech to a joint session of Congress less than two weeks after President Harry S. Truman* removed him from his position as commander of UN forces in the Korean War. Truman's recall of MacArthur* had ignited a firestorm of criticism in the United States, and the president's Republican critics had no trouble gaining approval for extending to the general an invitation to address Congress. On April 18, he left San Francisco for Washington, D.C., arriving shortly after midnight the following day at National Airport. On hand to greet him were 12,000 well-wishers who broke through the police line and forced cancellation of the welcoming ceremony. Also in attendance were the JCS, Secretary of Defense George C. Marshall*, and virtually the entire Republican membership of Congress. When MacArthur walked to the front of the House chambers twelve hours later, he received a wildly enthusiastic reception, as both the members of Congress and the people who had packed into the gallery to hear him speak clapped and cheered. For thirty minutes, the charismatic MacArthur spoke with force and eloquence, outbursts of applause interrupting his presentation on numerous occasions.

In his speech, MacArthur repeated arguments he had advanced before, most notably in his VFW message* and his letter to Joseph Martin*. The general insisted that the United States "courted disaster" by considering its security interests in Europe and Asia separately because the "Communist problem is a global one." In Korea, the UN had achieved complete victory and its goal was within grasp, when Chinese military intervention* created a "new war" and the need for an entirely new strategy, which MacArthur said had "not been forthcoming." After lecturing his listeners about "Asia's past and the revolutionary changes which have marked her course up to the present," he restated his position that the United States could not allow Taiwan to fall to the Communists. According to MacArthur, the administration was waging "only an indecisive campaign, with its terrible and constant attrition upon our forces." As an alternative, he outlined his plan for victory*, calling for applying greater military pressure on the Chinese Communists. He warned against allowing the People's Republic of China* to escape unpunished from its act of aggression in Korea, declaring that "history's clear lesson" was that appeasement would fail. As for the Soviet Union, it "will not necessarily mesh its actions with our moves."

Two portions of MacArthur's speech would make it memorable. First, the general declared that "once war is forced upon us, there is no other alternative than to apply every available means to bring it to a swift end. War's very object is victory—not prolonged indecision. In war, indeed, there can be no substitute for victory.'' Second, for his peroration, he recalled a refrain in an old army barrack ballad, stating, ''Old soldiers never die, they just fade away. And like the old soldier of that ballad, I now close my military career and just fade away—an old soldier who tried to do his duty as God gave him the light to see that duty.'' MacArthur's speech established a starting point for the investigation of his firing in the Senate's MacArthur Hearings* beginning in May, because he asserted that his ''views have been fully shared in the past by practically every military leader concerned with the Korean campaign, including our own Joint Chief of Staff.'' Following his address, MacArthur received the key to the city of Washington and then led a motorcade down Pennsylvania Avenue as a quarter of a million people watched and jet fighters and bombers flew overhead.

   N. A. Graebner, *Ideas and Diplomacy* (New York, 1964); B. I. Kaufman, *The Korean War* (Philadelphia, 1986); M. Schaller, *Douglas MacArthur: The Far Eastern General* (New York, 1989).

MACARTHUR'S SURRENDER ULTIMATUM TO NORTH KOREA
(October 9, 1950)

   CINCUNC General Douglas MacArthur's* call for the immediate surrender of North Korean forces came after he had initiated the UN offensive across the thirty-eighth parallel*. This was because the Truman administration feared that open talk of reunification might alienate members of the UN and prevent approval for operations northward. As a result of the success of the Inch'ŏn landing* and recapture of Seoul operation*, the 8th Army* and the X Corps* had destroyed Communist military power in South Korea. On October 1, MacArthur informed the JCS of his desire to issue a dramatic statement announcing his intention to pursue and destroy all remaining North Korean forces throughout the peninsula. The proclamation would warn the enemy that ''the field of our military operations is limited only by military exigencies and the international boundaries of Korea.'' The JCS cabled the general immediately to inform him that they considered ''it unwise to issue your statement. . . . We desire that you proceed with your operation without any further explanation or announcement and let action determine the matter.'' The U.S. government, the JCS continued, ''desires to avoid having to make an issue of the 38th parallel until we have accomplished our mission of defeating the North Korean forces.''

   Washington undoubtedly was following the advice of its allies in adopting this approach. In the end, the Truman administration's patience was rewarded when the General Assembly passed the UN resolution of October 7, 1950*, which instructed the UNC* to ''ensure conditions of stability throughout Korea.'' On October 9, MacArthur, ''for the last time,'' called upon Communist forces to surrender immediately so that the ''decisions of the United Nations may be carried out with a minimum of further loss of life and destruction of property.'' He asked the people to cooperate with the UN in creating a ''unified, independent and democratic government of Korea.'' The UN, he pledged, would ''act to relieve and rehabilitate'' the nation following an end to hostilities. In a radio message on October 10, Kim Il Sung*, commander in chief of the Democratic People's Republic of Korea's* military forces, rejected MacArthur's ultimatum, thus providing justification for continuing the UN offensive to the Yalu River. The JCS handling of MacArthur's ultimatum, however, also provided reason for the general to believe that his objective in Korea was political reunification.

Foreign Relations of the United States, 1950, vol. 7: *Korea* (Washington, D.C., 1976); J. I. Matray, "Truman's Plan for Victory: National Self-Determination and the 38th Parallel Decision in Korea," *Journal of American History* (September 1979).

MACARTHUR'S VFW MESSAGE (August 20, 1950)

This message caused a clash early in the Korean War between CINCUNC General Douglas MacArthur* and President Harry S. Truman* over U.S. policy in East Asia that led eventually to Truman's recall of MacArthur*. Following the flap over MacArthur's visit to Taiwan*, President Truman dispatched W. Averell Harriman* early in August 1950 to discuss China policy with the general. Although MacArthur pledged to "obey any orders he received from the President" and assured the emissary he would not conspire with Chiang Kai-shek* to drag the United States into a war with Peking, Harriman noted he seemed to speak "without full conviction." The Taiwan issue exploded again in mid-August 1950 when the Veterans of Foreign Wars (VFW) asked MacArthur to send a message to the group's upcoming convention in Chicago. On August 20, he responded with a bitter critique of administration policy designed to dispel "misconceptions currently being voiced concerning the relationship of Formosa to our strategic potential in the Pacific." Drawn largely from earlier, classified reports, he described Taiwan as an "unsinkable aircraft carrier and submarine tender" and Chiang as a vital ally. MacArthur attacked the "threadbare argument" of officials who advocated appeasement and defeatism in the Pacific, defined by him as a refusal to defend Taiwan or challenge Communist power in China. As America's greatest expert in "Oriental psychology," he claimed that Asians admired his "aggressive, resolute and dynamic leadership."

The White House staff learned of the statement on August 25 as it went to press in American news weeklies. The implicit challenge to administration policy outraged Truman's civilian advisers, and the Joint Chiefs bristled at the general's lifting text from classified messages. Following a meeting the next day, the president "decisively repudiated the [VFW] statement" as a "direct contradiction" of administration policy. Truman, Secretary of State Dean G. Acheson*, and Harriman considered the bellicose message an attempt by MacArthur to bully the United States into making an "unlimited commitment toward Formosa." Acheson reported his fear that the Soviets and Chinese would use the VFW message as an anti-imperialist rallying cry among neutral Asians. Meanwhile, U.S. allies would conclude "we have an uncontrollable military commander" eager to "deliver U.S.-China policy over to the Kuomintang." Chiang would be encouraged to carry out some "provocation" against China while the Communists would conclude that Washington intended to use Taiwan as a "springboard for an American or American-backed attack."

President Truman insisted that Defense Secretary Louis A. Johnson* order MacArthur to withdraw his message, despite Johnson's fear of confronting the general. MacArthur complied with the order, even while defending his remarks as "personal opinion." Privately, MacArthur threatened to "blast" the administration "wide open," while an equally bruised Truman contemplated removing the general. *See also* Harriman's Visit to Tokyo; Johnson's Resignation as Secretary of Defense; MacArthur's Memorandum on Taiwan's Strategic Significance.

D. C. James, *The Years of MacArthur*, vol. 3: *Triumph and Disaster, 1945–1964* (Boston, 1985); M. Schaller, *Douglas MacArthur: The Far Eastern General* (New York, 1989).

Michael Schaller

MACARTHUR'S VICTORY PROPOSAL (December 1952)

On December 5, 1952, during President-elect Dwight D. Eisenhower's* trip to Korea*, Douglas MacArthur* told an audience of American industrialists that he had a plan to end the Korean War. Eisenhower quickly agreed to meet with MacArthur at John Foster Dulles's* New York City town house to listen to this proposal. At the meeting on December 17, 1952, MacArthur presented Ike with a fourteen-point memorandum. The new president, MacArthur proposed, should arrange a conference with Joseph Stalin* at which he would demand the unification and neutralization of Korea. If the Soviet leader refused, the United States should proceed "to clear North Korea of enemy forces" by "the atomic bombing of enemy military concentrations" and "the sowing of fields of suitable radioactive materials, the by-product of atomic manufacture." Eisenhower received this astonishing proposal with little comment, telling MacArthur only that he would have to consider its effects on relations with U.S. allies. Although Eisenhower never gave serious thought to implementing MacArthur's recommendations, he did finally resort to more subtle forms of nuclear pressure to help persuade the People's Republic of China* to accept an armistice in Korea. *See also* Dulles's Atomic Warning to China.

S. E. Ambrose, *Eisenhower, the President* (New York, 1984); D. C. James, *The Years of MacArthur*, vol. 3: *Triumph and Disaster, 1945–1964* (Boston, 1985); B. I. Kaufman, *The Korean War* (Philadelphia, 1986); W. Manchester, *American Caesar* (Boston, 1978).

Robert A. Divine

MACARTHUR'S VISIT TO KOREA OF JUNE 29, 1950

The first of seventeen trips to Korea which General Douglas MacArthur* made during the conflict, this visit had threefold significance. By providing immediate evidence of U.S. support, it bolstered South Korean morale; by allowing MacArthur to report authoritatively on the situation to Washington, it would eventually tip the balance in favor of the large-scale deployment of U.S. ground forces to Korea; and by encouraging MacArthur to reflect on the strategy of defending the Republic of Korea*, it provided the genesis of the Inch'ŏn operation.

MacArthur flew to Korea from Tokyo in his personal aircraft (the *Bataan*), accompanied by five senior members of his staff and four pressmen. Although confessing later that his heart failed him "for a fleeting moment" at the outset, his spirits had soon revived. During the flight, he ordered the bombing of North Korean airfields, in advance of authorization from Washington to extend operations north of the thirty-eighth parallel. The *Bataan* landed at Suwŏn shortly after 11 A.M. on an airfield that had been strafed by enemy planes earlier in the morning and was to be again that afternoon. MacArthur was met by Brigadier General John H. Church*, Ambassador John J. Muccio*, and ROK president Syngman Rhee* and conveyed to Church's nearby headquarters, where he was briefed on the desperate position of the South Korean forces, with only 16,000 men accounted for. With MacArthur insisting on making a personal inspection of the front, the party then drove north to the south bank of the Han River through retreating troops and refugees. MacArthur spent about an hour observing enemy-occupied Seoul before returning to Suwŏn. He departed for Japan on the *Bataan* at about 6:00 P.M. and reached Tokyo some four hours later.

Although MacArthur was reported to have reached "certain momentous decisions" as he viewed the evidence of defeat, his initial report to Washington, curiously, downplayed the need for the commitment of U.S. troops. Not until 12:50 P.M. the next day (June 30, Tokyo time), perhaps after General Church had indicated a further deterioration in the situation, did he dispatch the pessimistic report on his impressions, which, according to his staff, he had composed on the flight back to Tokyo. Without the introduction of U.S. ground forces, he warned, there could be no assurance of holding the line or of later recovering the lost territory. Received in Washington shortly after midnight, June 30, this message precipitated President Harry S. Truman's* decision later that morning to commit substantial ground combat forces to Korea. *See also* Church Survey Mission; Han River Operations; Truman's Commitment of Ground Troops.

D. MacArthur, *Reminiscences* (London, 1964); J. I. Matray, *The Reluctant Crusade* (Honolulu, 1985); J. F. Schnabel, *Policy and Direction* (Washington, D.C., 1972); J. F. Schnabel and R. J. Watson, *History of the Joint Chiefs of Staff*, vol. 3: *The Korean War* (Wilmington, 1979); C. Whitney, *MacArthur: His Rendezvous with History* (New York, 1956).

Ian C. McGibbon

MACARTHUR'S VISIT TO TAIWAN (July 31–August 1, 1950)

Shortly after the Korean War began, CINCUNC General Douglas MacArthur* informed the JCS (though not, officially, the State Department) of his intention to visit Taiwan as part of his overall effort to contain the threat of communism around Korea. Although President Harry S. Truman* had ordered the "neutralization" of Taiwan*, the U.S. government had not committed itself to the maintenance of Chiang Kai-shek's* clique in power. Yet, as MacArthur told diplomat William J. Sebald*, even if Chiang "has horns and a tail," so long as he was "anti-communist, we should help him." Ever since late 1949, MacArthur had urged the JCS to permit him to "survey" Taiwan's defense needs and assist the Republic of China's* efforts to deter an expected Communist invasion. During 1949 and possibly early in 1950, the general had, without authorization, dispatched some U.S. weapons and Japanese veterans to the island to buttress its defenses and provide psychological support.

On July 31, 1950, the general and a dozen U.S. officers arrived in Taiwan and closeted themselves for two days with Chiang's entourage. At the end of the talks, MacArthur announced that he had come to assess the island's defense needs. Praising the generalissimo's "indomitable determination to resist Communist domination," he announced, "arrangements have been completed for effective coordination between American forces under my command and those of the Chinese Government" to meet any attack. Although there is no evidence that MacArthur made any secret military commitments to the generalissimo, his cavalier style enraged many in Washington. The general told aides that he had "no intention of providing details" to the State Department since the talks were his "sole responsibility." He even waited several days before reporting the visit to the Joint Chiefs. Perhaps more important, MacArthur's highly visible embrace of Chiang undermined ongoing efforts by U.S. and Taiwanese officials to replace the generalissimo with a moderate leader. Chiang used MacArthur's blessing to convince wavering supporters that his rule was actually a prerequisite for U.S. assistance.

Suspicion of a MacArthur-Chiang deal increased when, following the general's return to Tokyo, he recommended sending jet fighters to the island, possibly to attack Chinese forces on the opposite side of the Taiwan Strait. Fearful he would provoke an incident, Truman rejected the idea, sternly informing MacArthur that "no one other than the President" possessed "authority to order or authorize preventive action against" the Chinese mainland. The visit left a legacy of suspicion in Washington regarding MacArthur's motives in possibly expanding the scope of the Korean War. *See also* Harriman's Visit to Tokyo; Johnson's Visit to Tokyo; MacArthur's Memorandum on Taiwan's Strategic Significance; Truman's Recall of MacArthur.

D. C. James, *The Years of MacArthur,* vol. 3: *Triumph and Disaster, 1945–1964* (Boston, 1985); M. Schaller, *Douglas MacArthur: The Far Eastern General* (New York, 1989).

Michael Schaller

MAKIN, NORMAN J. O. (1889–1982)

Ambassador from Australia in Washington from 1946 to 1951, Norman John Oswald Makin served as the principal channel for Australian-U.S. diplomatic communications during the Korean War. He had a long career as an Australian Labour party member of the federal parliament from 1919 to 1946. Makin was speaker of the House of Representatives from 1929 to 1931 and, during the wartime government of John Curtin, minister for the navy and munitions from 1941 to 1946. He was then appointed ambassador in Washington, the first person to hold that post after it had been upgraded from a legation to an embassy. After Australia was elected to the first UN Security Council in 1946, Makin served as its first president. When the Labour party was defeated in December 1949, Makin was not replaced by the new conservative administration under Robert G. Menzies* until May 1951.

In June 1950, Makin reported that the United States had been grateful for Australia's prompt assistance in Korea and that it was an appropriate time to suggest to Washington that a regional arrangement between the two nations would have been helpful in meeting such a crisis. Thereafter, the embassy's reporting was important in the moves toward the creation of the Australian–New Zealand–United States alliance under the ANZUS Treaty*. In late 1950, Makin expressed Australian concern over the suggestions of U.S. retaliation against the People's Republic of China* after Chinese military intervention* in the war. He reported on British prime minister Clement R. Attlee's* visit to the United States* of December 1950 and expressed Australian views on the possible use of the atomic bomb, which were generally in accordance with Attlee's. At this time he also explored with U.S. officials the proposal by Percy C. Spender*, Australian minister for external affairs, that diplomatic recognition should be withdrawn from the Nationalist Chinese government of Chiang Kai-shek* as part of a peace settlement with the PRC. In February 1951 Makin told the State Department of Australia's concern over suggestions that UN forces might cross the thirty-eighth parallel and drive far into North Korea. After Spender replaced him in May 1951, Makin resumed his political career, sitting in the House of Representatives from 1954 to his retirement in 1963.

R. J. O'Neill, *Australia in the Korean War 1950–53* (Canberra, 1981, 1985).

Peter Edwards

MAKINS, ROGER M. (1904–   )

At the start of the Korean War, Sir Roger M. Makins was Britain's deputy under secretary of state and one of its most able economists. He accompanied Prime Minister Clement R. Attlee* during his visit to the United States* in December 1950 after Chinese military intervention*. After graduating from Oxford with a history degree in 1925, Makins read law in London and was called to the bar in 1927. He joined the foreign service in 1928, serving thereafter in the United States, Norway, and at the League of Nations. Deeply involved in postwar economic planning, Makins played a significant role in the negotiations over Britain's posture toward the European Recovery Program. He supported efforts to retain Britain's status as the "third world power" by a close affiliation with the United States. Service at Allied Forces headquarters, Algiers, in 1943 and 1944 and as minister of the British embassy in Washington, D.C., from 1945 to 1947 prepared Makins well to succeed Sir Oliver Franks* as British ambassador to the United States in 1953.

During the Korean War, Makins served in the governments of both the Labour and Conservative parties, consistently representing the outlook that stipulated an active role for Britain in the Commonwealth, Europe, and, with U.S. support, world affairs. In pursuit of that goal, Britain had to keep the Americans, who

tended to adolescent excess, from overreacting in Korea and thus forgetting that
their chief obligation resided with the Atlantic Alliance. A diplomat of vast
experience and ability, he stood high in the ranks of that distinguished though
little-known group of British civil servants who worked so effectively during
World War II and over the next decade to maintain Britain's influence in world
affairs. Makins was British ambassador in the United States for three years
before becoming joint permanent secretary of the treasury until 1959. He subsequently retired in 1964 to a life of peerage as Lord Sherfield, remaining active
in the field of corporate finance.

D. Acheson, *Present at the Creation* (New York, 1969); A. Bullock, *Ernest Bevin,
Foreign Secretary, 1945–1951* (New York, 1983); *Current Biography*, 1953; M. Gilbert,
Winston S. Churchill (Boston, 1988).

Theodore A. Wilson

MALENKOV, GEORGI (1902–1988)

The top member of a collective leadership in the Soviet Union immediately
after Joseph Stalin* died on March 5, 1953, Georgi Malenkov launched a "peace
offensive" (as it was termed by the Western press) that made possible the
armistice agreement* ending the Korean War. After fighting with the Red Army
as a teenager in 1920, Malenkov became a favorite of Stalin, especially when
he helped brutally purge persons the dictator targeted in the 1930s. In the confused, supercharged days after the death of Stalin*, Malenkov obtained the two
pivotal offices of first party secretary and prime minister. Although he soon
began losing power, he, along with other Kremlin leaders, realized that Stalin's
policies had stultified the Soviet economy and society, ruined relations with
Yugoslavia, and taken the country uncomfortably close to war with the United
States.

In mid-1953 speeches, Malenkov announced the Soviets now had a hydrogen
(or "super") bomb, then denied that war was inevitable (as Stalin had claimed),
and asked for talks to end the Korean conflict and negotiate a German settlement.
He especially hoped to free Soviet resources for badly needed domestic economic
reform. In 1954, Nikita Khrushchev accused Malenkov of appeasing capitalists
and neglecting basic Soviet industry for the sake of producing consumer goods.
Malenkov resigned from the leadership in February 1955 and two years later
was exiled to supervise a hydroelectric plant in Kazakhstan, where he remained
for the next thirty years.

D. J. Dallin, *Soviet Foreign Policy After Stalin* (Philadelphia, 1961); *New York Times,*
February 2, 1988.

Walter LaFeber

MALIK, JACOB A. (1906–1980)

Soviet diplomat and permanent UN representative, Jacob A. Malik is perhaps
best known for his televised confrontations with U.S. and British diplomats over
matters relating to Korea and China during the Korean War. A native of the
Ukraine, he attended the Institute of People's Education in his home city of

Kharkow, majoring in economics. In 1937, he graduated from the Soviet Institute for Foreign Affairs at the University of Moscow. After holding several minor diplomatic posts, Malik became ambassador to Japan in 1942. Following Japan's surrender in August 1945, he was stationed in Moscow for several months, participating in the Council of Foreign Ministers meeting there in December. He returned briefly to Tokyo in January 1946 as a political advisor to the chief delegate to the Allied Council for Japan. Eight months later, Malik assumed the post of deputy foreign minister of the Soviet Union. In May 1948, he replaced Andrei A. Gromyko* as the permanent Soviet representative at the UN.

In January 1950, Malik stormed out of a Security Council meeting, announcing a Soviet UN Security Council boycott* to protest the body's refusal to grant China's seat to the newly formed People's Republic of China*. By the time he returned in August, the Security Council still had not admitted the PRC but had passed resolutions supporting efforts to repulse the North Korean invasion of South Korea* and for creation of a UN Command* under the United States. As Security Council president during August, replacing Arne Sunde of Norway, Malik attempted to move the China question to the top of the agenda, but a majority blocked his effort after a furious debate before a national television audience.

Although always a strict adherent to the official Soviet line, Malik could be affable in private, and he often served as a primary instrument for Soviet overtures to the West, especially on Korea. In late September and early October 1950, he probed the Western position through shows of friendliness on the UN social circuit and in a private meeting with Dean Rusk*, a U.S. assistant secretary of state. In May and June of the following year, he held private conversations with American diplomats Thomas J. Cory*, Frank Corrigan, and George F. Kennan*. These led eventually to Malik's radio address of June 23, 1951*, which ended with the statement that an armistice in Korea was possible through a mutual withdrawal of forces from the thirty-eighth parallel. The Americans reacted favorably, and the Kaesŏng truce talks* began on July 10. Malik remained in his UN post until October 1952, when he assumed the position, previously held by Gromyko, of first deputy foreign minister. After the death of Joseph Stalin* in March 1953, Malik was appointed ambassador to the United Kingdom, where he served until 1960. In 1968, he returned to his old post at the UN, staying on until 1976. See also Kennan-Malik Conversations.

Current Biography, 1949; New York Times, February 13, 1980; W. W. Stueck, The Road to Confrontation (Chapel Hill, 1981); United Nations, Official Records, 1950.

William Stueck

MALIK'S RADIO ADDRESS OF JUNE 23, 1951

On the evening of Saturday, June 23, 1951, Jacob A. Malik*, the Soviet UN ambassador, delivered a speech as part of a series sponsored by the UN Department of Public Information on the theme "The Price of Peace." The significance of his address lay in the closing paragraphs, which stated that the Soviet people wanted to strengthen peace and believed that the most acute problem of the day, Korea, could be settled. As a first step, discussions should be started among the belligerents for a cease-fire and an armistice providing for the mutual withdrawal of forces from the thirty-eighth parallel. The statement attached no political conditions to the armistice and made public the position adopted by Malik in an unofficial talk with George F. Kennan* of the State Department of June 5.

On June 27, in a conversation with the U.S. ambassador to Moscow, Alan G. Kirk*, the Soviet first deputy minister for foreign affairs, Andrei A. Gromyko*, confirmed Malik's words and suggested that the military representatives of the belligerents should meet to conclude an armistice limited to military matters. Political issues should not be raised. Although the Soviet Union refused to speak for the People's Republic of China* or the Democratic People's Republic of Korea*, these statements defined the Communist position and opened the way for the Kaesŏng truce talks*, which began shortly afterward. In adopting this line, the Soviet Union repudiated the previous insistence of China and North Korea on linking political and military issues and placed negotiations on a basis acceptable to the United States. Although both followed the Soviet lead, there were signs that neither Peking nor P'yŏngyang was happy about this retreat. *See also* Kennan-Malik Conversations; Ridgway's June 30, 1951, Armistice Message.

D. Acheson, *Present at the Creation* (London, 1969); B. I. Kaufman, *The Korean War* (Philadelphia, 1986); R. R. Simmons, *The Strained Alliance* (New York, 1975).

Callum A. MacDonald

MANCHURIAN SANCTUARY

CINCUNC General Douglas MacArthur's* military directive of September 27, 1950, for the invasion of North Korea following the Inch'ŏn landing* forbade operations across the Chinese or Soviet borders. These limitations continued to operate despite Chinese military intervention*, although the administration briefly considered hot pursuit* of Communist aircraft across the Yalu. In an interview with *U.S. News and World Report* on December 1, 1950, MacArthur condemned the restrictions that prevented air attacks on Chinese bases in Manchuria as an "enormous handicap, without precedent in military history." It was a theme to which he returned during the MacArthur Hearings* in May 1951, claiming that the Chinese could have been thrown back had the restrictions on bombing been lifted in November 1950 and U.S. air power used to its full potential. The view of the Truman administration was that to bomb Manchuria would be to fall into a Soviet trap, sucking U.S. strength into a struggle with a secondary enemy. As Air Force Chief of Staff General Hoyt S. Vandenberg* emphasized at the MacArthur Hearings, the FEAF could devastate Manchuria, but only at the expense of unacceptable attrition, which would weaken it against the main enemy, the Soviet Union. Moreover sanctuary operated both ways, since the Communists had not attacked U.S. bases and lines of communication in Japan and the Republic of Korea*. As long as this situation continued, the Truman administration preferred to fight it out with the Chinese inside Korea under existing restrictions.

Despite these reservations, consideration was given to attacking the Manchurian sanctuary in certain circumstances. In April 1951, Lieutenant General Matthew B. Ridgway*, MacArthur's replacement as the CINCUNC, was authorized to retaliate against Manchurian airfields in the event of an air attack that threatened the UNC*. Attacks on airfields were also considered as a possible option by the JCS during the summer of 1951 in the event that the Kaesŏng truce talks* failed but rejected on the grounds of attrition. In May 1953, the NSC considered a JCS plan to break the deadlock at the P'anmunjŏm truce talks* by widening the war, employing tactical atomic weapons against Manchurian targets. Although President Dwight D. Eisenhower* expressed concern about retaliation against Japan, he agreed that if circumstances arose that forced the United States into an expanded war in Korea, the JCS plan "was most likely to achieve the objectives we sought." See also Chinese Military Disengagement of November 6, 1950; Yalu Bridges Controversy.

R. Foot, The Wrong War (Ithaca, N.Y., 1985); B. I. Kaufman, The Korean War (Philadelphia, 1986); D. MacArthur, Reminiscences (New York, 1964).

Callum A. MacDonald

MAO TSE-TUNG (MAO ZEDONG; 1893–1976)

Mao Tse-tung, as chairman of the government of the People's Republic of China* and the Chinese Communist party (CCP), was the final decision maker in the PRC's policy toward the Korean War. Mao was a native socialist, accepting Marxism in China and attending the First National Congress of the CCP in 1921. While other Communists were busy cooperating with the Kuomintang (KMT) in urban revolution, Mao was more interested in peasant uprisings. After Chiang Kai-shek* abandoned the CCP-KMT coalition in 1927, Mao made his famous observation that "political power comes from the barrel of a gun." He established Soviet bases in the countryside and fought against Chiang's troops in defiance of party rivals, who removed Mao from power in 1933. After the Moscow-oriented Wang Ming was unable to halt advancing KMT forces during Chiang's fifth campaign, the Red Army embarked on the Long March. In 1935, Mao regained power and led the Red Army to north Shensi province. Two years later, the Sino-Japanese War broke out, and the CCP and the KMT formed the second United Front. For the next eight years, Mao developed his political theories while his generals expanded the CCP's influence in rural areas beyond Japanese control. With this foundation, Mao directed the Chinese Civil War from 1946 to 1949, expelling Chiang's Nationalist government from mainland China.

Historians still debate Mao's role in the planning and execution of the North Korean invasion of South Korea*. It is probable that Joseph Stalin* informed Mao of Kim Il Sung's* plans when the Chinese leader visited Moscow in 1949. However, Mao could not have been enthusiastic, given the fact that his country was just beginning economic recovery after years of war and the CCP was still consolidating its power. And then the United States denied him the ability to eliminate Chiang's regime with its neutralization of Taiwan*. When the UN indicated its intention to carry the Korean War to the Chinese border, Mao became alarmed. For Mao, the loss of North Korea would expose China directly to the threat of foreign invasions. In a war with the United States, he thought China would promote its international position if it won. China also would benefit in a peace without victory because the PRC would have shown itself able to match the power of the strongest country in the world. Even if China experienced defeat, the outcome would be the same as the anti-Japanese war. Mao therefore decided to order Chinese military intervention*. A million Chinese ''volunteers'' crossed the Yalu River. Before their departure, Mao warned them not to take anything from the Korean people. Mao's eldest son, An-ying, went to the front and died in the first month of fighting. After the failure of the Chinese spring offensives of 1951*, Mao pledged that China would keep fighting until the American imperialists chose to stop.

In November 1953, Kim Il Sung visited China. Mao claimed that China would not demand repayment of the war debt North Korea owed and also would provide 800 million Chinese dollars to the Democratic People's Republic of Korea* for the postwar reconstruction. Mao's generosity resulted in increasing the PRC's already large debt to the Soviet Union. Setting the stage for the Sino-Soviet split, Stalin demanded repayment for the materials China had received from Moscow to fight in Korea. After the Korean War, Mao turned to China's socialist construction. He made many errors, particularly the anti-rightism movement and the Great Leap Forward. In foreign relations, Mao remained hostile to the West while gradually moving away from his alliance with the Soviet Union. In 1966, Mao launched the Great Proletarian Cultural Revolution, and China experienced great political and economic chaos. After Lin Piao's* failed coup attempt in 1971, Mao attempted to restore order, including his approval for U.S. president Richard M. Nixon* to visit China as the first step toward normalization of Sino-U.S. relations. Nevertheless, when Mao died in 1976, he left behind a nation exhausted and without any positive plans for the future.

History Division, *Ci Hai* (Shanghai, 1980); Huang Yu-ch'uan, *Mao Tse-tung: A Chronology of His Life* (Hong Kong, 1970); Mao Zedong, *Selected Words of Mao Zedong*, vols. 1–5 (Beijing, 1965, 1977).

Li Yi

MARCH FIRST MOVEMENT (1919)

Also known as the *Manse* (Long Live Korea) incident, this popular uprising against Japanese colonialism was perhaps the most significant event in the history of the Korean nationalist movement. During World War I, President Woodrow Wilson had proclaimed U.S. support for advancing the principle of national self-determination. This naturally appealed to the Korean people, who had watched Japan formally annex their nation in 1910 and then systematically integrate the peninsula into its imperial structure during the next decade. In January 1919, when the former Yi Dynasty (1392–1910) ruler died, rumors spread that a Japanese physician had poisoned him. Korean nationalists decided to issue a declaration of independence and appeal for foreign assistance to oust the Japanese on March 1, two days before the dead king's funeral. On that date, Japanese authorities in Seoul arrested leading organizers, while police used gunfire to disperse demonstrators. The movement quickly spread to the countryside, as an estimated 500,000 people actively joined mass parades, marching and shouting *Manse*. Using brute force, Japan violently suppressed the uprising in March and April, killing nearly 2,000 Koreans and imprisoning countless others.

Although the March First Movement failed, it awakened a rebellious Korean nationalism and created many new leaders in the quest for independence. Following the incident, Korean exiles, in search of foreign support for the liberation of their nation, scattered to China, the Soviet Union, and the United States. In Shanghai, several of the leaders of the March First Movement created the most well-known organization, the self-styled Korean Provisional Government (KPG), electing Syngman Rhee* as its first president. While the KPG utterly failed to enlist support from an isolationist United States after 1919, Korean radicals turned to a sympathetic Soviet Union. Thus, Communist revolutionary ideology emerged as a popular and powerful force, both among Korean exiles and inside Korea itself. Nevertheless, the KPG continued to insist that the March First Movement made it the legitimate heir to political authority in Korea. During World War II, KPG president Kim Ku, residing in China and receiving financial backing from Chiang Kai-shek*, appealed to the United States for recognition and Lend-Lease aid. But President Franklin Roosevelt, aware of the factionalism in the Korean independence movement, refused to sponsor any exile group and developed a trusteeship plan to bring Korea's postwar independence. *See also* Cairo Declaration.

Takashi Hatada, *A History of Korea* (Santa Barbara, Calif., 1969); C. Lee, *The Politics of Korean Nationalism* (Berkeley, 1963); J. I. Matray, *The Reluctant Crusade* (Honolulu, 1985).

MARSHALL, GEORGE C. (1880–1959)

One of the most respected figures in twentieth-century America, General George C. Marshall served as secretary of defense during most of the first year of the Korean War. Born in Uniontown, Pennsylvania, and educated at Virginia Military Institute, he was commissioned in the U.S. Army in 1902 and rose steadily through the ranks. Marshall served in World War I and after several postwar assignments was appointed chief of staff of the army in 1939 with the rank of general. He guided military strategy during World War II and after the war served as special envoy to China (1945–1946) and as President Harry S. Truman's* secretary of state (1947–1949), where he established the Marshall Plan for European economic revival. He also delivered a speech to the UN General Assembly in September 1947 placing the Korean issue on the agenda, resulting in passage of the UN resolution of November 14, 1947*.

Marshall served only a year as secretary of defense, taking office in September 1950 following Louis A. Johnson's* resignation*. But in that brief time, he handled a number of pressing issues. His first order of business was to restore communication and cooperation between the State and Defense departments, which had been hampered by the policies of his predecessor. This was essential to coordinate the diplomatic and military conduct of the Korean War. At the time Marshall took over, CINCUNC Douglas General MacArthur* had turned back the North Korean People's Army and was preparing for the UN offensive across the thirty-eighth parallel*. As a military man, Marshall knew that a field commander needed the freedom to follow up a victory. But when the Home-by-Christmas offensive* failed, Marshall became more cautious. He concurred with the Truman administration's decision to pursue a political settlement through the UN, and he agreed that the United States should not hold the Soviets directly responsible, despite his personal belief that the North Koreans made no pretense of their alignment with Moscow. In December 1950, he argued that the United States could not abandon the Republic of Korea* and that a cease-fire at that time would be a sign of weakness. At the same time, he advocated reasonable steps to avoid global war.

Marshall did not pretend to have a solution to the conflict. He ordered MacArthur to fall back to a more defensible position. He sympathized with his field commander's position, but he was becoming concerned about MacArthur's public criticism of administration policy, especially since MacArthur was defying the direct orders of his commander in chief and the JCS directive of December 6, 1950*. When on April 5, 1951, Congressman Joseph W. Martin* read a letter from MacArthur on the floor of the House in which the general criticized administration policy, Marshall realized MacArthur would have to be removed. Marshall continued as secretary of defense until Robert A. Lovett* replaced him in the fall of 1951, pursuing efforts to secure a cease-fire while at the same time trying to maintain U.S. strength and credibility on the battlefield. *See also* Truman's Recall of MacArthur.

R. Foot, *The Wrong War* (Ithaca, N.Y., 1985); L. Mosley, *Marshall: Hero for Our Times* (New York, 1982); F. Pogue, *George C. Marshall: Statesman, 1945–1959* (New York, 1987).

T. Michael Ruddy

MARTIN, JOSEPH W. (1884–1968)

Beginning in 1939, Joseph W. Martin, served in the U.S. House of Representatives as Republican minority leader and later as Speaker. He was "amiable, hard-working and ploddingly conscientious," an observer noted, and an example of the typical "party wheelhorse." During the Korean War, he gained fame when CINCUNC General Douglas MacArthur* wrote him a letter criticizing the strategy of limited war, thereby contributing to President Harry S. Truman's* recall of MacArthur*. Born in North Attleboro, Massachusetts, Martin became a reporter for his home-town newspaper rather than accepting a scholarship to Dartmouth College. With others, he purchased the *North Attleboro Evening Chronicle* in 1908, serving as its editor and publisher. Three years later, Martin was elected to the Massachusetts legislature and in 1914 to the state senate. After working from 1917 to 1922 in the insurance business, he became the executive secretary for the Massachusetts Republican party and in 1924 won election to the U.S. House of Representatives. Not only was Martin a close ally of President Calvin Coolidge, but he developed a friendship with Franklin D. Roosevelt as well.

As a politician, Martin was no ideologue, advising his colleagues to "vote your district." According to one critic, he "had a firm grip on the obvious but no profound understanding or new thoughts." After entering Congress, Martin helped organize a coalition against the New Deal, which he labeled fascism, persuading southern Democrats to join with Republicans in blocking passage of further reform measures. Martin was an isolationist prior to U.S. entry into World War II, voting against aid to Britain and for an impartial arms embargo. For Roosevelt, he symbolized Republican reaction, referring to him in 1940 as a member of "that great historic trio . . . Martin, Barton and Fish." When Martin became Speaker in 1947, he was pragmatic and ruled with a gentle hand, but he clashed with Truman on domestic issues. He endorsed a bipartisan foreign policy but also was one of Chiang Kai-shek's* strongest supporters in Congress and criticized Truman for not using Nationalist troops to fight in Korea.

An old friend of MacArthur, Martin wrote a letter to the general on March 20, 1951, requesting comments on his recent speech advocating U.S. support for a Nationalist attack on the Chinese mainland. Truman recalled MacArthur six days after Martin read the general's reply in the House of Representatives. The minority leader then helped arrange for MacArthur to address a joint session of Congress and for the MacArthur Hearings*. When Dwight D. Eisenhower* became president, Martin again assumed the position as Speaker for two years. Thereafter, he developed a close relationship with Sam Rayburn, the Democratic Speaker of the House, which alienated many of his colleagues. In a move toward younger leadership, the Republicans ousted him as minority leader in 1959. After his defeat in the Republican primary election of 1966, Martin retired from politics. *See also* MacArthur's Letter to Joseph Martin.

C. Blair, *The Forgotten War* (New York, 1987); *Current Biography*, 1948; *New York Times*, March 7, 1968; E. W. Schoenebaum (ed.), *Political Profiles: The Truman Years* (New York, 1978).

MATTHEWS, FRANCIS P. (1887–1952)

Francis P. Matthews was appointed secretary of the navy on May 25, 1949, and held the post at the outset of the Korean War. A corporate executive and attorney from Omaha, Nebraska, Matthews had little prior training or preparation for his post. He became known as the "rowboat secretary" because that was the only vessel he confessed ever to have sailed. Matthews had to administer his department according to the new reorganization plan for the armed forces, which weakened the role of the service secretaries and strengthened the role of the secretary of defense. He was deeply involved in the navy–air force debate over the capabilities of B-36 aircraft and a related debate over whether a supercarrier should be built.

Although he was present at the first Blair House meeting*, Matthews did not have a major role in the planning of the Korean War. Along with the other service secretaries, he was invited to hear the daily briefings on the war given by one of the Joint Chiefs, usually the chairman General Omar N. Bradley*. Before the war started, Matthews had presided over a curtailment of naval functions resulting from President Harry S. Truman's* austere defense budgets. At the outbreak of the war, Matthews took the opportunity to request additional funds for improving naval readiness and combat capabilities. The Truman administration and Congress responded without delay, quickly adding over $10 billion to defense appropriations. Matthews now presided over rapid naval expansion.

Matthews achieved an embarrassing notoriety in the Truman administration as a result of a highly controversial speech he gave on August 25, 1950, at the Boston Navy Yard's sesquicentennial celebration. The outbreak of war had led to much concern in the United States about the Communist threat and how to handle it. In his speech, Matthews offered the radical option of waging a preventive war. He stated that the United States should be willing to pay any price to achieve a world at peace, "even the price of instituting a war to compel cooperation for peace." The State Department criticized the speech, and President Truman gave Matthews a firm lecture but stopped short of firing him. In the summer of 1951, Truman ended Matthews's tenure as secretary of the navy by appointing him ambassador to Ireland. He served in Dublin for about a year before suffering a fatal heart attack while on a return trip to the United States in October 1952. *See also* Preventive War Scare.

P. E. Coletta (ed.), *American Secretaries of the Navy*, vol. 2: *1913–1972* (Annapolis, 1980); *New York Times,* August 26, 27, September 1, 1950; R. Schaffer, *Wings of Judgement* (New York, 1985); H. S. Truman, *Years of Trial and Hope* (Garden City, N.Y., 1956).

Tami D. Biddle

MATTHEWS, H. FREEMAN (1899–1986)

H. Freeman Matthews, in the position of deputy under secretary of state, served as a close adviser to Secretary of State Dean G. Acheson* during the Korean War. An experienced diplomat, he was born in Baltimore, and educated at Princeton University. His career spanned the years from 1923 to 1962. Beginning in 1944, Matthews played an increasingly important role in shaping U.S. foreign policy when he was appointed director of the Office of European Affairs in the State Department. In this capacity, he advised Presidents Franklin D. Roosevelt and Harry S. Truman* at the wartime conferences and also participated in the postwar foreign ministers' conferences. In 1947, Matthews was named ambassador to Sweden, a post he held until 1950 when Acheson appointed him deputy under secretary of state. Working closely with Under Secretary James E. Webb*, he served in this office until 1953.

As deputy under secretary, "Doc" Matthews participated in many of the discussions surrounding the policymaking and diplomatic maneuvers during the war. In addition, he served as liaison between the State and Defense departments, a difficult responsibility while Louis A. Johnson* was secretary of defense. Besides the advice Matthews contributed to discussions on the conduct and diplomacy of the Korean War, many credit him with conceiving one initiative that led toward an ultimate cease-fire and armistice. In May 1951, when diplomatic efforts were languishing, Matthews recalled how a similar stalemate during the Berlin crisis had been overcome by an informal approach to the Soviet ambassador to the UN. He recommended to Acheson that perhaps George F. Kennan* might approach Jacob A. Malik*, Soviet UN representative. Acheson approved and dispatched Kennan, who received a reply from Malik on June 5 that the Soviets did indeed want a peaceful solution but that approaches had to be made to the Chinese and North Koreans. Then Malik made his radio address of June 23, 1951*, in which he proposed that both sides withdraw to the thirty-eighth parallel and pursue cease-fire and armistice talks. The Soviet position was still somewhat ambiguous and an armistice still lay in the future, but Matthews's ploy contributed to getting the Kaesŏng truce talks* underway. See also Kennan-Malik Conversations.

D. Acheson, Present at the Creation (New York, 1969); R. Foot, The Wrong War (Ithaca, N.Y., 1985); J. C. Goulden, Korea: The Untold Story of the War (New York, 1982); H. F. Matthews, oral history interview, Harry S. Truman Library, Independence, Missouri.

T. Michael Ruddy

MCCLURE, ROBERT A. (1897–1957)

Born in Matoon, Illinois, Major General Robert A. McClure was chief of the U.S. Army's psychological warfare division during the Korean War and the founding father of the concept of voluntary repatriation* of POWs. After attending Kentucky Military Institute from 1912 to 1915, he received his commission as a second lieutenant in 1916 and then served with the Philippine Constabulary army and in China. McClure underwent additional training after World War I at Infantry School (1923–1924), Cavalry School (1924–1926), Command and General Staff School (1930–1932), and the Army War College (1935). After serving as an instructor at the Infantry School (1926–1930) and the Army War College (1936–1940), he was military attaché at the U.S. embassy in London when the United States entered World War II. McClure spent the rest of the war years at Supreme Headquarters of Allied Forces in Europe (SHAFE), holding positions as chief of intelligence and chief of the Psychological Warfare Division. In 1945, he became director of the Information Control Division of the U.S. military government in Germany and was responsible for approving all newspaper and magazine publications. From 1947 to 1950, McClure was chief of the Civil Affairs Division of the U.S. Army and commandant at Fort Ord in California.

Having risen through the ranks to brigadier general, McClure became head of the Psychological Warfare Division in 1950 and played a leading role in persuading the Truman administration to adopt a position against forcible repatriation of POWs at the P'anmunjŏm truce talks*. In the fall of 1951, he began to voice concern about the fate of those Chinese POWs who had fought under Chiang Kai-shek* in the Chinese Civil War. McClure feared that harsh punishment or execution awaited them upon their return to China. He therefore recommended that the United States make arrangements for sending those POWs resisting repatriation to Taiwan. In defense of his proposal, McClure stressed that voluntary repatriation was not only humanitarian but would encourage enemy soldiers to surrender, thereby weakening the Communist war effort. When the Communist delegation at P'anmunjŏm refused to accept the idea of voluntary repatriation, McClure proposed in February 1952 that the postwar political conference should handle the disposition of those POWs seeking asylum. Following the Korean War, McClure became chief of the U.S. military mission to Iran, remaining in this position until his retirement in 1956. *See also* UN POW Administration.

B. J. Bernstein, "The Struggle over the Korean Armistice: Prisoners of Repatriation?" in B. Cumings (ed.), *Child of Conflict* (Seattle, 1983); W. G. Hermes, *Truce Tent and Fighting Front* (Washington, D.C., 1966); *New York Times*, January 5, 1957; *Who Was Who in America*, vol. 3: *1951–1960* (Chicago, 1960).

"MEAT GRINDER" STRATEGY

Lieutenant General Matthew B. Ridgway*, as commander of the 8th Army*, developed this long-range approach in January 1951 to offset the numerical superiority of the Chinese Communists and force them to evacuate South Korea. American soldiers dubbed it the "meat grinder" strategy because its primary objective was to inflict maximum casualties on Communist forces, thereby compelling the enemy to retreat north of the thirty-eighth parallel. Ridgway's strategy emphasized positional warfare to seize territory that would improve the 8th Army's ability to trap and destroy enemy forces. It relied as well on the employment of long-range artillery coupled with air attacks using napalm and rockets. With the support of tanks, ground troops then would advance with heavy machine gun and mortar fire. Ridgway was interested in inflicting maximum punishment but without sustaining losses sufficient to undermine the basic security of the UNC*. Also, he acted on the assumption that the People's Republic of China* would maintain its offensive aimed at conquering the peninsula, while the 8th Army would receive neither reinforcements nor a change in its directive.

Ridgway implemented the meat grinder strategy for the first time in Operation Killer* and then in Operation Ripper* and Operation Courageous*. After less than three months, the UNC had returned to the thirty-eighth parallel, having moved northward 70 air miles in a careful and cautious advance. Although

Chinese forces had withdrawn entirely from the Republic of Korea* by March 1951, Ridgway acknowledged that the meat grinder strategy had produced only a "qualified success." The 8th Army had neither killed nor captured large numbers of enemy forces, and far too many Communist soldiers had escaped into North Korea. Thus, the UNC had not punished the Chinese enough to persuade them to accept a negotiated settlement. Perhaps worse, there was considerable criticism in the American press of a strategy that seemed excessively brutal. The State Department complained that the term *meat grinder* had reduced the entire meaning of the U.S. venture in Korea to one word—*killing. See also* JCS Directive of January 12, 1951.

D. Acheson, *Present at the Creation* (New York, 1969); C. Blair, *The Forgotten War* (New York, 1987); D. Rees, *Korea: The Limited War* (New York, 1964); M. B. Ridgway, *The Korean War* (Garden City, N.Y., 1967); J. F. Schnabel, *Policy and Direction* (Washington, D.C., 1972).

MENON, K. P. S. (1898–1982)

K. P. S. Menon was chairman in 1947 and 1948 of the UN Temporary Commission on Korea (UNTCOK). Born in the southern Indian state of Kerala, Menon attended Madras Christian College and Oxford University. He joined the Indian civil service under British colonial rule in 1921 and held a variety of posts at home and abroad. In 1945, he attended the UN Conference at San Francisco as chief adviser to the Indian delegation. After a brief tenure as India's ambassador to China in 1947, Menon was tapped by Prime Minister Jawaharlal Nehru* to serve as a representative for newly independent India on the UNTCOK. The commission had been formed in accordance with the UN resolution of November 14, 1947*, after the breakdown of Soviet-U.S. negotiations over plans for a Korean trusteeship. The UNTCOK's membership consisted of representatives from Australia, Canada, the Republic of China*, El Salvador, France, the Philippines, Syria, and India. It was charged with the difficult task of establishing a general plan for the withdrawal of U.S. and Soviet troops, the supervision of elections for a National Assembly, and the creation of a unified national government.

The UNTCOK actually had little chance of successfully bringing about Korea's peaceful unification. Since the Soviet Union refused to cooperate with the UN, the commission had no means of exercising its power in Soviet-occupied northern Korea. In southern Korea, Menon and the UNTCOK found a fractious political party structure and despaired of the possibility of creating order out of chaos. According to his memoirs, Menon was especially skeptical of Syngman Rhee's* ability to fashion a viable political solution to Korea's problems. Rhee's reliance on violence and intimidation to constrain leftist and liberal opposition to his rule, Menon recalled, had helped to create a police state in the south. Given these conditions, the commission initially refrained from following its mandate to supervise national elections. To the chagrin of the United States and Rhee, Menon's commission concluded that separate elections would probably harden the division of the nation and might lead to a bloody civil war.

On February 6, 1948, the commission decided to refer the matter to the Interim Committee of the UN. After Menon presented the UNTCOK's report, however, the United States pressed both the Indian and British representatives to reconsider their position and to accept elections only in the south as the most likely avenue to peaceful reunification. Both the Indians and the British consequently reversed their earlier stands, and under Menon's leadership, the UNTCOK endorsed the call for separate elections in southern Korea. Menon resigned his chairmanship before the May 1948 elections took place, but the decision to forgo the goal of reunification meant that the UN would have a moral obligation to defend the government emerging from those elections.

J. I. Matray, *The Reluctant Crusade* (Honolulu, 1985); K. P. S. Menon, *Many Worlds* (New York, 1965); W. W. Stueck, *The Road to Confrontation* (Chapel Hill, 1981).

Dennis Merrill

MENON POW SETTLEMENT PROPOSAL (November 17, 1952)

This proposal, set forth by Indian UN representative V. K. Krishna Menon*, helped to end the impasse at the P'anmunjŏm truce talks* over agenda item 4*, POW repatriation, paving the way for the Korean armistice agreement*. The Communist belligerents demanded the forcible repatriation of all POWs in keeping with the Geneva Convention of 1949* on prisoners of war. The United States had introduced the unorthodox principle of voluntary repatriation* whereby POWs would be screened to determine whether they preferred to return to their native countries. Many of Washington's allies, who hoped to bring a rapid conclusion to the war and to prevent its widening, urged the Truman administration to compromise. But none had publicly taken issue with the U.S. position, and in early October 1952, Secretary of State Dean G. Acheson* persuaded twenty nations to cosponsor with the United States a resolution that endorsed voluntary repatriation. The consensus broke down quickly in early November when Menon presented a compromise.

Evasive, flexible, and shrewd—and well known for his distrust of the United States—Menon kept his proposal imprecise. For a time, he even refused to put it in writing. As formally introduced to the UN, the Menon resolution included provisions for a cease-fire, an exchange of willing prisoners, and the establishment of a four-member Neutral Nations Repatriation Commission* to supervise the remaining POWs. Once armistice arrangements had been made, prisoners resisting repatriation would be turned over to a postwar Korean political conference. Acheson initially condemned the proposal as a "dangerous idea" that left the question of repatriation unsolved at the time of the armistice. Ironically, the Soviet Union—which initially suspected India of harboring Anglo-American sympathies—issued the first public rejection of the plan. In the face of Soviet opposition and strong allied support for the measure, Acheson decided to support Menon's resolution after winning approval for several amendments, the most important of which assured that the political conference would release all remaining prisoners within four months of the armistice signing.

The revised resolution, which now guaranteed voluntary repatriation, passed the General Assembly on December 3, 1952, with the Soviet bloc in sole opposition. Although Menon had provided a foundation for a POW agreement, Washington's insistence on voluntary repatriation probably served to prolong the war. Finally, in June 1953—after a period of negotiation, military escalation, and the death of Joseph Stalin*—the Democratic People's Republic of Korea* and the People's Republic of China* accepted a modified version of Menon's resolution. The signing of an armistice quickly followed in July. *See also* Chou En-lai POW Settlement Proposal; Twenty-one Power UN Resolution; UN Resolution of December 3, 1952.

D. Acheson, *Present at the Creation* (New York, 1969); B. J. Bernstein, "The Struggle over the Korean Armistice: Prisoners of Repatriation?" in B. Cumings (ed.), *Child of Conflict* (Seattle, 1983); S. Gopal, *Jawaharlal Nehru: A Biography* (London, 1979); B. I. Kaufman, *The Korean War* (Philadelphia, 1986).

Dennis Merrill

MENON, V. K. KRISHNA (1896–1974)

As Indian representative to the UN, Menon played a key role in the diplomacy that led to the Korean armistice agreement*. Born at Panniankara, Calicut, in India's southern state of Kerala, Menon undertook studies in England during the 1920s, graduating from the London School of Economics. During the 1930s, he steeped himself in Labour party politics, became an ardent supporter of India's independence movement, and acquired a status as de facto ambassador in London for the Indian Congress party. He also struck up a close friendship with Jawaharlal Nehru* during these early years. When Nehru emerged as prime minister of newly independent India in 1947, he tapped Menon to be his high commissioner in London. Menon served his government in a variety of capacities during the late 1940s and the 1950s, becoming well known in international circles for his spirited nationalism, his role in helping to frame India's nonaligned foreign policy, and his frequent verbal attacks against U.S. cold war policies. Menon's acid tongue and vain personal demeanor deeply alienated most U.S. policymakers, who mistakenly viewed his outbursts as evidence of a pro-Soviet bias.

In spite of his abrasive style, Menon demonstrated political savvy in his Korean War diplomacy. Prime Minister Nehru in early 1952 appointed Menon to the Indian delegation as a special assignment. In keeping with the fundamental goals of India's nonaligned foreign policy, Menon hoped to prevent any further escalation of the conflict while bringing the major belligerents and their allies to the negotiating table. By late 1952, the war had stalemated, and the P'anmunjŏm truce talks* had stalled over the single issue of agenda item 4*, POW repatriation. The Indian delegate immediately set to work to mold a compromise. Formally introduced to the UN in November 1952, the Menon POW settlement proposal*, after significant modification, laid the foundation for the June 8, 1953, POW agreement between the belligerents and the July armistice. When the projected Korean political conference failed to materialize in early 1954, Menon once more facilitated the peace process by suggesting that nonrepatriated prisoners simply be returned to their original custodians for release. *See also* UNC Final POW Settlement Proposal of May 25, 1953.

B. J. Bernstein, "The Struggle over the Korean Armistice: Prisoners of Repatriation?" in B. Cumings (ed.), *Child of Conflict* (Seattle, 1983); M. Brecher, *India and World Politics: Krishna Menon's View of the World* (London, 1968); S. Gopal, *Jawaharlal Nehru: A Biography* (London, 1979).

Dennis Merrill

MENZIES, ROBERT G. (1894–1978)

Prime minister of Australia during the Korean War, Robert Gordon (from 1963 Sir Robert) Menzies was an outstanding barrister before entering politics. He had been prime minister from 1939 to 1941 and then in opposition until his reelection in December 1949. His government regarded the conflict in Korea as part of the worldwide struggle against communism. Its immediate reaction on June 27, 1950, was to send a squadron of heavy bombers to Malaya to assist the British Commonwealth forces fighting a Communist insurgency there. Menzies consulted both London and Washington, but his instinct was to keep as close as possible to British policy. On June 29, after hearing that the United Kingdom had committed Royal Navy vessels for service in Korea, Menzies similarly committed a destroyer and a frigate of the Royal Australian Navy. After General Douglas MacArthur* had let the press know that he was seeking the commitment of a fighter squadron of the Royal Australian Air Force, then serving with the British Commonwealth Occupation Force in Japan, the squadron of Mustangs was committed on June 30.

Menzies shared the initial British reluctance to commit ground troops, a reluctance confirmed in discussions he held with the British cabinet in London in July. The British changed their minds while Menzies was at sea en route from Britain to the United States, and the Australian decision to commit the 3d Battalion, the Royal Australian Regiment, was taken in his absence, largely at the instigation of the minister for external affairs Percy C. Spender*. Menzies discovered this decision on his arrival in the United States and immediately put it to effect in improving Australian prestige in Washington, where he addressed both houses of Congress and secured a loan of $250 million from the World Bank. Menzies was doubtful about the need for, or the possibility of, a security pact between Australia and the United States, but the ANZUS Treaty*, negotiated in 1951, was closely related to the Australian commitment to Korea.

Thereafter Menzies and the governments he led until his retirement in 1966 acted as loyal allies of the United States, as well as of the United Kingdom. Nevertheless, he was not uncritical of the U.S. conduct of the Korean War. The Menzies government shared British concerns over possible U.S. retaliation against the People's Republic of China* and supported British prime minister Clement R. Attlee's* bid, in his visit to the United States* in December 1950, to dissuade Washington from any use of the atomic bomb. In February 1951,

Australia expressed concern at the possibility that UN forces might drive far into North Korea. Australian attempts to restrain the United States were generally expressed within a British Commonwealth framework, and Menzies was content to allow Britain, Canada, or India to take the lead in order not to damage the new Australian-American alliance.

R. J. O'Neill, *Australia in the Korean War 1950–53* (Canberra, 1981, 1985).

Peter Edwards

MERCHANT, LIVINGSTON T. (1903–1976)

Livingston T. Merchant was deputy assistant secretary of state for Far Eastern affairs when the Korean War broke out. If the old idea that foreign service officers were bred to the job has any validity, "Livy" Merchant was a case in point. He was educated at Hotchkiss School and graduated cum laude from Princeton University. Merchant joined the investment banking firm of Scudder, Stevens & Clark in Boston and became a partner in 1926. With U.S. entry into World War II, Merchant joined the Department of State with responsibilities for coordinating war materials. After the war, he entered the foreign service and served as counselor of the U.S. embassy at Chungking, the wartime capital of the Republic of China*. Like many other officials who later served in the Far Eastern Bureau, Merchant had some experience in China but not enough to be labelled a "China hand." Merchant went on to have a long and distinguished career in the foreign service and held high posts in the Department of State. Throughout his career, he was a skillful bureaucratic practitioner who was well versed in the techniques of international relations rather than a strategic thinker or policymaker.

Merchant attended many of the crucial policy meetings on Korea during 1950, but his second rank and personal inclination meant that he was more an observer than participant. Serving as the principal lieutenant to Assistant Secretary of State for Far Eastern Affairs Dean Rusk*, Merchant handled much of the day-to-day diplomacy of the war and participated in the Korean War briefing meet-ings*. Like his immediate superior, Merchant kept a relatively low profile. By the end of his tour in the Far Eastern Division, Merchant had taken a larger role in Korean policy formulation. After a short stint on mutual security affairs and a posting in Paris, Merchant became the Eisenhower administration's assistant secretary of state for European affairs in March 1953. As head of the European bureau, his role was two-fold: he was part of Secretary of State John Foster Dulle's* circle of close advisers, and he presented the views of the European Affairs Bureau on Korean policy. NATO allies, such as Great Britain, Canada, and Turkey, had made major troop contributions to the UN effort in Korea, and they pressed the Eisenhower administration to sign an armistice. Merchant ef-fectively made sure that Europe's concern with a speedy end to the war got a fair hearing in Washington.

Foreign Relations of the United States, 1950, vol. 7: *Korea* (Washington, D.C., 1976), *1951,* vol.7: *Korea and China* (Washington, D.C., 1983), and *1952–1954,* vol. 15: *Korea* (Washington, D.C., 1984).

                                                                            Edward C. Keefer

MEXICAN POW SETTLEMENT PROPOSAL

On September 2, 1952, Luis Padilla Nervo*, the Mexican ambassador to the United Nations, handed Secretary-General Trygve Lie* a proposal by Mexican president Miguel Alemán that was intended to serve as a means of breaking the deadlock at the P'anmunjŏm truce talks* over agenda item 4*, POW repatriation. Alemán proposed that the combatants agree to an armistice and that all POWs who so desired be immediately repatriated. To resolve the touchy question of what to do with those who resisted repatriation, they would be allowed to enjoy temporary asylum in the territory of a UN member nation that had accepted his plan. While at a neutral site, a POW would be granted immigration status and allowed to take employment. POWs who changed their minds during this period of temporary asylum could request repatriation under UN auspices. This apparently meant that the UN would prohibit forcible repatriation of POWs, but the vague wording would leave that question until after an armistice, thus allowing the Communist negotiators to save face.

The proposal's outlines became public knowledge a week after the letter was handed to Lie, thus generating considerable discussion long before Mexico offered it as an official resolution. The State Department and JCS initially welcomed Alemán's proposal—not as a solution in itself but because the plan afforded President Harry S. Truman* an opportunity to respond to it with a general armistice proposal before the UN General Assembly opened on October 14. On October 6, Warren R. Austin*, the U.S. ambassador to the UN, publicly offered his cautious welcome to the proposal. Nevertheless, Soviet officials at the UN made it clear in private discussions with American counterparts that they did not trust the Mexicans. And Truman made no new proposal because CINCUNC General Mark W. Clark* persuaded the JCS that an armistice at that time might allow the Communists to rebuild their military strength for a renewal of hostilities later.

The UN General Assembly was left to pick up the question after the truce talks suspension of October 8, 1952*. A succession of proposals were offered in late October and early November to revive the armistice process. Mexico formally offered the Alemán plan in more detailed form as a draft resolution on November 1. By this time, the United States was cool to the idea, and Soviet foreign minister Andrei Y. Vyshinsky* rejected it as unacceptable in a speech on November 10. In the end, the General Assembly turned to the V. K. Krishna Menon* POW settlement proposal* of November 17 as the rough model for the eventual solution to the POW problem. Alemán's plan thus did not figure in the final settlement.

Department of State Bulletin, November 3, 24, 1952; *Foreign Relations of the United States, 1952–1954,* vol. 15: *Korea* (Washington, D.C., 1984); C. A. MacDonald, *Korea:*

The War Before Vietnam (New York, 1986); New York Times, September 10, 11, 1952; J. F. Schnabel and R. J. Watson, History of the Joint Chiefs of Staff, vol. 3: The Korean War (Wilmington, 1979).

Jeffrey G. Mauck

MEYER, CLARENCE E. (1891–1965)

In 1952, President Harry S. Truman* appointed Clarence E. Meyer as the head of a mission to the Republic of Korea* to resolve a dispute over the currency exchange rate and suspense account controversy*. Meyer was born in East Ashford, New York, and graduated from Syracuse University in 1913. Thereafter, he worked for Vacuum Oil Company as a marketer of petroleum products, making several trips to China and Japan. In 1932, Meyer's firm, now Socony-Vacuum Oil Company, appointed him to supervise a joint venture with Standard Oil Company for the production, refining, and marketing of oil in Indonesia. Following a merger the next year, Meyer assumed control over all Standard Vacuum Oil Company's holdings in East Asia, including Australia, New Zealand, and parts of Africa.

In 1941, Meyer had been Standard Vacuum's general manager in Japan since 1934. Following Japan's attack on Pearl Harbor, he was arrested and spent seven months in solitary confinement. After returning to the United States aboard the Gripsholm, Meyer spent the remainder of World War II serving as petroleum attaché at the U.S. embassy in London. In 1945, he rejoined Standard Vacuum as a director, becoming a vice-president the next year. When he retired in 1950, "C. E." was director of his company's tanker operations and employee and public relations programs in China and Japan. Meyer then went to Taiwan and the Philippines as a representative of the U.S. government to evaluate economic conditions, before becoming chief of the Economic Coordination Administration (ECA) mission in Korea. In 1952, his special mission to Korea was a success largely because Meyer had extensive knowledge of and experience on Asian affairs. Subsequently he served as the ECA's mission chief in Vienna until 1954, later working for the Mutual Security Agency. From 1955 to 1957, Meyer was director of economic aid and chief of economic affairs at the U.S. embassy in Japan.

National Cyclopedia of American Biography, vol. 51 (New York, 1969); New York Times, March 17, 1965; Who Was Who in America, vol. 6: 1961–1968 (Chicago, 1968).

MEYER MISSION (April 10–May 24, 1952)

The basic objective of this special mission to Korea, appointed by President Harry S. Truman* and headed by Economic Cooperation Administration official Clarence E. Meyer*, was to establish joint machinery with the Republic of Korea* to stabilize the South Korean economy through better use of U.S. economic aid, adoption of anti-inflationary measures, and an agreement on the reimbursement and rate of exchange of advances of South Korean won to UN forces. At the time of the mission, South Korea was experiencing massive wartime inflation. Prices in early 1952 rose to approximately forty times the

1947 level. The South Korea government, which had balanced its budget and tightened credit, saw the advances of its currency, the won, for use by UN forces as the basic cause of inflation. To avert hyperinflation and potential financial disaster, South Korea recommended immediate and full settlement of outstanding won advances (some $70 million) so as to pay for imports, which could then be sold to Koreans. The proceeds from the sales of these imports would be withdrawn from circulation, and inflation would be curbed. In addition, the government of President Syngman Rhee* opposed as an infringement on its sovereignty UNC* joint control of all its foreign reserves. Finally, the ROK was anxious to retain the present conversion rate of won to dollars (6,000 to 1) for future transactions.

Washington officials considered it unwise to remit to the ROK the $70 million during the war because of the budgetary uncertainties of future aid to Korea. The $70 million could be used more effectively after the war for basic rehabilitation. Washington agencies were split on whether ROK foreign exchange should be under joint UNC-ROK control, but since South Korea was prepared to accept joint control of foreign exchange arising from UN operations (the principal source for ROK foreign exchange), the issue was essentially moot. All government experts in Washington agreed that the current won-to-dollar rate of 6,000 to 1 was unrealistic and should at least be 10,000 to 1.

On May 24, 1952, Meyer and his South Korean counterparts concluded an Agreement on Economic Coordination, which created a Combined Economic Board consisting of an ROK representative and a UNC representative. The board was to coordinate the use of ROK foreign exchange for both financial stabilization and reconstruction of the Korean economy. Under the terms of the agreement, the UNC agreed to repay to the ROK all won sold to the UN troops at the 6,000-to-1 rate for the period January 1952 through May 1952 and thereafter to pay $4 million per month to South Korea on account to be applied against an eventual settlement after March 31, 1953. These foreign exchange payments were used with some success by the ROK to curb inflation. Also included in the agreement was the understanding that as soon as possible after March 31, 1953, all outstanding won balances drawn since June 1, 1952, would be settled based on a realistic conversion rate. While the agreement and the board it created had responsibilities for economic coordination and reconstruction, in practice, the board concentrated its efforts primarily on the financial relations between the UNC and the ROK. *See also* Suspense Account Controversy.

Foreign Relations of the United States, 1952–1954, vol. 15: *Korea* (Washington, D.C., 1984).

Edward C. Keefer

MiG ALLEY

U.S. pilots called the area of northwest Korea between the Yalu River and Sinanju MiG alley because this was where the Soviet MiG–15 fighters intercepted U.S. B–29 bombers as they approached the Yalu River bridges. With the retreat of the U.S. 8th Army* south of Seoul in January 1951 after Chinese military intervention*, the UN forces lost dominance of the air over North Korea. The Chinese brought with them the Soviet MiG–15 fighter aircraft, the world's most advanced fighter plane. The plane was maneuverable at high speeds and able to outclimb and outrun at 25,000 feet the F–86 Sabre, the only allied aircraft able to challenge it. The MiG–15s, while frequently shot down by better-trained U.S. fighter pilots, nevertheless changed the air war. By November 1951, after the Battle of Namsi*, Air Force Chief of Staff General Hoyt S. Vandenbuerg* admitted that U.S. control of the air over northwest Korea, while by no means lost, was "not as firm as it was." The MiGs, which ultimately numbered some 800, combined with a network of anti-aircraft artillery and road-repair labor gangs, defeated U.S. attempts to cut supply lines (Operation Strangle*). By the end of January 1952, the United States had lost more than 600 bomber and fighter aircraft.

C. Blair, *The Forgotten War* (New York, 1987); M. Hastings, *The Korean War* (New York, 1987); B. I. Kaufman, *The Korean War* (Philadelphia, 1986).

William B. Pickett

MILITARY ARMISTICE COMMISSION

According to the terms of the armistice agreement* ending the Korean War, the Military Armistice Commission (MAC) was the primary agency for ensuring maintenance of the cease-fire. For U.S. military leaders, creation of this body was fundamental to its plan for preserving postwar peace in Korea. The JCS first referred to the necessity for a MAC in its directive of May 31, 1951*, to CINCUNC General Matthew B. Ridgway*. At the first session of the Kaesŏng truce talks* on July 10, the chief negotiator for the UNC*, Vice-Admiral C. Turner Joy, included in his proposed agenda, as item 6, the determination of the composition, authority, and function of a military armistice commission. Later Joy provided details, recommending a body with equal representation from both sides and the power to carry out its task of ensuring respect for the armistice terms. There also would be military observation teams to serve as the eyes and ears for the MAC with the right of free and unlimited access to all of Korea. In conjunction with the settlement of the agenda controversy*, the negotiators agreed to establish the MAC, adding this provision under agenda item 3*, cease-fire arrangements and inspection provisions.

On December 4, 1951, the subdelegations at the P'anmunjŏm truce talks* met to discuss the details of the MAC. While the UNC continued to insist on access throughout Korea and a predominant role for the MAC in monitoring the armistice, the Communists wanted the MAC's functions limited to the DMZ and proposed creation of a supervisory body comprised of neutral nations to monitor the cease-fire elsewhere. In sharp contrast to agenda item 4*, repatriation of POWs, and the airfield rehabilitation controversy*, the negotiators engaged in genuine bargaining with respect to the MAC. This resulted in agreement that the MAC would contain ten senior officers, five from each side, with overall responsibility for implementation of the terms of the armistice. Its main task was to ensure that neither side exploited the cease-fire to improve its military position preparatory to a resumption of the fighting. Under its supervision would be ten joint military observation teams composed of four to six representatives. The MAC could meet daily but would convene at least once a week to consider reports of violations inside the DMZ, while forwarding those occurring outside the DMZ to the Neutral Nations Supervisory Commission*.

On July 28, 1953, the MAC met formally for the first time on the day after the belligerents signed the armistice agreement. Initially the body worked as anticipated and with good results. It helped to determine the exact boundaries of the DMZ and to supervise withdrawal of troops from that area. The MAC also established procedures for identification and checking credentials of those individuals entering the DMZ. Finally, it helped in the removal of hazardous items like mines and unexploded bombs. But the MAC was unable to deal with violations, and cooperation on this issue soon disappeared. Whenever an incident occurred, the delegates would always hand down a split decision, guaranteeing inaction. Nor did the joint observation teams operate jointly. Ultimately the UNC representatives reported that the MAC was incapable of enforcing the equilibrium, and the truce provisions were useless as a means to preserve the cease-fire. By 1968, there had been 250 meetings, with each following a familiar pattern. The representatives would hear complaints of patrols' violating the truce terms without authorizing a response and then devote their energies to delivering charges and countercharges with denials and insults. But the MAC continued to have value as a conduit for communications between the commanders in times of crisis to prevent miscalculation. For example, it performed this function well in 1972 when North Koreans killed American soldiers during the famous axe murder incident at P'anmunjŏm.

C. Blair, *The Forgotten War* (New York, 1987); J. L. Collins, *War in Peacetime* (Boston, 1969); W. G. Hermes, *Truce Tent and Fighting Front* (Washington, D.C., 1966); W. H. Vatcher, *Panmunjom: The Story of the Korean Military Armistice Negotiations* (New York, 1958).

MINES, BATTLE OF THE
   See Wŏnsan Landing

MOLOTOV, VYACHESLAV M. (born Scriabine; 1890–1987)
   During most of the Korean War, Vyacheslav Mikhailovich Molotov did not hold the post with which he is most identified, Soviet foreign minister. After occupying this office from 1939 to 1949, he was succeeded as foreign minister in 1949 by Andrei Y. Vyshinsky*. After the death of Joseph Stalin* in March 1953, Molotov resumed his tenure as foreign minister and held this office during the final stages of the negotiations of the Korean armistice agreement*. From 1949 to 1953, Molotov was deputy chairman of the Council of Ministers. Of greater significance was his closeness to Stalin, shown, for example, by his

appointment as Soviet representative at the eleven-day conference with Communist Chinese leaders in August 1950 to discuss contingency plans in the event of UN forces' crossing the thirty-eighth parallel.

Molotov's influence within the Soviet government in Stalin's last years is difficult to gauge. Many regarded him as Stalin's right-hand man and natural successor, but Stalin sent Molotov's wife into exile in Siberia, and there were reports that Stalin intended to have Molotov killed. The lack of Soviet sources makes conclusions on Soviet policy in the Korean War speculative and renders impossible an informed assessment of the role of particular members of the Soviet government such as Molotov. In 1957, Molotov was one of the anti-party group in the abortive effort to overthrow Nikita Khrushchev. Unlike Stalin's time, Molotov's punishment was not execution but appointment from 1957 to 1960 as Soviet ambassador to Outer Mongolia.

B. Bromage, *Molotov* (London, 1956); R. D. Buhite, *Soviet-American Relations in Asia, 1945–1954* (Norman, Okla., 1981); R. A. Medvedev, *All Stalin's Men* (Oxford, 1983).

Peter G. Boyle

MORRISON, HERBERT S. (1888–1965)

Herbert Stanley Morrison became foreign secretary in Clement R. Attlee's* government in March 1951 when ill health forced Ernest Bevin* to retire. Although he was an experienced politician and a senior figure in the Labour party, his experience had been almost entirely in domestic affairs, and his short period at the Foreign Office was not a happy one. Attlee soon viewed his appointment as a mistake and remarked on Morrison's ignorance of world affairs, an opinion shared by Secretary of State Dean G. Acheson*, who discovered during talks on Korea in September 1951 that the foreign secretary was unfamiliar with the composition and role of the JCS.

Despite these failings, friction between the United States and Britain over East Asia, which had reached its height with Chinese military intervention*, was reduced under Morrison, partly because of President Harry S. Truman's* recall of CINCUNC General Douglas MacArthur*, which calmed immediate fears that Britain might be dragged into a wider war with the People's Republic of China*. It also stemmed from Morrison's preoccupation with the Iranian crisis, which made Britain less critical of U.S. policy in Asia in the hope of receiving U.S. support in the Middle East. Last, there was the intransigence of the PRC, which in the spring of 1951 seemed to reject all offers of a peaceful settlement in favor of an attempt to drive the UNC* from Korea by force. It was against this background that Britain voted in favor of a selective UN embargo against the PRC in May 1951 and accepted Acheson's proposal for a moratorium on the troublesome PRC UN representation question*. Morrison also agreed in principle that the UN commander should have the authority to retaliate against Manchurian bases in the event of a sudden air attack on his forces, though reserving Britain's right to prior consultation. The same month, he made a speech supporting the

Cairo Declaration* but denying that Britain wanted to hand over Taiwan to the Communists as long as the Korean War lasted.

Differences, however, still remained. Morrison, like Acheson, doubted that an armistice would be followed by a political settlement in Korea, but if talks did occur, he refused to rule out a comprehensive approach to the problems of East Asia. As for further moves against the PRC if armistice negotiations failed, Morrison was prepared to approve certain limited actions, such as bombing the Yalu power plants, but he emphasized British reluctance to widen the war. He stressed the vulnerability of Hong Kong and the importance of not driving Communist China entirely into Soviet hands. This reflected the lingering British fear that Washington might go too far under domestic political pressures and echoed the disagreement over China that had marked Attlee's visit to the United States* in December 1950. Morrison's "familiar exegesis" irritated Acheson, who considered Peking already a part of the Soviet conspiracy. When Labour lost the general election of October 1951, Morrison was succeeded as foreign secretary by Anthony Eden*. *See also* Acheson-Morrison Meeting; Manchurian Sanctuary.

D. Acheson, *Present at the Creation* (London, 1970); C. A. MacDonald, *Korea: The War Before Vietnam* (London, 1986); K. O. Morgan, *Labour in Power* (London, 1985).

Callum A. MacDonald

MU CHŎNG (KIM MU-CHŎNG; 1905–1951?)

Commander of the Second Corps of the North Korean People's Army (NKPA) at the start of the Korean War, Mu Chŏng was born at Kyŏngsŏng, North Hamgyŏng province. His family name may have been Kim but has been usually omitted. He went to China in 1922 and graduated from Henan Military Academy. Mu Chŏng began his military career under the warlord Yen Hsi-shan and developed an expertise in artillery warfare. He was an artillery lieutenant during the Northern Expedition and joined the Chinese Communist party (CCP) in 1926 in Shanghai. Thereafter, Mu Chŏng reportedly became chief of artillery in the Chinese Communist army. He was the only Korean to survive the Long March. In 1939 and 1940, Mu Chŏng established a Korean unit within the Chinese Communist army. Early the following year, this unit was developed into the North China Korean Youth Federation. Six months later, in combination with new arrivals from the Korean Volunteer Corps, which was receiving Nationalist backing in Nanking, the federation was reorganized into the North China Korean Independence League with Kim Tu-bong* as its chairman. Under the league, the Korean Volunteer Army was established with Mu Chŏng as its commander.

After liberation, Mu Chŏng was elected in absentia a member of the Central People's Committee for the Preparation of Korean Independence organized in Seoul, but he returned to northern Korea. In the initial period, he was regarded highly as the "vice-commander" of the 8th Route Army or "the Chinese Communist choice to assume leadership" in Korea, to the great displeasure of Kim Il Sung*. However, Mu Chŏng would hold no official position in the northern leadership until the fall of 1946, when he became deputy chief for artillery in the peace preservation corps, from which the NKPA would develop. Evidently, Kim Tu-bong served as the principal spokesman for the Yenan (Chinese exile) faction in northern Korea. Mu Chŏng was elected a member of the Central Committee of the North Korean Workers' party in March 1948.

Mu Chŏng's activities in the Korean War are unknown. However, at the third regular meeting of the Central Committee of the Korean Workers' party held on December 4, 1950, he was removed from the body on charges that he was responsible for the loss of P'yŏngyang in the fall. It was believed that Kim Il Sung purged him since Mu Chŏng's Chinese connection might heighten his politico-military position following Chinese military intervention* in the Korean War. The Chinese leadership helped him to be returned to China, where he reportedly died in the summer of 1951.

B. Cumings, *The Origins of the Korean War* (Princeton, 1981, 1990); D. Suh, *Kim Il Sung: The North Korean Leader* (New York, 1988).

Hakjoon Kim

MUCCIO, JOHN J. (1900–1989)

John Joseph Muccio was the U.S. ambassador to the Republic of Korea* during the first twenty-six months of the Korean War. Born near Naples, Italy, he was brought by his parents as an infant to Rhode Island, grew up in Providence, served briefly in the U.S. Army in 1918, and graduated from Brown University in 1921. On receiving naturalization papers, he entered the foreign service, earned an M.A. degree from George Washington University, and in 1924 went off to Hamburg in Germany to be vice-consul. He thereupon received a succession of assignments in China and, in 1935, began nine years of service in Latin America. In 1945 and 1946, he was again in Germany, this time as an assistant to Robert D. Murphy*, the U.S. political advisor on German affairs. The following year, he traveled over China and Manchuria while assigned to the inspector corps of the foreign service. In August 1948, when the United States accorded conditional recognition to the ROK, he became the head of the U.S. diplomatic mission in Seoul. When Washington raised its mission in South Korea to embassy rank in March 1949, Muccio became the first U.S. ambassador. In the latter position, he vigorously advocated expanded U.S. economic and military assistance for the ROK, in both private cables and testimony before congressional committees.

It was Muccio who notified leaders in Washington on June 25, 1950 (Korean time), of the North Korean invasion of South Korea*. In the hectic days that followed, as North Korean regiments pressed southward, he arranged for the U.S. evacuation of Seoul*. Suspecting that duty required that he stay at his post in the embassy, Muccio considered remaining in the beleaguered capital but departed on June 27 when advised by Secretary of State Dean G. Acheson* that he should follow ROK president Syngman Rhee* and his government, which had already departed for Taejŏn. In the desperate weeks that followed, Muccio may have performed the most important service of his long career. By insisting that the war was not lost and victory was indeed possible, he reinforced the morale of the despairing men of the Rhee government, including the president himself. Muccio's embassy meanwhile persuaded the U.S. Army to accept organized Korean combat police battalions in U.S. divisional areas to detect infiltrators and fight as light infantry. He was also instrumental in persuading the U.S. Army to fill out its understrength battalions with Korean soldiers. Finally, serving as a liaison between the two, it allayed suspicions and reduced friction that threatened in those critical weeks to undermine relations between the U.S. Army and Rhee's government.

Following the Inch'ŏn landing* and the subsequent recapture of Seoul operation*, in September 1950, Muccio returned his embassy to the capital, flew to the Wake Island Conference* the following month with CINCUNC General Douglas MacArthur*, and then traveled to Washington to confer with leaders of the government in November 1950 regarding U.S. policy in Korea when the UNC* completed its occupation of North Korea*. In January 1951, when Chinese forces swarmed toward Seoul, Muccio again found it necessary to take his embassy southward, this time directly to Pusan, where it would remain for the balance of Muccio's tenure as ambassador. In the months that followed, Muccio brought all of his skill to bear in a futile effort to persuade the Rhee government that a negotiated settlement of the Korean War was in its interests and that the United States would not abandon the ROK. In August 1952, Ellis O. Briggs* replaced Muccio, who a short time later received appointment to the UN Trusteeship Council. Muccio's final posts included envoy extraordinary to Iceland from 1954 to 1956 and ambassador to Guatemala from 1959 to 1961.

Foreign Relations of the United States, 1950, vol. 7: *Korea* (Washington, D.C., 1976), *1951,* vol. 7: *Korea and China* (Washington, D.C., 1983), and *1952–1954,* vol. 15: *Korea* (Washington, D.C., 1984); J. C. Goulden, *Korea: The Untold Story of the War* (New York, 1982); H. J. Noble, *Embassy at War* (Seattle, 1975); R. T. Oliver, *Syngman Rhee and American Involvement in Korea, 1942–1960* (New York, 1978).

John Edward Wilz

MURPHY, CHARLES S. (1909–1983)

Charles S. Murphy was a close confidant of President Harry S. Truman*, serving as special counsel and speechwriter during the Korean War. As a member of Truman's "little cabinet," he attended many late-night meetings where a small group of the president's advisers and friends would develop political and legislative strategy. Though lacking flair and imagination, Murphy had the talent for putting to paper the simple words and phrases Truman found appealing. His papers at the Harry S. Truman Library include much valuable information related to the Korean War.

Born on a farm near Wallace, North Carolina, Murphy passed the civil service exam in 1928 and went to work at the Wilmington Post Office. Eight months later, he enrolled in Duke University, earning a B.A. (1931) and a law degree (1934). Until 1947, he was an assistant counsel in the office of the legislative counsel of the U.S. Senate. There, Murphy was responsible for ensuring that draft bills contained suitable legal language. As a senator, Truman consulted him when he wrote the bill creating the defense industry investigation committee he would chair. As president, Truman selected Murphy in 1947 to serve as an administrative assistant with responsibility for shepherding bills through Congress.

In February 1950, Murphy became special counsel and assumed primary responsibility for monitoring the legislative progress of administration programs. As Truman's chief political lieutenant, he was influential in establishing policy in both domestic and foreign affairs. Self-effacing and inconspicuous, many observers considered Murphy to be the most able member of the president's staff. He was an excellent speechwriter and astute politician who earned a reputation for being meticulous.

From 1953 to 1960, Murphy practiced law but returned to government service in 1961 as under secretary of agriculture. Under President Lyndon B. Johnson, he would serve as special counselor and supervise the transition following the election of Richard M. Nixon* as president in 1968. Murphy resumed his private law practice in 1969 but remained influential in Democratic party politics. He also was a trustee for Duke University until he resigned in protest over plans to house Nixon's papers there.

Current Biography, 1950; *New York Times,* August 30, 1983; E. W. Schoenebaum (ed.), *Political Profiles: The Truman Years* (New York, 1978).

MURPHY, ROBERT D. (1894–1978)

Robert D. Murphy served as ambassador to Japan (1952–1953) during a critical stage of the P'anmunjŏm truce talks*. An experienced diplomat, he was born in Milwaukee, Wisconsin, and attended Marquette University. With previous service in the government, he joined the State Department in 1917 when the United States entered World War I and subsequently served in a number of European posts. Murphy's diplomatic expertise honed over twenty-three years brought him to President Franklin D. Roosevelt's attention in 1940 soon after the outbreak of World War II in Europe. He was appointed the president's personal representative and General Dwight D. Eisenhower's* political adviser in North Africa, and he played a role in the surrender of both Italy and Germany. After the war, President Harry S. Truman* named Murphy the U.S. civilian representative to the Allied Control Council in Germany. In 1949, as a reward for his work, Murphy was appointed ambassador to Belgium.

In something of a surprise move, Murphy was reassigned as ambassador to Japan in 1952, the first U.S. ambassador to Tokyo since the end of the war. In his new post, Murphy worked with CINCUNC General Mark W. Clark* to arrange an armistice in the Korean War. Murphy believed that the Soviet Union and the People's Republic of China* were using the Democratic People's Republic of Korea* for their own purposes. The Chinese, he speculated, did not want to extend the war to the Chinese mainland. The United States was being bluffed out of victory because he was certain it had the capacity to drive the

Chinese People's Volunteers Army* back into Manchuria. As ambassador, Murphy was frustrated by what he considered the recalcitrant and volatile maneuverings of President Syngman Rhee* of the Republic of Korea*. Rhee not only refused to moderate his position, but, in opposition to Murphy's efforts, he stubbornly resisted improving relations with Japan. In the face of all of this, Murphy tried to conduct himself as a professional diplomat.

Eleven months after his assignment to Tokyo, President Dwight Eisenhower reassigned Murphy as assistant secretary of state for UN affairs, but the transfer was delayed until the armistice was concluded. As Clark's political adviser in the final stages of negotiation, Murphy found the U.S. position particularly difficult. In similar situations he had been familiar with during World War II, the United States had victory as a base to work from. Such was not the case in Korea. After the completion of the armistice agreement*, Murphy returned to Washington in August 1953 and with little enthusiasm assumed his UN duties, believing that the United States should have fought the war to win. He partially blamed the United Nations for America's failure to do so since he perceived that body as a major "restraining influence" on the conduct of the war.

B. Alexander, *Korea: The First War We Lost* (New York, 1986); R. Foot, *The Wrong War* (Ithaca, N.Y., 1985); R. D. Murphy, *Diplomat among Warriors* (Garden City, N.Y., 1964).

T. Michael Ruddy

N

NAKTONG BULGE, BATTLE OF THE
See Battle of the Naktong Bulge

NAM IL (1913–1976)
Lieutenant General Nam Il was chief of staff of the North Korean People's Army (NKPA) during the Korean War and also served as North Korea's senior delegate at the Korean armistice negotiations. Nam was a Soviet Korean, born in Russia of Korean immigrant parents. He graduated from a teachers' college in Tashkent and may have taught school for a while. He also attended Smolensk Military School and served as an officer in the Soviet Army during World War II. Nam came to Korea with the Soviet forces that liberated Korea from Japanese rule in 1945. He served as deputy minister of education in the Soviet-occupied north and, though the Democratic People's Republic of Korea* replaced the Soviet occupation in 1948, continued in that post until the outbreak of the Korean War. Nam was appointed deputy chief of staff of the NKPA in July 1950 and then was named chief of staff in December of that year to replace Lieutenant General Kang Kŏn*, who had died in battle.

When the Kaesŏng truce talks* began in July 1951, Nam Il, now a lieutenant general, was appointed the head of the North Korean negotiating team, a position he held for the duration of the talks. U.S. officials believed that at the same time Nam was negotiating with the UNC* for a cease-fire, he also instigated and directed from afar the Kŏje-do POW uprising*. Shortly before he signed the armistice agreement*, Nam was promoted to general so that he would outrank Lieutenant General William K. Harrison, Jr.*, who signed on behalf of the UNC. In August 1953, Nam became the foreign minister of the DPRK and in that capacity he represented the DPRK at the Geneva Conference of 1954*, which failed to achieve its goal of a peace treaty providing a permanent settlement to the Korean conflict.

Nam was one of the few Korean officials of Russian background to survive Kim Il Sung's* purge of Soviet Koreans after the war. He rose to vice-premier in 1957, a post he held until his death, and also served at various times as chairman of the state construction commission, minister of railroads, and chairman of the light industry commission.

A. E. Goodman (ed.), *Negotiating While Fighting: The Diary of Admiral C. Turner Joy at the Korean Armistice Conference* (Stanford, Calif., 1978); W. G. Hermes, *Truce Tent and Fighting Front* (Washington, D.C., 1966); C. Lee and K. Oh, "The Russian Faction in North Korea," *Asian Survey* (1968); R. Scalapino and C. Lee, *Communism in Korea* (Berkeley, 1972); D. Suh, *Kim Il Sung: The North Korean Leader* (New York, 1988).

Don Baker

NAMSI, BATTLE OF
See Battle of Namsi

NATIONAL GUARD MOBILIZATION

Less than two months after the Korean War began, President Harry S. Truman* approved mobilizing selected divisions in the U.S. National Guard. This contrasts sharply with President Lyndon B. Johnson's consistent refusal to follow the same course in the Vietnam War. Administration officials first raised the issue at the second Blair House meeting*. Thereafter, it was Lieutenant General Charles E. Bolté*, the U.S. Army vice-chief of staff, who was the most vocal advocate of mobilization. However, Chief of Staff General J. Lawton Collins* hoped to find some other way to deal with the manpower shortage, fearing an adverse impact on the economy and the morale of home areas of selected divisions. While not wanting to act prematurely, he also believed it would violate the traditional purpose of the National Guard to maintain internal security within the states except in times of general mobilization. His colleagues on the JCS agreed, although they did obtain approval for the activation of National Guard units with specialized signal, medical, and police functions. But Collins changed his mind and on July 31 persuaded the JCS to submit a recommendation for the activation of four National Guard divisions and two regimental combat teams (RCTs). Truman approved this proposal, authorizing calling these troops into federal service on September 1. Over the next two months, these units would be brought to full strength through conscription and be ready for combat by April 14, 1951.

U.S. military leaders then had to determine which National Guard divisions to activate. Collins had inaugurated a study of this matter on July 21 when he requested recommendations from General Mark W. Clark*, the head of Army Field Forces. Clark solicited information from continental army commanders regarding which divisions were best trained, equipped, and prepared for war. After careful study, he submitted a priority list for selection: the 28th Division (Pennsylvania), the 29th Division (Virginia and Maryland), the 31st Division (Mississippi and Alabama), the 37th Division (Ohio), the 45th Division (Oklahoma), and the 50th Armored Division (New Jersey). Collins immediately expressed concern about the political repercussions of this uneven geographic spread, particularly the absence of units from the West Coast. Clark replied that while aware of this problem, he believed maximizing effective leadership and minimizing the number of filler replacements should be the key factors determining inclusion on the selection list. Nevertheless, his final recommendation substituted the 40th Division from California for the New Jersey unit.

On September 1, Truman called to active service the 28th, the 40th, the 45th, and the 43d (Rhode Island and Connecticut) divisions, along with the 196th (South Dakota) and the 278th (Tennessee) RCTs. With battle lines stabilizing in Korea, Collins thought that these units might not have to fight and soon would revert to inactive status. But Chinese military intervention* thoroughly changed the situation; the National Security Council approved the JCS request to mobilize two additional National Guard divisions to defend Japan if the 8th Army* halted the Communist advance. That same month, Collins decided against recommending approval of this proposal after his trip to Tokyo because the 8th Army had stabilized its defensive positions. Responding to continued military progress in Korea, the JCS obtained approval in February for sending the 40th and 45th National Guard divisions to Japan, and they arrived in April. In the fall of 1951, Collins recommended the rotation of these two units to Korea to replace the 1st Cavalry and 24th Infantry divisions, but CINCUNC Lieutenant General Matthew B. Ridgway* objected, recommending instead the individual replacement of these untried soldiers. Insisting on the right of the National Guard to fight as units, Collins prevailed, and the first divisions arrived in Korea during February 1952.

J. L. Collins, *War in Peacetime* (Boston, 1969); J. F. Schnabel, *Policy and Direction* (Washington, D.C., 1972); J. F. Schnabel and R. J. Watson, *History of the Joint Chiefs of Staff*, vol. 3: *The Korean War* (Wilmington, 1979).

NECK OF KOREA
See Waist of Korea

NEHRU, JAWAHARLAL (1889–1964)

Prime Minister Nehru of India emerged as a key actor in Korean War diplomacy. Born in the city of Allahabad in India's northern state of Uttar Pradesh, Nehru was the son of an upper-caste lawyer who had achieved prominence as a nationalist leader in the Indian Congress party. After receiving his education at Harrow and Cambridge in England, the younger Nehru returned to his native land and immersed himself in India's struggle for independence from British colonial rule. By the mid–1930s, he had emerged as Mahatma Gandhi's chief lieutenant in the movement. After India acquired independence in 1947, he was chosen prime minister and served in that capacity until his death in 1964. In foreign affairs, Nehru adopted a policy of cold war nonalignment. This posture reflected India's intense nationalism, its location near Soviet borders, its position of relative weakness, and its inclination to focus on regional issues in Asia rather than global politics. India's nonalignment received little support from either Washington or Moscow, each of which urged India to declare its true allegiance.

Nehru took a deep interest in the Korean War, and his nonaligned orientation shaped his attitude toward the conflict. When the fighting broke out in June 1950, India's chief delegate at the UN, Sir Benegal N. Rau*, voted for the UN Security Council resolution of June 25, 1950*, that condemned North Korean aggression. While New Delhi belatedly approved Rau's action, it instructed him to avoid any further commitments. After two cabinet meetings, and discussions between Nehru and the U.S. ambassador, Loy W. Henderson*, the Indian government issued a statement supporting a second UN Security Council resolution of June 27, 1950*, that directed member states to furnish assistance to the Republic of Korea*. Although Nehru accepted the two resolutions, he never adhered to the American thesis that the North Korean invasion of South Korea* had been directed by the Kremlin. In fact, he criticized the Truman administration for overreacting to a war of local origins.

Throughout the war, Nehru sought to exploit his open lines of communication to Washington, Moscow, and Peking in order to help mediate a negotiated settlement. The Nehru initiatives, however, never won full support from either of the Communist powers and often incurred the wrath of the Truman administration. The Indian prime minister also failed to prevent the expansion of the war in the fall of 1950 when London and Washington downplayed warnings from Chinese foreign minister Chou En-lai*, passed on by India's ambassador in Peking, K. M. Panikkar*, that the movement of UN troops north of the thirty-eighth parallel would provoke Chinese intervention. In late 1952, when the war had stalemated and the P'anmunjŏm truce talks* had become bogged down, Nehru allowed India's representative at the UN, V. K. Krishna Menon*, to fashion a compromise to agenda item 4*, the thorny POW repatriation issue. This Indian initiative successfully laid the foundation for the July 1953 armistice agreement*. It has long been speculated that the armistice came about largely due to Secretary of State John Foster Dulles's* atomic warning to China*, transmitted by Nehru after the secretary's visit to New Delhi in May 1953. Recent declassification of Dulles's notes of his talks with Nehru and the testimony of Indian officials, however, does not substantiate the story. *See also* Indian Peace Initiatives; Menon POW Settlement Proposal.

M. Brecher, *Nehru: A Political Biography* (New York, 1959); S. Gopal, *Jawaharlal Nehru: A Biography* (New Delhi, 1979).

Dennis Merrill

NEUTRAL NATIONS REPATRIATION COMMISSION

This was a UN commission created under the Korean armistice agreement* of July 27, 1953, to oversee the controversial process of prisoner of war repatriation. Armistice negotiations had been stalled for months when in November 1952 Indian representative to the UN, V. K. Krishna Menon* made his POW settlement proposal* calling for a resolution to establish a Neutral Nations Repatriation Commission (NNRC) to supervise prisoners who did not wish to return to their native lands following an armistice. After passage, the UN resolution of December 3, 1952*, provided a foundation for a June 8, 1953, POW agreement that named two nations friendly to the United States—Sweden and Switzerland—and two Soviet satellites—Poland and Czechoslovakia—to the five-member commission. The commission was headed by nonaligned India's General K. S. Thimayya*, who commanded a custodial force of 5,000 Indian troops to maintain order in the POW camps and to oversee the repatriation process. To ensure the voluntary disposition of nonrepatriated prisoners within a fixed period, Washington insisted on the provision that nonrepatriates would be transferred to the custody of the NNRC no later than sixty days following an armistice. They would remain under NNRC authority for another sixty days while the respective combatants attempted to persuade them to return home. Following these procedures, the postwar Korea political conference would hold them for thirty more days, after which the NNRC would be disbanded and the remaining POWs would become civilians.

After the signing of a formal armistice, the belligerents carried out Operation Big Switch whereby willing POWs were exchanged. This left more than 22,600 Communist nonrepatriates (the majority of whom were Chinese) and 359 UN nonrepatriates (23 American, 1 British, and 333 South Koreans). These POWs were turned over to the NNRC at the end of September and subsequently screened by their own nationals, who strongly encouraged them to return home. As the process of screening got underway, a number of prisoners assaulted their guards and attempted mass breakouts. In mid-October, about 1,000 North Korean prisoners refused to appear before the Communist "explainers." In response, the Indian government authorized General Thimayya to employ force if necessary to prevent an outbreak of violence, but the crisis soon passed. Although the NNRC received criticisms from all sides, including CINCUNC General John E. Hull*, it managed to maintain order and ultimately concluded its assignment with efficiency and dispatch. By the end of the assigned period, only 137 of the Communist nonrepatriates and 10 of the UN nonrepatriates had opted to return home. The remaining POWs were released in January 1954 after the NNRC delivered them back to their original custodians. On February 1, the NNRC voted to dissolve itself. *See also* Agenda Item 4; Communist POW Settlement Proposal of May 7, 1953; POW Transfer Location Question; UNC Final POW Settlement Proposal of May 25, 1953.

S. Gopal, *Jawaharlal Nehru: A Biography* (New Delhi, 1979); B. I. Kaufman, *The Korean War* (Philadelphia, 1986).

Dennis Merrill

NEUTRAL NATIONS SUPERVISORY COMMISSION

This was a commission of neutral nations organized to inspect and supervise the terms of the Korean War cease-fire and armistice agreement*. The idea of a Neutral Nations Supervisory Commission (NNSC) first developed in December 1951 at the P'anmunjŏm truce talks*. By April 1952, however, negotiations had become deadlocked over the composition of the proposed commission. The

Communists wanted to include the Soviet Union, and the United States refused to permit the Soviets a seat on a commission identified as "neutral." Instead, the United States insisted that membership include three neutrals friendly to the UNC*—Norway, Sweden, and Switzerland—and two neutrals friendly to Communist forces—Poland and Czechoslovakia. In early May, the chief UNC negotiator, Vice-Admiral C. Turner Joy*, attempted to break the impasse by offering the package proposal* for dealing with the NNSC and the unresolved matters of agenda item 3* and agenda item 4*, cease-fire inspections and POW repatriation, respectively. Under Joy's proposal, the UNC abandoned its previous insistence on a ban on new military airfields in exchange for Communist concessions on the thorny issue of voluntary repatriation* of POWs. In regard to the neutral commission, the UNC dropped Norway from membership in exchange for the omission of the Soviet Union. After several days of discussion, the Communist delegation announced on May 7 that it accepted all of these provisions except for the voluntary repatriation of prisoners. The POW issue continued to block armistice negotiations for the next year, but when the armistice was finally signed in July 1953, it included provisions for a four-member NNSC.

Once the armistice went into effect, the NNSC undertook the inspection of force levels and equipment in both North and South Korea. Its activities soon became shrouded in controversy. U.S. officials and the Republic of Korea* in particular protested that Communist members of the commission (Poland and Czechoslovakia) exploited their status as inspectors in order to carry out intelligence and propaganda operations. CINCUNC General John E. Hull* and President Syngman Rhee* further complained that the North Koreans had imposed restrictions on commission travel and successfully evaded inspection of their forces. At one point in 1954, the South Koreans went so far as to threaten to demand that Communist members of the NNSC immediately leave their country. Weary of the NNSC but hoping to forestall a unilateral breach of the armistice, the State Department persuaded the South Koreans against such drastic action and attempted to convince the Swiss and the Swedes to withdraw from the NNSC as a first step toward its dissolution. Committed to the maintenance of their role as a neutral overseer and skeptical that inspection teams could effectively engage in espionage activities, the Swiss and Swedish governments refused Washington's request. The NNSC remained in operation until 1957, when the United States announced that it would no longer recognize the commission's authority and began to bring in new armaments to Korea.

Foreign Relations of the United States, 1952–1954, vol 15: Korea (Washington, D.C., 1984); J. Halliday and B. Cumings, Korea: The Unknown War (New York, 1988); W. G. Hermes, Truce Tent and Fighting Front (Washington, D.C., 1966); B. I. Kaufman, The Korean War (Philadelphia, 1986).

Dennis Merrill

NEUTRALIZATION OF TAIWAN (June 27, 1950)

President Harry S. Truman* decided at the second Blair House meeting* to order the neutralization of Taiwan, sending the 7th Fleet to the Taiwan Strait to prevent the Chinese Communists from invading the island and to bar Chiang Kai-shek's* Nationalist forces from attacking the mainland. The president sought to block a widening of the Korean War, but this step also signaled a major shift in his policy toward China. On January 5, 1950, Truman had declared publicly that the United States "will not pursue a course which will lead to involvement in the civil conflict in China." Also, it would not "provide military aid or advice to Chinese forces on Formosa." Privately, administration officials expected the People's Republic of China* to invade Taiwan in the near future and destroy Chiang's regime. However, General Douglas MacArthur* and the JCS believed that Communist control over the island would seriously damage U.S. security interests in the Pacific. During Secretary of Defense Louis A. Johnson's* visit to Tokyo* in June 1950, MacArthur submitted to him his memorandum on Taiwan's strategic significance* in an effort to change Truman's policy.

Secretary Johnson returned to Washington on the day of the North Korean invasion of South Korea*. At the first Blair House meeting* the following night, he discussed Taiwan with Truman privately before dinner and gave him MacArthur's memorandum. The State Department had included neutralization in its initial recommendations for responding to the Korean crisis, but the president did not approve the proposal until the next night after the Democratic People's Republic of Korea*, in defiance of the UN Security Council resolution of June 25, 1950*, had refused to cease fire and withdraw from the Republic of Korea*. The following day, Truman announced the neutralization of Taiwan in his June 27, 1950, statement* outlining to the American people his Korean decisions. As to the future status of Taiwan, he said that it "must await the restoration of security in the Pacific, a peace settlement with Japan, or consideration by the United Nations." The PRC responded with a public denunciation of Truman's action. Foreign Minister Chou En-lai* branded it "an armed invasion of the Chinese territory and a complete infringement on the U.N. Charter."

Neutralization was a purely U.S. initiative and had no relationship to the UN Security Council resolution of June 27, 1950*, calling upon members to provide assistance in defending the ROK. The administration believed North Korea's attack was part of a coordinated Soviet plan that might spark a world war. It wanted to send a signal that the United States would respond to Communist probes elsewhere and thereby avert an unwanted escalation. Domestic political considerations also played a role. It would have been difficult for Truman to justify to Republican critics the commitment of U.S. military power in Korea while leaving Taiwan undefended. Truman still wanted to limit the U.S. commitment to Taiwan, declaring disdainfully at the second Blair House meeting that he would not give Chiang "a nickel" because previous U.S. aid had been "invested in United States real estate." Nevertheless, at the NSC meeting on June 27, the president approved substantial increases in U.S. military aid to the Nationalists, the dispatch of a survey mission to Taiwan, and U.S. reconnaissance flights over the Chinese mainland. Thus, the flexibility of Truman's China policy, which Secretary of State Dean G. Acheson* had been struggling to retain, was one of the first casualties of the Korean War.

Truman's neutralization of Taiwan had momentous consequences. By the spring of 1951, the president had approved NSC–48/5*, providing for even more assistance to Taiwan and a commitment to prevent Communist control over the island indefinitely. Neutralization was unpopular with U.S. allies and later became an issue complicating efforts to obtain a cease-fire. MacArthur apparently misinterpreted Truman's action, falsely concluding that the president had decided to support Chiang's aspirations to return to the mainland. This would result in Truman's recall of MacArthur*, inflicting major political damage on the administration. Saving Chiang and denying the PRC control over a highly visible part of China provided fresh evidence for the Chinese Communists of U.S. hostility, contributing to Mao Tse-tung's* decision for Chinese military intervention* in Korea. Early in 1953, President Dwight D. Eisenhower* would remove the 7th Fleet from the Taiwan Strait and announce the "unleashing" of Chiang*. Later, the United States would negotiate a mutual defense pact with Taiwan while strengthening its political ties to Chiang's regime. As a result, Sino-U.S. relations would remain frozen until President Richard M. Nixon* made his historic visit to the PRC in 1972. *See also* MacArthur's Visit to Taiwan.

D. M. Condit, *History of the Office of the Secretary of Defense,* vol. 2: *The Test of War, 1950–1953* (Washington, D.C., 1988); R. J. Donovan, *Tumultuous Years* (New York, 1982); T. H. Etzold (ed.), *Aspects of Sino-American Relations Since 1784* (New York, 1978); Okonogi Masao, *Chosen Senso* (Tokyo, 1986); W. W. Stueck, *The Road to Confrontation* (Chapel Hill, 1981).

Hajime Izumi

NEW ZEALAND AND THE KOREAN WAR

New Zealand was one of the first countries to answer the UN call for assistance in Korea, offering to send a naval contribution on June 29, 1950. Two frigates, HMNZS *Pukaki* and HMNZS *Tutira,* departed for the war zone on July 3, beginning a naval deployment that was maintained for the duration of the war. On July 26, in response to an appeal by the UN Secretary-General Trygve Lie*, New Zealand decided to send a ground combat force as well, despite practical difficulties. An artillery regiment and transport platoon, some 1,000 men in all, was recruited, trained, and equipped. This force left New Zealand on December 11, reaching Pusan on the last day of the month. By January 23, New Zealand gunners were in action as part of the 27th Commonwealth Brigade. In response to renewed U.S. calls for assistance, New Zealand sent a transport company to reinforce its force in Korea, all of which became part of the 1st Commonwealth Division*, on July 28, 1951. While dwarfed by the forces of the United States and the Republic of Korea*, New Zealand's military contribution on a per-head-of-population basis was second only to that of the United States of all the UN members.

The roots of New Zealand's response lay in the conviction that the Soviet Union was behind the North Korean invasion of South Korea* and that a line had to be drawn against aggression. A longstanding belief in the collective security principles embodied in the UN Charter, a desire to keep in step with the United Kingdom, and, in the case of the ground forces, concern at the implications for New Zealand's relations with the United States of a decision to stand aside—all played a part in encouraging New Zealand's active participation. With the United Kingdom also participating, New Zealand was able to promote its long-term political objective of securing a U.S. commitment to its security within a comfortable Commonwealth framework, as well as supporting an ideal long espoused. In offering New Zealand the opportunity to demonstrate its value as an ally and later, after Chinese military intervention*, creating a sense of urgency in Washington about a Japanese Peace Treaty*, the Korean War helped pave the way for the ANZUS Treaty* concluded on September 1, 1951.

I. C. McGibbon, "New Zealand's Intervention in the Korean War, June-July 1950," *International History Review* (1989).

Ian C. McGibbon

NITZE, PAUL (1907–   )

Paul Nitze helped formulate U.S. national security policy both before and after the Korean War. Under his supervision, the State Department's Policy Planning Staff (PPS) in 1949 produced NSC-68*, which after the start of the Korean War became the basis for U.S. military strategy in the cold war. Nitze's education and early business career provided entry into government service. He attended Harvard University, majoring in economics and receiving the B.A. degree cum laude in 1928. He became a vice president of Dillon, Read, & Company, the New York investment banking firm. There he met James V. Forrestal. When the latter in 1940 became under secretary of the navy, Nitze became his assistant. During World War II and after, Nitze served in a variety of government posts. By 1948, he was deputy to the assistant secretary of state for economic affairs and in August 1949 assistant to George F. Kennan*, director of the newly created PPS. When Kennan resigned in 1950, he became director.

Nitze's concern about a Soviet threat was the basis for U.S. foreign policy during the Korean War. NSC-68 stemmed from his view that Joseph Stalin's* Soviet Union was a global military danger. Experts on the Soviet Union, including Kennan and Charles E. Bohlen*, disagreed with this assessment, but Secretary of State Dean G. Acheson* accepted it. Accordingly, after the outbreak of war in Korea, the United States intervened militarily, and its defense budget, previously around $13 billion, soared to over $50 billion. Nitze thereafter was cautious but flexible in his recommendations. At first he argued against crossing the thirty-eighth parallel because he thought an invasion of a Soviet satellite would bring a reaction from the Soviet Union or the People's Republic of China*. Later, however, the PPS heard a presentation by John M. Allison*, director of the Office of Northeast Asian Affairs, calling North Korea a puppet state that Moscow had established in violation of UN resolutions. PPS China expert John Paton Davies* also doubted that the PRC would intervene. After the Inch'ŏn landing*, a new memorandum from Nitze's PPS declared that the United States should help bring about the "complete independence and unity of Korea." President Harry S. Truman*, accepting it only partially, directed CINCUNC General Douglas MacArthur's* forces to pursue North Korean troops to the Yalu River but not to occupy or unify the peninsula. Nitze was cautious again after Chinese military intervention* in November 1950. He believed, correctly, that the Soviet Union would intervene only if the overthrow of the Chinese government appeared likely or if some point close to the Soviet border were attacked.

Nitze left government service for a time after the inauguration of President Dwight D. Eisenhower* in 1953 and served as president of the Foreign Service Educational Foundation. In 1960, he headed John F. Kennedy's preelection committee on national defense problems and then was assistant secretary of defense for international security affairs. Over the next three decades, Nitze served successively as secretary of the navy; deputy secretary of defense; a member of the U.S. negotiating team at the Strategic Arms Limitation Talks; head of the U.S. delegation to the Geneva arms control talks; and special adviser to the president and secretary of state on arms control matters. In 1987, U.S. negotiators under his direction obtained an intermediate-range nuclear force reduction treaty with the Soviet Union.

C. Blair, *The Forgotten War* (New York, 1987); *Current Biography,* 1962; R. J. Donovan, *Tumultuous Years* (New York, 1982); R. Foot, *The Wrong War* (Ithaca, N.Y., 1985); J. C. Goulden, *Korea: The Untold Story of the War* (New York, 1982).

William B. Pickett

NIXON, RICHARD M. (1913–)

At the outbreak of the Korean War, Richard Nixon was beginning his successful campaign for the Senate against California congresswoman Helen Gahagan Douglas. From his seat in the House of Representatives, Nixon joined in the almost unanimous congressional support for U.S. action against the North Korean invaders. His stance, however, in accordance with the general line he was taking in his campaign, was in support only of the Truman administration's commitment to an anti-Communist Korea, not of its specific policies in the war. Korea was from the start a convenient issue with which to lash the Democrats, for Nixon could support the objectives of the war while simultaneously blaming President Harry S. Truman* and his party for policies that allegedly brought it about, chief among them the decision not to intervene in the Chinese Civil War. His criticisms grew more strident after the failure to hold North Korea following Chinese military intervention* and culminated in the national debate of April 1951 after Truman's recall of CINCUNC General Douglas MacArthur*. It was Nixon who introduced for the Republicans an unsuccessful Senate resolution calling on Truman to restore MacArthur to his commands. During the 1952 presidential campaign, in which the Republican nominee, Dwight D. Eisenhower*, took the high road and Nixon, as his running mate, the low, Korea was featured as the primary issue. Nixon also used the war as a shorthand symbol of the futility of containment. Eisenhower forced him, however, to modify his prescription for the future conduct of the war. He stated that with P'anmunjŏm truce talks* already underway, it was now too late to go for total victory.

In private correspondence, Nixon claimed that he agreed with a column in which Joseph Alsop asserted that the Korean truce of July 1953 had deprived the UN of victory. Recently published portions of discussions in the National Security Council, however, do not show Nixon's arguing very hard on the issue, either before or after the truce, perhaps because of the precarious nature of his relationship with Eisenhower. Ironically, at the time he endorsed Alsop's sentiments, Nixon had just completed his November 1953 mission to the Republic of Korea*, during which he first extracted from President Syngman Rhee* a promise "not to take any unilateral action" against North Korea without first informing Eisenhower. Pressed harder by Nixon, Rhee made vague statements about the necessity for the two countries to "travel together" and even, according to Nixon's memoirs, admitted that in his heart he knew that South Korea "could not possibly act alone." An ensuing letter from Rhee to Eisenhower, however, merely repeated the assurance that he would not act unilaterally without first informing the president. Rhee and Nixon agreed that Rhee should go on making belligerent statements in public. It is not clear whether this tactic represented Eisenhower's wishes.

S. E. Ambrose, *Nixon: The Education of a Politician, 1913–1962* (New York, 1987); *Foreign Relations of the United States, 1952–1954*, vol. 15: *Korea* (Washington, D.C., 1984); R. M. Nixon, *RN: The Memoirs of Richard Nixon* (New York, 1978).

David W. Mabon

NO NAME LINE

The Fifth Chinese Offensive, which began on the night of April 22–23, 1951, was the largest battle of the war. Although the UNC* held on to Seoul, it had to give ground farther east. On April 29, 1951, Lieutenant General James A. Van Fleet*, the 8th Army* commander, established a new defensive line. It ran just north of Seoul and then curved up to the northeast on the eastern half of the peninsula, running through Sabangu in central Korea to the coastal town of Taep'o-ri, just north of the thirty-eighth parallel. This new defensive position was called the No Name Line because, unlike other control measures farther north, staff officers had not assigned it a cover name. As such, the term *No Name Line* suggests a desperate, last-minute defense. In fact, however, it was a successful step in Van Fleet's policy of using firepower and flexible resistance to blunt enemy attacks.

The renewed Chinese offensive of May 15, 1951, penetrated the No Name Line in the mountains of east-central Korea, causing the UNC front to bulge southward for 35 miles. Despite this, UNC artillery and air power halted the Chinese spring offensives of 1951* far short of Communist objectives. On May 20, 1951, UN forces began the counteroffensive that left No Name Line behind.

C. Blair, *The Forgotten War* (New York, 1987); J. Miller, Jr., O. J. Carroll, and M. E. Tackley, *Korea: 1951–1953* (Washington, D.C., 1956); M. B. Ridgway, *The Korean War* (Garden City, N.Y., 1967).

Jonathan M. House

NOBLE, HAROLD J. (1903–1953)

From August 1949 to January 1951, Harold J. Noble was attaché and first secretary in the U.S. embassy in the Republic of Korea* and also served as a close personal adviser and speechwriter for President Syngman Rhee*. Opposition to North Korean communism and unwavering support for the ROK were the basic elements in his assessments of events in Korea. Born in P'yŏngyang, his parents were Methodist missionaries, and Rhee learned English from Noble's father. After earning an A.B. at Ohio Wesleyan (1924) and an M.A. at Ohio State University (1925), Noble was an instructor for three years at Ewha College in Seoul. In 1929, he became a teaching fellow at the University of California at Berkeley, completing his doctorate there two years later in history. Noble joined the faculty of the University of Oregon in 1931, subsequently establishing a reputation as an expert on the languages, culture, and history of East Asia. He also taught at the 3d College in Kyoto, Japan. In 1942, he enlisted in the U.S. Marine Corps and served during World War II in the Pacific as a company commander, a combat intelligence officer, and a Japanese-language specialist.

Following his discharge, Noble spent 1946 in China, Korea, and Japan as a correspondent for the *Saturday Evening Post,* predicting in one article that there would be a war in Korea. He then was chief of the publications branch of the civilian intelligence section of the Far Eastern Command from 1947 to 1948. After a brief posting in Seoul as chief political liaison, Noble was a member of the U.S. delegation at the UN General Assembly before returning to Korea as political attaché and first secretary in 1949. Just prior to the war, he worked to ensure that President Rhee would allow free elections in the ROK during May 1950. Noble was not in Korea when North Korea launched its invasion of South Korea*. After hurrying back to the ROK, U.S. ambassador John J. Muccio* instructed him to travel southward and serve as the embassy's chief liaison officer to Rhee. During July, he received a mild reprimand after urging in a published interview that the UN cross the thirty-eighth parallel in pursuit of forcible reunification. Noble viewed the Democratic People's Republic of Korea* as illegitimate, justifying its destruction. In June 1951, he left Korea and joined the Committee for a Free Asia, serving in a variety of capacities until his death from a heart attack. A prolific writer, Noble contributed many articles to the *Pacific Historical Review, Far Eastern Quarterly,* and *Current History,* while authoring in 1946 *What It Takes to Rule Japan.*

Foreign Relations of the United States, 1950, vol. 7: *Korea* (Washington, D.C., 1976); *New York Times,* December 24, 1953; H. J. Noble, *Embassy at War* (Seattle, 1975); *Who Was Who in America,* vol. 3: *1953–1960* (Chicago, 1960).

NORSTAD, LAURIS (1907–1988)

When the Korean War began, General Lauris Norstad was U.S. Air Force deputy chief of staff for operations and acting vice-chief of staff. He accompanied W. Averell Harriman* during his visit to Tokyo* in August 1950, returning with a recommendation for the replacement of Lieutenant General Walton W. Walker* with Lieutenant General Matthew B. Ridgway* as commander of the 8th Army*. A minister's son, Norstad was born in Minneapolis. He graduated from the U.S. Military Academy in 1930 and the following year, while stationed at March Field receiving training in the pursuit section of the U.S. Army Air Corps Flying School, transferred from the cavalry to the air corps. When the United States entered World War II, he was the assistant intelligence officer at Bomber Command headquarters, later helping to plan Allied landings in North Africa, Sicily, and Italy. After promotion to brigadier general in 1944, Norstad planned the B-29 raids against Japan, climaxing in the atomic bombings in 1945. During the immediate postwar period, he served as assistant chief of air staff and played a leading role in shaping an independent U.S. Air Force. In 1951, Norstad became commander of Allied Air Forces in Europe and, with promotion the following year, the youngest four-star general in U.S. history. From 1956 until his retirement in 1963, he was NATO commander, working for conventional military preparedness coupled with an independent nuclear capability in NATO. Norstad then joined Owens-Corning Fiberglass Corporation, becoming president in 1972.

C. Blair, *The Forgotten War* (New York, 1987); *Current Biography,* 1948; N. Lichtenstein (ed.), *Political Profiles: The Kennedy Years* (New York, 1976); *New York Times,* September 14, 1988; E. W. Schoenebaum (ed.), *Political Profiles: The Eisenhower Years* (New York, 1977); *Who's Who in the World, 1974–1975* (Chicago, 1975).

NORTH KOREA

See Democratic People's Republic of Korea

NORTH KOREAN INVASION OF SOUTH KOREA (June 25, 1950)

This event signaled the start of the Korean War. At approximately 4:00 A.M. on June 25, 1950, North Korean artillery fire blasted South Korean military positions on the Ongjin peninsula. Two hours later, the North Korean People's Army (NKPA) launched military assaults at seven different points along the thirty-eighth parallel while staging amphibious landings near Kangnŭng and Samch'ŏk on the east coast. The NKPA was composed of roughly 135,000 well-trained troops organized into two corps consisting of seven assault infantry divisions, a tank brigade, and two independent infantry regiments (89,000). These forces included approximately 38,000 Koreans recently returned from fighting in the Chinese Civil War. In addition, the army had 23,000 men in three reserve divisions and about 18,000 in its border constabulary unit. It had an estimated 150 Soviet-built T–34 tanks and 110 combat planes. The NKPA had large amounts of heavy artillery, and nearly all of it outranged that of South Korea.

By contrast, the army of the Republic of Korea* consisted of eight combat divisions totaling 65,000 soldiers plus 33,000 headquarters and service troops. The South Korean army had no tanks or planes and little heavy artillery. To stop tanks, it only had flat-trajectory anti-tank guns and rocket-launching bazookas. Four of the ROK's eight infantry divisions were deployed a few miles south of the thirty-eighth parallel. The 1st Division guarded the Kaesŏng corridor, a wide valley leading to Seoul without any natural barriers except the Imjin River. Past a series of mountains and ridges to the east, the 7th Division held the Ŭijŏngbu corridor. The 6th Division protected the Ch'unch'ŏn corridor in the center of the peninsula, while the 8th Division guarded the rest of the border eastward to the coastal road. At Seoul, the ROK Capital Division was in reserve, except for the 17th Regiment on Ongjin with no land connection to the rest of South Korea. Two of the three remaining divisions were stationed at Taejŏn and Taegu. North Korean forces exploited superior firepower and the element of surprise to advance easily against the ROK soldiers, who found it nearly impossible to stop the tanks. The main thrust of its offensive sent four NKPA divisions and 120 tanks toward Ŭijŏngbu and Kaesŏng, the Communists seizing the latter city three hours after the first assault. There was a lesser effort directed at Ch'unch'ŏn involving two divisions and the remainder of the tanks.

To halt the advance, General Chae Byung Dok*, the ROK chief of staff, ordered Brigadier General Lee Hyung Keun* to move his 2d Division 120 miles northward from Taejŏn to a location east of Ŭijŏngbu where, as part of a planned envelopment operation, his unit would counterattack with Brigadier General Yu Jai Hyung's* 7th Division, which had retreated southwest of Ŭijŏngbu, the next morning. Lee tried but failed to persuade Chae that because of insufficient time, his plan was flawed and would result in disaster. On the morning of June 26, Yu's 7th Division attacked but fought alone. Lee had moved his troops into position but without informing Chae decided not to engage the enemy. The NKPA shattered the 7th Division; most of the South Korean soldiers fled into the hills, and Yu led the remainder in retreat to positions south of the Han River. Amid panic and confusion, the South Koreans abandoned large amounts of mortars, machine guns, howitzers, and anti-tank guns. Although Seoul was now open to invasion, the North Koreans did not completely occupy the city until 1:00 A.M. on June 28. Subsequently, General Yu and Major General Kim Hong-il reorganized the remnants of the ROK's forces, perhaps 20,000 troops, and managed during the Han River operations* to slow the Communist advance; the NKPA did not break the ROK defensive line until July 3. Meanwhile, South Korean forces at Ch'unch'ŏn staged a spirited defense for five days, in part because one NKPA division had no tanks. Eventually they withdrew south to Wŏnju to avoid being flanked from the west after the North Koreans had lost 40 percent of its troops and most of its artillery. Isolated along the east coast, the 8th Division fought effectively as well and delayed the NKPA advance.

News of the invasion reached the U.S. military attaché at 6:30 A.M. After obtaining confirmation from a Korean Military Advisory Group* officer, he contacted Everett F. Drumright* at 8:15, but the embassy counselor dismissed it as a rumor. The arrival of further reports persuaded him to notify Ambassador John J. Muccio* around 9:30. It was not until 10:36 that Muccio cabled Washington. Because of the thirteen-hour time differential, it was 9:36 P.M. on June 24 that official word arrived of the start of the Korean War (a newspaper report of the attack already had appeared). For the United States, North Korea's attack came as a surprise, although intelligence reports in the spring of 1950 indicated that North Korea was evacuating civilians and staging a military buildup in the area just north of the thirty-eighth parallel. But the Truman administration was convinced that the Soviet Union would not engage in overt aggression across an established boundary line. This assumption provides a partial explanation for Secretary Dean G. Acheson's* exclusion of the ROK from the U.S. defensive perimeter in his National Press Club speech*. The United States was more concerned that Syngman Rhee* would order an invasion northward. On many occasions, the ROK's president had stated publicly his determination to achieve forcible reunification. As a result, the United States had purposely limited the military potential of South Korea.

Rather than immediately resorting to U.S. military power to defend the ROK, the administration, in accordance with prior plans, went to the United Nations and gained passage of the UN Security Council resolutions of June 25* and 27, 1950*, authorizing military assistance to the ROK. At the first Blair House meeting*, President Harry S. Truman* approved the use of naval and air support for South Korean forces. Acting on instructions, General Douglas MacArthur* dispatched Brigadier General John H. Church* to Korea. The Church survey mission* arrived at Suwŏn on June 27 and played an important role in reorganizing and bolstering the morale of the ROK's forces. Then MacArthur made his visit to Korea of June 29, 1950*, which resulted in Truman's commitment of ground troops*. By July 3, the NKPA had rebuilt the bridges over the Han River and was advancing toward Suwŏn, seizing the city the next day. At the Battle of Osan*, the North Koreans easily swept aside Task Force Smith*. The city of Taejŏn fell during the Battle of the Kŭm River*, as UN forces were pushed back to a rectangular area in the southeastern corner of Korea known as the Pusan Perimeter*. At that point, the ROK army was composed of five reorganized divisions, while the NKPA had increased to ten divisions with the addition of South Koreans who had been impressed or had voluntarily enlisted. Communist conquest of all Korea was a real possibility until September 15, 1950, when the Inch'ŏn landing* led to the near destruction of the NKPA and reversed the course of the war.

For forty years, historians have disagreed about the circumstances surrounding the outbreak of the Korean War. Truman, in his June 27, 1950, statement*, offered a simple explanation for the conflict, implying that the Soviets had ordered North Korea to attack. In his memoirs, Nikita Khrushchev confirms that Joseph Stalin* was aware of North Korea's plans but insists that Kim Il Sung* persuaded him to approve the invasion through arguing that the people of South Korea would welcome liberation and the NKPA would conquer the peninsula before the United States could intervene. While the Soviet Union did provide a good deal of military hardware early in 1950, some writers have claimed that the Democratic People's Republic of Korea* launched the attack prematurely, pointing to the Soviet UN Security Council boycott* that prevented Moscow from vetoing international action. Speculation aside, one point seems beyond dispute: if the North Koreans were not determined to achieve reunification, there would have been no war. Whether the People's Republic of China* was involved in approving Kim's plans remains a mystery. The DPRK has always maintained that the ROK attacked first and thus initiated the hostilities. Revisionists agree, claiming that the Fierce Tiger unit of Colonel Paek In-yŏp's 17th Regiment on Ongjin, under the command of Kim Chong-wŏn*, launched an assault northward around 2:00 A.M. on June 25. These writers, reviving an argument that I. F. Stone advanced in 1952, contend that Rhee set a trap for the DPRK, anticipating that the attack would bring U.S. military intervention and open the way to conquest of North Korea.

For most historians, the size and scope of the NKPA offensive argues powerfully that the North Korean leaders planned the invasion in advance. In addition, Kim Il Sung later purged Foreign Minister Pak Hŏn-yŏng* as punishment for falsely predicting an internal uprising in South Korea after the invasion, even though he had sold that bill of goods to Stalin. Although the border clashes* of 1948 and 1949 meant that a kind of Korean war was already underway by June 1950, Kim's resort to conventional warfare following the failure of the Fatherland Front unification proposal* constituted a key change in the nature of the conflict. Several factors explain his decision, but all suggest that Truman's policy of containment in Korea, which sought to destabilize the Communist regime in the north through economic means, was succeeding. First, the ROK army had destroyed the Communist guerrilla movement in South Korea by the spring of 1950. Second, the May 1950 elections brought the defeat of Rhee's allies, showing progress toward achieving genuine political democracy in the ROK. Third, economic conditions in the south had improved markedly, and the Rhee government was implementing strong measures to end persistent financial distress. Finally, the United States recently had proposed a sizable increase in military aid to the ROK, which meant that delay would raise the odds for the DPRK against conquering the south. It also is conceivable that Kim Il Sung decided to attack because he feared that a U.S. policy of rollback eventually would succeed as the people of North Korea voluntarily rejected his rule and sought amalgamation with the ROK. *See also* Battles of Wonju; CIA Report: Current Capabilities of the Northern Korea Regime; Occupation of South Korea; Taejŏn Agreement; UNCOK Report on North Korean Attack; U.S. Evacuation of Seoul; Withdrawal from Seoul of June 1950.

J. Halliday and B. Cumings, *Korea: The Unknown War* (New York, 1989); B. I. Kaufman, *The Korean War* (Philadelphia, 1986); Kim Chum-kon, *The Korean War* (Seoul, 1983); J. Merrill, *Korea: The Peninsular Origins of the War* (Newark, Del., 1989); R. R. Simmons, *The Strained Alliance* (New York, 1975).

NORTH KOREAN PEOPLE'S ARMY
See North Korean Invasion of South Korea

NORTH KOREAN POLITICAL PRISONER EXCHANGE PROPOSAL OF 1950

On June 7, 1950, the Democratic Fatherland Front made its unification proposal* calling for general, all-Korean elections on August 5, 1950. South Korea ignored the proposal. Three days later, Radio P'yŏngyang made a proposal to exchange Communist leaders Kim Sam-yŏng and Yi Chua-ha held by the Republic of Korea* for nationalist leader Cho Man-sik held by the Democratic People's Republic of Korea*. Kim was the head and Yi the military chief of the underground South Korean Workers' party before being arrested in February 1950. Cho was chairman of the Chosŏn Democratic party before being arrested in December 1945 because of his opposition to Soviet occupation policies in northern Korea.

On June 16, President Syngman Rhee* of the ROK approved his government's considering the proposal on the condition that Cho be returned to Seoul in sound physical condition. He also suggested that the UNCOK should be asked to act as the intermediary. The North Korean authorities rejected this conditional approach of South Korea. The South Korean government, anxious to have Cho returned to Seoul, repeated on June 23 its earlier proposal for Cho's repatriation, promising to release the two Communists. There was no response from North Korea. The sudden DPRK overture apparently was nothing but a tactical gesture to camouflage the impending North Korean invasion of South Korea*.

S. Cho, *Korea in World Politics, 1940–1950* (Berkeley, 1967); P. Han, *The Problem of Korean Unification* (Seoul, 1987).

Hakjoon Kim

NSC-8: POSITION OF THE UNITED STATES WITH RESPECT TO KOREA (April 2, 1948)

In anticipation of the creation of the Republic of Korea* following UN-supervised elections scheduled for May 1948, President Harry S. Truman* approved this paper as the basis for U.S. policy toward Korea. Replacing SANACC 176/35*, NSC-8 attempted to satisfy the demands of U.S. military leaders for early withdrawal of U.S. occupation forces from southern Korea but without abandoning the entire peninsula to Communist domination. After passage of the UN resolution of November 14, 1947*, the Army Department had completed a tentative timetable for withdrawal, providing for a series of troop reductions over three months beginning on August 15, 1948, with the projected creation of a Korean provisional government. Army Department planners began pressing the State Department in January 1948 to finish a detailed financial aid program for Korea, arguing that if Congress did not receive the request by March 1, military withdrawal could not proceed on schedule. Truman's diplomatic advisers were suspicious of this apparent willingness to disengage regardless of conditions at the time of departure. The JCS, however, supported the Army Department's position, relying on the arguments contained in the September 1947 JCS report on Korea's strategic significance*. Truman therefore authorized the JCS to begin preparations for disengagement from Korea before the end of 1948.

State Department officials remained dissatisfied, arguing that if the United States shunned its commitments in southern Korea, this would damage U.S. international credibility and prestige. Truman was sensitive to these concerns and approved NSC-8 because it offered a formula for achieving withdrawal without abandonment. The proposal outlined steps for the creation of a separate and independent South Korea. To abandon southern Korea to Communist domination, the paper declared, would improve the Soviet political and strategic position with respect to China and Japan. Thus, NSC-8 recommended that the United States provide $185 million in economic aid to South Korea for fiscal 1949 and create a small constabulary army capable of defending itself "against any but an overt act of aggression by north Korea or other forces." The paper projected U.S. military withdrawal from Korea* no later than December 31, 1948. NSC–8 ended with a warning that the United States should "not become so irrevocably involved in the Korean situation that any action taken by any faction in Korea or by any other power in Korea could be considered a *casus belli* for the U.S." Choosing to pursue a middle course in responding to the Soviet challenge in Korea, the United States would try to foster indigenous economic strength, political stability, and military power in South Korea so that it could protect itself. Truman's pursuit of this objective would lead to approval of NSC-8/2*, which delayed military withdrawal until June 1949.

Foreign Relations of the United States, 1948, vol. 6: *The Far East and Australasia* (Washington, D.C., 1974); J. I. Matray, *The Reluctant Crusade* (Honolulu, 1985).

NSC-8/2: POSITION OF THE UNITED STATES WITH RESPECT TO KOREA (March 23, 1949)

This revision of NSC-8* provided the foundation for U.S. policy toward Korea until the North Korean invasion of South Korea*. NSC-8/2 became necessary after President Harry S. Truman*, responding to the Yŏsu-Sunch'ŏn rebellion* in the Republic of Korea*, decided to postpone total withdrawal of U.S. forces from Korea beyond the December 31, 1948, deadline specified in NSC-8. At the National Security Council meeting of March 22, 1949, the administration discussed NSC-8/1, a reappraisal of U.S. policy in Korea. Despite aid and advice, the paper began, the ROK had not developed the military and economic strength necessary to defend itself against the challenge of the Soviet puppet regime in North Korea. If the United States withdrew abruptly from Korea at that time, this "disengagement would be interpreted as a betrayal by the U.S. of its friends and allies in the Far East and might contribute substantially to a fundamental realignment of forces in favor of the USSR throughout that part of the world." Premature U.S. withdrawal would shatter as well the confidence of South Korea and thus guarantee the rapid demise of the ROK. Such a dramatic Communist victory would damage U.S. interests because it would destroy the viability of the UN and force smaller countries to seek an accommodation with Moscow. NSC-8/1 thus concluded that despite the risks, Washington had to provide the ROK with continued economic, technical, and military assistance.

NSC-8/1 acknowledged, however, that U.S. military withdrawal from Korea* was essential, concluding that safe disengagement was possible if Washington satisfied certain conditions. First, the administration had to train, equip, and supply a security force with sufficient power to maintain internal order and deter an open attack from the north. Second, the United States had to implement a three-year program of technical and economic aid for recovery and self-sufficient growth. Finally, the UN had to continue its policy of diplomatic and political support as a boost to South Korea's morale. NSC-8/1 closed with the ominous prediction that if the United States delayed departure, the "occupation forces remaining in Korea might be either destroyed or obliged to abandon Korea in the event of a major hostile attack, with serious damage to U.S. prestige." After some key revisions, NSC-8/1 received Truman's approval.

In final form, NSC-8/2 represented a compromise between the conflicting desires of military and diplomatic leaders. The administration now resolved to gain congressional approval for a three-year program of economic aid to the ROK and enough military equipment and arms to maintain a security force of more than 100,000 men. NSC-8/2 also established June 30, 1949, as a firm date for complete withdrawal of U.S. combat forces but emphasized that departure should in no way imply any lessening of the U.S. commitment to the ROK's future survival. During the subsequent fifteen months until the outbreak of the Korean War, the Truman administration diligently attempted to realize the three conditions NSC-8/2 identified as essential for a safe withdrawal. *See also* Korean Aid Bill of 1949–1950.

Foreign Relations of the United States, 1949, vol. 7: *The Far East and Australasia*, pt. 2 (Washington, D.C., 1976); J. I. Matray, *The Reluctant Crusade* (Honolulu, 1985).

NSC-48/5: UNITED STATES OBJECTIVES, POLICIES, AND COURSES OF ACTION IN ASIA (May 17, 1951)

This paper affirmed limited U.S. objectives with respect to the war in Korea but represented a significant hardening of U.S. policy toward the People's Republic of China*. The only general policy paper on Asia to receive NSC approval during the Korean War, it consolidated and put the NSC imprimatur on several changes that the Truman administration had adopted in policy since the North Korean invasion of South Korea* and Chinese military intervention*. The previous policy paper on Asia, NSC-48/2, "The Position of the United States With Respect to Asia, December 30, 1949," had called for efforts to exploit Sino-Soviet differences, implied that recognition of the newly established PRC would not be long delayed, and specifically rejected intervention to prevent the anticipated capture of Taiwan by the Communists. NSC-48/5 approved U.S. encouragement of resistance to the Communist Chinese government through the support of anti-Communist elements, as well as continued protection of Taiwan by the 7th Fleet, recognition of the Republic of China*, opposition to PRC membership in the United Nations, and intensified economic restrictions against the PRC.

Approved during the controversy following President Harry S. Truman's* recall of CINCUNC General Douglas MacArthur* from command in Korea, NSC-48/5 affirmed administration policy to limit the Korean War to the Korean peninsula and to seek to avoid expansion of the war. It declared that the United States should pursue the ultimate objective of a united, independent, and democratic Korea through political rather than military means. As a short-term objective, it should at a minimum seek a settlement ending hostilities with a defensible boundary at least as far north as the thirty-eighth parallel, permitting the withdrawal of non-Korean armed forces from Korea. In the meantime, it should continue to wage a war of attrition. NSC-48/5 also supported plans for a peace treaty and a security treaty with Japan and called for assistance to the countries of Southeast Asia and to the French in Indochina. The NSC discussed a draft paper, NSC-48/3, in May and approved a revised draft, NSC-48/4, with some additional revisions on May 16. Truman approved NSC-48/5 the following day. *See also* Japanese Peace Treaty; JCS Directive of May 31, 1951.

Foreign Relations of the United States, 1951, vol. 6: *Asia and the Pacific* (Washington, D.C., 1977); J. F. Schnabel and R. J. Watson, *History of the Joint Chiefs of Staff*, vol. 3: *The Korean War* (Wilmington, 1979).

Harriet D. Schwar

NSC-68: UNITED STATES OBJECTIVES AND PROGRAMS FOR NATIONAL SECURITY (April 14, 1950)

This policy document, formally approved by President Harry S. Truman* in September 1950, served as the first comprehensive statement of U.S. national security policy in the postwar era. Written by a team of State and Defense department specialists headed by Paul Nitze*, director of the State Department's Policy Planning Staff, NSC-68 depicted the Soviet menace in grave terms. "In the face of obviously mounting Soviet military strength," it said, "ours has declined relatively." As a result of the Kremlin's growing boldness, "the integrity and vitality of our system is in greater jeopardy than ever before in our history." In order to counter what it characterized as a global Soviet threat, NSC-68 recommended that the Truman administration engage in "a rapid and sustained build-up of the political, economic, and military strength of the free world." Specifically, it called for a tripling of the U.S. defense budget.

NSC-68 marked a significant departure for U.S. strategic thinking in a number of areas. First, its authors judged Soviet military power and political influence as much more threatening to U.S. interests than had previous policy assessments. Second, they identified a Soviet threat that, since it was worldwide in scope, required a global U.S. response. Third, they insisted that the U.S. ability to meet the Soviet challenge could be substantially enhanced through increased defense spending without harming the domestic economy. Finally, the policy paper emphasized the necessity of meeting any threat, ranging from propaganda to covert action and from local conflict to general war.

Although NSC-68 almost certainly exaggerated Soviet capabilities and misread Moscow's intentions, the document nonetheless exerted a profound influence on U.S. foreign and defense policies. The Korean War seemed to validate for the Truman administration many of the assumptions that underlay NSC-68's analysis, as it appeared to Truman and his senior advisors to herald a new, more aggressive phase in the Soviet quest for world domination. Consequently, Truman's formal approval of NSC-68 in September 1950 was probably hastened by the North Korean invasion of South Korea* several months earlier. By the end of the year, the administration had greatly expanded U.S. worldwide commitments and had asked for and received a vast increase in defense appropriations. Whether approval of those measures would have been possible without the Korean War, especially given the budgetary restrictions imposed by Congress prior to the conflict, is a question that continues to be hotly debated by historians. *See also* Defense Appropriations Acts (1951–1953).

J. L. Gaddis, *Strategies of Containment* (New York, 1982); S. F. Wells, Jr., "Sounding the Tocsin: NSC-68 and the Soviet Threat," *International Security* (1979).

Robert J. McMahon

NSC-76: U.S. COURSES OF ACTION IN THE EVENT SOVIET FORCES ENTER KOREAN HOSTILITIES (July 21, 1950)

On June 30, 1950, Secretary of Defense Louis A. Johnson* requested the JCS to submit recommendations as to the course of action that the United States should adopt if Soviet forces intervened in the Korean conflict. In its response on July 10, the JCS warned against excessive commitments of U.S. military forces in areas that would not be decisive. Should the Soviet Union decide on global war, it would be able to exploit U.S. deployments and commitments in Korea and thus render more effective its overall war strategy. Should it become apparent that the Soviet Union entered the Korean struggle, the United States should minimize its commitment to Korea and prepare to execute its war plans, including full mobilization. After Secretary Johnson forwarded this memorandum to the NSC, the paper was designated NSC-76.

On July 25, the State Department presented its comments on NSC-76. It agreed that the entry of any major Soviet combat units into the Korean hostilities would demand a full-scale mobilization of U.S. forces. Such a decision involved the country's most basic national policies and therefore could be taken only at the highest level. It was also essential that the evaluation of a Soviet military presence in Korea be accurate. The State Department argued that such phrases as "prepare to minimize its commitments in Korea" and "prepare to execute war plans" were not precise when NSC-76 seemed to mean the evacuation of Korea and the initiation of full-scale mobilization. Before executing war plans, moreover, the United States would need to give consideration to appropriate action by the UN, to the effect of any decision on the NATO allies, to the impact of a Soviet military presence in Korea on world opinion, to whether the United States itself was prepared to carry out its war plans, and whether Congress was ready to support a decision that anticipated a general war. At its meeting on July 27, the NSC authorized the aerial reconnaissance of all North Korea, including coastal waters, but not across the frontiers of Manchuria and the Soviet Union. That meeting referred NSC-76 to the NSC staff for the preparation of recommendations for NSC action. Subsequently, this instruction was cancelled in the light of action taken on NSC-81* in September.

Foreign Relations of the United States, 1950, vol. 7: *Korea* (Washington, D.C., 1976).

Norman A. Graebner

NSC-80: PEACE OFFENSIVE CONCERNING KOREA (September 1, 1950)

Even before the 8th Army* had broken out of the Pusan Perimeter*, the Truman administration anticipated that the UNC* soon would reverse the course of the Korean War. This raised the question of a quick settlement of the conflict. To meet the challenge of an incipient peace movement, the secretaries of the army, navy, and air force presented a memorandum to the secretary of defense on August 24 that advocated a strong counteroffensive, based on thoroughly examined policy alternatives:

We strongly urge that you request the National Security Council staff to prepare a report on the courses of action to be taken to offset the psychological and diplomatic effects of a stalemate in Korea. Such actions would be taken, on the President's approval, with a view to bridging the gap until sufficient military force is available to launch a successful offensive in Korea.

This memorandum, supported by Secretary of Defense Louis A. Johnson* and with the concurrence of President Harry S. Truman*, was submitted to the NSC on September 1 as NSC-80 and referred to the NSC staff for use in preparing a policy statement. On October 12, the NSC, on the advice of the NSC senior staff, cancelled this proposal as no longer necessary. The Inch'ŏn landing* on September 15, followed by the UN decision to carry the war into North Korea, had eliminated the issue of a compromise peace.

Foreign Relations of the United States, 1950, vol. 7: *Korea* (Washington, D.C., 1976).

Norman A. Graebner

NSC-81: U.S. COURSES OF ACTION WITH RESPECT TO KOREA (September 1, 1950)

This paper was an attempt to define the policies that the United States should pursue to restore peace and security in Korea after the aggression had ended, either through a defeat of the North Korean forces or their voluntary withdrawal north of the thirty-eighth parallel. Any policy, the report began, must advance the interests of the United States. UN action in Korea continued to follow the UN Security Council resolutions of June 25* and June 27, 1950*; therefore any movement of troops north of the thirty-eighth parallel required UN approval. UN objectives in Korea, as outlined in General Assembly resolutions of November 14, 1947*, December 12, 1948*, and October 21, 1949*, comprised essentially the independence and unity of Korea. The achievement of that goal would indeed serve U.S. interests but not at the risk of a general war with the People's Republic of China* or the Soviet Union.

As UN forces approached the thirty-eighth parallel, Soviet actions would determine whether an advance into North Korea would pose a substantial risk of war. The NSC report, like previous State Department recommendations, doubted that the Soviet Union would accept a change of government in North Korea. Because of the danger of Soviet or Chinese entry into the war, UN forces must not approach the Manchurian border. The NSC report concluded that the course of action in Korea would serve the interests of the United States only if it considered the future actions of China and the Soviet Union, had the support of UN allies, and weighed the risks of a general war. Under no circumstances should the United States permit itself to become engaged in a war with China or the Soviet Union. NSC-81 recognized the legality of UN operations north of the thirty-eighth parallel to defeat the forces of North Korea but advised against any UN-authorized actions in areas near the Soviet and Manchurian borders of North Korea. The National Security Council submitted NSC-81/1, dated September 9, to the president. Two days later the president approved the conclusions of the report and directed their implementation by the appropriate executive agencies.

Foreign Relations of the United States, 1950, vol. 7: *Korea* (Washington:, D.C., 1976).

Norman A. Graebner

NSC-92: THE POSITION OF THE UNITED STATES REGARDING A BLOCKADE OF TRADE WITH CHINA (December 4, 1950)

Chinese military intervention* into the Korean War in late November 1950 raised the issue of U.S. commercial and financial relations with that country. On December 3, the Commerce Department adopted an export licensing system to control the flow of U.S. strategic materials into the People's Republic of China*. It requested that the National Security Council, in NSC-92, formalize this interim decision without addressing the larger question of a trade embargo. The Treasury Department on December 6 informed the NSC staff that any U.S. decision to impose a trade embargo must include one to block Communist Chinese assets in the United States. To institute an embargo without freezing assets would permit the Chinese to transfer dollars to import similar goods from other countries.

Meanwhile, Ambassador at Large Philip C. Jessup*, responding to a series of State Department reports, recommended to the NSC that the United States avoid a unilateral trade embargo and the freezing of Chinese assets, inasmuch as such action would have little effect on China and would antagonize many governments friendly to the United States. To State Department officials, it appeared essential that the United States make no decisions regarding mainland China that would undermine the UN majority that supported the war. On December 8, Jessup recommended the following conclusion to NSC-92:

The United States should continue, for the moment, its present policies regarding the placement of all exports under license to China and the NSC should keep under review the questions of a trade embargo, a blocking of assets of Communist China and action to prevent American shipping from calling at China mainland ports.

This statement did not terminate the conflict within the U.S. government. Treasury objected to the paragraph because it did not acknowledge the inconsistency between imposing an embargo and permitting the Chinese to utilize dollar assets for the purchase of goods, prohibited by U.S. trade policy, in third countries. Whereas the State Department insisted that any embargo and freezing measure should have the previous approval of the principal countries of Western Europe, the JCS on December 13 argued for total economic sanctions against Communist China, to be adopted immediately and unilaterally. State and Treasury officials now agreed that President Harry S. Truman* should authorize both departments to adopt freezing procedures at the appropriate time. On December 16, the U.S. government placed all Chinese assets within the United States under control; it prohibited all vessels of U.S. registry to enter the ports of Communist China. U.S. exports to China would require validated export licenses. At the same time, the State Department sought to assure the rest of the world that the United States would not permit its economic restrictions to draw it into a general war with the mainland Chinese. *See also* Truman's Declaration of a National Emergency.

Foreign Relations of the United States, 1950, vol. 6: *East Asia and the Pacific* (Washington, D.C., 1976).

Norman A. Graebner

NSC-95: UNITED STATES POSITION REGARDING A CEASE-FIRE RESOLUTION FOR THE KOREAN WAR (December 13, 1950)

This paper was in response to Secretary of State Dean G. Acheson's* announcement at the NSC meeting of December 11, 1950, that several Asian countries were planning to bring the issue of a cease-fire in Korea before the UN General Assembly. The proposed resolution would request the president of the General Assembly to appoint a committee to negotiate the conditions for a cease-fire. Acheson reminded the JCS that a cease-fire resolution could encompass a variety of military decisions affecting the security of UN forces. Because it appeared certain that the UNC* would be unable to hold a position north of the thirty-eighth parallel, members of the JCS recommended the acceptance of a cease-fire along the thirty-eighth parallel as the status quo position. President Harry S. Truman* directed the JCS to define the conditions for an acceptable cease-fire in Korea—one that did not place UN forces at a military disadvantage and did not offer political concessions.

On December 12, the JCS presented to the secretary of defense their terms for a Korean cease-fire. James S. Lay, Jr.*, the NSC executive secretary, circulated the JCS memorandum on December 13 as NSC-95. For the JCS, an acceptable arrangement, one confined to Korea, would include the cessation of all fighting, the establishment of a DMZ across Korea, and a prohibition against the introduction of new personnel, including volunteers, or equipment during the cease-fire period. The DMZ, to be honored by all ground, air, and naval forces, would cover approximately 20 miles, with its southern limit generally following the thirty-eighth parallel. Any armed forces in advance of the DMZ would be moved back through the area assigned to the main forces. All commanders in the field would provide for the security of their troops and installations but not within the DMZ. A commission supervising the terms, conditions, and arrangements of the cease-fire would have access to the whole of Korea; it would report all violations of the resolution to the General Assembly. The commission would need sufficient numbers of military observers to carry out its functions. The Joint Chiefs warned that any cease-fire along the thirty-eighth parallel would probably eliminate possibilities for achieving the UN objective of a free and united Korea. In acknowledging the necessity of reduced war aims, the JCS did not advocate a continuation of the war but sought rather to remind national leaders of the certain price of a cease-fire negotiation. *See also* Agenda Item 3; Kaesŏng Truce Talks; UN Resolution of December 14, 1950.

Foreign Relations of the United States, 1950, vol. 7: *Korea* (Washington, D.C., 1976).

Norman A. Graebner

NSC-101: U.S. ACTION TO COUNTER CHINESE COMMUNIST AGGRESSION (January 15, 1951)

During the early weeks of 1951, U.S. officials pondered the effect of the threat of Chinese military intervention* on the future of UN operations in Korea. After examining the military possibilities remaining to the United States, the JCS, in a document of January 12 that circulated as NSC-101, recommended a detailed military program aimed at the People's Republic of China* itself. The JCS advocated policies to protect the offshore defense line from Japan to the Philippines, as well as the independence of Taiwan; to stabilize Korea militarily but without an increase in U.S. forces; to support the Republic of Korea* wherever its government might exist; and to avoid war with the Soviet Union. Toward the Asian mainland, the JCS favored a more aggressive policy designed to prevent the extension of communism into Southeast Asia and to establish a friendly government in China. To achieve such purposes, the JCS proposed the buildup and employment of Japanese forces in Korea as a necessity for the defense of Japan; the establishment of a naval blockade of China; the removal of all restrictions on the operations of the Nationalist Chinese, including guerrilla warfare on the mainland; the pursuit of a UN vote to brand Communist China an aggressor; and the launching of naval and air attacks against mainland targets in retaliation should the Chinese attack U.S. forces outside Korea. Army Chief of Staff General J. Lawton Collins* and Air Force Chief of Staff General Hoyt S. Vandenberg* discussed the contents of this paper with CINCUNC General Douglas MacArthur* during their visit to Tokyo in January 1951. Later, MacArthur would claim that this showed that the JCS supported implementation of his plan for victory*.

On January 15, James S. Lay, Jr.*, the executive secretary of the NSC, presented NSC-101/1, a report based on the JCS recommendations, to the NSC. The staff report accepted the courses of action recommended by the JCS. It advocated a broadening of the war against mainland China, largely through the greater employment of air and naval power, as well as the introduction of additional forces from other countries. At the NSC meeting two days later, Secretary of State Dean G. Acheson* declared NSC-101/1 inadequate because it did not examine critically the questions raised by a naval blockade of China, the extension of air reconnaissance over Chinese territory, and the removal of restrictions on the Republic of China* to attack the mainland. The State Department memorandum of January 17, on which Acheson based his criticism, argued that a unilateral U.S. blockade could result in a general war with Communist China. To be effective, a blockade would require the inclusion of British Hong Kong, Portuguese Macao, and Soviet Dairen and Port Arthur. It was not clear that any blockade could terminate the junk traffic along the China coast. State Department officials doubted that a blockade could achieve more than the economic restrictions already in place. Finally, a blockade would strain U.S. relations with its allies; none of them favored any direct action against mainland China. Because of improved conditions on the battlefield, confirmed as a result of the Collins-Vandenberg visit to Tokyo in January 1951*, the Truman administration decided against implementing the measures outlined in the NSC-101/1.

At the January 17 NSC meeting, Acheson also asked the Joint Chiefs what they believed Chiang Kai-shek's* forces could accomplish on the mainland. Secretary of Defense George C. Marshall* wondered, in response, when the United States would agree to some offensive against Communist China. Finally, on March 14, the JCS submitted their report on the anti-Communist Chinese. The JCS agreed that mainland China was vulnerable to clandestine operations and that any Soviet decision for war would not come in response to Nationalist Chinese activity on the mainland. The report recognized the weakness of the Nationalist armed forces and the continued need of the 7th Fleet to protect Taiwan from the mainland Chinese. At the same time, the JCS believed Nationalist offshore raids could be effective in direct proportion to the level of U.S. support. Still, the report concluded that even U.S. air and naval support could guarantee no ultimate success to military operations against the mainland. Only in conjunction with other courses of action could the Nationalist Chinese effect some reduction of Communist China's military effectiveness. *See also* CIA Report: Position of the United States with Respect to Communist China; NSC-92.

Foreign Relations of the United States, 1951, vol. 7: *Korea and China* (Washington, D.C., 1983).

Norman A. Graebner

NSC-118: U.S. COURSES OF ACTION IN KOREA (November 9, 1951)

In response to the slow progress in the Kaesŏng truce talks*, this policy paper considered changes in U.S. military policy in the Korean War if the armistice negotiations failed. Presented to the NSC on November 9 as NSC-118, this document again was a revision of a JSC memorandum of July 13 to the secretary of defense. It emphasized the JCS belief in the need for greater military pressure on the enemy should the armistice negotiations fail. Because the increase in Communist fighter strength in Manchuria rendered U.S. air action above the Yalu too costly, the concept of hot pursuit* should receive no further consideration. The JCS advised, however, that the U.S. air force, unilaterally and on short notice if necessary, should attack selected Chinese air bases when "the scale of enemy air activity is such as seriously to jeopardize the security of United States forces in the Korean area."

To force a political settlement on the enemy satisfactory to the United States, the JCS concluded, would require additional U.S. forces and weaponry. Should the limitations on the use of ground, air, and naval forces result in inconclusive operations and the continuing attrition of manpower, the United States, the JCS warned, should not respond to the demand for a satisfactory military conclusion of the war by increasing the scale of war without reviewing its objectives in Korea as well as its global strategy. Fundamentally, the government had to determine whether its goals in Korea merited the commitment of additional resources or whether it should extend the war into Manchuria and China. Any extension of the war would require the support of the UN. The JCS requested the NSC to determine the country's objectives and courses of action in Korea should the armistice negotiations fail.

In its review of policy in Korea, the NSC staff, in NSC-118/1, recommended some minor changes in the NSC-118 draft. With the approval of President Harry S. Truman*, the NSC adopted the final text of NSC-118/2 on December 20. NSC-118/2 stated as a minimum U.S. objective in Korea a settlement of the conflict that would not jeopardize the position of the United States with respect to the Soviet Union, Taiwan, or the seating of the People's Republic of China* in the UN. Satisfactory armistice arrangements should guarantee the authority of the Republic of Korea* with defensible boundaries not south of the thirty-eighth parallel, the gradual withdrawal of all non-Korean troops, and the building of sufficient power in the ROK forces to enable them to repel any renewed aggression from North Korea alone. To avoid war with China or the Soviet Union, the NSC recommended limited military action until a minimum settlement was achieved. To maintain UN capabilities, the United States should continue all political and economic sanctions against Communist China and seek the maximum support of its UN allies, especially the ROK.

Should the armistice negotiations fail, the United States would prepare for the possibilities of a wider war, increase the scale of military operations consistent with available forces, and remove restrictions against military advances into North Korea, the bombing of targets on the Korean side of the Yalu, and attacks on Chinese air bases when enemy air activity threatened the security of the U.S. forces in Korea (but only with the specific authorization of the president). As much as possible the United States would seek the diplomatic isolation of Communist China. The statement favoring a naval blockade of mainland China by the major maritime powers and a complete embargo of shipments to Communist China was returned to the NSC staff for review. Should Soviet forces appear in Korea, the United States would immediately withdraw its forces and prepare for general war. *See also* P'anmunjŏm Truce Talks.

Foreign Relations of the United States, 1951, vol. 7: *Korea and China* (Washington, D.C., 1983).

Norman A. Graebner

NSC-147: ANALYSIS OF POSSIBLE COURSES OF ACTION IN KOREA
(April 2, 1953)

This paper, discussed by President Dwight D. Eisenhower* and his NSC in April-May 1953, presented policy choices should the United States decide to expand the Korean War militarily to gain a satisfactory outcome. It was organized into two main strategies: to fight the war south of the Yalu River or to carry it to the Chinese mainland. Within each of the two strategies, three military options were presented in order of ascending intensity. Options A-C fell within the first strategy. Option A called for fighting the war as President Harry S. Truman* had done, hoping in time that South Koreans could take over the major burden of the fighting. Option B contemplated increased ground operations with continuing aggressive air and naval support against North Korea. Option C suggested a coordinated ground offensive to the waist of Korea* and assumed that such a decisive military victory would force the People's Republic of China* and the Democratic People's Republic of Korea* to sign an armistice on UN terms. In the second unrestricted strategy, option D envisioned phased military escalation against China or Manchuria, including air and naval attacks, thus coercing Peking and P'yŏngyang to sign a truce. Option E added to option D a coordinated ground offensive to the Korean waist. Finally, there was option F, providing for a large-scale offensive in Korea combined with a naval blockade and air attacks on China designed to eliminate all Communist forces in the Korea peninsula.

When the planning board prepared NSC-147 in late March and early April 1953, the new administration was seriously examining the potential use of atomic weapons to end the war in Korea. The interagency drafters of NSC-147 gingerly approached this controversial issue by noting that atomic weapons could be used in all options except A and suggesting that the full NSC should make the ultimate decision. NSC-147 did not provide analysis on how China and the Soviet Union would react to an atomic attack nor did it raise the danger of global war.

Before the president and the NSC considered NSC-147, State Department advisors argued to Secretary of State John Foster Dulles* that the unrestricted options against China would seriously strain U.S. relations with European and British Commonwealth allies and risk global war. State officials also noted that attacking China contradicted a basic understanding between Moscow and Washington that neither would use Korea as a basic test of strength. The JCS also disliked NSC-147 but for very different reasons. They believed that to be effective, the options against China would require considerable use of tactical nuclear weapons. Furthermore, the JCS argued that tactical atomic targets would not be effective against the massive dugouts that characterized North Korean defensives along the front. The JCS favored a combination of air and naval operations against China with sufficient tactical atomic weapons to ensure success and a conventional ground offensive to the waist of Korea, close to option E of NSC-147 but with a definitive atomic strategy. Although not convinced that atomic weapons were inappropriate for Korea, Eisenhower agreed that for planning purposes, the JCS modification was the best plan.

NSC-147 was only a contingency plan. The Eisenhower administration hoped it would never have to be used. Nevertheless, the paper contained seriously flawed analysis, in good part because of the speed with which it was prepared and the inchoate nature of Eisenhower's strategic thinking on Korea. While hardly a clear blueprint on how to end the war militarily, NSC-147 nonetheless raised the issue and forced the bureaucracy to examine the options in Korea, including atomic war. Discussions of NSC–147 sent signals to hardliners in and outside the Republican administration that the president was trying to make good his campaign promises to end the war in Korea. Press accounts of NSC meetings on NSC-147 leaked out and served to put China and North Korea on notice that Eisenhower was considering dire means to end the war. *See also* Dulles's Atomic Warning to China.

Foreign Relations of the United States, 1952–1954, vol. 15: *Korea* (Washington, D.C. 1984); E. C. Keefer, ''Eisenhower and the End of the Korean War,'' *Diplomatic History* (Summer 1986).

Edward C. Keefer

NSC-148: UNITED STATES POLICY IN FAR EAST (April 6, 1953)

NSC-148 was an unsuccessful attempt to draw together various approved NSC papers on Korea, Southeast Asia, Taiwan, and Japan and create a general policy paper on East Asia. It characterized Soviet aims in East Asia as the domination of mainland Asia, Japan, and ultimately the offshore islands of the western Pacific. The mechanism for the Kremlin's hegemony was to be the ''development of the resources of communist China.'' Noting that U.S. and French forces were tied down in Korea and Indochina fighting ''indigenous Communist'' forces, the paper recommended the increased support and use of anti-Communist indigenous forces in Asia to create pro-American, non-Communist governments able to withstand Communist influence. NSC-148 recommended the defection of the People's Republic of China* from its alignment with the Soviet Union but called for its eventual overthrow and replacement by a non-Communist regime. How to mesh these apparently contradictory goals was one of the principal weaknesses of the paper.

When the NSC discussed NSC-148 on April 8, the general feeling of the council was that the paper attempted to cover too much ground too quickly. President Dwight D. Eisenhower* and Secretary of State John Foster Dulles* stressed that the recommendations of NSC-148 represented merely working hypotheses and the council need not think of them as cast in stone. Eisenhower suggested that the "Far East Financial Summary," an estimate of the cost of U.S. economic and military assistance in East Asia, which was attached to NSC-148, should be used as a tool for the upcoming budget presentation to Congress. For Korea specifically, the financial summary anticipated that the United States would spend $323 million and $279 million for economic and military assistance for 1953 and 1954, respectively, and estimated costs of about $4 billion to almost $10 billion for the various options of NSC-147's* different strategies of fighting the Korean War if no satisfactory peace was attainable.

The NSC postponed consideration of NSC–148 pending further study, but the paper was never revised. Having moved too fast, the Eisenhower administration allowed NSC-148 to wither on the bureaucratic vine. Under heavy pressure to cut defense spending, facing opposition from Republican conservatives in Congress for its willingness to accept an armistice in Korea, and jittery in the face of rampant McCarthyism at home, the Eisenhower administration was unprepared to undertake a major review of U.S. policy in East Asia. NSC-148 was eventually superseded by a new NSC paper on the Far East drafted and approved in late 1954.

Foreign Relations of the United States, 1952–1954, vol. 12: *East Asia and the Pacific* (Washington, D.C., 1984); P. Lyon, *Eisenhower: Portrait of a Hero* (Boston, 1974).

Edward C. Keefer

NSC-154/1: UNITED STATES TACTICS IMMEDIATELY FOLLOWING AN ARMISTICE IN KOREA (July 7, 1953)

This paper outlined interim U.S. policy after the anticipated signature of the Korean armistice agreement*. It assumed that notwithstanding their apparent willingness to sign the armistice, the Chinese Communists had not abandoned the use of armed force to achieve their objectives in Asia. NSC-154 warned that Chinese aggression would continue, particularly in Southeast Asia, even after a Korean armistice. The paper foresaw difficulty for the United States in convincing its allies to support continued political and economic pressures against the People's Republic of China* after the armistice and therefore called for a continuation of recognition and support of Taiwan as the sole representative of China, the total U.S. trade embargo, and maintenance of controls on Western trade with the PRC and the Democratic People's Republic of Korea*. NSC-154 also suggested placing Peking on notice that further armed conflict in Asia would not be tolerated by endorsing such international warnings as the Joint Policy (Greater Sanctions) statement* and a combined declaration with France, the United Kingdom, Australia, New Zealand—and as many other countries as possible—linking the Korean armistice to Communist "aggression" elsewhere in Asia. When the NSC discussed the paper, Acting Secretary of State Walter B. Smith* warned that the United States would be fortunate to induce its allies to hold the line on trade controls with China. President Dwight D. Eisenhower* balked at a suggestion that the United States institute a blockade of China, favoring instead heavy pressure on U.S. allies to support and even extend trade controls.

NSC-154 also outlined interim actions to be followed regarding Korea, including an endorsement of a security treaty and economic and military aid package to strengthen the Republic of Korea* in the postarmistice period. The JCS objected to such concessions without a prior specific assurance from President Syngman Rhee* on cooperation with the armistice. They also maintained that the language of NSC-154, guaranteeing the political independence of South Korea and the integrity of territory under its control, was too broadly stated. Therefore, the NSC insisted on receiving proper assurance of the ROK's acceptance of the armistice, and it substituted vaguer language on guarantees of South Korean integrity in the approved version, NSC-154/1, dated July 7, 1953. The drafters of NSC-154 had also recommended full U.S.-ROK consultation before and during the postarmistice political conference to ensure that Washington and Seoul dominated the UN delegation and limited discussion to Korean problems.

Foreign Relations of the United States, 1952–1954, vol. 15: *Korea* (Washington, D.C., 1984).

Edward C. Keefer

NSC-156/1: STRENGTHENING THE KOREAN ECONOMY (July 17, 1953)

NSC-156/1 was a promise of U.S. economic and military assistance to the Republic of Korea* so long as President Syngman Rhee* was prepared to abide by the terms of the armistice. A direct result of the Tasca Mission's* survey of war-torn Korea, it concluded that in order to defend itself from the external threat from the north and from the danger of internal subversion, the South Korean living standard had to be raised, and ultimately the ROK economy should become self-sufficient. The latter goal was out of the question for the time being, so NSC-156/1 recommended that the United States fill the breach with substantial outlays of military assistance, economic aid, and economic reconstruction assistance totaling over $1 billion. The money would be earmarked to support a twenty-division army, small increases in the ROK's marine, navy, and air force personnel, and a massive program of economic aid for reconstruction. For the long term, Henry J. Tasca* recommended a three-year plan for modernization, industrialization, and commercialization of Korean society that emphasized investments in agriculture, mining, cottage industry, and transportation. While advocating a jump start for the Korean economy, U.S. immediate objectives were modest: merely to raise standards of living and production to the 1949–1950 prewar levels.

The NSC planning board accepted the conclusions of the Tasca report as a framework for an expanded program of assistance to South Korea, but representatives from the Treasury Department and the Mutual Security Agency (MSA) differed on how to pay for the program. MSA director Harold Stassen believed that it would be impossible to finance expanded assistance to Korea through reductions or elimination of other country programs of lower priority within the mutual security program. Stassen stated that the administration would have to

obtain additional congressional authorization or authority to use funds appropriated for general expenditures by the Department of Defense or the MSA.
Secretary of the Treasury George Humphrey believed that the program could be
financed from funds already requested from Congress for security programs or
from savings in aid programs from other areas. By the time the president and
the NSC discussed NSC-156/1 on July 23, 1953, a consensus had emerged to
use savings from MSA and defense expenditures anticipated by the end of
hostilities in Korea to finance the program as recommended in NSC-156/1.
Eisenhower himself pushed this idea and chided the bureaucracy to "quit dal-
lying." The president also approved a request by Secretary of State John Foster
Dulles* to inform Rhee immediately upon signature of the armistice that the
United States would initiate an assistance program as recommended by Tasca.
The program initiated by NSC-156/1 acted as an economic lifeline to the ROK
in the immediate postwar years and no doubt helped set the stage for the later
indigenous Korean economic miracle. *See also* Robertson Mission.

   Foreign Relations of the United States, 1952–1954, vol. 15: *Korea* (Washington, D.C.,
1984).

                                                              Edward C. Keefer

NSC-157/1: U.S. OBJECTIVE WITH RESPECT TO KOREA FOLLOW-
ING AN ARMISTICE (July 7, 1953)

   Drafted in the Department of State and submitted to the NSC planning board
on June 15, 1953, this paper discussed possible outcomes of the political conference mandated by the armistice agreement*. It projected two alternatives: a
Korea divided indefinitely with the Republic of Korea* tied into the U.S. military
security system or a unified, neutralized, and non-Communist Korea oriented
toward the West. State Department policy planners argued that the People's
Republic of China* and the Soviet Union might sacrifice the Democratic People's
Republic of Korea* in return for removal of U.S. bases and forces from the
Korean peninsula and suggested that a neutralized Korea would be strategically
advantageous to the United States and Japan.

   The JCS did not see how neutralization would work except to create a "military
vacuum." On June 30, the JCS formalized their response into a long rebuttal,
which argued that NSC-157 was based on faulty assumptions. The DPRK, the
JCS argued, would never accept neutralization and its own demise, while Moscow and the PRC would not observe the provisions of an agreement setting up
a unified, non-Communist, neutral Korea under Syngman Rhee*. The JCS saw
a neutralized Korea going the way of Czechoslovakia in 1948, and a Communist-
dominated Korea would pose a serious threat to Japan. The JCS also worried
that neutralization would spread to Germany, Indochina, and even Australia,
with serious consequences for U.S. security. At the NSC meeting on July 2,
1953, chairman of the JCS, General Omar N. Bradley*, reiterated these views.
He also stated that while a neutralized, unified Korea might be conceivable, he
thought it would be "bad tactics" to begin the political conference with this

proposal as an"opening gun." Acting Secretary of State Walter B. Smith* took exception, asserting that Rhee could handle the problem of Communist subversion, neutralism would not spread, and U.S. bases in South Korea were not necessary for the defense of Japan. When asked if Moscow would accept neutralization of Korea, Smith responded that the Soviet Union's sensitivity to hostile forces near its borders might induce Soviet acceptance of a non-Communist neutral Korea based on free elections.

At least on an intellectual level, the State Department's idea of a neutralized Korea appealed to Eisenhower, who believed that air power, not troops on the ground, was the real deterrent in East Asia. As approved, NSC-157/1 set as an objective of U.S. policy a unified and neutral Korea under the ROK with—and here the language was suggested by the president himself—military forces sufficient for internal security and capable of defending Korean territory short of an attack by a major power. NSC-157/1 was an example of the Eisenhower administration's tendency to be unrealistic, since there was little chance that Moscow or Peking would accept a unified Korea under Syngman Rhee—let alone the idea that Kim Il Sung* would allow himself to be sacrificed. The Geneva Conference of 1954* failed to achieve a political settlement regarding Korea, and NSC-157/1 remained on the bureaucratic shelf, unrealistic and unrealized.

Foreign Relations of the United States, 1952–1954, vol. 15: *Korea* (Washington, D.C., 1984).

Edward C. Keefer

O

OCCUPATION DIRECTIVE FOR NORTH KOREA (October 28, 1950)

CINCUNC General Douglas MacArthur* received this directive providing guidance for the occupation of North Korea more than three weeks after the start of the UN offensive across the thirty-eighth parallel*. On October 3, 1950, U.S. military planners had finished drafting a preliminary directive outlining steps for the formation of a "military government," but final approval awaited action at the United Nations. For many UN members, the government of President Syngman Rhee* emerged as a source of embarrassment as victory seemed near. Rhee's unscrupulous and dictatorial behavior had been unwelcome since the start of the war because this contradicted the idea that the UN was fighting a crusade against tyranny and aggression. As a result, international opinion ran strongly against allowing the Republic of Korea* automatically to assume control of North Korea after liberation. Conscious of this attitude, the JCS advised MacArthur on September 27 that "political questions such as the formal extension of [the ROK's] sovereignty over North Korea should await action by the United Nations to complete unification of the country." When the General Assembly passed the UN resolution of October 7, 1950*, the measure created a body to supervise the occupation of North Korea: the UN Commission for the Unification and Rehabilitation of Korea* (UNCURK).

Despite these plans, after South Korean forces crossed the parallel on September 30, Rhee immediately set about establishing governmental control in the north. In response, the JCS informed MacArthur on October 9 that he was not to recognize the ROK's authority. Three days later, the UN Interim Committee formally resolved that the UN recognize no government as having "legal and effective control" over all Korea. It asked that the UNC* assume provisional responsibility for the government and civil administration of those areas of North Korea coming under its military control "pending consideration" by the UNCURK of the ultimate disposition of these territories. MacArthur was not pleased with the Interim Committee's action, telling President Harry S. Truman* at the Wake Island Conference* that it might damage relations between the ROK and the UN. "I have been shaking in my boots," the general said, "ever since I saw the United Nations resolution which would treat [the South Koreans] exactly on the same basis as the North Koreans." Although Truman responded that the United States was "supporting the Rhee regime and propaganda can go to hell," he made no effort to gain recognition of the Rhee government's authority in North Korea.

On October 28, Washington dispatched a final occupation directive to MacArthur reflecting the desire of the UN to prevent a mere extension of the ROK's control over the north. The UNC was to occupy North Korea "in the name of and on behalf of the United Nations," and MacArthur's mission was "to facilitate public order, economic rehabilitation and the democratic mode of life . . . and to prepare the way for unification of a free and independent Korea." The twelve-point directive on civil affairs provided for an occupation in three phases. First, MacArthur would act as supreme authority, subject to the control of the UN and the United States, until he restored internal security. Second, he would retain complete power until national elections occurred throughout Korea and a united government assumed responsibility. A UN commission would furnish advice and recommendations that MacArthur would honor if they did not undermine the security of his forces. Third, all non-Korean troops would withdraw from the peninsula gradually and MacArthur would have responsibility only for such missions as might be assigned to him.

Washington's instructions called for MacArthur to dissolve the Communist government of North Korea. But the directive stated that while the ROK

has been accepted as the only lawful government in Korea, its authority over that part of the country north of the 38th parallel has not been recognized. Although you are not authorized to recognize such authority, it is desirable that in matters of national scope you consult with the government of the Republic of Korea through the United States Ambassador to facilitate eventual reunification.

MacArthur would create no central government but would "establish and maintain supervision and controls over North Korean *de facto* provincial and local government." In addition, he was to "change as little as possible the fundamental structure" in North Korea, retaining "land reform measures, nationalization and socialization of industries and other matters which have a serious impact on individuals." The directive covered war crimes trials*, relief and economic rehabilitation, the administration of justice, organizational control, and authorization to "initiate and conduct an intensive re-education and re-orientation program designed to . . . expedite the unification of Korea under a freely elected government." During November, the occupation directive for North Korea became irrelevant when Chinese military intervention* reestablished the authority of the Democratic People's Republic of Korea* north of the thirty-eighth parallel. *See also* Occupation of North Korea.

Foreign Relations of the United States, 1950, vol. 7: *Korea* (Washington, D.C., 1976); C. A. MacDonald, *Korea: The War Before Vietnam* (New York, 1986); J. F. Schnabel, *Policy and Direction* (Washington, D.C., 1972).

OCCUPATION OF NORTH KOREA (October–November 1950)

On September 30, 1950, South Korean forces crossed the thirty-eighth parallel in pursuit of forcible reunification of the peninsula. For Syngman Rhee* of the Republic of Korea*, this offensive would result in the fulfillment of his dream to rule a united Korea. However, the UN Interim Committee formally resolved on October 12 that the UN would recognize no government as having "legal and effective control" over all Korea. This reflected widespread dissatisfaction in the international organization with Rhee's unsavory and dictatorial behavior before and during the Korean War, as well as unhappiness over the circumstances surrounding implementation of the UN resolution of November 14, 1947*, and the creation of the ROK in 1948. When Rhee received word of the Interim Committee's decision, he delivered an angry protest to CINCUNC General Douglas MacArthur*. He accused the UN of wanting to revive and protect the political power of the Communists in North Korea. His government, the South Korean president declared, was "taking over the civilian administration whenever hostilities cease." MacArthur forwarded Rhee's comments to Washington. However, the Truman administration supported the Interim Committee's position in its occupation directive for North Korea*, which called for the holding of nationwide elections under UN supervision, with North Korea under military control until the formation of a new national government.

Meanwhile, Rhee's government had begun to extend the ROK's control northward in defiance of the UN and the United States. On October 10, Home Minister Cho Pyŏng-ok* announced that the National Police controlled nine towns north of the parallel, with a special force of 30,000 being recruited for occupation duty. State Department officials wanted to establish some method for supervising the administrative behavior of the South Koreans to ensure that they would "be kept under control." But the United States was overtaken by events as some 2,000 National Police crossed the parallel. In P'yŏngyang, the notorious "Tiger" Kim Chong-wŏn* was in charge of the military police, and rightist youth groups held political indoctrination sessions. Some writers claim that as part of this right-wing counterrevolution, the ROK, as a matter of official policy, sought to "hunt out and destroy Communists and collaborators." The Democratic People's Republic of Korea* later reported that Rhee's agents executed "hundreds of thousands" of North Koreans. Fearing "an international scandal of a major kind," British foreign minister Ernest Bevin* informed the United States on October 28 that it could not allow Rhee to present the UN with a fait accompli. In reply, Assistant Secretary of State Dean Rusk* confirmed that South Korean officials had committed "atrocities" and promised to have U.S. military officers attempt to control the situation.

But the Truman administration evidently was not entirely displeased with the extension of the ROK's political authority northward. For example, Washington became upset when it appeared that MacArthur was prohibiting South Koreans from participating in civil affairs matters in North Korea. On November 2, the JCS cabled MacArthur that it "is not intended that pertinent directives . . . prohibit the use of ROK administrators, police, military forces, or any other ROK asset in North Korea as long as it is clearly and publicly understood that such resources are not under control of ROK but rather are designated as . . . under CINCUNC's control." But the United States, on MacArthur's advice, did not release the occupation directive because of possible adverse effects on the battlefield. Thus, when the UNC* used South Korean officials, it seemed to advocate an extension of the ROK's authority over North Korea. Worse, these South Korean agents remained loyal to Rhee. The UN would have had trouble reversing the trend had the issue not become moot with Chinese military intervention*. As the UNC withdrew from North Korea, reimposition of Communist rule on North Korea was unpleasant. Distrustful of the loyalty of the people, the DPRK executed, imprisoned, or ostracized countless individuals in those areas that the ROK's officials had occupied. *See also* UN Commission for the Unification and Rehabilitation of Korea.

Foreign Relations of the United States, 1950, vol. 7: *Korea* (Washington, D.C., 1976); J. Halliday and B. Cumings, *Korea: The Unknown War* (New York, 1989); C. A. MacDonald, *Korea: The War Before Vietnam* (New York, 1986); J. F. Schnabel, *Policy and Direction* (Washington, D.C., 1972).

OCCUPATION OF SOUTH KOREA (July–September 1950)

For two months in 1950, the Democratic People's Republic of Korea* possessed administrative control over most of the Republic of Korea*. While the North Korean People's Army (NKPA) attempted to overrun the Pusan Perimeter* and complete the conquest of the peninsula, thousands of northern and southern Korean Communists worked to reshape the political, social, and economic structure south of the thirty-eighth parallel. The first objective was to reestablish the people's committees that the U.S. military government had forced to disband during the first two years of U.S. occupation (1945–1946). Kim Il Sung*, the premier of the DPRK, called for the restoration of the people's committees in his first radio address after the North Korean invasion of South Korea*. Throughout the period of the NKPA occupation, North Korean propaganda in the south emphasized consistently the democratic and popular nature of the committee form of government, contrasting it with what the DPRK labeled the "ruling organs of Japanese imperialism."

Undoubtedly, many South Koreans were receptive to North Korean propaganda, believing the United States had imposed a colonial state on the south and welcoming an end to the rule of President Syngman Rhee*. During the retreat southward, Rhee had ordered the execution of 50,000 political prisoners. The NKPA uncovered mass graves at Taejŏn revealing one particularly brutal atrocity. A majority of the workers and half the students in Seoul rallied behind the DPRK, many voluntarily enlisting in the NKPA. In late July, nearly fifty members of the ROK National Assembly, who had remained in Seoul after the war began, held a meeting and declared their allegiance to the DPRK. Under the leadership of Yi Sŭng-yŏp*, a Politburo member of the Korean Workers' party,

South Korean Communists exploited this popular support to form quickly a Seoul people's committee. By early July, the administration had confiscated all Japanese property, as well as that belonging to the ROK goverment, its officials, and "monopoly capitalists." The NKPA distributed surplus rice to the poor, and Communist cadres prepared to implement a system of radical land redistribution. The DPRK also released political prisoners, many of whom then assumed responsibility for administering local justice. Not surprisingly, a reign of terror followed, as those recently imprisoned gained retribution from their former oppressors, especially police and youth groups.

Elsewhere in the ROK, the reemergence of local people's committees was less spontaneous. North Korean cadres maintained firm procedural control, ensuring that the membership conformed to the DPRK's practice and discipline. Restoring the people's committees was relatively simple compared with implementing land reform in the midst of war. The DPRK portrayed South Korea's landed class as the primary enemy of its revolutionary program, which it defined as anti-feudal and anti-colonial in character. Redistribution occurred in every province outside the Pusan Perimeter. Though hasty and done in wartime conditions, it swept away class structures and power.

North Korea's occupation of South Korea ended within two weeks after the Inch'ŏn landing* as a result of the recapture of Seoul operation*. Previously the DPRK had not condoned a systematic policy of terror, but now there were large-scale massacres as law and order disappeared. There also was widespread vandalism as the NKPA apparently encouraged vagrants and children to burn buildings. When the Rhee government regained control in South Korea, there was a new round of violent and bloody retribution against those who had collaborated with North Korea. The DPRK again occupied the northern half of the ROK during the winter of 1950 and 1951, but Chinese military intervention* made this possible and the Chinese People's Volunteers Army* was in charge. This second occupation also was too brief for the implementation of well-conceived or long-range programs. *See also* Secret Ceasefire Negotiations of 1951.

Foreign Relations of the United States, 1950, vol. 7: *Korea* (Washington, D.C., 1976); J. Halliday, "The Korean War: Some Notes on Evidence and Solidarity," *Bulletin of Concerned Asian Scholars* (July-September, 1979); J. Halliday and B. Cumings, *Korea: The Unknown War* (New York, 1989); C. A. MacDonald, *Korea: The War Before Vietnam* (New York, 1986), J. W. Riley and W. Schram, *The Reds Take a City* (New Brunswick, N.J., 1951).

O'DONNELL, EMMETT, JR. (1906–1971)

General Emmett O'Donnell, Jr., was commander of the Far East Air Force (FEAF) Bomber Command in Korea from 1950 to 1951. Born in Brooklyn, New York, O'Donnell graduated from the U.S. Military Academy in 1928 and the U.S. Army Air Corps Primary Flying School in 1929. During the 1930s, "Rosy" flew air mail and coached football at the U.S. Military Academy at West Point. After spending time with the 18th Reconnaissance Group on Long Island, he became a squadron commander in 1940 with the 11th Bombardment

Group in Hawaii. On December 7, 1941, the Japanese attack on the Philippines nearly wiped out a group of bombers and other aircraft O'Donnell had secretly moved there earlier that year. After a daring escape to Australia, he commanded the 10th Air Force operations in the India-Thailand-Burma theater, flying goods "over the hump" to China. In 1943, he returned to the United States where he would supervise training of the 73d Air Wing for the bombing campaign against Japan. In November 1944, O'Donnell, now a brigadier general, led the first major air raid on Tokyo, commanding over 100 B-29s. Following World War II, he was in charge of transporting supplies to Japan during the occupation. Upon his return to Washington, D.C., in 1946, O'Donnell became director of information for the air force, campaigning for unification of the services. He then served from 1947 to 1948 as deputy director of public relations in the Office of the Secretary of the Air Force, serving on joint boards in Canada, Mexico, and Brazil.

When the Korean War began, O'Donnell had been commanding general of the 15th Air Force at March Air Force Base since 1948. He immediately received appointment as head of the FEAF Bomber Command and during the next six months was responsible for conducting bombing operations against the North Koreans in accordance with instructions from CINCUNC General Douglas MacArthur*. O'Donnell was one of the few lower-ranking officials to appear at the MacArthur Hearings*. "Everything is destroyed," he testified. With no strategic targets left in Korea, B-29s could only "blow up haystacks." While bombing the Manchurian sanctuary* might have been wise in November 1950, O'Donnell emphasized that conditions had changed because the Chinese now had the capability of offering "heavy air opposition." Implementing MacArthur's plan for victory* would be too costly and would run the risk of undermining the U.S. deterrent capability against the Soviet Union. O'Donnell served until 1959 as deputy chief of staff for U.S. Air Force personnel. After earning a fourth star, he was commanding general of the U.S. Pacific Air Forces. In 1963, O'Donnell retired, working thereafter as president of the USO and a consultant for Marriot Corporation and Martin Marietta.

Current Biography, 1948; *Military Situation in the Far East*, 5 vols. (Washington, D.C., 1951); *New York Times*, December 27, 1971; D. Rees, *Korea: The Limited War* (New York, 1964); *Who Was Who in America*, vol. 5: *1969–1973* (Chicago, 1973).

OLD BALDY, BATTLE OF
See Battle of Old Baldy

OLIVER, ROBERT T. (1909–   )
Robert Tarbell Oliver, a teacher, scholar, and communication specialist, was one of the closest American associates and most loyal friends of Syngman Rhee*, first president of the Republic of Korea*. A professor of communications at Bucknell, Syracuse, and Penn State universities and one of the leading Korean advocates in the United States, he has written dozens of articles, essays, and

books about Korea. Oliver describes his relationship with President Rhee as follows: "For a quarter of a century, while he was coming into power and then exercising it, it was my privilege to be both his personal friend and his intimate counselor on international affairs. During all that period, we exchanged ideas and sentiments freely and frequently, without reserve, concerning the problems and the personalities with which he had to deal."

Oliver first met Rhee in Washington, D.C., during World War II while Rhee was lobbying the U.S. government to support postwar independence for Korea under the Korean Provisional Government. Thereafter, until Rhee was forced from office as a result of the April 1960 student uprising, he worked closely with him, first for Korean independence and then for creating a separate, "free yet dependent" Korean government. As a top public relations specialist and enthusiastic advocate for the Korean cause, he helped Rhee before and during the Korean War. From 1945 to 1948, he often angered State Department officials when vigorously lobbying on behalf of Rhee. After the creation of the ROK, Oliver pressed the United States to increase economic and military aid to the Rhee government. He was involved, directly or indirectly, in such thorny matters as Rhee's release of North Korean POWs* in 1953, negotiations at the P'anmunjŏm truce talks*, and postwar reconstruction through foreign aid and assistance.

R. T. Oliver, *Syngman Rhee: The Man Behind the Myth* (New York, 1955); R. T. Oliver, *Syngman Rhee and American Involvement in Korea, 1942–1960* (New York, 1978).

Sung Chul Yang

OPERATION ALBANY
See UNC POW Administration

OPERATION BIG SWITCH
See Neutral Nations Repatriation Commission; POW Transfer Location Question

OPERATION BLUEHEARTS
This was General Douglas MacArthur's* plan for a counteroffensive against North Korean forces in early July 1950. Though not executed, it called for an amphibious assault on the northwest coast of Korea. MacArthur's objective, which he had envisaged far in advance of the offensive initiated by the North Koreans on July 3, 1950, was to land elements of the U.S. 1st Cavalry Division, an amphibious engineering brigade, and a marine regimental combat team somewhere on the west coast close to the cities of Inch'ŏn and Seoul. This combined force was to be charged with capturing the city of Inch'ŏn and then proceeding on to retake Seoul. Preparations for Operation Bluehearts went into effect almost immediately after the North Korean invasion of South Korea* on June 25. On July 5, Major General Edwin K. Wright's 8th Army* planning group began to devise the operational guidelines for the invasion, with D day tentatively scheduled for July 22. Meanwhile, the 1st Cavalry Division, which was in Japan,

began amphibious training along the coast of Chigasaki in preparation for a landing at Inch'ŏn.

North Korean military successes, and especially the results of the Han River operations*, prompted the scrubbing of Operation Bluehearts. The forces that were to be employed in the amphibious operations were sent to reinforce Lieutenant General Walton H. Walker's* 8th Army, which was holding on to the Pusan Perimeter*. The 1st Cavalry Division landed at P'ohang-dong on the southeast coast to search out any North Korean forces operating in the southern sector of the defensive perimeter around Pusan, but it met with little opposition. Although Operation Bluehearts had to be put aside, General MacArthur remained convinced that the only way to stop the North Korean southward advance, and to relieve the pressure on the 8th Army, was an amphibious landing on the west coast that would cut off the flow of enemy troops and supplies headed south. In September 1950, Operation Bluehearts would serve as the blueprint for Operation Chromite*, the plan for the eventual Inch'ŏn landing*.

D. Rees, *Korea: The Limited War* (New York, 1964); J. F. Schnabel, *Policy and Direction* (Washington, D.C., 1972); W. Sheldon, *Hell or High Water* (New York, 1968).

David J. Wright

OPERATION CHROMITE

Once the Pusan Perimeter* was secure, CINCUNC General Douglas MacArthur* returned to his long-held strategy, which called for an amphibious landing on the northwest coast of the Republic of Korea* first outlined in a plan code-named Operation Bluehearts*. With the guidance of the newly formed X-force planning group, a new, more detailed proposal for a massive amphibious assault on the harbor city of Inch'ŏn began to take shape. MacArthur's objective was to cut the supply lines of the North Korean People's Army (NKPA), as well as access routes to the south. He planned to achieve this by seizing Inch'ŏn and then moving the balance of this assault force east to recapture Seoul and the strategically important Kimp'o Airfield. When these immediate goals were accomplished, the forces responsible for the Seoul campaign would then turn south and pursue the retreating NKPA units. Meanwhile, Lieutenant General Walton H. Walker's* 8th Army* and accompanying ROK forces were to break out of the Taejŏn-Taegu-Pusan Perimeter and head north toward the Han River. The descending forces would act as the anvil, while the 8th Army would be the hammer smashing the remnants of the enemy caught between them.

The order of battle was planned as follows. On D day, the 5th Marine Division (portions of it formed into several battalion-strength landing teams) was responsible for landing on Red Beach (adjacent to Inch'ŏn's industrial center) and Green Beach (on the island fortress of Wolmi-do) with instructions to secure the northwest sectors of the city. The remainder of the 5th Marine Division was divided into regimental combat teams (RCTs), which were to land at Blue Beach with the objective of securing the southwest sectors of Inch'ŏn, as well as all the important roads leading to Seoul. Finally, the newly formed X Corps*, which was comprised of the 1st Marine and the 7th Infantry divisions, was given the task of recapturing Seoul.

In late August 1950, MacArthur presented his plan in Tokyo to representatives of the JCS as well as commanding officers in charge of various theater operations. Operation Chromite, however, was ill received, largely because of the dangerous shifting tides and mud flats at Inch'ŏn. Even some of the more notable line officers under his command, such as Major General Doyle O. Hickey*, balked at the riskiness of the plan. Only after a remarkable oral presentation was MacArthur able to convince Army Chief of Staff General J. Lawton Collins* and Navy Chief of Staff Admiral Forrest P. Sherman* of the urgency and importance of his proposed assault. Thereafter, MacArthur proceeded with his preparations and set D day at September 15, 1950. On August 30, he gained approval from the JCS to implement Operation Chromite. With the planning done, its validity would soon be tested with the actual Inch'ŏn landing*. *See also* Collins-Sherman Visit to Tokyo.

R. E. Appleman, *South to the Naktong, North to the Yalu* (Washington, D.C., 1961); R. F. Futrell, *The United States Air Force in Korea* (New York, 1961); H. J. Middleton, *The Compact History of the Korean War* (New York, 1965); L. Montross and N. A. Canzona, *United States Marine Operations in Korea, 1950–1953,* vol. 2: *The Inchon-Seoul Operations* (Washington, D.C., 1955).

David J. Wright

OPERATION CLAM-UP (February 10–15, 1952)

Hoping to deceive the enemy, the UNC* implemented this plan for the purpose of capturing large numbers of enemy soldiers. From February 10 to 15, 1952, there would be no patrolling, artillery fire, or air support in an area 20,000 yards from the front. Theoretically, this strategy of silence would arouse the curiosity of the Communists, making them think that the UNC had withdrawn its forces to rear areas. Ambush and capture would await the surprised enemy when he ventured forward to investigate. But the Communists were not fooled and used the respite in fighting to strengthen their defensive positions. Operation Clam-Up illustrates well how the UNC was becoming frustrated with its inability to discover effective ways of fighting the stalemated Korean War. *See also* Active Defense Strategy.

W. G. Hermes, *Truce Tent and Fighting Front* (Washington, D.C., 1966).

OPERATION COMMANDO (October 3–8, 1951)

This was the Commonwealth Division* action taken during the UNC's* establishment of the Jamestown Line. The operation was intended to increase the strength of the UN defensive line. To this end, the corps commander, Lieutenant General J. W. O'Daniel, utilized three divisions—1st Commonwealth, 1st Cavalry, and 3d Infantry—with the aim of clearing the enemy in front and inflicting heavy losses while ensuring that the capture of the high ground, which he currently occupied, would make it more difficult for him to mount a large offensive. The task assigned to the Commonwealth Division was the capture of the dominating features Maryang-san, Kowan-san, and the mass of smaller hills running to the southwest of these. This was a two-brigade operation, because the headquarters and units of the 29th British Brigade were in the process of rotation and replacement. The attack was divided into three phases. Phase 1 involved the 28th Commonwealth assault upon Kowan-san, followed by the 25th Canadian Brigade's securing its objectives the next day. This was to be followed by a general exploitation of the ground gained, the whole operation to involve an advance of between 6,000 and 8,000 yards to the new line.

Kowan-san was not secured until the morning of the second day, after fierce fighting, and the Canadians met heavy resistance in attempting to take their objectives also. Maryang-san was the scene of heavy fighting for four days before the Chinese were finally driven off it. The Canadians secured their objectives by the afternoon of the third day, and by October 9, the Commonwealth units were able to consolidate their positions. Divisional casualties were moderate, around 420, the bulk of them suffered by the 28th Brigade. The enemy lost an estimated 1,000 killed, and 100 prisoners were taken. The success of Operation Commando led to the overextension of the Commonwealth Division's position. As a result, in the fierce counterattacks in early November, the Chinese recaptured Maryang-san, which they held then in strength for the rest of the war.

C. N. Barclay, *The First Commonwealth Division* (Aldershot, 1954); R. J. O'Neill, *Australia in the Korean War 1950–53* (Canberra, 1985); G. Taylor, "The 28th British Commonwealth Brigade in the Battle of Kowan San and Maryang San," in A. Cunningham-Boothe and P. Farrar (eds.), *British Forces in the Korean War* (Halifax, 1988).

Jeffrey Grey

OPERATION COURAGEOUS (March 22–29, 1951)

After Operation Ripper* had forced the Communists to evacuate Seoul, Lieutenant General Matthew B. Ridgway*, 8th Army* commander, developed this plan to compel the enemy to withdraw farther to a position just south of the thirty-eighth parallel. The new front would extend from the confluence of the Han and the Yesŏng rivers on Korea's west coast to the town of Yang-yang on the Sea of Japan in the east. Ridgway wanted to trap the fleeing Communist troops and therefore instructed the 187th Airborne to stage a parachute drop behind enemy lines, code-named Operation Tomahawk, while the I Corps mounted a frontal ground assault on enemy positions. Lieutenant General Edward M. Almond* and the other unit commanders involved received specific instructions not to cross the thirty-eighth parallel without approval. The objective of Operation Courageous was not to seize additional territory but to inflict maximum destruction on enemy troops and supplies in accordance with Ridgway's "meat grinder" strategy*. CINCUNC General Douglas MacArthur* approved the plan without obtaining approval from Washington and apparently expected a continuation of the offensive into North Korea, informing Ridgway that the 8th Army should cross the parallel. In response to the assault, Communist forces withdrew intact and avoided Ridgway's trap, retaining control over only a small amount of land below the thirty-eighth parallel in the west. The completion of Operation Courageous made possible implementation of Operation Rugged*.

C. Blair, *The Forgotten War* (New York, 1987); J. F. Schnabel, *Policy and Direction* (Washington, D.C., 1972).

OPERATION DAUNTLESS (April 6–11, 1951)

After the success of Operation Rugged*, the U.S. I Corps, in conjunction with other 8th Army* evolutions above the thirty-eighth parallel, was charged with moving into the Iron Triangle* area to create an offensive bulge. Upon clearing the triangle of enemy concentrations, the I Corps was to advance to the Kansas-Wyoming Line*. This operation, code-named Dauntless, began April 6. CINCUNC General Douglas MacArthur* initially had hoped that the I Corps, after breaching the Iron Triangle, could advance above the Wyoming Line. By April 11, the UNC* forces reached Wyoming. Because the I Corps overextended its forces and began to experience problems with logistics and supply, MacArthur decided to have the I Corps settle down along the Wyoming Line and link up with the IX and X Corps*, already dug in on the Kansas Line. This was the last military operation that MacArthur was involved in prior to his being relieved of command and replaced by his subordinate, Lieutenant General Matthew B. Ridgway*.

C. Blair, *The Forgotten War* (New York, 1987); J. F. Schnabel, *Policy and Direction* (Washington, D.C., 1972).

David J. Wright

OPERATION EVERREADY

As the United States completed the armistice agreement* in the spring of 1953, it faced one final serious obstacle to peace: South Korean opposition to a truce arrangement. First developed in the midst of the South Korean political crisis of 1952*, Operation Everready was a plan the United States revived to ensure South Korean compliance with the truce agreement, including the possibility of establishing a military government under the UNC*. President Syngman Rhee* in fact mobilized almost all South Koreans to oppose an armistice that failed to unify Korea. Rhee made his position public that he would never accept an armistice that did not guarantee the complete withdrawal of all Chinese forces from Korea, the total disarmament of North Korea, full participation of South Korea in any postwar political conference, and the complete protection of Republic of Korea's* sovereignty. Too, Rhee demanded a unilateral U.S. commitment to defend South Korea against any future Communist aggression by concluding, before an armistice with the Communists, a mutual defense treaty between the United States and South Korea. Washington frowned at Rhee's demands but considered South Korean cooperation necessary for the implementation of an armistice.

For the worst contingency, the 8th Army* had prepared Operation Everready. It outlined separate courses of action to deal with three different ways that the

ROK might try to undermine the armistice. First, "ROK troops, while not overtly hostile, are not responsive to UN directive"; second, "ROK government and military units proceed along an independent course of action"; third, "ROK government, military units or people are hostile to UN troops." Under the first two contingencies, precautionary measures were to be taken, including disarming disloyal ROK units and restricting civilian and military movements. Under the third condition, however, the 8th Army planned to execute a military coup d'état in South Korea through a proclamation of martial law in the name of the UN involving the seizure of dissident military and civilian leaders to secure the armistice. CINCUNC General Mark W. Clark* forwarded this plan to Washington on May 22, 1953.

Civilian and military policymakers in Washington held meetings on May 29 and 30 mainly to discuss alternatives for dealing with South Korean opposition to the impending armistice. The conferees agreed to recommend to President Dwight D. Eisenhower* that the United States enter into a mutual security arrangement with the ROK, similar to the ANZUS Treaty*, provided that the Rhee government would agree to the armistice, cooperate in carrying out the armistice arrangements, and leave its forces under UN control. American policymakers, however, balked at the proposal to establish a military government in Korea in order to enforce the armistice terms. They decided that the U.S. government could not concur in that part of Operation Everready that would replace the Rhee regime with a UNC military government. President Eisenhower readily approved, and Clark received instructions in accordance with these recommendations.

CINCUNC General John E. Hull* submitted a revised plan to Washington in October 1953, enumerating several countermeasures for dealing with possible South Korean actions to undermine the armistice signed less than three months earlier. These contingencies included the 8th Army's enforcing UN countermeasures through the ROK army, relieving disloyal ROK commanders, withdrawing all logistical and air support, securing custody of dissident military and civilian leaders, and obtaining control of Korean transportation and electric power. The 8th Army commander was also authorized to recommend several measures, including a naval blockade of South Korea, blocking Korean dollar and sterling accounts, and proclaiming martial law, as he judged fit for the situation that had evolved. The United States, especially the military, was ready to take all necessary measures to secure the armistice obtained after three years of bloody fighting and tortuous negotiations.

Foreign Relations of the United States, 1952–1954, vol. 15: *Korea* (Washington, D.C., 1984).

Chang-il Ohn

OPERATION HOMECOMING
See Civilian Internee Issue

OPERATION HUDSON HARBOR
This operation was part of U.S. preparations for the possible use of nuclear weapons in Korea to break the military deadlock that developed following the

Chinese spring offensives of 1951*. Conducted in the fall of 1951, it involved simulated atomic strikes in support of UNC* ground offensives into North Korea. Operation Hudson Harbor was significant for at least three reasons. First, it provides an excellent example of how the Truman administration seriously considered employing nuclear weapons to achieve a satisfactory military outcome in the Korean War. Second, U.S. officials undoubtedly hoped that the operation would have a positive impact on the armistice negotiations. Atomic intimidation might persuade the Communists to return to the bargaining table following the truce talks suspension of August 23, 1951*. Finally, Operation Hudson Harbor set the stage for subsequent discussions about ways to end the Korean War without risking huge ground casualties or unacceptable air force attrition. In April 1953, President Dwight D. Eisenhower* approved a contingency plan— NSC-147*—providing for atomic attacks on Communist air bases and lines of communication and transportation to force acceptance of a favorable settlement at the P'anmunjŏm truce talks*.

Immediately after the North Korean invasion of South Korea*, U.S. military planners began to consider employing nuclear weapons in Korea, but the United States possessed only a limited number of bombs designed for strategic use in a global war. Early in 1951, the U.S. Air Force conducted the first tests of tactical nuclear weapons and then initiated a program to provide its fighter-bombers with delivery capability. In June, Army Chief of Staff General J. Lawton Collins* submitted for discussion a plan calling for the identification of targets and authorization for FEAF crews to begin practicing atomic attacks. An Army Operations Division memorandum supported the proposal, arguing that it might become necessary to resort to nuclear weapons if the upcoming Kaesŏng truce talks* failed. "In the event of a stalemate in Korea in which the Communist forces pit manpower against our technological advantages," the report advised, "use of the atomic bomb to increase our efficiency of killing is desirable."

Although the JCS endorsed the Collins plan, they favored employing nuclear weapons only if the 8th Army* faced extinction. After receiving the final proposal, Secretary of Defense George C. Marshall* obtained President Harry S. Truman's* approval for Operation Hudson Harbor. In September and October 1951, the FEAF, in extreme secrecy, conducted a series of practical experiments involving the dropping of dummy atomic bombs on North Korea. The results demonstrated that the ability to use tactical nuclear weapons was quite limited because timely identification of large masses of enemy troops in Korea was very difficult. But U.S. military planners refused to abandon consideration of the nuclear option. During 1952, they continued to insist on the viable delivery capability of fighter-bombers, while developing plans for the use of tactical atomic weapons in the form of artillery shells.

R. Foot, *The Wrong War* (Ithaca, N.Y., 1985); J. Halliday and B. Cumings, *Korea: The Unknown War* (New York, 1988); C. A. MacDonald, *Korea: The War Before Vietnam* (New York, 1986); J. F. Schnabel and R. J. Watson, *History of the Joint Chiefs of Staff*, vol. 3: *The Korean War* (Wilmington, 1979).

OPERATION KILLER (February 21–March 1, 1951)

This operation marked the beginning of the 8th Army's* successful counter-offensive in the Korean War following Chinese military intervention* that would restore battle lines just north of the thirty-eighth parallel and open the way to armistice negotiations. After halting and putting to rout the Communist Chinese invasion of the Republic of Korea* at the Battle of Chip'yŏng* in February 1951, Lieutenant General Matthew B. Ridgway*, the 8th Army commander, put forth a plan for an assault against Communist forces in the eastern corps sector, above the Han River line. The earlier enemy offensive left the Chinese People's Volunteers Army* (CPVA) weakened and in want of fresh supplies. Not waiting for the enemy to regroup for a new offensive, Ridgway ordered the X Corps*, under the command of Lieutenant General Edward M. Almond*, and supported by elements of the U.S. IX Corps, to "kill or destroy" the enemy in the area above the town of Hoengsŏng. Ridgway emphasized the attrition aspects of the operation (code-named Killer for that reason) to his field commanders but cautioned them not to push too far north, for the operation was not a general advance to the Yalu River.

Operation Killer got underway on February 21. Logistics and supply problems combined with bad weather to hamper the efforts of the X Corps. By the end of the month, the X Corps had pushed out the Chinese forces that had held the town of Hoengsŏng. But these troops amounted only to rear-guard units left behind to cover the retreat of the main body of the CPVA forces. In fact, Operation Killer fell far short of its objective in killing the enemy. Nevertheless, it did reestablish and strengthen the UNC* positions along the Yangp'ŏng-Hoengsŏng-Pangnim line, which had been forfeited during the last enemy offensive. Finally, it left 8th Army forces in a position to launch Operation Ripper*, a more massive and ambitious offensive operation. *See also* "Meat Grinder" Strategy.

C. Blair, *The Forgotten War* (New York, 1987); J. F. Schnabel, *Policy and Direction* (Washington, D.C., 1972).

David J. Wright

OPERATION LITTLE SWITCH (April 20–May 3, 1953)

This was the exchange of sick and wounded POWs between the UNC* and the Communists prior to the signing of the armistice agreement* in July 1953. It had been proposed by the UNC and, to the surprise of many observers, accepted by the Communists. UN authorities turned over 6,670 POWs: 5,194 North Korean People's Army (NKPA) and 1,030 Chinese People's Volunteers Army* troops, as well as 446 civilian internees. The Communists released 684 POWs: 471 Republic of Korea*, 149 U.S., 32 British, 15 Turks, and 17 miscellaneous prisoners. Some of these Communist prisoners made propaganda statements during their release, with demonstrations, chants, songs, and refusal of dusting for removal of body parasites. Many also threw away their UN-supplied uniforms and toilet articles to indicate poor treatment by their captors. UN POWs were more quietly repatriated, although the emaciated appearance of many made a vivid statement about Communist POW administration*. They were quickly transported to processing areas in the ROK. U.S. POWs were flown to Japan for rest and initial treatment and then on to the United States.

A basic principle of the UNC, one that had prolonged the war by two years, remained in effect: no POW would be repatriated against his will. That the Communists had agreed to an exchange of sick and wounded POWs without forcing the UNC to abandon the principle of voluntary repatriation* demonstrated the UNC's success in establishing this point. The agreement at the P'anmunjŏm truce talks* resulting in Operation Little Switch was a key breakthrough in the deadlocked negotiations over agenda item 4*, POW exchanges. Perhaps a re-action to the death of Joseph Stalin*, Communist acceptance of the exchange of sick and wounded POWs would set in motion progress in negotiations leading to the final armistice agreement. *See also* Truce Talks Resumption of April 26, 1953.

B. Alexander, *Korea: The First War We Lost* (New York, 1986); W. G. Hermes, *Truce Tent and Fighting Front* (Washington, D.C., 1966); United Nations, *Report of the Neutral Nations Repatriation Commission Covering the Period Ending 9 September 1954* (New York, 1954).

Stanley Sandler

OPERATION MiG

This operation was the result of U.S. efforts to obtain intelligence about the MiG, about which little was known in the West. Not only did the jet represent a challenge to UNC* air superiority in Korea, but it was also the main threat to the bombers of Strategic Air Command in the event of global war with the Soviet Union. Since the pilots never flew across the front lines or over the offshore islands under UNC control, the difficulties were formidable. The FEAF estab-lished a special guerrilla unit targeted on MiGs, which obtained some parts from crashes. In April 1951, air intelligence landed a technical team by helicopter beside a wreck, but it was quickly driven off. That same month, the U.S. Navy launched an unsuccessful search for an aircraft that had crashed in the sea near the mouth of the Yalu River. The first real breakthrough occurred on July 9, 1951, when a pilot ejected from a damaged MiG northwest of P'yŏngyang. His aircraft flew out to sea and crashed on a sandbar off the island of Sinmi-do in the Yalu Gulf, where it was exposed at low tide. Operation MiG was immediately launched to recover the wreck. The size of the task force assigned to the operation, which included two aircraft carriers and a cruiser, was an index of its importance to the United States. The MiG was lifted in two parts on July 20 and 21, 1951, under cover of a heavy shore bombardment and flown to the United States for testing. The main information gained from Operation MiG was on engine per-formance and air frame construction. Air force intelligence, however, remained anxious to capture an intact aircraft for combat evaluation. *See also* Operation Moolah.

Aerospace Studies Institute, *Guerrilla Warfare and Airpower in Korea, 1950–1953* (Alabama, 1964); D. Lankford, *I Defy* (London, 1954); E. Linklater, *A Year of Space* (London, 1954); C. A. MacDonald, *Korea: The War Before Vietnam* (London, 1986).

Callum A. MacDonald

OPERATION MOOLAH

Operation Moolah offered $100,000 and political asylum to the first pilot who landed a MiG at Kimp'o Airfield and $50,000 to each subsequent defector. Launched in April 1953, Operation Moolah had two main purposes: to wage psychological warfare against the enemy during the final stages of the P'an-munjŏm truce talks* and to acquire a MiG for combat evaluation, a goal long pursued by U.S. Air Force intelligence. According to CINCUNC General Mark W. Clark*, the idea came from the United Press correspondent in Seoul, Dick Applegate; others believe the scheme originated at the Russian Research Center at Harvard. Operation Moolah was cleared by the JCS on March 20, 1953, and approved in its final form by the Joint Psychological Warfare Committee in Tokyo on April 1. The Department of the Air Force allocated $250,000 to Operation Moolah, and in the next six weeks almost 2 million reward leaflets printed in Chinese, Korean, and Russian were dropped along the Yalu River and over North Korean airfields. The offer was also broadcast in the same three languages by the UNC*.

Clark believed that the operation forced the Communists to ground their MiGs in late April and early May 1953 while the pilots underwent loyalty checks. The FEAF was more cautious, attributing the lull to bad flying weather, though speculating that the offer might have led the Soviets to withdraw their pilots from combat. No MiG appeared, however, until after the armistice. On September 21, 1953, Lieutenant No Kŏm-sŏk of the North Korean Air Force landed a MiG-15 BIS at Kimp'o Airfield. No had heard nothing about a reward and had defected for personal reasons. President Dwight D. Eisenhower* disliked the idea of paying bribes, preferring to emphasize ideological conviction. As a result, No was persuaded to reject the money but was provided with technical education and financial support totaling the same amount by the Committee for Free Asia, a CIA front. At the same time, the offer of $50,000 to subsequent defectors was withdrawn. According to Clark, the MiG was a valuable acquisition since it was the first combat model available to the U.S. Air Force for flight testing. No also provided intelligence on Communist violations of the armistice terms. *See also* Operation MiG.

S. E. Ambrose, *Eisenhower, the President* (New York, 1984); M. W. Clark, *From the Danube to the Yalu* (London, 1954); R. F. Futrell, *The United States Air Force in Korea* (New York, 1961); C. A. MacDonald, *Korea: The War Before Vietnam* (London, 1986); D. Rees, *Korea: The Limited War* (London, 1964).

Callum A. MacDonald

OPERATION PILEDRIVER (June 1–13, 1951)

This was the UNC's* last-ditch effort to solidify its position along the Kansas-Wyoming Line* in the area known as the Iron Triangle*. The plan called for

U.S. I Corps to advance on the triangle area and take and hold as much territory as possible. From June 11 to 13, I Corps had captured and held the towns of Ch'ŏrwon and Kŭmhwa and had entered the abandoned remnants of P'yŏngyang. Because the high ground above the burned-out city of P'yŏngyang was controlled by numerically superior Chinese forces, the I Corps elements there withdrew from the town. The significance of Operation Piledriver was twofold. First, it was the last offensive of the Korean conflict, prior to the settling down of lines just north of the thirty-eighth parallel. Second, the Iron Triangle from then on would become a kind of a no-man's-land, belonging to neither side.

H. J. Middleton, *The Compact History of the Korean War* (New York, 1965); D. Rees, *Korea: The Limited War* (New York, 1964).

David J. Wright

OPERATION PUNCH (February 5–9, 1951)

This operation began on February 5, 1951, the same day that the X Corps* implemented Operation Roundup* in the area of Hongch'ŏn, above the town of Hoensŏng. However, Operation Punch was an extension of the I and IX Corps push on the Seoul area in late January, code-named Operation Thunderbolt*, and not part of the X Corps offensive. The operation consisted of a task force comprised of the U.S. 25th Division, which was augmented by heavy artillery and armored units and by tactical close-air support. The mission of this task force was to destroy all the enemy troops that had defensive positions in the Hill 440 complex just south of the city of Seoul. From February 5 to 9, Operation Punch forces pounded Hill 440. By February 9, the Communist Chinese defenders had retreated across the Han River. More than 4,200 Chinese were killed (that number only includes the battlefield count and not those casualties that were carried from the field or the wounded). The UNC* forces suffered only 70 casualties. More important, Operation Punch had cleared the way for I Corps' final assault on Seoul.

C. Blair, *The Forgotten War* (New York, 1987); D. Rees, *Korea: The Limited War* (New York, 1964).

David J. Wright

OPERATION RATKILLER (December 2, 1951–March 15, 1952)

General James A. Van Fleet*, 8th Army* commander, approved the implementation of this plan to kill or capture bandits and guerrillas operating in the Republic of Korea*. Insurgent activity behind the UNC* lines had been a constant irritant from the outset of the Korean War. This problem became more acute after the Inch'ŏn landing* trapped large numbers of the North Korean People's Army (NKPA) in the south. In November 1951, there had been an upsurge of well-coordinated raids in South Korea against rail lines and military installations. At the same time, there was a lull in fighting at the front, as the UNC was following its active defense strategy*. Therefore, Van Fleet decided that it was a good time to eliminate this potential threat to communication and supply lines before the enemy staged a new offensive.

Conducted in four stages, the ROK army was in charge of the operation, often using excessive force and brutality to destroy the guerrillas. On December 1, 1951, President Syngman Rhee* declared martial law in the southwest part of Korea, establishing a curfew and restricting the movement of civilians. General Paik Son-yup* was in charge of the first phase of the operation, which lasted until December 14. First, Task Force Paik established a perimeter around Chiri-san, about 20 miles northwest of the city of Chinju. Then the ROK 8th Division moved into the area from the north while the Capital Division advanced from the south, flushing out the insurgents in groups of 10 to 500. To prevent any escape, Paik stationed police, youth groups, and security forces around the perimeter. Phase 1 produced 1,612 dead and 1,842 captured insurgents.

Operation Ratkiller's second stage focused on the mountainous area around the city of Chŏnju in Chŏllapukdo and lasted from December 19 to January 4, 1952. This time, South Korean forces trapped around 8,000 guerrillas and bandits, killing roughly half of them. During phase 3, with the 8th Division back at the front, the Capital Division returned to the Chiri-san area and by the end of January had killed or captured 19,000 more. Continuing until March 15, 1952, the last stage involved an attempt to eliminate the final remnants of the insurgency. The extent of Operation Ratkiller's success remains in doubt. There is evidence that major guerrilla activity in the south continued, suggesting the persistence of widespread opposition to Rhee's government and support for Communist rule in the ROK. *See also* Occupation of South Korea.

J. Halliday and B. Cumings, *Korea: The Unknown War* (New York, 1989); W. G. Hermes, *Truce Tent and Fighting Front* (Washington, D.C., 1966); M. B. Ridgway, *The Korean War* (Garden City, N.Y., 1967).

OPERATION RIPPER (March 7–15, 1951)

This was an offensive operation utilizing the IX and X Corps* with the objective of forming a bulge just east of the city of Seoul along what was known as Line Idaho. Line Idaho ran down from the town of Ch'unch'ŏn to the Han River just a few miles east of Seoul. As the commander of the 8th Army*, Lieutenant General Matthew B. Ridgway's* strategy was for the I Corps, which had retaken Kimp'o Airfield and Inch'ŏn, to remain in its defensive positions just west and south of Seoul and wait for the final assault on the capital of the Republic of Korea*. Meanwhile, the X and IX Corps was to advance to Line Idaho and continue its westward sweep until Seoul was completely surrounded by the three U.S. Army corps. With this objective accomplished, the 8th Army could retake the southern capital at its own pace, thus minimizing the prospect of sustaining an unnecessary number of UN casualties. By March 14, Seoul was once again in the hands of the UNC*. On March 15, the town of Hongch'ŏn was captured by elements of the X Corps. Finally, UNC forces comprised of the U.S. 1st Cavalry Division and the U.S. 187th Airborne RCT took the town of Ch'unch'ŏn on March 21. That final victory put the U.S. 8th Army on an offensive-defensive line, just a few miles south of the thirty-eighth parallel.

R. F. Futrell, *The United States Air Force in Korea* (New York, 1961); H. J. Middleton, *The Compact History of the Korean War* (New York, 1965); D. Rees, *Korea: The Limited War* (New York, 1964).

David J. Wright

OPERATION ROUNDUP (February 5–11, 1951)

This was a limited offensive in central South Korea following the successful implementation of Operation Thunderbolt* that had left the 8th Army* in control of the Han River on its left flank. Its primary objective was to advance the central front northward in preparation for a coordinated assault on Seoul, compelling the Communists to evacuate the capital of the Republic of Korea*. Even if it failed, the advance would disrupt any enemy plans for an offensive while revealing the disposition and intentions of the Communists. Prior to undertaking Operation Roundup, Lieutenant General Matthew B. Ridgway* moved troops from the western sector to reinforce the X Corps* and the ROK's III Corps in the center of the peninsula. Beginning on February 5, the UNC* forces advanced northward from Hoengsŏng toward Hongch'ŏn for several days, but resistance grew as they came closer to the main enemy positions. Meanwhile, one North Korean and two Chinese divisions had moved from Seoul to halt the advance. Intelligence reports warned that a counterattack was possible but Lieutenant General Edward M. Almond*, the X Corps commander, pressed forward. On the night of February 11, Communist forces counterattacked in force, breaking through to set up roadblocks behind UN lines. The X Corps was able to retreat to Wŏnju, but the ROK's 8th Infantry suffered annihilation, losing 7,500 men and all its equipment. Ridgway ordered the establishment of defensive positions to halt the retreat, setting the stage for the Battle of Chip'yŏng*.

C. Blair, *The Forgotten War* (New York, 1987); D. Rees, *Korea: The Limited War* (New York, 1964); J. F. Schnabel, *Policy and Direction* (Washington, D.C., 1972).

OPERATION RUGGED (April 3–6, 1951)

This was the operational designation for the 8th Army's* advance to what would later become the Kansas-Wyoming Line* above the thirty-eighth parallel. According to CINCUNC General Douglas MacArthur's* general orders, the U.S. 187th Airborne RCT, 1st Cavalry Division, and 3d, 24th, and 25th divisions were to advance from positions between Munsan and Ch'unch'ŏn north across the thirty-eighth parallel. These troops, accompanied by other UNC* forces attached to the U.S. IX Corps, began to advance slowly northward on April 3. Three days later, these forces had crossed the thirty-eighth parallel and, in accordance with their operational orders, had dug in along defensive Line Kansas.

C. Blair, *The Forgotten War* (New York, 1987); J. F. Schnabel, *Policy and Direction* (Washington, D.C., 1972).

David J. Wright

OPERATION SCATTER

In response to a Communist proposal of April 2, 1952, at the P'anmunjŏm truce talks*, CINCUNC General Matthew B. Ridgway* asked the JCS for authority to begin screening the prisoners held by the UNC*. Permission was received on April 3 to start the process at once, and two days later, Ridgway ordered General James A. Van Fleet*, the 8th Army* commander, to begin the screening under a plan code-named Operation Scatter. The plan was designed to determine the actual number of prisoners available for repatriation and to secure the maximum number of prisoners to be returned. Every prisoner was asked to ponder his own future and the fate of his family before reaching a final decision. Each prisoner was required to carry all his belongings with him so that he would not need to return to his former camps should he decide not to return.

On April 8, 1952, the UNC began the screening and separation of the non-repatriates from those who desired to be returned, an operation that proceeded without much difficulty. But there were seven compounds with over 37,000 determined North Korean Communists who did not allow the UN teams to interview and screen them, causing the UNC automatically to put the prisoners in these compounds into the list of the repatriates. The result of the first three days of screening showed that 40,000 of the 132,000 prisoners interviewed had declared that they would resist repatriation. By April 15, 1952, the screening was complete. Only about 70,000 of the over 170,000 military and civilian prisoners in the UNC hands had indicated their desire to return to the Communist side. This figure was much lower than the UNC's estimate of 116,000 previously presented at the P'anmunjŏm at the insistence of the Communists. Since he realized that the Communists would challenge the accuracy of these figures, Ridgway proposed to permit either an international neutral body or Red Cross teams to rescreen all of the non-repatriates if the Communists so desired.

As was expected, the Communists reacted vehemently against such a low estimate. At the meeting of the staff officers on April 19, the UNC representative informed his Chinese counterpart that 7,200 civilian internees, 3,800 South Korean prisoners, 52,900 North Korean, and 5,100 Chinese—a total of 70,000—would be available for repatriation. The Communists were shocked and asked for an immediate recess. On the following day, the Communists mounted a full-scale assault on the UN, claiming that "you flagrantly repudiated what you said before," and refused to authorize a rescreening of POWs* by neutral or Red Cross teams. Rather than breaking the deadlock over agenda item 4*, Operation Scatter had hardened the stalemate. The result of the process was detrimental to the Communists in their propaganda campaign and led to the Communist prisoners' instigating more acts of violence, climaxing in the Kŏje-do POW uprising* in May 1952. *See also* UN POW Administration.

M. W. Clark, *From the Danube to the Yalu* (New York, 1954); W. G. Hermes, *Truce Tent and Fighting Front* (Washington, D.C., 1966).

Chang-il Ohn

OPERATION SHOWDOWN (October 13–November 8, 1952)

This was a limited offensive evolution utilizing 2 battalions from the U.S. IX Corps, 1 Republic of Korea* division, 16 artillery battalions, and 200 fighter-bomber sorties. The objective was to assault and capture the hilly country just northeast of Kŭmhwa in the Iron Triangle*. General James A. Van Fleet*, the 8th Army* commander, believed that in the absence of this offensive operation, casualties would be greater if his forces remained in a defensive posture. Beginning five days after the P'anmunjŏm truce talks* suspension of October 8, 1952*, Operation Showdown also sought to send a message to the enemy that failure to reach an agreement on agenda item 4*, POW repatriation, would be costly on the battlefield. Communist forces reacted violently to the UNC's* advance, inflicting 9,000 casualties on the U.S. and ROK units in the heaviest fighting since late 1951. Achieving minor gains, Operation Showdown underscored the futility of such limited ground assaults on enemy positions, causing CINCUNC General Mark W. Clark* to revive the air pressure strategy in the spring of 1953 as a way to break the deadlock at P'anmunjŏm. *See also* Battle of Triangle Hill.

D. M. Condit, *History of the Office of Secretary of Defense,* vol. 2: *The Test of War, 1950–1953* (Washington, D.C., 1988); R. F. Futrell, *The United States Air Force in Korea* (New York, 1961); J. F. Schnabel and R. J. Watson, *History of the Joint Chiefs of Staff,* vol. 3: *The Korean War* (Wilmington, 1979).

OPERATION SMACK (January 25, 1953)
This was a failed U.S. 7th Infantry Division experiment in air-tank-artillery offensive coordination that produced extremely negative repercussions in the United States. The operation was organized to take the bothersome enemy-held Spud Hill, located in the west-central segment of the UNC* line. An unusually large number of high-ranking U.S. Army and U.S. Air Force officers and press reporters had been invited, and the division had thoughtfully provided a six-page, three-color informational brochure for their convenience, containing the word *scenario,* a regrettable choice, on the title page.

For a week before D day, the hill had been bombarded by air strikes and artillery. But from the start, things began to go wrong for this publicized operation. The FEAF's jets and Marine Corps prop-driven fighter-bombers missed their carefully prearranged targets. The first infantry assault was blocked and the troops trapped in a defile. Flamethrowers and automatic weapons jammed. All of the leaders of the three-platoon were wounded, and the troops were called off the hill well before the end of D day.

For a prodigal expenditure of 224,000 pounds of bombs on the first day alone, and over 12,000 rounds of 105mm and 155mm ammunition, 10,000 rounds of 40mm and 50-calibre ammunition, 650 grenades, and 2,000 rounds of 90mm ammunition fired from fifteen tanks, the 7th Division could claim a mere sixty-five enemy casualties. For a far less prodigal expenditure, and, of course, no air power whatsoever, the enemy had inflicted seventy-seven U.S. casualties. Operation Smack might well have faded into the realm of forgotten fiascos were it not for one enterprising reporter, recently arrived in Korea, who had not been in on the detailed pre-briefing. He wrote home that U.S. soldiers had died in a "demonstration" for the brass. While this was undoubtedly an exaggerated interpretation, there was indeed something of Madison Avenue about this over-planned, seemingly bloodless operation, apparently more suited to an advertising campaign for, say, the "all-new" 1953 Studebaker, than for a battle in which men were mutilated and killed. *See also* Army–Air Force Close Support Controversy.

W. G. Hermes, *Truce Tent and Fighting Front* (Washington, D.C., 1966).

Stanley Sandler

OPERATION STRANGLE

Operation Strangle was launched against the North Korean road network in June 1951 and was extended to the railway system in August to maintain military pressure on the Communists during the Kaesŏng truce talks* and to prevent them from building up sufficient supplies for a major new offensive. Some FEAF officers went even further, predicting that interdiction would isolate the battlefield and force the enemy to withdraw northward. In fact, the campaign failed in both respects. The FEAF planners underestimated the ability of the enemy to repair bomb damage and to move supplies, particularly by night, despite total UN air control. The logistics requirements of Communist divisions were low, and since Operation Strangle was not coordinated with a UN ground offensive, the enemy could dictate the rate at which he used up his available supplies. As a naval study emphasized, at no time were Communist military operations limited by logistic considerations.

Almost 100 percent of the carrier effort and 70 percent of air force operations were devoted to attacks on enemy lines of communication. The interdiction campaign was also supported by naval bombardment and commando raids on coastal targets. Operation Strangle was able to impose attrition on the enemy by destroying supplies, trucks, and rolling stock but only at the expense of valuable pilots and aircraft. The Communists responded to the campaign by improving the flak defenses around interdiction targets. By February 1952, there were 398 heavy anti-aircraft guns in North Korea and over 1,000 automatic weapons, most of them concentrated along the lines of communication. The FEAF lost 343 aircraft during Operation Strangle and 290 damaged, while only 131 replacements were received, a toll considered unacceptable. Moreover, the strain of daily interdiction raids against heavily defended targets with no apparent results affected the morale of pilots. By the spring of 1952, the campaign had reached stalemate, and the FEAF, embarrassed by the results, was looking for new and more decisive ways of employing air power. *See also* Air Pressure Strategy; Operation Hudson Harbor; Rashin Bombing Controversy.

M. W. Cagle and F. A. Manson, *The Sea War in Korea* (New York, 1980); R. F. Futrell, *The United States Air Force in Korea* (New York, 1961); W. G. Hermes, *Truce Tent and Fighting Front* (Washington, D.C., 1966).

Callum A. MacDonald

OPERATION TAILBOARD

See X (Tenth) Corps; Wŏnsan Landing

OPERATION THUNDERBOLT (January 25–February 1, 1951)

This was the operational prelude to the recapture of Seoul, the capital of the Republic of Korea*, for the fourth time since the initial commitment of UN forces in Korea. Early in January, the 8th Army* commander, Lieutenant General Matthew B. Ridgway*, ordered a large-scale reconnaissance operation, Operation Wolfhound*, to probe the Communist Chinese forces' strengths along the Suwŏn-Osan highway. These forces, predominantly comprised of elements of the U.S. I Corps, met with stiff enemy resistance at Suwŏn. Ridgway, fearing that the troops might be cut off and destroyed by the numerically superior Communist Chinese forces, withdrew UNC* forces to a defensive position just south of Osan. However, the Communist Chinese did not pursue and instead moved east into the hills around the Yŏju-Wŏnju area and dug in. This led Ridgway to believe that the Chinese were not strong enough, in numbers and materiel, to launch a major attack on UNC lines. In late January, Ridgway began to consider taking a calculated risk, devising a plan for a new offensive against Chinese defensive lines along the Seoul-Chip'yŏng-Hoengsŏng axis. On January 23, 1951, he constituted Operation Thunderbolt.

The plan for Thunderbolt called for the I, IX, and X Corps* to advance northward abreast of each other along the Han River. The I Corps had the responsibility of recapturing the port of Inch'ŏn and the Kimp'o Airfield, west of Seoul. On the eastern flank, the X Corps, commanded by Lieutenant General Edward M. Almond*, was ordered to advance on the town of Hoengsŏng and the surrounding area, via the town of Wŏnju. The center corps sector was the responsibility of the IX Corps. The IX Corps was charged with advancing northward along the Ich'ŏn-Yŏju-Wŏnju axis to attack enemy positions in the Chip'yŏng area, southeast of Seoul. IX Corps had the added responsibility of lending support to the efforts of the two flanking corps because it had elements on both sides of the Han River.

Operation Thunderbolt began on January 25. Two days later, CINCUNC General Douglas MacArthur's* seventy-first birthday, the I Corps captured the town of Suwŏn, 30 miles south of Seoul. Upon receiving the news, General MacArthur exclaimed that Ridgway had given him the best birthday gift in the seventy years of his life. By February 1, the I Corps had realized its objectives of recapturing Inch'ŏn and Kimp'o Airfield and set up a defensive line 6 miles south and west of the southern capital. On February 2, after utterly destroying the town of Wŏnju, the X Corps captured the town of Hoengsŏng. Meanwhile, the IX Corps was tied down fighting the stubbornly entrenched Chinese forces in the hills surrounding the Chip'yŏng area. To relieve the pressure on Seoul-Chip'yŏng sectors, while hoping to divert to the east as many of the enemy as possible, Ridgway on February 5 ordered the X Corps to make a limited offensive, code-named Operation Roundup*, on the Hongch'ŏn area, above the town of Hoengsŏng. *See also* Battles of Wŏnju.

C. Blair, *The Forgotten War* (New York, 1987); J. F. Schnabel, *Policy and Direction* (Washington, D.C., 1972).

Richard Dean Burns

OPERATION TOUCHDOWN
See Battle of Heartbreak Ridge

OPERATION WOLFHOUND (January 15–25, 1951)

In early January, the 8th Army* had received intelligence reports indicating that North Korean and Chinese Communist forces were building up along the southern banks of the Han River just below the city of Seoul. What was not known by the army staff and Lieutenant General Matthew B. Ridgway*, the commander, through these reports was precisely where the enemy lines were and in what concentrations. By mid-January, the 8th Army had advanced northward, up the Osan-Seoul highway, to within miles of the town of Suwŏn, just 30 miles south of the southern capital. On January 14, Ridgway, before deciding whether to withdraw 8th Army elements in the western (I Corps) sector to defensive positions at Osan or to advance farther north toward Seoul, ordered a limited reconnaissance offensive on the Suwŏn area. The operation was code-named after the Wolfhound Regiment of the U.S. 27th Infantry Division, which spearheaded the operation. The objectives of Operation Wolfhound were for the armor-supported 27th Infantry to advance on the town of Suwŏn and kill as many of the enemy's numbers as possible and to probe the enemy's strengths and weaknesses.

Operation Wolfhound got underway on January 16 and continued to the end of the month. As it progressed northward, the UNC* forces met with no real opposition until they had reached Suwŏn. At Suwŏn, Operation Wolfhound forces engaged Communist units and inflicted great damage on them without sustaining any serious casualties of their own. It was at this point that Ridgway wanted the 27th Division and its support to withdraw to more defensible positions south of Suwŏn while leaving a covering force to protect its retreat. Before the withdrawal began, the Communist forces withdrew to positions just south of Seoul. As Operation Wolfhound was in progress, a general relaxing of enemy pressure could be felt in all 8th Army corps sectors. The success of Operation Wolfhound led Ridgway to believe that the Communist forces were not strong enough yet to force a general offensive against UNC lines. Not waiting for a new enemy counterattack before acting, Ridgway ordered a general three corps, 8th Army offensive on January 25 code-named Operation Thunderbolt*.

C. Blair, *The Forgotten War* (New York, 1987); D. Rees, *Korea: The Limited War* (New York, 1964); J. F. Schnabel, *Policy and Direction* (Washington, D.C., 1972).

Richard Dean Burns

OSAN, BATTLE OF
See Battle of Osan

P

PACE, FRANK (1912–1988)

Frank Pace, Jr., served as secretary of the army from April 1950 to January 1953. Born in Little Rock, Arkansas, he graduated from Princeton University in 1933 and earned an LL.D. from Harvard Law School in 1936. Pace returned to Little Rock and worked in his father's law practice until entering the U.S. Army Air Corps as a second lieutenant during World War II. Following the war, he held several positions in the executive branch of the federal government before being appointed assistant director of the Bureau of the Budget in 1948 and then budget director in 1949. Pace's administrative skill and his fiscal conservatism impressed President Harry S. Truman,* who as a senator had chaired an oversight committee on military spending during World War II. In 1950, Pace was Truman's choice to help Secretary of Defense Louis A. Johnson* keep the lid on the defense budget.

On the job for barely two months before the North Korean invasion of South Korea*, Pace had little input into the decisions made during the early weeks of the crisis, although he voiced opposition to committing ground troops at the first Blair House meeting*. He later admitted that he "wasn't a military expert at all," and his influence on policymaking during the war appears to have been slight. Pace attended the Wake Island Conference* and backed the president's later decision not to fight for Korean unification after Chinese military intervention*.

Under Pace, the army grappled with manpower problems created by the requirements of mobilization, the need to maintain reserves in the event of a crisis elsewhere, and the perceived inequities of the selective service system. In 1951, Pace implemented a rotation of troops system* in which soldiers from reserve and National Guard units accumulated points for each month they served in Korea (four per month on the front lines, three for each month in the combat zone, and two for duty elsewhere in Korea). Soldiers with thirty-six points were rotated out of Korea and into units at home. Although the system spread the burden of the war among the eligible male population while building up a sizable pool of combat-trained reserves, it also undermined unit cohesion and hindered the development of an esprit de corps among the divisions in Korea. In January 1953, Pace resigned as army secretary to make way for the incoming Eisenhower administration. He became the director and then chief executive officer of General Dynamics, a major defense contractor.

C. Blair, *The Forgotten War* (New York, 1987); *Current Biography, 1950*; F. Pace, Jr., oral history interview, Harry S. Truman Library, Independence, Missouri; R. F. Weigley, *History of the United States Army* (New York, 1967).

Marc Gallicchio

PACIFIC PACT

Influenced by the negotiation of the North Atlantic Treaty early in 1949, a number of Asian and Pacific leaders proposed a military alliance to complement the one being formed in Europe. Prime Minister Joseph Chifley of Australia and Presidents Elpidio Quirino of the Philippines, Chiang Kai-shek* of the Republic of China*, and Syngman Rhee* of the Republic of Korea* all endorsed a Pacific Pact, though there was great variation in what each hoped to achieve thereby. Chifley and later Australian leaders wanted not only military cooperation in the Pacific but a vehicle that would link them to NATO planning. Quirino was in greater need of U.S. military assistance than an additional security guarantee. Chiang hoped that a multilateral Pacific linkage might somehow serve as an avenue to increased U.S. support of his crumbling regime on Taiwan.

For Syngman Rhee, the Pacific Pact was an idea that might offset the U.S. military withdrawal from Korea*, scheduled to be completed before July 1949. In statements the previous May, Rhee indicated that if his government could not get a bilateral U.S.-ROK mutual defense arrangement, it would like some form of a multilateral one, possibly a Pacific Pact similar to the Atlantic Pact. Subsequent developments dampened his enthusiasm, however. Only two days after one of Rhee's statements, Secretary of State Dean G. Acheson* stated categorically that a Pacific Pact was not "in the stage of any official consideration." When Chiang visited Quirino early in July and the two issued a communiqué endorsing a "Pacific Union," Washington was stonily hostile. Finally, during Chiang-Rhee discussions at Chinhae, Korea, in August, the Koreans, who wanted to talk about a Pacific Pact, were put off by Chinese Nationalist proposals for Korean base rights. Rhee wanted no involvement in the Chinese Civil War. Although he and Chiang endorsed the Pacific Pact concept in a joint communiqué, Rhee simultaneously assured the U.S. embassy that he would have nothing to do with a narrow Philippine-Kuomintang-Korea grouping.

This assurance was satisfactory to Washington, for around the time of the Chinhae meeting, the U.S. position on Pacific groupings entered a new phase. The United States let it be known that it would welcome moves toward Asian economic and political cooperation provided Washington would not have to take the lead, a stance embodied in policy paper NSC 48/2 approved by President Harry S. Truman* in December 1949. From time to time in 1950 and 1951, Rhee and other ROK officials brought up the Pacific Pact question with U.S.

representatives, but Rhee no longer mounted a public campaign. The North Korean invasion of South Korea* in June 1950 made the original ROK motives for desiring a Pacific Pact moot. When the United States floated a Pacific Pact proposal in January 1951 as a tentative solution to the security side of the Japanese Peace Treaty* negotiations, both Rhee and Washington understood from the outset that such a grouping would not involve the ROK.

   Foreign Relations of the United States, 1949, vol. 7: *The Far East and Australasia*, pt. 2 (Washington, D.C., 1976), *1950*, vol. 7: *Korea* (Washington, D.C., 1976), *1951*, vol. 6: *East Asia and the Pacific* (Washington, D.C., 1977), and vol. 7: *Korea and China* (Washington, D.C., 1983); D. W. Mabon, "Elusive Agreements: The Pacific Pact Proposals of 1949–1951," *Pacific Historical Review* (May 1988).

David W. Mabon

PACKAGE PROPOSAL (April 28, 1952)

   The UNC* delegation at the P'anmunjŏm truce talks* presented this proposal to settle the three still-unresolved issues in the armistice negotiations. Under the terms of this package proposal, the UN would place no restrictions on the rehabilitation of airfields in North Korea, both sides would return only POWs who did not object to repatriation, and the Soviet Union would not be a member of the neutral nations supervisory body. Instead the neutral nations would be Switzerland, Sweden, Poland, and Czechoslovakia. The lack of airfields restriction was a concession to the North Koreans and Chinese, but the criteria for return of POWs and the elimination of the Soviet Union as a member of the supervisory body clearly upheld previous U.S. positions at P'anmunjŏm. This inequity alone might have doomed the package proposal, but the POW issue proved an intractable, added complication. UN negotiators at P'anmunjŏm had given their Chinese and North Korean counterparts preliminary indications that approximately 116,000 of the 132,000 POWs the UNC held would want to return to China or North Korea. After screening the POWs, the UNC discovered that only 70,000 prisoners wished to return. When informed of this new figure, the Communist negotiators complained of a double cross.

   CINCUNC General Matthew B. Ridgway* had unsuccessfully warned his superiors in Washington that the two-for-one bias of the package proposal would be a mistake and had suggested that the issue of Soviet representation on the Neutral Nations Supervisory Commission* should be settled before delivery of the proposal. Yet Ridgway was unwilling to accept the Soviet Union as a member of a supervisory body, causing many officials in Washington to ponder just how the issue could be settled in advance. Ridgway also wanted to present the package proposal as an ultimatum, with the clear implication that Communist rejection would result in increased military pressure against them. While most of President Harry S. Truman's* key advisers favored a package presentation, none wanted it presented as an ultimatum.

   When the UNC negotiators presented the proposal in executive session, the Communists rejected it summarily without explanation. Days later when the Communists finally responded in detail to the package proposal, they accepted the non-restrictions on airfield rehabilitation and elimination of the Soviet Union as a potential neutral but insisted on return of all POWs without exception. While the failure of the package proposal was a disappointment, the Truman administration could at least claim a tactical advantage from the Communist rejection. Most important, the proposal reduced the issues separating the two sides in Korea to a single one—agenda item 4*, repatriation of POWs—clearing the way for eventual resolution of the most difficult confrontation of the truce talks. *See also* Airfield Rehabilitation Controversy.

Foreign Relations of the United States, 1952–1954, vol. 15: *Korea* (Washington, D.C., 1984); W. G. Hermes, *Truce Tent and Fighting Front* (Washington, D.C., 1966); B. I. Kaufman, *The Korean War* (Philadelphia, 1986).

Edward C. Keefer

PADILLA NERVO, LUIS (1898–   )

Luis Padilla Nervo of Mexico was elected president of the Sixth General Assembly of the UN in late 1951. Padilla Nervo, a former poet, professor, and labor mediator, was a veteran diplomat, who had served in the UN since 1945. Latin Americans had wanted to nominate him for the post of secretary-general but were confidentially informed by U.S. representatives that the United States would veto his candidacy. The United States wanted Trygve Lie* to be reelected secretary-general in appreciation for Lie's support for UN actions in Korea. As president, Padilla Nervo adopted a neutral position on cold war issues and worked to achieve a settlement of the Korean conflict. He served as a link between the U.S. and the Asian-Arab delegations, who proposed various formulas to resolve the outstanding Korean issues. In particular, Padilla Nervo urged a resolution of agenda item 4*, POW repatriation, suggesting prisoners be given temporary asylum in neutral countries. During late 1952, President-elect Adolfo Ruiz Cortines appointed Padilla Nervo foreign minister of Mexico. *See also* Arab-Asian Peace Initiatives; Mexican POW Settlement Proposal.

J. A. Houston, *Latin America in the United Nations* (New York, 1956); L. Padilla Nervo, *Discursos y declaraciones ante la organización de las Naciones Unidas, 1945–1958* (Mexico City, 1958).

Stephen G. Rabe

PAEK SŎNG-UK (1897–1981)

Republic of Korea* home minister Paek Sŏng-uk was born in Seoul and educated at Buddhist Central School, which would develop into Tong'guk University. After joining the March First Movement* of 1919, he exiled to Shanghai, China, and participated in the Korean independence movement there, through which he met Syngman Rhee*. Soon Paek went to France and to Germany, earning a doctorate in Buddhism at the University of Würzburg in 1925. After returning home, he settled down at a temple at the Kŭmgang mountain for ten years. Following liberation in 1945, Paek was reunited with Rhee, who had just returned home, and encouraged his political cause. When Rhee was in serious conflict with the U.S. occupation commander, Lieutenant General John R.

Hodge*, he strongly supported Rhee, declaring that only Rhee could be president of a future government in southern Korea.

By February 1950, Rhee had become president of the ROK and consulted Paek on the prospects for a parliamentary system, which the opposition forces in the National Assembly had proposed. Paek voiced strong opposition. Rhee immediately appointed him home minister, thereby giving him control over the central and local governmental employees, as well as the police. Paek then organized and directed the anti-parliamentary system campaign throughout the nation, while Rhee threatened to postpone the legislative elections scheduled for May 1950. This campaign may have contributed to the defeat of the proposed constitutional amendment calling for a parliamentary system in the National Assembly. However, the United States threatened to withhold economic and military aid if the elections were not held on schedule, forcing the acceptance of a compromise and thereby ending the crisis.

When the Korean War broke out, he was the only cabinet member who did not leave his office until the government as a whole officially left Seoul. One month later, he was fired and replaced by Cho Pyŏng-ok*. According to Harold J. Noble*, the U.S. embassy's first secretary at the start of the Korean War, Paek was "a combination of fatalist and military pessimist, who is said to have made most of his decisions from the early morning horoscopes cast especially for him by his mistress of younger days." Noble recalled that Paek had "a gloomy effect" on Rhee the day the war began, causing the ROK's president "to ask for Paek's resignation because of his dangerous defeatism." In 1952, he ran for vice-president unsuccessfully. From 1953 until 1961, he was president of Tong'guk University. After retiring from the university, he spent his last years as a private lecturer on Buddhism.

H. J. Noble, *Embassy at War* (Seattle, 1975); personnel records, Tong'guk University, Seoul, Korea.

Hakjoon Kim

PAIK SON-YUP (PAEK SON-YŎP; 1920–   )

Paik Son-yup was commanding officer of the Republic of Korea's* 1st Division, one of the four divisions defending the thirty-eighth parallel when the Korean War broke out. He graduated from the Manchurian Military Academy and served as a junior officer in the Japanese Manchurian army before the liberation of Korea. Paik worked briefly for the staunch anti-Japanese nationalist leader Cho Man-sik as his personal secretary after the liberation of Korea in 1945 until Cho was put under house arrest by the Soviet occupation authorities. After the North Korean invasion of South Korea*, he put up a good fight and defended his positions for four days against overwhelming odds at the beginning of the war. Apart from vast inferiority in equipment and number of soldiers, half of his troops were on weekend leave. Paik himself had been away from his post for ten days attending a three-month course of high-level military education. Only after he ran out of ammunition and learned that the North Korean People's

Army (NKPA) had taken Seoul early on the morning of June 28, 1950, along with the destruction of the Han River bridge, did he retreat south of the river.

Through his high-spirited wartime leadership, Paik left behind a number of legendary anecdotes. Once at a critical moment during the battle to defend the Pusan Perimeter*, he personally led a charge at the head of a battalion to retake a position occupied by NKPA soldiers, ordering his soldiers to shoot him if he himself retreated. Better known is the race toward P'yŏngyang between the ROK 1st Division he still commanded and the U.S. 1st Cavalry Division. Paik won, ultimately entering the capital of the Democratic People's Republic of Korea* on October 19. Between December 1951 and April 1952, he was the commander of Task Force Paik during Operation Ratkiller*, which dealt a crushing blow to the Communist guerrillas in the south.

General James A. Van Fleet*, the 8th Army* commander, considered Paik the best fighting general of the ROK, recommending him to President Syngman Rhee* for the post of chief of staff in the summer of 1952. He represented the South Korean side in the military armistice talks too. Paik was the chief of staff twice from 1952 to 1954 and again from 1957 to 1959. In 1953, he was made the first general of the ROK army at the age of 33. Paik became chairman of the ROK joint chiefs of staff in 1959 but resigned from the post and retired from active service the next year in the aftermath of the "purification campaign," a rebellious action taken by a group of lieutenant colonels to purge the army of "corrupt" elements. Since then, he has filled various high posts, including ambassadorships to Taiwan, France, and Canada and president of Korea General Chemical Corporation.

Chung Il Kwon, *Chŏnjaeng kwa Hyuchon* (Seoul, 1986); S. Kim, *Politics of Military Revolution in Korea* (Chapel Hill, 1971); Kukbang-bu chŏnsa p'yŏnch'an wiwŏn-hoe, *Han'guk Chŏnjaeng P'yŏngyang Tal Hwan Changch'ŏn* (Seoul, 1986); Paik Son-yup, "Kun Kwa Na," *Kyŏng Hyang Sinmun*, June 24, 1988.

J. Y. Ra

PAIK TU CHIN (PAEK TU-JIN; 1908–   )

Paik Tu Chin was finance minister and prime minister of the Republic of Korea* during the Korean War. As a technocrat on economic matters, he held the trust of President Syngman Rhee* for an unusually long period of time and frequently played the role of mediator in the strained relationship between Rhee and the United States. The wartime reconstruction measures that he worked out with the United States laid the foundation for the future economic growth of the ROK. Born at Shinch'ŏn, Hwanghae province (now in the Democratic People's Republic of Korea*), Paik grew up in Seoul. Upon graduation from the Tokyo College of Commerce in Japan in 1934, he joined the Bank of Korea in Seoul and worked there until January 1949, when he became the director of the foreign aid management agency. In 1950, after the outbreak of the Korean War, he became the president of the Korean Industrial Bank. In March 1951, he was appointed finance minister, thus becoming the chief economic adviser to Rhee during the remainder of the Korean War.

When Paik became the finance minister, Korea's economic condition was in shambles, the most serious problem being runaway inflation. To counter the hyperinflation, Paik employed strong measures, including the forceful collection of taxes and the drastic reduction of non-military expenditures. But both Rhee and Paik believed that the chief cause of the inflation was the advance of Korean currency, won, made available to the UNC* for maintenance costs in Korea, and they demanded repayment. This led to the suspense account controversy*. Paik later negotiated and signed with Clarence E. Meyer* in May 1952 the Agreement on Economic Coordination. The Meyer Mission* also resulted in the creation of the Combined Economic Board to coordinate all aspects of economic assistance and programs in Korea. Paik served as the Korean coordinator of this body until 1956.

In February 1953, Paik carried out a controversial currency reform, replacing the old won with the new *hwan* at the rate of 100 to 1, with the intention of bringing inflation under control and securing reserve funds for industrial development. When Henry J. Tasca* visited Korea as President Dwight D. Eisenhower's* special representative for the Korean economy, Paik worked closely with Tasca to help him formulate a long-range economic reconstruction program for Korea. In April 1952, Paik was given the concurrent post of acting prime minister and a year later was formally appointed prime minister. In June 1953, after attending the coronation of Queen Elizabeth II, he visited Washington for a meeting with Eisenhower, on which occasion he emphasized the importance of U.S. economic aid and expressed his strong opposition to the P'anmunjŏm truce talks*. In June 1954, he resigned the post of prime minister. In 1961 and again in 1967, Paik was elected to the National Assembly. In 1971, he became prime minister for the second time under President Park Chung Hee. *See also* Tasca Mission.

G. M. Lyons, *Military Policy and Economic Aid: The Korean Case, 1950–1953* (Columbus, Ohio, 1961); Paek Tu-jin, *Paek Tu-jin Hoegorok* (Seoul, 1975).

Yŏng-ho Ch'oe

PAK HŎN-YŎNG (1900–1955)

Pak Hŏn-yŏng, one of the key leaders of the Korean Communist movement, was born in Yesan, South Ch'ungch'ŏng province in southern Korea. He began his anti-Japanese Communist activities by joining in the Koryŏ Communist Youth League in Shanghai as early as 1919 and was one of the original members of the Koryŏ Communist party in Shanghai in 1921. He succeeded in forming the Korean Communist party and creating the Korean Communist Youth League in Seoul in 1925. The Japanese arrested him in 1921, 1924, and 1933 in connection with his Communist activities.

After the Japanese surrender in 1945, Pak was destined to be the key leader in the short-lived, stormy history of Communist ascendancy in southern Korea. He took the lead in the inauguration of the Democratic National Front, an instrument of the Left in southern Korea, in February 1946 and the creation of the South Korean Workers' party, a merger organ of the southern Left, in the fall of 1946. As the leader of the domestic faction, Pak was thus the logical choice as national leader of post–1945 Korean communism because of his indigenous support, long party experience, and strong intellectual qualifications. One obvious and crucial factor, however, intervened decisively: it was the Americans who occupied southern Korea. Since their fundamental objectives and the means they used in reaching them differed so radically, the U.S. occupation authorities and the Communists in southern Korea were destined to come into conflict. Pak and other southern Communist leaders were forced to move north and to be fixed in secondary positions there.

When the Democratic People's Republic of Korea* was established in September 1948, Pak became a vice-premier and minister of foreign affairs. He was also made vice-chairman of the Korean Workers' party and a member of the all-important seven-man military committee of the party. According to some writers, Pak urged the North Korean invasion of South Korea* in an effort to advance his political fortunes against his archrival, Kim Il Sung*. In March 1950, a secret conference reportedly was held in P'yŏngyang attended by top leaders of North Korea. Kim Il Sung is said to have opened for discussion the possibility of military action against the Republic of Korea*. Pak allegedly spoke strongly in favor of a militant course, asserting that if the North Korean People's Army invaded the south, 200,000 underground South Korean Communists would emerge to fight with the northern forces. Pak's fate was sealed by the North Korean failure to conquer the south. After the war, Pak, loser in the power struggle with Kim Il Sung, was purged. He was executed by Kim's *Kapsan* (Soviet exile) faction in December 1955.

Chungang Ilbo (ed.), *Pukhan Inmyong Sajŏn* (Seoul, 1981); R. Scalapino and C. Lee, *Communism in Korea* (Los Angeles, 1972).

Jinwung Kim

PANDIT, VIJAYA LAKSHMI (1900–1990)

Indian ambassador to the United States and chief delegate to the UN, Vijaya Pandit served as a spokesperson for India in the United States throughout the period of the Korean War. She was the sister of Prime Minister Jawaharlal Nehru* and, like her brother, entered politics as a participant in the Indian movement for independence from British colonial rule. After India gained nationhood in 1947, Pandit served her government in a variety of capacities, including appointments as ambassador to both the Soviet Union and the United States and high commissioner in England. She also gained election as president of the UN General Assembly and as a member of the Indian Parliament.

As ambassador in Washington, D.C., Pandit advanced India's nonaligned perspective on the Korean War, which emphasized the local roots of the conflict and sought to prevent a great power confrontation. More skeptical of Soviet leadership and friendlier toward the West than her brother, she tried to place her personal stamp on India's relations with the United States and worked to soften some of the prime minister's criticisms of the Truman administration. In July 1950, for example, the ambassador met personally with Secretary of State Dean G. Acheson* to explain her brother's call for the seating of the People's Republic of China* in the UN as a first step toward a negotiated settlement in Korea. Well aware of Acheson's strong opposition to linking Korean negotiations and the China matter, Ambassador Pandit urged the secretary to consider the public relations benefits that Washington might derive from a willingness to reach out to the PRC.

Although Pandit won the personal respect of Acheson and many other U.S. officials, the State Department and the White House viewed Indian policies as being either dangerously naive or perilously close to the Communist position. Indo-U.S. relations consequently suffered severe strains throughout Pandit's tenure. Pandit played little role in the V. K. Krishna Menon* POW settlement proposal* that in late 1952 helped to bring an end to the war. While she served as chief of the Indian delegation to the UN, Nehru assigned Menon the task of dealing with the Korean issue. Pandit, moreover, personally disliked Menon and doubted his ability to forge a compromise on the difficult agenda item 4, POW repatriation. *See also* Indian Peace Initiatives.

V. L. Pandit, *The Scope of Happiness: A Personal Memoir* (London, 1979); E. Reid, *Envoy to Nehru* (Delhi, 1981); W. W. Stueck, *The Road to Confrontation* (Chapel Hill, 1981).

Dennis Merrill

PANIKKAR, SARDAR K. M. (1893–1963)

As India's ambassador to the People's Republic of China*, K. M. Panikkar provided an important channel of communication between the Western nations and the diplomatically isolated PRC during the early stages of the Korean War. Panikkar was a historian by training who had worked in the courts of several of India's regional princes prior to the nation's independence. After India gained its freedom from British colonial rule in 1947, he served as ambassador to China, Egypt, and France. Panikkar quickly won a reputation in international circles as a brilliant, but rarely objective, scholar-diplomat who championed the cause of Afro-Asian nationalism. Prime Minister Jawaharlal Nehru* asked Panikkar in early 1950 to represent India in the PRC. Emphasizing the newly established Communist regime's independence from Moscow, the Indian government had granted diplomatic recognition to the PRC in December 1949. Panikkar's credentials as an Asian scholar, his support for India's nonaligned foreign policy, and his sympathy for China's revolution made him a logical choice for the post. He became one of the few non-Communist diplomats in Peking to enjoy friendly personal relations with China's leaders.

Panikkar regularly reported his conversations with Foreign Minister Chou En-lai* and other Chinese officials regarding the Korean conflict to Sir Girja Bajpai*, secretary-general of the Indian Ministry of External Affairs, who dutifully relayed the reports to the British and U.S. governments. Although London treated Panikkar's observations with a reasonable degree of caution, the State Department tended to view the Indian official as pro-Communist in his sympathies and thus as an unreliable source. During the early months of the fighting, Panikkar observed that the Chinese showed little interest in Korea and seemed unlikely to intervene. In late September, however, the Chinese evidenced increased concern as it became apparent that UN forces might cross the thirty-eighth parallel and enter North Korea. On September 30, 1950, Chou En-lai advanced the first of two warnings to the Indian ambassador that "if America extends her aggression China will have to resist." Prime Minister Nehru immediately passed the ominous message on to London and Washington, but the importance of India's entreaties was downplayed, and planning continued for carrying the war northward.

On October 3, Chou En-lai had Panikkar awakened and summoned to an emergency midnight meeting, where he reiterated China's threat. While some officials in the State Department, most notably U. Alexis Johnson* and O. Edmund Clubb*, and British Foreign Office counseled that the warning should be taken seriously, Secretary of State Dean G. Acheson* and other senior officials rejected any course of action that might be viewed as a sign of hesitation or weakness. After Chinese military intervention*, Panikkar's presence in Peking became less strategic. He returned to New Delhi in 1952 and was assigned to head the Indian embassy in Cairo.

S. Gopal, *Jawaharlal Nehru: A Biography* (New Delhi, 1979); P. Lowe, *The Origins of the Korean War* (London, 1986); S. K. M. Panikkar, *In Two Chinas: Memoirs of a Diplomat* (London, 1955); W. W. Stueck, *The Road to Confrontation* (Chapel Hill, 1981).

Dennis Merrill

P'ANMUNJŎM SECURITY AGREEMENT OF OCTOBER 22, 1951

Prior to the truce talks resumption of October 25, 1951*, the liaison officers negotiated this arrangement to provide for security at the new conference site at P'anmunjŏm. Its purpose was to avoid a repetition of the Kaesŏng neutral zone controversy* that had resulted in the Kaesŏng truce talks* suspension of August 23, 1951*. Since the start of the negotiations, the liaison officers had met regularly at P'anmunjŏm, located on the main road 5 miles east of Kaesŏng and about 15 miles west of Munsan. Discussions regarding the security agreement began on October 10. After several meetings, negotiators finished work on an eight-point agreement, with five associated "mutual understandings" embodying most of the features the UNC* desired. This accord would govern the security arrangements at P'anmunjŏm for the remainder of the Korean War.

Under the terms of the agreement, P'anmunjŏm was designated as the center of a circular neutral zone with a radius of 1,000 yards. It neutralized a 3-mile radius around Munsan and Kaesŏng, as well as 200 meters on either side of the Kaesŏng-Munsan road. In the P'anmunjŏm area, each side agreed to station two military police officers and fifteen men armed with small arms while the talks were in session and one officer and five men during other periods. The Communists accepted the UNC's position on violations of air space over the neutral zone, recognizing that there might be weather or technical conditions beyond human control causing aircraft to fly over the conference area but without any intent to attack or damage it. The UNC also was able to except itself from responsibility if irregular or partisan forces not under its control violated the security agreement. Finally, the Communists agreed to build tents for the delegates and the conference sessions, while the UNC provided flooring, lighting, and heat plus four captive balloons floating at 1,000 feet altitude to mark the periphery of the neutral zone. The UNC's chief delegate, Vice-Admiral C. Turner Joy*, dispatched a letter to Lieutenant General Nam Il*, his Communist counterpart, ratifying the liaison officer's accord. Nam signed the agreement on October 24, and the first meeting of the P'anmunjŏm truce talks* was scheduled for the next day.

   Foreign Relations of the United States, 1951, vol. 7: *Korea and China* (Washington, D.C., 1983); W. G. Hermes, *Truce Tent and Fighting Front* (Washington, D.C., 1966); D. Rees, *Korea: The Limited War* (New York, 1964); W. H. Vatcher, *Panmunjom: The Story of the Korean Military Armistice Negotiations* (New York, 1958).

P'ANMUNJŎM TRUCE TALKS (October 25, 1951–July 27, 1953)

   These negotiations between the UNC* and the Communists began with the truce talks resumption of October 25, 1951*, and ended with the signing of the armistice agreement* on July 27, 1953. CINCUNC General Matthew B. Ridgway* insisted upon moving the negotiating site to P'anmunjŏm following the Kaesŏng neutral zone controversy* that resulted in the truce talks suspension of August 23, 1951*. During the first session, the negotiators resumed discussions to break the deadlock over agenda item 2*, relating to the establishment of a demarcation line and DMZ. By November 27, 1951, both sides had reached agreement that the cease-fire would be coterminous with the battle lines as opposed to the thirty-eighth parallel. Negotiators then turned their attention to agenda item 3*, cease-fire arrangements and inspection provisions, but were unable to resolve the matter quickly. To speed the achievement of an armistice, the UNC proposed simultaneous discussion of agenda item 5*, covering postwar political arrangements, an issue that was more easily settled; the UNC accepted the Communist proposal of February 16, 1952, calling for the convening of a political conference after the achievement of a cease-fire. The truce talks at P'anmunjŏm then reached an impasse over agenda item 4*, repatriation of POWs. While the UNC delegation insisted on voluntary repatriation*, the Communists demanded the forcible return of all prisoners of war. In April 1952, discussion of the package proposal* left repatriation as the only issue preventing an end to the war.

   From the start, the government of the Republic of Korea* opposed the armistice negotiations. President Syngman Rhee* wanted to reunify his country with the UNC's assistance, therefore anticipating that the deadlock over the POW issue might result in the U.S. undertaking another military offensive into North Korea. Beginning in the summer of 1951, the South Korean demonstrations for unification* indicated considerable popular support for Rhee's position. Although the Truman administration refused to compromise on the repatriation issue, leading to the truce talks suspension of October 8, 1952*, it never acted on the plans it had under consideration to widen the war. When the Eisenhower administration assumed office in January 1953, it was anxious to obtain a cease-fire as soon as possible. It responded favorably to new Communist peace initiatives, especially the Chou En-lai* POW settlement proposal*, resulting in the truce talks resumption of April 26, 1953*. Once again, demonstrations of anti-Americanism erupted in the ROK, especially after the Communists accepted the UNC final POW settlement proposal*. Far worse was Rhee's release of North Korean POWs* in June 1953 to scuttle the armistice agreement. With this unilateral action, the South Korean president partially implemented his demand that prisoners ''detained in South Korea will be freed immediately with the beginning of the truce.''

Once the Communist delegation agreed to drop its demand for forcible repatriation of POWs, nothing stood in the way of completing a settlement at the P'anmunjŏm truce talks. The United States was anxious for a cease-fire after nearly two years of simultaneously talking and fighting. The Eisenhower administration therefore rejected Rhee's demands that the war continue until the achievement of reunification. However, the United States, as a result of the Robertson Mission*, assured the Rhee government in July 1953 that it would conclude a mutual defense treaty with the ROK, provide long-term economic aid, build South Korea's army to twenty divisions, and cooperate with the ROK in negotiations at the political conference. In response, Rhee promised the United States that he would not take steps to undermine the armistice agreement, which was signed on July 27, 1953, and remains in effect. *See also* Dulles's Atomic Warning to China; NSC-118; NSC-147; NSC-154/1; NSC-157/1; Operation Little Switch; UNC POW Administration.

W. G. Hermes, *Truce Tent and Fighting Front* (Washington, D.C., 1966); S. Y. Kim, *Panmunjom* (Seoul, 1972); ROK Ministry of Defense, *Korea in War, July 1952-July 1953* (Seoul, 1953); W. H. Vatcher, *Panmunjom: The Story of the Korean Military Armistice Negotiations* (New York, 1958).

                                                                                      Woo Chul-koo

PARTRIDGE, EARLE E. (1900–1990)

On June 25, 1950, Major General Earle E. Partridge was in command of the U.S. 5th Air Force stationed at Nagoya, Japan. His pilots and planes were the first U.S. military forces to see action in the Korean War, as the Truman administration resorted to air power in its initial attempt to halt the North Korean invasion of South Korea*. Partridge was born in Winchendon, Massachusetts. He enlisted in the U.S. Army in 1918 and fought with the 79th Division in France, participating in the Argonne offensive. Enrolling in Norwich University after the war, Partridge decided in 1920 to reenlist and, after serving briefly as an enlisted man at West Point, graduated from the U.S. Military Academy in 1924. He received flight training at Kelly Field in Texas, staying there as an instructor for three more years. After teaching math at West Point, Partridge spent time in the Panama Canal Zone and graduated from the Air Corps Tactical School in 1937. He then organized single engine airplane training schools until the United States entered World War II. In 1942, he served at the War Department General Staff and on the joint strategic committee, gaining promotion to brigadier general. Partridge fought in Europe during 1943, flying combat missions in Sicily, Italy, and Austria. He directed the strategic bombing operations against Nazi Germany before becoming chief of staff and deputy commander for Jimmy Doolittle's 15th Air Force. After other assignments, Partridge rejoined Doolittle as his deputy and helped to recognize the 8th Air Force and move it to Okinawa in 1945.

In 1946, Partridge became assistant chief of staff for air operations. Following reorganization and the establishment of an independent air force department, he was director of training and requirements in the office of the deputy chief of staff. When Partridge assumed command of the 5th Air Force in 1948, the first jet fighters were beginning to arrive in Japan, and he implemented a system for rapid movement and rear maintenance of the new aircraft. As a result, the United States could fully exploit its air superiority during the first year of the Korean War. But Partridge's vigorous advocacy of an interdiction strategy led to a dispute with Major General Oliver P. Smith* the commander of the 1st Marine Division, who favored close air support. Despite Smith's objections, the FEAF absorbed the 1st Marine Air Wing, but the stage now had been set for the army–air force close support controversy* later in the war. In 1951, Partridge earned his third star and then temporarily replaced Lieutenant General George E. Stratemeyer* as the FEAF commander. With the arrival of Stratemeyer's permanent replacement, Lieutenant General Otto P. Weyland*, Partridge returned to the United States as head of the air research and development command at Wright-Patterson Air Force Base for two years before becoming deputy chief of staff for air force operations. In 1954, Partridge assumed command of the FEAF and inspected the French air base at Dienbienphu. The following year, Partridge became head of the U.S. Continental Air Defense Command.

C. Blair, *The Forgotten War* (New York, 1987); *Current Biography,* 1955.

PEARSON, LESTER B. (1897–1972)

Lester B. Pearson was Canada's secretary of state for external affairs during the Korean War in the government of Prime Minister Louis S. Saint Laurent*. Acknowledged as one of the architects of the Atlantic Alliance and by many as Canada's greatest diplomat, ''Mike'' worked to build a strong Canada capable of using its influence to advance the cause of world peace. Born in Newtonbrook, Ontario, he earned a B.A. in history from the University of Toronto in 1919 and an M.A. from Oxford in 1925. After teaching at Toronto until 1928, he served as first secretary in Canada's Department of External Affairs until 1935. Pearson then spent six years in London before returning to Ottawa in 1941 as assistant under secretary of state for external affairs. For the remainder of World

War II, he served in Washington, D.C., as minister-counselor and then ambassador. In this capacity, he emphasized the importance of cooperation between the governments of Canada and the United States. Regarding Korea, he urged Prime Minister Mackenzie King to support implementation of the UN resolution of November 14, 1947*, calling for nationwide elections.

In the fall of 1948, Pearson returned to Ottawa as secretary of state for external affairs, subsequently participating in the establishment of the European Recovery Program and NATO. He campaigned for expansion of NATO's functions beyond purely military concerns. Although generally sympathetic to U.S. foreign policy objectives, Pearson early challenged the U.S. tendency after the North Korean invasion of South Korea* to view the war as a litmus test of anti-communism. Sharing the anxieties of many U.S. allies, he noted that by 1950 the issue was not whether the United States would commit fully its enormous power but how that power would be employed. Thus, Pearson openly criticized CINCUNC General Douglas MacArthur's* bellicose posturing and advocated an end to the fighting as a member of the UN Ceasefire Group* to prevent any dangerous escalation or expansion of the Korean conflict.

After the start of armistice negotiations, Pearson continued to search for a peaceful settlement, taking a leading part in the struggle at the UN to unsnarl the P'anmunjŏm truce talks* by finding a compromise on agenda item 4*, the prisoner repatriation issue. In the fall of 1952, alarmed by the U.S. military's hawkish stance, Pearson worked closely with British Foreign Minister Anthony Eden* and V. K. Krishna Menon*, India's UN representative, to break the POW deadlock. These efforts strained relations with Secretary of State Dean G. Acheson*, but the newly elected Eisenhower administration would prove more receptive to Pearson's advocacy of the Menon POW settlement proposal*. Ultimately, the UN resolution of December 3, 1952*, which Pearson helped to pass, provided the foundation for achieving an armistice ending the Korean War. His activism at the UN made him a logical candidate to replace Trygve Lie* as secretary-general in the spring of 1953, but the Soviet Union blocked his nomination for "the job I really wanted." Three years later, Pearson earned the Nobel Peace Prize for his mediation efforts in the Suez crisis. The Conservative electoral victory in 1957 left Pearson as head of the Liberal opposition until 1963 when he began five years of service as prime minister. In retirement, the "happy warrior" lectured at Carleton University and later became its chancellor.

D. Acheson, *Present at the Creation* (New York, 1969); *Current Biography*, 1963; C. A. MacDonald, *Korea: The War Before Vietnam* (New York, 1986); D. A. Munro and A. I. Inglis (eds.), *Mike: Memoirs of the Right Honourable Lester B. Pearson* (London, 1974); *New York Times*, December 28, 1972.

Theodore A. Wilson

PENG TEH-HUAI (PENG DEHUAI; 1898–1974)

Peng Teh-huai, a top Chinese Communist military official from 1928 to 1959, commanded the Chinese People's Volunteers Army* (CPVA) in the Korean

War. He was born in Hunan province into what he later described as a "lower-middle peasant" background. In 1913, Peng participated in demonstrations against wealthy merchants but two years later joined the army of Hunan's military governor. In 1921, he became a commissioned officer. Upon graduation from the Hunan Provincial Military Academy in 1923, Peng returned to his provincial army, which in 1926 joined the army of the Kuomintang (KMT). In 1928, after the KMT showed decreasing concern about conditions among the peasants, he joined the Communist party. In early 1937, Peng became vice-commander in chief of the Red Army and between 1942 and 1945 assumed increasing political responsibilities, winning election to the Politburo in 1945. In the spring of 1946, he assumed command of the Northwest Field Army and helped defeat Chiang Kai-shek's* forces in the Chinese Civil War, leading to the creation of the People's Republic of China* in 1949.

On October 5, 1950, Peng received orders to lead the Chinese forces intervening in the Korean War after Lin Piao* had declined the appointment. After some initial skirmishes with UN forces later in the month, the Chinese military disengagement of November 6, 1950*, gave the UNC* a chance to reconsider its push to the Yalu. In response to the Home-by-Christmas offensive* of November 24, Peng counterattacked with the full force of over 400,000 soldiers, driving UN units southward across the thirty-eighth parallel. On New Year's Eve, he opened an offensive into South Korea but proved unable to sustain the advance. By the end of January 1951, his armies were in retreat. After the UNC repulsed the massive Chinese spring offensives of 1951*, the Communists entered into the Kaesŏng truce talks* in July. From this point on, Peng concentrated first on the construction of an elaborate system of tunnels and trenches for defense and then on what he later called an "active defense in positional warfare."

In July 1953, Peng signed the armistice agreement*, conceding substantial territory above the thirty-eighth parallel to the anti-Communist Republic of Korea*, as well as the principle of voluntary repatriation* of POWs. His wartime experiences apparently convinced Peng that the Chinese army needed modernization of its equipment, professionalism, and new training for modern combined operations. After the war, he became first vice-chairman of the party Central Committee's Military Commission and, later, minister of national defense. In these top positions of the PRC's defense apparatus, he instituted a series of reforms, with the army of the Soviet Union providing the model. Peng's outspoken criticism of Mao Tse-tung's* growing personality cult and his Great Leap Forward during 1958 and 1959 led to his fall from favor in the latter year. During the Great Proletarian Cultural Revolution, Peng was imprisoned and tortured. Western historians have generally regarded Peng as a straightforward, hard-working, courageous man who was genuinely committed to the well-being of the peasants and the rank and file of his armies but lacked depth of training in Marxist-Leninist theory and was a mediocre military strategist.

J. Domes, *Peng Teh-huai: The Man and the Image* (Stanford, Calif., 1985); R.

MacFarquhar, *The Origins of the Cultural Revolution*, 2 vols. (London, 1974); Peng Dehuai, *The Memoirs of a Chinese Marshal (1898–1974)* (Beijing, 1984); W. Whitson and C. Huang, *The Chinese High Command* (New York, 1973).

William Stueck

PEOPLE'S REPUBLIC OF CHINA

On October 1, 1949, Mao Tse-tung* declared the founding of the People's Republic of China (PRC) in the traditional capital of Peking (Beijing). This declaration signaled the victory of Communist forces against those of the Nationalists under Chiang Kai-shek* and an approaching end to the Chinese Civil War. This government, like its rival, the Republic of China*, claimed to rule all of China and recognized no division of territory or authority. As a result, the PRC considered the U.S. neutralization of Taiwan* on June 27, 1950, an intervention in its internal affairs. Ostensibly, the PRC entered the Korean War at the request of the Democratic People's Republic of Korea*. However, the intervention was not only in support of a fraternal socialist nation but to maintain a socialist buffer between Manchuria, the major area of Chinese heavy industrial development, and the forces of imperialism represented by the U.S.-sponsored Republic of Korea*. The intervention placed a great strain on China's economic and military resources, but it also allowed an appeal to Chinese nationalism, with its underlying anti-Western base, to unite the Chinese people, regardless of politics, against Western military adventurism near China's borders.

It was this perceived threat to China that was responsible for the participation by the Chinese People's Volunteers Army* in the Korean War. China had repeatedly warned the United States, through third parties and directly, that if U.S. troops (not their South Korean allies) crossed the thirty-eighth parallel, China would intervene to protect itself. These warnings were discounted by most U.S. officials, both civilian and military, as an empty threat. U.S. troops crossed the parallel, and, on October 19, the first reports of Chinese troops were received in Washington but also discounted. These troops were identified as units of Lin Piao's* 4th Field Army. For China, a defense of its territory was imperative. This was especially true for the new government in Peking, which was not yet in firm control of China and faced a threat to its stability in Chiang's redoubt across the Taiwan Strait. Chinese military intervention*, and from the PRC's perspective victory, in defeating the forces of imperialism, has been and continues to be a source of national pride. *See also* China's Resist America Aid Korea Movement; People's Republic of China UN Representation Question.

E. P. Hoyt, *The Bloody Road to Panmunjom* (New York, 1985); I. C. Y. Hsu, *The Rise of Modern China* (New York, 1975); B. I. Kaufman, *The Korean War* (Philadelphia, 1986).

Katherine K. Reist

PEOPLE'S REPUBLIC OF CHINA UN REPRESENTATION QUESTION

During the Korean War, the People's Republic of China* controlled the mainland of China but did not occupy China's seat in the UN. Exercising its dominance of international affairs, the United States had secured for China a permanent seat on the UN Security Council when that organization was established in 1945. Few countries agreed with President Franklin D. Roosevelt's description of China as a great power, and Winston Churchill* contemptuously characterized Chinese representation as a faggot vote for the United States given the political dependence of the Republic of China* on U.S. support.

The issue became more complex when in 1949 the Chinese Communists drove the Nationalists from the mainland and on October 1 established a new government in Peking. Foreign Minister and Premier Chou En-lai* demanded that the PRC be given China's UN seat. Initially Washington decided not to block a vote to admit China to the UN, although it opposed this turn of events. In January 1950, however, the Soviet Union escalated the controversy by insisting on instant action and then beginning a boycott designed, presumably, to force the seating of Chinese Communist representatives. Moscow's actions actually delayed serious consideration of the Chinese admission issue, serving Moscow's desire to keep China isolated and dependent on the Soviet Union.

When the Korean War broke out, the Soviets, still boycotting the UN, were unable to veto the UN Security Council resolutions of June 25* and June 27, 1950*, to oppose the Democratic People's Republic of Korea*. Historians have pointed to Moscow's absence as evidence that the Soviets had not ordered the North Korean invasion of South Korea*. Moreover, the war lessened China's chances of entering the organization. The United States became determined to keep Peking out and proved able to rally sufficient votes to prevent expulsion of the Nationalist regime. *See also* Soviet UN Security Council Boycott.

N. B. Tucker, *Patterns in the Dust: Chinese-American Relations and the Recognition Controversy, 1949–1950* (New York, 1983).

Nancy Bernkopf Tucker

PERUVIAN POW SETTLEMENT PROPOSAL

On November 3, 1952, Peru submitted a draft resolution to the UN General Assembly intended to serve as a basis to break the deadlock in the P'anmunjŏm truce talks* over agenda item 4*, repatriation of POWs. The Peruvian plan was one of a succession of unsuccessful resolutions offered in the General Assembly in late October and early November to achieve an armistice in the Korean War. It called for the UN to appoint a five-member commission "on which each of the parties to the conflict shall be represented by one delegate." The General Assembly was then to appoint two delegates and invite the collaboration of one neutral state that was "not a member of the United Nations" to be a member and serve as chairman. The commission would take the necessary steps to ensure that all prisoners be immediately repatriated "in accordance with their freely expressed wishes." POWs who resisted repatriation were to be offered protection in a "neutralized zone," possibly in UN nations or trust territories, until some provision was made for their ultimate disposition. The commission would recommend to the UN, as soon as possible, a suitable program for their final release.

The Peruvian initiative went nowhere. Soviet foreign minister Andrei Y. Vyshinsky* rejected it as unworkable in a speech at the UN on November 10. As for the Truman administration, it was reticent to accept any neutral commission's handling the question of repatriation. Nothing came of this vague proposal, which was probably presented to stimulate discussion rather than as a definitive solution. The UN soon turned to discussion of the V. K. Krishna Menon* POW settlement proposal* on November 17 that, as matters turned out, provided the rough basis of an eventual settlement.

Department of State Bulletin, November 24, 1952; C. A. MacDonald, Korea: The War Before Vietnam (New York, 1986); D. Stairs, The Diplomacy of Constraint (Toronto, 1974); H. S. Truman, Years of Trial and Hope (Garden City, N.Y., 1956); United Nations General Assembly Official Records: Annexes, Seventh Session, 1952–1953.

Jeffrey G. Mauck

PLIMSOLL, JAMES (1917–1987)

Plimsoll was the Australian representative on the UN Commission for the Unification and Rehabilitation of Korea* (UNCURK) from 1950 to 1952. After working for a bank and service during World War II in the Australian army, James (from 1962, Sir James) Plimsoll began his diplomatic career as a member of the Australian delegation to the Far Eastern Commission from 1945 to 1948. His appointment as Australian representative on UNCURK became the foundation of his reputation as an outstanding diplomat, particularly highly regarded in the United States.

Soon after Plimsoll's arrival in Korea in November 1950, his influence was crucial in ensuring that UNCURK did not leave Korea following Chinese military intervention*. Plimsoll rapidly demonstrated a rare ability to exert some influence on President Syngman Rhee* of the Republic of Korea*, whose authoritarian policies caused grave concern to Australia, the United States, and other UN members. He played a significant part in the UNCURK's attempts to exert a moderating influence on South Korean police and prison administration while retaining contact with Rhee. Plimsoll initiated the proposal that following the occupation of North Korea*, the UNC*, rather than Rhee's government, should administer those parts of the Democratic People's Republic of Korea* from which the Communists had been driven. The high point of his role came in the South Korean political crisis of 1952* after Rhee's declaration of martial law* and his arrest of National Assembly members in order to force through a constitutional amendment that would prolong his presidency. Plimsoll personally confronted Rhee, told him that public opinion throughout the world would be shocked by his actions, and warned him of the effects on UN support for the ROK. Plimsoll subsequently played an important role in the exchanges between the Western powers and Rhee.

Plimsoll worked closely with U.S. ambassador John J. Muccio*, helping to cement the Australian-U.S. alliance being created at this time. Australian attempts to remove Plimsoll from Korea for other duties met strong U.S. resistance. The State Department believed that UNCURK could carry out its practical and symbolic functions only if it included representatives of high personal capacity. In deference to this view, the Australian government kept Plimsoll in Korea until the end of 1952. Plimsoll subsequently held virtually every major post open to an Australian diplomat, including those of secretary of the Department of External Affairs and head of diplomatic missions to the United States, the Soviet Union, the United Nations, the United Kingdom, Japan, and the European Communities.

R. J. O'Neill, *Australia in the Korean War 1950–53* (1981, 1985).

Peter Edwards

POLICE ACTION (June 29, 1950)

A term selected by President Harry S. Truman's* opponents as a means of criticizing his conduct of the Korean War, it finally contributed to a precipitous fall in the president's public opinion rating. During the last week in June 1950, Truman ordered U.S. military action, with UN approval, to meet the North Korean invasion of South Korea*. Truman might have asked for a joint congressional resolution endorsing his decision but knew that he already had support from Congress for military actions to contain the Communist advance. A declaration of war, while perhaps mobilizing Congress and the public, seemed inappropriate. The words *police action* had appeared earlier. The JCS had prepared a study during the summer of 1949 about possible U.S. action in the event of a North Korean invasion. It rejected large-scale military aid or unilateral intervention and recommended an appeal to the UN Security Council. Depending on the "council's decision," said the report, the United States might participate in a "police action." The term was a familiar one since it had been used to describe the Dutch police action of 1948 in Indonesia.

Truman's problem was his need to play down rather than dramatize U.S. efforts. One way of doing this was refusal to call his actions "war." On June 29, a reporter asked him, "Are we or are we not at war?" "We are not at war," he answered. "The members of the United Nations are going to the relief of the Korean Republic to suppress a bandit raid." "Mr. President," the reporter persisted, "would it be correct, against your explanation, to call this a police action under the United Nations?" "Yes," Truman replied quickly, "that's exactly what it amounts to." Interestingly, despite Republican claims to the contrary, Truman neither initiated nor volunteered the phrase *police action*. He had merely accepted it when offered. As it turned out, the controversy surrounding this term demonstrated that Truman had blundered by failing to make Congress an official partner in the Korean War. UN forces were unable to bring the fighting to a conclusion, and Truman decided not to introduce nuclear weapons or expand the war. The term *police action* became the means by which Republicans, following the lead of CINCUNC General Douglas MacArthur*, labeled Truman incompetent. Korea, they said, was "Mr. Truman's War." By 1952, a large percentage of the public agreed, persuading Truman not to run for reelection. *See also* Congress and U.S. Military Intervention; Congressional Meetings with Truman of June 1950.

R. J. Donovan, *Tumultuous Years* (New York, 1982); B. I. Kaufman, *The Korean War* (Philadelphia, 1986).

William B. Pickett

"A POLICY OF BOLDNESS" (May 19, 1952)

John Foster Dulles*, the leading Republican spokesman on foreign policy and future secretary of state under President Dwight D. Eisenhower*, offered a GOP alternative to the Democratic policy of containment, which presumably had led to the costly war in Korea, in this essay for *Life* magazine. Dulles stressed two concepts in "A Policy of Boldness." The first eventually became known as massive retaliation. Instead of depending on an increasingly expensive military buildup to counter Soviet aggression, Dulles favored a reliance on the threat of nuclear war. Stressing the concept of deterrence, Dulles spoke of the need to "organize the means to retaliate instantly against open aggression by Red armies." Although he avoided any direct reference to using the atomic bomb, he did talk about striking back "where it hurts, by means of our choosing." The second theme was liberation, defined as a political offensive to challenge the Soviet satellite empire and free the captive nations of Eastern Europe by peaceful means.

Despite the fact that Eisenhower had reservations about both aspects of Dulles's policy, he relied on liberation as a campaign issue in 1952 and later permitted Dulles to proclaim massive retaliation as the administration's primary defense policy. Although Dulles carefully defended President Harry S. Truman's* decision to fight in Korea, calling it "courageous," he and Eisenhower did rely on a form of massive retaliation to bring the fighting to an end. In May 1953, Dulles's atomic warning to China* sent via India helped break the deadlocked P'anmunjŏm truce talks* and led to the armistice on July 27, 1953. *See also* K1C2.

R. J. Caridi, *The Korean War and American Politics* (Philadelphia, 1968); J. F. Dulles, "A Policy of Boldness," *Life*, May 19, 1952; B. I. Kaufman, *The Korean War* (Philadelphia, 1986); D. Rees, *Korea: The Limited War* (New York, 1964).

Robert A. Divine

PONGAM-DO POW UPRISING (December 14, 1952)

The small island of Pongam situated near Kŏje-do became the detention camp for 9,000 Communist civilian Korean internees after the Kŏje-do POW uprising* of May 1952. Many of these POWs had previously participated in disturbances at the Kŏje-do POW camps in February 1952. There had been a series of disturbances in the camp throughout December 1952. On December 4, POWs in one compound refused to arrange their clothing and equipment for inspection. Two days later, camp authorities at Kŏje-do said they had uncovered evidence indicating that prisoners in the main camp and its branches, which included Pongam-do, might be planning a mass escape. On December 7, prisoners at Pongam-do defied camp authorities and conducted military drills at the three compounds. Three days later, a small group of Pongam prisoners assaulted an administrative soldier at a dispensary enclosure, and two prisoners attacked an enclosure commander.

On December 14, the brewing crisis reached a climax when the camp commander ordered around 3,600 internees in six compounds to terminate drilling and cease creating commotion. Instead, the internees joined in a mass demonstration that seemed to be in preparation for a breakout. They gathered together, locking arms, and from behind this protective human screen, other POWs hurled rocks and debris at the South Korean guards who were advancing to restore order. When the prisoners ignored warning shots, the South Korean soldiers fired at them, killing 85 internees and hospitalizing 113 others. Over 100 POWs sustained minor injuries, while only four South Korean personnel were wounded.

Responding to this tragedy, as well as other POW incidents such as the Chejudo POW uprising*, the Democratic People's Republic of Korea* charged that the "American brutality to POWs was aimed at damaging the prestige of North Korea and at blaming the system of People's Democracy in North Korea, detaining them under the guise of voluntary repatriation*." This uprising was planned and directed by Lieutenant General Nam Il*, chief delegate of the DPRK to the P'anmunjŏm truce talks*. The Communists exploited it for propaganda purposes. The UNC* also received criticism from the International Committee of the Red Cross. *See also* UNC POW Administration.

B. Alexander, *Korea: The First War We Lost* (New York, 1986); M. W. Clark, *From the Danube to the Yalu* (New York, 1954); A. E. Goodman (ed.), *Negotiating While Fighting: The Diary of Admiral C. Turner Joy* (Stanford, Calif., 1978); W. G. Hermes, *Truce Tent and Fighting Front* (Washington, D.C., 1966); ROK Ministry of Defense, *Korea in War: July 1952-July 1953* (Seoul, 1954).

Woo Chul-koo

PORK CHOP HILL, BATTLE OF
See Battle of Pork Chop Hill

POW POSTWAR CODE OF CONDUCT REGULATIONS

As a result of fears concerning the success of Chinese brainwashing* of UN prisoners of war, a number of countries instituted or tightened the provisions of code of conduct regulations designed to provide guidance on behavior to service personnel faced with capture. In the United States, this took the form of Executive Order 10631, issued by President Dwight D. Eisenhower* on August 17, 1955. It directed that U.S. service personnel be given training in resistance to interrogation, emphasizing the provision of "name, rank, number" as the only acceptable information to be given upon capture. The British also formed a committee to investigate the problem in consultation with American officials. This committee reported in the course of 1955 and reaffirmed the insistence upon "name, rank, number," but thirty-five years later its report remains classified. Other Commonwealth countries, such as Australia, based their policy on this report and instituted escape and evasion units within their military intelligence organizations.

A. D. Biderman, *March to Calumny* (New York, 1963); J. Grey, "Commonwealth Prisoners of War and British Policy during the Korean War," *RUSI Journal* (Spring 1988); U.S. Department of the Army, *Field Manual 21–77, Evasion and Escape* (Washington, D.C., 1965).

Jeffrey Grey

POW TRANSFER LOCATION QUESTION

Chou En-lai's* POW settlement proposal* in late March 1953 called for the transfer of non-repatriates to the custody of a neutral state after the armistice for a period of explanations, which presumably would persuade them to return home. Not only did Chou fail to nominate a neutral, but he did not make clear whether the POWs were to be transferred physically to the neutral state or to be handed over for explanations in Korea. When armistice talks resumed on April 26, 1953, the Communists made it clear that the POWs were to be sent out of Korea. The UNC* delegation opposed such a transfer and proposed Switzerland or Sweden as a neutral custodian. The Communists replied that an Asian country would be more appropriate, mentioning India, Pakistan, Indonesia, and Burma. They refused to nominate a neutral candidate, however, in advance of agreement on the principle of sending POWs directly to a neutral state for explanations.

On May 7, the Communists shifted their ground by proposing a Neutral Nations Repatriation Commission* (NNRC) to take custody of non-repatriates at their existing places of detention. The UNC final POW settlement proposal of May 25, 1953*, accepted this arrangement with the proviso that India alone among the members of the NNRC provide the custodial force. Although this modification was accepted by the Communist side on June 8, the arrangements had to be changed due to the opposition of President Syngman Rhee* of the Republic of Korea*. He refused either to allow the NNRC to operate on South Korean territory or to let Indian troops land there. His foreign minister, Pyun Yung Tai*, warned that the South Korean army would fire on the Indians if they tried to enter the ROK. As a result, new arrangements had to be made. By a temporary agreement supplementary to the armistice, the NNRC assumed custody of the non-repatriate POWs within the DMZ created under Article 1 of the armistice agreement*. The change involved the United States in the construction of a series of new compounds at a cost of $7,756,460. As for the Indian custodial force, the UNC had to fly it into the DMZ from the Han River estuary, a task that CINCUNC General Mark W. Clark* complained nearly wore out his helicopters. *See also* Communist POW Settlement Proposal of May 7, 1953; Truce Talks Resumption of April 26, 1953.

M. W. Clark, *From the Danube to the Yalu* (London, 1954); K. K. Hansen, *Heroes behind Barbed Wire* (Princeton, 1957); W. G. Hermes, *Truce Tent and Fighting Front* (Washington, D.C., 1966).

Callum A. MacDonald

POW UNILATERAL RELEASE PROPOSAL

For many U.S. officials, unilaterally releasing those POWs resisting repatriation offered the best method for resolving the dispute at the P'anmunjŏm truce talks* regarding agenda item 4*. Early in 1952, Major General John E. Hull*, U.S. Army vice-chief of staff, and Earl D. Johnson, the assistant secretary of the army, visited Tokyo and discussed the plan with CINCUNC General Matthew B. Ridgway*. They proposed that the UNC* reclassify as political refugees all POWs who refused to return home and then merely release them. This would present the Communists with a fait accompli, requiring the UNC to ride out the storm of criticism that would follow. Ridgway was unwilling to take this drastic step, preferring instead to exchange dropping the demand for prohibition against airfield rehabilitation for Communist acceptance of the principle of voluntary repatriation*. Implementing the Hull-Johnson plan, he argued, would bring charges that the UNC was guilty of treachery and deceit, thus destroying the prestige gained from opposing forcible repatriation. More important, it would endanger the lives of the UNC's prisoners of war.

After the Communists rejected the package proposal*, discussion of the unilateral release option resumed. To break the deadlock, General Mark W. Clark*, Ridgway's replacement, proposed in June 1952 taking all the POWs to the DMZ and releasing them without further screening or interviews, but the Truman administration refused to grant approval. Early in 1953, the Eisenhower administration revived the idea. In response to a request for his views on the plan, Clark stated that he favored unilateral release of the North Koreans because this would have no impact on the truce talks. However, disposition of the Chinese POWs was a more sensitive political issue. Subsequently, Clark developed a unilateral release plan, and the JCS approved its implementation if the Communists rejected the UNC final POW settlement proposal of May 25, 1953*. Shortly after, consideration for this option ended when the negotiators at P'anmunjŏm began to achieve progress toward resolving agenda item 4. Ironically, President Syngman Rhee* of the Republic of Korea* implemented this same plan in June 1953 when he ordered the release of North Korean POWs*.

J. L. Collins, *War in Peacetime* (Boston, 1969); J. F. Schnabel and R. J. Watson, *A History of the Joint Chiefs of Staff*, vol. 3: *The Korean War* (Wilmington, 1979); W. H. Vatcher, *Panmunjom: The Story of the Korean Military Armistice Negotiations* (New York, 1958).

PRESS COVERAGE OF TRUCE TALKS CONTROVERSY

At the first formal meeting of the Kaesŏng truce talks* on July 10, 1951, Communist newsmen and photographers were present to record the UNC* delegation's arrival in vehicles bearing white flags symbolizing surrender. Following the noon recess, Vice-Admiral C. Turner Joy*, the chief negotiator for the UNC, raised the issue of equal press coverage of the negotiations. He requested the right to bring to the conference area with the UNC delegation twenty newsmen and photographers for the next session, pointing out that Communist journalists already enjoyed full and free access. In addition, Joy protested Communist restriction on the movement of the UNC's couriers to the conference area. In response, Lieutenant General Nam Il*, the chief of the Communist delegation, seemed to agree to the principle of equality in press coverage but equivocated on the question of free movement for personnel, expressing concerns about safety. He then said that he would have to consult Kim Il Sung* before announcing a decision on either issue.

On July 11, at the second session, Nam Il approved free movement of properly marked UNC vehicles to the conference site but denied immediate press access. Meanwhile, CINCUNC General Matthew B. Ridgway* had gathered a contingent of newsmen at Munsan in anticipation of approval for coverage. He instructed Joy on July 12 to inform the Communists that the UNC delegation would return to Kaesŏng with the newsmen or not at all. The next day, the UNC liaison officer told his counterpart that newsmen would travel to the conference site that day as part of the UNC convoy. But the Communists stood firm and blocked passage to Kaesŏng, insisting that only military personnel could attend the conference. Press coverage would have to wait since the negotiators had not even agreed on an agenda. In response, the entire UNC delegation returned to Munsan. Having received approval from Washington, Ridgway now demanded not only the right to press coverage but also a more detailed agreement covering neutralization of the conference site. On July 14, the Communists relented, opening the way for resumption of the negotiations. The following afternoon, twenty newsmen accompanied the UNC delegation when it arrived for the third session. This dispute over press coverage of the truce talks provided an early indication that negotiating an armistice agreement would be neither quick nor easy. *See also* Kaesŏng Neutral Zone Controversy.

W. G. Hermes, *Truce Tent and Fighting Front* (Washington, D.C, 1966); D. Rees, *Korea: The Limited War* (New York, 1964); M. B. Ridgway, *The Korean War* (Garden City, N.Y., 1967); W. H. Vatcher, *Panmunjom: The Story of the Korean Military Armistice Negotiations* (New York, 1958).

PREVENTIVE WAR SCARE (August–September, 1950)

During each of the major crises of the cold war, a few Americans had talked about a "preventive" war with the Soviet Union. The Soviet explosion in 1949 of an atomic bomb had caused some Americans to advocate an attack on the Soviet Union while the United States still had overwhelming nuclear superiority. The North Korean invasion of South Korea* appeared to confirm the assessment of Soviet aggressive intentions as defined in NSC-68*, suggesting that Moscow would use even global war to attain its goals. The Korean War brought a renewal of such thinking in some circles and a discussion of it in the news magazines. Because some officials joined this debate, it created embarrassment for the Truman administration.

On August 25, Secretary of the Navy Francis P. Matthews* declared that the United States should be willing to pay any price to achieve world peace, "even the price of instituting a war to compel cooperation for peace." Not only did the State Department disavow these remarks the next day, but President Harry S. Truman* privately reprimanded Matthews. Truman speculated in his memoirs that Matthews had lost perspective after he had listened to "admirals and other high Navy people" speak often about the idea of "preventive war." But *New York Times* correspondent Hanson Baldwin* claimed that Secretary of Defense Louis A. Johnson* had persuaded Matthews to deliver the speech as a trial balloon.

A few days later, additional evidence surfaced that the United States might be contemplating preventive war. Major General Orvil Anderson, commandant of the Air War College, in an interview that appeared in the *Montgomery Advertiser*, said, "Give me the order to do it, and I can break up Russia's five A-bomb nests in a week." The general continued, "When I went up to Christ I think I could explain to him why I wanted to do it—now—before it's too late. I think I could explain to him that I had saved civilization." Newspapers across the country quickly printed Anderson's remarks. Coming in the wake of the Matthews speech and shortly after CINCUNC General Douglas MacArthur's* VFW message*, the Truman administration acted quickly to distance itself from such remarks. Air Force Chief of Staff General Hoyt S. Vandenberg* relieved Anderson, declaring that the mission of the U.S. Air Force was preserving peace, not starting war. Truman had already denounced the concept, ordering an end to such talk in his administration. Matthews's notion of the U.S. acting as an "aggressor for peace" was part of the atmosphere as Truman worked to limit the Korean conflict.

B. I. Kaufman, *The Korean War* (Philadelphia, 1986); R. Leckie, *Conflict: The History of the Korean War, 1950–1953* (New York, 1962); *New York Times*, August 1950; *Time*, September 18, 1950; H. S. Truman, *Years of Trial and Hope* (Garden City, N.Y. 1956).

William B. Pickett

"PRICE OF PEACE"
See Malik's Radio Address of June 23, 1951

PUNCHBOWL

This label referred to an area about 20 miles northeast of the Hwach'ŏn reservoir where a series of hills—numbers 983, 940, and 773—and their connecting ridges surround a circular valley. Punchbowl was the site of much heavy fighting after the summer and fall of 1951 when the Korean War developed into a bloody, positional, and stalemated conflict. *See also* Battle of Bloody Ridge; Battle of Heartbreak Ridge.

PUSAN PERIMETER

The Pusan Perimeter was a defensive area around the port of Pusan in the southeast corner of the Korean peninsula. It was established in late July 1950, as North Korean forces swept southward and threatened to overrun the whole of Korea. The perimeter was a rectangular area about 80 miles from north to south and 50 miles from east to west. The western boundary formed by the Naktong River from the vicinity of Sangju southward to the confluence of the Naktong and Namgang rivers where the defensive line ran across the hills to the

Korean Strait at Chindong. The northern boundary ran from Sangju on the Naktong to a little north of Yŏngdŏk on the Sea of Japan. In fierce fighting from late July to early September 1950, North Korean attempts to break through the perimeter line were beaten back by UNC* forces under the command of Lieutenant General Walton H. Walker*. The northern boundary was drawn back 15 miles by the end of August, but protection was provided for the government of the Republic of Korea* within the perimeter, first at Taegu and then at Pusan, while U.S. supplies and reinforcements were landed in Pusan. CINCUNC General Douglas MacArthur's* amphibious Inch'ŏn landing* assault on September 15, 1950, and subsequent interdiction of North Korean lines enabled Walker's forces to break out of the Pusan Perimeter on September 19, link up with Major General Edward M. Almond's* X Corps* on September 26, and rout the North Korean People's Army. *See also* Battle of the Naktong Bulge; Defense of Taegu; "Stand or Die" Order.

D. C. James, *The Years of MacArthur,* vol. 3: *Triumph and Disaster, 1945–1964* (Boston, 1985); C. A. MacDonald, *Korea: The War Before Vietnam* (New York, 1986); D. Rees, *Korea: The Limited War* (London, 1964).

Peter G. Boyle

P'YŎNGYANG BOMBING RAIDS OF 1952
See Air Pressure Strategy

PYUN YUNG TAI (PYŎN, YŎNG-T'AE; 1892–1969)

Pyun Yung Tai was minister of foreign affairs for the Republic of Korea* between 1951 and 1955, serving part of this period also as premier. During the P'anmunjŏm truce talks* and Geneva Conference of 1954*, he adhered strictly to President Syngman Rhee's* line in foreign policy, which was anti-Japanese and anti-Communist and against an armistice in Korea and any negotiations with the Communists. His assessment of the possibility of peaceful relations with Communist countries may be summarized in a quip he made at a press conference in June 1951: "When the Soviet Union talks war, it is bluffing. When it talks peace, it means war. When it means war, it strikes, not talks." On another occasion, he advocated a "moral totalitarianism" to counter threats of communism.

Before becoming minister of foreign affairs, Pyun was a professor of English literature at Korea University. But he also had worked for Rhee as a secretary after 1945. Concerned that a professor should not simultaneously serve in an official capacity, he resigned from Korea University when he was appointed the president's special envoy to the Philippines in 1949, his first experience in foreign affairs. Although he had never been abroad except to study briefly in China before 1949, he had a good reputation for his erudition and mastery of English. He held his own in exchanges with such international figures as Soviet foreign minister Andrei Y. Vyshinsky*, India's UN delegate V. K. Krishna Menon*, and Chinese foreign minister Chou En-lai*. He had somewhat the style of a traditional Korean scholar. To the end, he led an austere and frugal life, returning to the government what was left from meager expense allowances after his missions abroad. After resigning from the government, he taught English again in Seoul National University and Korea University. He ran for the presidency in the first election after Park Chung Hee's coup in 1961, but with poor results.

Oegyo Yŏrok (Seoul, 1959); Pyun Yong Tae, *Korea My Country* (Seoul, 1954).

J. Y. Ra

R

RADFORD, ARTHUR W. (1896–1973)

Admiral Arthur W. Radford was commander in chief in the Pacific (CINCPAC) and commander in chief of the Pacific Fleet (CINCPACFLT) from April 1949 to August 1953, when he was sworn in as chairman of the JCS. Born in Chicago, he graduated from the U.S. Naval Academy in 1916 and saw action aboard the battleship *South Carolina* during World War I. In the interwar period, Radford became a naval aviator and eventually commanded a fighter squadron on the carrier *Saratoga*. After Japan's attack on Pearl Harbor, Radford was chosen to oversee the expansion of the navy's flight training program. In April 1943, he was promoted to rear admiral and given command of a carrier division in the Pacific, participating in numerous amphibious operations, including the landings at Tarawa. After the war, Radford held a number of posts, including vice-chief of naval operations. He was a leader of the Revolt of the Admirals controversy that erupted in 1949 over navy opposition to the administration's emphasis on strategic air power.

Appointed CINCPAC in April 1949, Radford was a strong anti-Communist and a firm believer that the greatest threat to U.S. security was in Asia rather than in Europe. He did not, however, have any direct responsibility for U.S. forces in the Korean War because after the North Korean invasion of South Korea*, one of Radford's subordinate commands, the newly formed 7th Fleet, was placed under CINCUNC General Douglas MacArthur's* control. An advocate of an Asia First strategy and an admirer of General MacArthur, Radford supported the Inch'ŏn landing* plan (Operation Chromite*) and approved of the long-range goal of a military unification of Korea. He was present at the Wake Island Conference*, later recalling that he had interpreted MacArthur's assurance that U.S. forces could handle the Chinese if they intervened to mean that the Communists would not pose a problem so long as U.S. planes could strike their bases in Manchuria. Like MacArthur, Radford was frustrated by the restriction placed on U.S. forces after Chinese military intervention*. When MacArthur was relieved, he gave the returning general a hero's welcome in Hawaii.

In 1952, Radford joined President-elect Dwight D. Eisenhower* on his trip to Korea*. The admiral made a favorable impression on Eisenhower, who the following summer nominated Radford to head the JCS. As the new president considered alternatives for ending the war, he reportedly recommended threatening the Chinese with attacks on their Manchurian bases and using atomic weapons to end the war. After retiring from the navy in 1957, Radford served as a military adviser in the presidential campaigns of Vice-President Richard M. Nixon* in 1960 and Senator Barry Goldwater in 1964.

D. C. James, *The Years of MacArthur,* vol. 3: *Triumph and Disaster, 1945–1964* (Boston, 1985); S. Jurika, Jr. (ed.), *From Pearl Harbor to Vietnam: The Memoirs of Admiral Arthur W. Radford* (Stanford, Calif., 1980); E. Kemler, "Asia First Admiral," *Nation* (July 1954); *New York Times,* August 18, 1973.

Marc Gallicchio

RADHAKRISHNAN, SARVEPALLI (1888–1975)

As Indian ambassador to the Soviet Union, Sarvepalli Radhakrishnan sounded out Joseph Stalin* in July 1950 on the possibility of a negotiated settlement to the Korean War. Born into an upper-caste family in India's southern state of Madras, Radhakrishnan had accumulated very little political experience prior to India's independence in 1947. Instead, he had emerged as a renowned professor of philosophy, teaching at both Calcutta University and Oxford University in London as a specialist in Eastern religions. Impressed by Radhakrishnan's scholarship and liberal orientation, Prime Minister Jawaharlal Nehru* called upon the professor in 1949 to serve as India's ambassador in Moscow. Radhakrishnan maintained strong intellectual affinities to the West but was also a strong supporter of India's nonaligned foreign policy. Known for his idealism, the ambassador viewed India as a bridge between the two ideological camps in the cold war and as a major force for world peace.

When the Korean War broke out, Ambassador Radhakrishnan believed that India was perfectly positioned to play an important mediating role. Even before he was contacted by the Ministry of External Affairs in New Delhi, he inquired among Kremlin leaders and U.S. embassy officials in Moscow regarding the possibility of a negotiated settlement. He soon suggested to Prime Minister Nehru that the United States be urged to support the admission of the People's Republic of China* to the UN. In return, the Security Council, with Soviet support, would declare an immediate cease-fire in Korea, the withdrawal of North Korean troops above the thirty-eighth parallel, and the establishment of a united, independent Korea. These recommendations became the foundation for the Indian peace initiatives* of 1950 in which Prime Minister Nehru sent messages to Moscow, Washington, and Peking encouraging negotiations. In the end, nothing came of the efforts and Radhakrishnan returned to New Delhi in 1952 to serve as India's vice-president. After his departure for the Moscow post, his influence over India's Korea policy became minimal.

M. Brechner, *Nehru: A Political Biography* (London, 1959); S. Gopal, *Jawaharlal Nehru: A Biography* (New Delhi, 1979); E. Reid, *Envoy to Nehru* (Delhi, 1981); W. W. Stueck, *The Road to Confrontation* (Chapel Hill, 1981).

Dennis Merrill

RASHIN (NAJIN) BOMBING CONTROVERSY

This North Korean port city was a highly valued target for UNC* bombing because it housed a major port and extensive rail facilities. However, it was only 19 air miles south of the Soviet border on Korea's northeast coast, and the State Department therefore worried that air strikes on Rashin might provoke Soviet entry into the Korean War. Controversy within the administration over the wisdom of bombing Rashin began on August 10, 1950, when CINCUNC General Douglas MacArthur's* air forces bombed the city. State Department officials, concerned over possible violations of the Soviet border, were strongly opposed to further attacks, but President Harry S. Truman* overruled this objection on August 12, 1950. On September 4, 1950, U.S. Navy fighters shot down a Soviet aircraft in the Yellow Sea. A few days later, the JCS, with support from Secretary of Defense Louis A. Johnson*, asked the president to approve another bombing of Rashin, claiming that most Soviet armor for North Korea came through Rashin and that the city housed a quarter of North Korea's oil storage. This time the president viewed Secretary of State Dean G. Acheson's* objections more sympathetically. As a result, the JCS told MacArthur that no further attacks would be made on Rashin "at present," owing to tension caused by destruction of the Soviet aircraft and recent Manchurian border violations. MacArthur informed the JCS on September 10, 1950, that he concurred with their views and had issued appropriate orders to his command. The matter became academic with the military collapse of North Korea after the Inch'ŏn landing*.

On February 15, 1951, Communist military successes caused General MacArthur, on the recommendation of the FEAF commander, Lieutenant General George E. Stratemeyer*, to ask that the restrictions on bombing Rashin be removed. He called the city the keystone of the Democratic People's Republic of Korea's* logistics system and assured the JCS that his bombers could destroy Rashin without violating Soviet territory. Because the Department of State still objected strongly and because they did not believe that Rashin was as vital as MacArthur believed, the JCS turned down his request. But the bombing of Rashin became a live issue again on August 1, 1951, when CINCUNC General Matthew B. Ridgway* told the JCS that his air reconnaissance had discovered extensive military stockpiling at Rashin. Like his predecessor, MacArthur, Ridgway asked permission to bomb Rashin, saying that the FEAF could destroy it without violating Soviet territory. The JCS supported Ridgway's request, and Truman agreed with them. On August 25, 1951, B–29s bombed Rashin with "excellent results" and with no loss of aircraft. On December 9, 1952, Rashin was again attacked by U.S. carrier aircraft as part of a concerted air assault on rail facilities in northeastern Korea. *See also* Operation Strangle.

Command Report, COMNAVFE, December 1952; J. F. Schnabel, *Policy and Direction* (Washington, D.C., 1972); J. F. Schnabel and R. J. Watson, *History of the Joint Chiefs of Staff,* vol. 3: *The Korean War* (Wilmington, 1979).

James F. Schnabel

RAU, SIR BENEGAL N. (1887–1953)

Sir Benegal N. Rau, Indian permanent representative to the UN, played a central role in the Indian peace initiatives* of 1950 and later in the Korean War. Although Rau often irritated Americans at the UN with his independence and elaborate efforts at mediation, his charm and lack of personal vanity enabled him to get on well with diplomats of virtually all nations. He did have a tendency, nonetheless, to pursue courses that went beyond his instructions, which sometimes produced confusion as to the precise nature of Indian policy.

Son of a civil service official in British India, Rau received a B.A. in 1907 from Madras University and won a scholarship to study at Cambridge University in England. He passed the Indian civil service examination in 1909 and assumed his first position in Bengal as assistant collector and judge a year later. After many years as an adviser on legal affairs, he joined India's first delegation to the UN. In 1948, Rau became his nation's permanent representative to the young organization, a post he held until the end of 1951, when he was elected a judge of the International Court of Justice.

A gentle, patient man, Rau became an important figure in the diplomacy of the Korean War because, at the time of the North Korean invasion of South Korea*, his nation was a non-permanent member of the UN Security Council, and Rau held that body's rotating presidency. He promptly convened the Security Council in an emergency session and, though dubious about voting without instructions from home, supported the UN Security Council resolution of June 25, 1950*. However, he abstained on the UN Security Council resolution of June 27, 1950*, because of a lack of instructions. A staunch supporter of Prime Minister Jawaharlal Nehru's* "independent" foreign policy, he took the lead in August in an unsuccessful attempt to establish a subcommittee of non-permanent members of the Security Council to discuss UN aims in Korea.

During September and early October, Rau again provided leadership in efforts to slow the march of UN ground forces across the thirty-eighth parallel in Korea. In response to Chinese military intervention* in late November, the Indian representative avidly pursued a cease-fire in Korea. After attempting to persuade the Chinese not to cross the thirty-eighth parallel, Rau played a key role in drafting and guiding through the General Assembly the UN resolution of December 14, 1950*, establishing a three-man UN Ceasefire Group*. As a member of that group, he succeeded in focusing attention on possible negotiations for a cease-fire rather than on the American preference for resolutions attacking the People's Republic of China*.

When the Chinese crossed the thirty-eighth parallel at the beginning of the new year, U.S. insistence on a resolution condemning China eventually prevailed. But Rau's efforts helped to delay passage of the measure until February 1, by which time UN military prospects in Korea had begun to improve, and to tone it down sufficiently to discourage direct UN action against the mainland. Rau's role diminished after passage of the UN resolution of February 1, 1951*, as India refused to serve on the UN Good Offices Committee* established by it.

Current Biography, 1951; G. H. Jansen, Nonalignment and the Afro-Asian States (New York, 1966); New York Times, November 31, 1953; G. D. Paige, The Korean Decision (New York, 1968); "The Reminiscences of Ernest Gross," Oral History Project, Columbia University.

William Stueck

RECAPTURE OF SEOUL OPERATION (September 18–28, 1950)

After the Inch'ŏn landing* on September 15, the North Korean People's Army (NKPA) strongly contested the recapture of Seoul, the traditional capital of Korea. The burden of capturing the city, including crossing a major river, fell primarily on the 1st Marine Division, with supporting attacks by the 7th Infantry Division. After the capture of Kimp'o Airfield on the evening of September 17, 1950, the 1st Marine Division continued to push eastward from Inch'ŏn toward Seoul on two axes. The 1st Marine Regiment faced mounting resistance as it forced its way into Yŏngdŭngp'o, a separate suburb southeast of Seoul, but the North Koreans finally withdrew on September 22. Meanwhile, the 5th Marine Regiment advanced on the left (north) flank, crossing the Han River to approach Seoul from the northwest. The first attempt at this river crossing, a surprise attack on the night of September 20–21, was a costly failure, stopped by an NKPA battalion that had just occupied Hill 125 on the east bank of the river. The next morning, however, a conventional crossing using amphibian tractors supported by marine fighter aircraft succeeded. Thereafter, the 5th Marine advance was delayed for three days by carefully prepared NKPA defenses on the road from Kaesŏng to Seoul.

During these preliminary attacks, the 7th U.S. Infantry Division gradually came ashore at Inch'ŏn and began operations on the right (south) flank. The two divisions suffered from insufficient coordination and disagreements about map reading, so there were repeated incidents in which Major General Oliver P. Smith*, the 1st Marine commander, believed that the neighboring army units were not protecting his flank properly. The 7th Division attacked eastward to seize the road junction at Anyang on September 21, turned south to capture Suwŏn the next day, and finally linked up with elements of the 8th Army* advancing north from the Pusan Perimeter*. These attacks turned the 7th away from the axis of the marine advance on Seoul, increasing the possibility that the two would not be coordinated.

Major General Edward M. Almond*, the X Corps* commander, was dissatisfied at the rate of advance of the marines against heavy resistance in Seoul. Almond hoped to recapture the city by September 25, exactly ninety days after the North Korean invasion of South Korea*, and sought to do so by having the

7th Infantry Division make an additional attack across the Han River on September 25. This sudden change in plans involved a real danger of the two divisions' firing on each other in the city. Moreover, the way in which Almond made the change—talking directly to the regimental commanders involved rather than going through the marine division commander—increased friction. The two divisions finally linked up in eastern Seoul on September 28, but the mistrust between marine and army commanders continued for months.

R. E. Appleman, *South to the Naktong, North to the Yalu* (Washington, D.C., 1961); C. Blair, *The Forgotten War* (New York, 1987); R. D. Heinl, Jr., *Victory at High Tide* (Philadelphia, 1968).

Jonathan M. House

REPUBLIC OF CHINA

The government of the Republic of China (ROC) was reestablished on the island of Taiwan during the closing year of the Chinese Civil War (1946–1949). The Kuomintang (Nationalist) government and military leaders left the mainland as the Communist forces pushed them south. On Taiwan, they reconstituted their government, vowing to reorganize and reverse the military setbacks they had recently experienced. Meanwhile, they declared themselves to be the only legal government of all China. The government was headed by Chiang Kai-shek*, who had led the Chinese efforts against Japan in World War II and then against the Communist forces in the postwar struggle for power. Chiang was determined to lead his revitalized forces back to the mainland to defeat the Communists and regain actual control of China. However, the Truman administration's efforts to distance itself from the ROC early in 1950 convinced many that the People's Republic of China* soon would invade Taiwan and destroy Chiang's regime. The U.S. position seemed to be that whatever befell Taiwan was an internal Chinese matter. The thrust of the 1949 China White Paper had been that the ROC was not a U.S. problem.

U.S. policy toward China changed dramatically with the North Korean invasion of South Korea* as President Harry S. Truman* announced the neutralization of Taiwan*. Chiang offered to send troops to defend the Republic of Korea*, but this offer was not accepted. There were, however, consultations between Chiang and CINCUNC General Douglas MacArthur* during the general's visit to Taiwan* on topics of mutual interest. MacArthur was said to have advocated the "unleashing" of Chiang* and his anti-Communist forces for an assault on the southeast coast of China, while the UN forces passed from North Korea into Manchuria in a two-pronged attack, which would ultimately destroy the Communist governments of both the Democratic People's Republic of Korea* and the PRC. But during W. Averell Harriman's* visit to Tokyo*, MacArthur was told that Truman wanted him to avoid any actions risking a war on the Chinese mainland. Chiang's political allies in the United States were critical of the administration's refusal to provide more active support for the ROC. If the United States was committed to preventing a Communist triumph in South Korea, was not the spread of communism to Taiwan a parallel situation? The potential of a Nationalist attack was never discounted by the PRC, which stationed troops in likely attack zones. These forces were not available during Chinese military intervention* in the Korean War. *See also* Chiang's Offer of Chinese Troops.

D. Acheson, *The Korean War* (New York, 1971); I. C. Y. Hsu, *The Rise of Modern China* (New York, 1975); B. I. Kaufman, *The Korean War* (Philadelphia, 1986); P. Lowe, *The Origins of the Korean War* (New York, 1986).

Katherine K. Reist

REPUBLIC OF KOREA

The Republic of Korea (ROK) was formally inaugurated in Seoul on August 15, 1948. Claiming sovereignty over the entire country, the republic in fact exercised authority only south of the thirty-eighth parallel, containing two-thirds of the total Korean population. Its name dates back to the Korean Provisional Government (KPG) formed in 1919 following the March First Movement* the same year. The name *Republic of Korea* (*taehan Minguk*) was used for the first time on June 14, 1919, by Syngman Rhee*, then the president of the KPG, in a letter to the king of England notifying him of its establishment. The preamble to the constitution of the Republic of Korea ordained on July 12, 1948, makes the point clear that the republic upholds "the cause of the Provisional Government of Korea born of the March 1st Movement."

The republic was established through an election based on the UN resolution of November 14, 1947*, initiated by the United States after futile attempts to create a unified and democratic country through cooperation with the Soviet Union. Although the report of the UNTCOK was favorable on both the process and results of the election of May 10, 1948, it was marred by a large section of Koreans who tried to thwart it, because it perpetuated the division of the country, using various means, including terrorist attacks. Others boycotted the election. As these dissenters feared, three weeks after the ROK was established, the Supreme People's Assembly of Korea ratified the constitution of the Democratic People's Republic of Korea* in P'yŏngyang. Since then, Korea has been two separate countries, perpetuating the original division resulting from Soviet-U.S. occupation in 1945.

Born after three years of intensive political struggle between the Right and the Left, the republic was characterized by its hard-line anti-communism. Its constitution, however, adopted by the first National Assembly, incorporated many progressive elements regarding economic planning, social welfare, and the basic rights of the citizens. Even those representing the landowning class did not oppose the articles concerning redistribution of land, as Rhee, the ROK's first president, had expected that they would. As for the composition of the government, the majority of those at the top had good records as nationalists, but the civil service, particularly the national police, was largely filled by those who had served under the Japanese. It would thus appear that the legacies of the colonial past remained in considerable proportion, unpurged in the new government.

The republic faced staggering challenges from its inception. Its legitimacy was in doubt because of the election boycott by the moderates and leftists. The economy was near ruin due to mismanagement, social turmoil, and artificial division of the country, which left most of the industries, mineral resources, and electricity in the north. Serious threats to its security persisted in the form of civil unrest, guerrillas both indigenous and infiltrated from the north, and the preponderant military superiority of the North Korean People's Army (NKPA), which increasingly worried the government. There were also problems of political instability deriving from these factors and inexperience. Due to an influx of a large number of refugees from the north, it was suffering from overpopulation. However, the government managed to deal successfully with internal disturbances by the beginning of 1950. In some economic sectors, notably in cotton textiles, electricity, and coal, preliberation production standards were surpassed. It is possible that the ROK's economic and political progress persuaded the North Koreans to launch their invasion of South Korea*, fearing that any chance for reunification soon would be lost.

A decade after the Korean War, the Republic of Korea began to witness revolutionary changes led by success in economic development. There have been increasing demands for democratization in politics and social reform, especially after two decades of authoritarian rule under Park Chung Hee. Notably on two occasions, popular movements played crucial roles in bringing about progress toward democracy. In 1960, a revised constitution reflected greater democratization, and in 1987, protesters forced changes allowing for popular election of the president. Gradually anti-communism as an ideology and its presence in institutions and culture eroded. Leftist elements long suppressed have reemerged, led first by underground groups that have taken root or found expression in the academic community, journalism, and cultural movements. See also NSC-156/1; NSC-157/1.

S. Cho, *Korea in World Politics, 1945–1950* (Berkeley, 1967); B. Cumings, *The Origins of the Korean War* (Princeton, 1981; 1990); Lee Hyon-chong, *Han'guk ŭi Yŏksa* (Seoul, 1984); J. Merrill, *Korea: The Peninsular Origins of the War* (Newark, Del., 1988); Rhee In-soo, *Taehan Minguk ŭi Kŏnguk* (Seoul, 1988).

J. Y. Ra

RESCREENING OF POWS

Britain and India proposed impartial rescreening of Chinese and North Korean prisoners of war as a way to break the deadlock over agenda item 4*, repatriation of POWs, in May 1952. When the Truman administration began to consider supporting the principle of voluntary repatriation* late in 1951, the UNC* started preliminary screening of the POWs to determine how many would refuse to return home. During negotiations at P'anmunjŏm on agenda item 4, the UNC announced that it held 132,000 POWs and 38,500 civilian internees, speculating, after the Communists insisted, that probably 116,000 of these would request repatriation. On April 2, the Chinese, after firmly rejecting the concept of voluntary repatriation for weeks, suggested that to determine the number of POWs desiring repatriation, each side should prepare new lists of POWs, which involved the need for screening. Three days later, the UNC implemented Operation Scatter*, a process that in fact entailed a certain amount of rescreening. When CINCUNC General Matthew B. Ridgway* received word that only 70,000 POWs wanted repatriation, he knew that the Communists would protest. Therefore, he obtained approval from Washington to suggest at P'anmunjŏm that an international body or joint Red Cross teams conduct a rescreening of non-repatriates. Ridgway then instructed the UNC liaison officer to inform his counterpart on April 19 of the results of Operation Scatter. The Communist liaison officer was furious, insisting on receiving a more favorable figure and rejecting the alternative of a rescreening.

On April 28, the Communist delegation refused to accept the principle of voluntary repatriation as part of the package proposal*. When the P'anmunjŏm truce talks* resumed in open session on May 7, the Communists charged that the UNC was trying to bar the return of all prisoners. Following the Kŏje-do POW uprising*, the Communists exploited the Dood-Colson incident* to discredit the UNC's figures on repatriation while refusing to consider rescreening. By then, the UNC was less enthusiastic about impartial rescreening because of criticism from the International Red Cross regarding the Kŏje-do affair. Meanwhile, General Mark W. Clark*, Ridgway's replacement as CINCUNC, had ordered rescreening after discovering that many POWs had been victims of intimidation and coercion during Operation Scatter. Begun in late April, the Kŏje-do incident interrupted the rescreening, but the UNC ultimately determined that at least an additional 10,000 POWs favored repatriation. Vice-Admiral C. Turner Joy*, the chief of the UNC delegation, wanted to present this new information at P'anmunjŏm, but Washington feared that this might cause the Communists to delay longer in hopes of obtaining an even higher figure. Publicizing the new number, in combination with the Kŏje-do affair, would seem to verify charges that the UNC had purposely produced false figures, thus undermining international support for the U.S. position.

By the end of May, Charles E. Bohlen* and other U.S. officials were advocating an impartial rescreening as part of a final armistice agreement, hoping to break the deadlock in the negotiations. This proposal was the key element of an Anglo-Indian five-point plan for settling the POW controversy that British foreign secretary Anthony Eden* had sent to Washington on May 22. Eden had developed the proposal after receiving word from India that Chinese foreign minister Chou En-lai* wanted Britain to use its influence to end the stalemate. The United States responded positively and attempted to arrive at an agreement on the wording of a final proposal. However, K. M. Panikkar*, India's ambassador to the People's Republic of China*, presented Eden's original draft to the Chinese without obtaining British approval. He proposed also that a commission of belligerents with a neutral chairman conduct rescreening of the non-repatriates. On June 15, Chou approved Panikkar's plan with certain modifications, including that a neutral commission would supervise the rescreening in a neutral zone after the POWs had been released from military control and the influence of Kuomintang agents. Nothing came of the rescreening proposal, in part because the United States and Britain lost faith in India's reliability after Panikkar prematurely disclosed the Anglo-Indian five-point plan. Perhaps in response to the Suiho bombing operation*, the PRC announced on July 3 that while the Geneva Convention of 1949* did not apply to Korean POWs held in their own nation, it required the automatic return of all foreign troops to their home nation. *See also* UNC POW Administration.

Foreign Relations of the United States, 1952–1954, vol. 15: *Korea* (Washington, D.C., 1984); W. G. Hermes, *Truce Tent and Fighting Front* (Washington, D.C., 1966); C. A. MacDonald, *Korea: The War Before Vietnam* (New York, 1986); J. F. Schnabel and R. J. Watson, *History of the Joint Chiefs of Staff*, vol. 3: *The Korean War* (Wilmington, 1979).

RETURN-TO-SEOUL MOVEMENT

This was President Syngman Rhee's* campaign in late 1951 and 1952 to return his government from its temporary capital in Pusan to Seoul, the traditional capital of Korea since the beginning of the Yi dynasty (1392–1910). The return to Seoul had great political and psychological significance for Rhee. It imparted legitimacy to his government, provided a tangible demonstration to the Democratic People's Republic of Korea* that its invasion had failed, and bolstered Rhee's claims to represent all Koreans. CINCUNC's General Matthew B. Ridgway* and his successor, General Mark W. Clark*, opposed Rhee's plan, primarily for military reasons. They feared that they would be unable to defend Seoul, especially if there was a large-scale civilian return. Koreans' returning to Seoul would clog the roads and slow military movement in response to a potential Communist attack on the city. Furthermore, the UNC* specifically established the Korean Communications Zone in July 1952, which was responsible for rear-area activities. Moving the capital to Seoul would embroil the 8th Army* once again in civilian affairs and detract from its main task of fighting. Finally, the cost of rehabilitation of Seoul would siphon off economic aid required for more basic human relief.

Rhee was nevertheless determined to return to Seoul. After the South Korean presidential elections of August 1952*, he took up permanent residence in Seoul, which required key Republic of Korea* and U.S. officials to travel to the devastated capital to do business with him. By February 1953, the ROK government was shifting piecemeal to Seoul, and civilians were returning to the city. Ambassador Ellis O. Briggs* suggested that the United States accept Rhee's moving a few officials to Seoul, but Clark opposed even a partial return. The Department of State sent Clark and Briggs to Seoul in March 1953 in a failed effort to talk Rhee back to Pusan. Rhee stated that key officials from most ministries "would set up shop" in Seoul to do business with him, although the ministries would remain in Pusan. By May 1953, the locus of administration in Korea had shifted to Seoul, forcing Briggs himself to return. With the signing of the armistice agreement*, the rest of the ROK government, including the legislature, returned to Seoul.

Foreign Relations of the United States, 1952–1954, vol. 15: *Korea* (Washington, D.C., 1984); W. G. Hermes, *Truce Tent and Fighting Front* (Washington, D.C., 1966).

Edward C. Keefer

RHEE, SYNGMAN (YI SŬNG-MAN; 1875–1965)

Syngman Rhee was the first president of the Republic of Korea*, serving from 1948 to 1960. The Korean War was certainly the most trying period in Rhee's career, but it was also when he gained prominence as an unwavering anti-Communist and anti-Japanese fighter. Throughout the war, he had to lead multifronted struggles—not only against the Communists at the battlefront but also against the "appeasement tendencies" of his allies, the threat of Japan's reemergence, the U.S. policy of giving priority to the revival of the Japanese economy over that of Korea, and the growing opposition to him in domestic politics. On many occasions both public and private, he avowed that if he had to choose between Korea's two greatest enemies, he would fight the Japanese first even if he had to side with the Communists. Even bitter political opponents who suffered from Rhee's high-handedness gave him credit as a zealous guardian of Korean sovereignty.

Born into a noble family brought to near ruin, Rhee was one of those early Koreans who, after studying Western civilization, concluded that Korea had to modernize quickly. For his activities favoring radical reform of politics and society as one of the leaders of the Independence Club, he suffered torture and imprisonment. During his exile in the United States, he studied at George Washington and Harvard universities, earning his Ph.D. at Princeton, the first Korean who ever earned a doctorate. He was elected president of the Korean Provisional Government (KPG) formed in Shanghai following the March First Movement* of 1919, a national uprising against Japanese colonial rule in Korea. His anticommunism can be traced at least to the time of his presidency of the KPG when he strongly opposed cooperating with the Communists for independence, arguing that communism would mean another kind of slavery in the place of Japanese colonialism. He viewed the Soviet Union as a threat to Korea, a continuation of Russian expansionism, in the guise of a new ideology, which had earlier coveted the Korean peninsula as a route to the Pacific.

Rhee was undoubtedly the foremost national figure when Korea was liberated in 1945. Political support among the Koreans for Rhee was more complex than simply being confined to reactionary elements consisting of landlords and ex-collaborators. As a scholar-statesman and patriot who kept on with a lifelong struggle for Korean independence, he had a considerable appeal among the population. Besides, he was supported, in the beginning at least, by a wide range of people, including Christians, liberals, and traditionalists, who felt threatened by the vigorous leftist minority who avowedly aimed at nothing less than a total transformation of the society. Nevertheless, Rhee failed to compose various political forces competing for power and integrate them in a viable political structure. Engaging in political manipulation and often violence, he emerged as the leader of a separate South Korean government despite the objections of both the Soviet Union and the U.S. occupation commander, Lieutenant General John R. Hodge*.

For Rhee, his election as the first president of the ROK in 1948 did not constitute a complete victory because he had political authority over only half of his country. Rhee was determined to extend his control to northern Korea and made a series of public statements over the next two years about the need for reunification. His willingness to use force to achieve this objective caused the United States to limit South Korea's military capabilities. During the first weeks after the North Korean invasion of South Korea*, it appeared that reunification would result in the destruction of Rhee's regime. However, the Inch-'ŏn landing* reversed the course of the conflict and revived Rhee's ambition to rule a united nation, although there was strong opposition to such an outcome in the UN. Despite counsels to the contrary, he visited P'yŏngyang in October 1950 during the brief period of UNC* occupation of North Korea* and addressed a mass rally, where he was enthusiastically received. Chinese military intervention* brought an end to Rhee's hopes for an early reunification, as the United States sought a cease-fire in the vicinity of the thirty-eighth parallel. Thereafter, Rhee stridently opposed a truce if it left Korea divided, even attempting at the last minute to scuttle the armistice agreement* with his release of North Korean POWs* in June 1953. This angered the United States, as had Rhee's repression of political opponents throughout the war, most notably during the South Korean political crisis of 1952*. Both the Truman and Eisenhower administrations considered implementing Operation Everready*, a plan for removing Rhee from power.

Even Rhee's earliest writings show a paternalistic streak. As he confided to Robert T. Oliver*, his idea of good politics was more akin to the Confucian concept of an extended family led by a wise and devoted leader than to liberal democracy. Yet he failed to capitalize on the support he enjoyed to modernize the country and meet the expectations of the populace for political and economic development, adhering instead to a personalized style of rule that proved to be his ruin. Nevertheless, when he resigned following mass demonstrations in April 1960 and left the presidential palace for his private residence, citizens waved along the way and some even wept. He left Korea the next month for Hawaii, where he died in exile, yearning to the end to be back in Korea again.

B. Cumings, *The Origins of the Korean War* (Princeton, 1981; 1990); Q. Kim, *The Fall of Syngman Rhee* (Berkeley, 1983); R. T. Oliver, *Syngman Rhee and American Involvement in Korea, 1942–1960* (Seoul, 1978); S. Rhee, *Japan Inside Out* (New York, 1940); S. Rhee, *Tongnip Chŏngsin* (Seoul, 1947).

J. Y. Ra

RHEE ASSASSINATION ATTEMPT (June 25, 1952)

On June 25, 1952, during a ceremony attended by 50,000 people in Pusan marking the second anniversary of the outbreak of the Korean War, a 62-year-old gunman confronted President Syngman Rhee* of the Republic of Korea* at the podium where he was speaking, pointed a pistol at him at point-blank range, and pulled the trigger twice. The gun misfired both times, and the would-be assassin was overpowered by the director of the Korean National Police. The assassin was identified as Yu Sit'ae, an ultranationalist member of the Blood and Justice Association, whom police later claimed was acting as part of a larger plot by the opposition Democratic Nationalist party, which was opposed to Rhee's plans to change the ROK's constitution to ensure his reelection. South Korean security forces subsequently arrested two members of the Democratic Nationalist party.

The assassination had a stage-managed atmosphere with the probable intention of garnering public sympathy for Rhee and bolstering his claims that there was a plot against him. The attempt took place during the height of the bruising South Korean political crisis of 1952* in which Rhee charged that opposition National Assembly members were conspiring with the Democratic People's Republic of Korea* to bring him down. Rhee's conspiracy theories met with great skepticism among the foreign press and the diplomatic community. It seemed almost too fortuitous that an assassination would take place before the eyes of U.S. ambassador John J. Muccio*, the official diplomatic community, and most foreign journalists. In Washington, General Omar N. Bradley*, the chairman of the JCS, wondered if the empty-gun assassination was staged by Rhee himself. H. Freeman Matthews* of the State Department agreed that such a thought had "crossed our dirty minds too."

Foreign Relations of the United States, 1952–1954, vol. 15: *Korea* (Washington, D.C., 1984); *New York Times*, June 25, 1952.

Edward C. Keefer

RHEE-ROBERTSON COMMUNIQUÉ (July 11, 1953)

This press release summarized the results of the Robertson Mission* to the Republic of Korea*. Assistant Secretary of State Walter S. Robertson* suggested to President Syngman Rhee* that they issue this communiqué, which outlined in general terms the price the United States would pay to obtain South Korea's support for the armistice agreement* ending the Korean War. It described the two weeks of exchanges as "frank and cordial," achieving major strides toward a "mutual understanding" on "troubling questions."

First, the United States and the ROK reaffirmed their determination that "at the end of the specified period, all prisoners wanting to avoid returning to Communist jurisdiction shall be set free in South Korea," while Chinese POWs would proceed to the destination of their choice. Second, they agreed to enter "into a mutual-defense pact, negotiations for which are underway." Third, there were discussions related to "collaboration along political, economic, and defense lines" for the purpose of achieving "the realization within the shortest possible time of . . . a free, independent, and unified Korea." The communiqué ended confidently that there would be "continuing mutual consideration and . . . mutual accommodation'' between the two nations. Washington recommended issuing the communiqué to reassure the People's Republic of China* and U.S. allies that it had persuaded Rhee not to disrupt the armistice.

Department of State Bulletin, July 20, 1953.

RHEE'S DECLARATION OF MARTIAL LAW (May 25, 1952)

At one minute past midnight, May 25, 1952, President Syngman Rhee* declared martial law in Pusan, the Republic of Korea's* temporary capital, and in twenty-two neighboring counties. Rhee designated Major General Won Yong-duk*, a Rhee loyalist, as martial law commander with instructions to report directly to the president, thus bypassing military chains of command. Won Yong-duk issued proclamations limiting the carrying of firearms, restricting the holding of meetings, and instituting censorship, and claimed authority to arrest any government official. One of the general's first acts under martial law was to arrest So Min-ho, a leading independent member of the National Assembly and a critic of the Rhee administration. On the following day, military police detained forty-five members of the National Assembly. After two days of martial law, all but twelve assemblymen were released, but Rhee had passed his message to the legislature that its members were not safe from arrest.

While everyone realized that Rhee was using martial law as a screen to intimidate his opponents in the assembly, there was little agreement on how to stop him. During the remainder of the South Korean political crisis of 1952*, the United States, the UNCURK*, and other Western allies attempted without success various ploys to persuade Rhee to lift martial law. Even after July 3, when Rhee forced the assembly to pass his constitutional amendments, martial law remained in force. The use of martial law proved an effective mechanism for coercion against the National Assembly and a means of preventing potential popular opposition to rally to the support of the National Assembly.

Foreign Relations of the United States, 1952–1954, vol. 15: *Korea* (Washington, D.C., 1984); Report of the United Nations Commission for the Unification and Rehabilitation of Korea, U.N. Document A/2187 (New York, 1952).

Edward C. Keefer

RHEE'S RELEASE OF NORTH KOREAN POWS (June 18, 1953)

On June 18, 1953, President Syngman Rhee* released 27,000 North Korean POWs from four prison camps under the Republic of Korea's* control. Beyond his concern for the North Korean POWs, Rhee sought to use the release to prevent an armistice in the Korean War. The guards simply opened the gates and allowed the POWs to walk out. Most melted into South Korean society without a trace. Taken totally by surprise, the UNC* found itself virtually powerless to prevent the breakout. In April and May 1953, Rhee had pressed the United States to allow him to release North Korean POWs on the grounds that they should never be subjected to peacetime captivity under the supervision of the Neutral Nations Repatriation Commission*. Rhee feared that North Korean officials would take advantage of the commission and coerce non-repatriate North

Koreans to return to their homelands. First dismissing Rhee's strident opposition to including North Koreans in the complicated POW package as bluff, the Eisenhower administration came to take Rhee's threats of unilateral action more seriously. Nonetheless, President Dwight D. Eisenhower's* advisors convinced him that either to release the North Korean POWs unilaterally or even to reopen the negotiations on agenda item 4*, POW repatriation, might jeopardize the tentative POW settlement, which had virtually been agreed upon.

Rhee's unilateral action occurred just as the negotiators at the P'anmunjŏm truce talks* were polishing the final details of the armistice agreement*. In Washington, the NSC meeting to assess the damage was one of the grimmest of Eisenhower's presidency. The president was convinced that the armistice would collapse. Eisenhower wondered if the United States might not have to walk away from Korea after years of costly war. Secretary of State John Foster Dulles* stated that Rhee must be given stern private and public lectures, but he maintained that the United States could weather the storm because the Communists wanted an armistice so much that they would overlook the release. Other administration members supported Dulles, but Eisenhower judged such advice a "complete surrender to [Rhee's] blackmail." After cabinet and congressional leadership meetings on the next day, Eisenhower faced a clear consensus in Washington not to overreact but to convince Rhee to go along with the armistice.

Thereafter, the United States followed a policy of concession, persuasion, and hints of coercion to lead and push Rhee to accept an armistice. As Dulles had predicted, the Communist side returned to the negotiating table and signed the armistice. The POW release and Washington's surprised reaction to it demonstrated clearly that Rhee had acted on his own initiative, exploiting the defects of UNC POW administration*. While the release did no more than temporarily delay the armistice, it did force the Eisenhower administration to come to terms with Rhee's opposition to the peace agreement. The release also proved that the real POW issue all along had been Chinese, not Korean, prisoners. *See also* Robertson Mission.

B. I. Kaufman, *The Korean War* (Philadelphia, 1986); E. C. Keefer, "President Dwight D. Eisenhower and the End of the Korean War," *Diplomatic History* (Summer 1986).

Edward C. Keefer

RIDGWAY, MATTHEW B. (1895–   )

General Matthew Bunker Ridgway commanded the 8th Army* in Korea from December 1950 until April 1951 and then served as CINCUNC until May 1952. Born at Fort Monroe, Virginia, he graduated from the U.S. Military Academy in 1917. Thereafter, he rose through the ranks as an infantry officer. At the time of Pearl Harbor in December 1941, Ridgway was serving in the headquarters of Army Chief of Staff General George C. Marshall* in Washington. Ridgway commanded the 82d Airborne in Europe during 1943 and 1944 before taking over the 18th Airborne Corps. In 1946, he represented General Dwight D. Eisenhower*, then chief of staff, on the UN military staff committee. In September 1949, General J. Lawton Collins*, the new chief of staff, requested that Ridgway become his deputy in the Pentagon.

With the death in December 1950 of Lieutenant General Walton W. Walker*, commander of the 8th Army, Ridgway received the appointment as his successor. After examining U.S. lines on January 2, 1951, he ordered the 8th Army to fall back to the Han River, leaving Seoul, the capital of the Republic of Korea*, in enemy hands. Within weeks, the U.S. and the ROK forces were prepared to counterattack, implementing thereafter Ridgway's "meat grinder" strategy*. On March 14, the 8th Army reoccupied Seoul and continued north to the Kansas Line, roughly parallel to and north of the thirty-eighth parallel. Ridgway now prepared his forces to withstand a Chinese counterattack. Meanwhile, Ridgway rejected CINCUNC General Douglas MacArthur's* plan for victory* because it ran the risk of a world war without offering any possibility of success. Ridgway doubted that any effort to drive the Chinese People's Volunteers Army* back to the Yalu was worth the cost. With President Harry S. Truman's* recall of MacArthur* in April 1951, Ridgway became CINCUNC. During the fierce Chinese spring offensives in 1951*, Ridgway ordered his successor as 8th Army commander, Lieutenant General James A. Van Fleet*, to reinforce the Kansas Line (after adjustments, the Kansas-Wyoming Line*). Any northward advance, Ridgway cautioned, would create more casualties than the gains would justify.

In Tokyo, Ridgway continued to advocate a military stalemate in Korea. He assumed responsibility for opening the Kaesŏng truce talks* with the Chinese and North Koreans in July 1951. Despite the seemingly fruitless exchanges over the next nine months, Ridgway believed the negotiations were a necessary alternative to an endless and costly struggle for power for Korea. Throughout the negotiations, he revealed a tendency to be impatient, inflexible, and dogmatic. In May 1952, Ridgway succeeded General Eisenhower as supreme allied commander in Europe. During the Eisenhower administration, Ridgway, as U.S. Army chief of staff, would voice strong opposition to a U.S. military commitment to prevent a French defeat in Indochina at the hands of the Vietminh. His experiences in Korea also would cause him to advocate deescalation of the Vietnam War in 1968 as one of President Lyndon B. Johnson's "Wise Men." See also Active Defense Strategy; Ridgway's June 30, 1951, Armistice Message.

C. Blair, *The Forgotten War* (New York, 1987); M. B. Ridgway, *The Korean War* (Garden City, N.Y., 1967); M. B. Ridgway, *Soldier: The Memoirs of Matthew B. Ridgway* (New York, 1956).

Norman A. Graebner

RIDGWAY'S JUNE 30, 1951, ARMISTICE MESSAGE

Acting on instructions from Washington, CINCUNC General Matthew B. Ridgway* made this broadcast to the commanders of the Chinese People's Volunteers Army* (CPVA) and the North Korean People's Army (NKPA) proposing negotiations for an armistice in Korea. The message followed a speech by the Soviet UN ambassador, Jacob A. Malik*, on June 23, 1951, which had expressed

Soviet support for truce talks. Ridgway's statement was carefully drafted to avoid any implication that the UNC* was defeated or suing for peace and implied that the initiative had come from the other side. At the same time, it avoided humiliating the enemy, leaving the way open for the Communists to negotiate without loss of face. Ridgway noted that he had been informed that the Communists might wish a meeting to discuss an armistice that would end the fighting and contain adequate guarantees against a renewal of hostilities. If the opposing commanders sent word that they desired such an armistice, Ridgway was prepared to name a date for a meeting and to nominate his representative. He proposed that armistice negotiations take place in a Danish hospital ship in Wŏnsan harbor.

On July 2, 1951, Radio Peking broadcast a statement signed by Kim Il Sung*, the commander in chief of the NKPA, and Peng Teh-huai*, the commander of the CPVA, responding to Ridgway's proposal. The message noted that they were authorized to suspend military operations and to hold peace negotiations. They suggested that delegates from both sides should meet between July 10 and July 15 at Kaesŏng on the thirty-eighth parallel. The first meeting of liaison officers took place on July 8, and the Kaesŏng truce talks* began two days later. *See also* Malik's Radio Address of June 23, 1951.

D. Acheson, *Present at the Creation* (London, 1969); B. I. Kaufman, *The Korean War* (Philadelphia, 1986); H. S. Truman, *Years of Trial and Hope* (Garden City, N.Y., 1956).

Callum A. MacDonald

ROBERTS, WILLIAM L. (1891–1968)

Brigadier General William Lynn Roberts was the commanding officer of the Korean Military Advisory Group* (KMAG) from its creation until just before the start of the Korean War. He graduated from the U.S. Military Academy in 1913 and fought in France during World War I. During World War II, Roberts was tank commander of a combat unit in the 10th Armored Division. By 1944, he had attained only the rank of colonel, finishing the war as assistant commander of the 4th Armored Division. Entering the postwar era with an undistinguished record, Roberts soon faced mandatory retirement. In 1948, he arrived in southern Korea as an advisor to the director of the Department of Internal Security in the U.S. military government. With the formal establishment of the Republic of Korea* on August 15, Roberts became head of the Provisional Korean Military Advisory Group, then comprised of approximately 100 men. Five months later, U.S. military occupation of Korea formally ended, and Roberts replaced Major General John B. Coulter* as commander of the remaining U.S. military forces on the peninsula. His 5th Regimental Combat Team consisted of the 32d Infantry Regiment, the 48th Field Artillery Battalion, and the 7th Mechanized Cavalry Reconnaissance Team.

On June 29, 1949, complete U.S. military withdrawal from Korea* occurred, and two days later, the United States formally announced establishment of the KMAG. Its mission was to help train an army capable of defending the ROK without a guarantee of U.S. military protection. Roberts now was the commander of roughly 500 advisers and the main military adviser to Ambassador John J. Muccio*. Scheduled to leave Korea in one year, he was determined to field a credible army prior to his departure. Thus, in the spring of 1950, Roberts inaugurated a publicity campaign aimed at portraying the ROK's army as a more formidable force than circumstances warranted. He invited journalists and assorted politicians to South Korea and then escorted them to the field to witness the successful results of U.S. military advice and assistance. Ambassador Philip C. Jessup* and Senator William F. Knowland* were impressed, reporting that the South Korean army would shatter any North Korean invasion force. In March 1950, when a newsman asked about South Korea's lack of tanks, Roberts responded that Korea was ''not good tank country'' because of ''poor roads and bridges.'' Besides, it was ''good'' infantry that won wars and South Korean soldiers were superior to those in North Korea in ''training, leadership, morale, marksmanship, and better small arms equipment.''

Despite optimistic public pronouncements, Roberts had private doubts about South Korea's ability either to deter or repel an invasion from the north. He strongly endorsed Ambassador Muccio's forceful recommendations in the spring of 1950 to provide the ROK with aircraft, heavy artillery, anti-aircraft weapons, and tanks. Nevertheless, on June 5, 1950, Roberts, in an interview with *Time* magazine, declared flatly that the ROK army was the ''best doggone shooting army outside the United States.'' Consequently, the Truman administration instructed him to develop plans for the gradual curtailment of KMAG activities by the end of 1950. Less than a week before the war began, Roberts left Korea for the United States and retirement. On June 20, he stopped in Tokyo and there told General Omar N. Bradley*, the chairman of the JCS, that South Korea was capable of repelling any attack from the north. His replacement, Colonel W. H. Sterling Wright, echoed these sentiments in cables he sent to Washington during the last days prior to the North Korean invasion of South Korea*.

C. Blair, *The Forgotten War* (New York, 1987); J. I. Matray, *The Reluctant Crusade* (Honolulu, 1985); R. K. Sawyer and W. G. Hermes, *Military Advisors in Korea: KMAG in Peace and War* (Washington, D.C., 1962).

ROBERTSON, SIR HORACE C. H. (1894–1960)

Lieutenant General Sir Horace Clement Hugh Robertson was commander in chief, British Commonwealth Occupation Force and British Commonwealth Forces, Korea, from 1950 to 1951. A graduate of the second class at RMC Duntroon in 1914, Robertson served at Gallipoli and in Palestine during World War I. He attended the Staff College, Camberley (1923–1924), and then held a variety of staff and training posts in the small interwar Australian army. In early 1941, he led the 19th Australian Infantry Brigade during the highly successful campaign of the Australian 6th Division against the Italians in Libya. He returned to Australia in 1942, commanding Australian units in the final campaigns in the South West Pacific Area in 1945. He was appointed commander in chief of the British Commonwealth Occupation Force in Japan in April 1946, the most senior Allied officer in Japan after General Douglas MacArthur* himself.

One of the brightest Australian officers of his generation, Robertson was in a unique position in Japan as the first dominion officer to command a Commonwealth force containing British as well as dominion troops. His period of command in Japan was not easy, and he quarreled with both authorities in London and some of his British subordinates, disagreements not helped by his difficult personality. Many of the same disputes were to surface again after the Korean War began, when Robertson was made responsible for the non-operational, administrative, and logistical support of the Commonwealth Division* in Korea. Known as ''red Robbie''—for the color of his hair, not his temper—Robertson was a mercurial character about whom few of his contemporaries were neutral. A man of considerable intellect, his arrogance and tactlessness did not endear him to many, but he enjoyed good relations with successive CINCUNCs and was an effective advocate of Commonwealth interests within the U.S. command structure.

Roberton's achievements in Japan and Korea were considerable. The decision had been taken in May 1950 to withdraw the remaining Commonwealth units from Japan, and the outbreak of fighting in Korea found them understrength and ill prepared for operations. In the early months of the war, Robertson acted as a conduit for information between MacArthur and his superiors, successfully prevailing upon them to allow MacArthur to deploy the Royal Australian Air Force's No. 77 Squadron against the North Koreans within days of the northern invasion. At the same time, he oversaw the rapid reinforcement and training of the only Australian infantry battalion still in Japan, which was dispatched to join the UNC* forces in September 1950. Returned to Australia in November 1951, he held several senior appointments in Australia before retiring in 1954.

J. Grey, *The Commonwealth Armies and the Korean War* (Manchester, 1988); R. J. O'Neill, *Australia in the Korean War 1950–53* (Canberra, 1981, 1985).

Jeffrey Grey

ROBERTSON MISSION (June 22–July 12, 1953)

Assistant Secretary of State for Far Eastern Affairs Walter S. Robertson* went to the Republic of Korea* on June 22, 1953, to convince President Syngman Rhee* to agree to an armistice in the Korean War. Rhee's release of North Korean POWs* four days earlier added a sense of urgency to the mission. Robertson carried a stinging letter from Secretary of State John Foster Dulles* recalling U.S. sacrifices in defense of Korea and denying Rhee's contention that the Korean War had been fought to reunite Korea militarily. Nevertheless, Robertson was prepared to discuss concessions with Rhee. After Robertson's and Rhee's initial meetings, South Korea's terms for accepting an armistice became clear. Rhee insisted that the remaining North Korean non-repatriate POWs be turned over to the Neutral Nations Repatriation Commission* at the DMZ (not on South Korean soil), the political conference be limited to ninety days of discussion, Washington support an expanded twenty-division ROK army and augmented naval and air forces and provide massive U.S. economic aid, and the United States and the ROK sign a mutual defense treaty.

President Dwight D. Eisenhower* and Dulles accepted all of Rhee's terms with the exception of the ninety-day limit to the political conference, since they believed that an international conference could not have a time limit. However, if after ninety days it became clear that the conference was a mere propaganda exercise, the United States would consult with the ROK and then jointly withdraw. While the Eisenhower administration could not actually guarantee a mutual defense treaty prior to achieving Senate consent, Eisenhower and Dulles fully expected passage. When Robertson transmitted these views to Seoul, Rhee sensed an overeagerness and added two new conditions for an armistice: the possibility of an ROK army larger than twenty divisions and a promise that, if the political conference failed after ninety days, the United States and the ROK would resume military operations against the north.

Robertson rejected these new demands. He warned Washington to expect a long haggle with Rhee unless it was prepared to persuade and push him to realize that he had received Washington's last and best offer. To this end, the Eisenhower administration instituted a policy of planned leaks and feints indicating that the United States was prepared to leave Korea should the ROK fight on after the armistice. Washington also orchestrated a campaign by key U.S. congressional and private supporters of Rhee to press him to accept an armistice. The Eisenhower administration was under great international pressure to get an armistice, and it was prepared to pay Rhee his price so long as he accepted a divided Korea and did not disrupt the peace machinery. Rhee bowed to the inevitable with ill grace, but he made the best bargain he could. During the mission, Robertson displayed skill in persuasion and a penchant for hard bargaining. Both sides made concessions, but Rhee received the better deal. *See also* Dulles-Rhee Correspondence; POW Transfer Location Question; Rhee-Robertson Communiqué.

Foreign Relations of the United States, 1952–1954, vol. 15: *Korea* (Washington, D.C., 1984); B. I. Kaufman, *The Korean War* (Philadelphia, 1986).

Edward C. Keefer

ROBERTSON, WALTER S. (1893–1970)

Walter S. Robertson was appointed assistant secretary of state for Far Eastern affairs by President Dwight D. Eisenhower* in January 1953 and served in that post until he retired in June 1959. In this capacity, Robertson was the overall coordinator of Korean policy in the Department of State. Nonetheless, Robertson relied heavily on U. Alexis Johnson*, deputy assistant secretary of state for Far Eastern affairs, who had the day-to-day responsibility for Korea policy. Robertson travelled to the Republic of Korea* in June 1953 for negotiations with President Syngman Rhee* in what turned out to be part of a successful effort to persuade Rhee to pledge not to disrupt the armistice agreement*.

Robertson attended Hoge Military Academy, the College of William and Mary, and Davidson College. He left college to join the Richmond banking firm of Scott and Stringfellow. His banking career was interrupted when he enlisted in the U.S. Air Corps during World War II. During the war, Robertson transferred to the foreign service and became counselor for economic affairs at the U.S. embassy in Chungking, the wartime capital of the Republic of China*. Robertson became chargé of the embassy and served in that post until June 1946, when the embassy returned to Nanking. After he resumed his business career in late 1946, Robertson, a close friend of Chiang Kai-shek*, continued to be a vigorous public proponent of the view that the Chinese Nationalists on Taiwan comprised the only legitimate Chinese government.

Robertson's close ties to the China lobby made him a natural Eisenhower appointee for Far Eastern affairs at the State Department. Among his colleagues, Robertson was considered even more anti-Communist than his boss, Secretary of State John Foster Dulles.* Robertson therefore proved an acceptable substitute to Rhee when Dulles was unable to come to Korea to negotiate the conditions under which the Republic of Korea would accept the armistice. As it turned out, Rhee was surprised to find that Robertson was not more sympathetic to the calls to reunify Korea by force of arms under the anti-Communist banner. While Robertson was sympathetic to Rhee's concerns, he followed the Washington script by firmly informing the South Korean president that the United States was not prepared to continue the war to unify Korea. Still, Robertson administered this bitter pill to Rhee with a skillful mixture of persuasion, promise of future concessions, and threat of breaking off his mission if Rhee and he could not come to a tentative agreement. *See also* Robertson Mission.

Foreign Relations of the United States, 1952–1954, vol. 15: *Korea* (Washington, D.C., 1984); *New York Times,* January 20, 1970.

Edward C. Keefer

ROTATION OF TROOPS SYSTEM

Among the most serious criticisms of U.S. personnel practices in World War II had been the policy of replacing losses by individuals rather than by units and keeping divisions in action for extended periods. A policy of individual rotation on the basis of time in combat had been tested in 1944, but the number of men affected was small. During the Korean War, taking into account these criticisms and seeking to compensate for the problems occasioned by the harsh winters, the United States and Britain (and subsequently Canada) introduced a policy of individual rotation for soldiers who served a specified time in a combat theater. At first, the rotation policies appear to have been somewhat informal. Only after the armistice talks began in earnest were they codified. A point system was inaugurated. A total of thirty-six points was required for rotation home; a soldier earned four points for each month in the combat zone, three for being located from the line of emplaced batteries back through regimental headquarters, and two for rear echelon duty. Thus, the average infantryman could expect to return home within a year if he survived. The system proved controversial, some claiming—as later in Vietnam—that ''short timers'' became overly cautious in combat. Another criticism was that the policy of individual rotation weakened

RUSK, DEAN

morale by destroying unit cohesion. Certainly, the loss of savvy and battle toughness, as "reservists, National Guardsmen, and draftees" replaced experienced soldiers, had serious consequences by mid-1952. Nevertheless, troop rotation as a mechanism for equalizing sacrifice was highly popular among combat soldiers.

T. R. Fehrenbach, *This Kind of War* (New York, 1963); A. Kellett, *Combat Motivation* (Boston, 1982); R. Leckie, *Conflict: The History of the Korean War, 1950–1953* (New York, 1962).

Theodore A. Wilson

RUSK, DEAN (1909–   )

Dean Rusk was assistant secretary of state for Far Eastern affairs from the start of the Korean conflict until December 1951. Although influential in policymaking regarding Korea before and during the war, he would gain greater fame as secretary of state under Presidents John F. Kennedy and Lyndon B. Johnson. The son of an ordained Presbyterian minister who was also a tenant farmer, Rusk was born on a hardscrabble farm in Cherokee county, Georgia. He received a drive for success from his family that pushed him into a college education at Davidson. After a Rhodes Scholarship at Oxford, he served as a professor of international relations at Mills College and as dean of the faculty. Given his educational background, his interest in world affairs, and his reserve commission, Rusk rose during World War II to the position of deputy chief of staff for the China-Burma-India theater in 1944. His talents brought him to Washington in 1945, where, as a member of the operations division of the U.S. Army General Staff, he helped to choose the thirty-eighth parallel as a dividing line between U.S. and Soviet forces in liberated Korea.

Although tempted to remain in military service after World War II, he transferred to the State Department in March 1947, serving as director of UN affairs from 1947 to 1949. He was appointed deputy under secretary of state in 1949 and assistant secretary of state for Far Eastern affairs in March of the following year. In June 1950, before the Korean War began, he had presented his misgivings about the reduction in appropriations for Korea and the wisdom of U.S. military withdrawal from Korea*. Still, he claimed immediately prior to the invasion that the Republic of Korea* could resist incursions from the north but doubted the likelihood of a major attack. After the North Korean invasion of South Korea*, it was Rusk who was as responsible as any other official for making the resistance a matter for the UN. Rusk was also a key figure in preparing recommendations for the neutralization of Taiwan*, as a likely future victim of Communist aggression, without further involvement with the unreliable Chiang Kai-shek* regime.

After the Inch'ŏn landing*, Rusk worked for State Department support of a unified Korea and a UN offensive across the thirty-eighth parallel*. Consequently, Rusk had to bear part of the burden for the disaster in the winter of 1950–1951 after Chinese military intervention*. His response in a major speech in May 1951 was to castigate the People's Republic of China* as a puppet of the Soviet Union. In the short run, Rusk's hyperbole blunted some of the congressional criticism of the administration's policies in Korea; in the longer run, he may have made more difficult U.S. perceptions of genuine rift between the two Communist powers when they did take place a decade later. Before leaving office in December 1951, he claimed that major objectives had been won: containment in Korea without igniting a general war, support for the Republic of China*, and general assistance to "free nations" in Asia in the global spirit of the Truman Doctrine. Many of the positions he would take ten years later as secretary of state, especially regarding U.S. policy before and during the Vietnam War, were based on his experiences and conclusions drawn from them during the Korean War. *See also* Thirty-eighth Parallel Division.

W. Cohen, *Dean Rusk* (Totowa, N.J., 1980); T. J. Schoenbaum, *Waging Peace and War* (New York, 1988).

Lawrence S. Kaplan

S

___

SAINT LAURENT, LOUIS S. (1882–1973)

Louis S. Saint Laurent was Canada's prime minister from 1948 to 1957. Born in Compton, Quebec, he graduated from St. Charles College in 1902 and then earned a law degree from Laval University. Thereafter, until World War II, Saint Laurent spent most of his time pleading cases before the Canadian Supreme Court and the British Privy Council while teaching at Laval and campaigning for an end to Canada's dominion status. In 1941, Prime Minister Mackenzie King, needing help in his fight for conscription, asked Saint Laurent to become his minister of justice and attorney general because of his legal stature and French-Canadian background. Although non-political, Saint Laurent agreed to serve for the duration of World War II but could join the cabinet only after his election to Parliament in 1942 as a member of the Liberal party. He would retain these posts until 1946, attending the San Francisco Conference in 1945 and then successfully steering the UN Charter through Parliament. At the UN General Assembly's First Session in 1946, Sain Laurent was a member of the Canadian delegation and concentrated his efforts on strengthening the Security Council. That same year, he became secretary of state for external affairs, remaining in this position until he replaced King as prime minister in 1948.

For Saint Laurent, it was important for Canada to exert its influence in international affairs. He therefore advocated cooperation with the U.S. efforts to hold internationally supervised elections in Korea under the UN resolution of November 14, 1947*. Prime Minister King disagreed, insisting that Canada avoid any appearance of succumbing to U.S. dictation. But Saint Laurent prevailed, which perhaps contributed to Canada's election as a member of the Security Council in 1948. In response to the North Korean invasion of South Korea*, Saint Laurent, now prime minister, instructed the Canadian delegation to support the UN call for assistance in defending the Republic of Korea*. Also, he dispatched a Canadian destroyer and a brigade of ground troops to fight in Korea. After Chinese military intervention*, however, he worked with Lester B. Pearson*, his secretary of state for external affairs, to limit the conflict and attain an early cease-fire, opposing, for example, condemning the People's Republic of China* for aggression. A patient and genteel man, Saint Laurent retired after the Conservative party's electoral victory in 1957. He left behind a record reflecting his preference for conciliation, compromise, and constructive action.

Current Biography, 1948; Foreign Relations of the United States, 1947, vol. 6: The Far East (Washington, D.C., 1972); New York Times, July 26, 1973; Who Was Who in America, vol. 5: 1969–1973 (Chicago, 1973).

SANACC 176/35 (January 14, 1948)

This policy statement superseded SWNCC (State-War-Navy Coordinating Committee) 176/30* and remained the basic U.S. policy on Korea until approval of NSC-8* on April 2, 1948. The product of a review by the State–Army–Navy–Air Force Coordinating Committee (SANACC) of Korean policy, it centered around five key elements. First, SWNCC 176/30 specified that the United States should seek to reduce its commitment of men and money in Korea. Second, the JCS had recently issued a report (JCS 1483/44) stating that the United States had "little strategic interest in maintaining its present troops and bases in Korea." Third, at a meeting held on September 29, 1947, top State Department officials—including Secretary of State George C. Marshall*—concluded that because "ultimately the U.S. position in Korea" was "untenable," the United States should seek to "effect a settlement of the Korean problem which would enable the U.S. to withdraw from Korea as soon as possible with the minimum of bad effects." Fourth, while some earlier experts had contended that the economy of southern Korea could be rendered nearly self-sufficient, the new planners considered this impossible. Fifth, the UN resolution of November 14, 1947*, provided for the holding of elections in Korea no later than March 31, 1948, to form a unified provisional government.

Together, these five elements shaped the SANACC's thinking. In formulating the body of the new policy statement, the SANACC focused first on the upcoming UN-sponsored elections in Korea. It concluded that if the Soviets refused to allow elections in the north, the United States should use the elections to establish a more representative interim government in the south. Immediate U.S. withdrawal, the policymakers maintained, would result in the Communist domination of Korea and "serious damage to U.S. prestige," but they anticipated withdrawal in the future. Although they laid plans for "possible" U.S. aid following this withdrawal, they firmly ruled out any commitment to assistance beyond December 31, 1948. Despite the generally negative tone of their finished policy statement, the SANACC subcommittee concluded that the goal of U.S. policy remained a unified, independent Korea. Following its adoption, SANACC 176/35 gradually proved insufficient. Both the State Department and the Pentagon had already reached the conclusion that the U.S. position in Korea was untenable, and they wanted a policy even more clearly in line with that assessment, resulting in a new Korean policy—NSC-8. See also JCS Memorandum on Korea's Strategic Significance; Wedemeyer Report.

R. L. McGlothlen, "Acheson, Economics, and the American Commitment in Korea," *Pacific Historical Review* (February 1989); J. I. Matray, *The Reluctant Crusade* (Honolulu, 1985); W. W. Stueck, *The Road to Confrontation* (Chapel Hill, 1981).

Ronald L. McGlothlen

SCREENING OF POWS
See Operation Scatter

SEBALD, WILLIAM J. (1901–   )

William Sebald was political adviser to CINCUNC General Douglas MacArthur* before and during the Korean War. Born in Maryland, Sebald graduated from the U.S. Naval Academy in 1922, and three years later, the U.S. Navy assigned him to Japan as a language officer. After marrying while in Japan, he resigned from the navy, took a law degree at the University of Maryland, and returned to Japan in 1933. He remained until 1939 as a specialist in Japanese commercial law. In 1946, Sebald returned to Japan as a legal assistant to the acting political adviser to MacArthur. Upon the death of his chief in 1947, Sebald succeeded to three positions: political adviser (as representative of the State Department) to MacArthur, chief of the diplomatic section of MacArthur's headquarters, and chairman and U.S. member of the Allied Council for Japan, the international advisory body to the occupation.

During the Korean War, Sebald maintained the excellent relationship that he had built up with MacArthur since 1945, thus serving as an important channel of information for the State Department. It was to Sebald that MacArthur outlined on November 14, 1950—less than two weeks before the first major Chinese assault—his concept of what he thought would be the final stages of the Korean campaign. The plan included destruction of the bridges across the Yalu. Ominously, MacArthur added that if his concept failed, the bombing of "key points" in Manchuria might be necessary.

Sebald was not influential in policy decisions relating to the war, though he participated in many important meetings when emissaries from Washington made the pilgrimage to MacArthur. In July 1951, the JCS in effect vetoed Sebald's participation in the Kaesŏng truce talks*, on the grounds that it would indicate too plainly the political aspects of the talks and might even lead to speculation of a linkage between the truce talks and the Japanese Peace Treaty* preparations, in which Sebald was then involved. After President Harry S. Truman's* recall of MacArthur* in April 1951, Sebald retained his posts. He remained in Japan until shortly before the formal end of the occupation in April 1952. Thereafter, he became ambassador to Burma.

Foreign Relations of the United States, 1950, vol. 7: *Korea* (Washington, D.C., 1976) and *1951*, vol. 7: *Korea and China* (Washington, D.C., 1983); W. J. Sebald, *With MacArthur in Japan* (New York, 1965).

David W. Mabon

SECOND BLAIR HOUSE MEETING (June 26, 1950)

President Harry S. Truman* convened a second gathering of his top advisers to discuss possible additional steps to halt the North Korean invasion of South

Korea* after the Democratic People's Republic of Korea* ignored the UN Security Council resolution of June 25, 1950*, calling for a cease-fire and the withdrawal of the North Korean People's Army north of the thirty-eighth parallel. Following the pattern set at the first Blair House meeting*, Secretary of State Dean G. Acheson* opened the evening conversations and recommended removing all restrictions on the use of naval and air power in Korea. The president approved this proposal but emphasized that U.S. operations should not extend north of the thirty-eighth parallel. Returning to an issue discussed the prior night, Acheson raised the proposal for dispatching the 7th Fleet to the Taiwan Strait. Truman now decided to authorize the neutralization of Taiwan*. The participants then touched briefly on policy at the UN. Acheson explained that the United States would submit the next day what would become the UN Security Council resolution of June 27, 1950*. Truman stressed the importance of unqualified international support for the U.S. plan.

Discussions then shifted to the battlefield situation in Korea. Army Chief of Staff General J. Lawton Collins* reported pessimistically that the Republic of Korea* was on the verge of total collapse. Acheson commented that if Korean attempts at self-defense failed, the United States had to intervene more directly. Secretary of Defense Louis A. Johnson* disagreed, insisting that the United States had done enough. Truman spoke in favor of Acheson's position, declaring vaguely that "we must do everything we can for the Korean situation—for the United Nations." JCS Chairman General Omar N. Bradley* and Collins, assuming that Truman had just indicated his willingness to commit ground forces, reminded the president that such a decision would entail the need for mobilization. In reply, both Truman and Acheson voiced the hope that the United States could avoid this drastic step. At noon the next day, Truman, in his June 27, 1950, statement*, informed the American people of his actions. Truman's decisions at the second Blair House meeting represented only a minor change in tactics. Air and naval power still were the main ingredients in the U.S. response. The president continued to place faith in South Korea's ability to defend itself with limited assistance. See also Congress and U.S. Military Intervention; Congressional Meetings with Truman of June 1950.

J. I. Matray, *The Reluctant Crusade* (Honolulu, 1985); G. D. Paige, *The Korean Decision* (New York, 1968); H. S. Truman, *Years of Trial and Hope* (Garden City, N.Y., 1956).

SECRET CEASE-FIRE NEGOTIATIONS OF 1951

After the Chinese People's Volunteers Army* liberated Seoul, the capital of the Republic of Korea*, in January 1951, Pak Jin-mok, a former provincial cadre of the South Korean Workers' party, met Ch'oi Ik-hwan, a senior comrade, and agreed that cease-fire negotiations should be initiated by the Koreans themselves to avoid further national sacrifice. Later that month at Seoul, they were successful in meeting Yi Sŭng-yŏp*, chairman of the Seoul People's Committee and a Politburo member of the Korean Workers' party. Yi asked that either Pak or Ch'oi travel to Pusan and secure an official credential from the ROK showing its sincere desire for armistice negotiations.

Soon Operation Ripper* resulted in the UNC* recapturing Seoul. Through Yi Yong-kyŏm, a former translator of Lieutenant General John R. Hodge*, Pak and Ch'oi met U.S. embassy official Harold J. Noble*, who in turn informed the U.S. Department of Army liaison detachment of the proposal for armistice talks. The commander of the ROK army learned of the initiative and charged that Pak and Ch'oi were Communists working for the Democratic People's Republic of Korea*. Despite these allegations, the commander of the 705th U.S. Infantry concluded that this attempt at cease-fire was worth pursuing. However, it was only after the Kaesŏng truce talks* began that the American side sent Pak to North Korea with a "permit to pass the frontier," not credentials.

Pak left on July 28 pledging that he would return within ten days. In P'yŏn-gyang, it took more than ten days for Pak to meet Yi, who refused to discuss the issue on the grounds that Pak did not have credentials. Then the U.S. Army sent Kim Hae-suk, a former common-law wife of Yi Sŭng-yŏp, to discover Pak's fate. In early September, Pak returned to Seoul, but the new commander of the 705th, unaware of Pak's secret mission, immediately arrested him as a DPRK agent. Pak, in the subsequent investigation, reported that the DPRK was unable to continue the hostilities further despite Chinese military intervention*. Kim's return to Seoul and favorable testimony for Pak persuaded the Americans to release Pak. Kim relayed the North Korean message asking for the sending of Ch'oi as an official representative. The U.S. Army sent Ch'oi in late fall; however, the DPRK detained him until May 1953.

Secret cease-fire negotiations had repercussions on the domestic politics of the two Koreas. In the north, Kim Il Sung* utilized the case against Yi Sŭng-yŏp and his party superior, Pak Hŏn-yŏng*, alleging that they had attempted to overthrow the DPRK regime "in collusion with the American imperialists." In the south, the governmental authorities indicted Pak and attempted to implicate Cho Pong-am, a progressive political leader.

Pak Jin-mok, *Grassroots: A Memoir* (1983); Shin Bok-nyŏng, "A Study of Secret Armistice Negotiation in the Korean War," *Korean Political Science Review* (Winter Seoul, 1987).

Hakjoon Kim

SHERMAN, FORREST P. (1896–1951)

Chief of naval operations from November 1949 until his death in July 1951, Admiral Forrest Percival Sherman attended MIT for one year before accepting an appointment to the U.S. Naval Academy. He excelled at Annapolis, graduating second in his class of 1919. Viewed as somewhat aloof by his classmates, Sherman displayed the leadership, ambition, and intellectualism that marked his career. He developed an early interest in naval aviation and earned his wings in 1922. During the interwar years, he combined service in aircraft carriers with staff work. In 1940, Chief of Naval Operations Admiral Harold R. Stark placed Commander Sherman on the war plans board, where he displayed a talent for strategic planning and for mediating opposing views among board members. In

May 1942, Captain Sherman received command of the carrier *Wasp*. After the loss of the *Wasp* during the Solomons campaign, Sherman was appointed chief of staff of Pacific Fleet air forces. In November 1943, he was promoted to rear admiral and transferred to the staff of CINCPAC Admiral Chester W. Nimitz.

Following the war, Sherman, now a vice-admiral, became deputy CNO for operations and drafted a plan, presented to President Harry S. Truman* and defended before Congress, that was influential in the evolving U.S. strategic posture. Subsequently, in December 1947, Chief of Naval Operations Admiral Louis Denfeld named Sherman commander of what would soon become the 6th Task Fleet in the Mediterranean. On November 1, 1949, Sherman was recalled to Washington to succeed Denfeld. His return was not universally heralded within the navy, but he nevertheless proved to be an extremely effective spokesman for his own service. With the backing of the JCS, Sherman won congressional budget support for the development of the first nuclear-powered submarine, the modernization of ships needed for U.S.-NATO operations, and for the creation of a balanced naval force capable of meeting the global Soviet threat. Some analysts suggest that without Sherman's capable leadership during this period of fiscal retrenchment, the U.S. Navy would not have had a single aircraft carrier in the western Pacific at the onset of the Korean War.

With the outbreak of the Korean conflict in June, Sherman successfully pushed for further naval expansion. He was present at the first and second Blair House meetings* and traveled with Army Chief of Staff General J. Lawton Collins* to Tokyo for discussions with CINCUNC General Douglas MacArthur* in August 1950 regarding Operation Chromite*, the Inch'ŏn landing proposal. Seeking wartime command of the Pacific without sacrificing European priorities, Sherman won congressional authorization for construction of a supercarrier, a hotly debated issue that had contributed to Denfeld's demise. On July 15, 1951, Sherman left Washington for Europe to begin delicate negotiations with Spanish, French, and British officials regarding U.S. base rights in Spain and, most important, the NATO command structure. Tragically, on July 22, he suffered a series of heart attacks and died. Admiral William M. Fechteler* replaced him as CNO. *See also* Collins-Sherman Visit to Tokyo.

M. A. Palmer, *Origins of the Maritime Strategy: American Naval Strategy in the First Postwar Decade* (Washington, D.C., 1988); C. G. Reynolds, "Forrest Percival Sherman," in R.W. Love, Jr. (ed.), *The Chiefs of Naval Operations* (Annapolis, 1980).

Lynne K. Dunn

SHIN IK-HI (SIN IK-HŬI; 1894–1956)

Shin Ik-hi (whose name often appeared as Shinicky) was the Speaker of the National Assembly of the Republic of Korea* when the Korean War broke out. Having graduated from Waseda University, Japan, Shin taught for some time in a college in Korea before going into exile in Shanghai after participating in the March First Movement* in 1919. He successively filled important positions in the Korean Provisional Government in Shanghai, such as minister of home affairs, foreign minister, and minister of education. Returning to Korea after the liberation, he founded a college, now Kukmin University, ran a newspaper, and was active in politics with a consistent emphasis on anti-communism, anti-trusteeship, and immediate independence of Korea.

Shin gained election as Speaker in 1950 after forces critical of President Syngman Rhee* became the majority in the National Assembly. Though a member of the opposition, as speaker he often had to take a neutral position in the growing conflicts between the National Assembly on the one hand and President Rhee on the other. The climax came in the South Korean political crisis of 1952* when Rhee's term as president was nearing its end. His prospects of reelection being hopeless if the assembly made the choice, Rhee forced through the National Assembly a revision of constitution that provided for direct popular election of the president. Shin had to preside over the National Assembly during this trying period.

Shin was the opposition candidate in the 1956 presidential election against Rhee, who was by then aged and unpopular. He won enormous popularity but died suddenly at the peak of the election campaign of a stroke during his tour of Chŏlla province. His running mate, John M. Chang*, was ultimately elected as vice-president. Although he opposed Rhee during most of his political career, he still gave Rhee credit on occasion for his anti-Communist and anti-Japanese stance.

Kim Suk-young, *Shin Ik-hi Sŏnsaeng Ildaegi* (Seoul, 1956); H. J. Noble, *Embassy at War* (Seattle, 1975); Shin Jong-wan, *Haegong Geŭrigo Aboji* (Seoul, 1981); Sinmun Hakhoe, *Shin Ik-hi* (Seoul, 1956); Yoo Chi-song, *Haegong Shin Ik-hi Ildaegi* (Seoul, 1984).

J. Y. Ra

SHIN SUNG-MO (SIN SŎNG-MO; 1891–1960)

Shin Sung-mo, minister of defense for the Republic of Korea* during the Korean War, was born at Ŭiryŏng, South Kyŏngsang province, and educated at Posŏng College in Seoul. He fled to Vladivostok after the Japanese annexation of Korea in 1910 and participated in anti-Japanese activities. Shin then studied at Shanghai Commercial Steamship School and Nanking Navigation College. After graduating from the London School of Navigation with the certificate of first navigator, he worked as an officer for the British and Indian steamship companies until 1945, when he returned to Korea. His career was unique among Koreans. This and his good command of English attracted President Syngman Rhee*, who appointed him home minister in December 1948. Transferred to defense minister in March 1949, he retained this post until May 1951. During this period, he also was commandant of the Taehan Youth Corps*. From April to October 1950, he was concurrently acting prime minister. Reportedly many South Korean military professionals were highly skeptical of his capacity as defense minister. In early 1951, two unfortunate events occurred—the South Korean National Guard scandal* and the Kŏch'ang incident*. As defense minister, Shin received blame for both scandals, and Rhee was forced to remove him from the cabinet. He was soon transferred to chief of the ROK mission to Japan with the rank of ambassador, which would prove to be his last government post.

Widely viewed as Rhee's toady, he was said to have assured the ROK's president on many occasions before the Korean War of an easy South Korean military victory over the Democratic People's Republic of Korea* in the event of conflict. In 1949, he divulged that the South Korean secret intelligence agency found that the North Korean People's Army was moving heavy tanks, artillery, and large infantry units into what appeared to be attack positions just north of Kaesŏng. He also contended that new roads and airfields were being constructed just to the north of the thirty-eighth parallel. Americans brushed these reports aside as "mythical" before U.S. military withdrawal from Korea* in late June. Harold J. Noble*, who was first secretary at the U.S. embassy and observed the ROK cabinet members at the time of the Korean War, judged Shin to be

a man of the greatest personal courage, indefatigable in the face of danger. But he was always gravely apprehensive when the president was anywhere near a battle. Sin was concerned for the continuity of government, and partly, I think, he liked to be free to carry out his duties without having the president always breathing down his neck, asking questions, and issuing orders that showed he did not grasp the meaning of military affairs. I feel sure that this first Sunday afternoon of the war Sin Sŏng-mo was one of those who urged the President to get out of town, quickly.

H. J. Noble, *Embassy at War* (Seattle, 1975); R. T. Oliver, *Syngman Rhee and American Involvement in Korea, 1942–1960* (Seoul, 1978).

Hakjoon Kim

SHIN TAI-YONG (SIN TAI-YŎNG; 1891–1959)

Shin Tai-yong, minister of defense for the Republic of Korea* toward the end of the Korean War, was born in Seoul and educated in the same city at the Royal Boy's Military School and Royal Military School in the late Yi dynasty (1392–1910). In 1914, he graduated from the Japanese Military Academy and began his military career for Japan, reaching lieutenant colonel at the time of Japan's surrender in 1945. Shin renewed his military career with the rank of colonel in the fall of 1948, when the anti-government and leftist elements in the military staged the Yŏsu-Sunch'ŏn rebellion*. Promoted in May 1949 to brigadier general and five months later to major general, he was appointed commander for the defense of North Chŏlla province but fired in November 1949 because of conflicts with Defense Minister Shin Sung-mo*. In January 1952, he was reinstated and two months later promoted to lieutenant general. Soon Shin was appointed minister of defense, a post he retained until June 1952 when Sohn Won-il* replaced him. From 1954 to 1956, he was commander of the militia.
Republic of Korea, Ministry of Defense records.

Hakjoon Kim

SHORT, JOSEPH H., JR. (1904–1952)

Born in Vicksburg, Mississippi, Joseph Short was press secretary for President Harry S. Truman* for most of the Korean War. After developing an interest in journalism at Marion Institute, he became editor of *The Cadet* while attending Virginia Military Institute. Short graduated in 1925 and went to work as a reporter in his home state for the *Jackson Daily News*. Thereafter, he wrote for the *Vicksburg Post* and the *New Orleans Picayune*. In 1929, he joined the *Associated Press* and after spending two years at the Richmond bureau worked at the Washington bureau until 1941. When the United States entered World War II, Short was a reporter for the *Chicago Sun*, but in 1943, he began writing for the *Baltimore Sun*. He became acquainted with Senator Truman during the war, later covering his campaign for the vice-presidency in 1944 and then his presidency.

In December 1950, Truman's press secretary and boyhood friend Charles G. Ross died suddenly of a heart attack. Many observers were surprised when the president picked Short as his replacement because he was the first White House reporter to fill this post. In addition to speechwriting, his job required the development of diplomatic public explanations for the controversial issues surrounding the Korean conflict. Short gained some fame when he called together newsman early on the morning of April 11, 1951, to announce Truman's recall of CINCUNC General Douglas MacArthur*. Known for being hardworking and thorough, he was also personable and well liked. When Short suffered a fatal heart attack in September 1952, Truman replaced him with Roger Tubby, who served as press secretary for the remainder of his term in office.

Current Biography, 1952; *New York Times*, September 19, 20, 1952; *Who Was Who in America*, vol. 3: *1953–1960* (Chicago, 1960).

SHTYKOV, TERENTY F. (1907–1964)

From September 1948 until January 1951, Colonel General Terenty F. Shtykov was Soviet ambassador to the Democratic People's Republic of Korea*. Born in Vitebsk province, he went to work in a Leningrad industrial plant at age 18. In 1929, he joined the Communist party, thereafter holding various posts in the Communist Youth Organization and the party hierarchy. During World War II, Shtykov served as a political commander on several fronts, first in Leningrad and then in Soviet Asia. In 1945, he was political commissar for the Maritime Military District. In August, Shtykov went to Korea, spending the next three years as Moscow's political adviser in P'yŏngyang during the period of Soviet occupation.

Beginning in 1946, he was head of the Soviet delegation at the Joint Soviet-American Commission that attempted over the next two years to achieve Korea's reunification through implementing the Moscow Agreement. In his opening address, Shtykov declared that the Soviet government was committed to the realization in Korea of "a true democratic and independent country, friendly to the Soviet Union, so that in the future it will not become a base for an attack on the Soviet Union." In June 1947, after a group of Korean rightists pelted the Soviet delegation with stones and dirt, his demand for their exclusion from consultations led to a total breakdown in the negotiations. With the establishment of the DPRK, Joseph Stalin* appointed Shty-kov ambassador, but little is known of his activities in this capacity or following his return to Moscow early in 1951. After serving as party secretary in Novgorod province from 1954 to 1956, he again became political commissar of the Maritime Military District at Vladivostok. Shtykov's last posts were as chairman of the government and then party control commission of the Russian Republic (1961–1964).

J. I. Matray, *The Reluctant Crusade* (Honolulu, 1985); *New York Times,* October 28, 1964.

SICK AND WOUNDED POW EXCHANGE
See Operation Little Switch

SINO-SOVIET TREATY OF FRIENDSHIP AND ALLIANCE (February 14, 1950)

This treaty helped determine the Truman administration's response to the North Korean invasion of South Korea* in June 1950 and Chinese military intervention* the following November. Chinese Communist leader Mao Tse-tung*, on his first foreign journey, arrived in Moscow on December 16, 1949, for what he hoped would be quick negotiations with Joseph Stalin* over border issues and Soviet economic aid. Conflicting interests and heated arguments led to two months of talks. In the final pact, Mao persuaded Stalin to retreat from Soviet wartime claims to Manchurian railroads and the ice-free ports of Port Arthur and Darien. But in the vital border area of Sinkiang and elsewhere in Northeast Asia—where Russians and Chinese had clashed for centuries—Stalin insisted on Sino-Soviet joint stock companies as well as "independence" for Outer Mongolia, which in fact masked its subservience to Moscow. In return Stalin gave Mao only a five-year, $300 million credit (or about 50 cents per Chinese) and charged 1 percent interest. The Soviets pledged mutual assistance against aggression by Japan or "any other state which should unite with Japan directly or indirectly in acts of aggression." This clause, however, promised little if, for example, U.S. forces attacked the People's Republic of China* from Taiwan. Stalin did not even offer to give Mao modern arms but did, rumors insisted, try unsuccessfully to place Soviet "advisers" in Mao's police, army, and party.

U.S. officials, especially Secretary of State Dean G. Acheson*, understood the growing tensions between the two Communist giants but never found a policy to exploit them successfully during the Korean War. By its intervention in the Korean conflict, Washington hoped to show Mao that Stalin would not respond when U.S. troops landed on the Asian mainland. But throughout the autumn of 1950, top U.S. officials assumed that because of the treaty and the danger of Soviet involvement, Stalin could restrain Mao. When the Chinese intervened to protect their vital interests along the Korean-Manchurian border, Stalin at first helped little except by selling (not giving) arms and munitions to China. New U.S. uncertainty about the alliance and a possible Soviet response, however, greatly restrained Washington's reaction to Chinese military intervention. By late 1951–early 1952, moreover, as President Harry S. Truman* grew angry over the stalemated P'anmunjŏm truce talks*, superior Soviet MiG-15 fighters and Moscow's aid to the Chinese air defense system gave Mao some needed security. Such assistance, however, did little to heal the widening nationalist and party differences between the Soviet Union and the PRC that had been vividly demonstrated in the February treaty and, after 1957, became transformed into bitter confrontation between the neighboring Communist powers.

R. Foot, *The Wrong War* (Ithaca, N.Y., 1985); N. Mineo, "The Sino-Soviet Confrontation in Historical Perspective," in Y. Nagai and A. Iriye (eds.), *The Origins of the Cold War in Asia* (Tokyo, 1977); R. R. Simmons, *The Strained Alliance* (New York, 1975).

Walter LaFeber

SMITH, OLIVER P. (1893–1977)

As commander of the 1st Marine Division, Major General Oliver P. Smith was one of the leading U.S. combat officers during the Korean War. A deeply religious Christian Scientist, he neither drank nor swore. Smith graduated from the University of California at Berkeley in 1916, where he was a member of ROTC. He was working for Standard Oil Company when the United States entered World War I. In May 1917, after obtaining approval of his application for a commission in the Marine Corps Reserve, Smith went to Guam, freeing a more experienced officer for duty in France. From 1919 to 1921, he was stationed in San Francisco before serving as the commander of a marine detachment aboard the U.S.S. *Texas* until 1924. For the next four years, Smith was a personnel officer in Washington, D.C., and then devoted three years to occupation duty in Haiti before graduating from Infantry School in 1932. After serving two years in France, he taught amphibious operations at Quantico. When the United States entered World War II, Smith was executive officer at the division of planning and operations in Marine Corps headquarters. In 1944, he became assistant commander for the 1st Marine Division, later planning and leading the Peleliu operation.

After World War II, Smith's first assignment was as commander of the Marine Corps School at Quantico. In 1948, he became assistant commandant of the U.S. Marines and then chief of staff, devoting considerable time to developing battlefield uses for the helicopter. Smith resumed command of the 1st Marine Division in June 1950 following the North Korean invasion of South Korea*. Traveling with his unit to Korea in September, he led it in three major operations. Smith was a key figure in the planning and the execution of the Inch'ŏn landing*, though he had opposed the operation. Also, he had trouble working with Major General Edward M. Almond*, who was commander of the X Corps* and in charge at Inchŏn. His next success was the recapture of Seoul operation*. But then, after the Wŏnsan landing*, came the disastrous Chosin Reservoir Campaign*, which might have been worse had Smith not skillfully used helicopters for evacuation, reconnaissance, and resupply. In the midst of the Hŭngnam evacuation*, his alleged reply to a newsman's question became famous: "Retreat hell, we're just attacking in another direction." Reorganization of the UNC's* forces after Chinese military intervention* resulted in Smith briefly assuming command of the IX Corps. Upon his return to the United States, he became head of the marine forces in the Atlantic Fleet. Nicknamed the "professor," Smith earned a third star in 1953 and retired in September 1955.

C. Blair, *The Forgotten War* (New York, 1987); R. Spiller (ed.), *Dictionary of American Military Biography* (Westport, Conn., 1984).

SMITH, WALTER BEDELL (1895–1961)

Walter Bedell Smith was initially director of the Central Intelligence Agency (CIA) and then under secretary of state during the Korean conflict. He began his distinguished military career unassumedly as a member of the Indiana National Guard in 1911. He was commissioned a second lieutenant in the reserve army during World War I and joined the regular army in 1920. In 1939, when General George C. Marshall* became U.S. Army chief of staff, he appointed Smith as his assistant secretary and then as secretary of the War Department General Staff in 1941. In 1942, Smith attained the rank of brigadier general and became General Dwight D. Eisenhower's* chief of staff, where he served in the North African and Mediterranean theaters and then at the Supreme Headquarters, Allied Powers in Europe. President Harry S. Truman* later appointed Smith ambassador to the Soviet Union (1946–1949), where he frequently offered advice on how to break the Soviet-U.S. deadlock over Korea. In June 1950, Truman named Smith director of the CIA, hoping that the general could improve leadership and organization within the agency. The president was also concerned about charges of inept intelligence gathering contributing to the United States' not anticipating the North Korean invasion of South Korea*. Smith's reputation as a bureaucrat's bureaucrat and his firm, outspoken distrust of communism and the Soviet Union suited him for the task. He centralized and coordinated the intelligence community and prevailed upon CINCUNC General Douglas MacArthur* to accept the work of the CIA in Korea.

Smith's position on the Korean War was clear and simple: the Chinese Communists were primarily pawns of the Soviet Union; the Korean conflict was part of a global Soviet strategy. Although unprepared for or unwilling to risk war in Europe, the Soviets were willing to provoke a war between the United States and the People's Republic of China* in Asia, thus weakening the U.S. commitment to Europe and slowing Europe's rearmament. Smith advocated putting pressure on the PRC, even to the point of using the Republic of China's* forces, in order to bring a satisfactory settlement of the conflict. Because of his reputation and his close wartime relationship with Eisenhower, Smith was one of the few links of continuity between the Truman and Eisenhower administrations. In 1953, Eisenhower moved Smith from the CIA to the State Department, where he served as under secretary of state until his retirement in 1954. In this capacity, he helped Secretary of State John Foster Dulles* develop policy. He worked to devise a complicated compromise solution for agenda item 4*, POW repatriation, which paved the way for an armistice agreement* in 1953. As his last major responsibility, he was the U.S. representative to the Geneva Conference of 1954*, which was called to consider the reunification of Korea and to address the growing crisis in Indochina.

S. E. Ambrose, *Eisenhower, The President* (New York, 1984); S. E. Ambrose, *Ike's Spies* (New York, 1981); J. C. Goulden, *Korea: The Untold Story of the War* (New York, 1982).

T. Michael Ruddy

SOHN WON-IL (SON WŎN-IL; 1908–1980)

Admiral Sohn Won-il, defense minister for the Republic of Korea* late in the Korean War, was born in a rural area of South P'yŏng'an province near P'yŏng-yang. His father was a famous Methodist pastor and an independence movement fighter. After joining the March First Movement* of 1919, he went to Manchuria and studied at Yumin Middle School, where Kim Il Sung* had been a student. In 1930, Sohn graduated from the department of navigation, China Central University. He then worked for the Shanghai Coast Guard and an American steamship company at Hamburg at the recommendation of the Chinese navy. In 1934, Sohn returned to Korea, but the Japanese police arrested and tortured him on suspicion that he was an emissary sent by the Korean Provisional Government in China. He was soon released.

On November 11, 1945, Sohn initiated the organization of the Coastal Defense Army Unit with himself as its commander. This date has been celebrated as the founding of the Republic of Korea's navy. In June 1946, the Coastal Defense Army Unit became the South Korean Coastal Constabulary. Sohn was appointed its first commander and concurrently superintendent of the South Korean Coastal Constabulary School by the U.S. military government. In August 1948, with the establishment of the Republic of Korea, the Coastal Constabulary became a regular navy. He was appointed its chief of staff with the rank of brigadier general. At the time of the outbreak of the Korean War, Sohn "was in the middle of the Pacific Ocean, a passenger on one of three patrol crafts bought in the United States and being sailed to join the small ROK Navy." From June 1952 to May 1956, he was defense minister and later the first ambassador to West Germany. In 1967, Sohn joined the governmental Democratic Republican party and four years later became adviser to the National Unification Board. From 1972 to 1973, he was chairman of the Korean Anti-Communist League and chairman of the Korean Public Relations Association.

Han' guk Ilbo, September 30-December 21, 1976; H. J. Noble, *Embassy at War* (Seattle, 1975).

Hakjoon Kim

SOUTH KOREA
See Republic of Korea

SOUTH KOREAN ARMY
See North Korean Invasion of South Korea

SOUTH KOREAN DEMONSTRATIONS FOR UNIFICATION

Demonstrations erupted in the Republic of Korea* as the Kaesŏng truce talks* started in July 1951. A variety of groups, including students of all levels, youth corps members, and veterans, participated in the demonstrations opposing an armistice and clamoring for the immediate unification of the country by marching north. The U.S. embassy reported at the end of 1951 that anti-cease-fire demonstrations and parades occurred almost daily in Pusan. Foreign missions stationed in Korea were quick to claim that these demonstrations were inspired, facilitated, or even organized by the ROK government. As a report of the U.S. embassy had it, the masses of people were too absorbed in their own immediate daily survival.

Despite government encouragement, these demonstrations represented genuine sentiments on the part of the general public. There was in fact widespread dissatisfaction and even anger over the truce negotiations among all sectors of the public. There were feelings of frustration and indignation that the sufferings and sacrifices were all in vain, as the truce would end the war leaving the country still divided. The reaction was stronger on the part of those who had been separated from their families in North Korea. Many Koreans felt also that it was another betrayal of Korea by the big powers for their own interests—a feeling that has a deep root in Koreans. There was also concern about the possibility of a new North Korean invasion of South Korea*, in which case the prospect of another UN intervention would be by no means certain. Partly there was anxiety too over a rumor that the soldiers from the Chinese People's Volunteers Army* would settle permanently in North Korea after the war and marry Korean women to make up for the lack of male population, another traditional Korean fear.

Thus, on this particular issue of opposing the truce, there existed a virtual national consensus among the public and political leaders. The National Assembly, a large section of which was opposed to President Syngman Rhee*, was always unanimous in passing resolutions condemning "appeasements." Early in 1952, the U.S. embassy reported that even usually moderate and responsible elements of South Korean government seemed to support Rhee on this issue, with the National Assembly and newspapers all joining the chorus. Significantly,

Cho Pong-am, a leader of progressive groups who was later executed by the Rhee government, spoke against the truce and attacked Britain for appeasing the enemy. Even the North Koreans apparently disliked the truce initiative contained in Jacob A. Malik's* radio address of June 23, 1951*, but they did not publicly object to the negotiations.

C. Blair, *The Forgotten War* (New York, 1987); C. A. MacDonald, *Korea: The War Before Vietnam* (New York, 1986); J. Y. Ra, "Britain and the Korean War" (Ph.D. dissertation, Cambridge University, 1972).

J. Y. Ra

SOUTH KOREAN NATIONAL GUARD SCANDAL (January 1951)

In this incident, leaders of the Republic of Korea's* National Guard misappropriated government money and goods for themselves, and as a result, more than 1,000 enlisted guardsmen died of starvation, illness, and cold. After the Chinese military intervention*, the South Korean government enacted the National Guard Act in December 1950 to train reservists and mobilize them promptly at the time of national emergency. The act enrolled men from age 17 to 40 into the equivalent of second-class reserve forces. Immediately after the law was promulgated, President Syngman Rhee* reorganized his private army, the Taehan Youth Corps*, as the National Guard and appointed corps leaders to key posts of the newly formed organization. Kim Yun-gŭn, head of the Taehan Youth Corps, became commander, Yun Ik-hŏn deputy commander, and Pak Kyŏng-gu chief of staff. When the UN forces were in retreat, those men enlisted in the National Guard headed for North Kyŏngsang province on foot, where they were scheduled to be trained. The leaders of the organization seized this occasion to embezzle a large sum of public funds and materials. The consequent serious shortage of supplies brought about the death of many enlisted men, while others fell seriously ill.

The Korean National Assembly learned about the scandal and, after a close investigation, revealed that 2.4 billion won ($1 million) of government money and 52,000 *sŏk* (8,300 tons) of grain were illegally seized. The assembly passed a bill to dissolve the National Guard on April 30, 1951; the organization was finally disbanded on May 12. Minister of Defense Shin Sung-mo*, who had attempted to conceal the incident, was removed on May 7 and, ten days later, the new defense minister, Yi Ki-bung, announced the arrest of Commander Kim Yun-gŭn. The Korean provost marshal headquarters reinvestigated the scandal for about one month and brought eleven leaders of the National Guard, including Kim Yun-gŭn and Yun Ik-hŏn, before the military tribunal on June 15. The court-martial sentenced five of them to death on July 19, the incident ending with their execution on August 13, 1951. But the fact that money appropriated by them might have gone into the coffers of high-ranking government leaders, including Rhee, has not yet been disclosed.

Kukbang-bu p'yŏnch'an wiwŏn-hoe, *Han'guk Chŏnjaeng-sa* (Seoul, 1968); H. Yi (ed.), *Han'guk-sa Taesajŏn* (Seoul, 1976); Yŏrŭm Publishing Co. (ed.), *Han'guk Hyŏndae Sahoeundong Sajŏn* (Seoul, 1988).

Jinwung Kim

SOUTH KOREAN POLITICAL CRISIS OF 1952

An embarassment for the U.S and UN war effort, this test of strength between the National Assembly of the Republic of Korea* and President Syngman Rhee* occurred when the legislature in January 1952 soundly defeated Rhee's bill to amend the 1948 constitution from indirect election of the president by the National Assembly to direct election. Rhee then increased pressure on the assembly with a recall campaign against those members who opposed his bill (despite the fact there was no such provision in the constitution), stage-managed demonstrations, a declaration of martial law* in the temporary capital of Pusan, and the arrest of some assembly opponents on trumped-up Communist conspiracy charges. Rhee's extralegal methods caused the Truman administration to consider intervening in South Korean political affairs. To counter Rhee, U.S. embassy officials, especially E. Allan Lightner*, with strong backing from the UNCURK* under the leadership of Australian delegate James Plimsoll*, suggested physical protection of the assembly, a UNC* military takeover of the ROK government, or cooperation with an ROK army proposal for a military coup to replace Rhee and restore the balance between the executive and legislative branches. CINCUNC General Mark W. Clark* in Tokyo and General James A. Van Fleet*, the 8th Army* commander in Korea, feared that choosing any of these alternatives could cause potential UN armed conflict with forces loyal to Rhee. Already stretched in defending the front lines and guarding the unruly POW camps, the UNC was unprepared for action that might result in conflict with South Korean forces.

President Harry S. Truman* and his advisers weighed this conflicting advice and considered the political damage from the possible loss of another non-Communist state on the Asian mainland, especially just before the 1952 Republican presidential convention. Truman instructed the embassy in Pusan to try to promote a compromise between the two sides that would allow for direct election but retain for the assembly the responsibility for approving the cabinet and guarantee basic freedoms to the political opposition. The campaign of persuasion was ineffective. In early July 1952, Rhee's security forces held the assembly hostage until it passed his revised amendment on July 4. Potential political supporters of the assembly—Korean students and other members of the urban middle class—were so dislocated and weakened by the war and the wartime draft that they did not take sides during the crisis.

Rhee's triumph eliminated the assembly as a viable political institution and created a virtual presidential dictatorship. While the Truman administration was genuinely concerned about Rhee's illegal methods and seriously considered intervention, military and domestic political considerations combined to convince

Truman to limit the U.S. response to ineffective persuasion. Such a pattern generally characterized the ultimate response of the other Western democracies— Great Britain, Australia, Canada. The failure "to save democracy" has been laid to Truman and the Western allies, but the conflict between Rhee and the assembly had as much to do with access to power as with democratic government. Rhee sought direct election to free himself from control by the legislature, and the assembly leaders opposed Rhee in good part in the hopes of forcing him to grant them cabinet posts in return for his reelection.

G. Henderson, *Korea: The Politics of the Vortex* (Cambrige, 1968); J. B. Palais, "'Democracy' in South Korea, 1948–1972," in F. Baldwin (ed.), *Without Parallel* (Chicago, 1974).

Edward C. Keefer

SOUTH KOREAN PRESIDENTIAL ELECTIONS OF 1952

These were the spoils of the South Korean political crisis of 1952*. After bludgeoning the National Assembly to allow direct election of the president and vice-president, Syngman Rhee* decreed on July 18, 1952, that the elections would be held on August 5, 1952, thus allowing little time for opponents to organize or campaign. Nominated by the Liberal party, Rhee made a charade of reluctant acceptance. His reelection was a foregone conclusion because of his control of the Republic of Korea's* security forces and bureaucracy, his stature within South Korean society, and the wartime nature of the election. So strong were Rhee's assets that his political opponents struggled to find credible candidates willing to stand against him. Of the three who came forward, Cho Pongam (Rhee's former minister of agriculture and currently vice president of the National Assembly) had the best political profile based on his connection with land reform. Determined to win an overwhelming victory, Rhee's forces harassed Cho, who consequently spent much of the election campaign in hiding. When the final returns were tabulated, Rhee won over 5 million votes, while his three rivals received under 2 million. The UN Commission for the Unification and Rehabilitation of Korea* made spot observations of the election and concluded that election-day interference on behalf of Rhee had little appreciable effect on the outcome.

The real contest was in the separate but simultaneous vice-presidential election where the voters were, in effect, picking a potential successor to the 77-year-old Rhee. The Liberal party, in which the Taehan Youth Corps* had a strong influence, picked the founder of the corps and the current home minister, Yi Pŏm-sŏk*, as Rhee's vice-presidential candidate. Although Yi had just helped overcome the National Assembly, Rhee refused to endorse Yi and ensured his resignation as home minister, thus relieving him of command of the police, a valuable election asset. A week before the election, Rhee endorsed the Reverend Hahm Tae-yŏng, a North Korean Christian minister older than Rhee himself. Yi found himself in the unusual position of charging that the police and bureaucracy were interfering against his election and in favor of Hahm. When the votes were counted, Hahm received just under 3 million votes, Yi got 1.8 million, and seven other candidates split the rest of the just over 7.1 million cast. The vice-presidential election of August 1952 was the beginning of the elimination of Yi and his followers as a political force in South Korea, a process which was completed by 1954.

R. C. Allen, *Korea's Syngman Rhee: An Unauthorized Portrait* (Rutland, Vt., 1960); J. A. Kim, *Divided Korea* (Cambridge, 1975); Report of the U.N. Commission for the Unification of Rehabilitation of Korea (New York, 1952).

Edward C. Keefer

SOVIET MILITARY WITHDRAWAL FROM KOREA (December 31, 1948)

Although Moscow refused to permit UN verification, it claimed that it withdrew the last of its occupation forces from North Korea by the end of 1948. Soviet military withdrawal came in response to the formation of the Democratic People's Republic of Korea* the prior September. Premier Kim Il Sung*, as his first act, had addressed letters to both President Harry S. Truman* and Soviet leader Joseph Stalin*, requesting recognition and the removal of all occupation troops from the peninsula. On September 19, Stalin formally recognized the DPRK as Korea's legitimate government and pledged Soviet support. Complying with Kim's request, he also announced that the Soviet forces would leave North Korea before the end of the year. Stalin then invited the United States to follow suit.

This Soviet maneuver placed the United States in an embarrassing and dangerous position. The DPRK unquestionably was stronger militarily, economically, and politically than the newly created Republic of Korea* in the south. Although NSC-8* called for U.S. withdrawal by the end of 1948, disengagement would place the ROK's existence in grave jeopardy. On the other hand, South Korea's continued dependence on U.S. protection virtually precluded widespread international recognition of the ROK as the legitimate national government of Korea. Bowing to Soviet pressure, the administration incorporated a provision calling for Soviet and U.S. withdrawal from Korea in the UN resolution of December 12, 1948*. However, the Yŏsu-Sunch'ŏn rebellion* in the ROK caused Truman to retain U.S. troops in the south despite the Soviet Union's announced departure from the north. By January 1949, Moscow predictably was charging that continued U.S. occupation of South Korea proved that the United States was guilty of imperialism. Soviet military withdrawal from Korea played an important role in persuading the Truman administration to include a provision in NSC-8/2* requiring U.S. military withdrawal from Korea* no later than June 30, 1949.

C. Berger, *The Korean Knot* (Philadelphia, 1957); *Foreign Relations of the United States, 1948*, vol. 6: *The Far East and Australasia* (Washington, D.C., 1974); *New York Times,* December 31, 1948; H. S. Truman, *Years of Trial and Hope* (Garden City, N.Y., 1956).

SOVIET UN SECURITY COUNCIL BOYCOTT

The five permanent members of the UN Security Council are Great Britain, France, the Soviet Union, the United States, and China. In the period after 1949, there were two claimants to the Chinese seat, the Republic of China* and the People's Republic of China*, each claiming to be the sole government. The United States and its allies supported the seating of the ROC. The Soviet Union appeared to favor the PRC. Thus, the Soviet ambassador to the United Nations, Jacob A. Malik*, had been called back to Moscow for consultations in January 1950 after the seat remained assigned to the ROC. The Soviet government had apparently assumed that since the Republic of Korea* had not been named in Secretary of State Dean G. Acheson's* National Press Club speech* within the sphere of America's strategic interests, the United States would not become engaged in any conflict there.

On June 25, 1950, when the United States brought to the attention of the Security Council the North Korean invasion of South Korea* and asked for condemnation of this action with the possible formation of a security force to stem the aggression, the Soviet boycott meant that Malik was not present to vote on or veto the measure. The Security Council voted to condemn the North Korean action and take an active part in defending the ROK in the UN Security Council resolutions of June 25* and June 27, 1950*. The Soviet ambassador returned to the Security Council as its president in August, replacing Arne Sunde of Norway, to face a fait accompli. Many historians have pointed to the Soviet Security Council boycott as proof that Moscow had neither ordered the North Korean attack nor was aware of its timing. *See also* PRC UN Representation Question.

D. Acheson, *The Korean War* (New York, 1971); E. P. Hoyt, *The Bloody Road to Panmunjom* (New York, 1985); B. I. Kaufman, *The Korean War* (Philadelphia, 1986); P. Lowe, *The Origins of the Korean War* (New York, 1986).

Katherine K. Reist

SPENDER, PERCY C. (1897–1985)

Percy Claude Spender (from 1952, Sir Percy) was Australian minister for external affairs from 1949 to 1951 and ambassador to the United States from 1951 to 1958. A successful barrister before entering politics, he was appointed minister for external affairs in the government formed by Robert G. Menzies* in December 1949. From the outset, he sought to achieve a Pacific Pact* under which the United States would help to ensure Australian security. With this goal in mind, he was frustrated by the Anglophile Menzies's initial reluctance to commit ground troops in the Korean War. While Menzies was virtually incommunicado between London and Washington, Spender heard on July 26 that the British government had changed its mind and was about to announce that it would send troops. He immediately persuaded Acting Prime Minister A. W. Fadden to announce the commitment of Australian troops, an announcement that preceded the British statement by one hour. This initiative led to the commitment of an Australian battalion, which was later joined by a second battalion.

As minister for external affairs and as ambassador in Washington, Spender was an energetic participant in the diplomatic discussions at the Korean War briefing meetings*. He expressed Australian concern, for example, over the suggestions that the United States might retaliate directly against the People's Republic of China* after Chinese military intervention*. During British prime minister Clement R. Attlee's* visit to the United States* in December 1950, Australia supported British concerns over the possible use of the atomic bomb. Although Australia followed the U.S. policy of nonrecognition of the PRC, Spender raised with Washington the idea of withdrawing diplomatic recognition from the Republic of China* and Chiang Kai-shek* as part of a peace settlement with the Chinese Communists. On several other issues Spender raised questions and concerns over allied policy but always within the context of an overall commitment to a strong alliance between Australia and the United States.

Despite the skepticism of his prime minister regarding the need for or the possibility of obtaining a formal security guarantee from the United States, Spender skillfully used the prestige Australia had gained from its commitment of ground troops in Korea until, in 1951, he negotiated the Australia–New Zealand–United States security pact known as the ANZUS Treaty*. Later that year, he resigned from politics to become ambassador to the United States, in which capacity he signed the treaty for Australia. Spender's brief term as minister for external affairs was highly significant in shaping Australian foreign policy for the next quarter-century. Australian involvement in the Korean War helped to consolidate the foundations of that policy—close alliance with the United States and a concern to prevent the spread of communism in Asia.

R. J. O'Neill, *Australia in the Korean War 1950–53* (Canberra, 1981, 1985); P. C. Spender, *Exercises in Diplomacy* (Sydney, 1969); P. C. Spender, *Politics and a Man* (Sydney, 1972).

Peter Edwards

STALIN, JOSEPH (1879–1953)

Joseph Stalin was general secretary of the Soviet Union's Communist party from 1922 to 1953 and Soviet premier from 1941 to 1953. He accepted President Franklin D. Roosevelt's proposal of a postwar trusteeship over Korea at the 1945 Yalta Conference, but when the Pacific war suddenly ended in August, the United States unilaterally proposed the thirty-eighth parallel as the dividing point between occupying Soviet and U.S. armies, and Stalin readily accepted. His responses to Washington's requests for a united Korea remained flexible until mid-1947 when the cold war began to freeze affairs in both Europe and Asia. After Kim Il Sung* established the Democratic People's Republic of Korea* in 1948, Stalin ordered Soviet military withdrawal from Korea* in December, while maintaining Soviet advisers and continuing arms shipments.

As the Republic of Korea* suffered from civil war and internal economic and political weakness, Kim traveled to Moscow in late 1949 to request Stalin's support for a military campaign to unite the peninsula. The Soviet ruler had good reason to agree. Kim's success could help neutralize Japan (where the United States was planning to establish bases), tie Kim closer to Moscow instead of the People's Republic of China*, and lead to a Communist triumph without the danger of direct Soviet involvement. It might also compensate for the failure of Stalin's scheme with Chinese leader Kao Kang* to establish a special Soviet sphere of influence in Manchuria. The ever-cautious Stalin made Kim reconsider the plan carefully and then, some writers believe, requested Mao Tse-tung's* opinion and had a second meeting with Kim to consider his proposal. Kim and Mao apparently told Stalin that the North Koreans could make a quick "poke" and win before U.S. forces became involved. As Stalin gave a green light, he nevertheless pulled back Soviet advisors to ensure they would not be captured.

On June 29, 1950, four days after war erupted, the Soviets issued a statement that U.S. officials viewed as Stalin's determination to distance himself from the conflict. Throughout, he defined the struggle as a civil war in which the great powers (especially the United States) had no business. After the UN offensive across the thirty-eighth parallel* in October, Stalin apparently began to fear the possibility of escalation and a direct Soviet-U.S. confrontation, but he continued to distance himself from the war, even after the U.S. bombing of a Soviet airfield*. Chinese military intervention*, which he supported but aided with only supplies, not troops, eased the dictator's fears of a superpower confrontation. He sent advanced Soviet jets for North Koreans to use and then stood aside as UN and Chinese forces bogged down in bloody fighting. The stalemate and Sino-U.S. clash served Stalin's interests. In 1951 and 1952, he turned his attention to Western Europe to deal with what he considered to be the more important issue of Germany. Although he apparently authorized the Kennan-Malik conversations* in the spring of 1951 to investigate peace prospects in Korea, serious talks to end the Korean War did not begin until after his death in March 1953. *See also* Death of Stalin.

N. Khrushchev, *Khrushchev Remembers* (Boston, 1970); W. Taubman, *Stalin's American Policy* (New York, 1982); A. B. Ulam, *Stalin* (New York, 1973).

Walter LaFeber

"STAND OR DIE" ORDER (July 29, 1950)

This was a futile attempt by the UNC* to demonstrate its ability to hold defensive positions against the advancing North Korean People's Army (NKPA) and thus serve as a motivating factor for the 8th Army* (EUSAK). During the summer of 1950, North Korean infiltration techniques and flanking movements repeatedly forced the EUSAK to retreat. After meetings with CINCUNC General Douglas MacArthur* concerning recent NKPA advances, Lieutenant General Walton H. Walker*, the EUSAK commander, issued the infamous "stand or die" order. On July 29, 1950, in speeches to the EUSAK division chiefs, he stated that U.S. troops could no longer retreat and must hold their defensive positions at all costs. In reality, however, the order illustrated the expendability of the EUSAK. In the days that followed, Walker's statement proved to be meaningless as the EUSAK continued to yield ground during the Battle of the Naktong Bulge*. Eventually these readjustments led to the EUSAK's centralization in the Pusan Perimeter*, where environmental features created a definite fighting front and helped spread out and weaken the North Korean attack. *See also* Defense of Taegu.

R. E. Appleman, *South to the Naktong, North to the Yalu* (Washington, D.C., 1961); C. Blair, *The Forgotten War* (New York, 1987); J. C. Goulden, *Korea: The Untold Story of the War* (New York, 1982).

John Neilson

STEVENSON, ADLAI E. (1900–1965)

Adlai E. Stevenson was governor of Illinois when the Korean War began in 1950 and became the Democratic candidate for president in 1952. New Dealer, legal assistant to the secretary of the navy during World War II, and then senior adviser to the U.S. delegation to the UN, Stevenson gained election to the Illinois governorship in 1948 on a platform of good government and reform. After early successes, he and the Democrats in Illinois suffered a serious setback in the 1950 elections. Already Republicans were making the war in Korea an issue, blaming the Truman administration for the conflict there and linking it to the alleged loss of China and the perceived presence of Communists in the U.S. government. The Republican charges at the national level found their echoes in Illinois, where the GOP elected its entire slate of candidates for statewide offices and seized control of both houses of the legislature.

The Democratic defeat in Illinois contributed to Stevenson's decision to seek the presidency in 1952; not surprisingly, the Republicans during the presidential race reiterated the themes that had served them well two years before. Republican candidate Dwight D. Eisenhower*, implementing the K1C2* strategy, hit on the Korean issue in nearly every speech, charging the Truman administration with responsibility for the war and with mismanagement in its conduct. Stevenson faced the delicate task of distancing himself from the administration without appearing disloyal to the party. "Let's admit that mistakes were made," he said, suggesting that the United States might have given firmer guarantees of the Republic of Korea's* security and might have been slower to cross the thirty-eighth parallel. Stevenson's was an impossible job, and although he tried to make light of Eisenhower's pledge to go to Korea if elected (Stevenson countered, "If elected, I shall go to the White House"), the deadlocked war doomed his candidacy.

R. A. Divine, *Foreign Policy and U.S. Presidential Elections, 1952–1960* (New York, 1974); J. R. Greene, *The Crusade: The Presidential Election of 1952* (Lanham, M.D., 1985); J. B. Martin, *Adlai Stevenson of Illinois* (Garden City, N.Y., 1976).

H. W. Brands

STRATEMEYER, GEORGE E. (1890–1969)

Lieutenant General George E. Stratemeyer was commander of the U.S. Far East Air Force (FEAF) for the first sixteen months of the Korean War. Born in

Cincinnati, Ohio, he entered the U.S. Military Academy along with Dwight D. Eisenhower* and Omar N. Bradley* in 1910. Stratemeyer graduated in 1915 and, after serving briefly in the infantry, transferred to flight training. When the United States entered World War I, he became commander of the School of Military Aeronautics at Ohio State University, then chief test pilot at Kelly Air Force Base, and, until 1921, head of the Air Service Mechanics School at Chanute Field. After spending three years in Hawaii, he taught air tactics at West Point until 1929. Stratemeyer graduated from Command and General Staff School in 1932, remaining there as an instructor for four years before commanding the 7th Bombardment Group from 1936 to 1938.

During World War II, Stratemeyer was at the Army War College, served as chief of training and operations at Air Corps headquarters, and by 1943 had become chief of air staff. He spent the rest of the war in the China-Burma-India theater, first as air adviser to the commanding general and later as commander of the newly formed Eastern Air Command, the only completely integrated Anglo-American unit during World War II. Having risen through the ranks to lieutenant general, Stratemeyer's first postwar assignment was at Chungking, as commander of all U.S. air forces in China. In February 1946, he returned to the United States to supervise the new Air Defense Command, emerging as a strong campaigner for air force autonomy and a large Air National Guard. After reorganization in 1948, he became head of the Continental Air Command. In April 1949, Stratemeyer assumed command of the FEAF, which was comprised of the 5th Air Force in Japan, the 13th Air Force in the Philippines, and the 20th Air Force on Okinawa. His force contained eighteen groups of fighters and fighter-bombers and one wing each of B-26 and B-29 bombers. By then, he had a reputation for being able to get the most out of his subordinates without raising his voice.

When the Korean War began, the Truman administration resorted to air power in its initial attempts to halt the North Korean invasion of South Korea*. Stratemeyer's instructions were to attack advancing enemy forces and provide air cover for the U.S. evacuation of Seoul*. When General Douglas MacArthur* made his visit to Korea of June 29, 1950*, Stratemeyer was with him aboard the *Bataan*. While en route, MacArthur ordered air attacks on targets in North Korea, though his instructions restricted military operations to south of the thirty-eighth parallel. Stratemeyer's cable to Major General Earle E. Partridge*, commander of the 5th Air Force, stated succinctly:"Take out North Korean airfields. No publicity. MacArthur approves." Thereafter, the FEAF's mission was to "isolate the battlefield" through attacking North Korea's communication lines and all installations and factories in every city and village. It was a source of great pride for Stratemeyer that three-fourths of the men under his command in Korea were from the air force reserve training program he had established.

Stratemeyer later became more sensitive about MacArthur's exceeding his authority, especially after evidence began to emerge of Chinese military intervention*. In early November 1950, when MacArthur issued orders for the FEAF to bomb the Yalu bridges in clear violation of his instructions, Stratemeyer informed Air Force Chief of Staff General Hoyt S. Vandenberg*, causing the Truman administration to limit raids to the southern side of the river. MacArthur later pointed to these restrictions as responsible for the failure of his Home-by-Christmas offensive*. Much to the dismay of Secretary of Defense George C. Marshall*, Stratemeyer backed MacArthur and spoke in favor of unlimited military operations against the People's Republic of China*, later stating in a magazine interview that Washington had "handcuffed" the general. Once the UNC* had halted China's offensive southward, Stratemeyer advocated strategic bombing of industrial and supply centers in the north, rather than tactical support for ground troops, thus setting the stage for the army–air force close support controversy*. After suffering a heart attack in May 1951, he returned in November to the United States. Retiring the following year, Stratemeyer organized a campaign to persuade the U.S. Senate not to censure Joseph McCarthy in 1954. *See also* Chinese Military Disengagement of November 6, 1950.

C. Blair, *The Forgotten War* (New York, 1987); *Current Biography,* 1951; *New York Times,* August 11, 1969; J. F. Schnabel and R. J. Watson, *A History of the Joint Chiefs of Staff,* vol. 3: *The Korean War* (Wilmington, 1979); *Who Was Who in America,* vol. 5: *1969–1973* (Chicago, 1973).

SUIHO BOMBING OPERATION (June 23–26, 1952)

The UNC* attacked the Suiho hydroelectric plant in June 1952 as part of the greatest coordinated air offensive of the war in an effort to force the Communists to acquiesce in an acceptable armistice arrangement. Suiho lay on the Yalu River 36 miles northeast of Sinŭiji. Built by the Japanese, it was the biggest hydroelectric plant in East Asia and fourth largest in the world, its six generators producing 640,000 kilowatts of power. Between one-half and three-quarters of this output was used by Chinese industry in Manchuria. The dam was a massive structure, impervious to anything short of a tactical atomic weapon, but the powerhouses, which lay on the Korean side of the Yalu, could be destroyed by conventional bombing. Suiho was spared until 1952 because it was a politically sensitive target. Its importance to the People's Republic of China* meant that any attack might be taken as a symbol of U.S. determination to widen the war, something that would cause problems with the UN allies, particularly Great Britain. Washington also feared that it would increase the danger of war with the Soviet Union.

On April 29, 1952, General Otto P. Weyland*, FEAF commander, recommended attacks on the North Korean hydroelectric system, including Suiho, as a means of forcing concessions at the P'anmunjŏm truce talks*. Nothing was done, however, until General Mark W. Clark* became the CINCUNC, an appointment that coincided with the deadlock over agenda item 4*, repatriation of POWs. Seeking a means of putting pressure on the enemy without incurring the heavy casualties involved in a ground offensive, Clark turned to air power. He ordered the preparation of plans for a coordinated attack on the hydroelectric system and asked Washington for permission to include Suiho on the target list. The JCS approved the raid on June 19. Four days later, Suiho was bombed, along with the rest of the generating system, in attacks that continued for three days. Although Weyland called the raids spectacular, they failed to change the attitude of the Communists at P'anmunjŏm. The bombing may even have undermined tentative Anglo-American contacts with Chou En-lai* on the POW issue, which were then taking place through India.

There was a storm of protest in Britain over the Suiho bombing operation. When British Foreign Secretary Herbert S. Morrison* visited the United States for the Acheson-Morrison meetings* in September 1951, he consented to the destruction of Suiho but only if the armistice talks failed. However, the United States had not consulted the British about the Suiho bombing, although Defense Minister Lord Alexander had been in Tokyo when the operation was being planned. According to Clark, he did not raise the issue because Alexander had left before Washington authorized the raid. A more likely reason was that the Americans distrusted British security following the Burgess-MacLean spy scandal. Suiho lay close to Antung, the largest MiG base in Manchuria, and would be heavily defended if the Communists were forewarned. Although Prime Minister Winston Churchill* supported the U.S. action against the Labour party's criticism, the government privately asked Washington to spring no more surprises. *See also* Air Pressure Strategy; Alexander-Lloyd Mission of June 1952; Rescreening of POWs.

D. Acheson, *Present at the Creation* (London, 1969); M. W. Clark, *From the Danube to the Yalu* (London, 1954); R. F. Futrell, *The United States Air Force in Korea* (New York, 1961); W. G. Hermes, *Truce Tent and Fighting Front* (Washington, D.C., 1966); C. A. MacDonald, *Korea: The War Before Vietnam* (London, 1986).

Callum A. MacDonald

SUNG SHIN-LUN (SONG SHINLUN; 1907–   )

Sung was commander of the 9th Group Army of the Chinese People's Volunteers Army* (CPVA) and, although not always victorious, gained great fame during the Korean War. Stubborn and quick tempered, he gained a world reputation as one of the ablest Chinese Communist party (CCP) generals. He was born in Hunan province, entering the Huangpu Military Academy at age 18 in the same class as Lin Piao* and joining the CCP while at the school. After the CCP split with the Kuomintang (KMT), Sung led an uprising in Kiangsi province and became a Red Army commander. Becoming involved in political struggles with Mao Tse-tung*, he was once removed from the party. Although he repeatedly displayed outstanding military talent, his promotion was very slow, and by the end of World War II, he commanded only a division. During the Chinese Civil War, Sung finally had his chance. He fought many brilliant battles, capturing several large cities and obtaining command of a group army. His troops were the strongest in the 3d Field Army, and with the establishment of the People's Republic of China*, he became commissar of the East China military and administrative committee under Marshal Ch'en Yi*

In 1950, after the United States declared the neutralization of Taiwan*, Sung moved his 9th Group Army to Shantung province in preparation for possible entry into the Korean War. In October, his forces were among the first Chinese troops to cross the Yalu River, marching into North Korea over a period of fourteen days and carrying rifles, mortars, and machine guns but not heavy artillery because of the mountainous terrain. Sung was in charge of the eastern front, planning the counterattack that shattered the UNC's* forces during the Chosin Reservoir Campaign*. He employed more than 100,000 troops in a bold effort to encircle and destroy the U.S. 1st and 7th Marine divisions but lacked sufficient equipment and supplies to achieve complete victory. In 1952, Sung destroyed the Republic of Korea's* 3d Division and then turned to attack the U.S. 2d Division but failed to destroy either unit. After his forces stopped the UNC counterattack, the 9th Group Army returned to China.

In the summer of 1952, Sung was appointed the garrison commander of the city of Shanghai and then promoted to the post of vice-chief of the Nanking military zone. During the following years, Sung directed a series of attacks on the small KMT-occupied islands along the coast. In 1955, he gained promotion to general, becoming the president of the Military Science Academy and supervising its affairs. In 1973, he led a delegation to visit the Democratic People's Republic of Korea* and four years later became a member of the Central Committee of the CCP.

R. E. Appleman, *South to the Naktong, North to the Yalu* (Washington, D.C., 1961); Huang Chen-hsia, *Mao's Generals* (Hong Kong, 1968); Institute of International Relations, *Chinese Communist Who's Who* (Taipei, 1971); *Who's Who in Modern China* (Tokyo, 1978).

Li Yi

SUSPENSE ACCOUNT CONTROVERSY

This dispute was the result of problems arising from the advance of won, the Republic of Korea's* currency, to the UN Command* to finance its military operations during the Korean War. On July 28, 1950, at Taegu, U.S. and South Korean representatives signed the U.S.-ROK Expenditures Agreement to "govern the relationship with respect to provision and use of currency and credits between" the ROK and the UNC. Replacing an earlier arrangement of July 6, it stated that the ROK would provide won in amounts and types and at times and places that the CINCUNC requested to finance "expenditures arising out of [UNC] operations and activities in Korea." The date when the won was spent would determine the exchange rate. Although the CINCUNC could transfer currency and credits to forces from other nations fighting in Korea, he would inform the ROK. With regard to settlement of claims, the accord stated that negotiations would "take place directly between the Governments of the Forces concerned" and the ROK government but "shall be deferred to a time or times mutually satisfactory to the respective Governments." Subsequently, the UNC built a sizable suspense account at the Bank of Korea that eventually would require settlement. During 1951, the United States proposed that the relief goods it gave for the war refugees cancel out the suspense account, but Paik Tu Chin*, the ROK's finance minister, persuaded the United States to reimburse the won advance.

Controversy over the suspense account became serious in January 1952 when the ROK intimated that it would no longer be able to provide currency to the UNC. This was a response to uncontrollable inflation in South Korea. During the eight months after July 1, 1951, the amount of currency in circulation rose from 122 billion to 812 billion won. While the United States blamed inflation on the deficit spending and loose credit practices of President Syngman Rhee's* government, the South Koreans pointed to the won advances as the primary culprit. In addition, the ROK charged that the UNC was refusing to settle in U.S. dollars for the won issued thus far at a fair exchange rate. In response, CINCUNC General Matthew B. Ridgway* stated that he did not object to making monthly settlements in dollars for the won advances as long as the UNC retained some control over the ROK's foreign exchange. To counter inflationary pressures, he proposed that the UNC secure Korean currency by selling imported commodities to the Korean people and purchasing won at the best rate available. Also, Ridgway suggested book settlement for UNC services to restrict the amount of currency put into circulation.

In February 1952, negotiations to resolve the suspense account controversy reached an impasse. The ROK refused to permit the UNC to maintain control of its foreign exchange and wanted immediate and full settlement of won advances so as to pay for imports that could be sold to Koreans and the proceeds then withdrawn from circulation, thereby curbing inflation. Ridgway, while taking steps to limit expenditures of won, urged the Truman administration to send a high-level mission to reach an understanding on the entire field of ROK-U.S. relations. This would result in Washington's dispatch of the Meyer Mission* to South Korea. In March 1952, Clarence E. Meyer* successfully negotiated with the ROK the Agreement on Economic Coordination, which settled all advances since January 1952 and made provision for the future. However, the settlement of claims for the first eighteen months of the Korean War was deferred to a date as soon as possible after March 31, 1953. In June 1953, Paik Tu Chin, now prime minister, visited the United States, but his main concern was no longer the suspense account but gaining assurances about future economic aid for the ROK.

Foreign Relations of the United States, 1952–1954, vol. 15: *Korea* (Washington, D.C., 1984); W. G. Hermes, *Truce Tent and Fighting Front* (Washington, D.C., 1966); *United States Treaties and Other International Agreements,* vol. 1: *1950* (Washington, D.C., 1952).

SWNCC 176/30 (August 4, 1947)

This was the first report of the ad hoc subcommittee on Korea of the State-War-Navy Coordinating Committee (SWNCC) and remained the basic policy on Korea until the approval of SANACC 176/35* on January 14, 1948. Previously, an interdepartmental committee on Korea had framed a report on February 25, 1947, that had become both the basis of Korean policy and the impetus for the ill-fated Korean Aid Bill of 1947*. On July 29, 1947, John M. Allison*— the State Department's assistant chief of Northeast Asian affairs and the steering member of the SWNCC ad hoc subcommittee on Korea—issued a memorandum recommending that the United States seek a meeting with the Soviet Union, Britain, and the Republic of China* to arrange elections for a unified Korean government. If the Soviets blocked this move, Allison argued that the United States should take the issue to the UN. He also recommended that the United States move forward with a positive program of assistance for southern Korea, referring to the Korean aid bill then pending in Congress.

Starting with Allison's memorandum, the full subcommittee began drafting SWNCC 176/30. It included Allison's first two recommendations but recommended drafting new aid legislation, prefacing its policy statement with a series of conclusions, two of them central. First, the subcommittee concluded that the United States could not pull out of Korea at that time because withdrawal would lead to Communist domination and damage to U.S. prestige. Second, it stipulated that every effort should be made to "liquidate or reduce the U.S. expenditure of men and money in Korea as soon as possible without abandoning Korea to Soviet domination." This represented both a policy reversal and a victory for Secretary of War Robert P. Patterson. On April 4, 1947, Patterson wrote a memorandum to Under Secretary of State Dean G. Acheson* making clear both his reluctance to endorse the 1947 Korean aid bill and his preference for getting out of Korea at an early date.

By August, with Acheson out of the State Department, Patterson's views began to prevail. The new assistance legislation dropped the 1947 Korean aid bill's three-year $540 million economic rehabilitation program and slashed Korean aid for fiscal 1948. Drafted in accordance with SWNCC 176/30, the Korean aid bill now provided only $113 million for fiscal 1948, about half of what the prior legislation would have provided and far less than even the original War Department request of $137 million. Translating SWNCC 176/30 into action immediately after its approval, Secretary of State George C. Marshall* called for a meeting of the four powers to set up Korean elections, and when the Soviet Union blocked this move, Marshall took the Korean issue to the UN, resulting in the approval of the UN resolution of November 14, 1947*.

R. L. McGlothlen, "Acheson, Economics, and the American Commitment in Korea," *Pacific Historical Review* (February 1989); J. I. Matray, *The Reluctant Crusade* (Honolulu, 1985); W. W. Stueck, *The Road to Confrontation* (Chapel Hill, 1981).

Ronald L. McGlothlen

T

TAEGU, DEFENSE OF
See Defense of Taegu

TAEHAN YOUTH CORPS

This was an organization formed in December 1949 to absorb all the rightist youth groups that had been active in anti-leftist political repression in southern Korea since the end of World War II. After liberation in 1945, southern Korea was flooded with various rightist youth organizations, while leftist elements were soon unified as the Democratic Youth League. Shortly after the Republic of Korea* was established in August 1948, President Syngman Rhee* ordered all rightist youth organizations to be unified. Under Rhee's instruction, more than twenty youth bands combined to form the Taehan [Greater Korea] Youth Corps, including such powerful elements as the Taedong Youth Corps, the General League of Youth Korea, the National Society Youth Corps, the Korean Independence Youth Corps, and the Northwest Youth Society. The corps had Rhee as president and elected Chang T'aek-sang*, Lee Chong Ch'an*, Chŏn Chin-han, No T'ae-jun, Yu Chin-san, Sŏ Sang-ch'ŏn, Kang Nak-wŏn, and Shin Sung-mo* to a supreme committee.

The Taehan Youth Corps rallied 2 million members through its extensive national networks and exercised military training for the local defense. Reorganized as the National Guard in December 1950, it then incorporated all equivalents of the militia (second-class reserve forces) and exercised regular military training. An internal split in January 1950 replaced the supreme committee system with that of a commandant, and Shin Sung-mo was elected to the post. He was later succeeded by An Ho-sang*. After the South Korean National Guard scandal*, it remained only as a nominal body and was finally dissolved after the South Korean presidential elections of 1952*. A kind of private army for Syngman Rhee, it served thoroughly the cause of Rhee's regime from start to finish.

Kukbang-bu p'yŏnch'an wiwŏn-hoe, *Han'guk Chŏnjaeng-sa* (Seoul, 1968); H. Yi (ed.), *Han'guk-sa Taesajŏn* (Seoul, 1976); Yŏrŭm Publishing Co. (ed.), *Han'guk Hyŏn-dae Sahoeundong Sajŏn* (Seoul, 1988).

Jinwung Kim

TAEJŎN AGREEMENT (July 12, 1950)

Though often confused with the transfer to the UNC* of authority over South Korean military forces, this agreement between the Republic of Korea* and the United States in fact concerns the status and the rights of the U.S. armed forces stationed in Korea. It was completed with an exchange of notes between the Korean Ministry of Foreign Affairs and the U.S. embassy at Taejŏn, an interim capital city located about 100 miles south of Seoul, during the critical early point of the Korean War. In this agreement the United States obtained exclusive jurisdiction over all U.S. military personnel. The ROK also agreed that U.S. soldiers could not be requested to obey any order except those from U.S. military commanders. The U.S. side agreed that the U.S. military court in Korea would not have the right of jurisdiction over Korean civilians unless requested. This agreement became effective on the same day it was signed. Later, on July 9, 1966, the ROK and the United States modified the agreement, adding provisions concerning the status of the U.S. forces in Korea.

Some writers have confused the Taejŏn agreement with President Syngman Rhee's* transfer of authority over the ROK's military forces to the UNC. How-ever, this was an entirely different arrangement. On July 15, Rhee sent a letter to CINCUNC General Douglas MacArthur* stating that in response to "the joint military effort of the United Nations on behalf of the Republic of Korea, . . . I am happy to assign to you command authority over all land, sea, and air forces of the Republic of Korea during the period of the continuation of the present state of hostilities." "The Korean Army will be proud to serve under your command," he wrote, "and the Korean people and Government will be equally proud and encouraged to have the overall-direction of our combined effort in the hands of so famous and distinguished a soldier, . . . to resist the infamous Communist assault on the independence and integrity of our beloved land."

MacArthur replied three days later through U.S. Ambassador John J. Muccio*, declaring that "I am proud indeed to have the gallant Republic of Korea forces under my command." "Tell him also not to lose heart," the general concluded, because although "the way be long and hard, . . . ultimated [sic] result cannot fail to be victory." Since Rhee had transferred authority over the ROK's forces for the duration of the war, there was no change in the command relationship after President Harry S. Truman's* recall of MacArthur*. But when the United States indicated its intention to accept a cease-fire in 1953 without achieving reunification, Rhee threatened to remove the South Korean army from the UNC's control in a bold effort to scuttle the armistice. The Eisenhower administration was able to preserve the arrangement, which remains in existence in a revised form today. In recent years, the UNC's command relationship with the ROK's armed forces has been the focus of much criticism from student radicals in South Korea. For example, anti-government activists point to it as proof that the United States was responsible for the attack of ROK troops on demonstrators in May 1980, now known as the Kwangju incident. *See also* Korean Augmentation of the U.S. Army.

Defense Department of Korea, *The History of the Korean War* (Seoul, 1979); *Dictionary of Political Science* (Seoul, 1975); History Compilation Committee, Ministry of National Defense, *The Treaties of the National Defense* (Seoul, 1981); Y. M. Kim, *History of the Korean War* (Seoul, 1978).

Chull Baum Kim

TAEJŎN, BATTLE OF

See Battle of the Kŭm River

TAFT, ROBERT A. (1889–1953)

Senator Robert A. Taft of Ohio was the leading spokesman for the Republican party at the outbreak of the Korean War. Although Taft originally supported President Harry S. Truman's* decision to use force in Korea, he soon became a vocal critic of the administration's conduct of the war. The son of former president William Howard Taft, he was born in Cincinnati, Ohio, attended Yale University, and after a career as a state legislator and lawyer, won election to the Senate in 1938. A staunch opponent of the New Deal and an isolationist before Pearl Harbor, by the end of the 1940s he had won the nickname "Mr. Republican" for his devotion to his party. After Thomas E. Dewey's surprising defeat by Truman in 1948, Taft emerged as the leading GOP presidential contender.

Three days after the North Korean invasion of South Korea*, Taft gave a Senate speech in which he offered reluctant approval of Truman's decision to send U.S. troops into battle. While he endorsed that commitment as in the national interest, he criticized the president for failing to seek a declaration of war or at least a congressional resolution approving the use of force. The senator also held Truman responsible for the events leading to war, accusing him of pursuing a "bungling and inconsistent foreign policy" that gave "basic encouragement to the North Korean aggression," a reference among other actions to Secretary of State Dean G. Acheson's* National Press Club speech.*

During the course of the war, Taft exploited the administration's failure to win a clear-cut victory as a major campaign issue for the Republican party. The senator defended General Douglas MacArthur* after Truman's recall of MacArthur* in April 1951, going so far as to advocate using Chiang Kai-shek's* troops in Korea and bombing Chinese supply lines in Manchuria. When he sought the Republican nomination in the spring of 1952, Taft harped on Korea, asserting that Truman had gotten the nation involved in a costly war it could neither win nor end on honorable terms. Although he lost his bid for the GOP nomination, Taft could take solace in the fall campaign when Dwight D. Eisenhower* used the growing frustration over the Korean War to ensure the Republican victory in November.

R. J. Caridi, *The Korean War and American Politics* (Philadelphia, 1968); R. A. Divine, *Foreign Policy and U.S. Presidential Elections, 1952–1960* (New York, 1974); R. J. Donovan, *Tumultuous Years* (New York, 1982); J. T. Patterson, *Mr. Republican: A Biography of Robert A. Taft* (Boston, 1952).

Robert A. Divine

TAIWAN (FORMOSA)

See Neutralization of Taiwan; Republic of China

TASCA, HENRY J. (1912–1979)

In 1953, President Dwight D. Eisenhower sent Henry J. Tasca to the Republic of Korea* as his special representative to examine the Korean economy and make recommendations for future U.S. assistance to achieve reconstruction. Upon his return, he submitted a report that provided the foundation for the Eisenhower administration's program for the economic recovery of the ROK after the Korean War. Born in Providence, Rhode Island, Tasca graduated with a B.S. from Temple University in 1933. He then attended the University of Pennsylvania, earning an M.B.A. (1934) and a Ph.D. (1937). After a year at the London School of Economics, he joined the State Department's division of trade agreements as an economic analyst and then was a Penfield traveling scholar in Europe. From 1938 to 1941, Tasca was assistant director of the trade regulation and commercial policy project for the Rockefeller Foundation and economic advisor for trade with the National Defense Commission. In World War II, he served as a lieutenant commander in the U.S. Navy.

In 1945, Tasca became the Treasury Department's representative at the U.S. embassy in Rome, Italy, and special financial advisor to the Allied Commission. From 1948 to 1949, he was special assistant to the secretary of the treasury and alternate U.S. executive director at the International Monetary Fund. When the Korean War began, Tasca was in France as director of the plans and policy staff in the Department of Economic Affairs for the Marshall Plan. In 1951, he became W. Averell Harriman's* economic advisor at NATO and, the next year, deputy U.S. special representative in Europe. Following completion of the Tasca Mission* to Korea in 1953, he became the director of the foreign operations administration in Rome until 1956, when he went to Bonn, West Germany, where he served four years as minister of economic affairs. From 1960 to 1965, Tasca was at the State Department as deputy assistant secretary for African affairs before ending his diplomatic career as ambassador to Morocco (1965–1969) and Greece (1969–1974). During retirement, he lived in Rome, but remained active in international business affairs and served regularly as an advisor for the U.S. government on Third World and European economic matters. The author of two books on U.S. trade policy, Tasca died in an automobile accident.

New York Times, August 25, 1979; *Who Was Who in America,* vol. 7: *1977–1981* (Chicago, 1981); *Who's Who in the World, 1978* (Chicago, 1978).

TASCA MISSION (April 17–June 15, 1953)

The Tasca Mission was a presidential mission, headed by Henry J. Tasca*, sent in spring 1953 to survey the South Korean economy and make recommendations to the president and the NSC on U.S. aid levels for the Republic of Korea* and the postwar South Korean economy. Tasca's mission was the Eisenhower administration's successor to the Meyer Mission* appointed by President Harry S. Truman*. Whereas Clarence E. Meyer* concentrated on the wartime financial relationship between the ROK and the UN, Tasca examined the broader question of the South Korean economy with special emphasis on postwar reconstruction. Tasca's report became the basis of NSC–156/1*, discussed by the NSC on July 23, 1953, and approved by President Dwight D. Eisenhower* on that same day.

Tasca arrived in Korea on April 17, 1953, holding meetings with UNC* agencies, the UN Korean Reconstruction Agency*, members of the government of President Syngman Rhee*, the National Assembly, and the Korean Chamber of Commerce. Headquartered in Pusan, Tasca visited industrial, mining, and agricultural areas in South Korea, including Seoul. In a report to the NSC on June 15, 1953, Tasca stated that he had found a South Korea devastated by war with 2.5 million refugees, 5 million destitute civilians, and 60,000 houses destroyed. Tasca noted that war damages were $1 billion and production of rice was only two-thirds the 1949–1950 average. Per capita income had dropped from a prewar high of $90 in 1949–1950 to $60, and South Koreans were averaging only 1,500 calories daily food consumption. Tasca calculated that the ROK exports of the past year equalled little more than twice the total value of clothing and relief items provided by American charities to South Korea in that same year.

With soaring inflation and plans to expand the South Korean army from sixteen to twenty divisions, Tasca recommended that the United States make available to the ROK almost $975 million in economic aid over the next three years so as to support the expanded ROK armed forces and enable South Korea to return to its pre-invasion standard of living. Tasca's report gave focus to Eisenhower's belief that the United States should give special priority to South Korean reconstruction. The president became converted to the idea of massive rebuilding of the South Korean economic infrastructure by U.S. troops in Korea. Unfortunately Eisenhower's vision of employing the means of war for reconstruction proved to be too unorthodox and too costly. The Eisenhower administration requested and received from Congress large aid requests for South Korea—over $600 million from 1954 to 1956—but it was administered in the more traditional way. Still, it provided an economic lifeline to South Korea immediately after the armistice.

S. E. Ambrose, *Eisenhower, the President* (New York, 1984); *Foreign Relations of the United States, 1952–1954*, vol. 15: *Korea* (Washington, D.C., 1984); J. A. Kim, *Divided Korea* (Cambridge, 1975).

Edward C. Keefer

TASK FORCE SMITH

When President Harry S. Truman* committed U.S. ground forces to stop the North Korean invasion of South Korea*, General Douglas MacArthur* ordered the 8th Army's* 24th Infantry Division to proceed from Fort Wood, Japan, to Korea. The July 1, 1950, operations order provided for a delaying force to go to Pusan by air immediately. Named for its commander, Lieutenant Colonel Charles B. (Brad) Smith, Task Force Smith was assembled during the night of June 30 and then trucked to nearby Itazuke Air Base to be flown to Pusan in C-54s beginning at 8:45 A.M. on July 1. This initial commitment of U.S. ground troops in the Korean War consisted of 406 men: two understrength rifle companies, half of a battalion headquarters company, half of a communications platoon, a 75mm recoilless rifle platoon with two guns, and two 4.2-inch mortars. In addition, the two rifle companies had six 2.36-inch bazooka teams and four 60mm mortars. Each man carried 120 rounds of .30-caliber ammunition and two days of C rations. Some of the officer position gaps in the rifle platoons were filled from another battalion, but only about one-third of the officers and non-commissioned officers were World War II combat veterans. Only five years after the end of World War II, less than one-sixth of Task Force Smith had combat experience.

After their arrival at Pusan, Task Force Smith was trucked through cheering crowds to the train station where noisy bands celebrated its departure northward. This boosted the already high morale of the soldiers who thought that the North Koreans would stop as soon as they discovered that the "invincible" U.S. Army was committed. Smith chose an excellent infantry position 3 miles north of Osan to set up a roadblock for the first engagement on the morning of July 5. But he did not have the firepower to stop the Soviet-made T-34 tanks, nor did it seem to matter to the North Koreans at the Battle of Osan* that they were now fighting Americans.

General MacArthur called this small, ill-equipped unit an "arrogant display of strength." Like everyone else from President Truman to the lowliest privates, he thought that the mere presence of U.S. troops would "chill the enemy commander into taking precautionary and time-consuming" actions. He later claimed that although the first engagement at Osan did not cause the enemy to turn tail and run, Task Force Smith and the rest of Major General William F. Dean's* 24th Division forced the enemy to stop his tank column drive southward and deploy in a conventional line of battle across a 150-mile front, delaying the advance until the rest of the 8th Army could establish itself in Korea. *See also* Truman's Commitment of Ground Troops.

R. E. Appleman, *South to the Naktong, North to the Yalu* (Washington, D.C., 1961); T. R. Fehrenbach, *This Kind of War* (New York, 1963); D. MacArthur, *Reminiscences* (New York, 1964).

Larry R. Beck

TAYLOR, MAXWELL D. (1901–1987)

During the Korean War, Maxwell Davenport Taylor was 8th Army* commander and later replaced General John E. Hull* as CINCUNC. He entered the U.S. Military Academy at West Point in 1918 and became captain of the corps of cadets. He finished fourth in his class. After graduation, he served in the corps of engineers and the field artillery. After spending time as an instructor at West Point and studying the Japanese language in Japan, he was assistant military attaché in China and later part of a special mission to Latin America on hemispheric defense. During World War II, he traveled behind enemy lines in Italy to investigate the feasibility of an Allied airborne assault on Rome. He led the D-Day assault at Normandy as commanding general of the 101st Airborne Division. After the war, he returned to West Point as superintendent and then served in various commands in Europe. Before going to Korea in 1953, he was deputy army chief of staff for operations and administration.

As 8th Army commander, General Taylor's task in Korea was difficult. President Dwight D. Eisenhower* used a two-pronged approach to ending the war: he negotiated and at the same time used air attacks on North Korean rice fields and irrigation canals. He also considered using nuclear weapons. Beginning in late March 1953, the Chinese People's Volunteers Army* launched a series of attacks in the vicinity of Old Baldy and Pork Chop Hill, overrunning U.S. positions. Then President Syngman Rhee* of the Republic of Korea*, expressing his displeasure with negotiations, created another crisis with his release of North Korean POWs*. When the Chinese attacked again in July, Taylor, to limit casualties, ordered cessation of attacks on Old Baldy and withdrew UN forces from Pork Chop Hill. To bolster the ROK army and prevent loss of territory, however, he sent reinforcements. This was the heaviest fighting of the war, and casualties on both sides reached the tens of thousands.

After the armistice, Taylor instituted training programs for his troops and supervised the exchange of prisoners. He established a South Korean army of twenty active and ten reserve divisions and began rebuilding the South Korean economy. He became U.S. Army chief of staff in 1955 and retired in 1959. Returning to active duty after the failure of the Bay of Pigs invasion in April 1961, President John F. Kennedy appointed him military representative to the president and then asked him to be chairman of the JCS. He served in this capacity until President Lyndon B. Johnson named him U.S. ambassador in Saigon in 1964. It was after his return from Southeast Asia in the summer of 1965 that Taylor concluded his career in public service as special counsel to the president and chairman of the foreign intelligence advisory board. *See also* Chinese Summer Offensives of 1953.

C. Blair, *The Forgotten War* (New York, 1987); *Current Biography,* 1961; R. Foot,

The Wrong War (Ithaca, N.Y., 1985); "General Maxwell Davenport Taylor," June 1, 1964, U.S. Army Military History Institute, Carlisle Barracks, Pennsylvania; B. I. Kaufman, *The Korean War* (Philadelphia, 1986); *New York Times*, April 21, 1987.

William B. Pickett

TENG HUA (DENG HUA; 1910–1980)

Teng Hua was the vice-commander of the Chinese People's Volunteers Army* (CPVA)* during the Korean War. Born to a well-to-do family in Hunan province, Teng went to a missionary school. Instead of becoming a Christian convert, he accepted only the new Western ideas. In 1926, Teng joined the Northern Expedition as it passed his home town and became a Communist. He followed Chu Teh and Ch'en Yi* to the Chingkang Mountain in 1928. Teng showed great bravery in defending the Soviet base and, though only 20 years old, was appointed a division political commissar. In 1934, he entered Red Army University and was active during the Sino-Japanese War. He fought in the Battle of P'ing-hsing Pass, organized a large-scale uprising in Hupei province, and successfully established a resistance based behind the enemy lines. Following Japan's surrender, Teng was sent to Manchuria as the garrison commander of Shenyang. Soon after, he and his unit were organized into the 4th Field Army under the command of Lin Piao*. While Lin established his reputation as a brilliant leader of the Communist troops, Teng was his most able subordinate.

When Teng was fighting on Hainan Island as vanguard for the 4th Field Army, the Korean War broke out, and he was reassigned to the north and stationed along the Yalu River. The North Koreans appeared victorious, but Teng predicted that the UNC*, with its advantage in air and sea power, would land behind Communist lines and reverse the course of the war. After the Americans completed the recapture of Seoul operation*, some Chinese generals urged the government to intervene, but Teng advised delay until the UNC crossed the thirty-eighth parallel. In October 1950, after Mao Tse-tung* had ordered Chinese military intervention*, Teng's chance came when he was appointed the vice-commander of the CPVA.

Realizing that CINCUNC General Douglas MacArthur* was contemptuous of his Communist adversary and the UN forces were much better equipped, Teng developed a strategy with two basic elements: "night-fight" and "near-fight"— deeply penetrating enemy lines after dark and then attacking from the sides and the sea. In the first few battles, Teng's tactics experienced considerable success. Without modern weapons, however, Chinese victories were always limited and accompanied by heavy losses. After the UNC counteroffensive pushed the CPVA out of South Korea, Teng recognized that it was very difficult to destroy a whole enemy division in a mobile fight, so he devised the new tactic of tunnel warfare (building tunnels along the front to stabilize and strengthen the CPVA's positions), obtaining approval for implementing his proposal from Peng Teh-huai*, the CPVA commander. Known as "the underground China Wall," the tunnel strategy proved effective, as the Chinese established and held a defensive line just north of the thirty-eighth parallel. While China's losses declined, the UNC's advantage decreased.

In July 1951, the Kaesŏng truce talks* began, and Teng was the representative of the CPVA. However, Li K'e-nung* was chief of the delegation and directed the negotiations, although he remained in the background. In 1952, Peng returned home, and Teng acted as the commander. Mao called in Teng and warned him to be alert against another Inch'ŏn landing*. Teng therefore carefully studied the case of Normandy landing and spent great energy constructing coastal defenses. In 1954, the year after the Korean armistice agreement* was signed, he became the vice-commander of the Northeast Military Zone, earning the rank of general the next year.

Experiencing the whole of the Korean War, Teng came to the conclusion that China's army had to modernize, and he made every effort to achieve this goal. In 1959, Teng was involved in the political struggle between Mao and Peng. Siding with Peng, Teng was purged from the military and exiled to Szechwan province. "The hunting dog should be cooked," he complained, "since now [the] rabbits all [have] died." In 1977, he became vice-president of Military Science Academy.

Huang Chen-hsia, *Mao's Generals* (Hong Kong, 1968); Xinghuo Liaoyuan, *Jie Fang Jun Jinan Ling Zhuan* (Beijing, 1988);

Li Yi

X (TENTH) CORPS

This corps headquarters, independent of the 8th Army*, was created by CINCUNC General Douglas MacArthur* on August 26, 1950, to command the Inch'ŏn landing*. MacArthur chose to create this headquarters from the resources of his own staff in Japan, making Major General Edward M. Almond* simultaneously his own chief of staff and commander of the X Corps. MacArthur apparently believed that the operation would be so decisive that Almond could return to his staff duties in a matter of weeks. Built around the 1st Marine Division (with attached U.S. Army and Korean Marine units) and the 7th U.S. Infantry Division, the X Corps landed at Inch'ŏn on September 15, 1950. During subsequent operations to retake Seoul, the corps linked up with elements of 8th Army on September 27.

Following the recapture of Seoul operation*, most participants expected the X Corps to be placed under command of the 8th Army for the pursuit into North Korea. Instead, MacArthur chose to maintain the X Corps as an independent formation, in order to conduct a second combat landing (Operation Tailboard) farther north at the port of Wŏnsan on the east coast of the Korean peninsula. This decision had a number of consequences for the UNC* campaign. First, the continued pursuit north of Seoul was delayed by up to two weeks in early October 1950, while units of 8th Army conducted a passage of lines to take up the pursuit from the X Corps. Second, UN logistics were severely impeded; Inch'ŏn, the main supply port in the Seoul area, was virtually shut down while the 1st Marine

Division withdrew to the city and reloaded aboard ships for another amphibious landing. Many of the trucks on the peninsula were diverted to move the 7th Infantry Division by road from Seoul down to Pusan, where it, too, loaded aboard ship. All this made the 8th Army slower and weaker in its pursuit north and kept the X Corps out of battle.

By the time the X Corps was able to make the Wŏnsan landing* on October 26, 1950, the enemy had fled northward. For the next month, the corps spread out into central and eastern North Korea, pursuing the North Korean People's Army in a way that left units isolated from both each other and the 8th Army, far to the west. Beginning on November 7, the 3d U.S. Infantry Division landed at Wŏnsan to join the corps. Nevertheless, the X Corps units were severely damaged by the Chinese Communist offensive of November 25, 1950, forcing Almond's eventual withdrawal and the Hŭngnam evacuation* in December 1950. Under heavy pressure from Army Chief of Staff General J. Lawton Collins*, MacArthur had already decided on December 7 that the X Corps would fall under 8th Army control when it reentered the fight in South Korea. When Lieutenant General Matthew B. Ridgway* assumed command of the 8th Army in late December, he ended the special status and separate supply channels that the X Corps had previously enjoyed, making it the third corps in a consolidated 8th Army. As such, the X Corps remained throughout the rest of the war.

R. E. Appleman, *South to the Naktong, North to the Yalu* (Washington, D.C., 1961); C. Blair, *The Forgotten War* (New York, 1987); J. F. Schnabel, *Policy and Direction* (Washington, D.C., 1972).

Jonathan M. House

THIMAYYA, KADENDERA SUBAYYA (1906–1965)

K. S. Thimayya was chairman of the Neutral Nations Repatriation Commission* (NNRC) and therefore played a crucial role in carrying out the Korean War armistice agreement* terms on the repatriation of prisoners of war. Born into an elite landholding family in British India's southern territory of Coorg, he began his military career in 1922 when he became one of the first thirty-two entrants to the Royal Indian Military College (Sandhurst) in Dehra Dun, India. He graduated and was commissioned in 1926 and during World War II served against the Japanese in Burma. Brigadier Thimayya first caught the attention of Prime Minister Jawaharlal Nehru* immediately following India's independence from British colonial rule in 1947. During the hectic days of partition, he led the Indian Fourth Division in restoring order to the violence-plagued East Punjab, an area situated along the newly established Indian-Pakistani border, where millions of Hindu and Muslim refugees had migrated. After having emerged as a national hero, "Thimmy" was promoted to the rank of general and served with distinction later in 1947 in India's first war with Pakistan over the disputed state of Kashmir. When India was tapped in 1953 by the UN to head the NNRC and to provide a custodial force of 5,000 troops to maintain order in the POW camps, Nehru personally picked Thimayya to head the effort.

Initiating its work in September 1953, the NNRC had been charged with the task of supervising the screening of the 22,600 Communist and 359 UN prisoners who had declined repatriation to their countries of origin. Thimayya turned out to be perfectly suited for the assignment. Diplomatic but firm, he first won the trust of the Communist POWs—many of whom initially had refused to be screened by their own nationals out of fear of reprisal. Thimayya also dealt effectively with both Communist and UNC* charges of unfairness in the screening procedures. In one case, for example, he conceded the right to Communist observers to broadcast daily ten minute pleas for repatriation over camp loudspeakers, while at the same time accurately predicting to skeptical UNC officials that the Communists would fail to win converts. Thimayya proved to be especially adept at handling President Syngman Rhee* of the Republic of Korea*. When Rhee threatened to drive Indian troops out of Korea and liberate all prisoners, Thimayya simply persuaded CINCUNC General John E. Hull* to pull back South Korean marines from positions where they might have facilitated a breakout. Korean forces were subsequently replaced by U.S. Marines. Most important, Thimayya and the NNRC saw to it that the screening process was completed within its assigned eight-week schedule. In the end, only 137 of the Communist nonrepatriates and ten of the UN nonrepatriates opted to return home. The NNRC released the remaining POWs and dissolved itself on February 1, 1954. *See also* Menon POW Settlement Proposal.

S. Gopal, *Jawaharlal Nehru: A Biography* (New Delhi, 1979); B. I. Kaufman, *The Korean War* (Philadelphia, 1986); *Newsweek*, November 16, 1953; *Time*, November 9, 1953.

Dennis Merrill

THIRTY-EIGHTH PARALLEL CROSSING DECISION
See UN Offensive across the 38th Parallel

THIRTY-EIGHTH PARALLEL DIVISION
On August 15, 1945, President Harry S. Truman* proposed and received Joseph Stalin's* approval for General Order Number One, which included a provision for Korea's temporary division at the thirty-eighth parallel into two zones of military occupation, with the Soviet Union accepting the surrender of Japanese troops in the north and the United States in the south. This last-minute arrangement was necessary because the president had discarded the four-power trusteeship plan for Korea's postwar reconstruction that President Franklin D. Roosevelt had developed during World War II. Years later, Truman portrayed this decision as the product of military expediency and convenience. In reality, political and strategic considerations were primarily responsible for Korea's partition. When Truman became president in April 1945, Moscow's establishment of Communist governments in Eastern Europe persuaded him that Stalin would pursue the same objective in Korea. If the Soviet Union dominated Korea, it could undermine Chiang Kai-shek's* position in China and place the security

of Japan in jeopardy. Truman began to search for a way to occupy Korea unilaterally, thereby removing any chance for Sovietization. His decision to use the atomic bomb against Japan was in part aimed at forcing Tokyo to surrender quickly and thereby preempting Soviet entry into the Pacific war.

Truman's gamble failed. On August 8, Stalin acted to ensure that he would play a role in reconstructing East Asia after World War II, declaring war on Japan prior to its surrender and sending the Red Army into Korea. Two days later, the State-War-Navy Coordinating Committee (SWNCC) instructed Colonels C. H. Bonesteel and Dean Rusk* to find a line in Korea that would harmonize the political desire to have U.S. forces receive the surrender as far north as possible with the inability of the closest U.S. troops on Okinawa to reach the area before the Soviets occupied the entire Korean peninsula. Bonesteel and Rusk decided on the thirty-eighth parallel, and the SWNCC incorporated the line in General Order Number One. The JCS endorsed this decision, satisfied that the thirty-eighth parallel provided for U.S. control over both the capital at Seoul and sufficient land to apportion zones of occupation to China and Britain. Many American leaders doubted if Stalin would accept the proposal, but the Soviet leader agreed, probably in hopes of receiving a voice in the reconstruction of Japan. Truman's refusal to grant Stalin an equal role in determining Japan's future meant that Korea's reunification was unlikely from the start.

Scholars have criticized the decision to divide Korea into zones of military occupation. Certainly the line was ill advised as a permanent boundary since it cut across natural areas of geographic, cultural, and climatic continuity. On the west coast, for example, the Ongjin peninsula was part of the U.S. zone, yet the United States had no land connection to that area. But Truman did not think that the partition would become permanent. With the deterioration of relations in Europe, however, Korea became a captive of the cold war, as neither the Soviets nor the Americans would permit the removal of the thirty-eighth parallel division because this might allow its rival to dominate a reunited Korea. Given the alternative of complete Soviet control, Truman thought he had achieved a major success. The Red Army could have occupied the entire peninsula, and the president decided that it was politically and strategically important to avoid such a result. Only Stalin's willingness to accept the surrender agreement prevented Communist dominance throughout Korea. Under these circumstances, half of the Korean loaf was the most Truman or anyone else could have expected. Yet the thirty-eighth parallel division was responsible for the emergence of two Koreas, and the determination of each to achieve reunification would lead to the outbreak of the Korean War.

A. L. Grey, Jr., "The Thirty-Eighth Parallel," *Foreign Affairs* (April 1951); S. McCune, "The Thirty-Eighth Parallel in Korea," *World Politics* (January 1949); J. I. Matray, *The Reluctant Crusade* (Honolulu, 1985); M. Paul, "Diplomacy Delayed: The Atomic Bomb and the Division of Korea, 1945," in B. Cumings (ed.), *Child of Conflict* (Seattle, 1983); M. Sandusky, *America's Parallel* (Alexandria, Va., 1983).

TOMLINSON, FRANK S. (1912–   )

A career diplomat, Sir Frank Stanley Tomlinson was counselor in the British embassy in the United States from 1951 to 1953 and an active participant in the Korean War briefing meetings*. He was born in Sydney, Australia, and upon graduation from University College, Nottingham, joined the diplomatic service. From 1935 to 1941, he served in a variety of consular posts. For two years, Tomlinson was stationed at Saigon in French Indochina before transferring to the British embassy in Washington, D.C. In 1945, he became acting consul general in Manila and later chargé; he returned to Britain in 1947 to serve in the Foreign Office. Early in 1951, Tomlinson went back to the United States as counselor in the British embassy. He performed thereafter as a reliable conduit of information, faithfully presenting and explaining to U.S. officials Britain's position on issues related to the Korean War. Tomlinson was especially involved in policy regarding the People's Republic of China*, working in accordance with his instructions to achieve an early cease-fire and avoid a widening of the war. Tomlinson held various posts after leaving the United States, including counselor and head of the Southeast Asia Department. After serving from 1961 to 1964 as Britain's permanent delegate to NATO, he was consul general in New York City until 1966 and then spent three years as British High Commissioner in Ceylon, finishing his diplomatic career as deputy under secretary of state from 1969 to 1972.

Foreign Relations of the United States, 1951, vol. 7: *Korea and China* (Washington, D.C., 1983) and *1952–1954*, Vol. 15: *Korea* (Washington, D.C., 1984); *Who's Who, 1990* (New York, 1990); *Who's Who in America, 1974–1975* (New York, 1974).

TRIANGLE HILL, BATTLE OF

See Battle of Triangle Hill

TRIPARTITE MEETINGS OF NOVEMBER 1951

These meetings of the United States, Great Britain, and France took place during November 1951 as an adjunct to the meeting of the Sixth Session of the UN General Assembly (Paris) and the Eighth Session of the NATO Council (Rome). Secretary of State Dean G. Acheson* met throughout the month in bilateral and tripartite discussions with British foreign secretary Anthony Eden* and French minister of foreign affairs Robert Schuman on the subjects of Iran, NATO, Australia, Egypt, EDC, Germany, and Korea.

On November 28, 1951, Acheson and Eden met to discuss agenda item 3*, cease-fire arrangements in Korea, and a proposal to establish a supervisory organization to monitor the future terms of the agreement. The discussion centered around securing an agreement on inspection, which, they hoped, would minimize the military risk to troops engaged in the fighting. Five different types of inspection were proposed: full inspection behind the lines, selected inspection of key points, air inspection, inspection of only 25 miles beyond the armistice line, and inspection of only the DMZ. The problem, as viewed by Acheson and U.S. military leaders, was that a demand for acceptance of a strong system of inspection was not feasible at this juncture in the P'anmunjŏm truce talks*. Without this, however, the United States feared it would not be able to foresee and forestall a major Communist military offensive. Therefore, it proposed to Britain the issuance of a Joint Policy (Greater Sanctions) statement* stressing to the Communists the consequences of violation of the peace that would compensate for a less than adequate inspection system. This, it was thought, would give CINCUNC General Matthew B. Ridgway* the ability to bargain on the inspection issue in the peace talks with some assurance of security.

After lengthy discussion, Acheson and Eden reached agreement on several points. The British minister promised to consult Prime Minister Winston Churchill* on the feasibility of an Anglo-American declaration outlining the serious consequences of a ceasefire violation by the Chinese, including the possibility of bombing Communist airfields in Manchuria or implementing a naval blockade of the China coast. This public statement, it was also understood, would not be an unlimited future commitment. It was also agreed that a system of inspections was crucial to maintain a cease-fire and the UNC* had to continue to press for full joint inspections. Only if this could not be accomplished would the public statement be used. After discussions with Churchill and the chiefs of staff, Eden secured British agreement that Ridgway be authorized to conclude an armistice despite the problems with supervision, that a general statement be issued by participating countries warning of consequence if the peace was broken, and that although the British could not support an ineffective naval blockade or a general air attack on any Chinese town, they would favor a limited bombing plan as means of retaliation. *See also* NSC-118.

D. Acheson, *Present at the Creation* (New York, 1969); A. Eden, *Full Circle* (Boston, 1969); *Foreign Relations of the United States, 1951,* Vol. 7: *Korea and China* (Washington, D.C., 1983).

Kathleen F. Kellner

TRUCE TALKS RESUMPTION OF APRIL 26, 1953

On October 8, 1952, the P'anmunjŏm truce talks* were recessed by the UNC* side after reaching a deadlock on agenda item 4*, POW repatriation. No further progress was made until after the death of Joseph Stalin* on March 5, 1953. His successor, Georgi Malenkov*, emphasized the possibilities of peaceful coexistence with the United States, remarking on March 15 that there was no outstanding issue that could not be settled. On March 28, 1953, the Communists agreed to a proposal made by the UNC on February 22 for the exchange of sick and wounded prisoners (Operation Little Switch*). They expressed the hope that this would smooth the way to a solution of the entire POW question, proposing the resumption of negotiations. On March 30, the Chinese foreign minister, Chou En-lai*, elaborated on this proposal in a radio broadcast. According to the Chou En-lai POW settlement proposal*, prisoners who refused repatriation should be turned over to a neutral nation "so as to ensure a just solution to the question of their repatriation." This proposal was endorsed by North Korean premier Kim Il Sung* on March 31 and supported by the Soviet foreign minister, V. M. Molotov*, on April 1. The following day the Communists suggested a meeting of liaison officers at P'anmunjŏm to arrange the exchange of sick and wounded prisoners and to decide a date for the resumption of armistice negotiations, enclosing a copy of Chou En-lai's statement.

The United States was under pressure from its allies, particularly Britain, to make a positive response. On April 5, the UNC agreed to a meeting of liaison officers and requested clarification of the POW proposal. By April 11, an exchange of sick and wounded prisoners had been agreed. After further meetings of liaison officers, the full armistice negotiations reopened on April 26, and the Communists produced a six-point proposal on the POW question. It called for non-repatriate prisoners to be turned over to a neutral state within three months of the armistice. They would be subjected to six months of explanations by their own side to persuade them to return home. The fate of those remaining after this period would be decided by the political conference to be held under Article 4 of the armistice agreement*. This was unacceptable to the UN side because it did not provide for the automatic release of non-repatriate POWs within a fixed period, undermining the principle of voluntary repatriation*. *See also* Communist POW Settlement Proposal of May 7, 1953; Menon POW Settlement Proposal; Truce Talks Suspension of October 8, 1952.

M. W. Clark, *From the Danube to the Yalu* (London, 1954); W. G. Hermes, *Truce Tent and Fighting Front* (Washington, D.C., 1966); C. A. MacDonald, *Korea: The War Before Vietnam* (London, 1986); R. R. Simmons, *The Strained Alliance* (New York, 1975).

Callum A. MacDonald

TRUCE TALKS RESUMPTION OF OCTOBER 25, 1951

This event marked the beginning of the P'anmunjŏm truce talks*. Unable to persuade the UNC* to accept the thirty-eighth parallel as a demarcation line, the Communists had suspended the Kaesŏng truce talks* on August 23, 1951. The ostensible reason was the awkwardly fabricated evidence that UN planes had bombed Kaesŏng, when in reality the Communists were determined to force the UNC to accept their position on agenda item 2*, the thorny demarcation line issue. Then on September 10, a U.S. plane actually strafed Kaesŏng in error, providing a pretext for the Communists to justify their prior allegations. The UNC made an immediate apology, though there were no casualties reported. Being satisfied with this timely infraction and the UN apology, the Communists, probably having already decided to present an amended position on the issue of a demarcation line, showed willingness to resume the talks. It was CINCUNC General Matthew B. Ridgway* this time who was not willing to renew the talks at the old site under the old rules. He argued that the Kaesŏng arrangements could not guarantee the safety of the UN delegates because Kaesŏng was under Communist control.

When the liaison officers of both sides met on September 23, the UNC proposed a new meeting place, but the Communists were not prepared to discuss the matter. Subsequent meetings produced no progress on selecting a new place, and the delay in the resumption of truce talks aroused immediate attention in Washington. President Harry S. Truman* dispatched General Omar N. Bradley*, the chairman of the JCS, and Charles E. Bohlen* to Tokyo. Visiting Korea, they found that the battle situation was not alarming, persuading them that there was no need to resume the talks "so hurriedly." Acting on the results of the Bradley-Bohlen visit to Korea*, Washington radioed Ridgway on October 5 that "it is not intended to require you to return to Kaesong" but warned against announcing publicly that the UN delegation would not return to Kaesŏng under "any circumstances."

Meanwhile, UN forces did not slacken their efforts on the battlefield. On the eastern front, UN troops seized key positions in the Battles of Bloody Ridge* and Heartbreak Ridge*, while in the western and central fronts, they steadily advanced well beyond the Kansas-Wyoming Line* during the period of deadlock. The FEAF inflicted much damage upon North Korea itself, especially P'yŏngyang and Rashin. This punitive elbowing-forward tactic of UN forces from August through October inflicted severe losses on the Communists, undoubtedly enough to convince them that they could not win the war and should resume the armistice talks. For its part, the UNC was willing to return to the negotiating table because of pressure from U.S. allies, particularly the British, to achieve an early settlement. On October 25, both delegations met at P'anmunjŏm, a tiny village 6 miles east of Kaesŏng, which they had agreed upon as a new site for the talks in conjunction with a security agreement. Discussions at the first meeting on October 25, 1951, focused once again on agenda item 2, but the two delegations remained deadlocked on the demarcation line issue. *See also* Kaesŏng Neutral Zone Controversy; Kirk-Vyshinsky Discussion of October 5, 1951; P'anmunjŏm Security Agreement of October 22, 1951; Truce Talks Suspension of August 23, 1951.

D. Acheson, *The Korean War* (New York, 1971); *Foreign Relations of the United States, 1951*, Vol. 7: *Korea and China* (Washington, D.C., 1983); W. G. Hermes, *Truce Tent and Fighting Front* (Washington, D.C., 1966).

Chang-il Ohn

TRUCE TALKS SUSPENSION OF AUGUST 23, 1951

After resolution of the agenda controversy* at the Kaesŏng truce talks* on July 26, 1951, the armistice negotiators began discussion of agenda item 2*, the demarcation line and DMZ. It was immediately apparent that the difference between the UNC* and Communist positions on this issue was so great that agreement would be difficult. Initially, the UNC proposed a line far north of the thirty-eighth parallel, which the Communists angrily refused to accept. On August 10, 1951, however, the UNC delegation indicated its willingness to discuss a DMZ based on the existing battle line, but the Communists refused even to discuss any line other than the thirty-eighth parallel. As a result, there ensued "an unprecedented period of silence, lasting two hours and eleven minutes." The meeting was adjourned after this episode with the two delegations as far apart as ever.

Confronting the Communist intransigence on the issue, CINCUNC General Matthew B. Ridgway* requested Washington's approval to postpone the discussion of agenda item 2 and pass to the next one. Washington, however, favored a more patient approach. Policymakers in Washington anticipated a period of deadlock after adoption of the agenda, because U.S. officials had publicly stated that a truce along the thirty-eighth parallel would be acceptable and even desirable during the gloomy period of retreat after Chinese military intervention*. Thus, the UNC delegation was told to reiterate the UN position rejecting the thirty-eighth parallel, while continuing the talk with "calmness, firmness, and patience" until the Communists amended their position. In response to a UN initiative, the two delegations did choose a new method of negotiations, forming a subcommittee that would search for an equitable solution "in a more informal atmosphere." This subcommittee's effort was also short-lived. The meetings lasted for only six days from August 17 to 22, 1951, when the Communists suspended the truce talks.

On August 23, 1951, the Communists unilaterally adjourned the subcommittee meetings, charging that UN planes had bombed Kaesŏng. The clumsily fabricated evidence supporting the charge revealed that the real reason was their intention not to compromise on the demarcation line. The Communists instead inaugurated an intensive propaganda campaign to discredit the UNC for its alleged violation of the neutrality of the meeting zone. While the formal sessions of the two delegations were not convened for over two months, the UNC intensified its military operations to punish the Communists, ultimately resulting in the truce talks resumption of October 25, 1951*. *See also* Kaesŏng Neutral Zone Controversy.

D. Acheson, *The Korean War* (New York, 1971); *Foreign Relations of the United States, 1951,* vol. 7: *Korea and China* (Washington, D.C., 1983); W. G. Hermes, *Truce Tent and Fighting Front* (Washington, D.C., 1966); M. B. Ridgway, *The Korean War* (Garden City, N.Y., 1967).

Chang-il Ohn

TRUCE TALKS SUSPENSION OF OCTOBER 8, 1952

President Harry S. Truman* decided to suspend the P'anmunjŏm truce talks* in the fall of 1952 because of the unwillingness of the Communist delegation to drop its demand for forcible repatriation of POWs. In May 1952, the Communists rejected the principle of voluntary repatriation* as part of the package proposal*. Thereafter, discussion of a plan for rescreening of the POWs* failed to break the deadlock. On July 7, the Communists demanded once again the repatriation of all foreign troops in accordance with the Geneva Convention of 1949*. One week later, the UNC* announced that, as a result of rescreening, the number of repatriates had increased from 70,000 to 83,000. Major General William K.

Harrison, Jr.*, the UNC's chief negotiator, hoped that this larger figure would persuade the enemy to accept an agreement including voluntary repatriation. When this strategy failed, the UNC initiated a pattern of requesting weekly recesses, meeting only to ascertain whether the Communists had changed their position. To persuade the enemy to abandon its demand for forcible repatriation, the UNC resorted to an air pressure strategy*, anticipating that bombing the north would drive a wedge between China and North Korea.

Despite the acceleration of the air war, there was no progress in the negotiations. At this point, Vincent W. Hallinan, the Progressive party's presidential candidate in 1952, proposed that the UNC sign an armistice covering all settled issues, returning those POWs desiring repatriation and determining the fate of the remainder at a later date. Endorsing the idea, the State Department drafted a public statement for Truman containing the proposal. Harrison and CINCUNC General Mark W. Clark* strongly dissented, arguing that the bombing program was having a "material effect" and an armistice would eliminate any pressure on the Communists to accept the UNC position on repatriation. Labeling the plan an "obvious trap," they claimed it had surfaced because the enemy was losing the war. They urged instead authorization to suspend the talks if the Communists refused to accept one of a series of alternatives for resolving the POWs dispute. At first, the State Department did not press the issue, but then the Mexican POW settlement proposal*, which resembled the Hallinan initiative, seemed to provide an excellent opportunity for a presidential endorsement. But on September 24, after nearly a month of discussion, Truman rejected the State Department's plan, deciding against accepting an armistice that left the most important issue unresolved.

Four days later, Harrison outlined at P'anmunjŏm three ways to end the impasse and achieve an armistice "if you truly want one." All the options involved bringing the prisoners to the DMZ. First, after Red Cross and joint military teams had identified the POWs, each prisoner would be free to return to his captor and assume civilian status. Second, both sides would exchange those POWs wanting repatriation, while releasing the non-repatriates from military control to a group of neutral nations that would conduct interviews under observation of the Red Cross or joint military teams. After ten days, these POWs would be released to the nation of their choice. Third, both sides would follow the procedure outline in option 2 except non-repatriates would be released without questioning, interview, or screening. After presenting the choices, Harrison proposed a ten-day recess to permit the enemy to consider the alternatives, but the Communist delegation asked for an afternoon meeting. Upon reconvening, Lieutenant General Nam Il* stated that he would continue to demand full repatriation, agreeing to the recess so that the UNC could reconsider its position.

On October 8, the Communists accepted parts of the UNC plan for Korean POWs but demanded the return of all the Chinese prisoners. In response, Harrison delivered a blistering, denunciatory speech in excess of thirty minutes summarizing Communist responsibility for starting the Korean War and the UNC's efforts to negotiate a reasonable settlement. Branding the Communist position as "unreasonable, inconsistent, and inhumane," he announced that the UNC had no further proposals to offer and saw no reason to come to P'anmunjŏm just to listen to Communist propaganda and abuse. Harrison declared the talks in recess until the Communists were willing to accept one of the UNC's options or submit in writing a constructive alternative. The UNC delegation's departure from the conference site signaled the start of a long break in the negotiations. In Washington, Secretary of State Dean G. Acheson* issued a public statement declaring that the United States would not "trade in the lives of men" to gain a cease-fire. Acting swiftly to mobilize support for its position, the United States prepared for submission at the upcoming General Assembly its twenty-one-power UN resolution* advocating an inflexible stand on voluntary repatriation. The truce talks suspension of October 8, 1952, meant that the Truman administration would leave office without ending the Korean War.

J. L. Collins, *War in Peacetime* (Boston, 1969); W. G. Hermes, *Truce Tent and Fighting Front* (Washington, D.C., 1966); B. I. Kaufman, *The Korean War* (Philadelphia, 1986); D. Rees, *Korea: The Limited War* (New York, 1964); J. F. Schnabel and R. J. Watson, *History of the Joint Chiefs of Staff*, vol. 3: *The Korean War* (Wilmington, 1979).

TRUMAN, HARRY S. (1884–1973)

As president of the United States on June 25, 1950, Harry S. Truman was crucial in U.S. decisions throughout the Korean War. During the first six months, he decided to intervene with ground forces, to allow the war to be considered a police action* rather than going to Congress for a declaration of war, to refuse at the outset to ask for rationing and other economic controls that might have prevented the subsequent price inflation, and to reject British requests for negotiation late in 1950 following Chinese military intervention*. Born in Lamar, Missouri, Truman grew up in Independence, and from 1902 to 1917 was a bank teller and then a farmer until U.S. entrance into World War I. Enlisting, he emerged from the war a captain of an artillery battery, having seen heavy action in France. After an ill-starred effort in the clothing business, Truman turned to politics and spent ten years as a county executive in Missouri and then years as senator in Washington. After a few weeks as vice-president, he found himself in the nation's highest office upon the death of his predecessor, Franklin D. Roosevelt.

It is clear that Truman thought little about Korea prior to the North Korean invasion of South Korea* in June 1950. Anything he said or concurred in, prior to that time, was largely formality. He was certain that Europe was the prize in the cold war. He, of course, desired the security of Japan but by 1947 had written off China and presumably the Republic of Korea*. When the attack came, with a telephone call from Secretary of State Dean G. Acheson* to the president then vacationing in Independence, on Saturday evening, June 24 (U.S. time), followed by a second call about noon the next day, the president was thoroughly roused. Prior to that time, he had thought world peace momentarily secure. After his election in November 1948, the Berlin blockade had ended, and the Greek-Turkish dilemma had been resolved with economic and some military aid; the Marshall Plan, meanwhile, was beginning to strengthen the West European economies. NATO had been organized, although it was militarily very weak. The president's mind was turning to the need of worldwide economic measures; he in fact spoke of economics in addresses in St. Louis and Baltimore shortly before the Korean War. But the North Korean aggression was too much. In the limousine en route to the first Blair House meeting*, the president told Secretary Acheson, Under Secretary of State James E. Webb*, and Secretary of Defense Louis A. Johnson*, "By God, I'm going to let them have it!" Calmed down by Webb, upon arrival at Blair House, he thereafter consented to the series of more restrained measures hammered out at the conference that night and at a second Blair House meeting* the next evening.

In the years of retirement, Truman often told schoolchildren that his "toughest decision" was to enter the Korean War, but this seems not to have been true. He believed the credit of his country and of the United Nations demanded it. He believed that the Soviet Union was on the verge of world conquest and wrote in his diary for June 30, "Must be careful not to cause a general Asiatic war." Subsequent decisions were not always well taken, notably the decision not to ask for a declaration. Here he was persuaded by Senator Tom Connally*, chairman of the Senate Foreign Relations Committe, who, comparing the North Korean attack to a thief entering one's house, said that "you can shoot at him without going down to the police station and getting permission." At the first Blair House meeting, Webb wanted economic controls, and perhaps because the plane trip and evening's discussion had been tiring, the president put off economic questions. Speaker of the House of Representatives Sam Rayburn afterward advised against controls. A notable third presidential error was consenting to the UN offensive across the 38th parallel* in September 1950, a decision taken in the glow of the Inch'ŏn landing* and without serious thought.

In the crisis following China's entry into the war, the president stood firm, despite pressure from Prime Minister Clement R. Attlee*. The cause of Attlee's visit to the United States*, the presidential comment in a press conference stating that the United States contemplated use in Korea of all the weapons it possessed, including the atomic bomb, was a presidential gaffe, encouraged by reporters seeking to manufacture news; Truman did not really mean it. (Nor is there any evidence that a later diary entry, concerning the need to threaten the North Koreans, Chinese, and Soviets, was anything he meant to carry out.) On December 9, 1950, in his diary, the president showed the seriousness of the situation: "I have worked for peace for five years and six months and it looks like World War III is near." Not only did he refuse support for CINCUNC General Douglas MacArthur's* plan for victory*, but there is no serious evidence that he contemplated use of nuclear weapons. When in the spring of 1953 his successor, President Dwight D. Eisenhower*, used a threat of nuclear war to bring an armistice, Truman was appalled.

His dismissal of MacArthur was not a difficult matter. He had disliked MacArthur ever since the general's departure from the Philippines in 1942, believing that MacArthur should have "gone down with the ship." In the years prior to the Wake Island Conference*, he made innumerable private remarks about MacArthur. At Wake Island he found the general impressive. The Chinese intervention within weeks put MacArthur's stock down again. The general's insubordination then forced the decision of April 1951. He told Assistant Secretary of State Dean Rusk*, "I'll be darned if I will turn this office over to my successor with its prerogatives impaired by an American general." For the rest of the war, criticism continued, but the president doughtily persevered. His Gallup poll rating sank to 23, below that of President Richard M. Nixon* prior to his resignation of the presidency. This was undoubtedly the result of the prolonged P'anmunjŏm truce talks*, deadlocked primarily because of Truman's insistence on voluntary repatriation* of POWs. He took it as a dividend of what he always described as a necessary action, that is, intervention in a war that ended in stalemate rather than a global conflict. *See also* Congressional Meetings with Truman of June 1950; Truman's Atomic Bomb Press Conference Comment; Truman's Commitment of Ground Troops; Truman's Recall of MacArthur.

C. M. Dobbs, *The Unwanted Symbol* (Kent, Ohio, 1981); J. I. Matray, *The Reluctant Crusade* (Honolulu, 1985); M. B. Ridgway, *The Korean War* (Garden City, N. Y., 1967); W. W. Stueck, *The Road to Confrontation* (Chapel Hill, 1981); H. S. Truman, *Years of Trial and Hope* (Garden City, N.Y., 1956).

Robert H. Ferrell

TRUMAN-ATTLEE JOINT COMMUNIQUÉ (December 8, 1950)

This communiqué was issued at the close of Prime Minister Clement R. Attlee's* visit to the United States* occasioned by the deteriorating military position in Korea. The joint statement recorded that, over the course of six meetings, the two governments had reviewed the impact of the Chinese military intervention*, "discussed the problems of the Far East and the situation as it now presents itself in Europe," "surveyed the economic problems and the defense programs of our respective countries and particularly the existing and threatened shortages of raw materials," and "considered the arrangements for the defense of the Atlantic community, and our future course in the United Nations."

In a more specific reference to policies for the Korean War, the two governments agreed that, although they remained ready to seek a negotiated end to the hostilities, there could be "no thought of appeasement or of rewarding aggression." This phrasing reflected a victory for the Truman administration, because, unlike the British delegation, U.S. officials would not countenance UN recognition for the People's Republic of China* in exchange for an immediate cease-fire on the Korean peninsula. However, British officials ensured that the joint communiqué did spell out the Anglo-American differences on China policy, London (unlike Washington) having recognized the PRC and having remained wedded to the belief that a representative from Peking should occupy the UN seat.

More generally, the communiqué linked China's entry into the Korean War with a requirement for North Atlantic Treaty countries "to intensify their efforts to build up their defenses and to strengthen the Atlantic Community." With regard to joint control of atomic weapons, however, a British policy objective, the statement ended on a far more ambivalent note. President Harry S. Truman* recorded that "it was his hope that world conditions would never call for the use of the atomic bomb" and stated "his desire to keep the Prime Minister at all times informed of developments which might bring about a change in the situation." *See also* Truman's Atomic Bomb Press Conference Comment.

Foreign Relations of the United States, 1950, vol. 7: *Korea,* (Washington, D.C., 1976).

Rosemary Foot

TRUMAN-EISENHOWER TRANSITION MEETING (November 18, 1952)

This meeting between President Harry S. Truman* and President-elect Dwight D. Eisenhower* at the White House was dominated by discussions of the Korean War. Truman and Secretary of State Dean G. Acheson* hoped to use the meeting to gain the support of the president-elect in their effort to head off British and Canadian backing at the UN for the V. K. Krishna Menon* POW settlement proposal* of the day before. The administration feared that the vague nature of the proposal would circumvent its demand for voluntary repatriation* of prisoners.

Truman and Eisenhower held a private meeting in which Truman offered to make available during the interregnum any information that was requested. He also solicited support for his administration's position in Korea. The men then moved with their advisors to the cabinet briefing room, where Acheson went over several diplomatic problems but focused on the Korean situation. He suggested that the UN debate had reached a critical point and tried to persuade Eisenhower to sign a communiqué stating that he supported the administration's position on agenda item 4*, POW repatriation, that no POWs could be "forcibly repatriated." Eisenhower balked, agreeing instead to sign a vague statement saying that he and Truman were cooperating in the transition but that as the U.S. Constitution dictated, Truman would retain full control of the executive branch until inauguration day.

In his memoirs, Truman claimed that the president-elect was "overwhelmed" by what he had learned in the meeting. Eisenhower, on the other hand, recorded that the cabinet room briefing "added little to my knowledge." Still, Eisenhower apparently had second thoughts on the POW question, for the next day, November 19, he authorized Republican senator Alexander Wiley, a member of the Senate Foreign Relations Committee and a delegate to the UN, to make a statement saying that the president-elect supported the principle of "non-forcible repatriation." Bolstered by the Eisenhower's support and a foolish Soviet attack on the Indian plan, Acheson was able to obtain a modified form of the Indian proposal more in accord with administration wishes in the UN resolution of December 3, 1952*. Despite the critical nature of U.S. diplomacy regarding Korea, Truman and Eisenhower did not meet again during the interregnum.

C. M. Brauer, *Presidential Transitions: Eisenhower through Reagan* (New York, 1986); D. D. Eisenhower, *Mandate for Change* (Garden City, N.Y., 1963); *Foreign Relations of the United States, 1952–1954*, vol. 1: *General: Economic and Political Matters* (Washington, D.C., 1983); F. C. Mosher, W. D. Clinton, and D. G. Lang, *Presidential Transitions and Foreign Affairs* (Baton Rouge, La., 1987); H. S. Truman, *Years of Trial and Hope* (Garden City, N.Y., 1956).

Jeffrey G. Mauck

TRUMAN'S ADDRESS TO CONGRESS OF JULY 19, 1950

This speech sought to rally public support for additional forces, equipment, materiel, and funds after the UNC* proved unable to halt the North Korean invasion of South Korea* during the first weeks of the Korean War. The need became even more pressing when CINCUNC General Douglas MacArthur* called for an additional four divisions on July 7, 1950. Concerned with the growing need for more men and materiel and with the projected expense of the war, Secretary of State Dean G. Acheson* and others on July 14 urged President Harry S. Truman* to ask Congress for new appropriations to fund military production and for an increase in armed forces over the established limit of 2,005,802. Five days later, the president presented his address to Congress. He reviewed the history of the Republic of Korea* and U.S. and UN responsibility to that nation, condemning the North Koreans for their "deliberate, unprovoked aggression, breach of peace and challenge to the UN." He continued to stress that the United States would support the UN and summarized his actions to that point, which included sending U.S. troops, aircraft, and navy to Korea, neutralization of Taiwan*, and the strengthening of the security of the Philippines and Indochina.

The crux of his address dealt with his proposals for increased military production, armed forces, and funding. He urged Congress to remove the limitations on the size of the armed forces and to establish legislation that would authorize the allocation of materials to ensure procurement of new supplies and equipment. Additionally, he asked Congress to increase federal revenues to provide for these needs by raising taxes, restricting consumer credit, and setting price controls. Truman's address ended with the stirring reminder that the United States had to fulfill its responsibilities to preserve peace and protect the free world, which required bipartisan congressional support in a continuing battle for "liberty and peace."

Truman spoke at an opportune time, catching Congress on a wave of public support for the war and a U.S. commitment to containment in Asia. Although the MDAP bill for that year had been funded prior to the war for over $4 billion, Congress appropriated $11 billion more for defense spending and authorized the increase of military forces to 3.2 million. Passage of the Defense Production

Act* in September gave Truman economic powers to impose rationing, to commit large forces and supplies to the war effort, to impose credit restrictions, to direct allocation of strategic materials, and to control prices and wages—powers similar to those given President Franklin D. Roosevelt in World War II. *See also* Congress and the Korean War; Congress and U.S. Military Intervention; Defense Appropriations Acts (1951–1953).

D. Acheson, *Present at the Creation* (New York, 1969); R. J. Donovan, *Tumultuous Years* (New York, 1982); J. C. Goulden, *Korea: The Untold Story of the War* (New York, 1982); *New York Times,* July-August 1950; H. S. Truman, *Years of Trial and Hope* (Garden City, N.Y., 1956).

Kathleen F. Kellner

TRUMAN'S ATOMIC BOMB PRESS CONFERENCE COMMENT (November 30, 1950)

In response to Chinese military intervention* and the retreat of UN forces from the Yalu, President Harry S. Truman* on November 30 held a press conference. He said the United States would use every weapon at its disposal as needed to "meet the military situation in Korea." A reporter asked if this meant the atomic bomb. The president replied, "That includes every weapon we have." When asked whether this meant the United States was actively considering such use, Truman said there had "always been active consideration of its use." Later in the conference, he said that, as with other weapons, the "military commander in the field will have charge of the use of weapons, he always has." Truman's statements implied that he planned to violate the Atomic Energy Act of 1946, which provided that only the president may order the use of atomic weapons. Newspaper articles in Stockholm, Rome, Vienna, London, and Paris the next day expressed shock and outrage. In England, Labour prime minister Clement R. Attlee* received a letter from 150 members of his party in Parliament demanding withdrawal of British troops if the United States used an atomic bomb in Korea. Conservatives Winston Churchill* and Anthony Eden* were displeased. After calling an emergency meeting of his cabinet, Attlee traveled to Washington to obtain a clarification of U.S. policy.

Meanwhile, the JCS had been studying whether to use nuclear weapons in Korea but had reached no decision. The Pentagon's joint strategic survey committee, however, had submitted a report the day before Truman's comments to the press (November 29) that said a situation "might develop in which nuclear weapons would be necessary to save American troops in Korea from being overrun." The JCS report, submitted four days later, reached similar conclusions. Neither document brought action by the president. After Attlee's arrival and discussions in the oval office, he pursued negotiations at the United Nations, where a Chinese delegation had arrived. His object was a cease-fire as an avenue to negotiations. *See also* Attlee's Visit to the United States; Truman-Attlee Joint Communiqué.

C. Blair, *The Forgotten War* (New York, 1987); R. J. Donovan, *Tumultuous Years* (New York, 1982); J. C. Goulden, *Korea: The Untold Story of the War* (New York,

1982); M. Hastings, *The Korean War* (New York, 1987); B. I. Kaufman, *The Korean War* (Philadelphia, 1986).

William B. Pickett

TRUMAN'S COMMITMENT OF GROUND TROOPS (June 30, 1950)

Although the United States acted swiftly to assist the Republic of Korea* after the outbreak of the Korean War, President Harry S. Truman* did not commit ground combat forces until nearly a week after the North Korean attack. U.S. policy in Korea before June 1950 explains this hesitation. By 1949, Truman and his advisers had concluded that with U.S. economic aid, technical advice, and military assistance, the ROK would develop the capacity for self-defense and thereby deter an attack from the north. The North Korean invasion of South Korea* convinced Truman and his advisers that Moscow had altered its tactics for expansion and now would resort to military means to extend the area of Soviet control. Communist success in Korea would prompt the Soviets to instigate new acts of armed aggression elsewhere in the world, eventually threatening the United States itself. A global military threat of such monumental proportions seemed to demand drastic steps, yet the administration adopted a course of action commensurate with its own estimation of the danger only with great reluctance. Truman could have sent combat troops to the peninsula immediately to crush the aggressor swiftly and thereby show the extent of his resolve. Instead, at the first and second Blair House meetings*, the president and his advisers opposed using troops, hoping the ROK, with moral and material support from the UN, would be able to repel the assault.

General Douglas MacArthur*, in his initial report following his visit to Korea of June 29, 1950*, gave Truman reason to believe that U.S. ground forces would not be necessary. Despite 50 percent casualties, MacArthur explained, the South Korean army was beginning to regroup and soon might be able to halt the North Korean advance. In addition, the Soviet Union had announced its intention to avoid involvement in the Korean dispute. But just before dawn on June 30, the JSC received a more detailed report from MacArthur, including the general's request for immediate authorization to dispatch one regimental combat team (RCT) to the front line and introduce two more divisions as soon as practicable for use in a counteroffensive. When Secretary of the Army Frank Pace* telephoned to inform the president of MacArthur's recommendation, Truman's reply reflected his lingering desire to avoid making Korea a U.S. war. "Do we have to decide tonight?" he asked. Pace replied that in the general's judgment, the ROK would collapse without U.S. troops. Unwilling to accept a complete Communist victory, Truman, without obtaining the approval of Congress, authorized the immediate commitment of one RCT, approving the dispatch of two divisions later that morning. There can be no doubt that MacArthur's emphatic request was the key element in Truman's decision to send U.S. ground forces into the Korean War. Yet the president removed the final restrictions on Washington's commitment to defend the ROK only after it became clear that South Korea was thoroughly incapable of defending itself. *See also* Congress and U.S. Military Intervention; Task Force Smith.

Foreign Relations of the United States, 1950, vol. 7: *Korea* (Washington, D.C., 1976); J. I. Matray, *The Reluctant Crusade* (Honolulu, 1985); G. D. Paige, *The Korean Decision* (New York, 1968); J. F. Schnabel, *Policy and Direction* (Washington, D.C., 1972).

TRUMAN'S DECLARATION OF A NATIONAL EMERGENCY (December 16, 1950)

On December 15, 1950, President Harry S. Truman* on national television stated that he would "issue a proclamation tomorrow morning declaring that a national emergency exists." In the aftermath of the Chinese military intervention* and rout of the 8th Army* during the prior three weeks, Washington military authorities recommended that Truman declare a national emergency. This would activate statutory provisions and authorizations granted the president in wartime and would make it easier to expand the armed forces and the industrial base needed to support a stronger military effort. While this was important, Truman's main motive may have been psychological. As Assistant Secretary of State for Public Information Edward W. Barrett explained in a memorandum at that time, "The American people are getting the impression that their Washington leadership is utterly confused and sterile. They are saying in effect: 'Don't just sit there; do something!' " Congress had given Truman the authority to impose economic controls in the Defense Production Act*, but the president had hesitated to use these powers for fear of giving the impression that he was preparing for general war. Voluntarism had failed to limit inflation, and China's entry threatened greater economic instability. Thus, Truman decided to declare a national emergency to prepare the people for the onset of stronger measures to control the economy.

To mobilize the population behind a national effort to win an undeclared war in a remote area of the world, Truman resorted to exaggerated rhetoric. In his address of December 15, he argued that "our homes, our Nation, all the things we believe in are in great danger. . . . I summon our farmers, our workers in industry and our businessmen to make a mighty production effort to meet the defense requirements of the Nation and to this end to eliminate all waste and inefficiency and to subordinate all lesser interests to the common good." On the next day, he signed a proclamation which read, in part: "Now, therefore, I, Harry S. Truman, President of the United States of America, do proclaim the existence of a national emergency, which requires that the military, naval, air and civilian defenses of this country be strengthened as speedily as possible to the end that we may be able to repel any and all threats against our national security." The Truman administration subsequently found the declaration useful in facilitating the letting of contracts as it moved toward meeting the military manpower and procurement measures of NSC-68* by 1952, two years earlier than originally planned. This move toward total control of wages, prices, production, rents, and credit was politically risky because the United States was entering a period not of patriotism and willing sacrifice but frustrating and unpopular limited war. *See also* Congress and the Korean War.

R. J. Donovan, *Tumultuous Years* (New York, 1982); B. I. Kaufman, *The Korean War* (Philadelphia, 1986); J. F. Schnabel, *Policy and Direction* (Washington, D.C., 1972).

James F. Schnabel

TRUMAN'S PROPOSED CEASE-FIRE INITIATIVE (March 20, 1951)

CINCUNC General Douglas MacArthur* called upon the enemy to surrender on three occasions, the last time when President Harry S. Truman* was planning to propose publicly a truce in the Korean War; it was one of the major factors in Truman's decision to relieve him of his commands. By late March 1951, definite signs began to appear that MacArthur's forces were regaining the military initiative in Korea after the disastrous winter campaign. The 8th Army* under Lieutenant General Matthew B. Ridgway* was close to restoring the prewar boundary along to the thirty-eighth parallel. Encouraged, Truman's advisors proposed that he issue a public declaration inviting the enemy to join in a cease-fire and negotiate a settlement. In his message to the enemy, which would be cleared with other UN members having troops in Korea, the president would warn that if the Chinese and North Koreans refused to negotiate, the UNC* would be forced to continue fighting. On March 20, 1951, the JCS informed General MacArthur that such a statement was being prepared for presidential delivery.

Before the message had been put in final form, MacArthur issued his own cease-fire statement. Not content merely to call for enemy surrender, the general derided Communist China's military capabilities and reiterated his familiar view that "the fundamental questions continue to be political in nature and must find their answer in the diplomatic sphere." In the eyes of Truman and his advisors, this statement tacitly preempted the presidential prerogatives, contained implied criticism of the national policy, and vitiated the president's planned declaration. Truman later wrote that in this statement, MacArthur had threatened the enemy with an ultimatum, implying that the United States and its allies might attack the People's Republic of China* without restraint. He construed this action as a defiance of his orders as commander in chief and a challenge to his authority. Truman concluded he could no longer tolerate his field commander's insubordination. Secretary of Defense George C. Marshall* thought that this statement was the culminating factor in Truman's recall of MacArthur* in April 1951. *See also* MacArthur's "Pronunciamento."

J. F. Schnabel, *Policy and Direction* (Washington, D.C., 1972).

James F. Schnabel

TRUMAN'S RECALL OF MACARTHUR (April 11, 1951)

While the decision by President Harry S. Truman* to relieve General Douglas MacArthur* from his command of Korean forces and the Japanese occupation startled many Americans, the explosion had a long fuse. About the same time that Truman named MacArthur as CINCUNC in Korea (July 8, 1950), he told members of the White House staff that he had "little regard or respect" for the general. He was as "supreme egoist," a failed commander in the Philippines, and a "dictator" in Japan. The president told John Foster Dulles* that he would have removed MacArthur from Tokyo earlier except that he was "politically involved" with the Republican party and his removal would "cause a tremendous reaction" among GOP ranks. However, in August 1950, when MacArthur's controversial VFW message* was published, Truman contemplated bringing the general home.

Following Chinese military intervention* and the startling success of the Chinese People's Volunteers Army* in throwing back UN forces late in 1950, MacArthur publicly criticized the administration for denying him authority to strike back directly against the Manchurian sanctuary*. By granting China "privileged sanctuaries," he told Hugh Baille* and other American journalists early in December, Washington risked the "destruction" of his command. Truman later wrote that he "should have relieved General MacArthur then and there" but did not want to give the impression he was being fired because the Home-by-Christmas offensive* failed. The president believed he "must defend him and save his face even if he has tried on various and numerous occasions to cut mine off." Instead, Truman in the JCS directive of December 6, 1950*, instructed military officers not to comment publicly on sensitive issues. As the administration turned down successive pleas from MacArthur to adopt his plan for victory* and expand the war through attacking China, the general grew frustrated with the battlefield stalemate and the policy of settling for an armistice near the thirty-eighth parallel rather than the goal of Korean unification. In March 1951, MacArthur's "pronunciamento"* sabotaged Truman's proposed cease-fire initiative*.

Conferring in Washington, military officials admitted that if any other general had done what MacArthur had, "he would be relieved of his command at once." However, for a variety of reasons, many of them political, Truman and his aides reprimanded but did not recall the general. By early April 1951, a combination of factors sealed MacArthur's fate. The JCS worried about a Chinese and Soviet military buildup near Korea, fearing it might be unleashed against Japan as well as the UNC* in South Korea. The JCS believed that the CINCUNC should have standing authority to retaliate against any Communist escalation and even recommended deploying atomic bombs to forward Pacific bases. At the same time, they mistrusted MacArthur and guessed he might provoke an incident in order to widen the war. Then, on April 5, came MacArthur's letter to House Republican minority leader Joseph Martin* once again criticizing the administration's efforts to contain the war.

By now, the president and his advisers realized that MacArthur would play partisan politics and manipulate facts to get his way. The Joint Chiefs favored recalling MacArthur so that a more responsible successor could be granted authority to respond to the perceived Chinese-Soviet buildup. Secretary of State Dean G. Acheson* argued that MacArthur's behavior (his push for a wider war) threatened to destroy Western European and UN support for U.S. policy. Truman considered MacArthur's letter to Joseph W. Martin* "rank insubordination" and the "last straw." While awaiting the formal advice of his staff from April 5–9, he wrote in his diary that "the Big General in the Far East must be recalled." Truman believed that MacArthur provoked his own recall to escape from a war without glory and to achieve martyrdom. Then he would feel free to attack the administration's overall foreign policy and perhaps run for president. Acting on near-unanimous advice from his advisers, Truman signed the order to recall MacArthur on April 10, 1951. Although the White House tried to contact the general privately, fear of a news leak prompted the administration to announce the recall early in the morning of April 11, infuriating MacArthur and his supporters, who then accused Truman of consciously trying to humiliate a national hero. *See also* MacArthur's Visit to Taiwan; Wake Island Conference.

D. C. James, *The Years of MacArthur*, Vol. 3: *Triumph and Disaster, 1945–1964* (Boston, 1985); M. Schaller, *Douglas MacArthur: The Far Eastern General* (New York, 1989).

Michael Schaller

TRUMAN'S SPEECH OF SEPTEMBER 1, 1950

Two months after U.S. combat units had been dispatched to aid a beleaguered Republic of Korea*, President Harry S. Truman* went on radio and television to explain to the public "why we are there and what our objectives are." At that time, the military situation had stabilized along the Pusan Perimeter*, and secret plans were being made for the Inch'ŏn landing* that would take place in two weeks. Despite this improving situation, Truman clearly intended to gird Americans for greater sacrifices in Korea. The heart of his message was an analogy between the expansion of the fascist powers in the 1930s and the Communist North Korean invasion of South Korea*. In vintage cold war rhetoric, he told his listeners that "if aggression were allowed to succeed in Korea, it would be an open invitation to new acts of aggression elsewhere." At stake was nothing less than "the free way of life." Implying that the Kremlin was responsible for the attack on South Korea, Truman blamed "the Soviet Union and the nations it controls" for international tensions.

Truman then reviewed the major containment policies that his administration had implemented, including the aid to Greece and Turkey, the Rio Pact, Marshall Plan, Berlin airlift, and creation of NATO. The deployment of forces in Korea over the past six weeks was part of this continuing struggle between "freedom and communist imperialism." Bearing the greatest burden of this commitment, as he pointed out, were the U.S. and South Korean armies. But the resistance to aggression was also a collective effort by the UN to save the ROK, and growing support was apparent in Greece's promise, made that day, that it was sending troops to the Korean peninsula. To encourage the public further, Truman estimated that "the invasion has reached its peak." Still, he announced his plan to double the manpower of the U.S. armed forces from 1.5 million to 3 million.

He also signaled his intention to sign the Defense Production Act*. He promised that he would soon clarify his intentions in this regard (which he did in his speech of September 9 that covered the contents of the new legislation).

Truman then presented a list of U.S. objectives in East Asia. Noting that the United States hoped to avoid a general war or conflict with the People's Republic of China*, he stressed the limited nature of the military action. He stated that the mission of the 7th Fleet in the Taiwan Strait was "to keep Formosa out of the conflict" and that the future status of that island should be decided by international action. Regarding Korea, Truman called for the nation to be "free, independent, and united" under the direction of the UN. He concluded with a long platitudinal peroration on the necessity of the United States to take the lead in the worldwide effort to contain communism. *See also* Congress and the Korean War; Defense Appropriations Acts (1951–1953); NSC-81.

R. J. Donovan, *Tumultuous Years* (New York, 1982); *Public Papers of the Presidents of the United States: Harry S. Truman, 1950* (Washington, D.C., 1965).

Jeffrey G. Mauck

TRUMAN'S STATEMENT OF JUNE 27, 1950

President Harry S. Truman* noted in this statement that North Korean troops had not withdrawn north of the thirty-eighth parallel as requested in the UN Security Council resolution of June 25, 1950*, two days earlier, and declared that their attack "makes it plain beyond all doubt that Communism" now used armed invasion, not just subversion, "to conquer independent nations." He "ordered the U.S. Seventh Fleet to prevent any attack on Formosa" and warned the exiled Chinese regime on Taiwan to stop attacking the mainland. Truman also "accelerated the sending" of U.S. military aid to the Philippines, where the government fought Communist-led guerrillas. He "similarly directed acceleration in the furnishing of military assistance" to the French and Indochinese armies fighting Ho Chi Minh's Communist forces in Vietnam. That same day, at Truman's request, the UN Security Council resolution of June 27, 1950*, called on UN members to help "restore international peace and security in the area" of Korea. The U.S. press and leaders of both parties praised Truman's actions. The New York Stock Exchange reversed its panicky decline of June 26 as stocks rose the next day.

The day's declarations proved historic. After denying the People's Republic of China* victory in the Chinese Civil War with his neutralization of Taiwan*, Truman now began the commitment to defend the defeated Republic of China*. After trying to remain aloof from France's efforts to restore its colonial empire in Indochina from 1946 to 1948, U.S. officials had supported (albeit with reservations) that effort in later 1949 and early 1950. But Truman's statement opened the door for the first major, direct U.S. military involvement with French forces, including military missions and aid that by late 1950 already reached $133 million. Finally, the "in the area" phrase of the UN resolution was so general that some U.S. officials later used it to justify their policy of restoring such "peace" through the UN offensive across the thirty-eighth parallel* in September-October and attempting to unite Korea by force. *See also* Congress and U.S. Military Intervention; Congressional Meetings with Truman of June 1950; Second Blair House Meeting.

L. C. Gardner, *Approaching Vietnam* (New York, 1988); G. D. Paige, *The Korean Decision* (New York, 1968); H. S. Truman, *Years of Trial and Hope* (Garden City, N.Y.,1956).

Walter LaFeber

TRUMAN'S STEEL PLANTS SEIZURE

On April 8, 1952, President Harry S. Truman*, citing his constitutional powers as chief executive and commander in chief, ordered Secretary of Commerce Charles Sawyer to seize and operate the nation's steel mills after management refused to accede to a government-sponsored compromise meant to head off a strike by the United Steel Workers. Top advisers had told Truman that an extended halt in steel production would imperil the flow of critical war materials to Korea. But the president had failed to prevent a labor-management confrontation, largely because the undeclared and "limited" war in Korea had failed to generate the mobilization of industry and labor that had taken place during the world wars.

On November 1, 1951, the United Steel Workers had informed leaders of the industry management that they were ready to negotiate a new contract to replace the one that was to expire at the end of 1951. Early negotiations failed to produce a settlement and, faced with a possible strike, Truman managed to elicit from the workers an agreement to stay on the job if he would submit the problem to the Wage Stabilization Board (WSB), a federal agency specifically designed to resolve defensive-related labor disputes. Truman pursued this course instead of invoking the Taft-Hartley Act to keep the workers in the mills. He believed that invoking Taft-Hartley would provoke a confrontation with the workers and an immediate strike; moreover, the administration could ill afford to alienate an essential component of the Democratic coalition during an election year.

On March 20, the WSB presented Truman with its recommendations, which called for the union to be granted wage increases totaling 26.4 cents per hour in three stages over eighteen months. Industry representatives rejected the plan and then offered their own package, calling for a much smaller wage hike. Negotiations again failed, and as a strike loomed, Truman ordered the seizure. His action prompted outrage among business leaders and Republicans. Fourteen separate resolutions calling for his impeachment were introduced in Congress. Nevertheless, Truman was confident that the federal courts would uphold his actions because before moving, he had conferred secretly with Chief Justice Fred M. Vinson on his plans. But Vinson was in the minority when on June 2 the Supreme Court voted 6–3 in *Youngstown Sheet and Tube Co. v. Sawyer* that the seizure was unconstitutional and returned the mills to their owners.

After Truman failed on July 10 to obtain congressional sanction to seize the mills again, union members walked off the job and a fifty-three-day strike ensued. By late July, production of the F-86 Sabre jets had been interrupted, and critical shortages of artillery shells were appearing at the front. On July 24, Truman called management and union leaders to the White House for an emergency conference that resulted in a settlement that clearly favored management. Steel production resumed, and one of the pivotal constitutional crises of the century ended.

W. G. Hermes, *Truce Tent and Fighting Front* (Washington, D.C., 1966); R. A. Lee, *Truman and Taft-Hartley: A Question of Mandate* (Lexington, Ky., 1966); D. R. McCoy, *The Presidency of Harry S. Truman* (Lawrence, Ks. 1984); M. Marcus, *Truman and the Steel Seizure Case: The Limits of Presidential Power* (New York, 1977); J. E. Wilz, "The Korean War and American Society," in F. H. Heller (ed.), *The Korean War: A 25-Year Perspective* (Lawrence, Ks., 1977).

Jeffrey G. Mauck

TSAI CHENG-WEN (CAI CHENGWEN; 1915–   )

Born in Suiping, Hunan Province, Tsai Cheng-wen played a significant role as a liaison between the People's Republic of China* and the Democratic People's Republic of Korea* during the Korean War. He was also one of the chief Chinese negotiators of the Korean armistice negotiations. Commissioned a major general in 1961, Tsai retired from active service and is now a vice-president of the Beijing Society of International Strategic Problems. He became a revolutionary in 1936 and joined the 8th Route Army in 1937, serving as deputy chief of intelligence for the Kiangsi-Hupei-Shantung-Hunan military region during the Sino-Japanese War. Tsai became intelligence chief for the same region and for the 2d Field Army (Teng Hsiao-p'ing was the political commissar of both) during the Chinese Civil War, as well as section chief at the Kuomintang-Communist-U.S. Executive Headquarters. From 1950 to 1953, he served in North Korea as the primary coordinator of policy between the PRC and DPRK. After the Korean War, Tsai was minister at the Chinese legation in Denmark. His last posts before retirement were as the deputy chief of Chinese military intelligence and director of the foreign affairs bureau in the ministry of defense.

Tsai arrived in P'yŏngyang on July 10, 1950, as the first Chinese chargé in the Chinese embassy, also acting as a liaison for the Chinese military in North Korea. He continued his liaison work as the political counsellor of the embassy after Ni Chih-liang, the Chinese ambassador, arrived in Korea in August 1950. On September 1, he was summoned to Peking by Foreign Minister Chou En-lai* to report on the situation in Korea. He and Ambassador Ni prepared a memorandum emphasizing two essential points. First, the North Korean People's Army could not advance farther since they were in a stalemate with U.S. and South Korean troops. Second, a prolonged stalemate in a narrow peninsula without control of the air and sea likely would lead to disaster for the North Koreans. Replying to Chou's inquiry, Tsai said that the most difficult challenges for the Chinese troops fighting in Korea would be dealing with the problems of transportation and translation. He returned to Korea in mid-September with five military attachés who were to do topographical surveys to prepare for the Chinese troops fighting in Korea. Tsai and Ambassador Ni informed Kim Il Sung* on October 8, 1950, that China had decided to send the Chinese People's Volunteers Army* (CPVA) to fight in Korea. He also accompanied Marshal Peng Teh-huai*, the commander and political commissar of the CPVA, in Peng's first meeting with Kim on October 20, 1950. When the Kaesŏng truce talks* began in July 1951, Tsai became the chief secretary of the Chinese delegation and the Chinese liaison officer in the negotiations.

Cai Chengwen and Zhao Yongtian, *A Factual Record of the Korean War* (Beijing, 1987); Cai Chengwen and Zhao Yongtian, *Panmunjom Negotiations* (Beijing, 1990); Chinese People's Liberation Army Academy of Military Science, *A Military History of the Anti-U.S. Aid-Korea War* (Beijing, 1988); Yao Xu, *From the Yalu to Panmunjom* (Beijing, 1986).

Hua Qingzhao

TSARAPKIN, SEMYON K. (1906–1984)

During the Korean War, Semyon K. Tsarapkin was the Soviet Union's deputy permanent delegate on the UN Security Council. Because Jacob A. Malik*, Moscow's permanent representative, was ill frequently, he often served as his country's spokesman at the international body. Born in the Ukraine, Tsarapkin went to work in a smelting plant at age 17, later receiving advanced political training from the Communist party. He graduated from Moscow's Institute of Oriental Studies, receiving an assignment with the Soviet foreign service in 1937. In 1941, Tsarapkin helped negotiate the non-aggression pact between the Soviet Union and Japan. For the next three years, he was chief of the 2d Far Eastern Department in the Commissariat of Foreign Affairs. In 1944, Tsarapkin became head of the American Department. Subsequently, he attended the conferences at Dumbarton Oaks, San Francisco, and Potsdam, although he remained in the background. Following a brief assignment as minister in northern Korea in 1946, he became counselor at the Soviet embassy in the United States and a member of Moscow's UN delegation.

Prior to the outbreak of the Korean War, Tsarapkin, as a member of the UN Trusteeship Committee, was involved in a number of controversial issues, most notably Palestine in 1948. In addition, he was on the Atomic Energy Commission, helping to establish a position on this issue that would remain intact for a decade. In 1949, Tsarapkin often was in charge of Moscow's delegation in the absence of Malik and participated in the walkout that signaled the start of the Soviet UN Security Council boycott*. In March 1951, he became deputy permanent representative. The following May, Tsarapkin participated in private discussions between Malik and Thomas J. Cory*, a member of the U.S. delegation at the UN, that contributed to the start of the Kaesŏng truce talks*. In 1954, he returned to the Soviet Union to head the foreign ministry's international organizations division. Thereafter, Tsarapkin often provided advice regarding technical standards for nuclear testing control systems, such as in 1958 when he was chief Soviet delegate at the Geneva Conference called to discuss a nuclear test ban.

After his last diplomatic posting in Bonn, West Germany, he served until his death as a roving ambassador. Tsarapkin was known for being bright, aloof, and a stickler for detail.

Current Biography, 1960; *Foreign Relations of the United States, 1951,* vol. 7: *Korea and China* (Washington, D.C., 1983); *New York Times,* September 20, 1984; *Prominent Personalities in the USSR* (Metuchen, N.J., 1968).

TSIANG TING-FU (JIANG DINGFU; 1895–1965)

Born at Pao-ch'ing in Hunan province, T. F. Tsiang was permanent delegate at the UN for the Republic of China* (ROC) during the Korean War. After learning English from Presbyterian missionaries, he traveled to the United States in 1911. Then Tsiang went to France during World War I, where he was YMCA secretary for Chinese laborers working with the French army. After returning to the United States, he earned a B.A. in history at Oberlin College in 1918 and a Ph.D. at Columbia University in 1923, his doctoral dissertation entitled "Labor and Empire." Thereafter, Tsiang was assistant professor at Tientsin's Nankai University from 1923 to 1929 and professor of history at Peking's Tsinghua University from 1929 to 1935, serving as well as managing editor of the *Chinese Social and Political Science Review*. An expert on Sino-Russian relations, Chiang Kai-shek* appointed Tsiang in 1936 as ambassador to the Soviet Union. Two years later, he returned to Nanking as director of political affairs, a post he had held in 1935. After helping to fashion a budget that would control inflation, Tsiang in 1942 went to the United States to lobby for economic and military assistance. Later, he became head of UNRRA in China, attending various international conferences until his resignation in October 1946. During the Chinese Civil War, some Americans considered Tsiang an alternative to Chiang and Mao Tse-tung*. However, his loyalty to Chiang never wavered, as he criticized the U.S. for not providing sufficient financial support for the Nationalists.

In 1947, Chiang appointed Tsiang as the ROC's permanent UN delegate. He retained this position after the Kuomintang fled to Taiwan and despite the Soviet UN Security Council boycott* in 1950. Throughout this period, Tsiang faithfully supported U.S. policy with respect to Korea, including votes in favor of the UN resolutions of November 14, 1947*, December 12, 1948*, and October 21, 1949*. He also helped gain approval for the UN Security Council resolutions of June 25*, June 27*, and July 7, 1950*. In August, Tsiang worked to ensure continued representation for the Republic of Korea* at the Security Council, while urging that more Asian states contribute to the war effort. The North Korean invasion of South Korea* made Tsiang's job at the UN much easier because, in response to the war, the United States assumed responsibility for defending Chiang's regime on Taiwan and its UN seat. After the UN invitation to the People's Republic of China* to participate in debate* regarding Korea, Communist representative Wu Hsui-ch'uan* ridiculed Tsiang in November for speaking in English before the world body, pointing to this as proof that the ROC was not China's true representative. The following month, Tsiang was chair of the UN Security Council, creating some problems for the United States because, while several of its allies did not recognize Chiang's regime, the Soviet Union could justify using the veto with references to ROC's illegitimacy. In 1962, Tsiang left the UN to become the ROC's ambassador to the United States and retained that post until just before his death three years later.

Current Biography, 1948; *Foreign Relations of the United States, 1950*, vol. 7: *Korea* (Washington, D.C., 1976); *New York Times*, October 11, 1965; *Who Was Who in America*, vol. 4: *1960–1968* (Chicago, 1968).

TWENTY-ONE POWER UN RESOLUTION (October 24, 1952)

This was part of the Truman administration's attempt in October 1952 to achieve an endorsement at the UN of its firm stand at the P'anmunjŏm truce talks* on agenda item 4*, repatriation of POWs. When the UN General Assembly convened on October 14, several nations had been advocating compromise to break the deadlock that had emerged with the truce talks suspension of October 8, 1952*. But President Harry S. Truman* was determined to prevent any weakening of the UNC's* position at P'anmunjŏm. By October 24, the U.S. delegation had persuaded twenty other nations to join in sponsoring a resolution calling on the People's Republic of China* and the Democratic People's Republic of Korea* to recognize the right of the POWs to voluntary repatriation*. That day, Secretary of State Dean G. Acheson* delivered a speech to the UN Political Committee appealing for a continuation of the fight for a just peace. Responding to the Communist propaganda campaign denouncing the UNC for suspending the truce talks, he insisted that the UNC was prepared to reconvene the negotiations whenever the Communists were ready to drop their demand for forcible repatriation. Acheson declared that the UN faced a "test of its staying power." Support for the U.S. resolution evaporated in early November when India's representative, V. K. Krishna Menon*, proposed an alternative. Ultimately the Menon POW settlement proposal* led to passage of the UN resolution of December 3, 1952*, providing the framework for settling the dispute and ending the war.

Foreign Relations of the United States, 1952–1954, vol. 15: *Korea* (Washington, D.C., 1984); W. G. Hermes, *Truce Tent and Fighting Front* (Washington, D.C., 1966); C. A. MacDonald, *Korea: The War Before Vietnam* (New York, 1986); D. Rees, *Korea: The Limited War* (New York, 1964).

TWINING, NATHAN F. (1897–1982)

Born in Monroe, Wisconsin, General Nathan F. Twining continued family tradition and joined the profession of arms when he entered the U.S. Military Academy at West Point in 1917. Following several years of service as an infantry officer after graduation, he secured a transfer to the Army Air Service in 1923. After flight training, he served the remaining years until World War II in various materiel, tactical aviation, and staff assignments. During the war, his command experiences converted him to the philosophy of long-range, independent air power. After materiel and interservice postwar commands, Twining arrived in

Washington shortly before the outbreak of the Korean War to assume direction of air force personnel matters.

In the fall of 1950, Twining became vice-chief of staff, and for the next three years, he climbed the air force headquarters' ''greasy pole'' toward the position of chief of staff. Although he worked well with the current chief, General Hoyt S. Vandenberg*, Twining took full advantage of a tragic turn of events in May 1952. Vandenberg became gravely ill, and Twining served as acting chief of staff for the next four months. Although Twining had little to do with actually running the air war in Korea, he did represent the air force in the JCS and before Congress.

Twining, Secretary of the Air Force Thomas K. Finletter*, and several powerful uniformed and civilian subordinates in July 1952 produced a forty-page document, ''The New Era: A Statement of Policy,'' in which they asserted that ''land-based air power in the form of the United States Air Force is today recognized as the keystone of American military power.'' From then through Dwight D. Eisenhower's* election and inauguration, Twining maneuvered himself into position as the front-runner among the potential successors to Vandenberg, who planned to retire in May 1953. Early that month, he received the president's nomination as the next air force chief of staff. Shortly after, he announced publicly that the intercontinental air power mission was preeminent and that tactical air units would have to absorb air force budget cuts projected by the Eisenhower administration. Twining was sworn in as the air force's third chief of staff on June 30 and was about to lead it during a time when his philosophy was also that of the White House.

J. B. McCarley, ''General Nathan Farrugut Twining: The Making of a Disciple of American Strategic Air Power, 1897–1953'' (Ph.D. dissertation, Temple University, 1989); D. J. Mrozek, ''Nathan F. Twining: New Dimensions, A New Look,'' in J. L. Frisbee (ed.), *Makers of the United States Air Force* (Washington, D.C., 1987); N. F. Twining interviews, Oral History Project, Columbia University; N. F. Twining, *Neither Liberty Nor Safety: A Hard Look at U.S. Military Policy and Strategy* (New York, 1966); N. F. Twining papers, Library of Congress, Washington, D.C.

                                                                        J. Britt McCarley

U

UN ADDITIONAL MEASURES COMMITTEE

This committee was established by a resolution of the Political Committee of the UN General Assembly on January 30, 1951, which was confirmed by the General Assembly two days later. The resolution, which had been introduced by the United States, stated that the People's Republic of China* was engaged in aggression in Korea and requested a committee composed of the members of the UN Collective Measures Committee* "as a matter of urgency to consider additional measures to be employed to meet this aggression and to report thereon to the General Assembly." The committee was authorized to defer its report if the UN Good Offices Committee*, established by the same resolution, reported satisfactory progress in its efforts to end hostilities and realize UN objectives in Korea by peaceful means.

The UN Additional Measures Committee was composed of Australia, Belgium, Brazil, Britain, Canada, Egypt, France, Mexico, the Philippines, Turkey, the United States, and Venezuela. Of these, only the United States pressed for immediate action, the other members preferring to avoid anything that would complicate the work of the UN Good Offices Committee. Washington wanted the committee to recommend five minimum measures that combined political and economic sanctions. These included non-recognition of the PRC, its exclusion from all UN bodies, and an embargo on the export of strategic goods to China. The failure of the UN Good Offices Committee to produce results finally convinced the opponents of action that further measures were inevitable. Britain, however, opposed political sanctions. A special subcommittee was formed of Australia, Britain, France, and the United States, which agreed on April 17 to study proposals for economic sanctions. The final impetus towards action was provided by the Chinese spring offensives of 1951*, which made it difficult for Britain, the main advocate of delay, to maintain its opposition.

On May 14, 1951, the committee approved a U.S. proposal for a selective embargo against China. This was passed on May 17 by the UN Political Committee, 47–0, the Soviet bloc abstaining, and the General Assembly the following day. The resolution called on UN members to embargo the export to the PRC and the Democratic People's Republic of Korea* of "arms, ammunition and implements of war, atomic energy, materials, petroleum, transportation materials of strategic importance, and items useful in the production of arms, ammunition and implements of war." The resolution was less comprehensive than the United States would have liked and involved no change in the policy of major allies such as Australia, Canada, and Britain, which had already imposed such an embargo. *See also* NSC-92; NSC-101; UN Resolution of February 1, 1951.

J. A. Munro and A. I. Inglis (eds.), *Mike: The Memoirs of the Right Honourable Lester B. Pearson* (London, 1974); R. J. O'Neill, *Australia in the Korean War 1950–53* (Canberra, 1981); D. Stairs, *The Diplomacy of Constraint* (Toronto, 1974).

Callum A. MacDonald

UN APPEALS FOR ADDITIONAL TROOPS

UN Secretary-General Trygve Lie*, acting under the UN Security Council resolution of June 27, 1950*, made numerous appeals during the first year of the Korean War for military contributions to help defend the Republic of Korea*. From the outset, the U.S. government was anxious to secure support from as many UN members as possible regardless of kind or amount. Several factors limited the extent to which UN members could contribute to the UNC*. Although the size of each nation's military and its defense responsibilities at home played a role, political factors were perhaps more important. Obviously, the Soviet Union and its allies refused to support the UN war effort, but there were neutral nations who opposed international involvement in what they considered a civil war. Despite the fact that those UN members with forces in Korea had acted to defeat an act of aggression, many disagreed with the U.S. government on specific issues related to the conduct of the war. These differences became more serious after Chinese military intervention* when a consensus emerged in favor of achieving an early cease-fire. For example, on December 5, 1950, Secretary of State Dean G. Acheson* informed Secretary of Defense George C. Marshall* that the prospects for receiving more troops beyond those already pledged were not bright. Although he planned to approach the Latin American states and Pakistan, he was "not hopeful." During the next six months, Acheson approached several nations but was unable to secure any new contributions.

Another persistent problem concerned the size of the units that the UNC would accept for service in Korea. Although CINCUNC General Douglas MacArthur* initially had suggested accepting only units of about 1,000 men with equipment and artillery support, during the spring of 1951, Lieutenant General Matthew B. Ridgway*, MacArthur's successor, advocated encouraging UN members to increase their forces to not less than a brigade or a regimental combat team. Not only should these units have undergone full training prior to arrival in Korea, but they also should have their own integrated artillery, logistic, and administrative support. Ridgway's attempt to limit the U.S. responsibility for other UN forces significantly reduced the number of nations capable of making contributions. The issue became less important, however, when the belligerents agreed to negotiate an armistice. On the eve of the start of the Kaesŏng truce talks*, Ridgway recommended that no UN forces be materially increased until the results of the cease-fire negotiations became clear. Thereafter, the U.S. government increasingly emphasized the importance of building South Korea's military strength, thus creating the capacity for self-defense in the postwar era. *See also* Logistical Reimbursement Issue.

W. G. Hermes, *Truce Tent and Fighting Front* (Washington, D.C., 1966); J. F. Schnabel and R. J. Watson, *History of the Joint Chiefs of Staff*, vol. 3: *The Korean War* (Wilmington, 1979).

UN CEASEFIRE GROUP

On December 14, 1950, the Political Committee of the UN General Assembly passed a resolution sponsored by the Arab-Asian bloc calling on the president of the General Assembly "to constitute a group of three persons, including himself, to determine the basis on which a satisfactory cease-fire in Korea can be arranged and to make recommendations to the General Assembly as soon as possible." The Ceasefire Group, consisting of Nasrollah Entezam* of Iran, Lester B. Pearson* of Canada, and Sir Benegal N. Rau* of India, tried to take advantage of the presence of a Chinese Communist delegation at the UN to work out an armistice. On December 15, 1950, it secured a statement of the terms acceptable to the UNC*, but it had no success with the Chinese, who considered the UN Ceasefire Group illegal because the People's Republic of China* had not been involved in its establishment. Despite the efforts of the group and UN Secretary-General Trygve Lie*, the Chinese delegation left for Peking on December 19. On December 23, the PRC informed Lie that the United States supported a cease-fire only to avoid defeat and insisted that an armistice must be linked to wider political questions such as Taiwan and the PRC's right to a UN seat.

On January 3, 1951, the UN Ceasefire Group reported to the Political Committee that it had been "unable to pursue discussion of a satisfactory cease-fire arrangement." The Political Committee then asked the group to prepare a "statement of principles" on further steps that might be taken. On January 11, the UN Ceasefire Group produced a "Supplementary Report," which enumerated the five principles on which a Korean settlement might be based. The report called for a cease-fire, followed by arrangements to allow the carrying out of the UN resolution of October 7, 1950*, for an independent, democratic, and unified Korea. As soon as agreement had been reached on a cease-fire, the General Assembly should establish an appropriate body, including representatives of Britain, the United States, the Soviet Union, and the PRC, to achieve a settlement of "Far Eastern problems, including, among others, those of Formosa (Taiwan) and of representation of China in the United Nations." The United States accepted these principles reluctantly, and, on January 13, they were adopted by the Political Committee.

On January 17, the PRC rejected the five principles on the grounds that a cease-fire was to precede political negotiations and proposed a seven-nation conference to be held in China that would simultaneously discuss Korea, Taiwan, and the PRC UN representation question*. Although the United States called for immediate condemnation of China as an aggressor, Britain and others wanted clarification of the Chinese position. Exchanges with Peking continued until January 30 when the Political Committee passed a U.S. resolution condemning China as an aggressor and calling for the consideration of additional measures against Peking. The resolution, however, also called for a UN Good Offices Committee*, based on the old UN Ceasefire Group, to continue attempts to reach a peaceful settlement. *See also* Arab-Asian Peace Initiatives; NSC-95; UN Resolution of February 1, 1951.

D. Acheson, *Present at the Creation* (London, 1970); J. A. Munro and A. I. Inglis (eds.), *Mike: The Memoirs of the Right Honourable Lester B. Pearson* (London, 1974); D. Stairs, *The Diplomacy of Constraint* (Toronto, 1974).

Callum A. MacDonald

UN CIVIL ASSISTANCE COMMAND, KOREA

Establishment of this agency became necessary after Chinese military intervention* because continuation of the war prevented the UN Korean Reconstruction Agency* (UNKRA) from functioning effectively. Early in 1951, the UNC* created the UN Civil Assistance Command, Korea (UNCACK) under the 8th Army* to strengthen security inside the Republic of Korea*. To prevent unrest and disease in rear areas, the UNCACK provided emergency short-term relief, distributing consumer goods to meet the immediate needs of the civilian population. Late in 1951, after battle lines stabilized just north of the thirty-eighth parallel, the UNC worked out an arrangement with the UNKRA permitting it to start rehabilitation and reconstruction before the war ended. The UNCACK continued to operate, playing an important role in providing food and relocation assistance to South Korean civilian internees during June and July 1952. Performance of this liaison function meant that there was no interference with military operations. The UNCACK also attempted to encourage greater decentralization of the ROK's decision-making process but experienced little success. In April 1953, the UNCACK provided the headquarters for the Tasca Mission*. *See also* Civilian Internee Issue.

Foreign Relations of the United States, 1952–1954, vol. 15: *Korea* (Washington, D.C., 1984); W. G. Hermes, *Truce Tent and Fighting Front* (Washington, D.C., 1966); D. Rees, *Korea: The Limited War* (New York, 1964).

UN COLLECTIVE MEASURES COMMITTEE

A key provision of the UN Uniting for Peace resolution of November 3, 1950*, called for the creation of a UN Collective Measures Committee to study in consultation with the UN Secretary-General Trygve Lie* methods of strengthening international peace and security, including the use of armed force. It also recommended that member states establish and maintain military forces for deployment on behalf of the UN. Formed on November 3, the UN Collective

Measures Committee consisted of twelve states: Australia, Belgium, Brazil, Britain, Canada, Egypt, France, Mexico, the Philippines, Turkey, the United States, and Venezuela. In January 1951, after Chinese forces had pushed the UNC* south of the thirty-eighth parallel, the United States pressed for a resolution condemning the People's Republic of China* and requesting the UN Collective Measures Committee to recommend further punitive action. With authority granted under the Uniting for Peace measure, the General Assembly approved the UN resolution of February 1, 1951*, which branded the PRC an aggressor in Korea and established a UN Additional Measures Committee* "composed of the members of the Collective Measures Committee."

D. Acheson, *Present at the Creation* (London, 1970); T. Lie, *In the Cause of Peace* (New York, 1954); R. J. O'Neill, *Australia in the Korean War 1950–53* (Canberra, 1981).

Callum A. MacDonald

UN COMMISSION FOR THE UNIFICATION AND REHABILITATION OF KOREA

Creation of this body under the UN resolution of October 7, 1950*, reflected the General Assembly's optimistic expectation that the UN offensive across the thirty-eighth parallel*, which the measure authorized, would unite Korea. Although Chinese military intervention* made it impossible for the UN Commission for the Unification and Rehabilitation of Korea (UNCURK) to fulfill its primary mission, it continued to function and would play a central role in efforts to restrain the dictatorial actions of President Syngman Rhee* of the Republic of Korea*. The UNCURK consisted of representatives from Australia, Chile, the Netherlands, Pakistan, the Philippines, Thailand, and Turkey. Its mission was to "(i) assume the functions hitherto exercised by the [UN Commission on Korea], (ii) represent the United Nations in bringing about the establishment of a unified, independent and democratic Government of all Korea, (iii) exercise such responsibilities in connection with relief and rehabilitation in Korea as may be determined by the General Assembly." Pending the arrival of the UNCURK in Korea, the nations serving on the commission would form an ad hoc committee immediately "to consult with and advise the [UNC*] in light of the above recommendations." On October 12, the UN Interim Committee recommended that, preparatory to nationwide elections, the UNC "assume provisionally all responsibilities for" governing North Korea until the UNCURK considered the issue of future administration of these territories.

Upon receiving news of the UN's actions, Rhee sent an angry protest to CINCUNC General Douglas MacArthur*. Insisting that the ROK's authority was legitimate throughout Korea, he stated that "whenever hostilities cease," he was "dispatching governors appointed 2 years ago for 5 provinces of the north to restore peace and order." The Truman administration believed that the UNCURK could not ignore the ROK but hoped the Rhee government would agree voluntarily to support nationwide elections. However, "it will be up to

UNCURK, if after due study it finds complete national elections [to be] greatly preferable, to win ROK acquiescence [to] this course." When MacArthur received the occupation directive for North Korea* on October 28, it respected the UN position that Rhee's control did not automatically extend northward, but it also assumed close consultations between the UNCURK and the ROK. Rhee, in a press release issued two days later, pledged "to cooperate fully" with the UNCURK but promised elections only at the provincial level. He also stated that those who had fled northern Korea "will be going home" and "may be expected to play a significant role in the future affairs" of the north. Rhee intended to submit to MacArthur a list of "persons of North Korean origin" who would be "acceptable" candidates "for every post." Fearing that ROK agents would engage in political intimidation, the UN Interim Committee considered advising the UNCURK to recommend to MacArthur that "efforts be made to use local residents whenever possible before using Koreans from south of the 38th parallel."

Even before the UNCURK arrived in Korea, there was evidence that the People's Republic of China* had joined the fighting. On November 7, the UN Interim Committee resolved that the UNCURK should travel to the Yalu River and attempt to contact the PRC to determine its intentions. But after the Chinese military disengagement of November 6, 1950*, MacArthur said he did not think it was necessary for the UNCURK to "render any additional services." By November 20, the United States concluded that it was "possible to proceed now with the activities of the new UN Commission for the political and economic consolidation of existing gains," recommending a plan for neutralization of a united Korea. After the failure of the Home-by-Christmas offensive*, the UN compromised the UNCURK's authority. In addition to creating the UN Ceasefire Group* to end the fighting in Korea, it established the UN Korean Reconstruction Agency* (UNKRA). Thereafter, the UNKRA asserted increasing independence, though it was subordinate to the UNCURK. During the spring of 1951, the UNCURK considered issuing a radio appeal to the Democratic People's Republic of Korea* for a negotiated settlement, but UN Secretary-General Trygve Lie* saw this as "premature." It dropped the idea when the UN Good Offices Committee* said it would make its "task more difficult." Because of a "feeling of futility and a loss of morale," many members of the UNCURK wanted to leave Korea and disband the committee. This desire grew after the United States ruled out a role for the UNCURK in the Kaesŏng truce talks*.

Meanwhile, the UNCURK had been monitoring the activities of the Rhee government. During the occupation of North Korea*, James Plimsoll*, Australia's member on the commission, reported that South Korean troops were pillaging, looting, and engaging in general violence in the north. In December 1950, the UNCURK conducted an investigation of the ROK's policy of arresting, trying, and sentencing to death or imprisonment anyone suspected of Communist sympathies. It submitted a report to the UN criticizing in particular the Kŏch'ang incident* and the South Korean National Guard scandal*. While the United

States thought that the UNCURK had great symbolic, "political and psychological value," it was concerned about its "history of ineffectiveness and incompetence." Washington decided to recommend replacing the UNCURK with a single person after the commission complained about the UNKRA's autonomy. But then the UNCURK acted vigorously to restrain Rhee during the South Korean political crisis of 1952*, issuing a statement demanding an end to martial law and the release of arrested members of the National Assembly. Washington's plan for removing Rhee called for implementation of Operation Everready* in response to the UNCURK's request for action. After the crisis passed, Rhee took measures to limit the commission's interference in the ROK's internal affairs. Nevertheless, the UNCURK survived until 1972 because the United States insisted upon preserving the facade of UN interest in Korean affairs.

Foreign Relations of the United States, 1950, vol. 7: *Korea* (Washington, D.C., 1976), *1951*, vol. 7: *Korea and China* (Washington, D.C., 1983), and *1952–1954*, vol. 15: *Korea* (Washington, D.C., 1984); C. A. MacDonald, *Korea: The War Before Vietnam* (New York, 1986); J. F. Schnabel, *Policy and Direction* (Washington, D.C., 1972).

UN COMMISSION ON KOREA
See UN Resolution of December 12, 1948; UN Resolution of October 21, 1949; UNCOK Report on North Korean Attack

UN GOOD OFFICES COMMITTEE
The UN Good Offices Committee was established by a resolution of the Political Committee of the UN General Assembly on January 30, 1951, which was confirmed by the UN resolution of February 1, 1951*. The resolution, which had been proposed by the United States, condemned the People's Republic of China* as an aggressor and established a UN Additional Measures Committee* to consider sanctions against the PRC. It also affirmed, however, that UN policy remained "to bring about a cessation of hostilities in Korea and the achievement of United Nations objectives . . . by peaceful means" and requested the president of the General Assembly to "designate forthwith two persons who would meet with him at any suitable opportunity to use their good offices to this end." If the UN Good Offices Committee reported progress, the UN Additional Measures Committee was authorized to defer its report. This provision was designed to win support from those states, such as Britain and Canada, that were reluctant to support the U.S. demand for sanctions before every possibility of a settlement with China had been exhausted.

The UN Good Offices Committee was intended to be an extension of the old UN Ceasefire Group*. However, the Indian delegate, Sir Benegal N. Rau*, refused to serve because his government had voted against the resolution. The Canadian delegate, Lester B. Pearson*, also declined, feeling that his usefulness might have been compromised by his support of a resolution that condemned China as an aggressor. President of the General Assembly Nasrollah Entezam* of Iran filled their places with Sven Grafstrom* of Sweden and Luis Padillo

Nervo* of Mexico. The failure of the committee to make any progress in the next few months and the Chinese spring offensives of 1951* led the UN Additional Measures Committee to propose selective economic sanctions against China, a move approved by the UN General Assembly on May 18, 1951.

J. A. Munro and A. I. Inglis (eds.), *Mike: The Memoirs of the Right Honourable Lester B. Pearson* (London, 1974); R. J. O'Neill, *Australia in the Korean War 1950–53* (Canberra, 1981); D. Stairs, *The Diplomacy of Constraint* (Toronto, 1974).

Callum A. MacDonald

UN INVITATION TO THE PRC TO PARTICIPATE IN DEBATE (November 8, 1950)

The appearance of the Chinese People's Volunteers Army (CPVA)* in the Korean War caused the United Nations, in a reversal of its previous position, to invite representatives of the People's Republic of China* to join its deliberations. Early in August, after returning to the UN following a seven-month Soviet UN Security Council boycott*, Moscow's representative, Jacob A. Malik*, had introduced a resolution inviting representatives of the PRC and the Korean people, meaning the Democratic People's Republic of Korea*, to discuss the Korean question at the UN. On August 20, Premier and Foreign Minister Chou En-lai* welcomed Malik's resolution and demanded Chinese presence at UN Security Council discussions concerning Korea. But on September 6, the Security Council defeated Malik's resolution. Following evidence of China's entry into the war, the UN Security Council changed its mind. On November 8, it voted to discuss CINCUNC General Douglas MacArthur's* report on Chinese military intervention* and to invite the PRC to join in discussions scheduled to begin November 15 regarding the Draft Resolution on U.S. Aggression against Taiwan submitted by China and the Draft Resolution on Chinese Aggression against Korea proposed by the United States. The UN Security Council then considered a resolution calling upon the PRC to remove its troops from Korea and pledging, at the insistence of France, "to hold the Chinese frontier with Korea inviolate." On November 10, the Soviet Union vetoed the measure, arguing that there could be no discussion of the matter in the absence of the PRC's representative.

On October 23, Peking had named Wu Hsui-ch'uan* as its representative. In response to the UN Security Council's invitation to participate in debate on November 8, the PRC announced that while it would not discuss MacArthur's report, it would send Wu and a delegation of fourteen diplomats for talks on Taiwan. But Wu did not arrive at Lake Success until November 24. That very day, MacArthur had launched his Home-by-Christmas offensive*, which the CPVA met with a massive counterattack. The two-month hiatus has been a cause of speculation. Perhaps the PRC had set aside diplomacy until the military situation in Korea had improved. Possibly the invitation looked less appealing when given grudgingly rather than in recognition of

China's world status and sovereign rights. The United States, at the same time, did what it could to prevent Chinese participation. Wu addressed the UN for two hours and called for condemnation of the United States and resolutions demanding the withdrawal of its forces from Taiwan and Korea. In subsequent discussion, he berated the Republic of China's* representative, T. F. Tsiang*, for speaking English rather than Chinese, confirming, Wu suggested, that he was simply a puppet of the Americans. China's appearance at the UN did not resolve the conflict in Korea.

A. S. Whiting, *China Crosses the Yalu* (Stanford, Calif., 1960); Wu Xiuquan, *Eight Years in the Ministry of Foreign Affairs* (Peking, 1985).

Nancy Bernkopf Tucker

UN KOREAN RECONSTRUCTION AGENCY

This body was established under the UN resolution of December 1, 1950*, to help provide the Korean people with assistance in recovering from the devastation of the Korean War. Hundreds of thousands of refugees had fled southward during the North Korean invasion of South Korea*, and large numbers had been forced from their homes when UN forces counterattacked. Their plight had produced resolutions for the UN to assume responsibility for relief and rehabilitation efforts. Initially, the UNCURK* was responsible for economic reconstruction as part of its mission to establish a unified, independent government for Korea. However, political difficulties led to the desire for a sharper focus on rebuilding the Korean economy. On October 30, 1951, the UN Economic and Social Council, acknowledging the enormous devastation visited upon Korea, established the UN Korean Reconstruction Agency (UNKRA) and recommended a $250 million program to deal with immediate needs. On December 1, the General Assembly approved UNKRA's mission and authorized discussions to decide the voluntary contributions of each member to the program. Its first director was J. Donald Kingsley*, with Lieutenant General John B. Coulter* replacing him in the spring of 1953.

Massive Chinese military intervention* placed UNKRA in a new light, and efforts to meet Korea's most urgent needs were met primarily by the United States, Australia and other members of the British Commonwealth, and various European nations. Building on initiatives previously undertaken by the Economic Cooperation Administration (ECA), the UNC* acquired general responsibility for civilian relief and economic aid to Korea, fulfilling this mission through the activities of the UNCACK*. Despite obstructionist tactics by groups supporting President Syngman Rhee* of the Republic of Korea*, UNCACK and UNKRA teams contributed over the next three years to alleviation of disease, food shortages, lack of shelter, and economic dislocations throughout South Korea. At war's end, they mapped ambitious plans for Korea's reconstruction, ultimately establishing the foundation for the ROK's economic growth and prosperity.

L. M. Goodrich, *Korea: A Study of the U.S. Policy in the U.N.* (New York, 1956); USFFE, *United Nations Civil Affairs Activities in Korea* (Tokyo, 1952).

Theodore A. Wilson

UN OFFENSIVE ACROSS THE THIRTY-EIGHTH PARALLEL

President Harry S. Truman* approved this operation for the purpose of destroying the North Korean People's Army (NKPA) and reunifying Korea. His decision was unwise, if not disastrous, because it prompted Chinese military intervention* in the Korean War, transforming what might have been a brief conflict into one that would last more than three years. During the week after the North Korean invasion of South Korea*, U.S. leaders stated that their goal in Korea was a restoration of the status quo ante bellum. But following Truman's commitment of ground troops*, some administration officials, most notably John M. Allison*, began advocating a UN offensive across the thirty-eighth parallel in pursuit of reunification. General Douglas MacArthur* shared this view, submitting a plan (Operation Bluehearts*) early in July 1950 calling for a counter-offensive in coordination with an amphibious landing behind enemy lines allowing the United States to "compose and unite" Korea. Predictably, the Republic of Korea* also was urging the United States to adopt as a war aim the destruction of the Democratic People's Republic of Korea*, since this would extend the ROK's control to the entire peninsula. Other U.S. leaders, especially O. Edmund Clubb*, opposed crossing the parallel, fearing that this would bring the People's Republic of China* or the Soviet Union into the war. The JCS at first shared this concern, warning on July 21 against any "excessive commitment of United States military forces and resources in those areas of operations which would not be decisive."

Once MacArthur successfully halted the NKPA advance in later July, support within the administration for forcible reunification grew, as China expert John Paton Davies* and even the JCS advised that occupying the north was desirable. By the middle of August, Truman apparently agreed. At the UN, Warren R. Austin* indicated on August 17 that the president had authorized an offensive northward when he proclaimed, "Shall only a part of the country be assured this freedom? I think not." In NSC-80*, the administration revealed its concern that Indian peace initiatives* at the UN might delay offensive operations across the parallel. Truman's advisers therefore quickly completed work on plans for Korea's reunification (NSC-81*) and secured the president's approval on September 11. After the successful Inch'ŏn landing* and the recapture of Seoul operation*, UN forces were poised at the thirty-eighth parallel, ROK troops in fact moving into North Korea on September 30. After the General Assembly passed the UN resolution of October 7, 1950*, instructing the UNC* to "ensure conditions of stability throughout Korea," MacArthur launched his offensive northward.

Meanwhile, Chinese foreign minister Chou En-lai* had warned that if U.S. troops moved across the parallel, the Chinese would join the fighting. Although

U.S. leaders thought the PRC was bluffing, they succumbed as well to the irresistible temptation to reunify Korea, an objective the United States had sought since 1945. An offensive across the thirty-eighth parallel finally would destroy a regime that the Truman administration believed had denied the northern populace freedom of choice. Elections under UN supervision would allow rather than compel the Korea people to achieve independence, unity, and democracy. At first, the UNC* experienced little resistance as it advanced northward, capturing P'yŏngyang on October 19. MacArthur, upon arrival at the capital of the DPRK the next day, asked, "Are any celebrities here to greet me? Where's Kim Buck Too?" On October 28, Washington sent MacArthur an occupation directive for North Korea*, though the UNC already had captured Chinese soldiers. Then, at the Battle of Ŭnsan during the first week of November, two Chinese divisions inflicted major casualties on the ROK 1st Division and the U.S. 1st Cavalry Division, forcing a retreat south of the Ch'ŏngch'ŏn River. But the Chinese military disengagement of November 6, 1950*, restored MacArthur's confidence, setting the stage for launching his disastrous Home-by-Christmas offensive*. See also CIA Report: Factors Affecting the Desirability of a UN Military Conquest of All Korea; CIA Report: Threat of Full Chinese Communist Intervention in Korea.

J. L. Collins, *War in Peacetime* (Boston, 1969); *Foreign Relations of the United States, 1950*, vol. 7: *Korea* (Washington, D.C., 1976); L. C. Gardner, *The Korean War* (New York, 1972); J. I. Matray, "Truman's Plan for Victory: National Determination and the Thirty-eighth Parallel Decision in Korea," *Journal of American History* (September 1979); W. W. Stueck, *The Road to Confrontation* (Chapel Hill, 1981).

UN PEACE OBSERVATION COMMISSION
See UN Uniting for Peace Resolution of November 3, 1950

UN RESOLUTION OF APRIL 18, 1953
Passage of this resolution reflected rising optimism at the United Nations that there soon would be an armistice ending the Korean War. On April 11, 1953, negotiators at the P'anmunjŏm truce talks* agreed to the exchange of sick and wounded POWs (Operation Little Switch*). In anticipation of the truce talks resumption of April 26, 1953*, the General Assembly adopted UN Resolution 705 (VII) calling for reconvening the session and resuming consideration of the Korean question upon receiving notification from the UNC* that an armistice had been achieved. On July 27, the armistice agreement* was signed, and, after receipt of this news from CINCUNC General Mark W. Clark*, the president of the General Assembly informed the member states that the Seventh Session of the body would convene on August 17. In a brief plenary meeting on that date, the assembly voted to refer the Korean question to the First Committee, while the nations with troops in Korea submitted two draft resolutions. The first called for UN participation at the political conference limited to those nations "contributing armed forces under the Unified Command" that desired representation

and the Republic of Korea*. The second paid tribute to the soldiers and nations responsible for the UN effort in Korea.

Foreign Relations of the United States, 1952–1954, vol. 15: *Korea* (Washington, D.C., 1984).

UN RESOLUTION OF DECEMBER 12, 1948

With this resolution, the UN established a commitment to the survival of the Republic of Korea*, resulting in the international organization's military inter-vention in the Korean War. The UN resolution of November 14, 1947*, had called for internationally supervised elections for delegates to a Korean national assembly, but the Soviets had barred access to the north. Thus, the elections of May 10, 1948, were confined to the U.S. zone, as voters selected representatives who created a separate government for South Korea on August 15. At first, the Truman administration planned to ask the UN to recognize the ROK as the national government envisaged in the November 14 resolution. But Britain and Canada notified Washington that they could not support this position. Thus, the United States drafted a resolution providing for the UN to recognize the ROK as the only legitimate government on the Korean peninsula and allowing its representatives to participate in future UN deliberations. The Democratic Peo-ple's Republic of Korea*, by contrast, would not have a chance to present its case. Washington's revised proposal also called for the creation of a new UN Commission on Korea (UNCOK) to supervise the dissolution of all non-ROK administrative and military organizations in Korea and to report to the General Assembly on progress toward reunification. In its final form, the resolution provided that within ninety days after its adoption, the UNCOK would observe and verify Soviet-U.S. military withdrawal.

Once Washington abandoned its claim that the ROK constituted Korea's na-tional government, passage of the resolution was certain. On December 6, the UN Political and Security Committee voted overwhelmingly to reject the DPRK's claim to legitimacy and instead invited the ROK to send delegates to the UN. Two days later, it voted by a wide margin to recommend that the General Assembly adopt the U.S.-sponsored resolution. It amended the proposal to pro-vide for withdrawal of foreign troops from Korea "as soon as practicable" rather than ninety days after adoption. On December 12, the UN General Assembly easily approved the U.S. resolution, despite sharp criticism from the Soviet delegate. After rejecting Moscow's proposal to disband the UNTCOK, the Gen-eral Assembly voted to create a new commission that would be smaller than its predecessor, excluding both the Ukraine and Canada. Within thirty days, the UNCOK would arrive in Korea and begin to cooperate with the ROK in the achievement of reunification. For many UN members, passage of the December 12 resolution was a painful decision. Not only did this action alienate the Soviet Union, it also risked involvement in a brewing Korean civil war. However, the United States, exploiting its dominance over the international organization, con-vinced most members that the UN could not abandon its moral obligation to the ROK. *See also* UN Resolution of October 21, 1949.

Foreign Relations of the United States, 1948, vol. 6: *The Far East and Australasia* (Washington, D.C., 1974); L. Gordenker, *The United Nations and the Peaceful Reunification of Korea* (The Hague, 1959); J. I. Matray, *The Reluctant Crusade* (Honolulu, 1985).

UN RESOLUTION OF DECEMBER 1, 1950

This resolution established the UN Korean Reconstruction Agency* (UN-KRA). On October 15, 1950, at the Wake Island Conference*, President Harry S. Truman* asked CINCUNC General Douglas MacArthur* to comment on the need for the rehabilitation and reconstruction of Korea. MacArthur responded by suggesting that it would take about $500 million spread over three to five years to do the job. The next day, the U.S. delegation at the UN discussed a draft resolution dealing with the topic of Korean rehabilitation. It had been worked out with the British, French, Brazilians, and Canadians and had received their tentative approval. By the start of November, the UN Economic and Social Committee, in response to a request from the General Assembly, had taken action regarding the question of the relief and rehabilitation of Korea. It "adopted the substance of a U.S.-sponsored resolution to place the responsibility for these matters in the hands of an Agent General of the United Nations." There were further discussions in November of whether the U.S. or an Asian should administer the program. The United States also made efforts to convince other powers, especially Britain, of the need to help finance the Korean aid program. On December 1, 1950, by a vote of 51–0 with 5 abstentions, the UN General Assembly approved the resolution "providing for relief and rehabilitation of Korea and financial arrangements related thereto," thus creating UNKRA under the direction of a UN agent general. The resolution also established a negotiating committee whose purpose was "to consult with member and nonmember states concerning financial contributions for Korean relief."

Foreign Relations of the United States, 1950, vol. 7: *Korea* (Washington, D.C., 1976); R. J. O'Neill, *Australia in the Korean War 1950–53* (Canberra, 1981); D. Stairs, *The Diplomacy of Constraint* (Toronto, 1974).

Paul J. Morton

UN RESOLUTION OF DECEMBER 14, 1950

Passed by the General Assembly during the crisis following Chinese military intervention* in Korea, the resolution requested that body's president (Iran's Nasrollah Entezam*) to "constitute a group of three persons including himself to determine the basis on which a satisfactory ceasefire in Korea can be arranged and to make recommendations to the General Assembly as soon as possible." The resolution grew out of Arab-Asian efforts, led by India's Sir Benegal N. Rau*, to prevent a spreading of the conflict beyond Korea or, better, to resolve outstanding issues between the United States and the People's Republic of China*. Introduced in the First Committee on December 12, it had thirteen cosponsors, all of the Arab-Asian group that, from the fall of 1950 onward, made several attempts to mediate on Korea. Simultaneously, Rau introduced another resolution, this one with twelve co-sponsors (the same nations as on the other resolution minus the Philippines), implying that a settlement in Korea should be connected to agreements on other issues in East Asia, including the status of Taiwan and the PRC UN representation question*. The United States pressed successfully to table the latter proposal, thus giving priority to the former resolution. Given the American desire to push through a six-power resolution calling upon China to withdraw from Korea, this U.S. action represented a concession of sorts; yet it also involved pushing aside a Soviet resolution proposing total withdrawal of foreign forces from the peninsula.

The Soviet bloc opposed the thirteen-power resolution. The Chinese People's Volunteers Army* was still moving southward in Korea, and the Communists in New York showed little interest in establishing contact with the UN Ceasefire Group*, which was immediately established to implement the resolution. On December 15, the PRC delegation, which had arrived at the UN in late November to participate in discussions (subsequently postponed) on the Taiwan issue, informed Secretary-General Trygve Lie* that it would return home. A week later, Foreign Minister Chou En-lai* condemned the resolution as illegal in the light of his government's lack of "participation and concurrence" in its adoption. While acknowledging the sincerity of its Arab and Asian authors, he attacked the idea of a cease-fire followed by negotiations for a settlement on Korea and other issues as a U.S. scheme designed to give UN troops time to regroup and prepare for a renewed offensive. Despite continuing efforts by the cease-fire group during January 1951 and some indications from Peking of an interest in negotiations, continued U.S. resistance to any discussion on Korea alongside other Asian issues prevented the commencement of talks. Although the December 14, 1950, resolution did not lead to a cease-fire in Korea, it did create a process that, by delaying the U.S. campaign for sanctions against the PRC, reduced prospects for an expanded war. *See also* Arab-Asian Peace Initiatives.

Foreign Relations of the United States, 1950, vol. 7: *Korea* (Washington, D.C., 1976); UN documents A/C.1/SR. 415, A/C.641, A/C.1/642, A/PV.324, A/PV.325.

William Stueck

UN RESOLUTION OF DECEMBER 3, 1952

This resolution addressed the problem of POW repatriation (agenda item 4*) in an effort to remove the one major remaining obstacle to an armistice in Korea. At the Seventh Session of the General Assembly, Secretary of State Dean G. Acheson*, in late October and with the support of twenty other nations, put forward a draft resolution for an armistice agreement with the People's Republic of China* and the Democratic People's Republic of Korea*. The most important point in the resolution was a provision calling for no forced repatriation of POWs. But the Soviet Union supported compulsory repatriation, evidenced by its backing for a Polish resolution in mid-October addressing this issue. V. K. Krishna Menon*, India's delegate to the UN, proposed a compromise between the positions of the Americans and Soviets and found support for his POW settlement proposal* from the British and Canadian delegations. Acheson, however, argued against Menon's plan as simply another form of forced repatriation. Menon's effort came under more pressure on November 10 when Andrei Y. Vyshinsky* stated that the Soviets would not change their position on the repatriation issue. Acheson suggested that a subcommittee be formed to develop a compromise from the U.S. and Indian proposals, thus preventing any further deterioration of the U.S. position on repatriation. He was willing to use the subcommittee because the United States, as a member, would be in a position to influence the recommendations, while the chairman of the subcommittee was Percy C. Spender*, Australia's new head delegate, who was sympathetic with Acheson's position on the repatriation issue.

The subcommittee met on November 18, 19, and 21 but could not reach a compromise. On November 23, news of a disagreement among the British, Canadians, and Indians on the one side and the Americans on the other became public. After a quick trip to Canada, Acheson returned to New York. He again made it clear that he was willing to use the Menon proposal, but it had to be amended further. Menon did not go far enough for Acheson in ensuring voluntary repatriation*. On November 24, however, Vyshinsky's public rejection of Menon's original proposal made further efforts by the subcommittee of the twenty-one to find a compromise pointless. The Soviet delegate undercut Menon's position by seeming to indicate that the Communists had no intention of accepting a compromise on the repatriation issue. Menon's original proposal had apparently been shown to the Chinese, and they had not immediately rejected it. Vyshinsky's action indicated a possible difference of opinion between the PRC and the Soviet Union.

Acheson quickly took advantage of the situation by praising the efforts of the British and Indians and suggested a few amendments to the Menon proposal to prevent forced repatriation. On November 26, Menon agreed to the changes that were necessary for U.S. approval. By December 1, the First Committee had organized the proposal into a seventeen-point resolution. The key parts of the resolution called for repatriation to be supervised by a Neutral Nations Repatriation Commission*, ideally to be composed of the same four countries as the Neutral Nations Supervisory Commission* (already agreed to in the draft armistice agreement). Ninety days after the armistice was signed, if any POWs still had not been repatriated, their disposition was to be referred to a political conference arranged according to the terms of the armistice. If after thirty more days POWs still refused repatriation and no arrangements were made for them by the political conference, they were to be taken care of, and final determination of their disposition was to be assumed by the UN.

The General Assembly approved this proposal on December 3 by a vote of 54 to 5 with only the Republic of China* abstaining. Two days later, the president of the General Assembly sent the resolution to the PRC and the DPRK as a first step to a cease-fire agreement. The PRC rejected the proposal of ''forcibly'' retaining POWs, which was contrary to the Geneva Convention of 1949*. Three days later, the UN received a similar message from the DPRK. However, the main provisions of this resolution were revived in the spring of 1953 with the Chou En-lai* POW settlement proposal*. Ultimately, the UN resolution of December 3, 1952, would break the deadlock at the P'anmunjŏm truce talks*, opening the way to an armistice agreement*. *See also* Twenty-one Power UN Resolution.

D. Acheson, *Present at the Creation* (New York, 1969); R. J. O'Neill, *Australia in the Korean War 1950–53* (Canberra, 1981); D. Stairs, *The Diplomacy of Constraint* (Toronto, 1974); Tae-ho Yoo, *The Korean War and the United Nations* (Louvain, 1965).

Paul J. Morton

UN RESOLUTION OF FEBRUARY 1, 1951

This was the long-delayed response of the UN to the Chinese military intervention* in Korea. By a 47–7 vote, with 9 abstentions, the UN General Assembly condemned the People's Republic of China's* participation in North Korea's aggression, established the UN Additional Measures Committee* to consider new steps to deal with the situation, but provided for it to defer its report if a UN Good Offices Committee*, to be set up as well, reported satisfactory progress in its efforts to secure a cease-fire and peaceful settlement. This formulation, the product of intense diplomacy in the last ten days of January 1951, ensured the continued viability of the UN coalition.

The genesis of the resolution lay in the Truman administration's determination, especially for domestic political reasons, to secure a strong condemnation of the PRC by the UN. With great reluctance, it had held its hand in early January while attempts were made to find a basis for negotiation in the five principles drawn up by the UN Ceasefire Group*. When China rejected the principles, the United States lost no time in introducing a draft resolution to the UN General Assembly on January 20, condemning China as an aggressor and calling for agreement in principle on additional measures to meet the aggression. But at the same time, somewhat contradictorily, it reaffirmed the policy of bringing about a cease-fire, establishing the UN Good Offices Committee to this end. This placed most non-Communist members in a dilemma. To support the resolution on the terms proposed would be to increase greatly the danger of a general war, since additional measures, to be effective, would require direct action against China. But failing to support it would risk unilateral action by an exasperated and unrestrained United States, with perhaps the same result.

There was, in consequence, a determined effort to avoid the issue, reflected in the reluctance of many members to accept China's response to the five principles as barring the way to a negotiated cease-fire and a willingness to clutch at diplomatic straws offered by the Chinese. When it became apparent that many members, including Britain, would stand aside if pressed to vote on the original draft, the United States accepted two amendments that seemed to lessen the dangers. China's response was held to be not acceptance but not complete rejection of the five principles, and a buffer to immediate action by the UN Additional Measures Committee was introduced in the provision for it to defer its report while the UN Good Offices Committee was making progress. Even this formulation proved unacceptable to India, which with Burma joined the Communist powers in voting against the resolution. *See also* NSC-101.

D. Acheson, *Present at the Creation* (New York, 1969); *Foreign Relations of the United States, 1951*, vol. 7: *Korea and China* (Washington, D.C., 1983); L. M. Goodrich, *Korea: A Study of U.S. Policy in the U.N.* (New York, 1956); J. A. Munro and A. I. Inglis (eds.), *Mike: The Memoirs of the Right Honourable Lester B. Pearson* (Toronto, 1973); D. Stairs, *The Diplomacy of Constraint* (Toronto, 1974).

Ian C. McGibbon

UN RESOLUTION OF MAY 18, 1951
See UN Additional Measures Committee

UN RESOLUTION OF NOVEMBER 14, 1947

This resolution marked the beginning of UN involvement in the Soviet-U.S. dispute over Korea's future after World War II and created the foundation for its decision to intervene militarily in the Korean War. In August 1947, the Truman administration, responding to the failure of a Joint Soviet-American Commission to reunify Korea, approved SWNCC 176/30*, a policy paper outlining various methods for ending the deadlock. If Moscow was uncooperative, the plan provided for referral of the Korean issue to the UN. On September 4, the Soviet Union rejected Washington's proposal for a four-power conference to discuss steps toward achieving Korea's unity and economic recovery. Less than two weeks later, Secretary of State George C. Marshall* addressed the UN General Assembly and placed the Korean matter on its agenda. The State Department already had in hand a draft resolution calling for UN-supervised free elections for delegates to a national assembly within six months after adoption. This legislature, reflecting the two-to-one population superiority of southern Korea, would formulate a constitution and appoint officials to serve in a provisional government. Perhaps the most important provision provided for the creation of a UN Temporary Commission on Korea (UNTCOK), comprised of eleven nations, to supervise the elections, foster freedom of choice, and report its findings to the General Assembly.

Warren R. Austin*, in his capacity as U.S. permanent representative, presented a revised draft resolution on October 17, calling for elections no later than March 31, 1948, and incorporating Moscow's recent proposal for Soviet-U.S. military withdrawal ninety days after the formation of a provisional government. On November 14, the General Assembly passed the U.S.-sponsored resolution by a wide margin. Nine nations were to serve on the UNTCOK: Canada, the Republic of China*, Australia, France, El Salvador, the Philippines, Syria, India, and the Ukraine. Some members of the UNTCOK voiced misgivings about becoming involved in the dispute over Korea, especially after the Ukraine refused to participate. When the commission arrived in Korea, the Soviet occupation commander denied access to the north, causing the United States to urge the UNTCOK to supervise elections only in the U.S. zone. Bowing to U.S. pressure, the UN sanctioned an election confined to southern Korea. On May

10, 1948, the UNTCOK observed balloting for the selection of assembly delegates, leading to the formation of the Republic of Korea* the following August. The UNTCOK's judgment that the election results reflected the freely expressed will of the people gave the ROK an international stamp of legitimacy. UN involvement in creating the ROK established a moral commitment that would result in passage of the UN Security Council resolutions of June 25* and June 27, 1950*, calling on member nations to come to the assistance of the ROK after the North Korean invasion of South Korea*. *See also* UN Resolution of December 12, 1948; UN Resolution of October 21, 1949.

Foreign Relations of the United States, 1947, vol. 6: *The Far East* (Washington, D.C., 1972) and *1948*, vol. 6: *The Far East and Australasia* (Washington, D.C., 1974); L. M. Goodrich, *Korea: A Study of U.S. Policy in the U.N.* (New York, 1956); L. Gordenker, *The United Nations and the Peaceful Reunification of Korea* (The Hague, 1959); J. I. Matray, *The Reluctant Crusade* (Honolulu, 1985).

UN RESOLUTION OF OCTOBER 7, 1950

This resolution gave the UNC* forces authorization to advance into the Democratic People's Republic of Korea* and unify the Korean peninsula through military means in the fall of 1950. It was, of course, a sanction post factum. CINCUNC General Douglas MacArthur* had ordered his troops into North Korea on October 2, and the Republic of Korea* had done the same two days earlier. Thus, apart from providing the UNC with moral sanction, it carried little significance in practice. The problem of whether the UN forces should cross the thirty-eighth parallel and ultimately unify the whole of Korea had been under consideration within the Truman administration ever since the beginning of the war. It appears that the decision was reached at the highest level by the middle of August. MacArthur was authorized on September 27 to cross the thirty-eighth parallel and to destroy the North Korean People's Army. That the UN was not a major factor in this decision is clearly shown in another message two days later from Secretary of Defense George C. Marshall*, which instructed MacArthur to "feel unhampered tactically and strategically to proceed north of 38th parallel." The UN resolution itself owes much to British initiative for both its preparation and passage. In a paper prepared in the Foreign Office toward the end of August, it was suggested that a new UN resolution would be required for ground operations beyond the thirty-eighth parallel but without a specific commitment to the UN to unification by military means. Thus, the resolution would simply include a phrase recommending that "necessary steps should be taken . . . to promote conditions of stability and security" in the whole of Korea for the realization of long-term objectives of the UN with regard to the country.

Following the Inch'ŏn landing* and completion of the UNC's recapture of Seoul operation*, British foreign minister Ernest Bevin* in New York took the initiative in drafting the resolution and pushing it through the UN. The resolution adopted by the UN General Assembly underwent changes in the course of consultations with other powers. However, it was essentially based on the papers prepared in the Foreign Office reemphasizing the long-term objectives of the

UN in Korea but leaving the part authorizing military operations in North Korea deliberately vague. Throughout this initiative, both Bevin and Prime Minister Clement R. Attlee* believed that the "time factor" was most important "in order to forestall others and make sure that the Russians do not seize the initiative" to the extent of having to "forego the thornier problems." The British proposal for the establishment of a UN-supervised civil administration was left out of the final draft of the resolution due to U.S. objections. However, it did establish the UN Commission for the Unification and Rehabilitation of Korea* (UNCURK). In addition, on October 12, the UN Interim Committee resolved that the UN would recognize no government as having "legal and effective control" over all Korea. The UNC* would administer affairs in the north until the UNCURK was prepared to fulfill its mission. After passage of the resolution of October 7, Secretary of State Dean G. Acheson* expressed his "approval and appreciation" of the British efforts. *See also* MacArthur's Surrender Ultimatum to North Korea; Occupation of North Korea; UN Offensive across the Thirty-eighth Parallel.

P. Lowe, *The Origins of the Korean War* (London, 1986); C. A. MacDonald, *Korea: The War Before Vietnam* (London, 1986); J. I. Matray, "Truman's Plan for Victory: National Self-Determination and the Thirty-eighth Parallel Decision in Korea," *Journal of American History* (September 1979); J. Y. Ra, "Special Relationship at War: The Anglo-American Relationship during the Korean War," *Journal of Strategic Studies* (September 1984).

J. Y. Ra

UN RESOLUTION OF OCTOBER 21, 1949

Because of this resolution, UN representatives were present in Korea when the war began, and the UNCOK report on the North Korean attack* would provide evidence to justify passage of the UN Security Council resolution of June 27, 1950*. After the UN General Assembly recognized the Republic of Korea* as the only legitimate government on the Korean peninsula in the UN resolution of December 12, 1948*, the Truman administration pressed for the ROK's admission to the international organization. In February 1949, both the ROK and the Democratic People's Republic of Korea* made application for membership. Despite Soviet objections, the UN Security Council referred only the ROK's application to the UN Membership Committee. When the UN Membership Committee recommended approval, Moscow cast a veto on April 8 blocking the ROK's admission. Nevertheless, the UNCOK stayed in South Korea, submitting a report on progress toward peaceful reunification in September 1949. The commission informed the UN that without a Soviet-U.S. agreement, Korea never would reunify and probably would experience a barbarous civil war. The UNCOK blamed both the Soviet Union and the United States for posturing instead of working for a resolution of the impasse. These findings upset the Truman administration, as did the commission's criticism of ROK President Syngman Rhee* as an authoritarian leader.

Secretary of State Dean G. Acheson* was unhappy with the contents of the UN-

COK report but cleverly devised a strategy to use it for the creation of a new commission with expanded powers. Since there was a threat of war in Korea, international representatives had to be on the scene to observe and report any military activity leading to the outbreak of hostilities. On September 26, the United States, the Philippines, Australia, and the Republic of China* jointly submitted a resolution to the UN Ad Hoc Political Committee providing for maintaining a commission in Korea to observe conditions and report any developments "which might lead to or otherwise involve military conflict." Rather than merely being available for consultations, the new UNCOK would offer its "good offices" formally to both the ROK and the DPRK to achieve reunification. Moreover, the commission would be available to verify Soviet military withdrawal from Korea*.

On October 3, the Ad Hoc Committee overwhelmingly recommended adoption of the resolution, while rejecting a Soviet proposal to abolish the UNCOK and declare its prior activities an illegal interference in Korean internal affairs. The UN General Assembly on October 21 approved the U.S.-sponsored resolution by a wide margin. In February 1950, the new UNCOK, with Turkey replacing Syria, arrived in Korea and attempted to contact DPRK representatives at the thirty-eighth parallel, but North Korean soldiers fired on the commission members. Nervous about the possibility of invasion, the UNCOK requested trained military observers to monitor developments on the peninsula. UN Secretary-General Tryve Lie* complied, dispatching a team of eight experts to assist the commission in its efforts to fulfill the mission outlined for the UNCOK in the October 21 resolution.

Foreign Relations of the United States, 1949, vol. 7: *The Far East and Australasia*, pt. 2 (Washington, D.C., 1976) and *1950*, vol. 7: *Korea* (Washington, D.C., 1976); J. I. Matray, *The Reluctant Crusade* (Honolulu, 1985); *New York Times*, February 3, 12, 17, 1949.

UN SECURITY COUNCIL RESOLUTION OF JULY 7, 1950

This resolution established a unified command for UN forces in Korea under the direct administration of the United States. In recognition of the support for the UN Security Council resolutions of June 25* and June 27, 1950*, the council adopted formal measures outlining organization and management procedures for UN troops in Korea. All members of the UN offering military aid and assistance to the Republic of Korea* were united under U.S. authority. This new United Nations Command* (UNC), directed by a U.S.-appointed commander (CINCFE General Douglas MacArthur*), was authorized to use the UN flag in military operations. Although the UN Security Council also requested plans and progress reports, no provision was made for continuing UN supervision of military operations in Korea. In retrospect, by not stating guidelines and expectations and thus installing a more specific system of checks and balances, the UN Security Council left the conduct of UN military activities in Korea entirely to the U.S. government. *See also* MacArthur's Periodic Reports to the Security Council.

J. L. Collins, *War in Peacetime* (Boston, 1969); A. W. Cordier and W. Foote (eds.), *Public Papers of the Secretaries-General of the United Nations*, vol. 1: *Trygve Lie, 1946–1953* (New York, 1969); *Foreign Relations of the United States, 1950*, vol. 7: *Korea*

(Washington, D.C., 1976); L. M. Goodrich, *Korea: A Study of U.S. Policy in the U.N.* (New York, 1956).

John Neilson

UN SECURITY COUNCIL RESOLUTION OF JUNE 25, 1950

This resolution was the UN's initial response to the North Korean invasion of South Korea* and, with a further resolution two days later, provided the legal basis for UN intervention in the conflict. The UN Security Council met during the afternoon of June 25 (New York time) at the instigation of the United States, though with the UN Commission on Korea (UNCOK) urging similar action. At that time, the body consisted of representatives from the Republic of China*, Cuba, Equador, Egypt, France, India, Norway, the United Kingdom, the United States, and Yugoslavia. The Soviet Union also was a member but was then boycotting the UN Security Council's meetings. Sir Benegal N. Rau* of India was the UN Security Council's president that month. Seeing with grave concern "the armed attack upon the Republic of Korea* by forces from North Korea," it declared North Korea's action to constitute "a breach of the peace," calling for an "immediate cessation of hostilities" and for North Korea "to withdraw forthwith" north of the thirty-eighth parallel. In addition, it requested the UN-COK to submit its recommendations and to keep the UN Security Council informed of developments. Members were urged to render "every assistance" to the UN in the execution of the resolution and to refrain from assisting the Democratic People's Republic of Korea*

The resolution was a diplomatic triumph for the United States. Although there were other possible approaches to the situation, such as under U.S. responsibilities as an occupying power pending the peace settlement with Japan, successful recourse to the UN Security Council ensured wide international backing for U.S. policy. U.S. determination to support South Korea was matched by that of UN Secretary-General Trygve Lie*, who saw disaster for the UN in a failure to do so. Before the meeting, he was an active lobbyist in support of the U.S. draft resolution, particularly among delegations uneasy with the wording, which referred to "an unprovoked act of aggression" (removed from the final version). Lie also made a strong speech when the council met. But all this effort would have been in vain had it not been for the Soviet UN Security Council boycott* since January 1950 because of the failure to seat the People's Republic of China*. The Soviet delegate, Jacob A. Malik*, did not attend the meeting where he might have vetoed the resolution (though action would undoubtedly have been taken in the UN General Assembly had he done so). It was left to Yugoslavia's Ales Bebler* to provide the only serious resistance to the U.S. proposal, urging unsuccessfully that North Korea be heard and abstaining from voting for the resolution, which was adopted by a 9–0 vote. *See also* First Blair House Meeting; UN Security Council Resolution of June 27, 1950.

D. Acheson, *Present at the Creation* (New York, 1969); *Foreign Relations of the United States, 1950*, vol. 7: *Korea* (Washington, D.C., 1976); L. M. Goodrich, *Korea: A Study of U.S. Policy in the U.N.* (New York, 1956); F. H. Heller (ed.), *The Korean*

War: A 25-Year Perspective (Lawrence, Ks., 1977); T. Lie, *In the Cause of Peace* (New York, 1954).

Ian C. McGibbon

UN SECURITY COUNCIL RESOLUTION OF JUNE 27, 1950

This resolution reinforced the action taken by the UN Security Council two days before by calling upon members for assistance in repelling the North Koreans, who, far from heeding the Security Council's call for withdrawal north of the thirty-eighth parallel, had pressed on with their offensive. As evidence mounted on June 26 that, contrary to hopes in Washington, South Korea could not throw back the invader unaided, the United States moved toward providing direct military assistance. Although such action was possible under the UN Security Council resolution of June 25, 1950*, President Harry S. Truman* accepted Secretary of State Dean G. Acheson's* recommendation at the second Blair House meeting* that a new resolution be submitted to the UN Security Council the next day with a view to reinforcing international support for the measures the United States intended to take and which were announced in Truman's statement of June 27, 1950*. When the Security Council met at 3 P.M., it had not only evidence of U.S. determination to act—the announcement had been deliberately made before the meeting—but also three communications from the UNCOK, including one suggesting urgent attempts to mediate and the most recent reporting its view that the Democratic People's Republic of Korea* was carrying out a "well-planned, concerted, and full-scale invasion of South Korea."

Although the U.S. draft resolution was supported by sufficient delegations to secure its passage (members then were the Republic of China*, Cuba, Equador, Egypt, France, India, Norway, the Soviet Union, the United Kingdom, the United States, and Yugoslavia), voting was delayed in the hope that the Indian and Egyptian delegates would receive instructions allowing them also to vote in favor. When, after an adjournment of more than five hours, such approval was not forthcoming, the council proceeded to adopt the resolution without amendment just before midnight. Members were urged to "furnish such assistance to the Republic of Korea* as may be necessary to repel the armed attack and to restore international peace and security in the area"—the recommendatory nature of the resolution necessitated by the failure to implement the provisions of the UN Charter giving the UN Security Council power to command action. With the Soviet Union still absent, Joseph Stalin* having rejected Foreign Ministry advice that the Soviet representative, Jacob A. Malik*, be instructed to attend, the only opposing vote was cast by Ales Bebler* of Yugoslavia, who put forward an alternative suggestion for mediation. The resolution's seven affirmative votes were reinforced by India's later announcement that it supported the resolution.

Subsequently, the Soviet Union maintained that the resolution had not passed because one of the seven votes was that of the Republic of China and that neither the Soviet Union nor the People's Republic of China*, as permanent members of the Council, had exercised their votes in favor of it. The Security Council's action was denounced as interference in the domestic affairs of Korea. These charges were firmly rejected by UN Secretary-General Trygve Lie* who lost no time in calling on members to provide assistance to the UN in terms of the resolution. *See also* UNCOK Report on North Korean Attack; Soviet UN Security Council Boycott.

D. Acheson, *Present at the Creation* (New York, 1969); *Foreign Relations of the United States, 1950,* vol. 7: *Korea* (Washington, D.C., 1976); L. M. Goodrich, *Korea: A Study of U.S. Policy in the U.N.* (New York, 1956); A. A. Gromyko, *Memories* (London, 1989).

Ian C. McGibbon

UN SECURITY COUNCIL RESOLUTION OF NOVEMBER 8, 1950
See UN Invitation to PRC to Participate in Debate

UN TEMPORARY COMMISSION ON KOREA
See UN Resolution of November 14, 1947

UN UNITING FOR PEACE RESOLUTION OF NOVEMBER 3, 1950

This resolution was the result of U.S. efforts to ensure that the veto provision in the UN Charter would not prevent international action to counter aggression following the return of the Soviet representative to discussions at the UN Security Council. Warren R. Austin*, the permanent U.S. representative at the UN, responded on July 27 to a suggestion from the State Department that commissions similar to the UNCOK would be beneficial for monitoring developments in trouble spots such as Yugoslavia. Austin recommended that the UN Security Council set up an observation commission with authority to visit an area where peace was threatened rather than a separate special commission for each emerging trouble spot. Secretary of State Dean G. Acheson* agreed with Austin and the next day sent a draft resolution calling for the establishment of a Security Council Fact-Finding and Observation Commission to Britain and France requesting comments. The British and French were quite apprehensive about the proposal because they believed it left too much initiative to the commission, seemed to bypass the Security Council, and did not follow the letter of the UN Charter. They were also worried that with the end of the Soviet UN Security Council boycott* on August 1, Moscow would surely use the proposal for propaganda value.

Lacking allied support, Acheson decided against introducing the resolution. But he made clear that the United States would continue to study methods for strengthening the peacekeeping abilities of the UN, including the possibility of using the General Assembly where peace was threatened if the Security Council proved unable to act. By August 9, Acheson had decided to introduce a resolution to achieve this purpose through the General Assembly. The Fifth UN General Assembly, he cabled London, could offer a unique opportunity for utilizing the lessons and psychological impact of Korean crisis "to strengthen UN system in order to meet possible future cases of aggression.'' Acheson believed that the General Assembly had both the obligation and the authority to act against aggression if the Security Council was paralyzed by a veto. Since UN action in Korea was possible only because the Soviets were boycotting, it was clear that a mechanism was necessary to prevent Moscow from creating a stalemate at the UN in situations similar to Korea.

At the opening of the Fifth UN General Assembly on September 19, the United States submitted for the agenda its proposal United Action for Peace. The British continued to express their concern, claiming the proposal did not follow the strict reading of the UN Charter. The French were leery about giving the initiative to the General Assembly because of its size and its ''occasional irresponsibility.'' Finally, toward the end of the month, the United States gained ''lukewarm'' allied support for its proposal. On September 25, it sent the text of its slightly redrafted resolution, Uniting for Peace, to other friendly delegations. By October 3, negotiations had produced agreement on a resolution that would have seven cosponsors: the United States, Britain, France, Canada, Turkey, Uruguay, and the Philippines. After the First Committee reviewed it and considered amendments, the UN General Assembly approved the Uniting for Peace resolution on November 3 by a vote of 52 to 5, with 2 abstentions. It had four major provisions. First, it authorized the calling of an emergency session of the UN General Assembly within twenty-four hours by agreement of a majority of the members. Second, it established a UN Peace Observation Commission to provide independent information about areas that threatened the international peace. Third, each member was encouraged to designate a portion of its armed forces for use as a UN unit to maintain the peace when suggested by the UN Security Council or the UN General Assembly. Finally, it provided for the formation of a committee that would advise the UN on how best to organize and use what was made available for collective action.

D. Acheson, *Present at the Creation* (New York, 1969); *Foreign Relations of the United States, 1950*, vol. 2: *The United Nations: The Western Hemisphere* (Washington, D.C., 1976); Tae-ho Yoo, *The Korean War and the United Nations* (Louvain, 1965).

Paul J. Morton

UNC FINAL POW SETTLEMENT PROPOSAL OF MAY 25, 1953

This formula represented the last UNC* effort to resolve the stalemate at the P'anmunjŏm truce talks* on agenda item 4*, POW repatriation. It came after the Communists rejected a UNC counterproposal to the Communist POW settlement proposal of May 7, 1953*. This UNC plan of May 13 accepted the creation of a Neutral Nations Repatriation Commission* (NNRC) to assume custody of non-repatriate POWs after the armistice but insisted that the NNRC must reach decisions on the basis of unanimity. Only the Chinese non-repatriates were to be turned over to the NNRC for explanations, the Korean non-repatriates being released as civilians on the signature of the armistice. The NNRC was to hold POWs for sixty days, after which they were to be released as civilians.

Indian troops alone were to guard the prisoners on behalf of the NNRC rather than a mixed force including soldiers from Czechoslovakia and Poland. These terms were condemned by the Communists as a step backward, and the negotiations faced deadlock.

The proposal seemed to depart from the terms of the UN resolution of December 3, 1952*, on POWs, and Washington was under great pressure from its allies to modify its position rather than risk a breakdown at P'anmunjŏm. On May 25, 1953, the chief UNC delegate, Major General William K. Harrison, Jr.*, put forward the final position of his side on the POW issue. The NNRC was to reach its decisions by a majority vote and was to assume custody of both Chinese and Korean non-repatriates. Ninety days were to be set aside for explanations, and the fate of any remaining non-repatriates after this period would be considered by the political conference to be held under Article 4 of the armistice agreement*. If no solution emerged within 120 days of the NNRC's assuming custody, the prisoners were to be released or the issue referred to the UN General Assembly. The NNRC was to release non-repatriate POWs and dissolve itself after 120 days if no other disposition of the prisoners had been agreed by the political conference. After the Communist delegation accepted this proposal, the final Terms of Reference were signed on June 8. This outcome caused a crisis with President Syngman Rhee* of the Republic of Korea*, who, with his unilateral release of North Korean POWs* on June 18, sought to sabotage the armistice. *See also* Dulles's Atomic Warning to China; Truce Talks Resumption of April 26, 1953.

M. W. Clark, *From the Danube to the Yalu* (London, 1954); W. G. Hermes, *Truce Tent and Fighting Front* (Washington, D.C. 1966); B. I. Kaufman, *The Korean War* (Philadelphia, 1986).

Callum A. MacDonald

UNC POW ADMINISTRATION

During the Korean War, the UNC's* administration of prisoners of war played a central role in the controversy at the P'anmunjŏm truce talks* over agenda item 4*, repatriation of POWs. Both the Communists and the UNC sought to exploit the issue to gain a propaganda advantage, delaying the achievement of an armistice for more than a year. The UNC's problems with the POWs began when it captured an unexpectedly large number of North Koreans during a short span of time after the Inch'ŏn landing*. On September 26, 1950, the 8th Army* assumed control over the administration of the prisoners. Washington wanted to comply with the Geneva Convention of 1949* and ensure humane treatment to prevent reprisals against captured UNC personnel, as well as winning the hearts and minds of the North Korean prisoners in anticipation of unification. By November 1950, the 8th Army held about 137,000 POWs in makeshift camps, but lacked the manpower to provide enough guards and allowed the passive prisoners, who thought the war was near an end, to run their own affairs. Conditions in these camps were awful, as POWs went without food, water, clothing, or medical care. Disease was prevalent and most prisoners suffered from malnutrition, while racist U.S. guards often practiced brutality against the "gooks."

Chinese military intervention* forced the UNC to devote more serious attention to the POW problem. Lieutenant General Matthew B. Ridgway* saw that the poorly supervised prisoners constituted a serious threat to his retreating 8th Army. Thus, he implemented Operation Albany, evacuating the POWs to Kŏje-do, an island twenty miles southwest of Pusan. Although conditions improved somewhat after the UNC constructed a permanent network of compounds, life was far from pleasant on what U.S. guards referred to as Beggar's Island. After the Chinese spring offensives of 1951*, about 2,000 new POWs arrived daily on Kŏje-do. Before long, over 130,000 Koreans and 20,000 Chinese crowded together in compounds intended to house between 700 and 1,200 prisoners, but actually holding roughly five times that number. Soon, poor sanitation, inadequate lodging and heating, inferior food, and the lack of proper medical care produced a rising incidence of dysentery, malaria, tuberculosis, and pneumonia. By December 1951, 6,000 Communist prisoners of war had died.

Meanwhile, the UNC was unable to provide adequate security, relying for guards on South Koreans to free U.S. soldiers for duty at the front. Lacking any training and disliking their task, guards confiscated the personal possessions of POWs and often shot prisoners for minor offenses such as singing, shouting insults, or throwing stones. The small number of U.S. military policemen on Kŏje were of inferior quality and there was a high turnover of camp commanders. Discipline was lax and morale among the officers was low. These personnel problems forced the UNC to rely on prisoner cooperation. Compound representatives maintained discipline, distributed supplies, and served as liaisons with the UNC administration. Since guards rarely entered the POW enclosures, political struggle rather than military discipline dominated camp life. Not all Korean prisoners were the same. Some were anti-Communists who had deserted to the UNC at the first chance, others were dedicated party members, and many were simply peasant conscripts without political convictions. Since there had been no effort made to segregate the prisoners, a bitter contest for political control emerged in each compound.

In the Korean Communist compounds, party cadre immediately exercised leadership and established an elaborate system of communications linking the compounds to each other and, through refugees on Kŏje-do, to the North Korean high command. They used threats, violence, and kangaroo courts to maintain discipline. Anti-Communist compounds held the majority of the Korean POWs. There, self-styled "youth leagues," following an existing pattern in South Korean society, exercised authority. Nightly beatings of those resisting control were routine. A special section of the War Ministry of the Republic of Korea* advised the "youth leagues," which received enthusiastic support from anti-Communist guards. In the Chinese camps, former Kuomintang soldiers, who the Communists had conscripted but remained loyal to Chiang Kai-shek*, provided leadership because the UNC chose them as "trusties." In addition to "beatings, torture, and threats of punishment," these Chinese trusties exploited their control over food, clothes, fuel, and access to medical treatment to force allegience.

Anti-Communist Chinese POW leaders maintained close contact with the Republic of China* through Kuomintang personnel who the UNC had brought to Kŏje-do. Following the example of Communist POW administration* but in reverse, the UNC wanted to demonstrate to their prisoners the bankruptcy of communism and the virtues of capitalism. Modeled on a pilot project implemented in September 1950, a new education and indoctrination program for all POWs became mandatory in April 1951, employing lectures, films, and assorted reading material to inculcate western concepts of democracy and justice. Along with religious services containing a heavy political message, there were literacy classes, as well as vocational training. Since NSC–48/5* had identified as a foreign policy aim creating domestic opposition to Communist rule, these efforts probably were not intended to persuade the POWs to refuse repatriation, but to return home after the war and create internal political unrest. But to administer the program, the UNC relied on more than seventy Chinese from Taiwan, who, according to U.S. ambassador John J. Muccio*, were "doubtless members of Chiang Kai-shek's Gestapo." Along with 2,500 recruits from the POWs, they reinforced the anti-Communist leadership in the POW compounds and shifted the reeducation program to increasingly focus on repatriation to Taiwan. Vice-Admiral C. Turner Joy*, the UNC's chief negotiator at P'anmunjŏm, later recalled one occasion when prisoners were asked to decide whether they wished to be repatriated to the mainland, "those doing so were either beaten black and blue or killed. . . . [Most] of the POWs were too terrified to frankly express their real choice. All they could say in answer to the question was 'Taiwan' repeated over and over again."

Conditions in the Communist compounds meant that UNC control was a virtual impossibility, while almost guaranteeing clashes between guards and POWs. As early as August 1951, a clash ended in the killing of three prisoners. However, camp administration encouraged the political unrest. For example, the anti-Communist POWs were able to hold demonstrations, fly national flags, celebrate national days, and display signs and placards proclaiming "Kick out the Communists." By contrast, the UNC used violence and shootings to end similar activity in the Communist Chinese and North Korean compounds. Such provocative behavior fueled a pattern of rising bloodshed on Kŏje-do. On February 18, 1952, 1,500 POWs used homemade weapons, including iron bars, clubs, and barbed wire, to attack guards entering their compound. Efforts to restore order led in the killing of 77 POWs and the wounding of 140 others. Similar prisoner riots took place in the weeks that followed.

Communist negotiators at P'anmunjŏm pointed to these incidents as proof of the barbarous treatment of POWs in the UNC camps. Ridgway warned the JCS that "a potentially explosive atmosphere" existed at Kŏje-do which was "capable of developing to such a point [that] it might result in heavy loss of life and great discredit to the US and the UNC.'' Despite these warnings, the UNC proceeded with Operation Scatter* in April 1952, which set the stage for the Dodd-Colson incident* and the Kŏje-do POW uprising*. Subsequently, the UNC moved the Korean non-repatriates to the mainland and the Chinese prisoners to other islands. The Cheju-do POW uprising* and the Pongam-do POW uprising* during late 1952 and Syngman Rhee's* release of North Korean POWs* in June 1953 showed that the UNC never was able to resolve the problems plaguing its administration of POWs. *See also* Rescreening of POWs; Voluntary Repatriation.

R. Foot, *A Substitute for Victory* (Ithaca, N.Y., 1990); J. Halliday and B. Cumings, *Korea: The Unknown War* (New York, 1989); W. G. Hermes, *Truce Tent and Fighting Front* (Washington, D.C., 1966); B. I. Kaufman, *The Korean War* (Philadelphia, 1986); C. A. MacDonald, *Korea: The War Before Vietnam* (New York, 1986).

UNCOK REPORT ON NORTH KOREAN ATTACK (June 26, 1950)

This report by UNCOK observers on military activity along the thirty-eighth parallel immediately prior to the outbreak of the Korean War later provided key evidence for the UN that the Democratic People's Republic of Korea* had initiated hostilities. At that time, the only members of the UNCOK military observers' team to have arrived in Korea were two Australians, squadron leader R. J. Rankin and Major F. S. B. Peach. These men made an inspection tour along the thirty-eighth parallel between June 9 and 23 in order to report to the commission the general military situation between the two zones. They reported no evidence of extensive military activity north of the parallel on the part of Republic of Korea's* forces and found that the general state of material preparedness of those forces did not support the view that they were planning any large-scale military activity in the near future. The attitude of the South Korean commanders was one of "vigilant defense," while there was clear evidence that units of the North Korean People's Army (NKPA) had established salients south of the thirty-eighth parallel in a number of areas.

The report was drafted on June 24 in Seoul but was not given wide circulation at that stage because of the rapid turn of events. The report was delivered to a meeting of the commission on June 26 and a precis cabled by the commission to Secretary-General Trygve Lie* on the same day, later reproduced as UN Security Council document S/1507, dated June 26, 1950. The report was given further consideration by members of the commission on June 29, after they had been evacuated from Seoul, and further decisions arising from those deliberations were also cabled to the UN Security Council and reproduced as UN Security Council document S/1518, dated June 29. It was on the basis of this report and the conclusions of UNCOK that arose from it that the Security Council determined that an act of aggression had been committed by the DPRK against the south, leading to passage of the UN Security Council resolution of June 27, 1950*, and from which all other UN intervention stemmed. The Peach-Rankin field trip accordingly may be described as one of the most momentous reconnaissance missions in recent history. *See also* North Korean Invasion of South Korea; UN Resolution of October 21, 1949.

F. S. B. Peach, "Cold War Hot War: A Review Article," *Defense Force Journal* (January/February 1986); R. J. O'Neill, *Australia in the Korean War 1950–53* (Canberra, 1981).

Jeffrey Grey

UNITED NATIONS COMMAND

This was the official title of the UN military force during the Korean War. The UN Security Council resolution of June 27, 1950*, asked its membership to support the Republic of Korea* against the invasion from North Korea. Ten days later, France and Britain sponsored the UN Security Council resolution of July 7, 1950*, that allowed for the consolidation of the UN forces in Korea under the United Nations Command (UNC). The United States was asked to name a commander (CINCFE General Douglas MacArthur*), who would report on developments to the UN. One week later, ROK forces were also placed under MacArthur with an exchange of letters that was later confused with the Taejŏn Agreement*.

By the middle of September, fifteen nations had contributed ground forces to the UNC. The UNC commander had control over the military forces of the contributing states with regard to military operation decisions and movements, but these national forces remained under their own discipline and regulations and were allowed to maintain contact with their own government regarding procedural questions. Reports on activities of the UNC were sent to the UN Security Council. In practice, however, this was not done until MacArthur's periodic reports to the UN Security Council* had first gone through the appropriate authorities in Washington. A UN Reception Center (UNRC) was established at Taegu University in October 1950. Its purpose was "to clothe, equip and provide familiarization training with U.S. Army weapons and equipment to UN troops as determined essential for operations in Korea." In the next eight months, troops from eight countries were processed through UNRC. British Commonwealth units did their own training and did not use the UNRC. The UNRC was also involved in retraining some U.S. troops and familiarizing U.S. and other UN commanders with combined allied forces before they went into battle.

Most UN units were available by the last months of 1950. Depending on their size, UN units were placed with U.S. regiments, corps, or divisions. A number of considerations were taken into account when placing UN units, though the most important factor usually remained the tactical situation. Gradually, to remove administrative and organizational stumbling blocks and to encourage morale and efficiency, the UNC decided to maintain UN units with the same U.S. unit. Decisions regarding all aspects of the UNC were dominated by the United States because of its overwhelming superiority in numbers committed to Korea as compared to any other UN member. The approximate breakdown of ROK and UNC forces combined for ground forces was: United States 50.3 percent; other UN member states, 9.6 percent; ROK, 40.1 percent. For naval forces, it was: United States, 85.9 percent; other UN member states, 6.7 percent; ROK, 7.4 percent. And for air forces, it was: United States, 93.4 percent; other member UN states, 1.0 percent; ROK, 5.6 percent.

During the three years and one month that marked the police action* in Korea, almost 160,000 casualties were suffered by the UNC, including over 50,000 deaths. Sixteen nations contributed military forces to the UNC: Australia, Belgium, Canada, Colombia, Ethiopia, France, Greece, Luxembourg, Netherlands, New Zealand, Philippines, Thailand, Turkey, South Africa, the United Kingdom, and the United States. Five nations contributed just medical units: Denmark, Italy, India, Norway, and Sweden. By the end of June 1951, the Eighth Army*, which constituted the ground weapon of the UNC in Korea, had a reported strength of 554,577 soldiers. Organized into 4 corps, seven of its 17 divisions were U.S. and the rest were from the ROK. In addition, there were 4 brigades, 1 separate regiment, and 9 separate battalions. The specific strength figures showed 253,250 U.S. troops, 28,061 other UN personnel, 260,548 ROK soldiers, and 12,718 Koreans who were part of the Korean Augmentation of the U.S. Army*. *See also* Colombian Battalion; Commonwealth Division; Logistical Reimbursement Issue; New Zealand and the Korean War; UN Appeals for Additional Troops.

B. F. Cooling, "Allied Interoperability in the Korean War," *Military Review* (June 1983); W. G. Hermes; *Truce Tent and Fighting Front* (Washington, D.C., 1966); P. Lowe, *The Origins of the Korean War* (New York, 1986); W. H. Vatcher, *Panmunjom: The Story of the Korean Military Armistice Negotiations* (New York, 1958); Tae-ho Yoo, *The Korean War and the United Nations* (Louvain, 1965).

                                                                    Paul J. Morton

"UNLEASHING" OF CHIANG (February 2, 1953)

This refers to President Dwight D. Eisenhower's* action ending the neutralization of Taiwan*. President Harry S. Truman's* June 27, 1950 directive that the 7th Fleet should protect Taiwan from any Communist invasion had also required the fleet to prevent Republic of China* attacks from Taiwan against the mainland. This aspect of the policy immediately became the target of intense criticism from Republican partisans and Chiang Kai-shek's* supporters. General Douglas MacArthur* called for its reversal during the MacArthur Hearings*, and John Foster Dulles* did so in a 1952 article, "A Policy of Boldness"*, in *Life*. Soon after Eisenhower assumed the presidency, he announced in his State of the Union address that he was "issuing instructions that the Seventh Fleet no longer be employed to shield Communist China." The instructions were issued in a directive of the same date to the CINCPAC, who assumed responsibility for the defense of Taiwan at this time.

Eisenhower later wrote that he was convinced that by increasing pressure on the People's Republic of China*, this step had helped to bring about a settlement in Korea, but historians have generally viewed it as a gesture to appease the Republican right wing. The policy change was symbolic rather than real. Truman's directive had not prevented Nationalist raids from the offshore islands, while Eisenhower had no intention of supporting a large-scale Nationalist attack on the mainland. Chargé Karl L. Rankin quickly obtained an informal assurance from Chiang that he would take no major action without consulting Washington. Two months later, at Washington's insistence, he obtained a formal commitment.

R. J. Caridi, *The Korean War and American Politics* (Philadelphia, 1968); D. D. Eisenhower, *Mandate for Change* (Garden City, N.Y., 1963); *Foreign Relations of the United States, 1952–1954,* vol. 14: *China and Japan,* pt. 1, (Washington, D.C., 1985); K. L. Rankin, *China Assignment* (Seattle, 1964).

Harriet D. Schwar

ŬNSAN, BATTLE OF

See Chinese Military Disengagement of November 6, 1950; UN Offensive across the Thirty-eighth Parallel

U.S. BOMBING OF SOVIET AIRFIELD INCIDENT (October 8, 1950)

On October 8, 1950, two U.S. jet fighter aircraft strafed a Soviet airfield in the Soviet Maritime Provinces near Sukhaya Rechk, about 60 miles north of the border between the Democratic People's Republic of Korea* and the Soviet Union. This attack, the result of navigational error, did considerable damage to Soviet aircraft on the ground. It was never determined whether there were Soviet casualties from the attack. U.S. officials in Washington and Tokyo did not learn of this attack until the Soviet government protested it. On October 10, the JCS ordered CINCUNC General Douglas MacArthur* to take "appropriate action" to ensure future compliance with their directives on operations near the Soviet border and instructed him to investigate the Soviet charges. His subsequent investigation showed that the attack had indeed occurred. The United States apologized on October 18, 1950, to the Soviet Union for the incident, explaining that it had resulted from faulty navigation and poor judgment. Disciplinary action had been taken against the two pilots involved, and the commander of their unit had been relieved. The United States expressed its deep regret and offered to pay for all damages to Soviet property. So far as can be determined, the Soviet Union did not acknowledge this offer. As a result of this incident, the Department of State proposed that a limiting line be established for U.S. air operations near the border. The JCS objected to such limitation. Secretary of Defense George C. Marshall* agreed and so informed the Department of State. The matter was dropped for the time being.

J. F. Schnabel, *Policy and Direction* (Washington, D.C., 1972); J. F. Schnabel and R. J. Watson, *History of the Joint Chiefs of Staff,* vol. 3: *The Korean War* (Wilmington, 1979).

James F. Schnabel

U.S. EVACUATION OF SEOUL (June 25–29, 1950)

The evacuation of American civilian personnel from the Republic of Korea* was about the only bright spot for the United States in the grim early days of the Korean War. An evacuation plan had been drawn up for an air and sea movement through a Seoul-Inch'ŏn route, but in the end, it was more often ad hoc improvisation that saved the day. As early as 10:00 P.M. on the first day of the North Korean invasion of South Korea*, Ambassador John J. Muccio* had ordered the evacuation to begin. By 9:00 A.M. the next day, all civilian evacuees had passed over the Han River bridges (blown up early on the morning of June 28 with catastrophic loss of life) and were subsequently embarked on an odoriferous Norwegian freighter whose fertilizer cargo had been hastily off-loaded. Enemy aircraft attempted to interfere with the American air evacuation but were shot out of the sky by covering U.S. fighters in the first air combat of the Korean War, as well as the first aerial clash between U.S. and Communist forces. By June 29, over 1,500 U.S. nationals had been evacuated, apparently without loss of life. *See also* Withdrawal from Seoul of June 1950.

R. E. Appleman, *South to the Naktong, North to the Yalu* (Washington, D.C., 1961); D. Detzer, *Thunder of the Captains* (New York, 1977); H. J. Noble, *Embassy as War* (Seattle, 1975); R. K. Sawyer and W. G. Hermes, *Military Advisors in Korea: KMAG in Peace and War* (Washington, D.C., 1962).

Stanley Sandler

U.S. MILITARY WITHDRAWAL FROM KOREA (June 29, 1949)

Withdrawal of the last U.S. forces from Korea ended a military occupation that had begun on September 8, 1945. Critics later would charge that this decision, coupled with Secretary of State Dean G. Acheson's* National Press Club speech*, gave a green light for the North Korean invasion of South Korea*. Yet disengagement came nearly two years after President Harry S. Truman* had received the JCS report on Korea's strategic significance*, advocating the prompt removal of U.S. troops. U.S. military leaders, including occupation commander Lieutenant General John R. Hodge*, in fact had begun to urge redeployment of the USAFIK almost from the moment of its arrival. The State Department, however, feared that leaving southern Korea would lead to Communist domination over the entire peninsula, thus damaging U.S. prestige and credibility in Asia. Attempting to achieve withdrawal without abandonment, Truman referred the Korean issue to the United Nations after the Soviets blocked reunification on U.S. terms. The UN resolution of November 14, 1947*, called for Soviet-U.S. military withdrawal following supervised elections. In April 1948, Truman approved NSC-8*, providing for the departure of U.S. troops before the year ended. But U.S. military planners wanted to leave sooner, setting November 15 as a target date—ninety days after the scheduled establishment of the Republic of Korea*. During June, the Army Department approved the shipment of six months of military supplies for the ROK's army. By the end of July, the United States had evacuated its last military dependents from Korea.

Several factors explain Truman's decision to postpone U.S. military disengagement from Korea until June 1949. First, the ROK's newly elected president, Syngman Rhee*, urged Washington to delay withdrawal until South Korea had the capacity to defend itself. Second, after Communist leaders in the north had built a large army and established the Democratic People's Republic of Korea*,

Joseph Stalin* announced that Soviet military withdrawal from Korea* would occur before the end of 1948. Third, and most important, the outbreak in South Korea of the Yŏsu-Sunch'ŏn rebellion* in October indicated that if U.S. troops left on schedule, the ROK would collapse quickly. Although Truman halted withdrawal in November, he understood that continued U.S. occupation gave credence to the Soviet claim that the ROK was illegitimate. Thus, in March 1949, the president approved NSC-8/2*, which provided for complete U.S. withdrawal no later than June 30 but only after the Rhee government had received sufficient military aid to build an army capable of defending the ROK. Rhee tried to delay disengagement throughout the spring of 1949 but without success. To reassure the South Koreans, the U.S. established a Korean Military Advisory Group* to improve the effectiveness of the ROK's army. This, along with Truman's subsequent efforts to obtain congressional approval for both military and economic assistance to South Korea, showed that U.S. military withdrawal was not an act of abandonment. Rather, the Truman administration was confident that with U.S. help, the ROK would be able to defend itself, thereby confirming its legitimacy. *See also* Korean Aid Bill of 1949–1950.

C. M. Dobbs, *The Unwanted Symbol* (Kent, Ohio, 1981); *Foreign Relations of the United States, 1947*, vol. 6: *The Far East* (Washington, D.C., 1972), *1948*, vol. 6: *The Far East and Australasia* (Washington, D.C., 1974), and *1949*, vol. 7: *The Far East and Australasia*, pt. 2 (Washington, D.C., 1976); J. I. Matray, *The Reluctant Crusade* (Honolulu, 1985); W. W. Stueck, *The Road to Confrontation* (Chapel Hill, 1981).

U.S.-ROK EXPENDITURES AGREEMENT OF JULY 28, 1950
See Suspense Account Controversy

U.S.-ROK MUTUAL DEFENSE TREATY (January 26, 1954)
The mutual defense treaty between the Republic of Korea* and the United States, ratified in January 1954, had a long, uncertain gestation. Its origins derived from ROK President Syngman Rhee's* threat to disrupt any armistice unless the United States made a formal commitment to guarantee South Korea's security and to compel the withdrawal of the Chinese People's Volunteers Army* from the peninsula. Washington had resisted Rhee's clamor for a bilateral defense pact because of the possible political difficulties of involving Congress, because it would weaken the Joint Policy (Greater Sanctions) statement* already approved, and, no doubt, because such an arrangement would tend to strengthen Rhee's authoritarian regime. But efforts to bribe Rhee with promises of lavish U.S. military aid for creation of a twenty-division ROK army failed. Relations in fact deteriorated to the point that CINCUNC General Mark W. Clark* revived Operation Everready*, a plan envisioning occupation of Seoul and establishment of a military government by the UNC*.

Finally, the Eisenhower administration agreed to meet Rhee's demand for a mutual security treaty. Justifying the policy change by linking such a pact with the ANZUS Treaty* and a similar arrangement with the Philippines, Secretary of State John Foster Dulles* met with Rhee in August 1953. With each side professing domestic political difficulties, Rhee capitulated on the issue of not undermining the armistice agreement*, and the mutual defense treaty was signed on August 8, 1953. Comprised of six articles, the U.S.-ROK Mutual Defense Treaty affirmed that each signatory would view an armed attack on the other in the Pacific area "as dangerous to its own peace and safety and declares that it would act to meet the common danger in accordance with its constitutional processes." Although the pact avoided the language of automatic response, this pledge meant that the United States had accepted, however reluctantly, unilateral responsibility for South Korea's security. Some thirty-five years later, U.S. forces remain in Korea as a result of that commitment. *See also* Dulles-Rhee Correspondence; NSC-156/1; NSC 157/1; Robertson Mission.

S. E. Ambrose, *Eisenhower, the President* (New York, 1984); B. I. Kaufman, *The Korean War* (Philadelphia 1986); Chang-il Ohn, *"The Joint Chiefs of Staff and U.S. Policy and Strategy Regarding Korea, 1945–1953"* (Ph.D. dissertation, University of Kansas, 1982).

Theodore A. Wilson

V

VAN FLEET, JAMES A. (1892–   )

General James Alward Van Fleet succeeded Lieutenant General Matthew B. Ridgway* as commander of the 8th Army* in Korea in April 1951 following Harry S. Truman's* recall of CINCUNC General Douglas MacArthur*. Van Fleet was born in Coytesville, New Jersey. After his graduation from the U.S. Military Academy in 1915, he served in the Mexican Border Campaign (1916–1917). When the United States entered World War II, Van Fleet held an assignment to the 8th Infantry Division. He moved to the 2d Division briefly in 1944, then commanding the 20th Division (1944–1945) and XXIII Corps (1945–1946). In 1947, Van Fleet became deputy chief of staff of the European Command at Frankfurt, Germany. From 1948 until 1950, he directed the joint military aid groups in Greece.

In Korea, Van Fleet inherited a stable battle line in the vicinity of the thirty-eighth parallel and a policy designed to strengthen that line against further attacks from the north. He was not to order an advance without specific orders from Tokyo, because, as Ridgway cautioned Van Fleet on April 25, the possibility always existed for an expansion of the Korean War into a worldwide conflagration. That possibility placed heavy responsibility on all officers capable of engaging in offensive operations. Early in his new command, Van Fleet, joined by Ridgway, pressed President Syngman Rhee* of the Republic of Korea* to reorganize and reform the South Korean military. Under Van Fleet's intensive training program, the South Korean army developed into an effective fighting force. By the end of 1952, almost three-fourths of Van Fleet's front-line troops were Korean.

During July 1951, the Kaesŏng truce talks* opened, but neither these negotiations nor fierce fighting ended the stalemated war. The battlefront soon resembled that of World War I, with deep implacements and trenches, barbed-wire fences, and well-protected outposts where the fighting was continuous and costly. Some critics of U.S. policy in Korea advocated a drive to the Yalu in pursuit of victory and a united Korea. At first, Van Fleet was not among them.

In time, however, he became frustrated by the limitations placed on his military operations. He complained that the static war was slowly destroying the morale of his troops. He endlessly planned offensives, only to have them rejected. Van Fleet left Korea in the spring of 1953 and resigned from the armed forces. Upon his return to the United States, he wrote two long articles for the May 11 and May 18 issues of *Life* magazine in which he argued that the United States could achieve total victory in Korea easily and cheaply if it chose to do so.

C. Blair, *The Forgotten War* (New York, 1987); C. A. MacDonald, *Korea: The War Before Vietnam* (New York, 1986); M. B. Ridgway, *The Korean War* (Garden City, N.Y., 1967).

Norman A. Graebner

VANDENBERG, HOYT S. (1899–1954)

Hoyt Sanford Vandenberg was chief of staff, U.S. Air Force, during the Korean War. Born in Milwaukee, Wisconsin, he was the nephew of Senator Arthur H. Vandenberg (Republican, of Michigan), who had cooperated with the Truman administration in matters of foreign policy. A widespread suspicion that he owed his appointment as air force chief staff in 1948 to his uncle's influence apparently had no foundation. Vandenberg, who ranked near the bottom of his class, entered the air service on graduating from the U.S. Military Academy at West Point in 1923, then earned a reputation as a ''hot pilot.'' In the European theater during World War II, he won acclaim for his skill in organizing and commanding tactical air forces. When promoted to full general in 1948, he was the youngest four-star officer in the national military-naval establishment.

A participant in both the first and second Blair House meetings*, Vandenberg opined that U.S. warplanes could knock out North Korea's tanks provided the Soviet air force stayed clear of the war. When President Harry S. Truman* determined to project U.S. air and naval power into the war, Vandenberg set about to strengthen what he would later describe in the MacArthur Hearings* as ''a shoestring air force'' that relied heavily on equipment left over from World War II. Persuaded that the U.S. Air Force could not meet global responsibilities if ordered to undertake a dramatic expansion of operations in East Asia, Vandenberg looked askance on CINCUNC General Douglas MacArthur's* appeals for adoption of his plan for victory* that provided for the UNC* to carry the war to the People's Republic of China*.

Overshadowed by Generals Omar N. Bradley* and J. Lawton Collins*, Vandenberg was an active and cooperative member of the JCS. He traveled with Collins to Tokyo in July 1950 and again in January 1951. He supported Truman's recall of MacArthur* and during the MacArthur Hearings gave perhaps the most impressive testimony in opposition to MacArthur's ideas about conducting a strategic bombing campaign against the PRC. The attrition resulting from such a campaign, he said, would leave the United States ''naked for several years to come.''

Vandenberg made yet another trip to East Asia in autumn 1951 and expressed dismay at the recent buildup of the Chinese air force. "Almost overnight," he told reporters, "Communist China has become one of the major air powers of the world." To retain the UNC's aerial supremacy, he ordered the shipment of scores of F-86 Sabre jets to Korea. As a consequence of impressive victories in a succession of classic aerial battles, the Sabres and their pilots terminated the threat that China's MiG fighters might gain command of the air over Korea. In May 1952, Vandenberg became gravely ill and General Nathan F. Twining* served as acting chief of staff for the next four months. When Vandenberg retired in May 1953, Twining replaced him. When the war ended in July 1953, he believed the U.S. Air Force had met the trial or test of battle magnificently.

See also Collins-Vandenberg Visit to Tokyo (January 15, 1951); Collins-Vandenberg Visit to Tokyo (July 13–14, 1950).

Current Biography, 1946; R. F. Futrell, *The United States Air Force in Korea* (New York, 1961); J. C. Goulden, *Korea: The Untold Story of the Korean War* (New York, 1982); *New York Times,* April 3, 1954; J. F. Schnabel, *Policy and Direction* (Washington, D.C., 1972).

John Edward Wilz

VOLUNTARY REPATRIATION

The U.S. decision that it would not allow force to be used to return home the POWs in its custody was controversial for three main reasons: because of the policy's doubtful compatibility with the Geneva Convention of 1949*; because conditions within UNC* POW compounds were not conducive to the making of a genuine choice concerning repatriation wishes; and because the impasse this position created regarding agenda item 4*, POW repatriation, caused a long delay in the conclusion of the Korean conflict, with all that meant for the UNC POWs held in Communist compounds and for the men who were fighting and dying at the front.

The Truman administration debated the policy of voluntary repatriation (or non-forcible repatriation, as it came to be called) intermittently between July 1951 and late February 1952 when it was finally decided to adopt this position for humanitarian and propaganda reasons. The U.S. public and the international community were informed that any use of force to repatriate prisoners in UNC hands would be "repugnant to the fundamental moral and humanitarian principles which underlie our action in Korea." On other occasions, the psychological warfare aspects of the policy were given greater emphasis when the position was projected as a valuable adjunct to the policy of containment. Major General Robert A. McClure*, the father of the voluntary repatriation concept, argued that Soviet bloc governments would be reluctant to engage in aggression in the future because men in their armed forces would probably take the first opportunity presented to them to seek asylum in the West.

Although the Communist negotiators at the P'anmunjŏm truce talks* were unwilling explicitly to accept the policy of voluntary repatriation, especially for the Chinese POWs, on receipt of information on April 1, 1952, from the UNC negotiating team that as many as 116,000 out of 132,000 Communist prisoners would probably elect to return home, they agreed tacitly to a screening of inmates. This UNC estimate turned out to be wildly inaccurate, with early results of Operation Scatter* showing that only some 70,000 (later increased to 83,000) would agree to return home willingly. Presented with these figures, the Chinese and North Koreans were outraged and charged the UNC with a breach of faith.

The factionalism that existed among prisoners prior to the official UNC poll was heightened by this screening operation, resulting in an increase in the numbers of riots, deaths, and woundings in UNC compounds. Although in receipt of information that the poll of prisoners had been preceded by "organized murders, beatings, threats, before and even during the polling process," neither this information nor the continuing inability to establish control within the POW camps was sufficient to make the Truman or Eisenhower administrations reconsider their stance on this policy or to soften its terms. The last major issue to be resolved at the armistice talks from April 1952, it was not settled until June 8, 1953, after the Communists accepted with some further adjustments the UNC final POW settlement proposal of May 25, 1953*. *See also* Kŏje-do POW Uprising; POW Unilateral Release Proposal; Rescreening of POWs; Truce Talks Suspension of October 8, 1952; UNC POW Administration.

B. J. Bernstein, "The Struggle over the Korean Armistice: Prisoners of Repatriation?" in B. Cumings (ed.), *Child of Conflict* (Seattle, 1983); R. Foot, *A Substitute for Victory* (Ithaca, N.Y., 1990); A. E. Goodman (ed.), *Negotiating while Fighting: The Diary of Admiral C. Turner Joy at the Korean Armistice Conference* (Stanford, Calif., 1978); C. A. MacDonald, *Korea: The War Before Vietnam* (London, 1986).

Rosemary Foot

VYSHINSKY, ANDREI Y. (1883–1954)

Andrei Yanuarievich Vyshinsky was Soviet foreign minister from March 1949 to March 1953. He led the Soviet Union's attack from the UN on U.S. and UN policy in Korea. Born in Odessa, he received his early education in Kiev. In 1902, he joined the Mensheviks. After graduating in jurisprudence from Kiev University in 1913, Vyshinsky became an assistant advocate in Moscow in 1915. Four years later, he entered the Red Army as a member of the food commissariat. The following year, he joined the Bolsheviks, and thereafter his career as a jurist progressed rapidly, becoming president of the Supreme Court of the Soviet Union in 1928. Appointed public prosecutor of the Soviet Union in 1935, four years later he became a member of the Central Committee of the Communist party. Vyshinsky entered the Soviet foreign ministry in 1940. He was a member of the Soviet delegation at the Yalta and Potsdam conferences. He headed the Soviet delegation to the First Session of the UN General Assembly in 1946 and also participated in the Paris Peace Conference. Appointed foreign minister in 1949, he held that position until 1953.

The outbreak of hostilities in Korea added to existing Soviet-U.S. tension at the UN. Vyshinsky criticized UN intervention in Korea. As UN forces neared the thirty-eighth parallel in early fall 1950, he warned that crossing the line would be an aggression against the Democratic People's Republic of Korea*. In early October, Vyshinsky introduced a seven-point proposal to the UN General Assembly's Political and Security Committee calling for a cease-fire and removal of all foreign troops in Korea; an election, under the watch of a UN commission that included a representative from the People's Republic of China*, might then be held for all Korea. This resolution was easily defeated, and a few days later, the UN forces crossed into North Korea. Vyshinsky continued to attack the UN and U.S. action in Korea, alleging that the United States was using Japanese troops and that the war was the result of a South Korean invasion.

Vyshinsky forcefully expressed the Soviet position on agenda item 4*, re-patriation of POWs, an issue that plagued the P'anmunjŏm truce talks* because of the refusal of some North Korean and Chinese prisoners to return home. Vyshinsky supported compulsory repatriation of prisoners and agreed with a Polish resolution in the General Assembly calling for this in October 1952. The United States firmly supported voluntary repatriation* of prisoners, though most of the other nations in Korea were less committed to the U.S. position. Vyshinsky attempted but failed to postpone the prisoner question until a cease-fire was put in place.

V. K. Krishna Menon*, leader of the Indian UN delegation, made an effort to work out a compromise between the two extreme positions. There was some thought that because of Menon's contact with the Chinese, his effort might be a signal by Peking of its willingness to find a solution to the problem. Vyshinsky made Menon's job more difficult on November 10, 1952, when he stated that the Soviets would not move from their position. Two weeks later, he condemned the Menon POW settlement proposal* and suggested that he was also speaking for the Chinese and North Koreans on this issue. Vyshinsky's action may have been directed at the Chinese to force them to adhere to the Soviet position. After the death of Joseph Stalin*, Vyshinsky was made deputy foreign minister and permanent representative of the Soviet Union to the UN, replacing Valerian A. Zorin*. He continued in this position until his death in New York City.

B. J. Bernstein, "The Struggle over the Korean Armistice: Prisoners of Repatriation?" in B. Cumings (ed.), *Child of Conflict* (Seattle, 1983); R. Leckie, *Conflict: The History of the Korean War, 1950–1953* (New York, 1962); *New York Times*, November 23, 1954; R. J. O'Neill, *Australia in the Korean War 1950–53* (Canberra, 1981); M. D. Shulman, *Stalin's Foreign Policy Reappraised* (Cambridge, 1963).

Paul J. Morton

W

WAIST OF KOREA

This label refers to a geographic line located roughly in the middle of North Korea where the width of the peninsula narrows to a distance considerably less than the average of 200 miles. It runs from the city of Wŏnsan on the Sea of Japan in the east to the capital of the Democractic People's Republic of Korea* at P'yŏngyang and the Yellow Sea on the west. Korea is about 480 miles in length, and this narrowing occurs approximately 120 miles south of the northern border at the Yalu River. Thus, the line more accurately constitutes Korea's "neck" rather than "waist." During the first six months of the Korean War, both the British and the Indian governments advanced cease-fire proposals that would have halted the UNC* offensive into North Korea at this line, thus establishing a buffer zone between Korea's waist and the Yalu. By allowing a Communist regime to occupy the area bordering China, Britain and India hoped to reassure the People's Republic of China* that UN operations in North Korea would not threaten its security, thus averting Chinese military intervention* in the Korean War. *See also* British DMZ Proposal; Indian Peace Initiatives.

WAKE ISLAND CONFERENCE (October 15, 1950)

This conference occurred between President Harry S. Truman* and CINCUNC General Douglas MacArthur* as the UNC* was advancing into North Korea. Speculation as to why Truman wanted to confer with MacArthur was rampant. Some observers found the answer in domestic politics, specifically, the electoral campaign to determine the composition of Congress during the next two years. Most appeared to assume that the president sought to engage the illustrious general in serious discussion about serious issues relating to the Korean War and East Asian affairs. While speculation continued, Truman flew to California, where he was joined by an entourage of officials of his administration that included W. Averell Harriman*, Philip C. Jessup*, Dean Rusk*, and JCS chairman General Omar N. Bradley*. After a stopover in Hawaii, the presidential party flew to Wake Island, where MacArthur awaited his arrival.

If nettled that he had been called away from his command center for political reasons, MacArthur greeted Truman warmly when the president descended a mobile stairway. The two men drove off to a tiny structure where they conferred for forty minutes. By the later accounts of both, the apparently rambling and inconsequential conversation was amicable. The president and general then joined their respective entourages in a concrete and frame building where, for a mere eighty minutes, the conferees, in an atmosphere of conviviality and informality, superficially touched on an array of topics from war crimes trials* and the rehabilitation of Korea when the war ended, presumably in six or seven weeks, to U.S. relations with Japan to the war in Indochina. Best remembered is MacArthur's assurance that, because of command of the air by UN forces, the People's Republic of China* would not intervene in the Korean War—"if the Chinese tried to get down to P'yŏngyang there would be the greatest slaughter."

At a few minutes after 9:00 A.M., Truman terminated the meeting, and staff people prepared a wordy and vacuous communiqué. After pinning a fourth oak leaf cluster on MacArthur's Distinguished Service Medal and a Medal of Merit on John J. Muccio*, the U.S. ambassador to the Republic of Korea*, Truman took off at 11:35 A.M. for Hawaii and the United States. Clearly the Wake Island conference did not constitute a serious attempt to deal with fundamental questions of policy. MacArthur's assurances that the PRC would not enter the Korean War merely confirmed a view that officials in the Truman administration had already adopted. Why, then, had the president summoned MacArthur to a meeting at Wake Island? Certainly not because of differences in matters of policy between the president and the general—rather, it would appear, because Truman, who was fond of travel and had never met MacArthur, thought it would be pleasant to make a trip to the Pacific and get acquainted with the general and also to share the public spotlight, which in those weeks was beaming down on MacArthur and perhaps provide a lift for Democrats during the current electoral campaign.

D. C. James, *The Years of MacArthur,* vol. 3: *Triumph and Disaster, 1945–1964* (Boston, 1985); *Log of President Truman's Trip to Wake Island, October 11–18, 1950,* H. S. Truman papers, Harry S. Truman Library, Independence, Missouri; J. W. Spanier, *The Truman-MacArthur Controversy and the Korean War* (New York, 1959); *Substance of Statements Made at Wake Island Conference on 15 October 1950, Compiled by General of the Army Omar N. Bradley,* MacArthur Memorial, Norfolk, Virginia; J. E. Wilz, "Truman and MacArthur: The Wake Island Meeting," *Military Affairs* (December 1978).

John Edward Wilz

WALKER, WALTON H. (1899–1950)

Lieutenant General Walton H. Walker was commanding officer of the U.S. 8th Army* from September 1948 until his death in a jeep accident in Korea on December 23, 1950. He was born in Texas and was a member of the U.S. Military Academy at West Point class of 1912. A combat veteran of World War I, Walker served as a corps commander during World War II in General George

S. Patton's 3d Army. "Johnnie" Walker, as he was known to his cohorts, earned high and rare praise from Patton and General Dwight D. Eisenhower*. This high esteem doubtlessly contributed to his selection as the principal troop commander in General Douglas MacArthur's* Far Eastern Command. Tough, aggressive, and somewhat flamboyant in the style of Patton, Walker disliked MacArthur and had a contentious relationship with MacArthur's chief of staff, Major General Edward M. Almond*.

When war erupted in Korea in 1950, the burden of battlefield command fell directly on Walker. Establishing his headquarters at Taegu on July 13, he was in charge of all U.S. ground forces in Korea and the troops of the Republic of Korea* and other members of the UN. His hastily assembled army was understrength, mediocre in performance, and lacking adequate air and logistic support. It retreated steadily southward until Walker finally stabilized a defense line around Pusan. Concurrent with the Inch'ŏn landing*, Walker's 8th Army began a breakout from the Pusan Perimeter* in September. With Almond in command of the independent X Corps* at Inch'ŏn and Walker leading the remaining forces, the two elements pushed into North Korea until Chinese military intervention* forced their retreat in late November. Walker was deploying his defenses along a line near the thirty-eighth parallel when he was killed.

The dramatically shifting fortunes of the 8th Army from June to December 1950 raised numerous questions about Walker's leadership. He made many mistakes, although various decisions by MacArthur and other generals and a host of difficult circumstances contributed to his problems. Some of Walker's errors cost the lives of his own soldiers, while lapses allowed enemy units to escape encirclement and destruction. At various times, MacArthur and officials in Washington considered relieving him from command. At other times, however, Walker maneuvered his troops masterfully, and he always displayed a tenacity in battle that favorably impressed, among others, Army Chief of Staff General J. Lawton Collins*. On balance, Walker was a competent, but not inspiring, commander. *See also* Home-by-Christmas Offensive; "Stand or Die" Order.

R. E. Appleman, *South to the Naktong, North to the Yalu* (Washington, D.C., 1961); C. Blair, *The Forgotten War* (New York, 1987); J.F. Schnabel, *Policy and Direction* (Washington, D.C., 1972).

David L. Anderson

WAR CRIMES TRIALS

Military occupation of North Korea* in the fall of 1950 caused the United States to consider whether to punish war criminals. On October 10, 1950, Assistant Secretary of State Dean Rusk* received recommendations on the issue in a memorandum from Arthur B. Emmons III*, who was in charge of the Korea desk. After noting that the Democratic People's Republic of Korea* "was established and has been maintained as a typical Soviet puppet state," he argued that "primary responsibility for the aggression should be placed at the door of the Kremlin.'' In addition, ''the aggressive and virulent propaganda of the Communists of North Korea . . . has had its effect upon the North Koreans themselves who . . . have fallen victim to Soviet propaganda concerning the alleged aggressive intentions and vices of the ROK and of the Western Powers which have backed it.'' Although not condoning the ''cynical and cold-blooded'' North Korean invasion of South Korea*, this ''does perhaps in some measure tend to relieve the North Korean leaders of what otherwise would have been their complete responsibility.''

In his recommendations, Emmons urged that ''a distinction should be drawn between the so-called *war crime* of aggression on the one hand and war *crimes* involving violation of *the law and customs of war* and *atrocities against the civilian population* on the other.'' With respect to the latter, CINCUNC General Douglas MacArthur* would receive a directive covering the occupation of North Korea with instructions to arrest and hold for trial those who had committed such crimes. But it was the responsibility of the United Nations to decide whether to charge the North Korean leaders with war crimes guilt for ''unleashing an unprovoked military aggression'' and then continuing it in defiance of the UN. Although the United States had supported trials for the crime of conducting aggressive warfare, Emmons pointed out that many officials doubted whether this had been ''advisable or successful'' in Germany and Japan. In Korea, it also would ''serve only to intensify the hatred already unfortunately engendered between the populations of north and south Korea by intensive Communist propaganda,'' thereby making it more difficult to achieve effective and peaceful reunification. He recommended that the United States use its influence so that discussion of such punishment in the UN be ''avoided or minimized.''

At the Wake Island Conference*, General MacArthur expressed agreement with the thrust of the Emmons memorandum. ''Don't touch the war criminals,'' he told President Harry S. Truman*. ''It doesn't work. The Nurnburg [*sic*] trials and Tokyo trials were no deterrent.'' MacArthur told Rusk later that he opposed the trial of political war criminals on general grounds and not because the North Korean leaders were Soviet puppets. His responsibility for the trial of Japanese war criminals ''was the most repugnant task he had ever had to perform.'' However, he qualified this by saying that ''military commanders obey the orders of their governments and have no option about waging war.'' In addition, ''the conduct of North Korean troops toward prisoners and civilians varied greatly from unit to unit and he therefore doubted that it was a matter of general policy.'' If there was evidence that Kim Il Sung* ordered atrocities as a matter of policy, he would catch, try, and execute him by military commission. In the final occupation directive for North Korea*, MacArthur received instructions to ''apprehend and hold for trial by appropriate tribunals, . . . all persons who are or may be charged with atrocities or violations of the law and customs of war.'' In the unlikely event that the UNC* was able to capture top North Korean leaders, ''The United States should not propose or support in the United Nations the holding of war crimes trials in Korea.'' With Chinese military intervention*, discussion of war crimes trials ended because the United States abandoned the goal of unifying Korea. Nor could the UNC retain war criminals when it became necessary to maximize the number of repatriates to achieve an armistice.

Foreign Relations of the United States, 1950, vol. 7: *Korea* (Washington, D.C., 1976).

WASHINGTON CONFERENCE (March 26–April 7, 1951)

This was the fourth meeting of consultation of ministers of foreign affairs of American states held in Washington, D.C., to discuss Latin America's contribution to the UN and U.S. war effort in Korea. Secretary of State Dean G. Acheson* asked for the meeting of hemispheric ministers on December 16, 1950, on the same day President Harry S. Truman* issued his declaration of a national emergency* following Chinese military intervention*. The three previous foreign ministers meetings had convened during the World War II era. During that war, Latin Americans had stoutly supported the Allied effort, supplying strategic materials, military bases, and, in the cases of Brazil and Mexico, military forces. The United States hoped that the Latin Americans would again follow U.S. leadership. But at the Washington Conference, the United States received only rhetorical support from its southern neighbors. Latin Americans approved general resolutions backing the UN but declined to make specific commitments. The conference's key resolution, calling for increased production of strategic materials, was tied to a statement citing Latin America's need for economic development. Moreover, only Colombia responded to requests for troops, and with only a token Colombian Battalion* of volunteers. Latin Americans did not rally behind the United States primarily because they believed that it had neglected them in the postwar period. They resented the lack of a Marshall Plan for Latin America. *See also* Latin America and the Korean War.

H. E. Davis and L. C. Wilson (eds.), *Latin American Foreign Policies* (Baltimore, 1975); Pan American Union, *Fourth Meeting of Consultation of Ministers of Foreign Affairs Held in Washington, March 26-April 7, 1951: Proceedings* (Washington, D. C., 1951); R. P. Stebbins, *The United States in World Affairs, 1951* (New York, 1952).

Stephen G. Rabe

WEBB, JAMES E. (1906–   )

James E. Webb was the under secretary of state from 1949 to 1952. Born in Granville Country, North Carolina, he completed an A.B. degree at the University of North Carolina in 1928, studied law at George Washington University, and was admitted to the bar of the District of Columbia in 1936. A naval and marine aviator from 1930 to 1966, Webb rose to the rank of lieutenant colonel. In 1946, he became the executive assistant to the under secretary of the treasury and then director of the budget. He steadily developed a close working relationship with President Harry S. Truman*, who made Webb his under secretary of state in 1949. Secretary of State Dean G. Acheson*, whose previous service had also been primarily in economic planning, got along well with Webb. Since Acheson too had developed a close friendship with the president, their combined influence was formidable. Under Acheson's direction, Webb helped to orchestrate the successful struggle for the Korean Aid Bill of 1949–1950*. After persuading Truman to send a special message to Congress supporting the bill, he carefully organized the testimony of a series of experts who spoke in favor of the plan.

When Truman returned to Washington on the second day of the Korean War, Webb, Acheson, and Secretary of Defense Louis A. Johnson* met him at the airport. According to Webb's own account, Truman joined them in the presidential limousine and, after expounding at length on the logistical limitations that the Siberian railroad would place on the North Koreans, ended by saying, "By God, I'm going to let them have it." Johnson shook Truman's hand, exclaiming, "I'm with you, Mr. President." Then Webb, aware of the hostility between Acheson and Johnson, interjected that Truman should consider the joint recommendations drawn up by State and Defense before deciding his course. When they arrived for the first Blair House meeting*, Webb took the president into the cloakroom and outlined the joint recommendations: additional military aid for the Republic of Korea*, air support for the evacuation of U.S. dependents, and the interposition of the 7th Fleet between Taiwan and the mainland. Webb added that both he and Acheson thought it best to approve the first two and delay the neutralization of Taiwan*. Truman followed this advice precisely. But when the former budget director also urged Truman to organize the U.S. economy for war immediately, Truman hesitated, later causing inflation and political difficulties.

At the insistence of President Lyndon B. Johnson, a longtime friend, Webb later became the administrator of the National Aeronautics and Space Administration, where he served with distinction from 1961 to 1968. Thereafter, he served on the boards of dozens of corporations, civic organizations, and scientific groups. Asked in 1986 about the State Department's involvement in the decision to intervene in the Korean War in June 1950, Webb replied, "South Korea, in the hands of the North, would have been a dagger pointed at Japan and would have affected the whole economy of that region."

R. J. Donovan, *Tumultuous Years* (New York, 1982); R. L. McGlothlen, "Acheson, Economics, and the American Commitment in Korea," *Pacific Historical Review* (February 1989); J. I. Matray, *The Reluctant Crusade* (Honolulu, 1985).

Ronald L. McGlothlen

WEDEMEYER REPORT (September 18, 1947)

Named after Lieutenant General Albert C. Wedemeyer, this report summarized the findings of the mission he headed to China and Korea during the summer of 1947. Drafted in Hawaii, the Chinese portion of the report initially was the primary focus of policymakers, congressmen, and the press alike, but both the China and Korea portions of the report became significant in U.S. politics and foreign policy.

Wedemeyer's report on Korea came at a time of great turmoil below the thirty-eighth parallel and when the Truman administration was searching for a method of graceful withdrawal from the peninsula. Wedemeyer offered his superiors limited reason for optimism on the latter point, recommending "moral, advisory, and material support" to southern Korea. Without economic aid, the U.S. occupation zone would deteriorate into "riots and disorder"; without U.S. troops, it would be overtaken by northern Korea, "the end result [being] . . . creation of a Soviet satellite Communist regime throughout the country." This "would cost the United States an immense loss of moral prestige [in Asia] . . . [,] would probably have serious repercussions in Japan," and would constitute a substantial advance for the Soviet Union, producing "opportunities for [its] . . . further . . . expansion" in the region. Wedemeyer proposed an enlarged relief program for southern Korea and a buildup of indigenous armed forces on a scale adequate to protect against anything short of "an outright Soviet directed or controlled invasion." U.S. troops should remain until arrangements for the mutual withdrawal of foreign units could be agreed upon with the Soviets. These proposals were based on Wedemeyer's assumption that the United States would move toward creation of an independent government below the thirty-eighth parallel. The Truman administration was slow in implementing Wedemeyer's proposals for military and economic aid, although in both cases, it eventually moved in their direction.

The Wedemeyer report was initially classified top secret, largely due to its recommendation of a UN trusteeship for Manchuria, which State Department officials feared would embarrass the beleaguered regime of Chiang Kai-shek* in China. The China portion, however, was published in August 1949 as part of the famous China White Paper prepared by the State Department. The Korea section did not surface until May 1951 when, in the midst of the controversy over President Harry S. Truman's* recall of CINCUNC General Douglas MacArthur*, the State Department permitted Senate committees to publish it. Republican partisans attempted to use the report to attack administration policy toward Korea prior to June 1950, but Wedemeyer undermined these efforts when he testified that, in early 1949, he had recommended U.S. military withdrawal from Korea*.

Department of State, *United States Relations with China with Special Reference to the Period 1944–1949* (Washington, D.C., 1949); J. I. Matray, *The Reluctant Crusade* (Honolulu, 1985); W. W. Stueck, *The Wedemeyer Mission* (Athens, 1984); U.S. Congress, Senate Committee on Armed Services, *Report to the President Submitted by Lieutenant General Albert C. Wedemeyer, September 1947, Korea* (Washington, D.C., 1951).

William Stueck

WEST, SIR MICHAEL M. A. R. (1905–1978)

General Sir Michael Montgomery Alston Roberts West was general officer commanding the Commonwealth Division* from 1952 to 1953. West was commissioned from RMC Sandhurst in 1925 and spent the interwar years in various postings in Germany, Britain, and India. He held a number of regimental and brigade commands in the European theater during World War II, gaining appointment as commander of British occupation troops in Austria in 1950. West succeeded Major General A. J. H. Cassels* as commander of the Commonwealth Division in September 1952. His period of command coincided with the drawn-out negotiations for a cease-fire at the P'anmunjŏm truce talks*, and, except for a two-month period at the beginning of 1953, the division was in the line for the whole of the static phase of the war.

West oversaw a number of changes to the organization and dispositions of the division. Friction between the brigades, and the continuing manpower crisis in the British army that meant that the British battalions were consistently under establishment, led him to vary the deployment of the brigades in November 1952. Previously, the brigades had rotated in and out of the line on the familiar "two up, one back" pattern. Under West, this was varied so that all three remained permanently in the forward area, and rotation was internal and on a battalion basis. The manpower problem also saw the implementation of the KATCOM program—Korean Augmentation Troops Commonwealth—modeled on the U.S. Korean Augmentation of the U.S. Army* scheme.

The hallmark of the physically imposing West was a large walking stick, which he carried always when visiting troops in the forward areas. Widely respected, he nonetheless had several altercations with senior U.S. commanders over British Commonwealth operational methods, principally in early 1953 when he strongly disagreed with the U.S. insistence on the need for a continuing high level of offensive activity. After service in Korea, he was successively director of the Territorial Army, GOC 1st Corps, British Army of the Rhine, GOC Northern Command in the United Kingdom, and chairman of the British Defense Staff in Washington, retiring in 1965.

C. N. Barclay, *The First Commonwealth Division* (Aldershot, 1954); J. Grey, *The Commonwealth Armies and the Korea War* (Manchester, 1988).

Jeffrey Grey

WEYLAND, OTTO P. (1902–1979)

In June 1951, Lieutenant General Otto P. Weyland became commander of the U.S. Far East Air Force (FEAF), replacing Lieutenant General George E. Stratemeyer*, and personally led an unescorted bomber formation against North Korean targets. Born in Riverside, California, "Opie" earned a degree in mechanical engineering at Texas A&M, as well as a commission in the U.S. Air Corps Reserve in 1923. He then was assistant commandant of the aviation division of the National Guard bureau in Washington, D.C. Weyland graduated from Air Corps Tactical School in 1938 and Command and General Staff School the following year. From 1941 to 1942, he was stationed in Panama with the 16th Pursuit Group before he returned to the United States as deputy chief of staff for the 6th Air Force. After serving on the Air Corps staff, Weyland received command of the 84th Fighter Wing. In 1944 and 1945, he was commander of the 19th Tactical Air Command and, as part of the 9th Air Force, provided air support for the General George S. Patton's 3d Army during fighting in France, Belgium, Luxembourg, and Germany.

In 1945, Weyland assumed command of the 9th Air Force and then became assistant commandant of the Command and General Staff School. Thereafter, he served as assistant chief of air staff for planning (1946–1947) and deputy commanding officer of the National War College (1947–1950). When the Korean War began, Weyland became the FEAF's vice-commander for operations and, after briefly returning to the United States, assumed command from Stratemeyer. His role in the Korean War became important when General Mark W. Clark* replaced General Matthew B. Ridgway* as CINCUNC because the new commander ordered the implementation of an air pressure strategy* to force the Communists to compromise at the P'anmunjŏm truce talks*. Like Stratemeyer, Weyland was a proponent of interdiction, arguing in favor of this approach during the army–air force close support controversy*. Returning to the United States in 1954, he was commander of the Tactical Air Command until his retirement in 1959. Weyland then was a consultant for McDonnell Aircraft Corporation and the director of a life insurance company.

C. Blair, *The Forgotten War* (New York, 1987); W. G. Hermes, *Truce Tent and Fighting Front* (Washington, D. C., 1966); *Washington Post,* September 6, 1979; *Who's Who in America, 1974* (New York, 1974).

WHITEHORSE HILL, BATTLE OF
See Battle of Whitehorse Hill

WHITNEY, COURTNEY (1897–1969)
Clay Blair, a leading authority on the Korean War, has called Major General Courtney Whitney "the most trusted sycophant" of CINCUNC General Douglas MacArthur*, serving after 1946 as his aide, adviser, and press secretary. In this capacity, he screened the people and information that reached MacArthur, later accompanying the general to the front during the Korean War. Born in Tacoma Park, Maryland, Whitney enlisted as a private in the National Guard in 1917. Transferring to the Signal Reserve Corps, he worked in the aviation section until 1918, when he received his commission. After attending aviation school, he was assistant adjutant and then adjutant at Payne Field in Mississippi until 1920. In 1923, Whitney earned a law degree from National University and two years later went to the Philippines as adjutant for the 66th Service Squadron. From 1926 to 1927, he was chief of the publications section of the information division in the Office of the Chief of the U.S. Army Air Corps. Resigning from the army and returning to the Philippines, Whitney spent the next thirteen years practicing corporate law in Manila and building his friendship with MacArthur, whom he had met while stationed in Washington, D.C.

In September 1940, Whitney accepted the offer to return to active duty as a major in the Reserve Officer Corps, serving as assistant chief in the legal division at air corps headquarters and in 1943 as assistant judge advocate. He went to the Philippines the next year to organize MacArthur's secret service as a member of the Allied intelligence bureau. Thereafter, he was chief of MacArthur's civil affairs section and helped to organize Filipino resistance fighters. Early in 1946, Brigadier General Whitney joined MacArthur's staff in Tokyo as chief of the government section. His main job during the occupation was supervising the purge of those Japanese deemed unfit for political office. Though criticized for unfairness, he was nevertheless a principal drafter of Japan's new constitution. By 1950, when the Korean War began, some considered Whitney the ''second most powerful man in Japan.'' After President Harry S. Truman's* recall of MacArthur*, he told newsmen that ''this has been his finest hour.'' He resigned from the army upon his return to the United States. During the MacArthur Hearings*, Whitney served as the general's press secretary, insisting on one occasion that Communist China would not have entered the Korean War had the United States made clear its intention to bomb Manchuria in response to Chinese military intervention*. Fiercely loyal and devoted to MacArthur, he was bedside when the general died in 1964 and spent the remainder of his life defending his former boss, including writing a book, *MacArthur: His Rendezvous with History*.

C. Blair, *The Forgotten War* (New York, 1987); *Current Biography, 1951; New York Times,* March 22, 1969; D. Rees, *Korea: The Limited War* (New York, 1964); *Who Was Who in America,* vol. 5: *1969–1973* (Chicago, 1973).

WILLOUGHBY, CHARLES A. (1892–1972)

When the Korean War began, Major General Charles A. Willoughby had been U.S. Army assistant chief of intelligence in the Pacific since 1941. He also was one of the close circle of advisors around General Douglas MacArthur* known as the ''Bataan Gang.'' Willoughby was born in Heidelberg, Germany, and became a naturalized U.S. citizen in 1910. Four years later, he earned a B.A. at Gettysburg College. In 1915, he received a U.S. Army commission, fighting thereafter in the Mexican Border Campaign (1916–1917) and then in France (1917–1918) with the American Expeditionary Force. Over the next decade, Willoughby was a military attaché in Venezuela, Colombia, and Ecuador. He graduated from Infantry School in 1929 and Command and General Staff School in 1931, then serving at the latter institution as instructor and head of the military history department. Willoughby also spent some time as a graduate student at the University of Kansas and later attended the Army War College. In 1941, he went to the Philippines to join MacArthur's staff as chief of intelligence. A veteran of Bataan and Corregidor, Willoughby was MacArthur's representative during discussions in Manila with the Japanese about surrender terms on August 15, 1945. Meanwhile, he had written two books, *U.S. Economic Participation in the World War, 1917–1918* and *Maneuver in War,* while serving as editor in chief for the *General Staff Quarterly* from 1931 to 1935 and rising to the rank of brigadier general.

Willoughby was a controversial figure in the Korean War because many American newsmen and politicians criticized him for failing to anticipate either the North Korean invasion of South Korea* or Chinese military intervention*. In response to the attack, his initial report that South Korea's army was showing high morale and withdrawing with "orderliness" encouraged the belief that defending the Republic of Korea* was possible without U.S. ground forces. Early in October, Willoughby stated that the threats from the People's Republic of China* about entering the war were "probably in the category of diplomatic blackmail." Even after the capture of Chinese prisoners, he dismissed the reality of intervention, declaring that the "most auspicious time" for China's entry had "long since passed." As late as November 1950, his intelligence reports estimated that there were no more than 71,000 Chinese troops in Korea. Lieutenant Colonel John H. Chiles, a staff officer for Lieutenant General Edward M. Almond*, later said that Willoughby wanted to maintain MacArthur's cult of invincibility and thus had to substantiate his claim at the Wake Island Conference* that the Chinese would not enter the war. "Anything MacArthur wanted," Chiles explained, "Willoughby produced intelligence for. . . . In this case, Willoughby falsified the intelligence reports. . . . He should have gone to jail." Instead, he retired voluntarily after President Harry S. Truman's* recall of MacArthur*, becoming editor of the *Foreign Intelligence Digest*. Willoughby also wrote *MacArthur: 1941–1951*, defending himself and his boss against "calculated treason and subversion" from their critics.

C. Blair, *The Forgotten War* (New York, 1987); *New York Times,* October 26, 1972; D. Rees, *Korea: The Limited War* (New York, 1964); *Who Was Who in America,* vol. 5; *1969–1973* (Chicago, 1973).

WILSON, CHARLES E. (1886–1972)

Charles Wilson headed the Office of Defense Mobilization from December 1950 until his resignation in March 1952. Born and raised in New York City's rough West Side, he left school for work at the age of 12 to ease the burden on his widowed mother. Wilson took a job as an office boy at Sprague Electric Company, which was later purchased by General Electric, and rose steadily over the next four decades to become president of GE in 1939. The press later dubbed him "Electric Charlie," to avoid confusion with the head of General Motors, Charles E. "Engine Charlie" Wilson. In 1942, at the request of President Franklin D. Roosevelt, Wilson left General Electric to serve on the War Production Board. Universally praised for his ability to increase production of vital war materials, especially aircraft, Wilson eventually left the board in 1944 because of disagreements with its director, Donald Nelson. Although a Republican, Wilson served on a number of presidential panels, and in 1947 President Harry S. Truman* named him to head the Commission on Civil Rights.

In December 1950, after issuing his declaration of a national emergency*, Truman appointed Wilson as director of the recently created Office of Defense Mobilization. Recalling his experience in the previous war, Wilson took the post only after he received broad powers that would make him subject to only the president's supervision. "He's a great team player," one observer said of Wilson, "so long as he can be the captain." As mobilization director, Wilson presided over a massive military buildup that was intended to rearm the nation for a possible global war while it fought a limited war in Korea. In one year, military expenditures quadrupled from $15 billion to $60 billion. During this period, Wilson's price and wage controls and Truman's decision to increase taxes were largely successful in limiting wartime inflation.

In early 1952, however, Wilson and Truman clashed over a War Stabilization Board (WSB) recommendation to raise pay for steelworkers by an average estimated at between 18 to 30 cents an hour. Never a friend of organized labor, Wilson opposed the raise, as well as the board's recommendation for a union shop. Truman did not believe that the WSB's recommendations required an increase in steel prices, and Wilson subsequently resigned after complaining that the president had made him look like a liar by reneging on a compromise that would have allowed a $5 per ton increase in the price of steel. Wilson returned to business and later headed the People-to-People Foundation begun by President Dwight D. Eisenhower*. *See also* Defense Appropriations Acts (1951–1953); Truman's Steel Plants Seizure.

R. J. Donovan, *Tumultuous Years* (New York, 1982); D. R. McCoy, *The Presidency of Harry S. Truman* (Lawrence, Kans., 1984) ; W. Millis, *Arms and Men: A Study in American Military History* (New York, 1981); *New York Times,* January 4, 1972.

Marc Gallicchio

WITHDRAWAL FROM SEOUL OF DECEMBER 1950–JANUARY 1951

The winter offensive launched by the Chinese People's Volunteers Army* forced the UNC* and the government of the Republic of Korea* to withdraw from Seoul, allowing the capital to fall into the hands of the Communist forces on January 4, 1951. Following the disastrous retreat from North Korea, the UNC in mid-December 1950 set up its main defense line along the Imjin River to head off the Communist advance toward Seoul. Demoralized and dispirited, the UN troops fearfully awaited the next Chinese attack. Assuming command of the 8th Army* in Korea on December 26, 1950, Lieutenant General Matthew B. Ridgway* frantically tried to restore confidence and to reinvigorate the spirit of the troops under his command. Despite his efforts, on New Year's Eve the Chinese forces launched a general offensive, swarmed across the Imjin River and, by January 2, had advanced to the northern vicinity of Ŭijŏngbu, about 18 miles north of Seoul.

On January 3, the Chinese broke through the UN defense line about 10 miles northeast of Seoul, taking Ŭijŏngbu and causing Ridgway to order the withdrawal of his troops from Seoul. The next morning, on January 4, as the last troops of the UN forces abandoned the city, the Chinese troops moved in. In the meantime, the civilian population in South Korea had been watching adverse military developments with alarm ever since Chinese military intervention*. When the Chinese troops crossed the thirty-eighth parallel and moved into the Yŏnan area on December 12, 1950, it became apparent to many people in Seoul that the city could not be defended. Worse, rumors circulated that the UN forces would not be able to stop the Communist advances and might withdraw from Korea entirely. Under such circumstances, a number of people began to flee the city.

The ROK government, on the other hand, was determined not to repeat the blunder it had made in its withdrawal from Seoul of June 1950*. To deny any possibility of North Korean access to manpower in South Korea in case of its occupation, the ROK government hurriedly organized all non-military men between the ages of 17 and 40 into a new National Guard for evacuation to the rear. The severe mistreatment of these men during the evacuation later became the single biggest scandal that rocked the Rhee government during the war. Subsequently, acting on the advice of President Syngman Rhee*, the National Assembly formally voted on December 24 to move the capital city to Pusan. The ROK government then issued a proclamation advising all non-essential civilians to leave the city. In the mass exodus that followed, people, carrying whatever they could, crammed into the trains provided by the government to head for the south, and those who could not get on the trains formed human columns treading on icy roads in bitter cold to escape the Communist occupation. President Rhee and his cabinet members were the last civilians to leave on January 3. *See also* South Korean National Guard Scandal.

C. Blair, *The Forgotten War* (New York, 1987); Chungang Ilbosa, *Minjok ŭi Chŭngŏn*, vol. 3 (Seoul, 1973); Kukbang-bu p'yŏnch'an wiwŏn-hoe, *Han'guk Chŏnjaeng-sa*, vol. 5 (Seoul, 1972); M. B. Ridgway, *The Korean War* (Garden City, N.Y., 1967).

Yŏng-ho Ch'oe

WITHDRAWAL FROM SEOUL OF JUNE 1950

Within four days of the outbreak of the Korean War, North Korean troops stormed into Seoul and occupied the city on June 28. With the collapse of the Republic of Korea's* defenses to the north of Seoul, the chain of command and communication broke down within President Syngman Rhee's* government. Following the fall of Ŭijŏngbu on June 26, some high government officials began to panic. Without consulting or even informing his own cabinet, Rhee fled Seoul, against the advice of U.S. ambassador John J. Muccio*, at 2:00 A.M. on June 27 by train for an unknown destination. The cabinet, meanwhile, held an emergency meeting at 3:00 A.M. and decided to relocate the seat of government to Suwŏn. Not knowing of these developments, the National Assembly met for an emergency session in the early morning hours of the same day and adopted a formal resolution calling for the defense of the capital city to the last man.

Within the military command, Defense Minister Shin Sung-mo*, who was concurrently the acting prime minister, and Major General Chae Byung Dok*, the army chief of staff, failed to provide firm leadership. Upon hearing the news of the fall of Ch'angdong on June 27, General Chae ordered the army headquarters moved to Sihŭng, south of the Han River. The U.S. Korean Military Advisory Group*, however, was not informed and did not know of this decision until the Korean officers and soldiers began to leave the headquarters. Within the U.S. embassy in Seoul, Ambassador Muccio ordered the U.S. evacuation of Seoul* on the early morning of June 26, Muccio and his entourage crossing the Han River on the afternoon of June 27.

Meanwhile, the general public in Seoul had not been fully informed of the adverse war situation. The only radio station in South Korea at the time put out news bulletins intermittently from the ROK military authorities reassuring the public that the military situation was under control. Then, at 6:00 A.M. on June 27, a radio news bulletin announced the transfer of the government to Suwŏn without further explanation. By the afternoon of June 27, panicked citizens began to crowd the streets of Seoul seeking refuge across the Han River. At 10:00 P.M., a radio message from President Rhee, taped—without telling the public—from the southern city of Taejŏn, appealed to the people to remain calm. Listeners in Seoul, however, could hear the bursts of artillery fire reverberating in the immediate vicinity, and many rushed to cross the only highway bridge over the Han River to escape the North Korean advance.

At about 2:30 A.M. on June 28, the most incredible and dramatic event of the withdrawal from Seoul took place. While the Han River bridge was still packed with pedestrians and vehicles fleeing the city, it was blown up without any prior warning by explosive charges detonated under the direction of the ROK army chief engineer, killing or wounding an untold number of people. The premature destruction of the bridge prevented the orderly retreat of the main bodies of the South Korean army, who were still north of the Han resisting the North Korean offensive. Their withdrawal route effectively sealed off, these ROK troops had to find other means to cross the river, abandoning most of their equipment. *See also* Han River Operations; North Korean Invasion of South Korea.

R. E. Appleman, *South to the Naktong, North to the Yalu* (Washington, D.C., 1961); *Choguk Haebang Chŏnjaeng-sa,* vol. 1 (P'yŏngyang, 1972); Chungang Ilbosa, *Minjok ŭi Chŭngŏn,* vol. 1 (Seoul, 1972); Kukbang-bu p'yŏnch'an wiwŏn-hoe, *Han'guk Chŏnjaeng-sa,* vol. 2 (Seoul, 1968); H. J. Noble, *Embassy at War* (Seattle, 1975).

                                                                    Yŏng-ho Ch'oe

WON YONG-DUK (WŎN YONG-DŎK; 1907–1968)

Lieutenant General Won Yong-duk was born in Seoul and educated at Severance Medical School (now the Medical School at Yonsei University) in Seoul. He was a surgeon with the rank of lieutenant colonel in the Manchukuo Army. After liberation, Won became an assistant to the superintendent of the Military English Language School, which was established to train officers destined for the constabulary army in southern Korea during the U.S. military occupation after 1945. In this capacity, he helped recruit officers for the school, and he himself graduated from the school in 1946 to become major. From February to June, Won was the first commander of the South Korean Constabulary army. In September 1946, he became superintendent of the Korean Military Academy. Four months later, he was transferred to commander of the 5th Brigade. Later he became a lieutenant general. Won distinguished himself by his slavish loyalty to President Syngman Rhee* during the South Korean political crisis of 1952* and especially martial law episode. In June 1953, he was promoted to provost marshal of the Republic of Korea's* army, navy, and air force and helped Rhee's release of North Korean POWs* from the detention of the UNC* forces. *See also* Rhee's Declaration of Martial Law.

B. Cumings, *The Origins of the Korean War* (Princeton, 1981); Ministry of Defense records, Republic of Korea.

Hakjoon Kim

WŎNJU, BATTLES OF
See Battles of Wŏnju

WŎNSAN LANDING (October 1950)

In mid-September 1950, following the Inch'ŏn landing*, CINCUNC General Douglas MacArthur* ordered his planning staff to complete preparations for the next operation. On September 27, Brigadier General Edwin K. Wright, MacArthur's operations officer, presented Operations Plan 9–50, calling for a two-pronged attack north of the thirty-eighth parallel. Lieutenant General Walton W. Walker's* 8th Army* would move northwestward from Seoul along a Kaesŏng-Sariwon-P'yŏngyang axis. Simultaneously, Major General Edward M. Almond's* X Corps* would sail from Inch'ŏn, disembarking at Wŏnsan on the eastern coast of North Korea (Operation Tailboard). Following the assault landing, X Corps would cross the waist of Korea*, link up with Walker's forces, and envelope P'yŏngyang, the capital of the Democratic People's Republic of Korea*. After receiving JCS approval, preparation began almost immediately despite the concerns of some planners. D day was only three weeks away, and the overriding advantage of opening an eastern port, and the logistical difficulty inherent in an overland assault on Wŏnsan, made the amphibious landing the preferable option.

On October 2, Vice-Admiral Arthur D. Struble ordered Joint Task Force Seven to prepare for the Wŏnsan assault. Although more than 300 mines had been sighted along the Korean coast, intelligence reports did not suggest a particularly heavy concentration around Wŏnsan. Struble dispatched Captain Richard T. Spofford's Mine Squadron Three, which arrived on October 10 and swept a 3,000-yard-wide channel, roughly 12 miles long. At dusk, Spofford received reports of an extensive minefield in the path of the flotilla. Since intelligence reports indicated the location of the navigational channel used by the Soviets, Spofford shifted the sweeping operation, hopeful that the Soviet channel would have fewer mines. He then concentrated on plans for the use of a relatively new technique: carrier aircraft would bomb the minefield. Japanese minesweepers participated in the operation, winning favor with the Truman administration and thereby hastening the negotiation of the Japanese Peace Treaty*.

Following the air attack, sweepers passed through the Soviet channel into unswept waters. The flagship *Pirate* hit a mine almost immediately. Undetected shore batteries on the island of Sin-do opened fire. As the destroyer minesweeper

Pledge came to aid *Pirate,* it struck a mine. Both vessels sank. Following reports of the action, Rear Admiral Allan Smith, advance force commander, sent a message that rocked the Pentagon: "The U.S. Navy has lost command of the sea in Korean waters." Mine Squadron Three ultimately accomplished its mission on October 25, and the troops landed. Since the Republic of Korea's* I Corps had captured the city overland on October 10, the amphibious landing was accomplished without casualties. Navy Chief of Staff Admiral Forrest P. Sherman*, responding angrily to the experiences at Wŏnsan, stated at the time that "when you can't go *where* you want to, *when* you want to, you haven't got command of the sea. . . . We've been plenty submarine conscious and air-conscious. Now we're going to start getting mine-conscious—beginning last week." Recommissioning several minesweepers, Sherman gave priority to the development of mine-countermeasure technology, which paid benefits in Korea and when the U.S. Navy confronted a sizable mine threat in Vietnam. *See also* UN offensive across the Thirty-eighth Parallel.

M. W. Cagle and F. A. Manson, *The Sea War in Korea* (New York, 1980); J. A. Field, *History of United States Naval Operations—Korea* (Washington, D.C., 1962); *Korean War U.S. Fleet Operations, Interim Evaluation Report: Mine Warfare* (Washington, D.C., 1951); L. Montross and N. A. Canzona, *U.S. Marine Operations in Korea 1950–1953, vol. 3: The Chosin Reservoir Campaign* (Washington, D.C., 1954).

Lynne K. Dunn

WRONG, HUME (1894–1954)

Throughout the Korean War, Humphrey Hume Wrong was Canada's ambassador to the United States. Son of a famous Canadian historian, he was born in Toronto, Ontario, and graduated with a B.A. from the University of Toronto in 1915. Although he earned a scholarship to study at Oxford, Wrong volunteered for the Canadian army but was rejected because of an injured eye. Traveling to England, he received a commission in the British infantry and was wounded at the Somme. Wrong served briefly in the administrative office of the Canadian section of the Royal Flying Corps before enrolling at Oxford. After earning a B.Litt. and an M.A. in history, he joined the faculty of the University of Toronto in 1921 and subsequently published two books. When Canada opened its first legation in Washington, D.C., in 1927, Wrong, who had joined the foreign service, gained appointment as first secretary, later serving as counselor (1931–1935) and chargé (1935–1936). In 1937, he became Canada's permanent delegate to the League of Nations. At the start of World War II, Wrong went to London to help with economic coordination but returned to the U.S. legation the next year as senior counsellor.

In 1942, Wrong returned to Ottawa to become assistant under secretary for external affairs in charge of Commonwealth and European relations. Two years later, he assumed responsibility for all political divisions as the associate under secretary. In 1945, Wrong was an alternate delegate at the San Francisco Conference, serving the next year as Canada's representative at the first UN General Assembly meeting. In September 1946, he gained appointment as ambassador in Washington, D.C., working thereafter to promote close economic integration between the United States and the Commonwealth. A supporter of U.S. economic assistance to Europe, he wanted a separate Marshall Plan for Canada. A consistent advocate of collective security, Wrong proposed to revise the UN Charter to restrict the use of the veto. In response to the North Korean invasion of South Korea*, he enthusiastically endorsed the decision of Prime Minister Louis S. Saint Laurent* to provide military assistance to defend the Republic of Korea* but urged autonomy for Canadian forces. He stressed the importance of broad UN participation in the war effort because this would underscore the international character of the UN Command*.

When evidence emerged in November of Chinese military intervention*, Wrong voiced concern that CINCUNC General Douglas MacArthur* was exceeding his authority and thereby risking the loss of support from nations with troops fighting in Korea. He was an active participant in the Korean War briefing meetings*, in fact hosting the first gathering at the Canadian embassy. Throughout the war, Wrong faithfully presented his government's positions to the United States but was not reluctant to express his own opinions. For example, he agreed that if Chinese forces invaded the ROK, it would be necessary to condemn the People's Republic of China* as an aggressor, though this did not reflect Canada's attitude at the time. Similarly, Wrong offered much personal advice on the Joint Policy (Greater Sanctions) statement*. However, he shared the views of his government and Britain that it was essential to achieve an early armistice, encouraging the United States to reassure the PRC and avoid any indication of a desire to widen the war. After the start of the armistice negotiations, he emphasized the need to consult with Canada about any shift toward a more aggressive military strategy, speaking against an advance into North Korea. In 1953, Wrong became under secretary of state for external affairs. He suffered a fatal heart attack the following year.

Current Biography, 1950; *Foreign Relations of the United States, 1950*, vol. 7: *Korea* (Washington, D.C., 1976), *1951*, vol. 7: *Korea and China* (Washington, D.C., 1983), and *1952–1954*, vol. 7: *Korea* (Washington, D.C., 1984); *New York Times*, January 25, 1954; *Who Was Who in America*, vol. 3: *1953–1960* (Chicago, 1960).

WU HSIU-CH'UAN (WU XIUQUAN; 1908–   )

Wu Hsiu-Ch'uan's place in the Korean War is in his representing the People's Republic of China* to the UN in New York soon after Chinese military intervention* into the war. The tone and substance of his appearance before the UN Security Council was confident and defiant, for he knew how badly the Chinese People's Volunteers Army* (CPVA) had just defeated the UN, largely U.S., forces in the hills of North Korea. Although the Korean War was prominently discussed by Wu and his delegation in the twelve-day visit, it was clearly secondary to Taiwan and the PRC UN representation question*. Thus, foremost on Wu's agenda and prominently featured in Chinese foreign policy as well as the press, was the protest against continuing U.S. support for the Republic of China* in the Chinese Civil War and as China's representative to the UN. Wu's protest was an appeal to international law prohibiting outside interference in the internal affairs of a sovereign state.

When the stalemate set in by the spring of 1951, Chinese confidence in any appeal to the UN and positive references to the UN soon disappeared. As if to seal the PRC's disappointment, the UN General Assembly, pressured by the United States, passed the UN resolution of February 1, 1951*, labeling China as an ''aggressor'' in the Korean War. Wu's visit and that vote are turning points in the mutual escalation of Sino-U.S. hostilities in the Pacific. Wu returned to Peking on December 30, 1950, via Europe, just as he was appointed vice-minister of foreign affairs.

Wu's career charts the dramatic shifts in Sino-Soviet relations from the early friendship toward the Soviet Union, reaching a high point on the eve of the Korean War, to the rift beginning in the mid–1950s, to the rapprochement today. Leaving China at the age of 18, Wu studied five years at the Sun Yat-sen University in Moscow. He later joined Mao Tse-tung* in Shensi province, serving as chief of staff of the Red Army headquarter there. He survived the Long March, became the director of the Foreign Affairs Department of the Chinese Communist party (CCP) at Yenan, represented the party to the Marshall Mission in China in 1946, headed the Soviet Union and East European Affairs Department in the foreign ministry after 1949, and accompanied Foreign Minister Chou En-lai* to Moscow in January 1950 to negotiate the Sino-Soviet Treaty of Friendship and Alliance*.

However close China and the Soviet Union were in policy at mid-century, the Korean War may have become an important factor in the Sino-Soviet dispute. The Soviet Union supplied material for the Chinese war effort, but at cost, and its support after the Chinese spring offensives of 1951* when the CPVA became overextended was largely rhetorical. Wu disappeared from official circles between 1967 and 1974 during the Great Proletarian Cultural Revolution. Since then, he has resumed his membership on the Central Committee of the party and has served as vice-minister of foreign affairs. *See also* UN Invitation to the PRC to Participate in Debate.

D. W. Klein and A. B. Clark (eds.), *Biographic Dictionary of Chinese Communism, 1921–1965* (Cambridge, 1971); *New York Times,* November 28–30, December 1–10, 1950; Renmin chuban she, *Weida de kangMei yuanChao yungdong,* vol. 1 (Peking, 1954); *United Nations Security Council Official Records,* 1950, meeting 527.

Philip West

Y

YALU BRIDGES CONTROVERSY

Bombing the Yalu bridges became an issue when evidence began to emerge of Chinese military intervention* in the Korean War. The People's Republic of China* warned the United States that crossing the thirty-eighth parallel by South Korean troops would be tolerated but if U.S. soldiers pushed into the Democratic People's Republic of Korea* the PRC would intervene. China's action would occur to protect its heavy industry zone in Manchuria; Korea had traditionally been the route of invasion of China through Manchuria.

As U.S. forces pushed past the parallel, North Korean troops were regrouping farther north or crossing the bridges into China. Some Chinese troops were crossing into Korea, though it was some time before the UNC* confirmed that fact. When CINCUNC General Douglas MacArthur* ordered bombing attacks on the bridges across the Yalu River, the JCS instructed the general to postpone the operation. They feared that possible bomb damage on the Chinese side would bring the PRC (and possibly the Soviet Union, since the Sino-Soviet Treaty of Friendship and Alliance* was in effect) into a widening war. MacArthur insisted on the need to eliminate the bridges to hamper the flow of men and material into North Korea and to protect American lives, since U.S. forces had advanced to within 35 miles of the border.

In time, permission to destroy the Korean end of the bridges was received. There were sixteen bridges across the Yalu and Tumen rivers (the latter was the border between Korea and the Soviet Union). Some were damaged or dropped during the bombing raids. Yet the problems of Chinese response, by anti-aircraft fire or the fighters of the Chinese air force, increased exponentially the possibility of a wider war. The bombing did not appreciably interrupt the flow of goods or men because half the bridges still stood and the rivers froze. The United States announced that it had no intention of invading Chinese territory, thereby hoping to ease tensions. Instead, the bombing of the Yalu bridges brought to the attention of the Chinese people the reality of the U.S. military threat to them. *See also* Chinese Military Disengagement of November 6, 1950.

D. Acheson, *The Korean War* (New York, 1971); S. B. Griffith, *The Chinese People's Liberation Army* (New York, 1967); E. P. Hoyt, *The Bloody Road to Panmunjom* (New York, 1985); B. I. Kaufman, *The Korean War* (Philadelphia, 1986).

Katherine K. Reist

YANG YOU CHAN (YANG YU-CH'AN; 1897–1975)

Yang You Chan was the Republic of Korea's* ambassador to the United States from 1951 to 1960. Born in Pusan, he moved in 1903 with his family to Hawaii, where he grew up. He attended the Korean Christian Institute in Honolulu, which was run by Syngman Rhee*, thus becoming Rhee's protégé. After studying at the University of Hawaii, Yang graduated from Boston University and its medical school in 1922 with an M.D. degree. In 1923, he opened a private practice in medicine in Honolulu, gaining wealth and prominence. In Hawaii, he worked closely with Rhee until Rhee's return to Korea in 1945 and was an active local leader in Korean-U.S. affairs.

When Yang became ambassador in March 1951, replacing John M. Chang*, the United States had already begun to pursue a cease-fire in the Korean War. Yang, however, was strongly opposed to any truce that did not bring the reunification of Korea under the ROK. He later recalled that his "most important task [in Washington] was to carry out diplomatic activities aimed at blocking the armistice negotiations that the United States was pursuing." Toward this objective, he spoke out forcefully and frequently against the P'anmunjŏm truce talks*, insisting that the Communists were not trustworthy and that any attempt to reach an agreement with them constituted appeasement. In July 1952, at Colgate University's Conference on American Foreign Policy, he stated that unless the "foreign-imposed line of artificial division" of Korea was eliminated, "the principle of collective security is flouted and no people anywhere can consider themselves safe." When the armistice negotiations were approaching the final agreement, Yang publicly stated that South Korea "will go it alone" and then charged that the UNC* "has sold us down the river." His outspoken criticism led the State Department to consider declaring Yang as persona non grata for having "far exceeded his functions as a foreign diplomat." Subsequently, he became the deputy head of the ROK delegation to the Geneva Conference of 1954*, which was held unsuccessfully in accordance with the Korean armistice agreement*.

Current Biography, 1953; *New York Times*, June 14, 1953; *Who Was Who in America*, vol. 7: *1979–1981* (Chicago, 1981); Yang Yu-ch'an, "Namgigo Sip'un Iyagi," in *Chungang Ilbo* (Los Angeles edition), November 17, 1987-January 12, 1988.

Yŏng-ho Ch'oe

YI PŎM-SŎK (LEE BUM SUK; 1900–1972)

Yi Pŏm-sŏk, founder of the Racial Youth Corps, served as ambassador to the Republic of China* in Taipei after the outbreak of the Korean War and also, briefly in 1952, as home minister of the Republic of Korea*. Born in Seoul, Yi spent most of his politically active years in China. He went to China in 1915 and graduated from the Yunnan Military Academy in 1919. The next year, he led a successful attack on Japanese forces in northeastern Manchuria, securing a reputation as a leading opponent of Japanese colonial rule over Korea. Yi remained in China, serving first as an instructor at Loyang Military Academy and officer for Chiang Kai-shek's* forces. From 1940 until 1945, he was chief of staff and later head of the Second Branch Unit of the Korean Restoration Army, the military arm of the Korean Provisional Government in exile in Nationalist China.

Yi returned to Korea soon after liberation and, with financial support from the U.S. Army in southern Korea, organized the Racial Youth Corps. Originally intended to provide an apolitical training ground for a future South Korean army, the Racial Youth Corps grew into a highly politicized organization that reminded many observers of the Hitler Youth Corps. In fact, Yi and his assistant, An Ho-sang*, made no secret of their admiration for Hitler's concept of a tightly disciplined, racially pure corps of anti-Communist political activists. After Yi became the first prime minister and, concurrently, defense minister of the ROK in 1948, President Syngman Rhee* forced him to dissolve his Racial Youth Corps, though it survived as one of the constituent elements of the Taehan Youth Corps*, which emerged in late 1949.

Yi was forced to step down as prime minister and then as defense minister in the first half of 1950, before the Korean War began. But in response to the North Korean invasion of South Korea*, Rhee asked him to participate in the initial military strategy sessions, though Yi was neither an active-duty military officer nor a member of the cabinet. Supporting the advice of John J. Muccio*, the U.S. ambassador to the ROK, he urged Rhee not to leave Seoul abruptly. Subsequently Yi would exercise political power as an organizer and vice-chairman of Rhee's Liberal party and was home minister for three months during the South Korean political crisis of 1952*. He used the police powers available to the home minister to coerce the National Assembly into accepting Rhee's demand for a shift from a cabinet to a presidential form of government. Yi subsequently became the scapegoat for the harsh measures taken against Rhee's opponents in the spring and summer of 1952. He sought but failed to win the vice-presidency of the ROK that year and again in 1956. His last public post was that of a member of the upper house of the National Assembly of the short-lived Second Republic from 1960 through 1961. *See also* South Korean Presidential Elections of 1952.

B. Cumings, *The Origins of the Korean War* (Princeton, 1981); M. Gayn, *Japan Diary* (Rutland, Vt., 1981); H. J. Noble, *Embassy at War* (Seattle, 1975); J. Oh, *Korea: Democracy on Trial* (Ithaca, N.Y., 1968).

Don Baker

YI SŬNG-YŎP (1905–1953)

Yi Sŭng-yŏp, minister of justice of the Democratic People's Republic of Korea*, was born on Tŏkjŏk island near Inch'ŏn and educated at Inch'ŏn Commercial School. In 1919, he participated in the March First Movement* and was expelled from the school. He joined the Korean Communist party in September 1925 and was a reporter for the *Chosŏn Ilbo*. His Communist activities led to his imprisonment in 1931, 1937, and 1940, each time for approximately four years. From 1941 to 1945, he was a board member of the Inch'ŏn District Rice Distribution Corporation, the post that would become a target for his opponents to label him pro-Japanese.

Immediately after liberation, Yi helped Pak Hŏn-yŏng* in reconstructing the Korean Communist party and became a member of its central committee. At the same time, he became a member of the Central People's Committee at the Committee for Preparation of Korean Independence. In November 1946, when the major leftist parties merged into a single South Korean Workers' party, he became a member of its central committee, chairman of its Kyŏnggi province branch, and editor in chief of the party organ, *Haebang Ilbo* ("Daily Liberation.") In early 1948, Yi fled to northern Korea and joined in the establishment of the DPRK, becoming minister of justice. In June 1949, the North Korean Workers' party absorbed the South Korean Workers' party, thus becoming the Korean Workers' party. Yi became its Politburo member and a secretary of its central committee. In this capacity, he was regarded as second to Pak Hŏn-yŏng in the South Korean Workers' party or domestic faction in North Korean politics.

On June 28, 1950, with the start of the North Korean occupation of South Korea*, Yi became chairman of the Seoul People's Committee. Six months later, he was engaged in secret cease-fire negotiations of 1951* with the South Korean leftists under U.S. auspices. About this time, the power struggle between the Kim Il Sung* *Kapsan* (Soviet exile) faction and the Pak Hŏn-yŏng domestic Communist faction became extremely intense. Indicative of Pak's impending demise, Yi was relieved in December 1951 as minister of justice. Five months later, he was ousted from the secretariat and demoted to chairman of the People's Inspection Committee, the sinecure post he lost ten months later. Immediately after the armistice, he was arrested with the other leaders of the South Korean Workers' party faction. At the military court in August 1953, he was sentenced to death and soon executed as a "state enemy who colluded with the American imperialists" to overthrow the North Korean regime.

D. Suh, *Kim Il Sung: The North Korean Leader* (New York, 1988).

Hakjoon Kim

YIM, LOUISE (IM YŎNG-SIN; 1899–1977)

Louise Yim, a pioneering woman leader in Korean education and a close political ally of Syngman Rhee*, was born into a relatively rich farming family in North Chŏlla province. She was educated at the Christian schools in Chŏnju, Korea, and Hiroshima, Japan, and at the University of Southern California, receiving her B.A. in 1950 and her honorary LL.D. in 1957. Yim founded Chung'ang Nursery School in 1932, which was developed into Chung'ang Women's College in 1946 and then Chung'ang University in 1953. She was chancellor of Chung'ang University from 1953 to 1971 and chair of the Korean Federation of Educators, a nationwide organization of teachers and professors at all levels.

An ardent lifelong supporter of Rhee, who called her "my daughter," Yim initially helped his anti-Japanese activities in the United States. Upon her return home in 1945, she engaged in anti-Japanese activities, maintaining contacts with Rhee. As the founder and president of the Korean Women's Nationalist party and a member of the South Korean Democratic Representative Council, she strongly supported Rhee's successful efforts to establish the Republic of Korea* in 1948. In 1946, Yim traveled to the United States in the capacity of the Democratic Representative Council's observer to the UN. In Rhee's first cabinet, she was appointed minister of commerce and industry, later being elected to the first National Assembly through by-election.

Only a month after Yim's reelection, the Korean War broke out. She campaigned in the United States in the capacity of the South Korean National Assembly's observer to the UN to mobilize U.S. public opinion for the cause of the ROK. In 1952, Yim ran for vice-president, supporting Rhee's candidacy for the president of the ROK, but was defeated. In the 1960s, she was adviser to President Park Chung Hee's Democratic Republican party. In the 1970s, Yim was a member of the National Council for Reunification, a rubber-stamp organ electing the president of the ROK under the *Yushin* constitution. However, she was still regarded in general as an educator rather than a politician.

New York Times, February 17, 1977; L. Yim, *My Forty Year Fight for Korea* (Seoul, 1951).

Hakjoon Kim

YŎNGCH'ŎN, BATTLE OF
See Battle of Yŏngch'ŏn

YŎSU-SUNCH'ŎN REBELLION (October 1948)

The government of President Syngman Rhee* was in office only two months when the army of the Republic of Korea's* 14th Regiment rebelled on October 19, 1948, at the southern port city of Yŏsu. The uprising, led by Communists among the regiment's senior non-commissioned officers, was touched off prematurely by a sudden order for part of the unit to move to Cheju-do to help suppress a rebellion on the island. Fearing that an investigation of the regiment's commander—who weeks earlier had been arrested on trumped-up charges of plotting against Rhee—was close to uncovering them, Communists in the regiment decided to rebel. The uprising began at regimental headquarters while troops and supplies were being loaded at the docks. Joined by local South Korean Labor party (SKLP) supporters, the rebels seized control of Yŏsu, moved by rail a few miles north to the city of Sunch'ŏn, and positioned themselves for further advances on two provincial capitals. Rightists and police in the two occupied cities were searched out and executed.

In its haste to suppress the Yŏsu-Sunch'ŏn rebellion, the Rhee government allowed many insurgents to escape into the nearby Chiri mountains, where they established themselves as guerrillas. The rebels did not attempt to hold Yŏsu and Sunch'ŏn, entrusting their defense to local Communists and youth group members. Sunch'ŏn was recaptured on October 23, but the government needed three more days to regain control of Yŏsu against much stiffer resistance. Although accurate casualty figures are unavailable, some 1,200 police, soldiers, and pro-government civilians were killed, as against 1,500 rebels and their supporters. Hundreds more suspected Communists were later executed or given long prison sentences (among them, Park Chung Hee, then a major and later president of the ROK, who though not directly involved in the rebellion, was a key leader in the Communist apparatus of the South Korean Constabulary army).

The Yŏsu-Sunch'ŏn rebellion created a tremendous sense of insecurity among the South Korean public. The military situation was precarious for the first few days; no one was sure whether the revolt was planned or whether it would spread to other constabulary units. Enough incidents occurred elsewhere to keep alive doubts about the loyalty of the security forces. Responding to pleas from Rhee, the Truman administration slowed the pace of U.S. military withdrawal from Korea*, thus squelching rumors that the United States was about to abandon the ROK. In the aftermath of the rebellion, Rhee imposed martial law on the southern provinces, passed a draconian national security law, and intensified the purge of Communists in the constabulary army.

It is unlikely that the uprising sought to overthrow Rhee's regime. The rebellion caught the SKLP by surprise, and in fact the Seoul branch of the party first heard of it from news reports. Although *Radio P'yŏngyang* had details of the rebellion on the air within hours, the thirty-eighth parallel—which the Democratic People's Republic of Korea* had just assumed responsibility for defending during Soviet military withdrawal from Korea*—remained quiet. It was not until a month later that the DPRK dispatched its first band of guerrillas across the parallel to relieve the pressure on the insurgents; the SKLP's turn to armed struggle did not come until the following spring. *See also* Cheju-do Rebellion.

Kim Sŏk-hak and Kim Chong-myŏng, *Kwangbok 30 Nyon, Chŏnnam ŭi Chuyo Sagon,* vol. 2: *Yŏsun Pallan* (Kwangju, 1975); J. I. Matray, *The Reluctant Crusade* (Honolulu, 1985); J. Merrill, *Korea: The Peninsular Origins of the War* (Newark, Del., 1989).

John Merrill

YOUNGER, KENNETH (1908–1976)

Sir Kenneth (Gilmour) Younger was minister of state at the British Foreign Office at the beginning of the Korean War. Because Foreign Minister Ernest Bevin* was often hospitalized, Younger had to handle on his behalf day-to-day business and some of the important issues related to the war. Educated in Winchester and Oxford, he served during World War II as an officer in the intelligence corps. Elected as a member of Parliament in 1945, he was regarded then as one of the most promising young Labour politicians. In his first year in the House,

Younger became minister of state. From 1946 to 1950, he was very active as a British representative at the UN. Among some senior Foreign Office officials, he was looked on as a "conceited young man" perhaps because of some of his views based on new Labour perspectives of foreign policy for Britain. Because of health reasons, Younger would retire from active politics in the 1960s and not become foreign minister as some expected.

Younger's role was particularly important in raising for the first time among the high-level officials within the Foreign Office the question of the next course of action after the UNC* restored the status quo ante bellum in the Korean War. He did this while pitched battles were still raging at the Pusan Perimeter*, to which Under Secretary of State William Strang answered, "smiling smugly," that he had not thought of the problem. Younger also took the initiative in raising the delicate issue of whether Britain should join forces with the United States in the event war broke out between the latter and the People's Republic of China* over Taiwan. The consensus among senior Foreign Office officials was that Britain could not remain aloof in a Sino-U.S. conflict and would have to join the United States against China. He brought the result to Bevin in the hospital, who freely expressed agreement but did not want to bring this matter to the cabinet because he wanted to "keep his hands free." Later he approached Minister of Labor Aneurin Bevan* with the same problem, who, somewhat to his surprise, expressed the opinion that in view of "world-wide alliance with the United States," he could not see any other choice, thus indicative of general mood in Britain in the summer of 1950. He played a most prominent role related to the Korean War when he led the British delegation in supporting the UN resolution of October 7, 1950*, which authorized the UN offensive across the thirty-eighth parallel*.

P. Lowe, *The Origins of the Korean War* (London, 1986); J. Y. Ra, "Britain and the Korean War" (Ph.D. dissertation, Cambridge, 1972).

J. Y. Ra

YU JAI HYUNG (YU CHAE-HŬNG) (1921–   )

At the time of the North Korean invasion of South Korea*, Brigadier General Yu Jai Hyung was commander of the army of the Republic of Korea's* 7th Division. His unit guarded the Ŭijŏngbu corridor, the closest and easiest invasion route to Seoul 30 miles to the south. A short, stocky man who gave the appearance of thorough competence, Yu was a graduate of the Japanese Military Academy (1940) and a former major in the Japanese army. After World War II, he graduated from the U.S. Military Government's English Language School in southern Korea and was the first commander of the South Korean Constabulary army. On June 25, 1950, Chief of Staff Chae Byung Dok* ordered Yu to move his forces northwest of Ŭijŏngbu in preparation to halt the North Korean advance and stage a counterattack the next morning. General Chae simultaneously ordered the 2d ROK Division, under the command of Brigadier General Lee Hyung Keun*, to provide military support in the area northeast of Ŭijŏngbu. On the morning of June 26, General Yu implemented his instructions, briefly halting the advance of North Korea's 3d and 4th Infantry Divisions, but Lee did not order his troops into battle. Without assistance, North Korean troops shattered the 7th Division. Yu led the soldiers who had not fled into the hills in a retreat south of the Han River, leaving the capital at Seoul open to occupation.

After promotion to major general, Yu assumed command of the ROK's II Corps and led his unit at the Battle of Yŏngch'ŏn* and during the UN offensive across the thirty-eighth parallel*. According to Major General Frank E. Lowe*, Yu "had exhibited superior leadership, possessed far more military knowledge than any other general officer in the Korean Army" but "has never been in favor with the high political officials in Korea." Consequently, he was relieved in late October 1950 just before the Chinese Communist troops shattered the ROK's II Corps. "Basing their decision on a quick and sudden victory," Lowe charged, "General Yu was relieved and replaced by a political favorite [Paik Son-yup*] in order to gain the glory." Lowe speculated that Defense Minister Shin Sung-mo* was responsible for this change of command. Yu then served on the UNC* delegation at the P'anmunjŏm truce talks*.

In 1954, Yu graduated from the U.S. Army's Command and General Staff School. Upon returning to Korea, he served as vice-chief of staff, commander of the 1st Army, and chairman of the ROK joint chiefs of staff. Yu retired from the military in 1960 with the rank of lieutenant general. During the next decade, he was ambassador to Thailand, Sweden, and Italy before become minister of defense in 1971.

R. E. Appleman, *South to the Naktong, North to the Yalu* (Washington, D.C., 1961); T. R. Fehrenbach, *This Kind of War* (New York, 1963); H. J. Noble, *Embassy at War* (Seattle, 1975); H. S. Truman papers, Harry S. Truman Library, Independence, Missouri; K. Yi, *Pigŭkŭi Kunindŭl* (Seoul, 1981).

Jinwung Kim

YUN CHI-YŎNG (1898–   )

Yun Chi-yoñg was vice-speaker and chairman of the Defense and Foreign Affairs Committee of the first National Assembly of the Republic of Korea*. Born to an illustrious family, Yun was educated in Japan (Waseda) and the United States (Hawaii, Princeton, George Washington, and American Universities). He worked for Syngman Rhee* in the United States after 1923, returning to Korea in 1937. He suffered imprisonment and torture in the hands of Japanese police. After Rhee's return to Korea in 1945, Yun worked again for him as his chief secretary until he was forced to resign as a result of Rhee's conflict with Lieutenant General John R. Hodge*, the U.S. occupation commander. He also became the first minister of home affairs when Rhee formed his cabinet but remained in the office for only five months. Yun failed to be reelected in the second parliamentary election held one month before the North Korean invasion of South Korea*. When the war broke out, he organized a volunteers' corps in Pusan to help government and UN forces. Yun also allegedly cooperated with the Americans in organizing special units to infiltrate North Korea. Yun was appointed minister to France in August 1950, but never assumed the post because he spent most of his time in New York after joining the Korean delegation to United Nations. In January 1951, he returned to Pusan.

Yun was elected to the National Assembly again in 1952, defeating a major political figure, Cho Pyŏng-ok*. He was outspoken in opposing the armistice agreement*, while backing Rhee in the South Korean political crisis of 1952* for constitutional revision and his reelection as president. According to his own account, he was against the idea of organizing in 1952 a new Liberal party for Rhee and did not join it, also opposing the high-handed methods employed by those around Rhee to force the hand of National Assembly. However, he was often regarded by the United States as one of the "trio clique" surrounding Rhee and exercising harmful influences, together with Yi Pŏm-sŏk* and Louise Yim*. Although he became alienated from Rhee, Yun never wavered in his personal loyalty to him to the end of his days. He remained independent in the National Assembly, isolated from main currents of politics. Yun participated in founding the Democratic Republican party after Park Chung Hee's military coup and became chairman of the party congress. He also worked for Park as his chief campaign manager in the presidential election of 1963. For two and a half years after the election, he served as mayor of Seoul. An active and energetic man, he has combined various functions and posts, which at one time amounted to thirty in number, apart from his activities in politics.

Yun Chi-yŏng, "Na ŭi Ilyŏk Sŏ," *Chungang Ilbo*, July 24, 1981.

J. Y. Ra

Z

ZINCHENKO, KONSTANTIN E. (1909–   )

Konstantin Zinchenko, the assistant secretary-general for Security Council Affairs at the UN from 1949 to 1952, served as an occasional conduit of feelers on Korea between UN officials and the Soviet government and vice-versa. A Soviet citizen, he was born and raised in the Ukraine and graduated in 1931 from the Mining Academy of Moscow. Zinchenko joined the Soviet Foreign Ministry in 1940 and became counsellor of his nation's embassy in London two years later. After serving in Moscow for three years, in June 1948 he became first counsellor and secretary-general of the Soviet Union to the UN. In April of the following year, he accepted appointment to the UN Secretariat. Although his position was supposed to be in service to the organization rather that to his country, his colleagues assumed that he reported everything of consequence to the Soviet mission.

Zinchenko's name first came up in relation to Korea in the spring of 1950, when the UNCOK proposed to Secretary-General Trygve Lie* that, on his upcoming visit to Moscow, he use his Soviet assistant to aid it in establishing contact with the Democratic People's Republic of Korea*. Lie declined, arguing that such a move might interfere with more pressing matters, such as the ongoing Soviet UN Security Council boycott*. In March 1951, Lie approached Zinchenko regarding the possibility of arranging talks on Korea through the Soviet Union. Zinchenko suggested raising the matter with Andrei A. Gromyko* and despite encouragement from Zinchenko to follow up a DPRK message to the UN of April 15, the United States backed off when the Communists launched the Chinese spring offensives of 1951*. In late June, Lie used Zinchenko to elaborate on the meaning of Jacob A. Malik's* radio address of June 23, 1951*. A year later, the Soviets appeared to be using Zinchenko to plant a feeler on agenda item 4*, POW repatriation, through the U.S. delegation at the UN, but an American follow-up led nowhere.

In June 1952, Zinchenko left New York on summer vacation and never came back. UN observers were puzzled over his failure to return, as he was considered

exceptional among Soviet diplomats for his ability to interact easily with West-
erners. Yet the last months of Joseph Stalin's* rule were ones of decreasing
contacts between U.S. and Soviet diplomats, and in that context, his abilities
may well have been regarded as liabilities. He formally resigned from his UN
post in May 1953 and did not resurface again until mid–1955, when he apparently
became a member of the staff of *News,* an English-language journal published
in Moscow. Rumors surfaced in 1957 that Zinchenko had spent the period from
his departure from New York in 1952 to his resurfacing almost three years later
in a prison camp, a victim of Stalin's last purge.

A. W. Cordier oral history, Oral History Project, Columbia University; *Foreign Relations of the United States, 1950,* vol. 7: *Korea* (Washington, D.C., 1976), *1951,* vol.
7: *Korea and China* (Washington, D.C., 1983), and *1952–1954,* vol. 15: *Korea* (Washington, D.C., 1984); *New York Times,* October 22, 1949, December 16, 1952, June 19,
1955, May 22, 1957; *U.N. Bulletin,* May 15, 1949.

                                                                    William Stueck

ZORIN, VALERIAN A. (1902–1986)

In October 1952, Valerian A. Zorin replaced Jacob A. Malik* as the Soviet
Union's permanent delegate at the UN, serving in this post until April 1953. He
joined the Communist party in 1924 and for the next decade was head of the
Comsomol Central Committee. Zorin graduated from the High Communist Institute of Education in 1933 and then engaged in two years of postgraduate study.
From 1935 to 1941, he held various party posts dealing with education and
helped to organize the Young Pioneers movement, a children's organization to
which most Soviet youngsters would belong. Zorin then gained appointment as
assistant general secretary at the Commissariat for Foreign Affairs. In 1943, he
began two years of service at the Central European section of the Foreign Ministry. He was Moscow's first postwar ambassador to Czechoslovakia and accompanied Eduard Benes on his return to Prague. In 1947, as a delegate to the
UN Economic Commission for Europe, Zorin criticized U.S. aid to Greece and
Turkey and then announced in July that the Soviets would not cooperate with
the Marshall Plan. That same year, he spent time with the Soviet delegation at
the UN.

Before the end of 1947, Zorin was back in Moscow serving as deputy foreign
minister. Reportedly he was in charge of the Communist coup in Czechoslovakia
in February 1948. With the outbreak of the Korean War, he was the primary
contact for Indian ambassador Sarvepalli Radhakrishnan* during the period of
Indian peace initiatives*. Zorin also informed U.S. representatives that the Soviet
Union had no intention of interfering in Korea's civil war. In October 1952, he
made his first appearance as Soviet permanent UN representative at the Disarmament Commission but failed to obtain approval for opening the discussions
to the public. When Zorin served as president of the UN Security Council in
November, Foreign Minister Andrei Y. Vyshinsky* spoke for Moscow during
debate over such key issues as the V. K. Krishna Menon* POW settlement
proposal*. One month after the death of Joseph Stalin*, Vyshinsky replaced

Zorin at the UN. After resuming his post as deputy foreign minister, Zorin was stationed from 1955 to 1956 in Bonn, West Germany, but then served again as deputy foreign minister for the rest of the 1950s. In 1960, he returned to the UN as Moscow's permanent representative. Two years later, Adlai E. Stevenson*, the U.S. permanent representative, told Zorin that he was prepared to wait ''until hell freezes'' for an answer to the question of whether the Soviets had placed missiles in Cuba. From 1965 to 1971, Zorin was ambassador to France, serving thereafter in retirement as ambassador at large on issues related to human rights.

Current Biography, 1953; *Foreign Relations of the United States, 1950,* vol. 7: *Korea* (Washington, D.C., 1976); *New York Times,* January 19, 1986; *Prominent Personalities in the USSR* (Metuchen, N.J., 1968).

Appendix A:
Statistical Information

Table A-1
Military Contributions to the United Nations Command[1]

Ground Forces (Personnel)

	30 Jun 51	30 Jun 52	31 Jul 53
United States[2]	253,250	265,864	302,483
Republic of Korea[3]	273,266	376,418	590,911
Australia	912	1,844	2,282
Belgium[4]	602	623	944
Canada	5,403	5,155	6,146
Columbia	1,050	1,007	1,068
Ethiopia	1,153	1,094	1,271
France	738	1,185	1,119
Greece	1,027	899	1,263
India[5]	333	276	70
Italy[5]	0	64	72
Netherlands	725	565	819
New Zealand	797	1,111	1,389
Norway[5]	79	109	105
Philippines	1,143	1,494	1,496
Sweden[5]	162	148	154
Thailand	1,057	2,274	1,294
Turkey	4,602	4,878	5,455
United Kingdom	8,278	13,043	14,198
Total	554,577	678,051	932,539

Air Forces (Squadrons)

	30 Jun 51	30 Jun 52	31 Jul 53
United States	58	67	66
Australia	1	1	1
Canada	1	1	1
South Africa	1	1	1
Total	61	70	69

Naval Forces (Ships)

	30 Jun 51	30 Jun 52	31 Jul 53
United States	186	195	261
Republic of Korea	34	67	76

	15 Jan 52	15 Oct 52
Australia	4	4
Canada	3	3
Colombia	1	1
Denmark	1	1
Netherlands	1	1
New Zealand	2	2
Thailand	2	2
United Kingdom	22	22

1. J. F. Schnabel and R. J. Watson, A History of the Joint Chiefs of Staff, Vol. 3: The Korean War (1979).
2. Includes marine and navy personnel under U.S. Army control.
3. Includes Korean Augmentation of the U.S. Army (KATUSA), ROK Marines, and civilian trainees.
4. Includes forty-four men from Luxembourg.
5. Contributed non-combat medical units only.

Table A-2
Battle Casualties[1]

Korean and Chinese

	Killed	Wounded	POW	Total
South Korea[2]	47,000	183,000	8,656	238,656
North Korea[3]	---	---	110,723	630,723
China[4]	---	---	21,374	381,374

United States

	Total	Army	Navy	USMC	Air Force
Total Casualties	142,091	109,958	2,087	28,205	1,841
Deaths	33,629	27,704	458	4,267	1,200
Killed in Action	23,300	19,334	279	3,308	379
Wounded in Action	105,785	79,526	1,599	24,281	379
Died	2,501	1,930	23	537	11
Other	103,284	77,596	1,576	23,744	368
Missing in Action	5,866	4,442	174	391	859
Died	5,127	3,778	152	391	806
Returned	715	664	13	0	38
Captured or interned	7,140	6,656	35	225	224
Died	2,701	2,662	4	31	4
Returned	4,418	3,973	31	194	220
Refused repatriation	21	21	0	0	0

United Nations (other than United States)

	Killed	Wounded	Missing/POW	Total
Australia	261	1,034	37	1,332
Britain	686	2,498	1,102	4,286
Canada	294	1,202	47	1,543
New Zealand	22	79	1	102
Others	1,931	6,484	1,582	9,997
Total	3,194	11,297	2,769	17,260

1. D. Rees, Korea: The Limited War (1964).
2. There were roughly one million South Korean civilian casualties.
3. There were roughly one million North Korean civilian casualties and the figure for total casualties includes estimates of dead and wounded.
4. Figure for total casualties includes estimates of both dead and wounded.

Table A-3
Prisoners of War[1]

Repatriates

Nationality	LITTLE SWITCH	BIG SWITCH	Total
Total.......	6,670	75,823	82,493
North Koreans....	5,640[2]	70,183[3]	75,823
Chinese..........	1,030	5,640[4]	6,670
Total.......	684	12,773	13,444
U.S..............	149	3,597	3,746
ROK..............	471	7,862	8,321
U.K..............	32	945	977
Turks............	15	229	243
Filipinos........	1	40	41
Canadians........	2	30	32
Colombians.......	6	22	28
Australians......	5	21	26
Frenchmen........	....	12	12
South Africans...	1	8	9
Greeks...........	1	2	3
Netherlanders....	1	2	3
Belgians.........	....	1	1
New Zealanders...	....	1	1
Japanese.........	....	1	1

Non-Repatriates

Held by UNC

Disposition	Total	Chinese	Korean
Total.....................	22,604	14,704	7,900
Returned to Communist control..	628	440	188
Escaped and missing............	13	2	11
Died in custody of Custodial Forces in India...........	38	15	23
Went to India with CFI.........	86	12	74
Returned to UNC control........	21,839	14,235	7,604

Held by Communists

Disposition	Total	U.S.	U.K.	Korean
Total.....................	359	23	1	335
Returned to Communist Control..	347	21	1	325
Went to India with CFI.........	2	....	....	2
Returned to UNC control........	10	2	....	8

1. W. G. Hermes, Truce Tent and Fighting Front (1966).
2. Includes 446 civilian internees (3 of them women) and 18 female POWs.
3. Includes 60,788 male POWs, 473 female POWs, 23 children, and 8,899 civilian internees.
4. Includes 1 female POW.

Appendix B: Summary of Personnel Changes

Table B-1
United Nations Command Senior Military Commanders[1]

Commander-in-Chief, United Nations Command (CINCUNC)

General of the Army, Douglas MacArthur	8 July 1950
Lt.-Gen. Matthew B. Ridgway	11 April 1951
(promoted Gen., 11 May 1951)	
General Mark W. Clark	12 May 1952

Commanding General, Eighth U.S. Army in Korea (EUSAK)

Lt.-Gen. Walton H. Walker	13 July 1950
Lt.-Gen. Matthew B. Ridgway	26 December 1950
Lt.-Gen James A. Van Fleet	14 April 1951
(promoted Gen., 1 August 1951)	
Lt.-Gen. Maxwell D. Taylor	11 February 1953
(Gen. 23, June 1953)	

Commanding General, US I Corps

Maj.-Gen. John B. Coulter [2]	2 August 1950
Maj.-Gen. Frank W. Milburn	11 September 1950
Maj.-Gen. John W. O'Daniel	19 July 1951
Maj.-Gen. Paul W. Kendall	29 June 1952
(Lt.-Gen., 16 September 1952)	
Maj.-Gen. Bruce C. Clarke	11 April 1953

Commanding General, IX Corps

Maj.-Gen. Frank W. Milburn	10 August 1950
Maj.-Gen. John B. Coulter	12 September 1950
Maj.-Gen. Bryant E. Moore	31 January 1950
(Moore died following a helicopter accident on 23 February)	
Maj.-Gen. Oliver P. Smith, USMC	24 February 1951
Maj.-Gen. William F. Hoge	5 March 1951
(Lt.-Gen., 3 June 1951)	
Maj.-Gen. Willard G. Wyman	24 December 1951
Maj.-Gen. Joseph P. Cleland	31 July 1952
Maj.-Gen. Reuben E. Jenkins	9 August 1952
(Lt.-Gen., 8 November 1952)	

Table B-1 (continued)

Commanding General, X Corps

Maj.-Gen. Edward M. Almond	26 August 1950
Maj.-Gen. Clovis E. Byers	15 July 1951
Maj.-Gen. Williston B$_3$ Palmer	5 December 1951
Maj.-Gen. I. D. White	15 August 1952
(Lt. Gen., 7 November 1952)	

Commanding General, Far East Air Forces (FEAF)

Lt.-Gen. George E. Stratemeyer	26 April 1949
Lt.-Gen. Earle E. Partridge (acting)	21 May 1951
Maj.-Gen. O. P. Weyland	1 June 1951
(Lt.-Gen., 28 July 1951;	
Gen., 5 July 1952)	

Commanding General, Fifth Air Force

Lt.-Gen. Earle E. Partridge	6 October 1948
Maj.-Gen. Edward J. Timberlake	21 May 1951
Maj.-Gen. Frank F. Everest	1 June 1951
Lt.-Gen. Glenn O. Barcus	30 May 1952
Lt.-Gen. Samuel E. Anderson	31 May 1953

Commander, Naval Forces Far East (COMNAVFE)

Vice-Adm. C. Turner Joy	26 August 1949
Vice-Adm. R. P. Briscoe	4 June 1952

Commander, Seventh Fleet, Task Force 70

Vice-Adm. A. D. Struble	6 May 1950
Vice-Adm. H. H. Martin	28 March 1951
Vice-Adm. R. P. Briscoe	3 March 1952
Vice-Adm. J. J. Clark	20 May 1952

Chief of Staff, ROK Army

Maj.-Gen. Chae Byung Dok	10 April 1950
Lt.-Gen. Chung Il Kwon	30 June 1950
Maj.-Gen Lee Chong Ch'an	23 June 1951
Lt.-Gen. Paik Son-yup	23 July 1952–
	5 May 1953

---

1. D. Rees, Korea: The Limited War (New York, 1964).
2. Milburn was acting CG, EUSAK, 23-26 December 1950 following Walker's death. The Corps was then commanded by Maj.-Gen. William B. Kean.
3. Maj.-Gen. I. P. Smith was acting CG, X Corps, 10-12 July 1952; Maj.-Gen. David L. Ruffner, acting CG, 12-14 August 1952; and Maj.-Gen. Joseph P. Cleland, acting CG, 1-7 April 1953.

Table B-2
Plenary Members of the Armistice Delegations[1]

<u>United Nations Command Delegation</u>

Vice-Adm. C. Turner Joy, USN	10 Jul 51-22 May 52
Maj.-Gen. Henry I. Hodes, USA	10 Jul 51-17 Dec 51
Rear-Adm. Arleigh A. Burke, USN	10 Jul 51-11 Dec 51
Maj.-Gen. Laurence C. Craigie, USAF	10 Jul 51-27 Nov 51
Maj.-Gen. Paik Son-yup, ROKA	10 Jul 51-24 Oct 51
Maj.-Gen. Lee Hyung Keun, ROKA	24 Oct 51-6 Feb 52
Maj.-Gen. Howard M. Turner, USAF	27 Nov 51-5 Jul 52
Maj.-Gen. Claude B. Ferenbaugh, USA	17 Dec 51-6 Feb 52
Rear-Adm. Ruthven E. Libby, USN	11 Dec 51-23 Jun 52
Lt.-Gen. William K. Harrison, Jr. USA	6 Feb 52-27 Jul 53
Maj.-Gen. Yu Jai Hyung, ROKA	6 Feb 52-28 May 52
Brig.-Gen. Frank C. McConnell, USA	22 May 52-26 Apr 53
Brig.-Gen. Lee Han Lim, ROKA	28 May 52-26 Apr 53
Brig.-Gen. Joseph T. Morris, USAF	5 Jul 52-26 Apr 53
Rear-Adm. John C. Daniel, USN	
Brig.-Gen. Ralph M. Oshborne, USA	23 Jun 52-27 Jul 53
Brig.-Gen. Choi Duk Shin, ROKA	26 Apr 53-16 May 53
Brig.-Gen. Edgar E. Glenn, USAF	25 Apr 53-20 June 53
Brig.-Gen. George M. Finch, USAF	20 Jun 53-27 Jul 53

<u>North Korean and Chinese Communist Delegation</u>

Lt.-Gen. Nam Il, NKPA	10 Jul 51-27 Jul 53
General Teng Hua, CPVA	10 Jul 51-24 Oct 51
Maj.-Gen. Lee Sang Cho, NKPA	10 Jul 51-27 Jul 53
Maj.-Gen. Hsieh Fang, CPVA	10 Jul 51-26 Apr 53
Maj.-Gen. Chang Pyong San, NKPA	10 Jul 51-24 Oct 51
General Pien Chang-wu, CPVA	24 Oct 51-26 Apr 53
Maj.-Gen. Chung Tu Hwan, NKPA	24 Oct 51-28 Apr 52
Rear-Adm. Kim Won Mu, NKPN	28 Apr 52-11 Aug 52
Maj.-Gen. So Hui, NKPA	11 Aug 52-26 Apr 53
General Ting Kuo-yu, CPVA	26 Apr 53-27 Jul 53
Maj.-Gen. Chang Chun San, NKPA	26 Apr 53-25 May 53
Maj.-Gen. Tsai Cheng-wen, CPVA	26 Apr 53-27 May 53
Admiral Kim Won Hu, NKPN	25 May 53-17 Jun 53
Maj.-Gen. Kim Dong Hak, NKPA	17 Jun 53-27 Jul 53

---

1. W. G. Hermes, <u>Truce Tent and Fighting Front</u> (1966).

Appendix C: Chronology of the Korean War

1882		Korean-American Treaty of Friendship and Commerce signed.
1919		March First Movement protests Japanese colonial rule in Korea.

1943

December	1	Cairo Declaration promises Korean independence ''in due course.''

1945

August	8	Soviet Union declares war on Japan and sends troops to occupy Korea.
	11	Soviet-U.S. agreement divides Korea at the thirty-eighth parallel into zones of military occupation.
September	2	Japan's formal surrender ends World War II.
	6	Creation of Korean People's Republic in Seoul.
	8	U.S. troops arrive in southern Korea to begin occupation.
December	21	Moscow Agreement provides formula for Korean reunification.

1946

May	8	Joint Soviet-American Commission adjourns after failing to agree on how to implement the Moscow Agreement.

1947

August	4	SWNCC 176/30 outlines steps to break Soviet-U.S. deadlock over Korean reunification.
September	17	United States refers issue of Korean independence to UN.

	29	JCS submits memorandum assessing Korea's strategic significance.
November	14	UN General Assembly approves resolution providing for a UN Temporary Commission on Korea (UNTCOK) to supervise national elections leading to reunification and independence.

1948

January	24	Soviet occupation commander refuses to permit UNTCOK entry into northern Korea, thus preventing national elections.
April	2	President Harry S. Truman approves NSC–8 as the basis for U.S. Korea policy.
May	10	Separate elections held under UN supervision in southern Korea.
August	15	Establishment of the Republic of Korea (ROK).
September	9	Establishment of the Democratic People's Republic of Korea (DPRK).
October	19	Outbreak of Yŏsu-Sunch'ŏn uprising in South Korea.
December	12	UN approves resolution recognizing the Republic of Korea as the only legitimate government on the peninsula, calling for Soviet-U.S. withdrawal as soon as practicable, and establishing a UN Commission on Korea (UNCOK)
	31	Soviet occupation forces withdraw from North Korea.

1949

March	23	President Truman approves NSC–8/2 as new U.S. Korea policy.
April	8	Soviet Union vetoes admission of the ROK to the UN.
May	2	Establishment of U.S.-Korean Military Advisory Group (KMAG).
June	29	U.S. occupation forces withdraw from South Korea.
October	21	UN passes resolution instructing the UNCOK to use its "good offices" to encourage Korean reunification, verify Soviet military withdrawal, and observe and report any developments contributing to the outbreak of hostilities.

1950

January	12	Secretary of State Dean G. Acheson excludes the ROK from U.S. defensive perimeter in National Press Club speech.
	19	House of Representatives defeats Korean aid bill of 1949–1950.

February	14	President Truman signs Far Eastern Economic Assistance Act.
		Sino-Soviet Treaty of Friendship and Alliance signed.
April	14	General Douglas MacArthur submits memorandum emphasizing Taiwan's strategic significance.
		NSC–68 recommends substantial increase in U.S. defense budget.
May	2	Senator Tom Connally predicts fall of the ROK to Communists.
	30	National Assembly elections in the Republic of Korea produce a majority of representatives opposed to President Syngman Rhee.
June	7	Democratic Fatherland Front proposes plan for reunification.
	15	John Foster Dulles arrives in South Korea on fact-finding mission and addresses National Assembly two days later.
	24	UNCOK surveys thirty-eighth parallel and finds ROK troops in defensive positions.
	25	North Korean army invades South Korea.
		UN Security Council approves resolution calling for cease-fire in Korea and withdrawal of DPRK forces north of thirty-eighth parallel.
		First Blair House meeting to discuss the crisis in Korea.
	26	Second Blair House meeting held.
	27	Arrival of Church survey mission in Korea and the creation of the Advance Command and Liaison Group in Korea (ADCOM).
		UN Security Council approves resolution calling upon members to provide assistance to the ROK in resisting aggression.
		President Truman announces U.S. air and naval assistance for the ROK and neutralization of Taiwan.
	28	Han River bridge destroyed prematurely trapping South Korean soldiers and civilians in Seoul.
		North Korean troops occupy Seoul, the capital of the ROK.

29   General MacArthur visits Korea and observes fighting at the Han River.

       Soviet Union informs the United States of intention to remain uninvolved in Korean civil war and declares UN Security Council resolutions illegal.

       President Truman at press conference agrees with a reporter's description of the Korean War as a "police action."

       Congress approves Deficiency Appropriations Act providing additional aid to the ROK.

30   President Truman commits ground forces in Korean War.

July

2   President Truman rejects Chiang Kai-shek's offer of Chinese troops for service in the Korean War.

5   Battle of Osan and first Battle of Wŏnju.

7   UN Security Council resolution establishes UN Command.

8   President Truman appoints General Douglas MacArthur commander in chief of UN Command (CINCUNC).

12   U.S. and the ROK sign the Taejŏn Agreements.

13   Army Chief of Staff General J. Lawton Collins and Air Force Chief of Staff General Hoyt S. Vandenberg visit Tokyo for discussions with MacArthur lasting until July 14.

       Indian prime minister Jawaharlal Nehru urges United States and Soviet Union to take steps to localize and terminate the Korean War.

14   Battle of the Kŭm River, lasting until July 20.

15   President Syngman Rhee transfers control of the ROK's military forces to the UNC for the duration of the Korean War.

19   President Truman addresses nation on the Korean crisis.

20   North Korean forces seize city of Taejŏn.

29   Lieutenant General Walton W. Walker, 8th Army commander, issues "stand or die" order.

31   MacArthur visits Taiwan until August 1 to discuss measures for defense of the island.

August

1   Soviet Union ends boycott of UN Security Council, as Jacob Malik assumes position as president of the body.

4   UN forces withdraw inside Pusan Perimeter.

5   Battle of the Naktong Bulge, lasting until August 19.

6   W. Averell Harriman visits Tokyo with Lieutenant General Matthew B. Ridgway for discussions with MacArthur until August 8.

9 Beginning of the defense of Taegu.

10 First bombing raid on Rashin (Najin).

15 Establishment of the Korean Augmentation of the U.S. Army (KATUSA).

17 U.S. permanent representative at UN, Warren R. Austin, calls for reunification of Korea.

19 General Collins and Navy Chief of Staff Admiral Forrest P. Sherman visit Tokyo to discuss plans for the Inch'ŏn landing with CINCUNC General Douglas MacArthur.

25 Publication of MacArthur's VFW message.

Secretary of the Navy Francis P. Matthews refers to the possibility of waging a preventive war against the Soviet Union.

26 Creation of the X Corps in preparation for the Inch'ŏn landing.

September 1 President Truman addresses Congress to explain U.S. policy the in Korean War.

Mobilization of four U.S. National Guard divisions.

4 U.S. Navy fighters shoot down Soviet aircraft over Yellow Sea.

5 Battle of Yŏngch'ŏn, lasting until September 13.

8 Congress approves Defense Production Act.

11 Truman orders implementation of NSC-81, the plan for the military offensive across the thirty-eighth parallel.

12 Secretary of Defense Louis A. Johnson resigns; General George C. Marshall is his replacement.

15 UNC stages Inch'ŏn landing.

18 UN forces recapture Kimp'o Airfield.

19 8th Army begins breakout from Pusan Perimeter.

25 JCS authorizes ground operations north of thirty-eighth parallel.

Acting Chief of Staff of Chinese People's Liberation Army warns that China will not "sit back with folded hands and let the Americans come up to the border."

27 8th Army and the X Corps link forces south of Seoul.

JCS directive forbids air operations beyond Yalu River.

29 UN forces complete recapture of Seoul operation.

30 South Korea's 3d Division crosses thirty-eighth parallel.

October 2 Chinese premier Chou En-lai warns Indian ambassador K. M. Panikkar that People's Republic of China will intervene in Korean War if U.S. forces cross thirty-eighth parallel.

7   UN resolution authorizes military operations to reunite Korea and establishes UN Committee for the Unification and Rehabilitation of Korea (UNCURK).

8   U.S. planes strafe Soviet air base in Siberia.

9   General MacArthur demands immediate North Korean surrender.

10 North Korean leader Kim Il Sung rejects surrender demand.

11 South Korea's 3d Division captures port of Wŏnsan.

12 UN Interim Committee resolves that the UN recognizes no government as having "legal and effective control" over North Korea and asks the UNC to assume administrative responsibility in the north pending arrival of the UNCURK.

15 President Truman and MacArthur meet at Wake Island Conference.

19 Chinese People's Volunteers Army crosses the Yalu.

    South Korean forces occupy P'yŏngyang.

24 MacArthur removes restrictions on movement of non-Korean forces to provinces bordering the Yalu River.

25 X Corps lands at Wŏnsan harbor.

    Opening of Chosin (Changjin) Reservoir Campaign.

27 China opens first offensive lasting until October 31, and UNC captures first Chinese "volunteers."

28 JCS sends MacArthur an occupation directive for North Korea.

November   1   Battle of Ŭnsan, lasting until November 6.

                  First Chinese MiGs appear along Yalu River.

              3   UN approves Uniting for Peace resolution to permit the General Assembly to act against an aggressor and to create a UN Collective Measures Committee.

              6   Chinese forces attack 8th Army north of Ch'ŏngch'ŏn River and then disengage, starting a three-week lull in the fighting.

              7   MacArthur requests approval for hot pursuit of Chinese planes into Manchuria and destruction of Yalu bridges.

              8   UN Security Council passes resolution inviting the PRC to participate in debate on the issues of Korea and Taiwan.

             10   Soviet Union vetoes UN Security Council measure calling upon the PRC to withdraw its forces from Korea.

British Foreign Minister Ernest Bevin submits "buffer zone" proposal to U.S.

24 MacArthur announces while visiting Korea the start of the Home-by-Christmas offensive.

PRC representative Wu Hsui-ch'uan arrives at UN for discussions.

26 Chinese launch second offensive lasting until December 9.

28 PRC's representative to the UN Wu Hsui-ch'uan denounces the United States for aggression in Korea.

30 President Truman's atomic bomb press conference comment.

First Korean War briefing meeting at the Canadian embassy.

December
1 MacArthur points to prohibitions on air strikes in Manchuria to explain the UNC retreat in *U.S. News and World Report* interview.

Passage of UN resolution establishing UN Korean Reconstruction Agency (UNKRA).

4 British prime minister Clement Attlee begins trip to United States.

5 UN forces evacuate P'yŏngyang.

6 JCS directive bans unauthorized public statements by government officials regarding the war.

8 Issuance of Truman-Attlee communiqué.

10 Hŭngnam evacuation of the X Corps and 7th Infantry Division begins, lasting until December 24.

14 UN resolution establishes UN Ceasefire Group.

15 UNC forces retreat below the thirty-eighth parallel.

16 President Truman declares state of national emergency.

19 PRC Delegation leaves UN.

20 Former President Herbert Hoover delivers "Gibraltar America" speech.

23 PRC premier Chou En-lai rejects UN Ceasefire Group's proposal, demanding U.S. withdrawal from Korea and Taiwan and the PRC's admission to the UN.

General Walker, 8th Army commander, killed in a jeep accident.

26   Lieutenant General Matthew B. Ridgway arrives in Korea to replace Walker.

31   China launches third offensive south of the thirty-eighth parallel.

1951

January

1   Mobilization of two more U.S. National Guard divisions.

3   UN Ceasefire Group reports failure of negotiations with PRC.

4   Chinese Communist forces capture Seoul.

11   UN Ceasefire Group proposes five principles as basis for a settlement of the Korean War.

12   JCS rejects MacArthur's plan for winning the Korean War.

13   U.S. votes in favor of UN cease-fire resolution that promises discussion of other Far Eastern issues.

15   Operation Wolfhound begins, lasting until January 25 and forcing Chinese retreat to Osan.

Generals Collins and Vandenberg visit Tokyo for discussions with General MacArthur.

17   China rejects UN Ceasefire Group's five principles because ''the purpose of arranging a ceasefire first [before negotiating] is merely to give the United States troops a breathing space.''

25   Operation Thunderbolt begins, lasting until February 1 and forcing Chinese retreat to the Han River.

February

1   Passage of UN resolution condemning China for aggression in Korea and establishing UN Additional Measures Committee and UN Good Offices Committee.

5   Operation Punch forces the Chinese to retreat north of Seoul.

Operation Roundup met with Chinese counterattack, forcing the X Corps on February 11 to retreat southward to Wŏnju.

10   South Korean National Guard units slaughter innocent civilians at the town of Kŏch'ang.

11   Fourth Chinese offensive to force UNC retreat from central Korea.

13   Battle of Chip'yŏng, lasting until February 15.

15   General MacArthur requests permission to bomb Rashin (Najin).

21   Operation Killer begins, lasting until March 1 and pushing Communist forces in central Korea north of Han River.

March	7	Operation Ripper begins, lasting until March 21 and forcing Chinese retreat north of thirty-eighth parallel.
		MacArthur makes "die for tie" statement at a press conference in Korea.
	14	UNC completes recapture of Seoul from the Chinese Communists.
	15	MacArthur advocates in a press interview crossing the thirty-eighth parallel to fulfill the UNC mission of reuniting Korea.
	20	JCS informs MacArthur of Truman's planned cease-fire initiative.
	22	Operation Courageous by March 29 moves the UNC to a position just south of the thirty-eighth parallel.
	24	MacArthur issues "pronunciamento" demanding Communist surrender.
	26	Washington Conference of foreign ministers of nations in the Western Hemisphere begins, lasting until April 7.
	29	PRC radio broadcast rejects MacArthur's ultimatum and calls for renewed military efforts.
April	3	Operation Rugged allows UNC forces to cross the thirty-eighth parallel and establish the Kansas Line on April 6.
	5	Republican House Minority Leader Joseph W. Martin, Jr., of Massachusetts reads letter from MacArthur dated March 20 in the House calling for victory in the Korean War.
	6	Operation Dauntless, lasting until April 11, results in the UNC's establishing the Kansas-Wyoming Line.
	11	Truman recalls MacArthur, replacing him with General Ridgway.
	14	Lieutenant General James A. Van Fleet arrives in Korea to replace Ridgway as 8th Army commanding general.
	19	MacArthur delivers "No Substitute for Victory" speech to a joint session of Congress.
	22	China opens first stage of fifth offensive, lasting until April 28.
		Battle of the Imjin River, lasting until April 25.
	23	Battle of Kap'yŏng, lasting until April 25.
	28	JCS authorizes UNC attacks on air bases in Manchuria if Chinese Communist planes threaten the security of UNC forces on the ground.
May	3	Senate MacArthur Hearings before Joint Committee of Armed Services and Foreign Relations commence, lasting until June 25.

	16	China opens second stage of fifth offensive, lasting until May 23.

16 China opens second stage of fifth offensive, lasting until May 23.

17 Truman approves NSC–48/5.

18 UN resolution calls for selective embargo against PRC.

Assistant Secretary of State Dean Rusk delivers speech referring to the PRC as "a Slavic Manchukuo on a large scale" and "not the Government of China."

30 UNC forces restore defensive positions at Kansas Line.

31 First meeting between George F. Kennan and Jacob A. Malik regarding possible cease-fire negotiations in Korean War.

JCS sends new directive to Ridgway on future conduct of the war.

June

1 Operation Piledriver moves UNC forces to Wyoming Line.

2 UNC implements Operation Strangle.

5 Second Kennan-Malik meeting.

15 UNC consolidates defensive position along Kansas-Wyoming Line.

23 Jacob Malik's radio broadcast suggests opening of truce talks.

29 CINCUNC General Ridgway offers to meet Communist commander in the field to discuss a cease-fire and armistice.

July

10 Opening session of Kaesŏng truce talks.

14 Communist delegation agrees to permit equal press coverage.

15 Governor Thomas E. Dewey visits Korea.

26 Approval of agenda for Kaesŏng truce talks.

28 Commonwealth Division established.

August

17 Communist delegation demands UNC apology for ambush near Kaesŏng.

18 Battle of Bloody Ridge, lasting until September 5.

23 Communists suspend truce talks because of alleged UNC strafing of Kaesŏng neutral zone.

25 U.S. bombing raid on Rashin (Najin).

September

1 ANZUS Treaty signed.

8 Japanese Peace Treaty signed in San Francisco.

11 Acheson meets with British foreign minister Herbert S. Morrison.

13 Battle of Heartbreak Ridge, lasting until October 15.

	28	JCS Chairman General Omar N. Bradley and State Department Soviet expert Charles E. Bohlen visit Tokyo and Korea until October 3.
October	3	Operation Commando, lasting until October 8.
	5	U.S. ambassador Alan G. Kirk meets Soviet foreign minister Andrei Y. Vyshinsky and urges him to persuade Chinese and North Koreans to resume armistice negotiations.
	22	Signing of the P'anmunjŏm security zone agreement.
	24	Battle of Namsi, largest air clash of the war.
	25	Truce talks resume at P'anmunjŏm.
		Winston Churchill replaces Clement Attlee as British prime minister following Labour Party's electoral defeat.
November	12	Ridgway orders 8th Army to implement active defense strategy.
		Operation Ratkiller begins to kill or capture guerrillas in South Korea, lasting until March 15, 1952.
	13	At P'anmunjŏm, the UNC proposes the battle line as the demarcation line for a DMZ if all other issues are settled in thirty days.
	27	Agreement reached at P'anmunjŏm truce talks on agenda item 2, demarcation line and DMZ.
	28	First Anglo-American discussion of Joint Policy (Greater Sanctions) statement.
December	3	Negotiators at P'anmunjŏm refer Communist proposal for settling agenda item 3, covering cease-fire inspection, to subdelegates to work out the details.
	20	Truman administration approves NSC-118/2.
	27	Agreement on demarcation line at P'anmunjŏm invalidated.

1952

January	2	UNC proposes voluntary repatriation of POWs at P'anmunjŏm.
	8	Communist delegation rejects voluntary repatriation principle.
	27	P'anmunjŏm negotiators agree to defer discussion of airfield rehabilitation.
	31	Negotiators shift to subdelegation discussion of agenda item 5, political consultations between governments.
February	10	Operation Clam-Up, lasting until February 15.

	16	Communist negotiators at P'anmunjŏm suggest that the Soviet Union should be a member of the neutral commission in charge of supervising the ceasefire.
	18	Soviet Union charges U.S. with waging biological warfare in North Korea.
	19	Agreement at P'anmunjŏm truce talks on agenda item 5 provides for political conference ninety days after the armistice to discuss withdrawal of foreign troops and Korean reunification.
March	26	U.S. delegate at UN denies charges of using biological warfare and criticizes Communists for refusing an impartial investigation.
April	2	Communist delegation at P'anmunjŏm recommends checking POW lists.
	5	Operation Scatter results in screening of POWs in UNC camps, lasting until April 15.
	8	Truman seizes U.S. steel mills.
	10	Meyer mission to Republic of Korea begins, lasting until May 24.
	20	UNC announces only 70,000 Communist POWs desire repatriation.
	28	UNC submits package proposal at P'anmunjŏm truce talks, but Communist delegation refuses to accept voluntary repatriation.
		Truman appoints General Mark W. Clark to replace Ridgway.
May	2	Communists partially accept package proposal, dropping the Soviet Union as a NNSC member for no limits on airfield rehabilitation.
	7	Kŏje-do POW camp uprising begins with seizure of camp commander, Brigadier General Francis T. Dodd, lasting until June 10.
	11	Communist POWs release General Dodd.
	12	General Clark formally assumes command as CINCUNC.
	19	Publication of John Foster Dulles's "A Policy of Boldness" article in *Life* magazine.
	22	Foreign Minister Anthony Eden sends draft of Anglo-Indian Five Point Plan for settling POW controversy to Washington.
	24	U.S. and ROK sign Agreement on Economic Coordination.
	25	President Syngman Rhee declares martial law in Pusan.

June	2	Supreme Court declares Truman's seizure of steel plants unconstitutional in *Youngstown Sheet and Tube v. Sawyer*.
	10	UN forces rout militant POWs, ending Kŏje-do uprising.
	22	Lloyd-Alexander mission to Tokyo.
	23	Suiho bombing raids begin, lasting until June 26.
	25	Assassination attempt on President Rhee.
		JCS authorizes General Clark to develop Operation Everready for removal of Rhee from power in South Korea.
	26	Battle of Old Baldy begins, lasting until March 23, 1953.
July	1	Operation Homecoming releases 27,000 civilian internees, lasting until the end of August.
	4	South Korean National Assembly passes amendment for popular election of the president, ending the political crisis.
	7	Communist delegation at P'anmunjŏm repeats its demand for the repatriation of all Chinese POWs.
	11	Massive UNC air raid on P'yŏngyang.
August	5	South Korean presidential elections produce victory for Rhee.
	27	Second UNC air raid on P'yŏngyang—largest of the war.
September	2	Mexican POW settlement proposal submitted to the UN.
	28	UNC presents final proposal to settle POW repatriation issue.
October	1	Cheju-do POW uprising.
	6	Battle of White Horse Hill signals Communist acceleration of ground war, lasting until October 15.
	8	UNC declares indefinite recess of the P'anmunjŏm truce talks.
	13	Operation Showdown reveals futility of ground assaults against entrenched Communist positions.
	14	Battle of Triangle Hill, lasting until November 5.
	24	Republican presidential nominee Dwight D. Eisenhower pledges to ''go to Korea'' if elected.
		U.S. introduces Twenty-one Power UN resolution, calling for a reaffirmation of support for voluntary repatriation concept.
	26	Battle of the Hook, lasting until July 25, 1953.
November	3	Peruvian POW settlement proposal submitted at the UN.
	4	Dwight D. Eisenhower elected president of the United States.

	10	General Van Fleet, the 8th Army commander, announces mobilization of two new South Korean divisions and six regiments.
	17	Menon POW settlement proposal submitted at the UN.
	18	Truman-Eisenhower transition meeting held at the White House.
December	2	President-elect Eisenhower tours Korea until December 5.
	3	UN resolution endorses Menon POW settlement proposal.
	9	U.S. bombing raid on Rashin (Najin).
	14	Pongam-do POW uprising.
	17	Eisenhower meets with MacArthur, who submits plan for victory.

1953

January	20	Eisenhower inaugurated president of the United States.
	25	Operation Smack tests close air support strategy.
February	2	"Unleashing" of Chiang in Eisenhower's State of the Union speech.
	7	Clark requests permission to bomb Kaesŏng.
	22	UNC proposes exchange of sick and wounded POWs.
		Lieutenant General Maxwell D. Taylor replaces Van Fleet as commander of the 8th Army.
March	5	Death of Soviet leader Joseph Stalin.
	15	Georgi Malenkov speech voices support for cease-fire in Korea.
	20	JCS approves Operation Moolah to encourage MiG pilots to defect.
	23	Battle of Pork Chop Hill, lasting until July 11.
	28	Communist delegation at P'anmunjŏm accepts UNC proposal for exchange of sick and wounded POWs.
	30	Chou En-lai radio broadcast outlines POW settlement proposal for exchange of sick and wounded plus non-repatriate POWs to a neutral state.
April	2	President Eisenhower approves NSC-147, a contingency plan to escalate military operations against the DPRK and the PRC.
	11	Operation Little Switch receives approval.
	17	Start of Tasca Mission to study Republic of Korea's economy, lasting until June 15.
	18	UN resolution calls for convening General Assembly after signing of a Korean armistice agreement.

20 Exchange of sick and wounded POWs, lasting until May 3.

22 Eisenhower approves arms and equipment for two new ROK divisions.

26 Resumption of P'anmunjŏm truce talks.

May 7 Lieutenant General Nam Il advances eight-point POW settlement proposal.

13 Start of UNC raids on dams in North Korea, lasting until May 16.

President Eisenhower approves arming four more South Korean divisions, to a total army strength of twenty divisions.

22 General Clark sends Operation Everready plan to Washington, D.C., for final approval.

Secretary of State Dulles warns China through India that United States might use atomic weapons if UNC POW settlement proposal is rejected.

25 Final UNC POW settlement proposal submitted at P'anmunjŏm with the intention to terminate truce talks if Communists reject plan.

June 4 At P'anmunjŏm, Communists accept UNC final POW settlement proposal.

8 Communists formally approve concept of voluntary repatriation.

10 Communist forces open offensive against South Korean troops.

15 President Eisenhower receives Tasca report.

17 Acceptance of revised demarcation line at P'anmunjŏm truce talks.

18 President Rhee releases 27,000 North Korean POWs.

20 UNC delegation gains approval for recess at P'anmunjŏm.

22 Start of Assistant Secretary of State Walter S. Robertson's mission to the ROK, lasting until July 12.

July 6 Communists stage new military thrust into Iron Triangle.

7 Eisenhower administration approves NSC-154/1 and NSC-157/1.

10 Rhee agrees not to disrupt armistice agreement.

11 Issuance of Robertson-Rhee communiqué.

13 Final Chinese offensive of the war inflicts heavy casualties on South Korean forces in Kŭmsŏng region.

17 Eisenhower administration approves NSC-156/1.

		19	Agreement reached on all substantive points at P'anmunjŏm.
		27	Signing of the Korean armistice agreement.
			Signing of the Joint Policy (Greater Sanctions) statement, issued publicly on August 7.
		28	Military Armistice Commission meets for the first time.
August		8	Dulles and Rhee approve terms of U.S.-ROK Mutual Defense Treaty.

1954

January		26	U.S. Senate ratifies U.S.-ROK Mutual Defense Treaty.
February		1	Neutral Nation Reparation Commission formally dissolves.
April		26	Opening at Geneva Conference of discussions regarding Korean reunification.

Selected Bibliography

ANTHOLOGIES

Baldwin, Frank, ed. *Without Parallel: The Korean-American Relationship since 1945.* 1973.

Bernstein, Barton J., ed. *Politics and Policies of the Truman Administration.* 1970.

Borg, Dorothy, and Heinrichs, Waldo, eds. *Uncertain Years: Chinese-American Relations, 1947–1950.* 1980.

Bradbury, William C.; Meyers, Samuel M.; and Biderman, Albert D., eds. *Mass Behavior in Battle and Captivity: The Communist Soldier in the Korean War.* 1968.

Cumings, Bruce, ed. *Child of Conflict: The Korean-American Relationship, 1943–1953.* 1983.

Guttman, Allen, ed. *Korea: Cold War and Limited War.* 1972.

Heller, Francis H., ed. *The Korean War: A 25 Year Perspective.* 1977.

Koo Young-nok, and Suh Dae-sook, eds. *Korea and the United States: A Century of Cooperation.* 1984.

Lee Yur-bok, and Patterson, Wayne, eds. *One Hundred Years of Korean-American Relations, 1882–1982.* 1986.

Nagai Yonosuke and Iriye Akira, eds. *The Origins of the Cold War in Asia.* 1977.

ARMISTICE NEGOTIATIONS

Acheson, Dean G. "The Truce Talks in Korea." *Harper's* 203 (January 1953).

Bacchus, Wilfred. "The Relationship between Combat and Peace Negotiations: Fighting While Talking in Korea, 1951–1953." *Orbis* 17 (Summer 1973).

Bernstein, Barton J. "Syngman Rhee: The Pawn as Rook: The Struggle to End the Korean War." *Bulletin of Concerned Asian Scholars* 10 (January-March 1978).

———. "Truman's Secret Thoughts on Ending the Korean War." *Foreign Service Journal* 57 (November 1980).

Brands, Henry W., Jr. "The Dwight D. Eisenhower Administration, Syngman Rhee, and the 'Other' Geneva Conference of 1954." *Pacific Historical Review* 56 (February 1987).

Bullen, Roger. "Great Britain, the U.S. and the Indian Armistice Resolution on the Korean War, November 1952." *International Studies* 1 (1984).

Cai Chengwen and Zhao Yongtian. *Panmunjom Negotiations.* 1990.

Dingman, Roger. "Atomic Diplomacy during the Korean War." *International Security* 13 (Winter 1988–1989).

Foot, Rosemary. "Nuclear Coercion and the Ending of the Korean Conflict." *International Security* 13 (Winter 1988–1989).

———. *A Substitute for Victory: The Politics of Peacemaking at the Korean Armistice Talks*. 1990.

Friedman, Edward. "Nuclear Blackmail and the End of the Korean War." *Modern China* 1 (January 1975).

Goodman, Allan E., ed. *Negotiating While Fighting: The Diary of Admiral C. Turner Joy at the Korean Armistice Conference*. 1978.

Keefer, Edward C. "President Dwight D. Eisenhower and the End of the Korean War." *Diplomatic History* 10 (Summer 1986).

Kim Suk Young. *Panmunjom*. 1972.

Vatcher, William H. *Panmunjom: The Story of the Korean Military Armistice Negotiations*. 1958.

Young, Kenneth T. *Negotiating with the Chinese Communists*. 1968.

BACTERIOLOGICAL WARFARE

Clews, John. *The Communists' New Weapon: Germ Warfare*. 1953.

Endicott, Stephen L. "Germ Warfare and Plausible Denial: The Korean War, 1952–1953." *Modern China* 5 (January 1979).

Gittings, John. "Talks, Bombs, and Germs: Another Look at the Korean War." *Journal of Contemporary Asia* 5 (1975).

Van Ginneken, Jaap. "Bacteriological Warfare." *Journal of Contemporary Asia* 7 (1977).

BIOGRAPHIES

Allen, Richard C. *Korea's Syngman Rhee: An Unauthorized Portrait*. 1960.

Ambrose, Stephen E. *Eisenhower, the President, 1952–1969*. 1984.

———. *Eisenhower, the Soldier, General of the Army, President-Elect, 1890–1952*. 1983.

———. *Nixon: The Education of a Politician, 1913–1962*. 1987.

Barclay, R. *Ernest Bevin: Foreign Office, 1932–1969*. 1975.

Barros, James. *Trygve Lie and the Cold War*. 1989.

Beal, John. *John Foster Dulles: A Biography*. 1957.

Blair, Clay. *MacArthur*. 1977.

Blumenson, Martin. *Mark Clark*. 1985.

Brecher, Michael. *India and World Politics: Krishna Menon's View of the World*. 1968.

———. *Nehru: A Political Biography*. 1959.

Bromage, R. *Molotov*. 1956.

Bullock, Alan. *Ernest Bevin: Foreign Secretary, 1945–1951*. 1983.

Callahan, Raymond A. *Churchill: Retreat from Empire*. 1984.

Carlton, David. *Anthony Eden: A Biography*. 1981.

Cohen, Warren I. *Dean Rusk*. 1980.

Domes, Jurgen. *P'eng Te-huai: The Man and the Image*. 1985.

Ebon, Martin. *Lin Piao: The Life and Writings of China's New Leader*. 1970.

Foot, Michael. *Aneurin Bevan, 1945–1960*. 1973.

Gerson, Louis L. *John Foster Dulles*. 1967.

Gilbert, Martin. *Winston S. Churchill*. 1988.

Goold-Adams, Richard. *John Foster Dulles: A Reappraisal*. 1962.

Gopal, Sarvepalli. *Jawaharlal Nehru, 1947–1956*. 2 vols. 1979.

Guhin, Michael A. *John Foster Dulles: A Statesman and His Times*. 1972.

Gunther, John. *The Riddle of MacArthur: Japan, Korea and the Far East*. 1951.

Harris, Kenneth. *Attlee*. 1982.

Hoopes, Townsend. *The Devil and John Foster Dulles*. 1973.

James, D. Clayton. *The Years of MacArthur*. 3 vols. 1970–1985.

Kim Quee-young. *The Fall of Syngman Rhee*. 1983.

Long, Gavin. *MacArthur as Military Commander*. 1969.

McLellan, David S. *Dean Acheson: The State Department Years*. 1976

———. "Dean Acheson and the Korean War." *Political Science Quarterly* 83 (March 1968).

———, and Acheson, David C., eds. *Among Friends: Personal Letters of Dean Acheson*. 1980.

Manchester, William. *American Caesar: Douglas MacArthur, 1880–1945*. 1978.

Mazuzan, George T. *Warren Austin at the U.N., 1946–1953*. 1977.

Miller, Merle. *Plain Speaking: An Oral Biography of Harry S. Truman*. 1973.

Moran, Lord. *Winston Churchill: The Struggle for Survival, 1940–1945*. 1968.

Mosley, Leonard. *Dulles*. 1978.

———. *Marshall: Hero of Our Times*. 1982.

Oliver, Robert T. *Syngman Rhee: The Man behind the Myth*. 1954.

———. *Syngman Rhee and American Involvement in Korea, 1942–1960: A Personal Narrative*. 1978.

Patterson, James T. *Mr. Republican: A Biography of Robert A. Taft*. 1972.

Pogue, Forrest. *George C. Marshall*. 3 vols. 1963–1973.

Pruessen, Ronald W. *John Foster Dulles: The Road to Power*. 1982.

Schaller, Michael. *Douglas MacArthur: The Far Eastern General*. 1989.

Schoenbaum, Thomas J. *Waging Peace and War: Dean Rusk in the Truman, Kennedy, and Johnson Years*. 1988.

Schram, Stuart. *Mao Tse-tung*. 1966.

Smith, Gaddis. *Dean Acheson*. 1972.

Suh Dae-sook. *Kim Il Sung: The North Korean Leader*. 1988.

Truman, Margaret. *Harry S. Truman*. 1972.

Uhalley, Stephen, Jr. *Mao Tse-tung: A Critical Biography*. 1975.

Whitney, Courtney. *MacArthur: His Rendevous with History*. 1956.

Willoughby, Charles A., and Chamberlain, John. *MacArthur 1941–1951: Victory in the Pacific*. 1956.

CHINESE INTERVENTION

Boardman, Robert. *Britain and the People's Republic of China, 1949–1974*. 1976.

Cohen, Warren I. *America's Response to China*. 1971.

Dingman, Roger. "Truman, Attlee, and the Korean War Crisis." In *The East Asian Crisis, 1945–1951*. Edited by *International Studies*. 1982.

Dulles, Foster Rhea. *American Policy toward Communist China: The Historical Record, 1949–1969*. 1972.

George, Alexander L. *The Chinese Communist Army in Action: The Korean War and Its Aftermath.* 1967.

Gittings, John. *The Role of the Chinese Army.* 1974.

———. *The World and China, 1922–1972.* 1974.

Griffith, Samuel B. *The Chinese People's Liberation Army.* 1967.

Hao Yufan and Zhai Zhihai. "China's Decision to Enter the Korean War: History Revisited." *China Quarterly* 121 (March 1990).

Huang Chen-hsia. *Mao's Generals.* 1968.

Nakajima Mineo. "The Sino-Soviet Confrontation: Its Roots in the International Background of the Korean War." *Australian Journal of Chinese Affairs* (1979).

O'Ballance, Edgar. *The Red Army of China.* 1962.

Spurr, Russell. *Enter the Dragon: China's Involvement in the Korean War, 1950–1951.* 1988.

Stueck, William W., Jr. *The Road to Confrontation: American Policy toward China and Korea, 1947–1950.* 1981

Tsou Tang. *America's Failure in China, 1941–1950.* 1963.

Tucker, Nancy Bernkopf. *Patterns in the Dust: Chinese-American Relations and the Recognition Controversy, 1949–1950.* 1983.

Whiting, Allen S. *China Crosses the Yalu: The Decision to Enter the Korean War.* 1960.

Whitson, William W., and Huang Chen-hsia *The Chinese High Command.* 1973.

Woodman, Dorothy. "Korea, Formosa, and World Peace." *Political Quarterly* 21 (October 1950).

Yao Xu. *From the Yalu to Panmunjom.* 1986.

Zelman, Walter A. *Chinese Intervention in the Korean War.* 1967.

COLD WAR IN ASIA

Aron, Raymond. *The Imperial Republic: The United States and the World, 1945–1973.* 1974.

Barnet, Richard J. *Intervention and Revolution: The United States and the Third World.* 1968.

Beloff, Max. *Soviet Foreign Policy in the Far East, 1944–1951.* 1953.

Blum, Robert M. *Drawing the Line: The Origin of the American Containment Policy in East Asia.* 1982.

Buhite, Russell D. *Soviet-American Relations in Asia, 1945–1954.* 1981.

Dallin, David J. *Soviet Russia and the Far East.* 1949.

Fleming, Denna F. *The Cold War and Its Origins.* 2 vols. 1961.

Gaddis, John L. *Strategies of Containment: A Critical Appraisal of Postwar American National Security Policy.* 1982.

Iriye Akira. *The Cold War in Asia: A Historical Introduction.* 1974.

Jervis, Robert. "The Impact of the Korean War on the Cold War." *Journal of Conflict Resolution* 24 (December 1980).

Kolko, Joyce, and Kolko, Gabriel. *The Limits of Power: The World and U.S. Foreign Policy, 1945–1954.* 1972.

Lafeber, Walter. *America, Russia, and the Cold War, 1945–1984.* 1985.

May, Ernest R. *"Lessons" of the Past: The Use and Misuse of History.* 1973.

———, and Thomson, James. *American-East Asian Relations: A Survey.* 1972.

Rose, Lisle A. *Roots of Tragedy: The United States and the Struggle for Asia, 1945–1953.* 1976.

Tompkins, Pauline. *American-Russian Relations in the Far East.* 1949.

Vinacke, Harold M. *The United States and the Far East, 1945–1951*. 1952.
Wehrle, Edmund S. *International Politics in East Asia since World War II*. 1975.

EISENHOWER ADMINISTRATION

Adams, Sherman. *Firsthand Report: The Story of the Eisenhower Administration*. 1961.
Childs, Marquis W. *Eisenhower: Captive Hero*. 1958.
Cook, Blanche Wiesen, ed. *The Declassified Eisenhower: A Divided Legacy*. 1981.
Divine, Robert A. *Eisenhower and the Cold War*. 1981.
Donovan, Robert J. *Eisenhower: The Inside Story*. 1956.
Ferrell, Robert H., ed. *The Eisenhower Diaries*. 1981.
Greenstein, Fred I. *The Hidden-Hand Presidency: Eisenhower as Leader*. 1982.
Hughes, Emmett J. *The Ordeal of Power*. 1963.
Lyon, Peter. *Eisenhower: Portrait of the Hero*. 1974.
Parmet, Herbert S. *Eisenhower and the American Crusades*. 1972.
Pusey, Merlo J. *Eisenhower: The President*. 1956.
Richardson, Elmo R. *The Presidency of Dwight D. Eisenhower*. 1979
Rovere, Richard H. *Affairs of State: The Eisenhower Years*. 1956.

GENERAL HISTORIES

Alexander, Bevin. *Korea: The First War We Lost*. 1986.
Bell, Coral. "Korea and the Balance of Power." *Political Quarterly* 25 (January-March 1954).
Bernstein, Barton J. "New Light on the Korean War." *International History Review* 46 (February 1977).
Blair, Clay. *The Forgotten War: America in Korea, 1950–1953*. 1987.
Cai Chengwen and Zhao Yongtian. *A Factual Record of the Korean War*. 1987.
Carpenter, William M. "The Korean War: A Strategic Perspective Thirty Years Later." *Comparative Strategy* 2 (1980).
Detzer, David. *Thunder of Captains: The Short Summer in 1950*. 1977.
Deweerd, H. A. "Lessons of the Korean War." *Yale Review* 40 (Summer (1951).
Dille, John. *Substitute for Victory*. 1954.
Fehrenbach, T. R. *This Kind of War: A Study in Upreparedness*. 1963.
Foot, Rosemary. *The Wrong War: American Policy and the Dimensions of the Korean Conflict*. 1985.
Gardner, Lloyd C., ed. *The Korean War*. 1972.
Goulden, Joseph C. *Korea: The Untold Story of the War*. 1982.
Halliday, Jon. "The Korean War: Some Notes on Evidence and Solidarity." *Bulletin of Concerned Asian Scholars* 11 (July-September 1979).
———, and Cumings, Bruce. *Korea: The Unknown War*. 1989.
Halperin, Morton H. *Limited War in the Nuclear Age*. 1963.
———. "The Limiting Process in the Korean War." *Political Science Review* 78 (March 1963).
Hastings, Max. *The Korean War*. 1987.
Kaufman, Burton I. *The Korean War: Challenges in Crisis, Credibility, and Command*. 1986.
Kim Chum-kon. *The Korean War*. 1973.

Kim Yang Myong. *History of the Korean War*. 1978.

"The Korean Experience." *Journal of International Affairs* 6 (Spring 1952).

Lawton, Don. *United States in the Korean War: Defending Freedom's Frontier*. 1964.

Leckie, Robert. *Conflict: The History of the Korean War, 1950–1953*. 1962.

Lowe, Peter. *The Origins of the Korean War*. 1986.

McCormack, Gavan. *Cold War, Hot War*. 1983.

MacDonald, Callum A. *Korea: The War Before Vietnam*. 1986.

McGovern, James. *To the Yalu*. 1972.

Middleton, Harry J. *The Compact History of the Korean War*. 1965.

Nagai Yonosuke. "The Korean War: An Interpretive Essay." *Japanese Journal of American Studies* 1 (1981).

O'Ballance, Edgar. *Korea: 1950–1953*. 1969.

Oliver, Robert T. *Verdict in Korea*. 1952.

Osgood, Robert E. *The Limited War: The Challenge to American Strategy*. 1957.

Park Chang Jin. "American Foreign Policy in Korea and Vietnam: Comparative Case Studies." *Review of Politics* 37 (January 1975).

———. "The Influence of Small States upon the Superpowers: United States–South Korean Relations as a Case Study, 1950–1953." *World Politics* 28 (October 1975).

Park Hong-kyu. "Korean War Revisited: Survey of Historical Writing." *World Affairs* 137 (Spring 1975).

Poats, Rutherford B. *Decision in Korea*. 1954.

Rees, David. *Korea: The Limited War*. 1964.

Sasaki Harutaka. *Hidden History of the Korean War*. 1977.

Simmons, Robert R. *The Strained Alliance: Peking, Pyongyang, Moscow and the Politics of the Korean War*. 1975.

Stairs, Denis. *The Diplomacy of Constraint: Canada, the Korean War, and the U.S.* 1974.

Stokesbury, James L. *A Short History of the Korean War*. 1988.

Stone, I. F. *The Hidden History of the Korean War*. 1952.

Stueck, William W., Jr. "The Korean War as International History." *Diplomatic History* 10 (Fall 1986).

Thomas, R. C. W. *The War in Korea, 1950–1953*. 1954.

Vorhees, Melvin B. *Korean Tales*. 1952.

Warner, Geoffrey. "The Korean War." *International Affairs* 56 (January 1980).

JOURNALIST ACCOUNTS

Beech, Keyes. *Tokyo and Points East*. 1954.

Burchett, Wilfred. *At the Barricades*. 1981.

Cutforth, Rene. *Korean Reporter*. 1955.

Gayn, Mark. *Japan Diary*. 1981.

Higgins, Marguerite. *War in Korea: Report of a Woman War Correspondent*. 1951.

Kahn, Ely Jacques. *The Peculiar War: Impressions of a Reporter in Korea*. 1952.

Knightley, Phillip. *The First Casualty*. 1975.

Thompson, Reginald. *Cry Korea*. 1951.

KOREAN HISTORY

Choi Bong-youn. *Korea—A History*. 1971.

Chung Kyung Cho. *Korea Tomorrow: Land of the Morning Calm*. 1956.

Grajdanzev, A. J. "Korea Divided." *Far Eastern Survey* 14 (October 10, 1945).
———. *Modern Korea.* 1944.
Green, A. Wigfall. *The Epic of Korea.* 1950.
Halliday, Jon. "What Happened in Korea? Rethinking Korean History, 1945–1953." *Bulletin of Concerned Asian Scholars* 5 (November 1973).
Han Pyo-wook. *The Problem of Korean Unification.* 1987.
Hatada Takashi. *A History of Korea.* 1969.
Henderson, Gregory. *Korea: The Politics of the Vortex.* 1968.
Kim Hakjoon. *Korea in Soviet East Asian Policy.* 1986.
Kim Hong-kyu. "From Pearl Harbor to Cairo: America's Korean Diplomacy, 1941–1943." *Diplomatic History* 13 (Summer 1989).
Kim Joungwon A. *Divided Korea: The Politics of Development, 1945–1972.* 1976.
Lee Chong-sik. *The Politics of Korean Nationalism.* 1963.
Lee Ki-baik. *A New History of Korea.* 1984.
McCune, George M., and Grey, Arthur L. *Korea Today.* 1950.
Oh, John Kie-chang. *Korea: Democracy on Trial.* 1968.
Scalapino, Robert A., and Lee Chong-sik. *Communism in Korea.* 1972.
Suh Dae-sook. *Documents of Korean Communism.* 1970.
———. *The Korean Communist Movement.* 1967.
Wilz, John E. "Did the United States Betray Korea?" *Pacific Historical Review* 54 (August 1985).

KOREAN-LANGUAGE STUDIES

Choguk Haebang Chŏnjaeng-sa [History of the Fatherland Liberation War]. 2 vols. 1972.
Chosŏn Chonsa [History of Korea]. 1981.
Chŏng Song-gwan. *P'anmunjŏm ŭi Pisa* [An Inside Story of P'anmunjom]. 1953.
Chungang Ilbosa. *Minjok ŭi Chungon [Testimonies of the People].* 3 vols. 1971–1973.
Kim Hui-il. *Mije ŭi Chosŏn Ch'imnnyak-sa* [History of the Invasion of American Imperialism in Korea]. 1962.
Kim Il Sung. *Chayu wa Tongnip ŭl wihan Chosŏn Inmin ŭi Choguk Haebang Chŏnjaeng* [Korean People's Liberation War for Fatherland's Freedom and Independence]. 1954.
Kukbang-bu p'yŏnch'an wiwŏn-hoe. *Han'guk Chŏnjaeng-sa* [History of the Korean War]. 5 vols. 1968–1972.
Pak Chan. *Han'guk Woegyo Pisa* [Secret History of Korean Diplomacy]. 1979.
Republic of Korea, Ministry of Defense. *Han'guk Chollan Chi* [The Korean War Records]. 5 vols. 1951–1955.
———. *Yugio Sabyŏn-sa* [A History of the Korean Conflict]. 1959.
Republic of Korea, Ministry of Foreign Affairs. *Han'guk Tongil Munje: Yoksa wa Munhon, 1943–1960* [Problems of Korean Unification: History and Documents, 1943–1960]. 1960.
Republic of Korea, Army Headquarters. *Yugio Sabyon Hubang Chŏnsa* [The Home Front of the Korean War]. 2 vols. 1955, 1956.
———. *Yugio Sabyon Yukkun Chŏnsa* [The Army's Battle History of the Korean War]. 6 vols. 1954–1957.
Rhee In-Soo. *Taehan Minguk ŭi Konguk* [Establishment of the Republic of Korea]. 1988.
Tonga Ilbosa. *Pihwa Cheil Konghwaguk* [Hidden History of the First Republic]. 5 vols. 1975.

Yi Chong-hak. *Han'guk Chonjaeng-sa* [The Military History of the Korean War]. 1969.
Yi H., ed. *Han'guk-sa Taesajŏn* [The Great Dictionary of Korean History]. 1988.

MEDIATION EFFORTS

Berkes, Ross N., and Bedi, Mohinder S. *The Diplomacy of India*. 1953.
Dayal, Shiv. *India's Role in the Korean Question*. 1959.
Dingman, Roger. "Truman, Attlee, and the Korean Crisis." *International Studies* (1982).
Farrar, Peter N. "Britain's Proposal for a Buffer Zone South of the Yalu in November 1950: Was It a Neglected Opportunity to End the Fighting in Korea?" *Journal of Contemporary History* 18 (1983).
Foot, Rosemary. "Anglo-American Relations in the Korean Crisis: The British Effort to Avert an Expanded War, December 1950–January 1951." *Diplomatic History* 10 (Winter 1986).
Jansen, G. H. *Non-Alignment and the Afro-Asian States*. 1966
Kundra, J. C. *Indian Foreign Policy, 1947–1954*. 1955.
Ra, J. Y. "Special Relationship at War: The Anglo-American Relationship during the Korean War." *Journal of Strategic Studies* 3 (1984).
Steinberg, Blema S. "The Korean War: A Case Study in Indian Neutralism." *Orbis* 8 (Winter 1965).
Stueck, William W. "The Limits of Influence: British Policy and American Expansion of the War in Korea." *Pacific Historical Review* 55 (February 1986).

MEMOIRS AND PERSONAL ACCOUNTS

Acheson, Dean G. *Present at the Creation: My Years in the State Department*. 1969.
Allison, John M. *Ambassador from the Prairie or Allison Wonderland*. 1973.
Attlee, Clement. *Twilight of Empire: Memoirs of Prime Minister Clement Attlee*. 1962.
Bohlen, Charles E. *Witness to History, 1929–1969*. 1973.
Bowles, Chester. *Ambassador's Report*. 1954.
———. *Promises to Keep: My Years in Public Life, 1941–1969*. 1971.
Bradley, Omar N., and Blair, Clay. *A General's Life: An Autobiography*. 1983.
Briggs, Ellis O. *Farewell to Foggy Bottom: The Recollections of a Career Diplomat*. 1964.
Clark, Mark W. *From the Danube to the Yalu*. 1954.
Collins, J. Lawton. *Lightning Joe: An Autobiography*. 1979.
———. *War in Peacetime: The History and Lessons of Korea*. 1969.
Connally, Tom. *My Name Is Tom Connally*. 1954.
Dean, William F. *General Dean's Story*. 1954.
Eden, Anthony. *Full Circle: The Memoirs of Anthony Eden*. 1960.
Eisenhower, Dwight D. *Mandate for Change: 1953–1956*. 1963.
Finletter, Thomas K. *Power and Policy: U.S. Foreign Policy and Military Power in the Hydrogen Age*. 1954.
Gromyko, Andrei A. *Memories*. 1989.
Gross, Ernest A. *The United Nations: Structure of Peace*. 1962.
Harriman, W. Averell. *America and Russia in a Changing World: A Half Century of Personal Observations*. 1971.
Jebb, H. M. Gladwyn. *The Memoirs of Lord Gladwyn*. 1972.

Johnson, U. Alexis. *The Right Hand of Power*. 1984.

Joy, C. Turner. *How Communists Negotiate*. 1955.

Jurika, Stephen, ed. *From Pearl Harbor to Vietnam: The Memoirs of Admiral Arthur W. Radford*. 1980.

Kennan, George F. *Memoirs, 1925–1963*. 2 vols. 1967, 1972.

Khrushchev, Nikita. *Khrushchev Remembers*. 1971.

Lie, Trygve. *In the Cause of Peace*. 1955.

Lodge, Henry Cabot, Jr. *As It Was*. 1976.

———. *The Storm Has Many Eyes: A Personal Narrative*. 1973

MacArthur, Douglas. *Reminiscences*. 1964.

Menon, K. P. S. *The Flying Troika*. 1963.

Munro, J. A., and Inglis, A. I., eds. *Mike: The Memoirs of the Right Honourable Lester B. Pearson, 1948–1957*. 2 vols. 1974.

Murphy, Robert D. *Diplomat among Warriors*. 1964.

Noble, Harold J. *Embassy at War*. 1975.

Pandit, Vijaya Lakshmi. *The Scope of Happiness: A Personal Memoir*. 1979.

Panikkar, K. M. *In Two Chinas: Memoirs of a Diplomat*. 1955.

Peng Dehuai. *Memoirs of a Chinese Marshal—The Autobiographical Notes of Peng Dehuai (1898–1974)*. 1984.

Ridgway, Matthew B. *The Korean War: History and Tactics*. 1967.

———. Soldier: The Memoirs of Matthew B. Ridgway. 1956.

Sebald, William J. *With MacArthur In Japan: A Personal History of the Occupation*. 1965.

Spender, Percy C. *Exercises in Diplomacy*. 1969.

———. *Politics and a Man*. 1972

Taylor, Maxwell D. *Swords and Plowshares*. 1972.

———. *The Uncertain Trumpet*. 1960.

Truman, Harry S. *Years of Trial and Hope*. 1956.

Vandenberg, Arthur H., Jr. *The Private Papers of Senator Vandenberg*. 1953.

Weyland, Otto P. *Airpower: The Decisive Force in Korea*. 1957.

Wu Xiuquan. *Eight Years in the Ministry of Foreign Affairs*. 1985.

MILITARY HISTORIES

Aerospace Studies Institute. *Guerrilla Warfare and Airpower in Korea, 1950–1953*. 1964.

Appleman, Roy E. *Disaster in Korea: The Chinese Confront MacArthur*. 1989.

———. *East of Chosin: Entrapment and Breakout in Korea, 1950*. 1987.

———. *Escaping the Trap: The U.S. Army X Corps in Northeast Korea, 1950*. 1990.

———. *Ridgway Duels for Korea*. 1990.

Barclay, C. N. *The First Commonwealth Division: The Story of British Commonwealth Land Forces in Korea, 1950–1953*. 1954.

Blair, Clay. *Beyond Courage*. 1955.

Cassels, A. J. H. "The Commonwealth Division in Korea." *Journal of the Royal United Services Institute* (April 1953).

Cunningham-Boothe, Ashley, and Farrar, Peter. eds. *British Forces in the Korean War*. (1988).

Geer, Andrew. *The New Breed: The Story of the U.S. Marines in Korea*. 1952.

Grey, Jeffrey. *The Commonwealth Armies and the Korean War*. 1988.

Hammel, Eric. *Chosin: Heroic Ordeal of the Korean War*. 1981.

Heinl, Robert D., Jr. *Victory at High Tide: The Inchon-Seoul Campaign*. 1968.

Hoyt, Edwin P. *The Bloody Road to Panmunjom*. 1985.

Jackson, Robert. *Air War over Korea*. 1973.

Knox, Donald. *The Korean War: An Oral History*. 2 vols. 1985, 1990.

Langley, Michael. *Inchon Landing: MacArthur's Last Triumph*. 1979.

Linklater, Eric. *Our Men in Korea*. 1952.

Marshall, S. L. A. *Pork Chop Hill: The American Fighting Man in Action, Korea, Spring 1953*. 1965.

————. *The River and the Gauntlet: The Defeat of the Eighth Army by the Chinese Communist Forces*. 1953.

Maurer, Maurer. "The Korean Conflict Was a War." *Military Affairs* 24 (Fall 1960).

Palmer, Michael A. *Origins of the Maritime Strategy: American Naval Strategy in the First Postwar Decade*. 1988.

Poole, Walter S. *History of the Joint Chiefs of Staff*. Vol 4: *The Joint Chiefs of Staff and National Policy, 1950–1952*. 1979.

Ramsey, Russell W. "The Colombian Battalion in Korea and Suez." *Journal of Inter-American Studies* (October 1967).

Russ, Martin. *The Last Parallel*. 1957.

Schnabel, James F., and Watson, Robert G. *History of the Joint Chiefs of Staff*. Vol. 3: *The Korean War*. 1979.

Sheldon, Walt. *Hell or High Water: MacArthur's Landing at Inchon*. 1968.

Skaggs, David C. "The Katusa Experiment: The Integration of Korean Nationals into the U.S. Army, 1950–1965." *Military Affairs* 38 (April 1974).

Stanton, Shelby Z. *America's Tenth Legion: X Corps in Korea, 1950*. 1989.

Thorgrimsson, Thor, and Russell, E. C. *Canadian Naval Operations in Korean Waters, 1950–1952*. 1966.

Wood, Herbert Fairlie. *Strange Battleground: The Operations in Korea and Their Effect on the Defense Policy of Canada*. 1966.

NORTH KOREA

Dubin, Paul S. "The Political Evolution of the Pyongyang Government." *Pacific Affairs*, 23 (December 1950).

Halliday, Jon. "The North Korean Phenomenon." *New Left Review* 127 (May-June 1980).

Kalinov, Kyril. "How Russia Built the North Korean Army." *Reporter*, September 26, 1950.

Koh Byung Chul. *The Foreign Policy of North Korea*. 1969.

Lee Chong-sik. "Kim Il-song of North Korea." *Asian Survey* 7 (June 1967).

————, and Oh K. "The Russian Faction in North Korea." *Asian Survey* (1968).

Nam Koon Woo. *The North Korean Communist Leadership, 1945–1965: A Study of Factionalism and Political Consolidation*. 1974.

Paige, Glenn D. "Korea." *In Communism and Revolution: The Uses of Political Violence*. Edited by Cyril E. Black and Thomas P. Thornton. 1964.

————. *The Korean People's Democratic Republic*. 1966.

Suh Dae-sook. "A Preconceived Formula for Sovietization: The Communist Takeover of North Korea." In *The Anatomy of Communist Takeovers*. Edited by Thomas T. Hammond. 1975.

Washburn, John N. "Russia Looks at North Korea." *Pacific Affairs* 20 (June 1947).

————. "Soviet Russia and the Korean Communist Party." *Pacific Affairs* 23 (March 1950).

OFFICIAL HISTORIES

Appleman, Roy E. *South to the Naktong, North to the Yalu.* 1961.
Cagle, Malcolm W., and Manson, Frank A. *The Sea War in Korea.* 1957.
Chinese People's Liberation Army Academy of Military Science. *A Military History of the Anti-U.S. Aid-Korea War.* 1988.
Condit, Doris M. *History of the Office of the Secretary of Defense.* Vol. 2: *The Test of War, 1950–1953.* 1988.
Field, James A., Jr. *History of United States Naval Operations, Korea.* 1962.
Futrell, Robert F. *The United States Air Force in Korea, 1950–1953.* 1961.
Gugeler, Russell A. *Combat Actions in Korea: Infantry, Artillery, and Armor.* 1970.
Hermes, Walter G. *Truce Tent and Fighting Front.* 1966.
Karig, Walter; Cagle, Malcolm W.; and Manson, Frank A. *Battle Report.* Vol. 6: *The War In Korea.* 1952.
Miller, John, Jr.; Carroll, Owen J.; and Tackley, Margaret E. *Korea: 1951–1953.* 1956
Montross, Lynn, and Canzona, Nicholas A. *U.S. Marine Operations in Korea.* 5 vols. 1954–1972.
Mossman, Billy C. *Ebb and Flow, November 1950-July 1951.* 1990.
O'Neill, Robert. *Australia in the Korean War.* 2 vols. 1981,1985.
Reister, Frank A. *Battle Casualties and Medical Statistics: U.S. Army Experience in the Korean War.* 1973.
Sawyer, Robert K., and Hermes, Walter G. *Military Advisors in Korea: KMAG in Peace and War.* 1962.
Schnabel, James F. *Policy and Direction: The First Year.* 1972.

ORIGINS OF THE KOREAN WAR

Berger, Carl. *The Korean Knot: A Military-Political History.* 1957.
Caldwell, John C. *The Korea Story.* 1952.
Cho Soon-sung. *Korea in World Politics, 1941–1950: An Evaluation of American Responsibility.* 1967.
Cumings, Bruce. *The Origins of the Korean War.* 2 vols. 1981, 1990.
Dobbs, Charles M. *The Unwanted Symbol: American Foreign Policy, the Cold War, and Korea.* 1981.
Gupta, Karunaker. "How Did the Korean War Begin?" *China Quarterly* 8 (October-December 1972).
Hitchcock, Wilbur. "North Korea Jumps the Gun." *Current History* 20 (March 1951).
Matray, James I. *The Reluctant Crusade: American Foreign Policy in Korea, 1941–1950.* 1985.
Merrill, John. *Korea: The Peninsular Origins of the War.* 1989.
Mitchell, C. Clyde. *Korea: Second Failure in Asia.* 1951.
Oliver, Robert T. *Why War Came in Korea.* 1950.
Stueck, William W., Jr. "Cold War Revisionism and the Origins of the Korean Conflict: The Kolko Thesis." *Pacific Historical Review* 42 (November 1973).

————. "The Soviet Union and the Origins of the Korean War." *World Politics* 28 (July 1976).

Swartout, Robert, Jr. "American Historians and the Outbreak of the Korean War: A Historiographical Essay." *Asia Quarterly* (1979).

POLITICS AND PUBLIC OPINION

Almond, Gabriel A. *The American People and Foreign Policy*. 1950.

Caridi, Ronald J. *The Korean War and American Politics: The Republican Party as a Case Study*. 1968.

Divine, Robert A. *Foreign Policy and U.S. Presidential Elections*. 1974.

Graebner, Norman A. *The New Isolationism: A Study in Politics and Foreign Policy since 1950*. 1956.

Hamby, Alonzo L. "Public Opinion: Korea and Vietnam." *Wilson Quarterly* 2 (Summer 1978).

Kepley, David R. "The Senate and the Great Debate of 1951." *Prologue: Journal of the National Archives* 14 (Winter 1982).

Lofgren, Charles. "Mr. Truman's War: A Debate and Its Aftermath." *Review of Politics* 31 (April 1969).

Lubell, Samuel. *The Future of American Politics*. 1965.

Mueller, John E. *War, Presidents, and Public Opinion*. 1973.

Neustadt, Richard E. *Presidential Power: The Politics of Leadership*. 1960.

Reichard, Gary W. "Divisions and Dissent: Democrats and Foreign Policy, 1952—1956." *Political Science Quarterly* 93 (Spring 1978).

Westerfield, H. Bradford. *Foreign Policy and Party Politics: Pearl Harbor to Korea*. 1955.

PRISONERS OF WAR

Biderman, Albert D. *March to Calumny: The Story of American POWs in the Korean War*. 1963.

Dean, Phillip. *I Was a Captive in Korea*. 1953.

Grey, Jeffrey. "Commonwealth Prisoners of War and British Policy during the Korean War." *RUSI Journal* (1988).

Hansen, Kenneth K. *Heroes behind Barbed Wire*. 1957.

Hunter, Edward. *Brainwashing: The Story of the Men Who Defied It*. 1958.

Kincaid, Eugene. *In Every War But One*. 1959.

Pasley, Virginia. *21 Stayed*. 1955.

United Nations Command. *The Communist War in POW Camps*. 1953.

Vetter, Hal. *Mutiny on Koje-do Island*. 1955.

White, William L. *The Captives of Korea*. 1957.

SOUTH KOREA

Bunce, Arthur C. "The Future of Korea: Part I." *Far Eastern Survey,* April 19, 1944.

————. "The Future of Korea: Part II." *Far Eastern Survey,* May 17, 1944.

Dull, Paul S. "South Korean Constitution." *Far Eastern Survey,* September 8, 1948.

Kim Se-jin. *Politics of Military Revolution in Korea.* 1971.

Lauterbach, Richard E. "Hodge's Korea." *Virginia Historical Review* 23 (June 1947).

McGlothlen, Ronald L. "Acheson, Economics, and the American Commitment in Korea." *Pacific Historical Review* 58 (February 1989).

Matray, James I. "Spoils of War: The Korean War as an American Case Study." *Prologue: Journal of the National Archives* 20 (Spring 1990).

Meade, E. Grant. *American Military Government in Korea.* 1951.

Merrill, John. "The Cheju-do Rebellion." *Journal of Korean Studies* 2 (1980).

Nam Joo-hong. *America's Commitment to South Korea: The First Decade of the Nixon Doctrine.* 1986.

Reeve, W. D. *The Republic of Korea: A Political and Economic Study.* 1963.

Riley, John W., Jr., and Schramm, Wilbur. *The Reds Take a City: The Communist Occupation of Seoul.* 1951.

Sarafan, Bertram D. "Military Government: Korea." *Far Eastern Survey,* November 20, 1946.

Weems, Benjamin. "Behind the Korean Elections." *Far Eastern Survey,* June 23, 1948.

THIRTY-EIGHTH PARALLEL DIVISION

Grey, Arthur L., Jr. "The Thirty-eighth Parallel." *Foreign Affairs* 29 (April 1951).

McCune, Shannon. "The Thirty-eighth Parallel Decision in Korea." *World Politics* 1 (January 1949).

Sandusky, Michael. *America's Parallel.* 1983.

THIRTY-EIGHTH PARALLEL CROSSING DECISION

Bernstein, Barton J. "The Policy of Risk: Crossing the 38th Parallel and Marching to the Yalu." *Foreign Service Journal* 54 (March 1977).

Lafeber, Walter. "Crossing the 38th Parallel: The Cold War in Microcosm." In *Reflections on the Cold War: A Quarter Century of American Foreign Policy.* Edited by Lynn H. Miller and Ronald W. Pruessen. 1974.

Lichterman, Martin. "To the Yalu and Back." In *American Civil-Military Decisions: A Book of Case Studies.* Edited by Harold Stein. 1963.

Matray, James I. "Truman's Plan for Victory: National Self-Determination and the Thirty-eighth Parallel Decision in Korea." *Journal of American History* 66 (September 1979).

TRUMAN ADMINISTRATION

Bundy, McGeorge, ed. *The Pattern of Responsibility.* 1952.

Cochran, Bert. *Harry Truman and the Crisis Presidency.* 1973.

Dalfiume, Richard M. *Fighting Two Fronts: The Desegregation of the U.S. Armed Forces.* 1968.

Donovan, Robert J. *Tumultuous Years: The Presidency of Harry S. Truman, 1949–1953.* 1982.

Ferrell, Robert H. *Harry S. Truman and the Modern American Presidency.* 1983.

———, ed. *Off the Record: The Private Papers of Harry S. Truman.* 1982.

Graebner, Norman A. "Global Containment: The Truman Years." *Current History* 57 (August 1969).

Hamby, Alonzo L. *Beyond the New Deal: Harry S. Truman and American Liberalism.* 1973.

Haynes, Richard F. *The Awesome Power: Harry S. Truman as Commander in Chief.* 1973.

McCoy, Donald R. *The Presidency of Harry S. Truman.* 1984.

Marcus, Maeva. *Truman and the Steel Seizure Case: The Limits of Presidential Power.* 1977.

Phillips, Cabell. *The Truman Presidency: The History of a Triumphant Succession.* 1966.

Purifoy, Lewis McCaroll. *Harry Truman's China Policy: McCarthyism and the Diplomacy of Hysteria, 1947–1951.* 1976.

TRUMAN-MacARTHUR CONTROVERSY

Higgins, Trumbull. *Korea and the Fall of MacArthur: A Precis on Limited War.* 1960.

Norman, John. "MacArthur's Blockade Proposals against China." *Pacific Historical Review* 26 (May 1957).

Rovere, Richard H., and Schlesinger, Arthur M., Jr. *The General and the President: The Truman-MacArthur Controversy and the Future of American Foreign Policy.* 1957.

Ruetten, Richard T. "General Douglas MacArthur's 'Reconnaissance in Force': The Rationalization of a Defeat in Korea." *Pacific Historical Review* 36 (February 1967).

Ryan, Halford R. "Harry S. Truman: A Misdirected Defense for MacArthur's Dismissal." *Presidential Studies Quarterly* 11 (Fall 1981).

Smith, Robert. *MacArthur in Korea: The Naked Emperor.* 1982.

Spanier, John W. *The Truman-MacArthur Controversy and the Korean War.* 1965.

Wilz, John E. "The MacArthur Hearings of 1951: The Secret Testimony." *Military Affairs* 39 (December 1975).

———. "Truman and MacArthur: The Wake Island Meeting." *Military Affairs* 42 (December 1978).

UNITED NATIONS

Bloomfield, Lincoln. *The United Nations and U.S. Foreign Policy.* 1967.

Cooling, B. F. "Allied Interoperability in the Korean War." *Military Review* (1983).

Goodrich, Leland M. "Efforts to Establish International Policy Force down to 1950." In *A United Nations Peace Force.* Edited by William R. Frye. 1957.

———. *Korea: A Study of U.S. Policy in the U.N.* 1956.

Gordenker, Leon. *The United Nations and the Peaceful Reunification of Korea, 1947–1950.* 1959.

Haas, Ernest B. "Types of Collective Security: An Examination of Operational Conceptions." *American Political Science Review* 44 (March 1955).

Hazzard, Shirley. *Defeat of the Ideal: The Self-Destruction of the UN.* 1973.

Luan, Evan. *A History of the United Nations.* Vol. 1: *The Years of Western Dominance, 1945–1955.* 1982.

McGibbon, Ian C. "New Zealand's Intervention in the Korean War, June-July 1950." *International History Review* (1989).

Riggs, Robert E. *Politics in the United Nations: A Study of United States Influence in the General Assembly.* 1958.

Russell, Ruth B. *The United Nations and United States Security Policy.* 1968.

Wint, Guy. *What Happened in Korea: A Study in Collective Security.* 1954.

Wolfers, Arnold. "Collective Security and the War in Korea." *Yale Review* 43 (June 1954).

Yoo Tae-ho. *The Korean War and the United Nations: A Legal and Diplomatic Historical Study.* 1965.

U.S. DEFENSE POLICY

Bell, Coral. *Negotiation from Strength: A Study in the Politics of Power.* 1977.

Gaddis, John L. "Was the Truman Doctrine a Real Turning Point?" *Foreign Affairs* 52 (January 1974).

————, and Nitze, Paul. "NSC-68 and the Soviet Threat Reconsidered." *International Security* 4 (Spring 1980).

Kaplan, Lawrence S. *A Community of Interests: NATO and the Military Assistance Program, 1948–1951.* 1982.

Kissinger, Henry. *Nuclear Weapons and Foreign Policy.* 1957.

Lafeber, Walter. "NATO and the Korean War: A Diplomatic Context." *Diplomatic History* 13 (Fall 1989).

Lyons, G. M. *Military Policy and Economic Aid: The Korean Case, 1950–1953.* 1961.

Rosenberg, David A. "The Origins of Overkill: Nuclear Weapons and American Strategy, 1945–1960." *International Security* 7 (Spring 1953).

Schilling, Warner; Hammond, Paul Y.; and Snyder, Glenn E. *Strategy, Politics, and Defense Budgets.* 1962

Wells, Samuel F. "The Origins of Massive Retaliation." *Political Science Quarterly* (Spring 1981).

————. "Sounding the Tocsin: NSC-68 and the Soviet Threat." *International Security* 4 (Fall 1979).

U.S. INTERVENTION

Bernstein, Barton J. "The Origins of America's Commitments in Korea." *Foreign Service Journal* 55 (March 1978).

————. "The Week We Went to War: American Intervention in the Korean Civil War." *Foreign Service Journal* 54 (January 1977).

Buhite, Russell D. "'Major Interests': American Policy toward China, Taiwan and Korea, 1945–1950." *Pacific Historical Review* 47 (August 1978).

Deweerd, H. A. "Strategic Surprise in Korea." *Orbis* 6 (Fall 1962).

George, Alexander L. "American Policy-Making and the North Korean Aggression." *World Politics* 7 (January 1955).

————, and Smoke, Richard. *Deterrence in American Foreign Policy.* 1974.

Hoare, Wilber W., Jr. "Truman." In *The Ultimate Decision: The President as Commander in Chief.* Edited by Ernest R. May. 1960.

Hoyt, Edwin C. "The United States Reaction to the Korean Attack." *American Journal of International Law* 55 (January 1961).

Mabon, David W. "Elusive Agreements: The Pacific Pact Proposals of 1949–1951." *Pacific Historical Review* 57 (1988).

May, Ernest R. "The Nature of Foreign Policy: The Calculated versus the Axiomatic." *Daedalus* 91 (Fall 1962).

Paige, Glenn D. *The Korean Decision, June 24–30, 1950.* 1968.

Pelz, Stephen E. "When the Kitchen Gets Hot, Pass the Buck: Truman and Korea in 1950." *Reviews in American History* (December 1978).

Smith, Beverly. "The White House Story: Why We Went to War in Korea." *Saturday Evening Post,* November 10, 1951.

Warner, Albert L. "How the Korean Decision Was Made." *Harper's* 202 (June 1951).

U.S. GOVERNMENT DOCUMENTS

U.S. Congress. Senate. Foreign Relations and Armed Services Committees. *Military Situation in the Far East,* 5 vols., 82d Cong., 1st sess., 1951.

U.S. Department of the Army. *Korea—1950.* 1952.

U.S. Department of State. *The Conflict in Korea: Events Prior to the Attack on June 25, 1950.* Far Eastern Series 45. 1951.

———. *Department of State Bulletin.* 1945–1953.

———. *The Fight against Aggression in Korea.* Far Eastern Series 37. 1950.

———. *Foreign Relations of the United States. 1945.* Vol. 6: *The British Commonwealth. The Far East.* 1969.

———. *Foreign Relations of the United States. 1946.* Vol. 8: *The Far East.* 1971.

———. *Foreign Relations of the United States. 1947.* Vol. 6: *The Far East.* 1972.

———. *Foreign Relations of the United States. 1948.* Vol. 6: *The Far East and Australasia.* 1974.

———. *Foreign Relations of the United States. 1949.* Vol. 7: *The Far East and Australasia.* Part 2. 1976.

———. *Foreign Relations of the United States. 1950.* Vol. 7: *Korea.* 1976.

———. *Foreign Relations of the United States. 1951.* Vol. 7: *Korea and China.* 1983.

———. *Foreign Relations of the United States. 1952–1954.* Vol. 15: *Korea.* 1984.

———. *Guide to the U.N. in Korea.* Far Eastern Series 47. August 1951.

———. *A Historical Summary of United States–Korean Relations, 1934–1962.* Far Eastern Series 11. November 1962.

———. *Korea.* August 1951.

———. *Korea 1945 to 1948: A Report on Political Developments and Economic Resources with Selected Documents.* Far Eastern Series 28. October 1948.

———. *Korea's Independence.* Far Eastern Series 18. October 1947.

———. *North Korea: A Case Study in the Techniques of Takeover.* Far Eastern Series 103. January 1961.

———. *The Record on Korean Unification, 1943–1960: Narrative Summary with Principal Documents.* Far Eastern Series 101. October 1960.

———. *United States Policy in the Korean Crisis.* Far Eastern Series 34. July 1950.

Index

Main entries indicated by **bold type**.

Acheson, Dean G., **1–2**, 13–14, 55, 56
115, 143, 169, 218, 286, 313, 371,
393, 480, 523; activities at the United
Nations, 26, 27, 328, 501–2; dealings
with Congress, 122, 124, 125, 135,
174; dealings with General Douglas
MacArthur, 196, 264, 268, 283, 470–
71; discussions with the British, 2–3,
19, 24, 25, 53, 54, 67, 107, 151, 164,
299, 300, 455, 456; National Press
Club speech, **3–4**, 76, 124, 126, 143,
218, 252, 262, 319, 433, 445, 510;
policy recommendations regarding
China, 4, 83–84, 90, 159, 201, 312,
330, 424; reaction to the North Korean
invasion of South Korea, 31, 163, 301,
418, 461, 462, 500, 523–24; relations
with Louis A. Johnson, 201–2, 203–4,
301; response to Menon POW settlement proposal, 21, 290, 376, 464,
465, 492, 493; role in prewar policy
toward Korea, 3–4, 232–33, 364, 442,
497–98; role in starting Kaesŏng truce
talks, 168, 219, 287
Acheson-Morrison meeting, **2–3**, 299,
439
active defense strategy, **4–5**
Advance Command and Liaison Group in
Korea (ADCOM), 103, 104
agenda controversy (agenda item 1), **5–7**,
11, 212–13, 297, 458

agenda items: 1, *see* agenda controversy;
2, *see* demarcation line; 3, *see* cease-
fire inspection provisions; 4, *see* repatriation of prisoners; 5, *see*, postwar
political conference
Agreement on Economic Coordination,
296, 369, 441
air pressure strategy, **12–13**, 113, 133,
359, 438–39, 460, 526
air war, 3, 344, 478, 526; against the
PRC, 269, 438; bombing of North Korea, 5, 120, 220, 238, 331; initial U.S.
response in Korean War, 104, 163,
172, 275, 374, 375, 418, 437, 514,
525; North Korean involvement in, 40,
275; PRC involvement in, 280–81,
331, 344, 515; relationship to the truce
talks, 209–11, 457, 459; role of MiGs
in, 40–41, 288, 296–97, 353–54, 425;
Soviet involvement in, 92, 331, 354,
435, 509; UNC close support operations, 17, 34–35, 42, 43, 45, 49, 99,
140, 288, 355, 359, 395, 438, 527;
U.S. policy regarding, 198, 204, 510.
See also air pressure strategy; Army-
Air Force close support controversy;
atomic attacks; dam raids of 1953; hot
pursuit; Kaesŏng bombing proposal;
Operation Strangle; Rashin bombing
controversy; Suiho bombing operation;
U.S. FEAF; Yalu bridges controversy
airfield rehabilitation controversy, 8, 9,
13–14, 297, 310, 365–66, 385

About the Editor and Contributors

DAVID L. ANDERSON is professor of history and chairman of the department of history and political science at the University of Indianapolis. He is the author of *Trapped by Success: The Eisenhower Administration and Vietnam, 1953–1961* and *Imperialism and Idealism: American Diplomats in China, 1861–1898*.

DON BAKER is assistant professor of Korean studies at the University of British Columbia in Vancouver, Canada. He has published several articles on Korean history, including "From Pottery to Politics: The Transformation of Korean Catholicism," in the forthcoming volume *Religion and Contemporary Society in Korea* from the Institute of East Asian Studies at the University of California in Berkeley.

LARRY R. BECK is a college instructor of history at New Mexico State University, Alamogordo branch campus. He became interested in Korean affairs while serving as a political-military affairs officer on the U.S. Forces Korea Intelligence Staff. Currently completing his doctorate in education at New Mexico State University, he has published a critical review in *Fletcher Forum*.

TAMI D. BIDDLE is a doctoral candidate in the department of history at Yale University and is currently a Smithsonian Fellow at the National Air and Space Museum. She has published several scholarly articles on military and diplomatic affairs and is currently writing about the history of strategic bombing.

PETER G. BOYLE teaches American history in the department of American studies at the University of Nottingham, England. He is author of several publications on relations between Britain, the United States, and the Soviet Union in the early Cold War years. He is currently editing *The Churchill-Eisenhower Correspondence, 1953–55*.

H. W. BRANDS is an associate professor of history at Texas A & M University. He is the author of *Cold Warriors: Eisenhower's Generation and American Foreign Policy*, *The Specter of Neutralism: The United States and the Emergence of the Third World, 1947–1960*, and *India and the United States: The Cold Peace*.

RICHARD DEAN BURNS is a professor of history at California State University, Los Angeles, where he also serves as department chair and director of the Center for the Study of Armament and Disarmament. His major publications include *A Guide to American Foreign Relations Since 1770*, *Harry S. Truman: A Bibliography of His Times and Presidency*, *The Indochina Wars: A Bibliographical Guide*, and *Disarmament in Perspective, 1919–1941*. Additionally, he is general editor of three book series: *War/Peace Bibliographies*, *Guides to Historical Issues*, and *Guides to Contemporary Issues*.

YǑNG-HO CH'OE is a professor of history at the University of Hawaii at Manoa specializing in pre-modern and modern Korean history. Author of *The Civil Examinations and the Social Structure in Early Yi Dynasty Korea: 1392–1600*, he has published a number of articles in such journals as *The Journal of Asian Studies* and *Korean Studies* among others.

ROBERT A. DIVINE received his Ph. D. at Yale University in 1954 and has taught diplomatic history at the University of Texas at Austin ever since. He has written extensively on 20th Century American foreign policy and is the author of *Foreign Policy and U.S. Presidential Election, 1952–1960*, which includes chapters on the political impact of the Korean War.

LYNNE K. DUNN is currently an assistant professor of history at Winthrop College, Rock Hill, South Carolina. Prior to accepting that position, she spent two years as an historian with the Contemporary History Branch of the Naval Historical Center, Washington, D.C., where she began work on a history of women and the United States Navy. In addition, Dunn is completing a study of the diplomatic career of Eleanor Lansing Dulles. A portion of this research has appeared in Edward Crapol's *Women and American Foreign Policy—Lobbyists, Critics, and Insiders*.

PETER EDWARDS received his B. A. from the University of Western Australia and his D. Phil. from Oxford University, where he was a Rhodes Scholar. He is the author of *Prime Ministers and Diplomats: The Making of Australian Foreign Policy 1901–1949*, the editor of *Australia Through American Eyes 1935–1945*, and one of the editors of *Documents on Australian Foreign Policy 1937–49*. He is currently official historian of Australia's involvement in the Malayan Emergency, the Indonesian-Malaysian Confrontation, and the Vietnam War.

RICHARD W. FANNING earned his doctoral degree at Indiana University in 1988, completing his dissertation on the Geneva Naval Conference of 1927 under the direction of Robert H. Ferrell. He is a contributor to *American Secretaries of State: A Biographical Directory* and has served as an editorial assistant for the *American Historical Review*. He is currently a visiting assistant professor in the department of history at Seattle Pacific University.

ROBERT H. FERRELL is professor of history emeritus at Indiana University. His publications deal with a variety of topics, including *Peace in Their Times: The Origins of the Kellogg-Briand Pact* and *Woodrow Wilson and World War I*. He is a past president of the *Society for Historians of American Foreign Relations*.

ROSEMARY FOOT is the John Swine Research Fellow in the international relations of the Far East at St. Anthony's College, Oxford. Earning her doctorate at the London School of Economics and Political Science, she is the author of *The Wrong War: American Policy and the Dimensions of the Korean Conflict, 1950–1953*, and most recently *A Substitute for Victory: The Politics of Peacemaking at the Korean Armistice Talks*.

MARC GALLICCHIO is an assistant professor of history at Villanova University. He is the author of *The Cold War Begins in Asia: American East Asian Policy and the Fall of the Japanese Empire*.

NORMAN A. GRAEBNER is the Randolph P. Compton professor of history and public affairs emeritus at the University of Virginia. He has authored or edited some twenty books and over one hundred articles on various aspects of American diplomatic history during his stellar forty year career. Former president of the *Society for Historians of American Foreign Relations*, he is the recipient of numerous awards and honors recognizing his excellence as teacher and scholar.

JEFFREY GREY is a member of the department of history, University College, at the Australian Defence Force Academy. He is the author of *The Commonwealth Armies and the Korean War: An Alliance Study* and *A Military History of Australia*.

JONATHAN M. HOUSE earned his doctoral degree at the University of Michigan in 1975, completing his dissertation entitled "Public Force in Paris, February 22 to June 26, 1848" under the direction of John Shy and John Bowditch. An intelligence officer in the U.S. Army, he served two years in Korea and currently is an historian at the military studies branch of the Center of Military History in Washington, D.C. House's articles have appeared in *Military Affairs* and *Military Review*, as well as a number of anthologies.

HUA QINGZHAO is a research professor at the Institute of World History, Chinese Academy of Social Sciences, Beijing. He is also the director of the Center of American Studies, Tianjin Academy of Social Sciences, and professor of diplomatic history, Nankai University, Tianjin, China. He has just completed a major work on the Truman diplomacy which is written in English and will be published in the United States.

HAJIME IZUMI is associate professor of Korean studies at the University of Shizuoka, Japan. He is author of several publications on international relations surrounding the Korean peninsula, including *North Korea at the Crossroads*. He is currently working on U.S. policy towards Korea.

LAWRENCE S. KAPLAN is university professor of history and director of the Lyman L. Lemnitzer Center for NATO Studies at Kent State University. Prior to coming to Kent State in 1954, he was with the Historical Office, Office of the Secretary of Defense. He has written numerous articles, monographs, and books on U.S. diplomatic history and NATO affairs, including *A Community of Interests: NATO and the Military Assistance Program, 1948–1951* and *The United States and NATO: The Formative Years*.

EDWARD C. KEEFER is an historian at the Department of State, Washington, D.C., and an editor of the *Foreign Relations of the United States* series, specializing in East and Southeast Asia. He is the editor of *Foreign Relations 1952– 1954*, XV: *Korea* and a co-editor or editor of many of the volumes on Vietnam, Laos, and Cambodia for the period 1955 to 1963. He has written journal articles on the United States and Korea during the Korean War. His entries contain personal opinions and not those of the U.S. government.

KATHLEEN F. KELLNER is a part-time associate professor of history at Kent State University and part-time lecturer at the University of Akron. She is the co-author with Lawrence S. Kaplan of a chapter on General Lyman L. Lemnitzer and the French withdrawal from NATO in Robert Jordan's *Generals in International Politics: NATO's Supreme Allied Commander, Europe*. Currently, she is working on revisions of her dissertation on Lemnitzer and on two articles on the introduction of Italian opera to America.

CHULL BAUM KIM is associate professor of international politics at the Research Institute on National Security Affairs at National Defence University, Seoul, Korea. He is author of several publications on U.S. relations with Korea and East Asia, including *U.S. Withdrawal Decision from Korea, 1945–1949*. He currently is working on *The Korean War and U.S.* and *U.S. Withdrawal Policy since the Carter Administration*.

HAKJOON KIM is special assistant to President Roh Tae Woo of the Republic of Korea. Formerly a professor of political science at Seoul National University, he is author of *Unification Policies of South and North Korea, 1945–1985: A Comparative Study* and *Korea in Soviet East Asian Policy.*

JINWUNG KIM is an associate professor at Kyungpook National University, Taegu, Republic of Korea. His publications include *Hyondae Miguk Oegyosa (contemporary American Diplomatic History).*

WALTER LAFEBER is the Noll Professor of History at Cornell University. He is the author of *America, Russia, and the Cold War, The American Age: U.S. Foreign Policy at Home and Abroad Since 1750,* and *"Korea Came Along and Saved Us:" Acheson, Tocqueville, and Origins of the Cold War,* among other publications.

LI YI finished his undergraduate study and then earned his first Master's degree in 1985 at Peking University in China. He taught for three years in the department of history at South China Normal University before coming to the United States in 1988, where he received his second Master's degree two years later at New Mexico State University. Currently, he is working toward a doctoral degree at the University of Washington.

DAVID W. MABON received a doctorate from the University of California at Berkeley. Since 1970, he has been with the Office of the Historian, Department of State, where he works on the documentary series *Foreign Relations of the United States.* His entries contain personal opinions and not those of the U.S. government.

CALLUM A. MacDONALD is senior lecturer in the department of history, University of Warwick, England. He is the author of various articles and books on modern international history including *The United States, Britain and Appeasement* and *Korea: The War Before Vietnam.* He is currently working on a book about Britain and the Korean War for the Institute of Contemporary British History.

JAMES I. MATRAY is associate professor of history at New Mexico State University. Author of several articles on U.S. policy toward Korea, his *The Reluctant Crusade: American Foreign Policy in Korea, 1941–1950,* won the Phi Alpha Theta book prize in 1986. Currently, he is writing a survey of U.S.-Korean relations since World War II and a study of American foreign policy in Korea from 1950 to 1953.

JEFFREY G. MAUCK earned his doctoral degree at Indiana University, completing his dissertation under the direction of David M. Pletcher. During the 1989–1990 academic year, he was a visiting instructor of history at the University of Texas, Pan American.

J. BRITT McCARLEY earned his doctoral degree at Temple University. Currently, he is command historian for the U.S. Army Air Defense Artillery (ADA) branch and teaches military history at the ADA School, Fort Bliss, Texas.

IAN C. McGIBBON is a senior historian in the Historical Branch of the Department of Internal Affairs, Wellington, New Zealand. He is the author of several publications on New Zealand's defense and foreign policy, including *Blue-water Rationale: The Naval Defence of New Zealand 1914–1942*. He is currently working on the official history of New Zealand's involvement in the Korean War.

RONALD L. McGLOTHLEN is a doctoral candidate at Northern Illinois University. He is the author of "Acheson, Economics, and the American Commitment in Korea, 1947–1950," published in 1989 in the *Pacific Historical Review* and winner of the Louis Koontz Award. He is currently working on a book on Dean Acheson and Asian foreign policy, as well as several articles in military and diplomatic history.

ROBERT J. McMAHON is an associate professor of history at the University of Florida. He has authored *Colonialism and Cold War: The United States and the Struggle for Indonesian Independence, 1945–49* and *Major Problems in the History of the Vietnam War*. His articles have appeared in the *Journal of American History, Pacific Historical Review, Diplomatic History*, and the *Political Science Quarterly*, among other journals.

DENNIS MERRILL received his Ph. D. from the University of Connecticut in 1986 and teaches at the University of Missouri-Kansas City as an assistant professor of history. He has written "A Missed Opportunity in Asia: Indo-American Relations, 1947–1950," published in 1987 in *Diplomatic History*, which won the Stuart L. Bernath article prize. His doctoral dissertation will soon be published under the title *Bread and the Ballot: The United States and India's Economic Development, 1947–1963*.

JOHN MERRILL is an analyst with the Bureau of Intelligence and Research of the U.S. Department of State. A specialist in Northeast Asian politics and former Fulbright Fellow at the Asiatic Research Institute of Korea University, Dr. Merrill has taught at Lafayette College and the University of Delaware. He is the author of *Korea: The Peninsular Origins of the War* and co-author of *The DPRK: Politics, Economics, and Society*. His entries contain personal opinions and not those of the U.S. government.

PAUL J. MORTON is a doctoral candidate at the University of Southern California studying under Roger Dingman. He received his M. A. from Villanova University. His research interests include recent American diplomatic history especially with Australia and New Zealand.

JOHN NEILSON is historian at Fort Concho National Historic Landmark in San Angelo, Texas. In 1989, he earned his Master's degree at New Mexico State University and received the Monroe Billington Award for Outstanding History Thesis.

CHANG-IL OHN is associate professor of military history and strategy and director of the division of humanities and social sciences at the Korean Military Academy. He is author of several articles on U.S.-Korean relations, including "The Korean War of 1950–1953: U.S. Joint Chiefs of Staff and U.S. Strategy," and "The Republic of Korea-United States Relations in the Korean Armistice Negotiations." He currently is working on an official history of the Korean War to be written in Korean.

KENNETH O'REILLY teaches history at the University of Alaska, Anchorage. He is the author of *Hoover and the Un-Americans* and *"Racial Matters"*.

WILLIAM B. PICKETT is professor of history at Rose-Hulman Institute of Technology. He is author or editor of several publications on recent United States history, including a biography of former U.S. Senator Homer E. Capehart. He has taught in Korea for the University of Maryland and has been a Fulbright visiting professor at Nanzan and Nagoya Universities in Japan. Currently, he is writing a brief biography of Dwight D. Eisenhower.

J. Y. RA is a professor of political science and dean of the graduate school at Kyung Hee University, Seoul, Korea. Earning his doctorate at Trinity College, Cambridge, he was a Fulbright senior fellow at the University of Southern California in 1987. In addition to an article in the *Journal of Strategic Studies*, he is author of *Cooperation and Conflict*.

STEPHEN G. RABE is professor of history at the University of Texas at Dallas. He is the author of *The Road to OPEC: United States Relations with Venezuela, 1919–1976* and *Eisenhower and Latin America: The Foreign Policy of Anticommunism*. He currently is working on a concise, interpretive history of U.S. policy toward Latin America since 1945.

KATHERINE K. REIST is assistant professor of history at the University of Pittsburgh at Johnstown. A specialist of East Asian history, she received her doctorate from the Ohio State University in 1983.

DAVID ALAN ROSENBERG is associate professor of history at Temple University. The author of numerous publications on the history of nuclear strategy and post-World War II naval history, he is completing a biography of Admiral Arleigh Burke and a book on U.S. nuclear strategy from 1945 to 1968. He was awarded a MacArthur Foundation five year fellowship in 1988.

T. MICHAEL RUDDY is professor of history at St. Louis University. He is author of *The Cautious Diplomat: Charles E. Bohlen and the Soviet Union, 1929–1969*, along with several other articles on the Cold War. Presently his research focuses on the foreign relations of Finland and Sweden toward the United States and NATO.

STANLEY SANDLER is command historian at the U.S. Army John F. Kennedy Special Warfare Center and School. He is the author of numerous publications on military and naval technology, including *The Emergence of the Modern Capital Ship*. He is currently completing a book on the all-black fighter squadrons of the USAAF during World War II.

MICHAEL SCHALLER is professor of history and head of the department of history at the University of Arizona. His *The U.S. Crusade in China, 1938–1945*, won the Stuart L. Bernath book award in 1980. In addition to several articles on U.S. foreign policy in East Asia during and after World War II, he is author of *The American Occupation of Japan: The Origins of the Cold War in Asia* and *Douglas MacArthur: The Far Eastern General*.

JAMES F. SCHNABEL served as an historian for the United States Army from 1949 until 1964 while an officer on active duty. He retired as a lieutenant colonel and served as a civilian historian for the Joint Chiefs of Staff from 1964 until 1983. As an historian in General Douglas MacArthur's Tokyo headquarters when the Korean War began, he started work on his definitive history of United States policy in the Korea War, *Policy and Direction: The First Year*, within three days of the war's outbreak. In conjunction with Robert J. Watson, he has also written a two volume history of the Joint Chiefs of Staff and the Korean War. Currently retired, he has recently published his first novel.

HARRIET D. SCHWAR is an editor of the series *Foreign Relations of the United States* at the Department of State Historian's Office. She has edited or co-edited a number of volumes on East Asia, primarily China. Her personal research interests focus on U.S. policy toward China in the 1950's. Her entries contain personal opinions and not those of the U.S. government.

WILLIAM STUECK is an associate professor of history at the University of Georgia. In addition to numerous articles on U.S. policy in Asia during the Cold War, he is author of *The Road to Confrontation: American Policy Toward China and Korea, 1947–1950* and *The Wedemeyer Mission*. Stueck received the Stuart L. Bernath lecture award in 1986 and is currently completing work on an international history of the Korean War.

ANN TROTTER is associate professor of history in the department of history at the University of Otago, Dunedin, New Zealand. She is author of a number of publications relating to international history in East Asia and the Western Pacific, including *Britain and East Asia, 1933–1937*. She is editor of the volumes *Asia 1914–1939* in the series *Reports and Papers from the Foreign Office Confidential Print* and is currently working on New Zealand's relations with Japan since 1945.

NANCY BERNKOPF TUCKER is an associate professor in the school of foreign service and the department of history at Georgetown University. She is author of *Patterns in the Dust: Chinese-American Relations and the Recognition Controversy, 1949–1950* and several articles on American foreign policy and American-Asian relations. In 1986 and 1987, she worked in the U.S. Department of State's Office of Chinese Affairs and the American Embassy in Beijing. She is currently writing on American-Chinese relations 1953–1966 and on U.S.-Taiwan-Hong Kong relations after 1945.

PHILIP WEST is the Mansfield professor of modern Asian affairs at the University of Montana. His *Yenching University and Sino-Western Relations, 1916–1952* was nominated for a Pulitzer Award in 1976 by Harvard University Press. His current research is on the impact of the war on Chinese culture and society.

THEODORE A. WILSON is professor of history at the University of Kansas. Among other works, he has written *The First Summit: Roosevelt and Churchill at Placentia Bay, 1941* and *The Marshall Plan: An Atlantic Venture, 1947–1951*. He is currently serving as Senior Research Professor, U.S. Army Center of Military History, while completing a history of postwar economic and military aid programs and a study of ground combat forces in World War II.

JOHN EDWARD WILZ is professor of history at Indiana University/Bloomington. He is the author of *In Search of Peace: The Senate Munitions Inquiry, 1934–36*, *From Isolation to War, 1931–1941*, and *Democracy Challenged: The United States Since World War II*. His essays on the Korean War include "The MacArthur Inquiry, 1951," in Arthur M. Schlesinger, Jr. and Roger Bruns, *Congress Investigates*, "The Korean War and American Society," in Francis H. Heller, *The Korean War: A 25-Year Perspective*, "The MacArthur Inquiry of 1951: The Secret Testimony" and "Truman and MacArthur: The Wake Island Conference" in *Military Affairs*, and "Did the United States Betray Korea in 1905?" in the *Pacific Historical Review*.

WOO CHUL-KOO is professor of political science at Yeungnam University, Taegu, Korea. He received his doctoral degree at the University of Paris in 1980 and his dissertation was entitled "Foreign Advisors to the Royal Court of Korea, 1882–1898." He has published articles in *The Journal of Social Science* and *The Journal of Korean Studies*.

DAVID J. WRIGHT earned his M. A. at California State University, Los Angeles, and is now a research associate at California State University's Center for the Study of Armament and Disarmament. Currently, he is engaged in research on NATO. He served in the U.S. Navy during the Vietnam War from 1969 to 1974. He plans to complete his doctoral degree in modern military history.

SUNG CHUL YANG is professor of political science and dean of academic affairs, the Graduate Institute of Peace Studies, Kyung Hee University, Seoul, Korea. He is author of several publications on North and South Korea and Korean relations with the United States, including *Korea and Two Regimes: Kim Il Sung and Park Chung Hee*. He is currently working on a book entitled *The North and South Korean Political Systems*.